THE
EMOTIONAL
BRAIN

THE EMOTIONAL BRAIN

The Mysterious Underpinnings

of Emotional Life

∽◦∾

JOSEPH LeDoux

WEIDENFELD & NICOLSON
LONDON

First published in Great Britain in 1998
by Weidenfeld & Nicolson

This edition published by arrangement with Simon & Schuster,
Rockefeller Center,
1230 Avenue of the Americas,
New York, NY 10020

A CIP catalogue record for this book
is available from the British Library.

ISBN 0 297 84108 4

Printed in Great Britain by Clays Ltd, St Ives plc

Weidenfeld & Nicolson
The Orion Publishing Group Ltd
Orion House
5 Upper Saint Martin's Lane
London, WC2H 9EA

For the people who have had the greatest influence

on my emotional brain:

Nancy, Jacob, and Milo

and

Pris and Boo

CONTENTS

PREFACE

•

I FIRST STARTED WORKING on the brain mechanisms of emotion in the late 1970s. At that time very few brain scientists were interested in emotions. In the intervening years, and especially recently, the topic has begun to be fairly heavily investigated, and a good deal of progress has been made. I thought it was time to share some of this information with the general public.

The Emotional Brain provides an overview of my ideas about how emotions come from the brain. It is not meant as an all-encompassing survey of every aspect of how the brain produces emotions. It focuses on those issues that have interested me most, namely, issues about how the brain detects and responds to emotionally arousing stimuli, how emotional learning occurs and emotional memories are formed, and how our conscious emotional feelings emerge from unconscious processes.

I tried to write *The Emotional Brain* so that it would be accessible to readers not trained in science or versed in scientific jargon. But I also tried not to water down the science. I hope I've been successful in making the book readable and enjoyable for lay persons and scientists alike.

I'm extremely grateful to my family for tolerating me while I struggled to write this book. I owe much to my wife, Nancy Princenthal, for her tireless reading of endless drafts of my book proposal, and then of the chapters, and for her many useful suggestions. Our two boys, Jacob and Milo, kept my emotional brain in tip-top shape throughout.

Many students and postdoctoral researchers have helped greatly in my past and current research on emotions in the brain: Akira Sak-aguchi, Jiro Iwata, Piera Chichetti, Liz Romanski, Andy Xagoraris, Christine Clugnet, Mike Thompson, Russ Phillips, Maria Morgan, Peter Sparks, Kevin LaBar, Liz Phelps, Keith Corodimas, Kate Melia, Xingfang Li, Michael Rogan, Jorge Armony, Greg Quirk, Chris Repa, Neot Doron, Gene Go, Gabriel Hui, Mian Hou, Beth Stutzmann, and Walter Woodson. I have also had some important collaborators, in-cluding Don Reis, David Ruggiero, Shawn Morrison, Costantino Iadecola, and Terry Milner at Cornell Medical School; David Servan-Schreiber and Jon Cohen at the University of Pittsburgh; Asla Pitkä-nen in Finland; and Chiye Aoki at NYU. And I will always be grateful to Claudia Farb for her many tangible and intangible contributions to my lab. Some of these people have had to do their work while I was writing the book. I apologize to them for being inaccessible, espe-cially during those last days when it seemed that I might never finish. I also owe a great deal to Irina Kerzhnerman and Annette Olivero, who helped with many aspects of the final preparation of the book. Jorge Armony and Mian Hou assisted with the illustrations.

I also want to thank Mike Gazzaniga, my Ph.D. advisor, for show-ing me how to have fun while being a scientist, and for teaching me how to think about the mind. He encouraged me to write a book on emotions years before I actually got around to it. I'm also grateful to Don Reis, who took me into his lab as a postdoc, taught me neurobi-ology, and provided me with the resources I needed to start pursuing the brain mechanisms of emotion.

The Neuroscience Research Branch at the National Institute of Mental Health has generously funded my work. The research that this book is based on could not have been done without this support. New York University, especially the Faculty of Arts and Science Dean's Of-fice, has also been very supportive. And I couldn't ask for better col-leagues than those I have in the NYU Center for Neural Science.

Katinka Matson and John Brockman of Brockman, Inc., have been wonderful as literary agents. They were instrumental in helping me shape my proposal and in signing me up with Simon & Schuster, where I'm pleased to have had the opportunity to work with Bob Asahina, who made only good editorial suggestions. I wish him luck in his new job, which took him away just as the book went into production. Bob Ben-der, who took over, has been wonderful as well, and Johanna Li.

Some people go on sabbatical to write books. I'm now going on one to recover.

1

WHAT'S LOVE GOT TO DO WITH IT?

"Our civilization is still in a middle stage, scarcely beast, in that it is no longer guided by instinct, scarcely human in that it is not yet wholly guided by reason."

Theodore Dreiser, *Sister Carrie*[1]

MY FATHER WAS A butcher. I spent much of my childhood surrounded by beef. At an early age, I learned what the inside of a cow looks like. And the part that interested me the most was the slimy, wiggly, wrinkled brain. Now, many years later, I spend my days, and some nights, trying to figure out how brains work. And what I've wanted to know most about brains is how they make emotions.

You might think that this would be a crowded field of research. Emotions, after all, are the threads that hold mental life together. They define who we are in our own mind's eye as well as in the eyes of others. What could be more important to understand about the brain than the way it makes us happy, sad, afraid, disgusted, or delighted?

For quite some time now, though, emotion has not been a very popular topic in brain science.[2] Emotions, skeptics have said, are just too complex to track down in the brain. But some brain scientists, myself included, would rather learn a little about emotions than more about less interesting things. In this book, I'll tell you how far we've gotten. Skeptics be warned, we've gotten pretty far.

Of course, at some level, we know what emotions are and don't need scientists to tell us about them. We've all felt love and hate and fear and anger and joy. But what is it that ties mental states like these together into the bundle that we commonly call "emotions"? What makes this bundle so different from other mental packages, ones that we are less inclined to use the term "emotion" for? How do our emotions influence every other aspect of our mental life, shaping our perceptions, memories, thoughts, and dreams? Why do our emotions often seem impossible to understand? Do we have control over our emotions or do they control us? Are emotions cast in neural stone by our genes or taught to the brain by the environment? Do animals (other than human ones) have emotions, and if so do all species of animals have them? Can we have unconscious emotional reactions and unconscious emotional memories? Can the emotional slate ever be wiped clean, or are emotional memories permanent?

You may have opinions, and even strong ones, about the answers to some of these questions, but whether your opinions constitute scientifically correct answers can't be determined by intuitions alone. Occasionally, scientists turn everyday beliefs into facts, or explain the workings of intuitively obvious things with their experiments. But facts about the workings of the universe, including the one inside your head, are not necessarily intuitively obvious. Sometimes, intuitions are just wrong—the world seems flat but it is not—and science's role is to convert these commonsense notions into myths, changing truisms into "old wives' tales." Frequently, though, we simply have no prior intuitions about something that scientists discover—there is no reason why we should have deep-seated opinions about the existence of black holes in space, or the importance of sodium, potassium, and calcium in the inner workings of a brain cell. Things that are obvious are not necessarily true, and many things that are true are not at all obvious.

I view emotions as biological functions of the nervous system. I believe that figuring out how emotions are represented in the brain can help us understand them. This approach contrasts sharply with the more typical one in which emotions are studied as psychological states, independent of the underlying brain mechanisms. Psychological research has been extremely valuable, but an approach where emotions are studied as brain functions is far more powerful.

Science works by experimentation, which, by definition, involves the manipulation of some variables and the control of others. The brain is an enormously rich source of variables to manipulate. By studying emotion through the brain, we greatly expand opportunities for making new discoveries beyond what can be achieved with psychological experimentation alone. Additionally, studying the way emotion works in the brain can help us choose between alternative psychological hypotheses—there are many possible solutions to the puzzle of how emotions might work, but the only one we really care about is the one that evolution hit upon and put into the brain.

I got interested in how emotions come from brains one day in New England. It was the mid-1970s, and I was a graduate student doing my Ph.D. research at the State University of New York at Stony Brook. A decade earlier, my advisor, Mike Gazzaniga, had made a big splash with his thesis research involving the psychological consequences of split-brain surgery in humans, work that he had done at Cal Tech with the late Nobel Laureate Roger Sperry.[3]

Split-brain surgery is a procedure in which the nerve connections between the two sides or hemispheres of the brain are severed in an attempt to control very severe epilepsy.[4] A brand-new series of patients was being operated on at Dartmouth and the surgeon had asked Gazzaniga to study them.[5] We built a laboratory inside a camper-trailer attached to a pumpkin-colored Ford van, and frequently traveled from Long Island to see the patients at their homes in Vermont and New Hampshire.[6]

The earlier studies that Gazzaniga had done showed that when the brain is split, the two sides can no longer communicate with each other. And because language functions of the brain are usually in the left hemisphere, the person is only able to talk about things that the left hemisphere knows about. If stimuli are presented in such a way that only the right hemisphere sees them, the split-brain person is not able to verbally describe what the stimulus is. However, if you give the right hemisphere the opportunity to respond without having to talk, it becomes clear that the stimulus was registered. For example, if the left hand, which sends touch information to the right hemisphere, reaches into a bag of objects, it is able to sort through them and pull out the one that matches the picture seen by the right hemisphere. The right hemisphere can thus match the way the object feels with a memory of the way it looked a few moments earlier and pull out the correct one. The right hand can't do this because its touch information goes to the left hemisphere, which didn't see the object. In the split-brain patient, information put into one hemisphere remains trapped on that side of the brain, and is unavailable to the other side. Gazzaniga captured the essence of this remarkable situation in an early article on the topic called "One Brain—Two Minds."[7]

The split-brain experiment that set my scientific compass in the direction of emotion involved the presentation of stimuli with emotional connotations to the two half-brains of a special patient known as P.S.[8] He was special because unlike most previous patients of this type, he was able to read words in both hemispheres, although, as with the others, he could only speak through his left hemisphere. So when emotional stimuli were presented to the left hemisphere, P.S. could tell us what the stimulus was and how he felt about it— whether it signified something good or bad. When the same stimuli were presented to the right hemisphere, the speaking left hemisphere was unable to tell us what the stimulus was. However, the left hemisphere could accurately judge whether the stimulus seen by the right was good or bad. For example, when the right hemisphere saw the word "mom," the left hemisphere rated it as "good," and when the right side saw the word "devil," the left rated it as "bad."

The left hemisphere had no idea what the stimuli were. No matter how hard we pressed, the patient could not name the stimulus that had been presented to the right hemisphere. Nevertheless, the left hemisphere was consistently on the money with the emotional ratings. Somehow the emotional significance of the stimulus had leaked across the brain, even though the identity of the stimulus had not. The patient's conscious emotions, as experienced by his left hemisphere, were, in effect, being pushed this way and that by stimuli that he claimed to have never seen.

How did this occur? Most likely, the path taken by the stimulus through the right hemisphere forked. One branch brought the stimulus to parts of the right hemisphere that identify what the stimulus is. The split-brain surgery prevented the identification made by the right hemisphere from reaching the left. The other branch took the stimulus to parts of the right hemisphere that determine the emotional implications of the stimulus. The surgery did not prevent the transfer of this information over to the left side.

The left hemisphere, in other words, was making emotional judgments without knowing what was being judged. The left hemisphere knew the emotional outcome, but it did not have access to the processes that led up to that outcome. As far as the left hemisphere was concerned, the emotional processing had taken place outside of its realm of awareness (which is to say, had taken place unconsciously).

Split-brain surgery seemed to be revealing a fundamental psychological dichotomy—between thinking and feeling, between cognition and emotion. The right hemisphere was unable to share its thoughts about what the stimulus was with the left, but was able to transfer the emotional meaning of the stimulus over.

By the way, this work was not at all about the issue of possible hemisphere differences in emotion.[9] We were simply examining the kinds of information that could and could not flow between the hemispheres when the brain was split.

Freud of course told us long ago that the unconscious is the home of our emotions, which, he said, were often dissociated from normal thought processes. However, decades later, we still had little understanding of how this might take place, and whether it was true at all was often questioned. I set as my goal figuring how the brain processes the emotional meaning of stimuli, a goal that I have since pursued.

After completing my graduate work, I decided that the techniques available for studying the human brain were too limited and that I would never be able to understand the neural basis of emotion by studying humans. I therefore turned to studies of experimental animals, rats, for the purpose of trying to unlock the brain's emotional secrets. As important as the human split-brain observations were in getting me going on this topic, it has been the animal studies that have really shaped my view of the emotional brain.

This book will tell you what I've learned from my researching and thinking about brain mechanisms of emotions. It gives a scientific account of what emotions are, how they operate in the brain, and why they have such important influences on our lives.

Several themes about the nature of emotions will emerge and recur. Some of these will be consistent with your commonsense intuitions about emotions, whereas others will seem unlikely if not strange. But all of them, I believe, are well-grounded in facts about the brain, or at least in hypotheses that have been inspired by such facts, and I hope that you will hear them out.

- The first is that the proper level of analysis of a psychological function is the level at which that function is represented in the brain. This leads to a conclusion that clearly falls into the realm of the bizarre at first—that the word "emotion" does not refer to something that the mind or brain really has or does.[10] "Emotion" is only a label, a convenient way of talking about aspects of the brain and its mind. Psychology textbooks often carve the mind up into functional pieces, such as perception, memory, and emotion. These are useful for organizing information into general areas of research but do not refer to real functions. The brain, for example, does not have a system dedicated to perception. The word "perception" describes in a general way what goes on in a number of specific neural systems—we see, hear, and smell the world with our visual, auditory, and olfactory systems. Each system evolved to solve different problems that animals face. In a similar vein, the various classes of emotions are mediated by separate neural systems that have evolved for different reasons. The system we use to defend against danger is different from the one we use in procreation, and the feelings that result from activating these systems—fear and sexual pleasure—do not have a common origin. There is no such thing as the "emotion" faculty and there is no single brain system dedicated to this phantom function. If we are interested in understanding the various phenomena that we use the term "emotion" to refer to, we have to focus on specific classes of emotions. We shouldn't mix findings about different emotions all together independent of the emotion that they are findings about. Unfortunately, most work in psychology and brain science has done this.

- A second theme is that the brain systems that generate emotional behaviors are highly conserved through many levels of evolutionary history. All animals, including people, have to satisfy certain conditions to survive in the world and fulfill their biological imperative to pass their genes on to their offspring. At a minimum, they need to obtain food and shelter, protect themselves from bodily harm, and procreate. This is as true of insects and worms as it is of fish, frogs, rats, and people. Each of these diverse groups of animals has neural systems that accomplish these behavioral goals. And within the animal groups that have a backbone and a brain (fish, amphibians, reptiles, birds, and mammals, including humans), it seems that the neural organization of particular emotional behavioral systems—like the systems underlying fearful, sexual, or feeding behaviors—is pretty similar across species. This does not imply that all brains are the same. It instead means that our understanding of what it means to be human involves an appreciation of the ways in which we are like other animals as well as the ways in which we are different.

- A third theme is that when these systems function in an animal that also has the capacity for conscious awareness, then conscious emotional feelings occur. This clearly happens in humans, but no one knows for sure whether other animals have this capacity. I make no claims about which animals are conscious and which are not. I simply claim that when one of these evolutionarily old systems (like the system that produces defensive behaviors in the presence of danger) goes about its business in a conscious brain, emotional feelings (like being afraid) are the result. Otherwise, the brain accomplishes its behavioral goals in the absence of robust awareness. And absence of awareness is the rule of mental life, rather than the exception, throughout the animal kingdom. If we do not need conscious feelings to explain what we would call emotional behavior in some animals, then we do not need them to explain the same behavior in humans. Emotional responses are, for the most part, generated unconsciously. Freud was right on the mark when he described consciousness as the tip of the mental iceberg.

- The fourth theme follows from the third. The conscious feelings that we know and love (or hate) our emotions by are red herrings, detours, in the scientific study of emotions. This will surely be hard to swallow at first. After all, what is an emotion but a conscious feeling? Take away the subjective register of fear and there's not much left to a dangerous experience. But I will try to convince you that this idea is wrong—that there is much more than meets the mind's eye in an emotional experience. Feelings of fear, for example, occur as part of the overall reaction to danger and are no more or less central to the reaction than the behavioral and physiological responses that also occur, such as trembling, running away, sweating, and heart palpitations. What we need to elucidate is not so much the conscious state of fear or the accompanying responses, but the system that detects the danger in the first place. Fear feelings and pounding hearts are both effects caused by the activity of this system, which does its job unconsciously—literally, before we actually know we are in danger. The system that detects danger is the fundamental mechanism of fear, and the behavioral, physiological, and conscious manifestations are the surface responses it orchestrates. This is not meant to imply that feelings are unimportant. It means that if we want to understand feelings we have to dig deeper.
- Fifth, if, indeed, emotional feelings and emotional responses are effects caused by the activity of a common underlying system, we can then use the objectively measurable emotional responses to investigate the underlying mechanism, and, at the same time, illuminate the system that is primarily responsible for the generation of the conscious feelings. And since the brain system that generates emotional responses is similar in animals and people, studies of how the brain controls these responses in animals are a pivotal step toward understanding the mechanisms that generate emotional feelings in people. Studies of the neural basis of emotion in humans vary from difficult to impossible for both ethical and practical reasons. The study of experimental animals is, as a result, both a useful and a necessary enterprise if we are to understand emotions in the human brain. Understanding emotions in the human brain is

clearly an important quest, as most mental disorders are emotional disorders.

- Sixth, conscious feelings, like the feeling of being afraid or angry or happy or in love or disgusted, are in one sense no different from other states of consciousness, such as the awareness that the roundish, reddish object before you is an apple, that a sentence just heard was spoken in a particular foreign language, or that you've just solved a previously insoluble problem in mathematics. States of consciousness occur when the system responsible for awareness becomes privy to the activity occurring in unconscious processing systems. What differs between the state of being afraid and the state of perceiving red is not the system that represents the conscious content (fear or redness) but the systems that provide the inputs to the system of awareness. There is but one mechanism of consciousness and it can be occupied by mundane facts or highly charged emotions. Emotions easily bump mundane events out of awareness, but nonemotional events (like thoughts) do not so easily displace emotions from the mental spotlight—wishing that anxiety or depression would go away is usually not enough.

- Seventh, emotions are things that happen to us rather than things we will to occur. Although people set up situations to modulate their emotions all the time—going to movies and amusement parks, having a tasty meal, consuming alcohol and other recreational drugs—in these situations, external events are simply arranged so that the stimuli that automatically trigger emotions will be present. We have little direct control over our emotional reactions. Anyone who has tried to fake an emotion, or who has been the recipient of a faked one, knows all too well the futility of the attempt. While conscious control over emotions is weak, emotions can flood consciousness. This is so because the wiring of the brain at this point in our evolutionary history is such that connections from the emotional systems to the cognitive systems are stronger than connections from the cognitive systems to the emotional systems.

- Finally, once emotions occur they become powerful motivators of future behaviors. They chart the course of moment-to-moment action as well as set the sails toward long-term achievements. But our emotions can also get us into trouble. When fear becomes anxiety, desire gives way to greed, or annoyance turns to anger, anger to hatred, friendship to envy, love to obsession, or pleasure to addiction, our emotions start working against us. Mental health is maintained by emotional hygiene, and mental problems, to a large extent, reflect a breakdown of emotional order. Emotions can have both useful and pathological consequences.

As emotional beings, we think of emotions as conscious experiences. But when we begin probing emotion in the brain, we see conscious emotional experiences as but one part, and not necessarily the central function, of the systems that generate them. This does not make our conscious experiences of love or fear any less real or important. It just means that if we are going to understand where our emotional experiences come from we have to reorient our pursuit of them. From the point of view of the lover, the only thing important about love is the feeling. But from the point of view of trying to understand what a feeling is, why it occurs, where it comes from, and why some people give or receive it more easily than others, love, the feeling, may not have much to do with it at all.

Our journey into the emotional brain will take us down many different paths. We start with the curious fact that the study of emotion has long been ignored by the field of cognitive science, the major scientific enterprise concerned with the nature of the mind today (Chapter 2). Cognitive science treats minds like computers and has traditionally been more interested in how people and machines solve logical problems or play chess than in why we are sometimes happy and sometimes sad. We will then see that this shortcoming has been corrected in an unfortunate way—by redefining emotions as cold cognitive processes, stripping them of their passionate qualities (Chapter 3). At the same time though, cognitive science has been very successful, and has provided a framework that, when appropriately applied, provides an immensely valuable approach for pursuing the emotional as well as the cognitive mind. And one of the major conclusions about cognition and emotion that comes from this approach is that both seem to operate unconsciously, with only the outcome of cognitive or emotional processing entering awareness and occupying our conscious minds, and only in some instances.

The next stop along the way takes us into the brain, in search of the system that gives rise to our emotions (Chapter 4). We'll see that there is no single emotion system. Instead, there are lots of emotion systems, each of which evolved for a different functional purpose and each of which gives rise to different kinds of emotions (Chapter 5). These systems operate outside of consciousness and they constitute the emotional unconscious.

We then concentrate on one emotion system that has been extensively studied, the fear system of the brain, and see how it is organized (Chapter 6). The relation between unconscious emotional memory and conscious memories of emotional experiences is then discussed (Chapter 7). The breakdown of emotion systems, especially the fear system, is then considered (Chapter 8). We see how anxiety, phobias, panic attacks, and post-traumatic stress disorders emerge out of the depths of the unconscious workings of the fear system. Psychotherapy is interpreted as a process through which our neocortex learns to exercise control over evolutionarily old emotional systems. Finally, we explore the problem of emotional consciousness, and the relation of emotion to the rest of the mind (Chapter 9). I conclude with the hypothesis, based on trends in brain evolution, that the struggle between thought and emotion may ultimately be resolved, not simply by the dominance of neocortical cognitions over emotional systems, but by a more harmonious integration of reason and passion in the brain, a development that will allow future humans to better know their true feelings and to use them more effectively in daily life.

2

SOULS ON ICE

"Think, think, think."

Winnie the Pooh[1]

"Ahab never thinks, he just feels, feels, feels."

Herman Melville, *Moby-Dick*[2]

THE HUMAN BRAIN CONTAINS about 10 billion neurons that are wired together in enormously complex ways. Although the electrical sparks within and chemical exchanges between these cells accomplish some amazing and perplexing things, the creation of our emotions stands out as one of their most amazing and perplexing feats.

When we turn our mind's eye inward on our emotions, we find them at once obvious and mysterious. They are the states of our brain we know best and remember with the greatest clarity. Yet, sometimes we do not know where they come from. They can change slowly or suddenly, and their causes can be evident or opaque. We don't always understand what makes us wake up on the wrong side of the bed. We can be nice or nasty for reasons other than the ones we believe are guiding our actions. We can react to danger before we "know" we are in harm's way. We can be drawn toward the aesthetic beauty of a painting without consciously understanding what it is we like about it. Although our emotions are at the core of who we are, they also seem to have their own agenda, one often carried out without our willful participation.

It's hard to imagine life without emotions. We live for them, structuring circumstances to give us moments of pleasure and joy, and avoiding situations that will lead to disappointment, sadness, or pain. The rock critic Lester Bangs once said, "The only questions worth asking today are whether humans are going to have any emotions tomorrow, and what the quality of life will be if the answer is no."[3]

Scientists have had lots to say about what emotions are.[4] For some, emotions are bodily responses that evolved as part of the struggle to survive. For others, emotions are mental states that result when bodily responses are "sensed" by the brain. Another view is that the bodily responses are peripheral to an emotion, with the important stuff happening completely within the brain. Emotions have also been viewed as ways of acting or ways of talking. Unconscious impulses are at the core of an emotion in some theories, while others emphasize the importance of conscious decisions. A popular view today is that emotions are thoughts about situations in which people find themselves. Another notion is that emotions are social constructions, things that happen between rather than within individuals.

A scientific understanding of emotions would be wonderful. It would give us insight into how the most personal and occult aspects of the mind work, and at the same time would help us understand what may go wrong when this part of mental life breaks down. But, as the above comments indicate, scientists have not been able to agree about what an emotion is. The careers of many a scientist have been devoted to, if not devoured by, the task of explaining emotions. Unfortunately, one of the most significant things ever said about emotion may be that everyone knows what it is until they are asked to define it.[5]

This state of affairs might seem to pose a major stumbling block for our attempt to understand the emotional brain. If we can't say what emotion is, how can we hope to find out how the brain does it? But this book is not about mapping one area of knowledge (the psychology of emotion) onto another (brain function). It is instead about how studies of brain function allow us to understand emotion as a psychological process in new ways. I believe that we can get a unique and advantageous view of this puzzling part of the mental terrain by peering at it from inside the nervous system.

But I don't intend to ignore the psychology of emotion. Psychologists have had lots of insights. The problem is deciding which are correct and which are clever but wrong. Studies of the emotional brain can give us additional insights, but can also help us pick and choose from the psychological offerings. Aspects of the psychology of emotion are discussed in Chapter 3.

Our pursuit of the psychology of emotion, though, needs to be prefaced with an exploration of how emotion fits into a larger view of the mind—we need to delve into the nature of cognition, emotion's partner in the mind. The study of cognition, or just plain thinking, has advanced amazingly far in recent years. These advances provide a conceptual framework and methodology that is useful as an approach to all aspects of the mind, including emotion. The business of this chapter will therefore be to see what cognition is and how emotion and cognition relate.

Reason and Passion

Since the time of the ancient Greeks, humans have found it compelling to separate reason from passion, thinking from feeling, cognition from emotion. These contrasting aspects of the soul, as the Greeks liked to call the mind, have in fact often been viewed as waging an inner battle for the control of the human psyche. Plato, for example, said that passions and desires and fears make it impossible for us to think.[6] For him, emotions were like wild horses that have to be reined in by the intellect, which he thought of as a charioteer. Christian theology has long equated emotions with sins, temptations to resist by reason and willpower in order for the immortal soul to enter the kingdom of God. And our legal system treats "crimes of passion" differently from premeditated transgressions.

Given this long tradition of separation of passion and reason, it should not be too surprising that a field currently exists to study rationality, so-called cognition, on its own, independent of emotions. This field, known as cognitive science, tries to understand how we come to know our world and use our knowledge to live in it. It asks how we recognize a certain pattern of visual stimulation falling on the retina as a particular object, say an apple, or determine the apple's color, or judge which of two apples is bigger, or control our arm and hand in the act of catching an apple falling out of a tree, or remember where we were or who we were with when we last ate an apple, or imagine an apple in the absence of one, or tell or understand a story about an apple falling out of a tree, or conceive of a theory of why an apple falling out of a tree goes toward the earth instead of the sky.

Cognitive science emerged recently, around the middle of this century, and is often described as the "new science of mind."[7] However, in fact, cognitive science is really a science of only a part of the mind, the part having to do with thinking, reasoning, and intellect. It leaves emotions out. And minds without emotions are not really minds at all. They are souls on ice—cold, lifeless creatures devoid of any desires, fears, sorrows, pains, or pleasures.

Why would anyone want to conceive of minds without emotions? How could such a field focused on emotionless minds be so successful? How do we get emotion and cognition back together? To answer these questions we need to see where cognitive science came from and what it's all about.

Thinking Machines

Throughout much of the first half of this century, psychology was dominated by behaviorists, who believed that the subjective inner states of mind, like perceptions, memories, and emotions, are not appropriate topics for psychology.[8] In their view, psychology should not be the study of consciousness, as had been the case since Descartes said "Cogito, ergo sum,"[9] but instead should be the study of observable facts—objectively measurable behaviors. Being subjective and unobservable (except by introspection), consciousness could not, in the behaviorists' mind, be examined scientifically. Mental states came to be known pejoratively as "ghosts in the machine."[10] Behaviorists were known to ridicule those who dared to speak of mind and consciousness.

By mid-century, though, the behaviorist stronghold on psychology began to weaken.[11] Electronic computers had been developed,

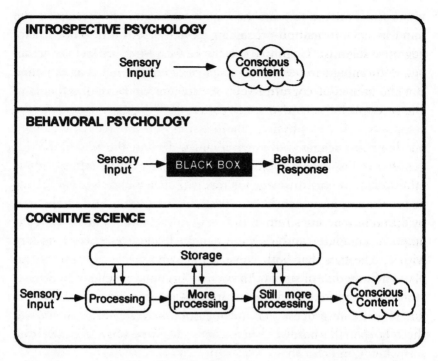

FIGURE 2-1
Three Approaches to the Science of Mind and Behavior.

Introspective psychology *is mainly concerned with the contents of immediate
conscious experience. Behaviorism rejected consciousness as a legitimate subject matter for psychology and treated the events occurring between stimuli
and responses as hidden in a black box. Cognitive science tries to understand
the processes that occur inside the black box. These processes tend to occur unconsciously. In focusing on processes rather than conscious content, cognitive
science did not exactly revive the view of the mind that the behaviorists rejected. More and more, however, cognitive scientists are beginning to try to understand the mechanisms of consciousness as well as the unconscious processes
that sometimes do and sometimes do not give rise to conscious content.* (Bottom panel is based on figure 1 in U. Neisser [1976], *Cognition and Reality.* San Francisco: W.H. Freeman.)

and engineers, mathematicians, philosophers, and psychologists
quickly saw similarities in the way computers process information
and the way minds work. Computer operations became a metaphor
for mental functions, and the field of artificial intelligence (AI),
which seeks to model the human mind using computer simulations,

was born. Pretty soon, anyone who bought into the notion of the mind as an information-processing device came to be known as a cognitive scientist. Cognitive science caused a revolution in psychology, dethroning the behaviorists and bringing the mind back home. But the impact of cognitive science reached far beyond psychology. Today, cognitive scientists can be found in linguistics, philosophy, computer science, physics, mathematics, anthropology, sociology, and brain science, as well as psychology.

One of the most important conceptual developments in the establishment of cognitive science was a philosophical position known as functionalism, which holds that intelligent functions carried out by different machines reflect the same underlying process.[12] For example, a computer and a person can both add 2 + 5 and come up with 7. The fact that both achieve the same answer cannot be explained by the use of similar hardware—brains are made of biological stuff and computers of electronic parts. The similar outcome must be due to a similar process that occurs at a functional level. In spite of the fact that the hardware in the machines is vastly different, the software or program that each executes may be the same. Functionalism thus holds that the mind is to the brain as a computer program is to the computer hardware.

Cognitive scientists, carrying the functionalist banner, have been allowed to pursue the functional organization of the mind without reference to the hardware that generates the functional states. According to functionalist doctrine, cognitive science stands on its own as a discipline—it does not require that we know anything about the brain. This logic was a shot in the arm to the field, giving it a strong sense of independence. Regardless of whether they do experiments on humans or use computer simulations of the human mind, many cognitive scientists today are functionalists.

It would be natural to presume that the cognitive revolution resulted in the return of consciousness as the number one topic of psychology. But this was not the case. The cognitive movement brought the mind back to psychology, but not exactly the all-knowing conscious mind that Descartes had popularized. For Descartes, if it wasn't conscious it wasn't mental: mind and consciousness became synonymous after him.[13] In contrast, as we'll soon see, cognitive scientists tend to think of the mind in terms of unconscious *processes* rather

FIGURE 2-2
Functionalism.

This is a philosophical position which proposes that mental functions (think-
ing, reasoning, planning, feeling) are functional rather than physical states.
When a person and a computer add 2 to 5 and come up with 7, the similar
outcome cannot be based on similar physical makeup, but instead must be due
to a functional equivalence of the processes involved. As a result, it is possible
to study mental processes using computer simulations. Minds might in princi-
ple even exist without bodies. (Based on J.A. Fodor, The Mind-Body Problem.
Scientific American [January 1981], Vol. 244, p. 118.)

than conscious *contents*. And in leaving out consciousness, cognitive
science left behind those conscious states called emotions. Later,
we'll see why this occurred. For now, we want to explore the unconscious nature of cognitive processes.

The Cognitive Unconscious

Rooted in the idea of mind as an information processing device, cognitive science has been geared toward understanding the functional organization and processes that underlie and give rise to mental events, and much less toward understanding the nature of consciousness and its subjective contents. In order for you to consciously perceive an apple in front of you in space, the apple must be represented in your brain and that representation must be made available to the conscious part of your mind. But the mental representation of the apple that you consciously perceive is created by the unconscious turnings of mental gears. As Karl Lashley long ago pointed out, conscious content comes from processing, and we are never consciously aware of the processing itself but only of the outcome.[14] These mental processes are the bread and butter of cognitive science. Cognitive scientists sometimes speak of consciousness as the end result of processing, but are usually far more interested in the underlying processes than in the contents of consciousness that occur during and as a result of the processing. This emphasis on unconscious *processes* as opposed to conscious *content* underlies much work in cognitive science.[15] And for adherents of strong versions of functionalism these processes can be studied equally well in any device that can solve the functional problem at hand, regardless of whether the device is made of neurons, electrical components, mechanical parts, or sticks and stones.[16]

The psychologist John Kihlstrom coined the term "cognitive unconscious" to describe the subterranean processes that have been the main preoccupation of cognitive science.[17] These processes span many levels of mental complexity, all the way from the routine analysis of the physical features of stimuli by our sensory systems, to remembrance of past events, to speaking grammatically, to imagining things that are not present, to decision making, and beyond.

Like Freud before them, cognitive scientists reject the view handed down from Descartes that mind and consciousness are the same. However, the cognitive unconscious is not the same as the Freudian or dynamic unconscious.[18] The term cognitive unconscious merely implies that a lot of what the mind does goes on outside of consciousness, whereas the dynamic unconscious is a darker, more malevolent place where emotionally charged memories are shipped to do mental dirty work. To some extent, the dynamic unconscious can be conceived in terms of cognitive processes,[19] but the term cognitive unconscious does not imply these dynamic operations. We are going to also discuss the dynamic unconscious in some detail in later chapters. But for now we are focused on the tamer cognitive unconscious, which consists of processes that take care of the mind's routine business without consciousness having to be bothered. Let's consider some examples.

The first level of analysis of any external stimulus by the nervous system involves the physical properties of the stimulus. These low-level processes occur without awareness.[20] The brain has, for example, mechanisms for computing the shape, color, location, and movement of objects we see, and the loudness, pitch, and location of sounds we hear. If we are asked to say which of two objects is closer or which of two sounds is louder, we can do so, but we cannot explain what operations the brain performed to allow us to reach these conclusions. We have conscious access to the outcome of the computation but not to the computation itself. The processing of physical stimulus features makes possible all other aspects of perception, including our conscious awareness of perceiving something. It is just as well that we are unaware of these processes, as we would be so busy doing the computations that we would never get around to actually perceiving anything if we had to do it all with deliberate concentration.

On the basis of its analysis of physical features of stimuli, the brain begins to construct meaning. In order to know that the object you are looking at is an apple, the physical features of the stimulus have to find their way into your long-term memory banks. Once there, the stimulus information is matched up with stored information about similar objects and is classified as an apple, allowing you to "know" that you are looking at an apple and perhaps even leading you to remember past experiences you've had that involved apples. The end result is the creation of conscious memories (conscious contents) but through processes that you have little conscious access to. Presumably you can remember what you had for dinner last night, but you are not likely to be able to explain the machinations your brain went through to pull that information out.

Even that most ghostly of cognitions, the mental image, is the product of unconscious processes. For example, the cognitive psychologist Stephen Kosslyn asked subjects to draw an imaginary island that contained certain objects (tree, hut, rock, etc.).[21] The subjects were then asked to imagine the map and focus on one of the objects. A test word was then given and the subjects had to press a button to indicate whether the word named one of the objects on the map. The amount of time taken to press the button was directly related to the distance between the object named by the test word and the object being imagined. This suggested to Kosslyn that the brain actually computes geometric distances in mental images. But the subjects did not deliberately perform these calculations. They just gave the answers by pressing a button. All the work was done by the brain operating unconsciously.

Just because your brain can do something does not mean that "you" know how it did it. If it seems odd that the brain can unconsciously solve geometric problems, imagine the kinds of automatic calculations that go on in the brain when we turn the steering wheel to navigate a curve at 60 mph, or better yet, the kinds of processes that go on in the nervous system of homing pigeons or honeybees as they fly out into the world in search of food and then effortlessly find their way home using an internal compass.

Speech, consciousness' favorite behavioral tool, is also the product of unconscious processes.[22] We do not consciously plan the grammatical structure of the sentences we utter. There simply isn't enough time. We aren't all great orators, but we usually say things that make sense linguistically. Speaking roughly grammatically is one of the many things that the cognitive unconscious takes care of for us.

The cognitive unconscious also extends to complex judgments about the mental origins of beliefs and actions. In 1977, Richard Nisbett and Timothy Wilson published an extremely interesting paper, "Telling More Than We Can Know: Verbal Reports on Mental Processes."[23] They created a number of carefully structured experimental situations in which people were required to do things and then say why they did what they did. In one study, they lined up several pairs of stockings on a table. Female subjects were then allowed to examine the stockings and to choose which one they liked best.

When the women were questioned, they had all sorts of wonderful answers about the texture and sheerness of the stockings that justified their choices. But unbeknownst to them, the stockings were identical. The subjects believed that they had decided on the basis of their internal judgments about the quality of the stockings. In this and a host of other studies, Nisbett and Wilson showed that people are often mistaken about the internal causes of their actions and feelings. Although the subjects always gave reasons, the reasons came not from privileged access to the processes that underlay their decisions, but from social conventions, or ideas about the way things normally work in such situations, or just plain guesses. Accurate introspective reports, Nisbett and Wilson say, often occur in life because the stimuli involved in causing the behavior or the belief are salient and plausible causes of these. But when salient and plausible stimuli are not available, people make up reasons and believe in them. In other words, the inner workings of important aspects of the mind, including our own understanding of why we do what we do, are not necessarily knowable to the conscious self.[24] We have to be very careful when we use verbal reports based on introspective analyses of one's own mind as scientific data.

Around the same time that Nisbett and Wilson were performing their studies, Michael Gazzaniga and I were engaged in studies of split-brain patients that led us to a similar conclusion.[25] It was well-known from earlier work by Gazzaniga and others that information presented exclusively to one hemisphere of a split-brain patient is unavailable to the other.[26] We capitalized on this as a model of how consciousness deals with information generated by an unconscious mental system. In other words, we secretly instructed the right hemisphere to perform some response. The left hemisphere observed the response but did not know why the response was performed. We then asked the patient why he did what he did. Since only the left hemisphere could talk, the verbal output reflected that hemisphere's understanding of the situation. Time after time, the left hemisphere made up explanations as if it knew why the response was performed. For example, if we instructed the right hemisphere to wave, the patient would wave. When we asked him why he was waving, he said he thought he saw someone he knew. When we instructed the right hemisphere to laugh, he told us that we were funny guys. The spoken explanations were based on the response produced rather than knowledge of why the responses were produced. Like Nisbett and Wilson's subjects, the patient was attributing explanations to situations as if he had introspective insight into the cause of the behavior when in fact he did not. We concluded people normally do all sorts of things for reasons they are not consciously aware of (because the behavior is produced by brain systems that operate unconsciously) and that one of the main jobs of consciousness is to keep our life tied together into a coherent story, a self-concept. It does this by generating explanations of behavior on the basis of our self-image, memories of the past, expectations of the future, the present social situation, and the physical environment in which the behavior is produced.[27]

Although a good deal remains uncertain about the cognitive unconscious,[28] it seems clear that much of mental life occurs outside of conscious awareness. We can have introspective access to the outcome of processing (in the form of conscious content), but not all processing gives rise to conscious content. Stimulus processing that does not reach awareness in the form of conscious content can nevertheless be stored implicitly or unconsciously (see chapter 7) and have important influences on thought and behavior at some later time.[29] Further, it is worth emphasizing that information can be simultaneously processed separately by systems that do and do not give rise to conscious content, leading to the conscious representation in some and the unconscious representation in other systems. We may sometimes be able to introspect and verbally describe the workings of the systems that create and use conscious representations, but introspection is not going to be very useful as a window into the workings of the vast unconscious facets of the mind. This will be an especially important point when we consider the emotional unconscious in the next chapter.

The field of cognitive science has been incredibly successful in its stated mission of understanding information processing, which turns out to mean the unconscious processing of information. We now have excellent models of how we perceive the world in an orderly fashion, remember events from the past, imagine stimuli that are not present, focus our attention on one stimulus while ignoring many others, solve logical problems, make decisions on the basis of incomplete information, make judgments about our beliefs, attitudes, and behaviors, and many other aspects of mental functioning.[30] That much of the processing involved in these functions occurs unconsciously has allowed cognitive science a luxury that earlier forms of mentalism did not have—the field could get on with the business of studying the mind without having to first solve the problem of consciousness.[31] This does not mean that consciousness is irrelevant or unimportant. It is so important that when it has come up in the past it has completely dominated the scientific pursuit of the mind. This time around, though, scientists have figured out that the unconscious aspects of the mind are also important. In fact, it is probably not too far off the mark to say that consciousness will only be understood by studying the unconscious processes that make it possible. In this regard, cognitive science seems right on track. We'll return to the topic of consciousness, and especially emotional consciousness, in Chapter 9.

The Mental Health of Machines

The *cognitive mind* (the mind being studied by cognitive scientists) can do some very interesting and complicated things. For example, it can play chess so well that real grand masters can be given a run for their money.[32] But the cognitive mind, when playing chess, does not feel driven to win. It doesn't enjoy putting its partner in checkmate, or feel saddened or annoyed if it loses a match. It is not distracted by the presence of an audience at a big game, by sudden anxiety over the realization that a mortgage payment is late, or by the need to go to the little chip's room. The cognitive mind can even be programmed to cheat at chess, but not to feel guilty when it does.

As one thumbs through some of the attempts to define cognitive science it is striking how often this field is characterized by saying that it is not about emotion. For example, in *The Mind's New Science: A History of the Cognitive Revolution*, Howard Gardner lists the deemphasis of affective or emotional factors as one of five defining features of cognitive science.[33] In his seminal 1968 textbook, *Cognitive Psychology*, Ulric Neisser states that the field is not about the dynamic factors (like emotions) that motivate behavior.[34] Jerry Fodor, in *The Language of Thought*, a groundbreaking book in the philosophy of cognitive science, describes emotions as mental states that fall outside the domain of cognitive explanation.[35] And Barbara von Eckardt, in a book titled *What Is Cognitive Science?* says that most cognitive scientists do not consider the study of emotions to be part of the field.[36] These cognitive scientists each pointed out that emotional factors are important aspects of the mind, but also emphasized that emotions are just not part of the cognitive approach to the mind.

What is it about emotion that has compelled cognitive scientists to separate it out from attention, perception, memory, and other bona fide cognitive processes? Why was emotion banned from the rehabilitation of the mind that took place in psychology's cognitive revolution?

For one thing, as we have seen, philosophers and psychologists have for millennia found it useful to distinguish thinking and feeling, cognition and emotion, as separate facets of mind. And following the work of philosophers like Bertrand Russell[37] in the early twentieth century, thinking came to be viewed as a kind of logic, now known, thanks to Fodor, as the language of thought.[38] When the computer metaphor came along, it was seen as more applicable to logical reasoning processes than to so-called *illogical* emotions. But, as we will see, cognition is not as logical as it was once thought and emotions are not always so illogical.

AI researchers realized early on that knowledge was needed in problem-solving machines—problem solvers with impeccable logic but without facts didn't get very far.[39] However, knowledge was a crutch to logic in these models. It is now believed that thinking does not normally involve the pure reasoned rules of logic.[40] This has been demonstrated in research by Philip Johnson-Laird.[41] He examined people's ability to draw logical conclusions from statements like: all artists are beekeepers, all beekeepers are chemists. He found that quite often people draw logically invalid conclusions, suggesting that if the human mind is a formal logic machine, it is a pretty poor one. People are rational, according to Johnson-Laird, they just don't achieve their rationality by following formal laws of logic. We use what Johnson-Laird calls mental models, hypothetical examples drawn from our past experiences in real life or from imagined situations. Other studies by Amos Tversky and Daniel Kahneman led to a similar view, but from a different angle.[42] They showed that people

use their implicit understanding of the way the world works, often relying on educated guesswork rather than formal principles of logic, to
solve the problems that they face in their daily lives. Economist
Robert Frank, however, goes further.[43] He argues that decision making is often not rational at all: "Many actions, purposely taken with
full knowledge of their consequences, *are* irrational. If people did not
perform them, they would be better off and they know it." He cites
examples such as battling endless red tape to get a small refund on a
defective product or weathering a snowstorm to cast a ballot that will
on its own have little impact in a race. Jorge Luis Borges' description
of the British and Argentine battle over the Falkland Islands, quoted
by Frank, says it all: "two bald men fighting over a comb." If cognition
is not just logic, and is sometimes illogical, then emotion might not
be as far afield from cognition as it was initially thought.

Many emotions are products of evolutionary wisdom, which
probably has more intelligence than all human minds together. The
evolutionary psychologists John Tooby and Leda Cosmides say that
the species' past goes a long way toward explaining the individual's
present emotional state.[44] What is irrational about responding to
danger with evolutionarily perfected reactions? Daniel Goleman
gives lots of examples of emotional intelligence in his recent book.[45]
Success in life, according to Goleman, depends on a high EQ (emotional quotient) as much or more than a high IQ. True, derailed emotions can lead to irrational and even pathological consequences, but
emotions themselves are not necessarily irrational. Aristotle, for example, saw anger as a reasonable response to an insult, and a number of philosophers have taken this view.[46] Antonio Damasio, a
neurologist, also stresses the rationality of emotion in his book
Descartes' Error.[47] He emphasizes the importance of *gut feelings* in
making decisions. And while early AI programs were most successful
at modeling logical processes, more recent models have gone far beyond this truly artificial approach and some even try to model aspects
of emotions. Some programs use emotional *scripts* or *schemas* (built-
in information that suggests what is likely to happen in certain situations: for example, in baseball games, classrooms, business meetings)
as aids to decision making and action, others try to simulate the
processes through which people evaluate or appraise the emotional
meanings of stimuli, and still others attempt to make use of our un-

derstanding of the emotional brain in order to model how emotions are processed.[48] The logical/illogical or rational/irrational distinction is not a very sharp one when it comes to separating emotion and cognition, and is certainly not a clean way of defining what a science of mind should be about.

The second reason why emotion was not rehabilitated in the cognitive revolution may have been because emotions have traditionally been viewed as subjective states of consciousness. To be afraid, angry, or happy is to be aware that you are having a particular kind of experience, to be conscious of that experience. Computers process information rather than have experiences (at least by most people's way of thinking). To the extent that cognitive science was the science of information processing, rather than a science of conscious content, then emotion, being an aspect of consciousness, did not necessarily fit comfortably in the program. Recently, though, as we'll see in Chapter 9, consciousness has come to be more and more a part of cognitive science. Consequently, the excuse that emotions are subjective states loses much of its appeal. But the subjective argument should have never carried much weight. There is really nothing more or less subjective about the experience of an emotion than about the experience of the redness of an apple or the memory of eating one. The study of visual perception or memory has not been held back simply because these brain functions have subjective correlates, and neither should the study of emotion.

As we will see in the next chapter, subjective emotional states, like all other states of consciousness, are best viewed as the end result of information processing occurring unconsciously. Just as we can study how the brain processes information unconsciously in perceiving visual stimuli and using visual information to guide behavior, we can study how the brain processes the emotional significance of stimuli unconsciously and uses this information to control behaviors appropriate to the emotional meaning of the stimuli. And just as we hope that studying how the brain processes visual stimuli will help us understand how it creates the accompanying subjective perceptual experiences, we hope that studying how the brain processes emotional information will help us understand how it creates emotional experiences. This does not mean that we will program computers to have these experiences. Instead, it means we can use information-processing ideas as the conceptual apparatus for understanding conscious experiences, including subjective emotional feelings, even if such experiences are themselves not computational states of computers.[49] More about this when we get to consciousness in Chapter 9.

So, emotion could have fit into the cognitive framework. The question is whether it should have been included in cognitive science, or, more to the point, whether the boundaries of cognitive science should now be expanded to include emotion, placing all of the mind under one big conceptual tent.

All along some cognitive scientists have recognized that emotion is important. AI pioneer Herbert Simon,[50] for example, argued in the early 1960s that cognitive models needed to account for emotions in order to approximate real minds, and around the same time social psychologist Robert Abelson[51] suggested that the field of cognitive psychology needed to turn toward "hot cognitions," as opposed to the "cold" logical processes that it had been focusing on. Philip Johnson-Laird and George Miller, two leading cognitive psychologists, made a similar point in the 1970s.[52] And recently, Alan Newell, another AI pioneer, writing about emotions, noted, "no satisfactory integration yet exists of these phenomena into cognitive science. But the mammalian system is clearly constructed as an emotional system."[53] These suggestions by leading cognitive scientists have finally begun to have an impact—more and more cognitive scientists are getting interested in emotions. The problem is, instead of heating up cognition, this effort has turned emotion cold—in cognitive models, emotions, filled with and explained by thoughts, have been stripped of passion (we're going to go into the cognitive theory of emotion and its unfortunate consequences in great detail in the next chapter).

In the final analysis, then, the processes that underlie emotion and cognition can be studied using the same concepts and experimental tools. Both involve unconscious information processing and the generation of conscious content (sometimes) on the basis of this processing. At the same time, though, it does not quite seem right that emotion should be subsumed under cognitive science. The experimental study of the mind should be done in a framework that conceives of the mind in its full glory. The artificial separation of cognition from the rest of the mind was very useful in the early days of cognitive science and helped establish a new approach to the mind. But now it is time to put cognition back into its mental context—to reunite cognition and emotion in the mind. Minds have thoughts as well as emotions and the study of either without the other will never be fully satisfying. Ernest Hilgard, an eminent psychologist, makes the point nicely when he says that sibling rivalry is as important a concept to child development as is the maturation of thought processes.[54] "Mind science" is the natural heir to the united kingdom of cognition and emotion. To call the study of cognition and emotion cognitive science is to do it a disservice.

Minds, Bodies, Emotions

The idea of what the mind is has changed a number of times since the early Greeks, many of whom were preoccupied with rationality, but tended to view the mind as having both knowable and unknowable facets. Descartes redefined the mind to include only what we are aware of, making mind and consciousness the same thing. Since consciousness was viewed as a unique human gift, other animals were treated as mindless creatures. Freud, in formalizing the unconscious as the home of primitive instincts and emotions, helped reestablish a mental link between animals and humans, and began to dethrone consciousness as the sole occupant of the mind. The behaviorists dismissed the whole idea of mind, and took a step that really put animals and people on the same continuum, but one involving behavioral rather than mental functions. Cognitive science resurrected the Greek idea of mind, mind as reason and logic. And because the kind of mental states that were being suggested in the earlier days were based on the rules of logic, which is closely tied up with the human capacity for language, cognitive science was, for some time, not very friendly to the idea of animal minds. The idea of the human mind as a carefully engineered machine seemed more appealing than the idea of the mind as a biological organ with an evolutionary history.

The emergence of ideas about unconscious processing, and the re-realization that mind is more than cognition, again puts major parts of the mental life of humans and other animals on a continuum and encourages cognitive scientists to study mental functions in the context of the machine in which the functions are housed rather than as complete abstractions. Reacting to the functionalist credo that the mind can be modeled independent of knowledge of how the brain works, philosopher Patricia Churchland and computational neuroscientist Terrence Sejnowski have argued, "Nature is more ingenious than we are. And we stand to miss all that power and ingenuity unless we attend to neurobiological plausibility. The point is, *evolution has already done it,* so why not learn how that stupendous machine, our brain, actually works?"[55]

The functionalist conception of mind as a program that can run on any machine (mechanical, electronic, biological) has been fairly easy to accept, or at least tolerate, in the area of cognition. The biological machine of relevance to cognition, of course, is the brain. And the idea that the brain is a cognitive computer is now commonplace. However, in emotions, unlike in cognitions, the brain does not usually function independently of the body. Many if not most emotions involve bodily responses.[56] But no such relation exists between cognitions and actions. In the case of cognitively driven responses, the response is arbitrarily linked to cognition. This is partly why cognition is so powerful—cognitions allow us to be flexibile, to choose how we will respond in a certain situation. Such responses are used by but are not essential to the cognition. The capacity to understand language, one of man's highest forms of cognition, and the form of cognition most closely tied to a specific set of expressive responses, works just fine in people who live their lives without being able to express this capacity in speech. In the case of emotion, though, the response of the body is an integral part of the overall emotion process. As William James, the father of American psychology, once noted, it is difficult to imagine emotions in the absence of their bodily expressions.[57]

We know our emotions by their intrusions (welcome or otherwise) into our conscious minds. But emotions did not evolve as conscious feelings. They evolved as behavioral and physiological specializations, bodily responses controlled by the brain, that allowed ancestral organisms to survive in hostile environments and procreate. If the biological machine of emotion, but not cognition, crucially includes the body, then the kind of machine that is needed to run emotion is different from the kind needed to run cognition. Even if the functionalist argument (that the hardware is irrelevant) could be accepted for mind as cognition (and it is not clear that it can), it would not seem to work for the emotional aspects of the mind (since the hardware does seem to make a difference when it comes to emotion).

Programming a computer to be conscious would be an essential first step toward programming it to have a full-blown emotional experience, since the feelings through which we know our emotions occur when we become conscious of the unconscious workings of emotional systems in the brain. However, even if a computer could be programmed to be conscious, it could not be programmed to have an emotion, as a computer does not have the right kind of composition, which comes not from the clever assembly of human artifacts but from eons of biological evolution.

3

BLOOD, SWEAT, AND TEARS

"My love was so hot as mighty nigh to burst my boilers."
Davy Crockett, *A Narrative of the Life of David Crockett.*[1]

IN SPITE OF THE benign neglect of the topic of emotion by cognitive science, scientists who study emotion have by no means ignored cognition. In fact, psychologists interested in emotion, seduced by the intellectual excitement and appeal of cognitive science, have for some time been preoccupied with attempts to explain emotions in terms of cognitive processes. By this way of thinking, an emotion is not different from a cognition—emotions are just thoughts about situations we find ourselves in. Although this approach has had its share of successes, these have come at a high price. In trading in the passion of an emotion for thoughts about it, cognitive theories have turned emotions into cold, lifeless states of mind. Lacking sound and fury, emotions as cognitions signify nothing, or at least nothing very emotional. Our emotions are full of blood, sweat, and tears, but you wouldn't know this from examining modern cognitive research on emotion. Emotion research wasn't always this way, so let's see how and why the transformation occurred.

Body Heat

Why do we run away if we notice that we are in danger? Because we are afraid of what will happen if we don't. This obvious (and incor-

rect) answer to a seemingly trivial question has been the central concern of a century-old debate about the nature of our emotions.

It all began in 1884 when William James published an article titled "What Is an Emotion?"[2] The article appeared in a philosophy
journal called *Mind*, as there were no psychology journals yet. It was
important, not because it definitively answered the question it raised,
but because of the way in which James phrased his response. He conceived of an emotion in terms of a sequence of events that starts with
the occurrence of an arousing stimulus and ends with a passionate
feeling, a conscious emotional experience. A major goal of emotion
research is still to elucidate this stimulus-to-feeling sequence—to figure out what processes come between the stimulus and the feeling.

James set out to answer his question by asking another: do we run
from a bear because we are afraid or are we afraid because we run?
He proposed that the obvious answer, that we run because we are
afraid, was wrong, and instead argued that we are afraid because we
run:

> Our natural way of thinking about . . . emotions is that the mental
> perception of some fact excites the mental affection called emotion,
> and that this latter state of mind gives rise to the bodily expression.
> My thesis on the contrary is that the bodily changes follow directly
> the PERCEPTION of the exciting fact, and that our feeling of the
> same changes as they occur IS the emotion.[3]

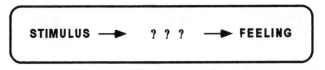

FIGURE 3-1
The Stimulus-to-Feeling Sequence.

*Identification of the processes that intervene between the occurrence of an
emotion-arousing stimulus and the conscious emotions (feelings) it elicits has
been one of the major goals of emotion research. Unfortunately, this goal has
often been pursued to the exclusion of some other equally important goals.*

The essence of James' proposal was simple. It was premised on the fact that emotions are often accompanied by bodily responses (racing heart, tight stomach, sweaty palms, tense muscles, and so on) and that we can sense what is going on inside our body much the same as we can sense what is going on in the outside world. According to James, emotions feel different from other states of mind because they have these bodily responses that give rise to internal sensations, and different emotions feel different from one another because they are accompanied by different bodily responses and sensations. For example, when we see James' bear, we run away. During this act of escape, the body goes through a physiological upheaval: blood pressure rises, heart rate increases, pupils dilate, palms sweat, muscles contract in certain ways. Other kinds of emotional situations will result in different bodily upheavals. In each case, the physiological responses return to the brain in the form of bodily sensations, and the unique pattern of sensory feedback gives each emotion its unique quality. Fear feels different from anger or love because it has a different physiological signature. The mental aspect of emotion, the feeling, is a slave to its physiology, not vice versa: we do not tremble

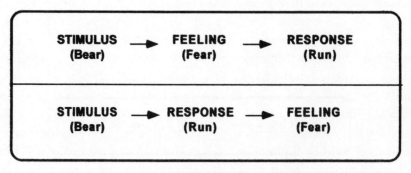

FIGURE 3-2
William James' Two Chains of Emotion.

The modern era in emotion research began when James asked whether feelings cause emotional responses or responses cause feelings. In answering that responses cause feelings, he started a century-old debate about where feelings come from. The question of what causes responses in the first place has, unfortunately, often been ignored.

```
STIMULUS ──► RESPONSE ──► FEEDBACK ──► FEELING
```

FIGURE 3-3
James' Feedback Theory.

James' solution to the stimulus-to-feeling sequence problem was that feedback from responses determine feelings. Since different emotions have different responses, the feedback to the brain will be different and will, according to James, account for how we feel in such situations.

because we are afraid or cry because we feel sad; we are afraid because we tremble and sad because we cry.

Fight or Flight

James' theory dominated the psychology of emotion until it was called into question in the 1920s by Walter Cannon, a prominent physiologist who had been researching the bodily responses that occur in states of hunger and intense emotion.[4] Cannon's research led him to propose the concept of an "emergency reaction," a specific physiological response of the body that accompanies any state in which physical energy must be exerted. According to Cannon's hypothesis, the flow of blood is redistributed to the body areas that will be active during an emergency situation so that energy supplies, which are carried in the blood, will reach the critical muscles and organs. In fighting, for example, the muscles will need energy more than the internal organs (the energy used for digestion can be sacrificed for the sake of muscle energy during a fight). The emergency reaction, or "fight-or-flight response," is thus an adaptive response that occurs in anticipation of, and in the service of, energy expenditure, as is often the case in emotional states.

The bodily responses that make up the emergency reaction were believed by Cannon to be mediated by the sympathetic nervous system, a division of the autonomic nervous system (ANS). The ANS is a web of neural cells and fibers located in the body that controls the activity of the internal organs and glands, the so-called internal milieu, in response to commands from the brain. The characteristic bodily signs of emotional arousal—like pounding hearts and sweaty palms—were known in Cannon's day to be the result of the activation of the sympathetic division of the ANS, which was believed to act in a uniform way, regardless of how or why it was activated. Given this supposed singularity of the sympathetic response mechanism, Cannon proposed that the physiological responses accompanying different emotions should be the same regardless of the particular emotional state that is experienced. As a result, James could not be right about why different emotions feel different, since all emotions, according to Cannon, have the same ANS signature.[5] Cannon also noted that ANS responses are too slow to account for feelings—we're already feeling the emotion by the time these responses occur. So even if different emotions had different bodily signatures, these would be too slow to account for whether we feel love, hate, fear, joy, anger, or disgust in a particular situation. The answer to the riddle of emotion, according to Cannon, is found completely within the brain, and does not require that the brain "read" the bodily response, as James had said.[6] We'll discuss the neural views espoused by James and Cannon in the next chapter, and we'll return to the issue of bodily feedback contributions to emotional experience in Chapter 9.

Cannon felt that while bodily feedback could not account for differences between emotions, it nevertheless played an important role, giving emotions their characteristic sense of urgency and intensity. Although James and Cannon disagreed about what distinguishes different emotions, they would seem to have agreed that emotions feel different from other (nonemotional) states of mind because of their bodily responses.

Passions as Reasons

During the behaviorists' reign in psychology, emotions, like other mental processes, were treated as ways of acting in certain situations.[7] There was little or no effort to explain what gives rise to conscious emotional experiences, as these were not recognized as legitimate phenomena for scientific investigation. The stimulus-to-feeling sequence was simply not an issue. In fact, the concept of emotion as a subjective state was often singled out by behaviorists as a prime example of the kind of fuzzy idea that needed to be dispensed with in a scientific psychology. It was one of the prime mental fictions, ghosts in the machine, created by psychologists to overcome their ineptness at explaining behavior.[8]

In the early 1960s, though, all this began to change. Stanley Schachter and Jerome Singer, social psychologists at Columbia University, revived the issue of where our feelings come from and proposed a new solution to the James-Cannon debate.[9] Like James, Schachter and Singer suggested that bodily arousal or feedback was indeed crucial in the genesis of an emotional experience, but not quite in the way that James had proposed. And, like Cannon, they believed that physiological feedback lacked specificity. Riding the tide of the cognitive revolution, which had begun to penetrate deep into the heart and soul of most areas of psychology by this time, they argued that cognitions (thoughts) fill the gap between the nonspecificity of feedback and the specificity of felt experiences.

Schachter and Singer started with the assumption that physiological responses in emotion (sweaty palms, rapid heart beat, muscle tension) inform our brain that a state of heightened arousal exists. However, since these responses are similar in many different emotions they do not identify what kind of aroused state we are in. Schachter and Singer suggested that, on the basis of information about the physical and social context in which we find ourselves, as well as knowledge about what kinds of emotions occur in these particular kinds of situations, we label the aroused state as fear or love or sadness or anger or joy. According to Schachter and Singer, this labeling of the aroused state is what gives rise to and accounts for the specificity of felt emotion. In other words, emotional feelings result when we explain emotionally ambiguous bodily states to ourselves on the basis of cognitive interpretations (so-called attributions) about what the external and internal causes of the bodily states might be.

The major prediction from the Schachter-Singer theory was that if ambiguous physiological arousal was induced in human subjects it should be possible to bias the kind of emotion experienced by arranging the social context in which the arousal occurs. Schachter and Singer tested this hypothesis by giving subjects injections of adrenaline, a drug that induces physiological arousal by artificially activating the sympathetic division of the ANS. The subjects were then exposed to either a pleasant, unpleasant, or emotionally neutral situation. As predicted, mood varied in accord with the context for the subjects given adrenaline but not for the control group that received placebo injections: adrenaline-treated subjects exposed to a joyful situation came out feeling happy, those exposed to an unpleasant situation came out feeling sad, and the neutral ones felt nothing in particular. Specific emotions were produced by the combination of artificial arousal and social cues. By inference, then, when emotionally ambiguous physiological arousal occurs naturally in the presence of real emotional stimuli, the aroused feeling is labeled on the basis of social cues. Emotions, in short, result from the cognitive interpretation of situations.

Stuart Valins, another social psychologist, performed a series of experiments to try to elucidate the nature of the cognition-arousal-emotion interaction.[10] Subjects were given inaccurate information about how their body was responding to some situation. For example, Valins showed male subjects pictures of partially nude women. The subjects were at the same time listening to a sound that was supposed to be indicative of the rate at which their heart was beating. Valins manipulated the sounds independent of true heart beat so that some

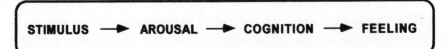

FIGURE 3-4
The Schachter-Singer Cognitive Arousal Theory.

Schachter and Singer, like Cannon, accepted that feedback is not specific enough to determine what emotion we feel in a given situation, but, like James they felt it was still important. Their idea was that feedback from bodily arousal is a good indicator that something significant is going on, even though it is not able to signal exactly what is happening. Once we detect bodily arousal (through feedback) we are then motivated to examine our circumstances. On the basis of our cognitive assessment of the situation, we then label the arousal. The labeling of arousal is what determines the emotion we feel. Cognitions thus fill the gap between the nonspecificity of bodily feedback and feelings for Schachter and Singer.

pictures were associated with high false heart rates and others with low rates. Later, the subjects judged as more attractive the pictures that had been associated with the high heart rate sounds, even though their actual heart rate was not high during exposure to these pictures. Valins concluded that in order for physiological activity to contribute to an emotional experience, the activity has to be represented cognitively. He argued that it is the cognitive representation of the physiological arousal, not the arousal itself, that interacts with thoughts about the situation in the generation of feelings.

The Schachter-Singer theory and the research that followed were criticized on many points.[11] The real impact of this work, though, was not so much that it explained where our emotions come from but instead that it revitalized an old notion, one that was implicit in the philosophical writings of Aristotle, Descartes, and Spinoza—that emotions might be cognitive interpretations of situations.[12] Schachter and Singer put the idea into a package that fit nicely into the cognitive pandemonium that was everywhere in psychology. The success of their efforts is exemplified by the fact that the psychology of emotion, to this day, is mostly about the role of cognition in emotion.

The Big Chill

Something was missing in the cognitive theory espoused by Schachter and Singer. They tried to explain how we deal with emotional responses once they occur (when you notice your heart beating and your forehead sweating as you begin to run away from a bear in the woods, you label the experience fear) but did not give an account of what generates the responses in the first place. Obviously, the brain has to figure out that the bear is a source of danger and has to arrange for the responses that are appropriate to danger to occur. The brain's emotional business is thus well underway by the time Schachter and Singer's mechanism kicks in. So what happens first? What makes us run from danger? What comes between the stimulus and the response? Cognitive evaluations, according to appraisal theorists, fill this gap.

The concept of appraisal was crystallized by Magda Arnold in an influential book on emotion published at about the same time that

Schachter and Singer were doing their experiments.[13] She defined appraisal as the mental assessment of the potential harm or benefit of a situation and argued that emotion is the "felt tendency" toward anything appraised as good or away from anything appraised as bad. Although the appraisal process itself occurs unconsciously, its effects are registered in consciousness as an emotional feeling.

Arnold's interpretation of James' bear-in-the-woods story would go like this: we perceive the bear and appraise it unconsciously, and our conscious experience of fear results from the tendency to run. In contrast to James, for Arnold the response does not need to occur in order to have the feeling—a feeling only requires an action tendency rather than an actual action. Emotions thus differ from nonemotional states of mind by the presence of appraisals in their causal sequence, and different emotions are distinguished from one another because different appraisals elicit different action tendencies, which give rise to different feelings.

In Arnold's view, once the appraisal outcome is registered in consciousness as a feeling, it becomes possible to reflect back on the experience and describe what went on during the appraisal process. This is possible because, according to Arnold, people have introspective access to (conscious awareness of) the inner workings of their mental life, and in particular access to the causes of their emotions. Arnold's approach assumes that we can, after an emotional experience, gain access to the unconscious processes that gave rise to the emotion. As we will see, this assumption is open to challenge.

The appraisal concept was adopted by other researchers in the 1960s. One of these was Richard Lazarus, a clinical psychologist who used the concept to understand the way people react to and cope with stressful situations.[14] Studies by Lazarus clearly showed that interpretations of situations strongly influence the emotion experienced. For example, in a classic experiment, subjects watched a gruesome film clip of a circumcision ritual involving teenage members of an aboriginal Australian tribe. For some subjects, the soundtrack verbally played up the gory details, whereas for others the episode was either minimized or intellectualized by the voice overlay. The group that had the first soundtrack, in which the gruesome details were emphasized, had stronger ANS responses and their self-reports suggested that they felt worse afterward than the other two

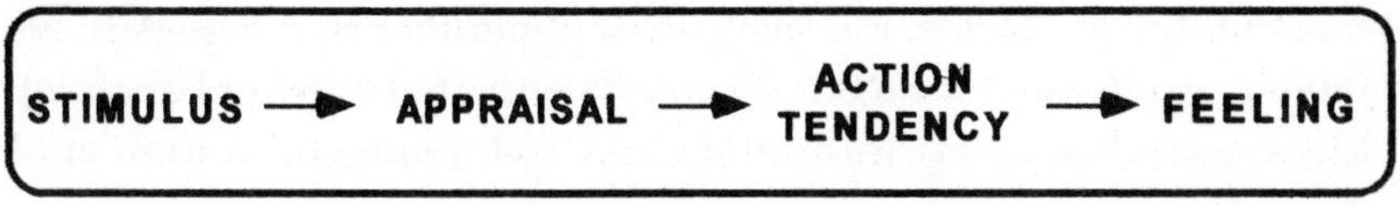

FIGURE 3-5
Arnold's Appraisal Theory.

Arnold argued that in order for a stimulus to produce an emotional response or an emotional feeling, the brain must first appraise the significance of the stimulus. Appraisals then lead to action tendencies. The felt tendency to move toward desirable objects and situations and away from undesirable ones is what accounts for conscious feelings in this model. Although appraisals can be either conscious or unconscious, we have conscious access to the appraisal processes after the fact.

groups, in spite of the fact that the arousing parts of the film were the same for all. Lazarus suggested that the different soundtracks caused the subjects to appraise the films in different ways and this led to different feelings about the situation. Lazarus argued that emotions can be initiated automatically (unconsciously) or consciously, but he emphasized the role of higher thought processes and consciousness, especially in coping with emotional reactions once they exist. Summarizing his position, he recently noted that "cognition is both a necessary and sufficient condition of emotion."[15]

Appraisal remains the cornerstone of contemporary cognitive approaches to emotion.[16] In the tradition started by Arnold, most work in this field has proceeded under the assumption that the best way to find out about appraisals is the old-fashioned way—to ask the subjects to introspect and figure out what went through their minds when they had some past emotional experience. For example, in a seminal study of these *emotion-antecedent appraisal processes* by Craig Smith and Phoebe Ellsworth, people were asked to recall a past experience implied by emotion words (pride, anger, fear, disgust, happiness, etc.) and to rate the recalled experiences on different dimensions (pleasantness, effort involved, self-other involvement, attentional activity, controllability, etc.).[17] They found that remembered experiences triggered by thoughts about emotion words could be accounted for by the interplay of several different appraisals. For example, pride was characterized as occurring in situations involving pleasantness associated with little effort but much concentration of attention and personal responsibility, whereas anger involved unpleasantness associated with much effort, lack of control, and someone else being responsible. Smith and Ellsworth concluded that people's emotions are intimately related to their cognitive appraisals of their circumstances and that it is possible to gain insights into them by asking people to reflect back on what different emotions are like. These and other researchers assume that the kind of information that subjects use when they reflect back on an emotional experience is the same kind of information that the brain uses in creating the emotional experiences.[18]

To my mind, appraisal theories came very close to getting things right: the evaluation of a stimulus is clearly the first step in the initiation of an emotional episode; appraisals occur unconsciously; emotion involves action tendencies and bodily responses, as well as conscious experiences. But appraisal theories took two wrong turns on the road to understanding the emotional mind. First, they based their understanding of appraisal processes largely on self-reports—introspective verbal reflections. As we saw in the last chapter, introspection is often a blurry window into the workings of the mind. And if there is one thing about emotions that we know well from introspection, it is that we are often in the dark about why we feel the way we do. Second, appraisal theories overemphasized the contribution of cognitive processes in emotion, thereby diminishing the distinc-

FIGURE 3-6
General Purpose Appraisal Model.

Following Arnold, many psychologists today recognize the importance of appraisal processes in emotional phenomena, but they do not necessarily accept Arnold's equation of emotional feelings with action tendencies. The general-purpose appraisal model shown here thus simply suggests that appraisals fill the stimulus-to-feeling gap.

tion between emotion and cognition. Given that a major failing of cognitive science as a science of mind is its lack of concern with emotion (see Chapter 2), it is not too surprising that the cognitive approach to emotion suffers from the same problem—in emphasizing cognition as the explanation of emotion, the unique aspects of emotion that have traditionally distinguished it from cognition are left behind.

The Psychologist Who Came in from the Cold

By 1980, the cognitive approach to emotion was just about the only approach. But this began to change with the publication of a paper by social psychologist Robert Zajonc (pronounced, zy-unce).[19] The paper was called "Feeling and Thinking: Preferences Need No Inferences." It very persuasively argued, on the basis of logic and clever experiments, that preferences (which are simple emotional reactions) could be formed without any conscious registration of the stimuli. This, he said, showed that emotion has primacy over (can exist before) and is independent of (can exist without) cognition. The net effect was a stall, rather than the demise, of the cognitive approach to emotion, as much appraisal research has occurred in the years following Zajonc's paper. Nevertheless, Zajonc had a major impact on the field, keeping alive the idea that an emotion is not just a cognition.

Zajonc summarized several experiments that he and his colleagues had performed using a psychological phenomenon, called the mere exposure effect, that he had discovered earlier. If subjects are exposed to some novel visual patterns (like Chinese ideograms) and then asked to choose whether they prefer the previously exposed or new patterns, they reliably tend to prefer the preexposed ones. Mere exposure to stimuli is enough to create preferences.

The twist to the new experiment was to present the stimuli subliminally—so briefly that the subjects were unable in subsequent tests to accurately state whether or not they had seen the stimulus before. Nevertheless, the mere exposure effect was there. The subjects judged the previously exposed items as preferable over the new (previously unseen) ones, in spite of the fact that they had little ability to consciously identify and distinguish the patterns that they had seen from those that they had not. As Zajonc put it, these results go against common sense and against the widespread assumption in psychology that we must know what something is before we can determine whether we like it or not. If in some situations emotion could be present without recognition of the stimulus, then recognition could not be viewed as a necessary precursor to emotion.

The subliminal mere exposure effect has been confirmed by many different laboratories and the idea that preferences can be formed for stimuli that do not enter consciousness seems rock solid.[20] However, Zajonc's interpretation was controversial. He argued that the absence of conscious recognition meant that preferences (emotions) were forming without the aid of cognition—that emotion and cognition are separate functions of the mind. As we saw in Chapter 2, many information-processing functions that are considered prototypical examples of cognition also occur without conscious awareness. The absence of conscious recognition is not, strictly speaking, a useful basis for exclusion of cognition from emotional processing. At the same time, although Zajonc's studies did not prove that emotion and cognition are separable aspects of the mind, this does not mean that the opposite is correct, a point that we will return to at the end of the chapter.

Regardless of the relevance of Zajonc's subliminal mere exposure studies for understanding whether emotion depends on cognition, the experiments provided incontrovertible evidence that affective re-

FIGURE 3-7
Zajonc's Affective Primacy Theory.

Contrary to much work in psychology, Zajonc has argued that affect precedes and occurs independent of cognition. This controversial hypothesis has been heatedly debated. What seems clear now is that emotional processing can occur in the absence of conscious awareness, but that this is a different issue from whether emotion and cognition are independent.

actions could take place in the absence of conscious awareness of the stimuli. Although some appraisal theories accept that appraisal is, or can be, unconscious, they have tended to also suggest that the individual has conscious access to the processes underlying appraisals (thus justifying the use of verbal reports to identify emotion-antecedent appraisal processes). If unconscious occurrences such as those found by Zajonc were commonplace, rather than esoteric outcomes of a clever experimental design, the conscious introspections that make up the database of appraisal theory would not be a very solid foundation for an understanding of the emotional mind.

The Emotional Unconscious

Zajonc was certainly not the first experimental psychologist to be interested in the emotional unconscious. There was a time, back around mid-century, when the emotional unconscious was quite the rage in psychology. It all began with the New Look movement,[21] which challenged the stimulus-response view of perception espoused by the behaviorists. The New Look argued that perceptions are constructions that integrate sensory information about physical stimuli with internal factors, such as needs, goals, attitudes, and emotions. When New Look psychologists started doing experiments showing that subjects could have ANS responses to emotionally charged stimuli in the absence of conscious awareness of the stimuli (see below), it seemed as though the gap between two strange (if not estranged) bedfellows, psychology and psychoanalysis, might be closing.[22] After all, the unconscious, and especially the emotional unconscious, is the linchpin of psychoanalytic theory.

After a brief period of enthusiastic reception, the unconscious perception studies of the New Look were extensively criticized and they were essentially dismissed. Unconscious perception just did not make sense to many psychologists, as there was no adequate framework for thinking about perception without awareness of the perceived stimulus. The cognitive movement and its emphasis on unconscious processing was knocking on the door, but psychology was still strongly behavioristic, and verbal responses were the primary behaviors of interest in research on humans. As one commentator,

Matthew Erdelyi of Brooklyn College, noted, there is a certain irony in this history.[23] Studies of unconscious processing were being buried at just the time that cognitive science was beginning to discredit the behaviorist preconceptions that made non-verbalizable perceptions seem impossible. But there is another irony here—that behaviorists, whose field was created to rid psychology of ghostly concepts like consciousness, should have befriended conscious introspections (verbal reports) as a method for validating psychological ideas.[24] Below, we will take a look at some early unconscious perception studies and the criticisms of them, and then turn to the new wave of research on this topic.

One of the major areas of research on unconscious processing to come out of the New Look involved *perceptual defense*, the demonstration that "dirty" words have a higher threshold for stimulus recognition than comparable words that lack sexual, scatological, or other taboo connotations. In a typical experiment, subjects were shown words on a screen. By varying the amount of time that the words were shown, it was possible to determine the amount of time a particular subject needed to recognize a given word. It was discovered that the exposure time required for "taboo" words (e.g., bitch, fuck, Kotex, cancer) was longer than for words lacking taboo connotations.[25] The results were interpreted in terms of Freudian defense mechanisms, particularly repression: the taboo words were perceived subconsciously and censured (prevented from entering consciousness) because their appearance in consciousness would have elicited anxiety.

A related line of work involved *subliminal perception*. One of the classic studies was performed by Richard Lazarus, before his appraisal theory days.[26] In that experiment, patterns of letters were briefly flashed on a screen using exposure durations that were determined to be too short to allow verbal identification. Some of the patterns had been previously paired with an electric shock in order to transform the meaningless letters into emotionally charged stimuli capable of eliciting ANS responses. When these conditioned emotional stimuli were presented subconsciously, but not when emotionally neutral stimuli occurred, the ANS responded, indicating that the emotional meaning of the conditioned stimuli had been registered, in spite of the fact that the subjects reported no awareness of the stimuli (ANS responses have been a favorite in this kind of work since they do not depend on verbal processes and can thus be used to track emotions that occur in the absence of the ability to verbally describe the stimulus).

Marketing experts seized upon the implications of subliminal perception research, hoping to surreptitiously influence consumers to buy products. A theater in New Jersey, for example, gave audiences quick flashes of the phrase "Drink Coke" or "Eat popcorn" in order to promote visits to the concession stand.[27] Whether the tactic actually worked or not is not clear, but the public was outraged over this unethical act of manipulation and the invasion of privacy.[28] In point of fact, though, the advertising industry uses emotional cues (implicitly and explicitly) to persuade consumers to buy products all the time. Persuasion is, after all, their business, as Vance Packard noted in a famous book, *The Hidden Persuaders*.[29] Persuasion always works better when the persuadee is not aware that he or she is being influenced.[30] Implicit messages are the bread and butter of many advertising campaigns.

In spite of a great deal of initial interest in the theoretical implications of the perceptual defense and subliminal perception experiments, the interpretation of the results in terms of unconscious perception of emotional meaning was called into question by Charles Eriksen in the early 1960s.[31] Eriksen believed that unconscious perception was a logical impossibility[32] and he challenged this interpretation of the findings. He argued that the failure of the subjects in perceptual defense studies to verbally identify the taboo stimuli was due, not to the failure of the stimulus to enter consciousness, but to an unwillingness of the subjects to say these embarrassing words in public. And the inability of subjects in the subliminal perception experiments to verbally identify the secret stimuli was due, not to a failure to consciously perceive the stimuli, but to imperfections of verbal processes when it comes to accurately characterizing perceptual experiences.

Widespread acceptance of Eriksen's critique sealed research on the emotional unconscious into what seemed to be a coffin, but turned out to be a time capsule. After somewhat of a hiatus in the 1960s and 1970s, a new surge of interest in unconscious emotional processes emerged, spurred on by Zajonc's studies and by Matthew Erdelyi's reinterpretation of the perceptual defense and subliminal perception work in terms of the principles of cognitive science.[33] Nevertheless, within the psychology of emotion, especially amongst the cognitively minded appraisal theorists, the emphasis has remained on the conscious, verbally accessible aspects of emotion. The evidence for the existence of unconscious aspects of emotion is often ignored or denied, or when accepted is given second billing to the conscious aspects. As several researchers who work on unconscious processes have stated, they are so busy trying to prove that unconscious processing exists that there is little time to actually explore how it works.[34] But due to the creation of new and improved techniques for studying unconscious processing,[35] the existence proofs now seem clear. Below I will review some of the evidence showing that emotional processing can take place outside of conscious awareness. Some of the work involves subliminal stimulation, whereas other studies utilize stimuli that are consciously perceived but their emotional implications are implicit and not noticed at the time the stimulus is seen or heard.

Zajonc's subliminal mere exposure studies were some of first to use the new techniques that made unconscious processing seem undeniable. In the wake of this research, many similar experiments were performed. In one particularly interesting variation by Robert Bornstein, subjects were brought into the laboratory and given very brief exposures to pictures of faces.[36] As expected, they were unable to identify which ones they had seen before, but when asked to rate how much they liked the pictures, the preexposed ones received more positive ratings. Mere exposure works for faces. In a second part of the study, the subjects were given brief (subliminal/unconscious) exposures to pictures of person A or of person B. Then, the subject, together with persons A and B, was asked to try to decide on the gender of the author of several poems. By a prearrangement unknown to the subject, A and B disagreed and the subject had to break the tie. As predicted by the mere exposure hypothesis, the subjects tended to side with the person whose face they had been unconsciously exposed to. Familiarity does not necessarily breed contempt. Bornstein later performed what is called a "meta-analysis" of subliminal mere exposure research, which means he analyzed the published data from many different studies.[37] This led him to conclude that the mere exposure effect is much stronger when the stimuli are subliminally presented than when the stimuli are freely available for conscious inspection. This turns out to be a common finding in a number of different kinds of studies of unconscious emotional processing, and it emphasizes a point that we will see time and again—our emotions are more easily influenced when we are not aware that the influence is occurring.

The emotional unconscious has also been studied with a procedure called subliminal emotional priming that has been used extensively by Zajonc and several of his associates in recent years.[38] In this kind of experiment, a priming stimulus with some emotional connotation, such as a picture of a frowning or smiling face, is presented very briefly (5 milliseconds, or 1/200th of a second) and is immediately followed by a masking stimulus, which eliminates the subject's ability to consciously recall the prime—the mask displaces the prime from consciousness, essentially blanking it out. Following a delay, a target stimulus pattern is presented. It remains on a comfortable amount of time (seconds) and is consciously perceived. After seeing many patterns in this way, the subject is asked to rate how much they liked the target stimuli. Zajonc found that whether the subjects liked or disliked a stimulus (for example, a Chinese ideogram) was related to whether the stimulus was primed by an unconscious smile or frown. The target stimulus acquired emotional significance by virtue of its relationship with an emotional meaning activated subliminally by the unconsciously processed smile or frown. And, as in the mere exposure work, the emotional priming was much more effective for subliminal (masked, thus unconscious) presentations than for presentations that were not masked and where conscious awareness of the stimulus was possible.

And then there is the Pöetzl effect.[39] Otto Pöetzl, a Viennese psychiatrist, performed studies in 1917 in which a complex visual picture, like a landscape, was shown to subjects subliminally. He then asked the subjects to draw as much of the picture as possible. Afterward, the subjects were instructed to go home and have a dream that night, and then come back the next day. When they returned to the laboratory, they were asked to report on the dream and draw pictures related to the dream. Poetzl claimed that features of the original picture that were not included in the first drawing emerged in the drawing of the dream.

Matthew Erdelyi has profitably exploited the Pöetzl effect to explore the nature of unconscious processes.[40] In one study Erdelyi presented subjects with a complex visual scene for 500 milliseconds. This is not a subliminal presentation, as there is plenty time for parts of the stimulus to enter into awareness. The purpose of using this duration was to allow some but not all of the scene to be consciously perceived. In fact, though, you can get the same result by allowing the subject to just look at the picture freely since in any complex scene there will always be stimulus elements that are noticed and others that are not,[41] and of those that are noticed some will be recalled and some not. In Erdelyi's study, after the flash, the subjects were then asked to draw as much of the scene as possible. Some then engaged in a period of free association and fantasy while others played a game of darts. They then made drawings of the picture again. Erdelyi found that the second drawings often reflected previously unremembered aspects of the stimulus for the subjects allowed to fantasize and free associate but not for the dart game group. Erdelyi calls this effect "hypermnesia," by which he means an improvement in memory—the recovery of a previously inaccessible memory. Hypermnesia has been shown by Erdelyi using his modified Pöetzl procedure and several other kinds of techniques, and he believes that the recovery of memory, by dreaming, and by fantasy and free association while awake, represents the release of memories from suppression by other factors.

Through therapeutic sessions with patients, psychoanalyst Howard Shevrin identified words related to their conscious experience of a symptom or to the unconscious conflict underlying the symptom.[42] For example, a patient may come to the analyst complaining of being extremely uncomfortable in social situations. The patient is thus fully conscious of this social phobia, but does not consciously know the cause of the problem. After the analytic sessions, Shevrin came up

FIGURE 3-8
Hypermnesia Stimulus:

Complex visual scene used by Erdelyi to study the effects of fantasy and dream-ing on memory recall. Subjects examined the picture briefly. The next day they were asked to recall as much as they could about the picture. See text for de-tails. (From *Psychoanalysis: Freud's Cognitive Psychology* by Erdelyi. Copyright © 1985 by Mathew Hugh Erdelyi. Used with permission of W.H. Freeman and Company.)

with a set of individually tailored words that he felt captured aspects of either the unconscious conflict or the conscious symptoms. He then presented them subliminally or openly to the patients while "brain waves" were recorded from their scalps. For the words related to the unconscious conflict (the underlying cause of the social pho-bia), the brain waves were more strongly elicited by subliminal pre-sentations, whereas for the words related to the conscious symptom (fear of social situations), the brain waves were more strongly elicited when the stimuli were consciously perceived. Again, the emotional mind seems to be particularly susceptible to stimuli that its conscious counterpart does not have access to.

Finally, social psychologist John Bargh has performed many ex-periments showing that emotions, attitudes, goals, and intentions can be activated without awareness, and that these can influence the way people think about and act in social situations.[43] For example, physical features (like skin color or hair length) are enough to activate racial or gender stereotypes, regardless of whether the person possessing the feature expresses any of the behavioral characteristics of the stereotype. This kind of automatic activation of attitudes occurs in a variety of different situations and appears to constitute our first reaction to a person. And once activated, these attitudes can influence the way we then treat the person, and can even have influences over our behavior in other situations. In one dramatic example, Bargh had subjects participate in what they thought was a language test. They were given words on cards and had to make sentences out of them. For some subjects, the sentences were about elderly people, whereas other subjects received sentences about other topics. After completing the task, the subjects left the room. Unbeknownst to them, the amount of time taken to walk down the hall to a designated location was timed by the experimenters. Remarkably, the subjects that had unscrambled sentences about elderly people took longer to cover the distance than the other subjects. The sentences did not include any specific statements about old people being slow or weak, but simply thinking (and pretty indirect thinking at that) about old people was enough to activate this stereotype and influence their behavior. In other studies subjects unscrambled sentences having to do with either "assertiveness" or "politeness." They were then told to walk down the hall and find the experimenter, who, by prearrangement, was involved in a conversation with someone. The amount of time the subjects waited before interrupting was recorded. Those primed with assertiveness interrupted sooner than those primed with politeness. Bargh notes that this automatic activation of unconscious processes has an upside and a downside. If we are nice to someone they may indeed be nice to us in return. On the other hand, if seeing someone from another racial group activates a negative attitude (e.g., that persons of that group are hostile and aggressive), we may act negatively toward them, prompting them in return to act negatively toward us, creating a vicious circle that further perpetuates the stereotype.

In the two studies described above, the priming stimuli were consciously available but their meanings were implicit. Nevertheless, other studies show similar effects when the social primes are presented subliminally. Bargh argues that whether the subjects are aware of the priming stimulus is less critical than whether they are aware of the ways in which the stimuli are implicitly (without awareness) categorized and interpreted. The fact that emotions, attitudes, goals, and the like are activated automatically (without any conscious effort) means that their presence in the mind and their influence on thoughts and behavior are not questioned. They are trusted the way we would trust any other kind of perception. In other words, the perception in oneself of an attitude (disguised as fact) about a racial group can seem to be as valid as the perception of the color of their skin. When one is aware of biases and possesses values against having these, he or she can exercise control over them. However, the ability to do this depends on being aware of the unconscious influences, which is quite another matter. As cognitive psychologist Larry Jacoby asks and answers: "When are unconscious influences expected to have their largest effects? . . . When you least expect them."[44] According to Bargh, a goal of social psychology should be to make people aware of these nonintuitive, scientifically discovered unconscious factors that affect thought and behavior. But he admits that this is an uphill battle: "Inasmuch as people check such a proposition against their own phenomenal experience to test its validity, we will never be persuasive, because by definition one can never have any phenomenal experience of perception without awareness."[45]

As we look back on almost a half a century of research on unconscious processing, it is fair to say that some of the early studies may indeed not have used techniques that allow one to completely rule out the possibility of some awareness of the stimuli. But science is progressive, and the mistakes of the past are part of the wisdom of the present. We have learned a great deal about how subliminal perception research should be conducted and interpreted, and research today has higher standards of what counts as an unconscious perception.[46] When we apply the new, clever, and strict ways of evaluating whether information processing takes place unconsciously, we still reach the conclusion that emotional meanings can be processed at subconscious levels. Just because the research methods of the past may have lacked perfection does not mean that the results were wrong. It now seems undeniable that the emotional meanings of stimuli can be processed unconsciously. The emotional unconscious is where much of the emotional action is in the brain.[47]

A Reappraisal

From James onward an important gap was left in the causal chain leading to emotional responses and emotional experiences, and something like appraisal was needed. The gap occurs between the arrival of the emotion-provoking stimulus and the resulting physiological responses and/or feelings. In James' theory, the perception of the stimulus automatically (without conscious participation) produces the responses that provide the feedback that defines the feeling. But not all stimuli that are perceived do this. Something else has to happen. The physical features of the stimulus have to be evaluated—appraised; their significance to the individual has to be determined. It is this computed significance that starts the emotion ball rolling. This is the case for all of the theories that have been described. The brain has to evaluate a stimulus and decide whether that stimulus should be ignored or should lead to some reaction. Appraisal, in other words, fills the gap between stimuli and responses and between stimuli and feelings. But, in my view, appraisal theories did not quite get it right, as they required that the appraisal mechanism get all involved in introspectively accessible levels of higher cognition from the start.

The inadequacy of any approach to emotion based solely or mainly on introspectively accessible aspects of the mind is apparent from the experimental studies described above showing that much of emotional processing occurs (or can occur) unconsciously, as well as by the fact that people often find their emotions puzzling. Consciously accessible appraisal processes cannot be the way, or at least not the only way, the emotional brain works. Even when we are conscious of the outcome of some emotional appraisal (for example, knowing that you dislike someone), this does not mean that you consciously understand the basis of the appraisal (knowing why you dislike the person). The conscious outcome might be based on nonverbalizable intuitions, so-called gut feelings,[48] rather than on some verbalizable set of propositions.

Proponents of folk psychology (a kind of introspective psychology), argue that people know what is in their minds and they use this information all the time.[49] They point out that people are very good at accounting for their mental life and behavior on the basis of self-knowledge and their general understanding of the way other people's minds work. For example, if I say I will pick up my son at school at a certain time, chances are I will do it. If I see you arguing with your spouse, chances are I'll be correct if I assume you are mad. The folk psychologist says that examples like this add proof to the idea that age-old wisdom constitutes a scientifically correct theory of mind that we all have in our heads. But even though I am consciously aware of my decision to pick my son up and may even consciously re-member to carry out the plan, this does not mean that I know how I remembered to do it. And even though I may be correct when I de-cide you are angry, that does not mean that I know how I made my decision or that I know what it is in your brain that accounts for your anger. The biologist Stephen J. Gould makes a good point: "Science is not 'organized common sense'; at its most exciting, it reformulates our view of the world by imposing powerful theories against the an-cient, anthropocentric prejudices that we call intuition."[50] When I say I'm angry, I may be, but I might also be wrong. I might really be afraid or jealous or some combination of all of these. Donald Hebb pointed out long ago that outside observers are far more accurate at judging a person's true emotional state than is the person himself.[51] I'm not denying that people are consciously aware of certain things and that they can consciously do things. All I'm saying is that some, perhaps many, of the things we do, including the appraisal of the emotional significance of events in our lives and the expression of emotional behaviors in response to those appraisals, do not depend on consciousness, or even on processes that we necessarily have con-scious access to.

Noting that emotions can sometimes be puzzling, the philoso-pher Amelie Rorty makes a distinction between the apparent cause of an emotion (the stimuli immediately available and consciously per-ceived) and the actual cause.[52] The real cause of an emotion is not necessarily some immediately present stimuli, but instead may involve the interaction of these with a causal history stored in memory. As we have seen, unnoticed events can activate memories, including emotional memories, implicitly (without awareness), and implicit and undetected meanings of consciously perceived stimuli can do the same. A father who yells at his children may rationalize his outburst by saying that the children were misbehaving. But the outburst may also be due in part to the fact that he had a bad day at the office, or even to the way his parents treated him as a child, and at the time he may not be consciously aware of these influences at all. The cause of an emotion can, in other words, be very different from the reasons we use to explain the emotion to ourselves or others after the fact. Appraisal theories have dealt with reasons rather than causes.

Two of the leading appraisal theorists, Nico Frijda and Klaus Scherer, have both recently acknowledged significant limitations of the research foundation of much of cognitive appraisal. Frijda says: "investigating the relationships between appraisals and emotion labels is research into emotion word meanings or into the structures of experience, as distinct from research that qualifies as investigation of emotion antecedents. . . . Emotions may well result from appraisal processes, but these need not be those suggested by the self reports."[53] Along similar lines, Scherer says that the emphasis of appraisal research on mapping emotion words onto emotion experiences has left the field concentrating on the content of experiences and the way experiences are verbally labeled to the exclusion of the true processes that give rise to appraisals.[54] And in an insightful discussion of unconscious processes, Kenneth Bowers makes the interesting point that if our understanding of the causation of thought and action were directly available to introspection, we would not need the field of psychology.[55] Indeed, it was the inadequacy of introspection that led to behaviorism, and the success of cognitive science as an alternative to behaviorism is due in large measure to its ability to investigate the mind without relying exclusively or mainly on introspection.

Some appraisals lead to conscious awareness of the appraisal outcome, whereas others do not. Introspections are often going to be a poor window into how processing that gives rise to conscious content works and are no window at all into processing that does not give rise to immediate conscious content. Although cognitive appraisal theorist Richard Lazarus has emphasized conscious appraisal processes in emotions, he has always accepted that unconscious appraisals occur and recently he argued: "although it is a daunting task, I believe we must . . . find effective ways of exploring what lies below the surface, how it relates to what is in awareness, and how it influences the entire emotion process."[56] Similarly, Klaus Scherer recently challenged his colleagues who study human appraisal processes to rely more on techniques that do not depend on verbal reports. Scherer also suggests that appraisal researchers turn to brain science to try to validate mechanisms that psychologists uncover.[57] I go one step further and argue that we might turn to brain research to find novel mechanisms that psychologists have not thought of or to find novel interpretations of existing mechanisms.

Introspective understanding of the causes of emotion states can be weak, especially when people are asked to reflect back on an episode after it is over.[58] And even if they are asked right away they may still not know the actual cause. There is much more to explain about an emotion than what one can get at from retrospective consciously accessible thoughts about the situation. But this does not mean that introspection is useless. There are some kinds of mental events that we have introspective access to and others that we do not. The trick, obviously, is to figure out where the dividing line is. However, the line is both thin and fuzzy—it may not be in the same place in different people and in a given individual it may move from moment to moment.[59] There is much to be learned about conscious experience by studying introspections. But if emotions reflect processes that also occur unconsciously, as it seems they do, then we need to take these into consideration as well.

Emotion and Cognition: Two Sides of the Same Coin, or Different Currency?

So far I have tried to present a strong case for the argument that much emotional processing occurs unconsciously and therefore that there is more to an emotion than what we can glean from our intro-spections about it. But the same argument was made about cognition in the previous chapter—that not all aspects of thinking, reasoning, problem solving, and intelligence can be understood on the basis of introspections. Given that emotional and cognitive processing both largely occur unconsciously, it is possible that emotional and cogni-tive processing are the same, or, as it is usually said, that emotion is just a kind of cognition.

There is a benign and a not-so-benign version of the idea that emotion is a kind of cognition. In both versions, the terms "cognitive" and "mental" are used interchangeably. This is clearly a departure from the approach of early cognitive scientists, who saw cognition as the part of the mind having to do with thinking and reasoning, but not with emotion and some other mental processes like motivation and personality (see Chapter 2).

In the benign version, the boundaries of cognition are moved so that, in addition to including thinking, reasoning, and intelligence, it also includes emotion. In this scheme, nothing fundamental changes in the way emotion is conceived—cognition and emotion are given equal billing in a field that studies both. This is simply a semantic is-sue about what the mind, and its science, should be called. I prefer the term "mind science" over "cognitive science" for this all-encompassing approach to the mind. Although this is somewhat a matter of prefer-ence, it is not an idle one. It is an attempt to prevent one from slid-ing from the benign to the not-so-benign version, in which emotion is perversely reconceived as thinking and reasoning.

In the not-so-benign version, then, "cognitive" and "mental" are equated by squeezing emotion into the traditional view of cogni-tion—cognition as thinking and reasoning. This, as we have seen, is the unfortunate way the study of emotion has gone since the early 1960s—the essence of an emotion has been altered in order that emotions could be conceived as reasoned thoughts about situations. It is this trend that Zajonc was reacting to when he proposed that emotion and cognition should be kept separate. But the heated de-bate over the relation of emotion to cognition got caught up in a va-riety of technical issues and this broader concern was lost.[60]

My desire to protect emotion from being consumed by the cogni-

tive monster comes from my understanding of how emotion is organized in the brain. Although the brain organization of emotion is the
subject of other chapters, I will summarize several key points that
justify my belief that emotion and cognition are best thought of as
separate but interacting mental functions mediated by separate but
interacting brain systems.

- When a certain region of the brain is damaged, animals or humans lose the capacity to appraise the emotional significance
  of certain stimuli without any loss in the capacity to perceive
  the same stimuli as objects. The perceptual representation of
  an object and the evaluation of the significance of an object are
  separately processed by the brain.
- The emotional meaning of a stimulus can begin to be appraised by the brain before the perceptual systems have fully
  processed the stimulus. It is, indeed, possible for your brain to
  know that something is good or bad before it knows exactly
  what it is.
- The brain mechanisms through which memories of the emotional significance of stimuli are registered, stored, and retrieved are different from the mechanisms through which
  cognitive memories of the same stimuli are processed. Damage
  to the former mechanisms prevents a stimulus with a learned
  emotional meaning from eliciting emotional reactions in us,
  whereas damage to the latter mechanism interferes with our
  ability to remember where we saw the stimulus, why we were
  there, and who we were with at the time.
- The systems that perform emotional appraisals are directly
  connected with systems involved in the control of emotional
  responses. Once an appraisal is made by these systems, responses occur automatically. In contrast, systems involved in
  cognitive processing are not so tightly coupled with response
  control systems. The hallmark of cognitive processing is flexibility of responses on the basis of processing. Cognition gives
  us choices. In contrast, activation of appraisal mechanisms
  narrows the response options available to a few choices that
  evolution has had the wisdom to connect up with the particu-

lar appraisal mechanism. This linkage between appraisal process and response mechanisms constitutes the fundamental mechanism of specific emotions.

- The linkage of appraisal mechanisms with response control systems means that when the appraisal mechanism detects a significant event, the programming and often the execution of a set of appropriate responses will occur. The net result is that bodily sensations often accompany appraisals and when they do they are a part of the conscious experience of emotions. Because cognitive processing is not linked up with responses in this obligatory way, intense bodily sensations are less likely to occur in association with mere thoughts.

The conversion of emotions into thoughts has allowed emotion to be studied using the tools and conceptual foundations of cognitive science. There are now numerous computer simulations of appraisal and other emotional processes[61] and some proponents of this AI approach to emotion believe that emotions can be programmed in computers.[62] The following limerick spun by an AI researcher summarizes the beliefs and hopes of the field:

A computer so stolid and stern
Can simulate man to a turn.
Though it lacks flesh and bones
And erogenous zones,
It can teach—but, oh can man learn?[63]

Simulations do indeed have much to offer as an approach to modeling aspects of the mind. However, as the next limerick (though tasteless) reminds us, minds feel as well as think, and feelings involve more than thinking.

There was once an ardent young suitor
Who programmed a female computer,
But he failed to connect
The affective effect,
So there wasn't a thing he could do to 'er.[64]

And, finally, we are also reminded by a limerick that there may be some things that a computer just can't do. This limerick needs to be prefaced with a reminder that in the old days computers were fed information on cards with holes punched out of them that were read by special sensing devices, and that some aspects of computer memory were stored on endless spools of magnetic tape.

> *There was once a passionate dame*
> *Who wanted some things made plain,*
> *So she punched up the cards,*
> *Filled tape by the yards,*
> *But—somehow—it just wasn't the same!*[65]

Where Do We Go from Here?

I have tried to make a clear statement about what emotion is not. It is not merely a collection of thoughts about situations. It is not simply reasoning. It cannot be understood by just asking people what went on in their minds when they had an emotion.

Emotions are notoriously difficult to verbalize. They operate in some psychic and neural space that is not readily accessed from consciousness. Psychiatrists' and psychologists' offices are kept packed for this very reason. Yet, much of our understanding of the way the emotional mind works has been based on studies that have used verbal stimuli as the gateway to emotions or verbal reports to measure emotions.

Consciousness and its sidekick, natural language, are new kids on the evolutionary block—unconscious processing is the rule rather than the exception throughout evolution. And the coin of the evolutionarily old unconscious mental realm is nonverbal processing. Given that so much work on unconscious processing (cognitive and emotional) has focused on verbal processes, we probably have a highly inaccurate picture of the level of sophistication of unconscious processes in humans. And we will not likely begin to fully understand the workings of human unconscious processes until we turn away from the use of verbal stimuli and verbal reports.

It is a testament to human vanity and linguistic chauvinism that the ancestral functions of the brain are characterized as the negation of newly evolved ones. Animals were unconscious and nonverbal long before they were conscious and verbal. Fortunately, ancestral functions, like certain emotional processing functions, are preserved in the human brain, and we can turn to studies of animals to discover how these work in humans as well.

Obviously, we cannot explain everything about human emotions by studying animals. But, as I hope to show you, we have been able to come to a very good understanding of some basic emotional mechanisms that are common to humans and other animals. With this information in hand, we are in a much better position to understand how newly evolved functions, like language and consciousness, contribute to emotions, and particularly how language and consciousness interact with the underlying nonverbal and unconscious systems that make up the heart and soul of the emotional machine.

4

THE HOLY GRAIL

ᠥᠣᠧ

The brain is my second favorite organ.
Woody Allen[1]

A MAJOR GOAL OF modern brain science is to figure out in as much detail as possible where different functions live in the brain. Knowing "where" a function is located is the first step toward understanding "how" it works. Not surprisingly, emotions are functions that scientists have traditionally been interested in localizing in the brain.

For more than a century, crusades have been made through the cerebral promised land in search of the emotional Holy Grail, the brain region or network that will explain where guilt and shame and fear and love come from. Around mid-century it seemed that the prize was finally in hand when the limbic system theory of emotion was proposed.[2] This remarkable conception gave an explanation of emotional life in terms of a brain network that evolved to subserve functions necessary for the survival of the individual and species. The limbic system theory claimed nothing short of having found the physical basis of the Freudian id.

But by the early 1980s, very little research on the brain mechanisms of emotion was being conducted. No doubt, the extension of the cognitive revolution (which excluded emotion as a research topic) into brain science contributed to this, but so too did the apparent thoroughness of the limbic system theory as an account of emotion. The emotional brain seemed, at least in general terms, to be understood.

It would be hard to overestimate the impact of the limbic system concept. It had a tremendous influence not only on the way we think of emotional functions but also on the way we think of the structural organization of the brain. Each year, legions of neuroscience students are taught where the limbic system is and what it does. Unfortunately, though, there is a problem. The limbic system theory is wrong as an explanation of the emotional brain and some scientists even say that the limbic system does not exist. So before I go further and give you my view of the emotional brain, I want to tell you where the limbic system idea came from and explain why it is inadequate as an account of emotional life.

Bumps on the Head

In many ways, we owe the notion that functions are localized to specific parts of the brain to a strange movement in the nineteenth century called phrenology.[3] Phrenologists were scientists, or some would say pseudoscientists, who analyzed personality traits and mental disorders by feeling the surface geography of the human skull.

Phrenology originated through the work of a respected scientist, Franz Josef Gall. Like many before and after him, Gall felt that the mind is composed of a variety of specific faculties (like sensing, feeling, speech, memory, intelligence). Gall went further and made the interesting suggestion that each faculty has its own "organ" in the brain. This was the birth of modern ideas about functional localization. So far so good.

Unfortunately, Gall, and especially his followers, took another step,[4] arguing that more developed faculties had larger brain organs, and that the skull above these protruded more than above less developed organs. As a result, it was possible to characterize personality traits and intellectual abilities by feeling the bumps on one's head, and to detect disorders of thinking and mood by finding deviations from the norm. Phrenologists cast caution to the wind, mapping the cranial location not only of regular old mental faculties (sensation, feeling, memory, and language) but also such exotic traits as veneration, benevolence, friendship, sublimity, suavity, and even philoprocentiveness (whatever that might be).

With so little known about the brain from a scientific point of view, phrenology captured the imagination of inquiring Victorian

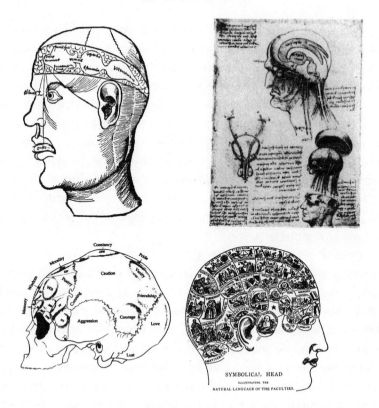

FIGURE 4-1
Localization of Brain Function Through the Ages.

Around A.D. *500, St. Augustine proposed that higher mental functions come from the brain's ventricles, the caverns that contain cerebrospinal fluid. This view persisted for centuries. A version of this idea from around 1500 is depicted in a drawing from Gregor Reisch's book (upper left). Around the same time, Leonardo sketched his view of brain function (upper right). With the emergence of phrenology in the late nineteenth century, localization of function came to be associated with specific areas of the brain, especially of the neocortex. By feeling the shape of one's skull, phrenologists proposed that they could tell the extent to which different parts of the underlying brain were developed (bottom left). Extremists amongst the phrenologists identified a great variety of skull locations with different psychological functions (bottom right).* (Left side illustrations reprinted with permission from M. Jacobson [1993], *Foundations of Neuroscience*. New York: Plenum [upper left reprinted from figure 1.7 and lower left from figure 1.11]. Right side illustrations reprinted with permission from F. Plum and B.T. Volpe [1987], Neuroscience and higher brain function: From myth to public responsibility. In F. Plum, ed., *Handbook of Physiology, Section 1: The nervous system*, vol. V. Bethesda: American Physiological Society.)

minds. It became the pop psychology of its day. And like most pop explanations of why we do what we do, phrenology was off the mark. Although the skull does indeed have bumps, these are just bumps, not indicators of the ups and downs of mental abilities. But since Gall was a scientist of some repute, his ideas warranted a challenge by other respectable men of learning. The result was a scientific backlash against the very idea of functional localization.[5] More as a reaction to phrenology's excesses than anything else, serious scientists adopted the belief that mental functions are distributed all over the brain rather than located in particular parts—a thought or an emotion, in this view, does not occur in one region, but involves all or at least many regions at once.

Ironically, it was Gall's insight, that functions are localized, that ultimately won out, though not in the way that Gall had proposed. Later workers found that different faculties or functions are localized in different regions of the brain, and functional localization is now taken as an accepted fact.[6] We can point to specific brain regions that are involved in the perception of the color and shape of visual objects, in the understanding and production of speech, in imagining what something looks like without actually seeing it, in producing accurate movements in space, in the laying down of memory traces, in smelling the difference between a rose and lilac, in detecting danger, finding food and shelter, selecting mates, and on and on.

Nevertheless, mental processes are not, strictly speaking, functions of brain areas. Each area functions by way of the system of which it is a part. For example, the visual cortex, a region in the rear of the cerebral cortex (the wrinkled outer layer of the brain), is crucially involved in our ability to see. If this region is damaged, you will, for all intents and purposes, be blind.[7] This does not mean that vision is localized to the visual cortex. It means that the visual cortex is a necessary part of the system that makes seeing possible. This system includes the visual cortex as well as a variety of other areas that transfer information from the eyes into the brain and ultimately to the visual cortex. And the visual cortex itself is a complicated structure, being composed of many subregions and subsystems that each contribute in unique ways to the act of seeing.[8] Damage anywhere along the path from the eye through the final stages of processing in the visual cortex can disrupt vision, just as removal of any link breaks a chain.

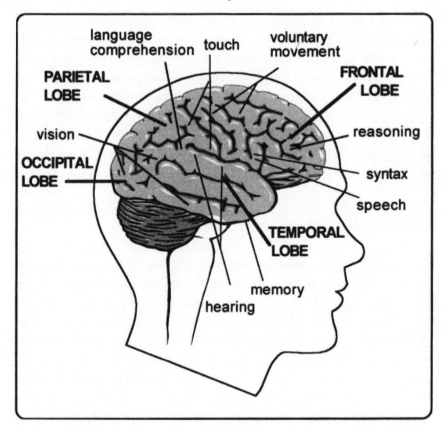

FIGURE 4-2
A Contemporary Map of Some Cortical Functions.

Contemporary understanding of cortical function is based on studies that show the effects of damage to specific regions on the ability to perform behavioral or mental tasks; that reveal behavioral or mental consequences of stimulating brain areas; or that record neural activity or image neural activity in different locations during the performance of behavioral or mental tasks. However, the identification of brain regions associated with specific functions should not be taken too literally. Functions are mediated by interconnected systems of brain regions working together rather than by individual areas working in isolation. In general, studies of experimental animals allow much more precision in identifying the functions to which specific brain regions contribute. In fact, without the animal research, it would be difficult to interpret some of the less precise findings from humans. Nevertheless, studies of the human brain make unique contributions, especially to our understanding of functions that are primarily present in the human brain. (Modified clipart from Canvass and Corel Draw.)

Brain regions, in short, have functions because of the systems of which they are a part. And functions are properties of integrated systems rather than of isolated brain areas. In this sense the truth lies somewhere between Gall and his detractors, but is more tilted toward Gall's view. That is, although mental functions involve many different regions working together, each function requires a unique set of interconnected regions, its own system. The system that allows us to see does not allow us to hear, and neither of these is very useful for feeling pain or walking.[9]

A Stimulating Time

Shortly after the debates between Gall and his detractors, brain researchers began to address questions about functional localization in the brain using experimental approaches. Darwin's theory of evolution[10] had given scientists strong reasons for believing that there was continuity between the biological (and even psychological) makeup of man and other animals, and researchers turned to studies of other species in the hope of revealing important insights into the human brain and its functions.

The main techniques used in these early pioneering studies involved stimulating cortical areas or ablating (removing) them surgically. Brain stimulation involves passing small amounts of electric current through an electrode, a tiny wire that is inserted in the brain. Since the brain operates on the basis of electrical signals transmitted from neurons (brain cells) in one area to neurons in another, electrical stimulation artificially reproduces the effects of natural information flow in the brain. Ablation studies reveal the functions of a brain region by the behavioral or mental capacities that are lost as a result of the damage, whereas with stimulations functions are suggested by responses that are produced. These were the yin and yang of early brain science methodology, and remain key techniques even today.

One of the first discoveries from experimental studies of the brain was that electrical stimulation of certain areas of the cortex elicited movements of specific bodily parts and that surgical lesions of the same regions produced deficits in performing movements of these same parts.[11] The areas in question were in the front part of the cortex, in a region now referred to as the motor cortex, which is known to be crucially involved in the control of voluntary movement. This region has connections with neurons in the spinal cord, which in turn send messages out that control the movement of limbs and other body parts. Stimulation of areas in the rear of the cortex produced no movements, but damage to these regions interfered with the normal perception of information from the eyes, ears, or skin, rendering the animals blind, deaf, or insensitive to touch, all depending on where the lesion was located. These areas are now known as the visual, auditory, and somatosensory regions of the cerebral cortex.

Early neurologists were making very similar discoveries on the basis of observations in brain-injured humans suffering from strokes or tumors.[12] The correspondence between the clinical observations in humans and the more exacting findings from animal experimentation provided strong evidence in support of a Darwinian continuity of brain organization across species.[13]

Quite the Rage

In the early explorations of the functions of the cerebral cortex it was noted that animals with massive ablations showed strikingly normal patterns of emotional reactivity.[14] For example, following removal of the entire cerebral cortex, cats still exhibited characteristic signs of emotional arousal. When provoked, they crouched down, arched their backs, retracted their ears, unsheathed their claws, growled, hissed, showed their teeth, and bit any object around.[15] In addition, they exhibited strong signs of autonomic arousal, including piloerection (puffing of the hair), pupil dilation, and elevations of blood pressure and heart rate. This was surprising given the belief at the time that the complex behaviors, including emotional behaviors, were controlled by the sensory and motor cortex. For example, in the neural version of his feedback theory, William James had proposed that emotions are mediated by sensory and motor areas of the cortex—the motor areas were needed for producing responses and the sensory areas for detecting the stimulus in the first place and then for "feeling" the feedback from the responses (see Figure 4-3). James got this one wrong, since cortical damage had no effect on emotional responses.

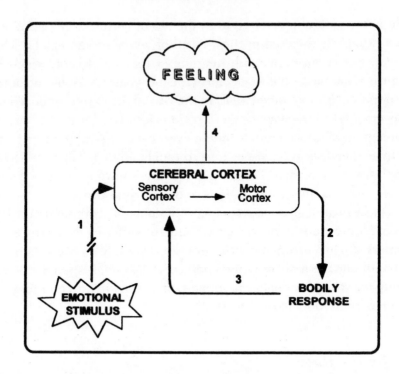

FIGURE 4-3
William James' Brain Pathways of Emotion.

An external stimulus, such as the sight of a bear, is perceived by the sensory areas of the cerebral cortex. Through the motor cortex, responses, such as running away, are controlled. Sensations produced by the responses are fed back to the cerebral cortex, where they are perceived. The perception of bodily sensations associated with the emotional responses is what gives the peculiar quality to the emotion in James' theory.

Yet, the emotional behavior of decorticate animals (animals in whom the cerebral cortex was removed) was not completely normal. These creatures were very easily provoked into emotional reactions by the slightest events. They seemed to be lacking any regulation of their rage, which suggested that cortical areas (like Plato's charioteer) normally rein in these wild emotional reactions and prevent their expression in inappropriate situations.[16]

Walter Cannon was famous not only for his attack on William James' theory, described in Chapter 3, but also for his own neural theory of emotion, which was based on research conducted in his laboratory by Philip Bard. Bard carried out a systematic series of lesion studies aimed at finding just what parts of the brain are required for the expression of rage.[17] He made larger and larger lesions, starting with the cortex and working his way down, until he found a pattern of destruction that eliminated rage responses. The critical lesion was one that encroached upon an area called the hypothalamus. In the absence of the hypothalamus, only fragments of emotional reactivity, rather than fully integrated reactions, could be mustered, and only in response to very intense, painful stimuli. The animals might crouch, snarl, hiss, unsheathe their claws, retract their ears, bite, and/or exhibit some autonomic reactivity, but these did not all occur together in coordinated fashion as they did when the hypothalamus was intact, and only very intense stimulations evoked the responses. Such findings suggested to Bard and Cannon that the hypothalamus is the centerpiece of the emotional brain (see Figure 4-4).

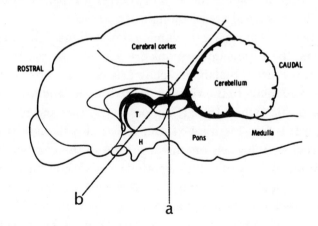

FIGURE 4-4
Lesion Strategy Used by Bard to Isolate the Hypothalamus as an Emotional Center.

First, Bard removed all brain areas above (to the left of) line "b." Included were the cerebral cortex and all other parts of the forebrain except the hypothalamus (H) and some portions of the thalamus. These lesions did not prevent emotional reactions. However, when the lesion was extended to include the areas between lines "b" and "a" as well as the areas rostral to "b," emotional reactions were essentially eliminated. Rostral = Front; Caudal = Back. (Based on J.E. LeDoux [1987], Emotion. In F. Plum, ed., Handbook of Physiology, Section 1: The nervous system, vol. V. Bethesda: American Physiological Society.)

The brain can be divided into three divisions along the vertical axis, the hindbrain, midbrain, and forebrain. As we ascend from hindbrain to forebrain, the functions represented go from psychologically primitive to psychologically elaborate. The hypothalamus, about the size of a peanut in the human brain, sits at the base of the forebrain and forms the interface between the psychologically sophisticated forebrain and the more primitive lower areas. In Cannon and Bard's day, the hypothalamus was known to be involved in the regulation of the autonomic nervous system,[18] and it made sense to them that the hypothalamus might be the place where bodily reactions occurring in strong emotions might be controlled by the forebrain.

The Cannon-Bard theory built upon the well-known fact that the sensory systems that take in information from the outside world send the information they receive to specialized regions of the cerebral cortex—information from the eyes goes to the visual cortex and information from the ears to the auditory cortex. In their travels toward the specialized cortical areas, though, the sensory messages make a stop in subcortical areas—in thalamic relay stations. Like their cortical partners, these thalamic regions are also specialized for sensory processing (the visual thalamus receives visual signals from receptors in the eyes and relays to the visual cortex while the auditory thalamus receives acoustic signals from receptors in the ears and relays to the auditory cortex) (see Figure 4-5). But it was also thought that some thalamic regions relay sensory messages not to the cortex but to the hypothalamus. As a result, the hypothalamus should have access to sensory inputs at about the same time as the cortex. And once the hypothalamus received these signals, it could then activate the body to produce the autonomic and behavioral responses characteristic of emotional reactions (see Figure 4-6). This explained to Cannon and Bard why decortication failed to prevent the expression of emotion and why James' cortical theory was therefore wrong (emotional responses are controlled by the hypothalamus, not the motor cortex, and sensations can activate the hypothalamus directly, without passing through the sensory cortex).

Although Cannon and Bard eliminated the cortex from the chain of events leading to emotional responses, they did not completely rule out a role for the cortex in emotion. In fact, Cannon and Bard felt that the conscious experiences of emotions, the feelings, depend

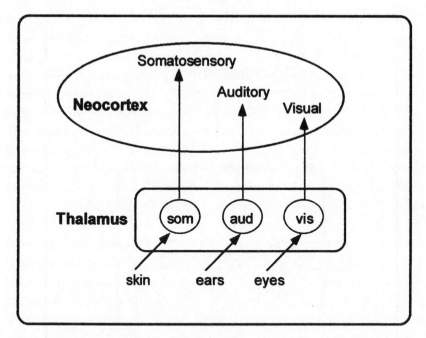

FIGURE 4-5
Relation of Sensory Thalamus and Sensory Cortex.

Sensory messages are transmitted from external receptors (e.g., in the eyes, ears, and skin) to specific areas of the thalamus that then process the signals and relay the results to specialized areas of the neocortex. Abbreviations of thalamic areas: som, somatosensory thalamus; aud, auditory thalamus; vis, visual thalamus.

upon the activation of the cortex by nerve fibers ascending from the hypothalamus. So in the absence of the cortex angry behavior is produced but is unaccompanied by the conscious feeling of rage. For this reason, Cannon used the term "sham rage" to describe the emotional outbursts of decorticate animals.[19]

For James, the peculiar quality of an emotional experience was determined by feedback to the brain from the bodily responses—responses thus occur before feelings. But for Cannon emotions are defined by processes completely contained within the brain and centered around the hypothalamus. The hypothalamus discharged to the body to produce emotional responses and to the cortex to pro-

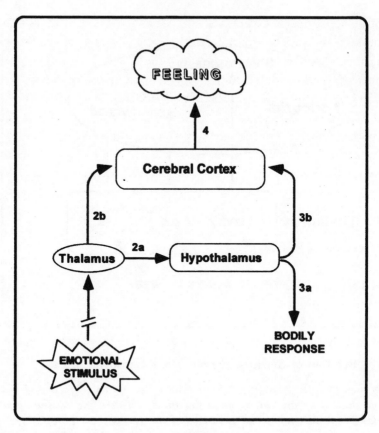

FIGURE 4-6
Cannon-Bard Theory of the Emotional Brain.

Cannon and Bard believed that external stimuli processed by the thalamus were routed to the cerebral cortex (path 2b) and to the hypothalamus (path 2a). The hypothalamus, in turn, sent messages to both bodily muscles and organs (path 3a) and the cortex (path 3b). The interaction of messages in the cortex about what the stimulus is (path 2b) and about its emotional significance (path 3b) results in the conscious experience of emotion (feelings). Emotional responses and feelings occur in parallel in this theory.

duce emotional experiences. And since the fibers descending to the bodily response systems and the fibers ascending to the cortex are activated simultaneously by the hypothalamus, emotional feelings and emotional responses occur in parallel, rather than in sequence.

Although Cannon disagreed with James on what causes emotional experiences, on another very important point, and one that is not often recognized, Cannon seems to have agreed with James—emotional responses (running from the bear) are not caused by conscious emotional experiences (being afraid). For James, emotional responses precede and determine conscious experiences, whereas for Cannon responses and experiences occur simultaneously. It thus seems likely that James and Cannon would both go along with the notion, developed in the last chapter, that conscious emotional experiences are a consequence of prior emotional processes (evaluations or appraisals) that occur outside of conscious awareness, which is to say, unconsciously.

The Stream of Feeling

James Papez, a Cornell University anatomist, never specifically did research on emotion, but in 1937 he proposed one of the most influential theories of the emotional brain.[20] Rumor has it that Papez found out that an American benefactor had donated a large sum of money to a British laboratory for the purpose of figuring out how emotions work.[21] In a stroke of national pride, he dashed off his famous article in a few days to show that Americans also had some ideas about emotions. However, had he known that his theory would sink into the back pages of science until rediscovered and revived around mid century, Papez might have developed his theory at a more leisurely pace.

Papez was strongly influenced by the work of C. Judson Herrick, an anatomist who specialized in brain evolution. Herrick had earlier pointed out a distinction between two parts of the cortex, the lateral and medial parts.[22] Imagine the brain as a hot dog bun, with the two halves of the bun being the two cerebral hemispheres. The brownish, toasted part of the bun that we can see from the outside is like the lateral part of the cerebral cortex. This is the part of the cortex that has all the sensory and motor functions that we've talked about and is generally believed to be the place where all our highest thought processes occur. Now, imagine prying the bun apart down the seam in the middle, pulling the two hemibuns away from each other. The white, untoasted part of hemibuns down the middle is like the medial part of the cortex. This part, according to Herrick, is evolutionarily older and is involved in more primitive functions than the newer cortex, known as the neocortex, a designation that reflects its supposedly more recent origin in evolution (see Figure 4-7).

Herrick's medial cortex had earlier been called *le grand lobe limbique* by the great French anatomist Paul Pierre Broca.[23] Broca noted that the medial cortical areas have an oval shape, almost like the rim of a tennis racquet. In fact, *limbique* is the French version of the Latin word *limbus*, which means rim. Broca had a structural description of the medial cortex in mind when he labeled the area, but somewhat later the limbic lobe was renamed the rhinencephalon, which

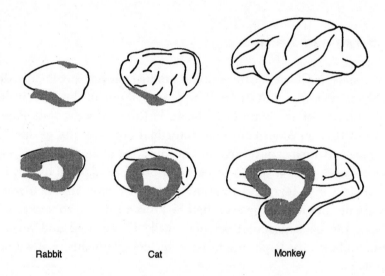

Rabbit   Cat   Monkey

FIGURE 4-7
Lateral and Medial Cortex in Mammalian Evolution.

The cerebrum of a rabbit (left), cat (center), and monkey (right), is shown in lateral (top row) and medial (bottom row) views. The so-called limbic lobe, supposedly made up of evolutionarily old cortex, is shown in gray, and the evolutionarily new cortex, the neocortex, is in white. The limbic lobe is mostly located in the medial wall of the cerebrum. In the rabbit, the limbic lobe accounts for most of the medial cortex. In cats and primates, the limbic lobe accounts for progressively less of the medial cortex, and thus for less of the cortical mass. The changes across mammals reflect the expansion of the neocortex. Cortical expansion reaches its greatest extent (so far) in humans. (Based on P.D. MacLean [1954], Studies on limbic system ["visceral brain] and their bearing on psychosomatic problems. In E. Wittkower and R. Cleghorn, eds., *Recent Developments in Psychosomatic Medicine.* London: Pitman.)

means "smell brain," to account for its apparent involvement in the perception of odors and in controlling behaviors guided by smell.

Herrick noted that in primitive animals smell plays an important role in feeding, sexual, and defensive behaviors. He proposed that the higher intellectual functions mediated by the lateral neocortex evolved from the sense of smell and that the lateral cortex itself is an evolutionary outgrowth of the smell brain. According to Herrick, the basic sensory and motor functions controlled by the medial cortex in primitive animals were transferred over to the newly evolved lateral cortex, allowing room for the elaboration of sensation into higher thought processes and the expansion of primitive motor functions of early vertebrates into complex human behaviors.

Papez was a great synthesizer and put together Herrick's idea about the evolutionary distinction between the medial and lateral cortex with two other kinds of findings—observations about the consequences of brain damage in the medial cortex in humans and research on the role of the hypothalamus in the control of emotional reactions in animals. The outcome was a theory that explained the subjective experience of emotion in terms of the flow of information through a circle of anatomical connections from the hypothalamus to the medial cortex and back to the hypothalamus. This is now known as the Papez circuit.

Papez, in the tradition of Cannon, emphasized the importance of the hypothalamus in the reception of direct sensory inputs about emotional stimuli from the thalamus, in the control of bodily responses during emotion, and in the regulation of emotional experience by ascending fibers to the cortex. However, Papez was particularly concerned with further illuminating how emotional experience might come out of the brain and proposed a more elaborate and detailed emotional network than Cannon.

The Papez hypothesis begins with the idea that sensory inputs transmitted into the brain are split at the level of the way stations in the thalamus into the *stream of thought* and the *stream of feeling*. The stream of thought is the channel through which sensory inputs are transmitted, by way of paths through the thalamus, to the lateral areas of the neocortex. Through this stream, sensations are turned into perceptions, thoughts, and memories. The stream of feeling also involved sensory transmission to the thalamus, but at that point the information was relayed, as Cannon proposed, directly to the hypothalamus, allowing the generation of emotions.

Cannon treated the hypothalamus as a homogeneous structure. But Papez pinpointed the hypothalamic mammillary bodies, so named because of their breastlike protrusion from the bottom of the brain, as the place that receives the thalamic sensory inputs and then relays the messages toward the cortex. And he was also quite specific about which part of the cortex was involved, proposing that the cingulate cortex (a part of the older, medial cortex) is the cortical region for the perception of emotion, just as the visual cortex is the region for visual perception. And pursuing the analogy with sensory systems, he proposed that the anterior thalamic nucleus, which connects the mammillary bodies to the cingulate cortex, is a thalamic relay in the emotional system. But the circuit did not stop there. The cingulate cortex then sends its outputs to the hippocampus, another old, medial cortical area, the output of which was directed back to the hypothalamus, thus completing the circle of emotion (see Figure 4-8).

In Papez's time, the actual connections of the brain were very poorly understood, as the methods for tracing connections between regions were crude. Papez therefore based his circuit partly on the known connections, but also on the clinical effects of damage to the various brain regions and speculation about what connections might exist. The hippocampus was included in the circuit because it was known to be a major site of brain damage associated with rabies, a disease characterized by "intense emotional, convulsive, and paralytic symptoms," in which the patient presents the "appearance of intense fright and of mingled terror and rage."[24] The cingulate was given a central role because damage there resulted in apathy, drowsiness, delirium, depression, loss of emotional spontaneity, disorientation in time and space, and sometimes coma.

Descartes had put the soul in the pineal gland, the only part of the brain not divided in two halves.[25] Papez was more sympathetic with the suggestion of a later Frenchman, La Peyronie, the professor of surgery at Montpellier, who located the seat of the soul near the cingulate region. But Papez had a more modest aim than La Peyronie, referring to the cingulate cortex as the place where "environmental events are endowed with an emotional consciousness."[26] If

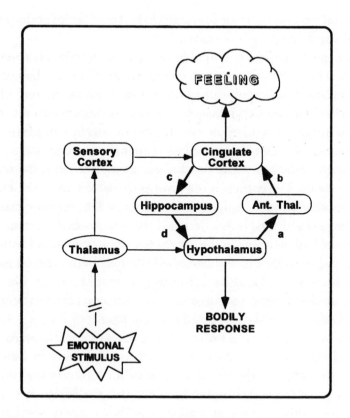

FIGURE 4-8
The Papez Circuit Theory.

Like Cannon and Bard, Papez believed that sensory messages reaching the thalamus are directed to both the cerebral cortex and the hypothalamus; the outputs of the hypothalamus to the body control emotional responses; and outputs to the cortex give rise to emotional feelings. The paths to the cortex were called the "stream of thinking" and the ones to the hypothalamus the "stream of feeling." Papez was considerably more specific than Cannon and Bard about how the hypothalamus communicates with the cortex and about which cortical areas are involved. He proposed a series of connections from the hypothalamus to the anterior thalamus, to the cingulate cortex (part of the evolutionarily old, medial cortex). Emotional experiences occur when the cingulate cortex integrates signals from sensory cortex (part of the evolutionarily new, lateral cortex) and the hypothalamus. Outputs from the cingulate cortex to the hippocampus and then the hypothalamus allow thoughts occurring in the cerebral cortex to control emotional responses.

the cingulate cortex was not the seat of the soul for Papez, it was at least the seat of the soul's passions.

Papez suggested that emotional experiences could be generated in two ways. The first was activation of the stream of feeling by sensory objects. This, as just described, involves the flow of inputs from sensory areas of the thalamus to the mammillary bodies, and then to the anterior thalamus and cingulate cortex. The second was by way of the flow of information through the stream of thought to the cerebral cortex, where the stimulus is perceived and where memories about the stimulus are activated. The cortical areas involved in perception and memory then, in turn, activate the cingulate cortex. In the first instance the cingulate cortex is activated by low-level subcortical processes through the stream of feeling, whereas in the other instance it is activated by high-level cortical processes in the stream of thought. This distinction between subcortical and cortical activation of emotion, which was also part of Cannon's theory, was forgotten for many years but has been revived recently and will be discussed in detail later.

The Papez circuit was a brilliant piece of anatomical speculation, as most of the anatomical paths proposed had not been identified at the time. Remarkably, almost all of them exist. With very few modifications, a set of connections closely resembling the Papez circuit has been found. Unfortunately, at least for the Papez theory of emotion, this circuit appears to have little involvement in emotion. Nevertheless, the Papez circuit theory is a crucial part of the history of the emotional brain, as it was the takeoff point for the limbic system theory, which will be considered shortly.

Psychic Blindness

Nineteen thirty-seven was a banner year for the emotional brain. Not only was the Papez theory published then, but so too was the first in a series of reports by Heinrich Klüver and Paul Bucy.[27] These investigators were involved in a study of the brain regions that mediate drug-induced visual hallucinations when they stumbled upon a remarkable set of observations on the effects of damage to the temporal lobes of monkeys.

The lateral cerebral cortex can be divided into four subparts, known as lobes. The occipital lobe is in the back and is where the visual cortex is located. The frontal lobe, obviously, is in the front, and rests just above the eyes on each side. Between the occipital and frontal lobes are the parietal and temporal lobes. The parietal lobe sits on top, and the temporal lobe is just below it, right behind and slightly above your ears (see Figure 4-2).

In their first report on one monkey, a case study of the effects of temporal lobe removal, Klüver and Bucy noted:

> the animal does not exhibit the reactions generally associated with anger and fear. It approaches humans and animals, animate as well as inanimate objects without hesitation and although there are no motor defects tends to examine them by mouth rather than by the use of the hands. . . . Various tests do not show any impairment in visual acuity or in the ability to localize visually the position of objects in space. However, the monkey seems to be unable to recognize objects by the sense of sight. The hungry animal, if confronted with a variety of objects, will, for example, indiscriminately pick up a comb, a bakelite knob, a sunflower seed, a screw, a stick, a piece of apple, a live snake, a piece of banana, and a live rat. Each object is transferred to the mouth and then discarded if not edible.[28]

They referred to this collection of symptoms as "psychic blindness," by which they meant that the animals had perfectly good visual acuity but were blind to the psychological significance of stimuli.

Later studies confirmed the major facets of what has come to be known as the Klüver-Bucy syndrome.[29] Animals with such lesions are "tame" in the presence of previously feared objects (people and snakes); they will put almost anything in their mouths, being unable to identify by sight alone whether something is edible; and they become hypersexual, attempting to copulate with other monkeys of the same sex or with members of other species (sexual activities seldom if ever practiced by "normal" monkeys).

In the wake of Klüver and Bucy's publications, a plethora of research was conducted to try to further understand the nature of the syndrome. This work had a significant impact on several areas of brain research, including the search for the brain mechanisms of visual perception, long-term memory, and emotion. But the impact of most relevance to us at the moment was its influence on Paul MacLean and his limbic system theory of the emotional brain.

The Emotional Keyboard

Research on the neural basis of emotion was interrupted by World War II. But things began to pick up steam again in 1949 when Paul MacLean revived and expanded the Papez theory, integrating it with the Klüver-Bucy syndrome and with Freudian psychology.[30] The Papez theory, in fact, might have faded quietly into the past had it not been a major inspiration for MacLean's treatise.

MacLean sought to construct an all-encompassing theory of the emotional brain. Drawing on the work of Cannon and Papez, as well as that of Klüver and Bucy, MacLean noted the importance of the hypothalamus in emotional expression and the importance of the cerebral cortex in emotional experience. He sought to identify some way in which these regions might communicate and thereby allow the affective qualities of experience to act on the autonomic and behavioral control systems in the generation of emotional responses and in the establishment and maintenance of psychosomatic diseases, such as hypertension, asthma, and peptic ulcers.

MacLean, like many others before him and since, believed that the capacity to appreciate all of the various affective or emotional qualities of experience and to differentiate them into feeling states (like fear, anger, love, and hate) required the cerebral cortex. At the same time, the newly evolved part of the cortex, the neocortex, was known to lack significant connections with the hypothalamus, and therefore could not act on the autonomic centers to produce visceral responses. However, as Papez and Herrick had argued, the evolutionarily older areas of the medial cortex, the so-called rhinencephalon, are intimately connected with the hypothalamus. That the rhinencephalon was not just a smell brain in higher mammals was evident from the fact that dolphins and porpoises, which have no sense of smell, have highly elaborate rhinencephalic regions, and that in humans the olfactory sense is of comparatively less importance but certain areas of the rhinencephalon (especially the hippocampus and cingulate regions) reach their greatest development.

Clinical evidence was added to the list supplied by Papez to support the role of the rhinencephalon in emotion. For example, MacLean noted that in temporal lobe epilepsy, which often involves pathology in the hippocampal region, the patient is sometimes in a "dreamy state" and can have a feeling of fear or even terror right before having a seizure. Further, patients with epilepsy may be afflicted with severe emotional and psychological disturbances (nervousness, obsessive thinking, depression) between seizures. The role of the mammillary bodies in emotion was further supported by the fact that damage to this region, often as a consequence of vitamin deficiencies resulting from poor dietary habits in prolonged and severe alcoholism, can result in psychotic behavior. Further, stimulation of the brain in the region of the mammillary bodies was known to produce blood pressure elevations, which MacLean took to mean that this region is involved in psychosomatic diseases, such as high blood pressure due to excess stress. And, as further support of importance of the cingulate cortex in emotion, he suggested that the changes in respiration elicited by stimulation of this region might be related to psychosomatic forms of asthma. And he also mentioned the case of a fifty-five-year-old woman with a tumor in the vicinity of the cingulate region. The main symptoms exhibited were nymphomania accompanied by a persistent passionate feeling, which was exaggerated by the smell of perfume, possibly because of the importance of the smell brain to emotion.

The accuracy of these anatomical correlations is, at this point, of less importance than their implications for MacLean. In his mind, all roads led to the smell brain as the seat of emotion. Noting that stimulation of the rhinencephalic areas, but not areas of the neocortex, typically produced autonomic responses (changes in respiration, blood pressure, heart rate, and other visceral functions), he renamed the rhinencephalon the visceral brain. MacLean suggested that, "although, in the ascension to higher forms, the rhinencephalon yields more and more control over the animal's movements to the neocortex, its persistent, strong connections with lower autonomic centers suggests that it continues to dominate in the realm of visceral activity." While the neocortex "holds sway over the body musculature and subserves the functions of the intellect," the visceral brain is the region involved in "ordering the affective behavior of the animal in such basic drives as obtaining and assimilating food, fleeing from or orally disposing of an enemy, reproducing, and so forth."[31]

MacLean's basic idea was that in primitive animals the visceral brain was the highest center available for coordinating behavior, since the neocortex had not yet evolved. In these primitive creatures, the visceral brain took care of all the instinctual behaviors and basic drives underlying the survival of the individual and the species. With the emergence of the neocortex in the mammals, the capacity for higher forms of psychological function, like thinking and reasoning, began to emerge and reached its zenith in man. But even in man, the visceral brain remains essentially unchanged and is involved in the primitive functions that it carried out in our distal evolutionary ancestors.

MacLean believed that emotional feelings involve the integration of sensations arising from the external environment with visceral sensations from within the body and proposed that these integrations take place in the visceral brain. His theory was in essence a feedback hypothesis about the nature of emotion, not unlike James'. That is, emotional stimuli in the external world produce responses in the visceral organs. Messages from these internal organs then return to the brain, where they are integrated with ongoing perceptions of the outside world. This integration of the internal and external worlds was viewed as the mechanism that generates emotional experience:

> The problem pertaining to emotional mechanisms is basically one of communication in the nervous system. It may be assumed that messages from both without and within the organism are relayed to the brain by nervous impulses traveling along nerve fibers and possibly by humoral agents carried in the blood stream. Ultimately, however, any correlation of these messages must be a function of a highly integrated body of neurones capable of sorting, selecting, and acting upon various patterns of bioelectrical activity. The indications are that both the experience and the expression of emotion are the resultant of the association and correlation of a wide variety of internal and external stimuli whose messages are transmitted as nervous impulses in cerebral analyzers.[32]

The cerebral analyzers underlying emotion were, in MacLean's view, located in the visceral brain, and particularly in the hippocampus, so-named for its sea horse shape—in Greek mythology, *hippokampos* was a horse-shaped (*hippo*) sea monster (*kampos*).

MacLean poetically described the large nerve cells in the hippocampus as an emotional keyboard. The keyboard idea comes from the fact that cells in this region are very orderly arranged, side by side. When the elements of the sensory world activate these cells, the tunes they play are the emotions we experience (see figure 4-9).

MacLean proposed that our emotions, in contrast to our

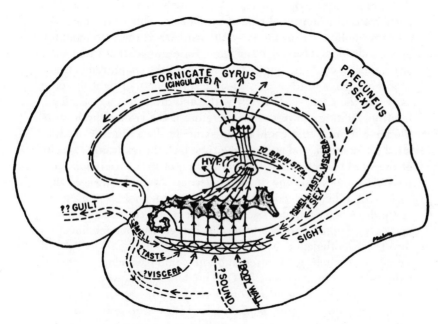

FIGURE 4-9
MacLean's Visceral Brain (Limbic System) Theory.

The centerpiece of the limbic system was the hippocampus (shown as a seahorse). It was believed to receive inputs from the external world (sight, smell, hearing, touch, taste) as well as from the internal or visceral environment. The integration of internal and external sensations was viewed as the basis of emotional experience. The pyramidal cells of the hippocampus (black triangle inside the seahorse) were viewed as the emotional keyboard (see text). (Reprinted from P. MacLean [1949], Psychosomatic disease and the "visceral brain." Recent developments bearing on the Papez theory of emotion. *Psychosomatic Medicine* 11, 338–53.)

thoughts, are difficult for us to understand precisely because of structural differences between the organization of the hippocampus, the centerpiece of the visceral brain, and the neocortex, the home of the thinking (word) brain: "the cortical cytoarchitecture of the hippocampal formation indicates that it would have little efficiency as an analyzer compared to the neocortex." Further elaborating this idea, he said:

> one might infer that the hippocampal system could hardly deal with information in more than a crude way, and was possibly too primitive a brain to analyze language. Yet it might have the capacity to participate in a nonverbal type of symbolism. This would have significant implications as far as symbolism affects the emotional life of the individual. One might imagine, for example, that though the visceral brain could not aspire to conceive of the colour red in terms of a three-letter word or as a specific wavelength of light, it could associate the color symbolically with such diverse things as blood, fainting, fighting, flowers, etc. Therefore if the visceral brain were the kind of brain that could tie up symbolically a number of unrelated phenomena, and at the same time lack the analyzing capacity of the word brain to a nice discrimination of their differences, it is possible to conceive how it might become foolishly involved in a variety of ridiculous correlations leading to phobias, obsessive-compulsive behavior, etc. Lacking the help and control of the neocortex, its impressions would be discharged without modification into the hypothalamus and lower centers. Considered in light of Freudian psychology, the visceral brain would have many of the attributes of the unconscious id. One might argue, however, *that the visceral brain is not at all unconscious (possibly not even in sleep), but rather eludes the grasp of the intellect because its animalistic and primitive structure makes it impossible to communicate in verbal terms.*[33] [MacLean's italics]

MacLean pursued the hypothesis, and a very radical one at the time, that psychiatric problems might be attributable to disorders of the visceral brain, and particularly that the visceral brain might be the source of pathology in patients with psychosomatic symptoms:

> so much of the information obtained from these patients has to do with material which in a Freudian sense is assigned to the oral and oral-anal level, or, as one might say all inclusively, the visceral level. In practically all the psychosomatic diseases such as hypertension,

peptic ulcer, asthma, ulcerative colitis, that have been subject to fairly extensive psychiatric investigation, great emphasis has been placed on the "oral" needs, the "oral" dependencies, the "oral" drives, etc., of the patients. These oral factors have been related to rage, hostility, fear, insecurity, resentment, grief, and a variety of other emotional states. In certain circumstances, for example, eating food may be the symbolic representation of psychologic phenomena as diverse as 1) the hostile desire to eradicate an inimical person, 2) the need for love, 3) fear of some deprivation or punishment, 4) the grief of separation, etc. . . . Many of the seemingly paradoxical and ridiculous implications of the term "oral" result from a situation, most clearly manifest in children or primitive peoples, where there is a failure or inability to discriminate between the internal and external perceptions that make up the affective qualities of experience. . . . [The] emotional life [of psychosomatic patients] often becomes a matter of "invisicerating" or "exviscerating." It is as if the person never "learned to walk" emotionally. . . . In the psychosomatic patient it would almost seem that there was little direct exchange between the visceral brain and the word brain, and that emotional feelings built up in the hippocampal formation, instead of being relayed to the intellect for evaluation, found immediate expression through autonomic centers.[34]

He goes on to suggest that one would not expect to accomplish a great deal with words at the beginning of psychotherapy and that the most important first steps would be for the therapist to relate to the patient's visceral brain.[35]

In 1952, three years after publication of the visceral brain hypothesis, MacLean introduced the term "limbic system" as a new name for the visceral brain.[36] Limbic, you will recall, comes from Broca's description of the rim of medial cortex that later became the rhinencephalon. But in contrast to Broca, MacLean had function, not structure, on his mind when he packaged Broca's limbic cortex and related cortical and subcortical regions into the limbic system. In addition to the areas of the Papez circuit, MacLean included regions like the amygdala, septum, and prefrontal cortex in the limbic system. He then proposed that the structures of the limbic system comprise a phylogenetically early neural development that functions in an integrated way, in fact as a system, in maintaining the survival of the individual and the species. This system evolved to mediate visceral functions and affective behaviors, including feeding, defense, fighting, and reproduction. It underlies the visceral or emotional life of the individual.

MacLean has continued to develop and embellish the visceral brain/limbic system theory over the years. In 1970 he introduced his theory of the triune brain.[37] The forebrain, according to MacLean, has gone through three stages of evolution: reptilian, paleomammalian, and neomammalian. He notes, "there results a remarkable linkage of three cerebrotypes which are radically different in chemistry and structure and which in an evolutionary sense are eons apart. There exists, so to speak, a hierarchy of three-brains-in-one, or what I call, for short, a *triune brain*."[38] Each of the cerebrotypes, according to MacLean, has its own special kind of intelligence, its own special memory, its own sense of time and space, and its own motor and other functions. In humans, other primates, and advanced mammals, all three brains exist. Lower mammals lack the neomammalian brain, but have the paleomammalian and reptilian brain. All other vertebrate creatures (birds, reptiles, amphibians, and fishes) have only the reptilian brain. The paleomammalian brain, present in all mammals, is essentially the limbic system. The triune brain thus puts the limbic system into a broader evolutionary context to account for behaviors and mental functions of all levels of complexity.

Trouble in Paradise

What a synthesis! Reading MacLean's original writings, it is easy to see why the problem of the emotional brain seemed, by 1952, all wrapped up. The theory was far reaching and covered the latest in brain science, psychology, psychiatry, and even managed to talk about the new emerging ideas about computer modeling of neural activity. It was an amazing achievement. There have been few if any theories in neuroscience that have been as broad in their scope, as wide ranging in their implications, and as long-lived. The limbic system concept survives to this very day as the major view of the emotional brain. Textbooks of neuroanatomy routinely include a chapter on the structural organization and function of the limbic system. It is a household concept in the mind of every brain scientist. Lay dictionaries have an entry for the term, describing the limbic system as a circle of connections that mediates emotions.

Unfortunately, the idea that the limbic system constitutes the emotional brain is, for a variety of reasons, not acceptable. But before explaining why, I'd like to separate MacLean's fascinating and penetrating ideas about the nature of emotion and emotional disorders from the limbic system theory. I think he did an incredible job of conceptualizing the general way in which emotions might come out of brains. Like MacLean, and unlike many contemporary cognitive and social constructivist theorists, I believe that it is essential that the emotional brain be viewed from an evolutionary perspective.[39] I am very fond of his idea that the emotional brain and the "word brain" might be operating in parallel but using different codes and thus are not necessarily able to communicate with each other. And I also think that his idea that some psychiatric problems might represent the operation of the emotional brain independent of the "word brain" is on the mark. But these gems need to be separated from the rest of the limbic system theory.

The limbic system theory was a theory of localization. It proposed to tell us where emotion lives in the brain. But MacLean and later enthusiasts of the limbic system have not managed to give us a good way of identifying what parts of the brain actually make up the limbic system.

MacLean said that the limbic system is made up of phylogenetically old cortex and anatomically related subcortical areas. Phylogenetically old cortex is cortex that was present in very old (in an evolutionary sense) animals. Although these animals are long gone, their distal progeny are around and we can look in the brains of living fish, amphibians, birds, and reptiles and see what kinds of cortical areas they have and compare these to the kinds of areas that are present in newly evolved creatures—humans and other mammals. When anatomists did this early in this century, they concluded that the lowly animals only have the medial (old) cortex, but mammals have both the medial and lateral (new) cortex.[40]

This kind of evolutionary neurologic carried the day for a long time, and it was perfectly reasonable for Herrick, Papez, MacLean, and many others to latch on to it. But, by the early 1970s, this view had begun to crumble. Anatomists like Harvey Karten and Glenn Northcutt were showing that so-called primitive creatures do in fact have areas that meet the structural and functional criteria of neocortex.[41] What had been confusing was that these cortical areas were not exactly in the place that they are in mammals so it was not obvious that they were the same structures. As a result of these discoveries, it is no longer possible to say that some parts of the mammalian cortex were older than other parts. And once the distinction between old and new cortex breaks down, the whole concept of mammalian brain evolution is turned on its head.[42] As a result, the evolutionary basis of the limbic lobe, rhinencephalon, visceral brain, and limbic system concepts has become suspect.[43]

Another idea was that the limbic system might be defined on the basis of connectivity with the hypothalamus. After all, this is what led MacLean to the medial cortex in the first place. But with newer, more refined methods, it has been shown that the hypothalamus is connected with all levels of the nervous system, including the neocortex. Connectivity with the hypothalamus turns the limbic system into the entire brain, which doesn't help us very much.

MacLean also proposed that areas of the limbic system be identified on the basis of their involvement in visceral functions. While it is true that some areas traditionally included in the limbic system contribute to the control of the autonomic nervous system, other areas, like the hippocampus, are now believed to have relatively less involvement in autonomic and emotional functions than in cognition.[44] And other areas not included in the limbic system by anyone (especially areas in the lower brain stem) are primarily involved in autonomic regulation. Visceral regulation is a poor basis for identifying the limbic system.

Involvement in emotional functions is, obviously, another way the limbic system has been looked for. If the limbic system is the emotion system, then studies showing which brain areas are involved in emotion should tell us where the limbic system is. But this is backward reasoning. The goal of the limbic system theory was to tell us where emotion is in the brain on the basis of knowing something about the evolution of brain structure. To use research on emotion to find the limbic system turns this criterion around. Research on emotion can tell us where the emotion system is in the brain, but not where the limbic system is. Either the limbic system exists or it does not. Since there are no independent criteria for telling us where it is, I have to say that it does not exist.

But let's consider the issue of using research on emotion to define the limbic system a little further. MacLean had proposed that the limbic system was the kind of system that would be involved in primitive emotional functions and not in higher thought processes. Recent research, which we will discuss in detail later, is very problematic for this view. For example, damage to the hippocampus and some regions of the Papez circuit, like the mammillary bodies and anterior thalamus, have relatively little consistent effect on emotional functions but produce pronounced disorders of conscious or declarative memory—the ability to know what you did a few minutes ago and to store that information and retrieve it at some later time and to verbally describe what you remember. These were exactly the kinds of processes that MacLean proposed that the visceral brain and limbic system would not be involved with. The relative absence of involvement in emotion and the clear involvement in cognition are major difficulties for the view that the limbic system, however one chooses to define it, is the emotional brain.

How, then, has the limbic system theory of emotion survived so long if there is so little evidence for its existence or for its involvement in emotion? There are many explanations that one could come up with. Two seem particularly cogent. One is that, though imprecise, the limbic system term is a useful anatomical shorthand for areas located in the no-man's-land between the hypothalamus and the neocortex, the lowest and highest (in structural terms) regions of the forebrain, respectively. But scientists should be precise. The limbic system term, even when used in a shorthand structural sense, is imprecise and has unwarranted functional (emotional) implications. It should be discarded.[45]

Another explanation for the survival of the limbic system theory of emotion is that it is not completely wrong—some limbic areas have been implicated in emotional functions. Given that the limbic system is a tightly packaged concept (though not a tightly organized, well-defined system in the brain), evidence that one limbic area is involved in some emotional process has often been generalized to validate the idea that the limbic system as a whole is involved in emotion. And, by the same token, the demonstration that a limbic region is involved in one emotional process is often generalized to all emotional processes. Through these kinds of poorly reasoned associations, involvement of a particular limbic area in a very specific emotional process has tended to substantiate the view that the limbic system is the emotional brain.

Like other theories that preceded it, the limbic system theory of the emotional brain was meant to apply equally to all emotions. It was a general theory of how feelings come from the brain. This general explanation was based on a specific functional hypothesis—when information about the external world is integrated with sensations arising from within the body, we have feelings. While the general limbic system concept has been adopted by many subsequent researchers and theorists, the specific hypothesis about integration of internal and external senses that led MacLean to the general theory has been left behind. The general theory, that the brain has a limbic system and that our emotions come out of this system, took on a life of its own and has survived, and even thrived, independent of its conceptual origins. Even as research has shown that classical limbic areas are by no means dedicated to emotion, the theory has persisted. Implicit in such a view is that emotion is a single faculty of mind and that a single unified system of the brain evolved to mediate this faculty. While it is possible that this view is correct, there is little evidence that it is. A new approach to the emotional brain is needed.

One of MacLean's many important insights was his emphasis on the evolution of the brain as a key to understanding emotions. He saw emotions as brain functions involved in maintaining the survival of the individual and the species. From the vantage point of hindsight, it seems that his mistake was to package the entire emotional brain and its evolutionary history into one system. I think that his logic about emotional evolution was perfect, he just applied it too broadly. Emotions are indeed functions involved in survival. But since different emotions are involved with different survival functions—defending against danger, finding food and mates, caring for offspring, and so on—each may well involve different brain systems that evolved for different reasons. As a result, there may not be one emotional system in the brain but many.

5

THE WAY WE WERE

⌒∞⌒

"Human subtlety . . . will never devise an invention more beautiful, more simple or more direct than does nature."

Leonardo da Vinci, *The Notebooks* (1508–1518)[1]

WHEN ENGINEERS SIT DOWN to design machines, they start off with some function they want to implement and then figure out how to make a device that will accomplish the task. But biological machines aren't assembled from carefully engineered plans. The human brain, for example, happens to be the most sophisticated machine imaginable, or unimaginable, yet it wasn't predesigned. It is the product of evolutionary tinkering, where lots of little changes over extremely long periods of time have accumulated.[2]

Organisms, according to Stephen J. Gould, are Rube Goldberg devices, patchworks of quick fixes and partial solutions that shouldn't work but somehow do the trick.[3] Evolution works with what it has, rather than starting from scratch. As evolutionary biologist Richard Dawkins points out, this is horribly inefficient on small time scales— it would have been foolish to try and construct the first jet engine by modifying an existing gasoline engine.[4] But, as Dawkins notes, evolution's strategy of tinkering works pretty well over the huge spans of time on which it operates. Besides, there's no alternative.

The problem of figuring out how a brain works has been described by the linguist Steven Pinker as "reverse engineering."[5] We've got the product and we want to know how it functions. So we pick the brain apart in the hope that we will see what evolution was up to when it put the device together.

Although we often talk about the brain as if it has a function, the brain itself actually has no function. It is a collection of systems, sometimes called modules, each with different functions.[6] There is no equation by which the combination of the functions of all the different systems mixed together equals an additional function called brain function.

Evolution tends to act on the individual modules and their functions rather than the brain as a whole. For example, there is evidence that specific brain adaptations underlie certain capacities, like song learning in birds, memory for food location in foragers, sex differences, hand preferences, and language skills in humans.[7] It is true that at times evolution might act globally,[8] say increasing the size of the entire brain, but by and large most evolutionary changes in the brain take place at the level of individual modules. These modules accomplish such mental exotica as having thoughts or beliefs, but also activities as mundane as breathing. Evolutionary improvements in our ability to believe do not necessarily help us breathe any better. They may, but they don't necessarily.

Admittedly, breathing and believing are pretty distinct functions, clearly mediated by different brain regions. Breathing is controlled in the medulla oblongata, that utility station down in the subbasement of the brain, whereas believing, like all good higher cognitive functions, goes on up in the neocortical penthouse. Contrasting these is not so interesting.

So let's consider functions that are more similar, like different emotions. Do changes in our ability to detect danger and respond to it help us in our love life or make us less prone to anger or depression? They could, especially if there was a universal emotional system in the brain, a system dedicated to emotional functions and within which all emotional functions are mediated. A general improvement in the operation of this system would probably impact across the board on all emotions. We could certainly concoct an explanation for why feeling good and bad may have been beneficial to survival to our ancestors, and theirs, and therefore why an all-purpose emotion system might have evolved. In the last chapter, though, we saw that attempts to find a single unified brain system of emotion have not been very successful. It is possible that such a system exists and that scientists just haven't been clever enough to find it, but I don't think that's the case. Most likely, attempts to find an all-purpose emotion system have failed because such a system does not exist. Different emotions are mediated by different brain networks, different modules, and evolutionary changes in a particular network don't necessarily affect the others directly. There might of course be indirect effects—an increased ability to detect danger and defend against it might leave more time and resources for pursuing romantic interests—but this is a different matter.

If I'm correct, the only way to understand how emotions come out of brains is to study emotions one at a time. If there are different emotional systems and we ignore this diversity we will never make much sense of the brain's emotional secrets. If I'm wrong, though, we've lost nothing by taking this approach. We can mix the findings from fear, anger, disgust, and joy back together anytime.

For these reasons, my research on the emotional brain has been focused on the neural basis of one particular emotion—fear, and its various incarnations. Much of the remainder of this book is aimed at explaining what we know about the brain mechanisms of fear, especially what we've learned from research on fear behavior in nonhuman animals, and then seeing to what extent this knowledge can help us understand "emotion" in the broader sense of the term (especially human emotion). But before going further, I need to convince you that the study of fear behavior in animals is a good starting point. And before doing this, I need to go through some ideas about the evolution of emotions, some criticisms of them, and my take on where the balance lies.

To Change or Not to Change, That Is the (Evolutionary) Question

For some mental functions, like language, the job facing evolutionary theorists is to try to understand how the function came to be in humans. Our species seems to be the only one living now that is endowed with natural language.[9] So the big question, in terms of origins, is what did language evolve from—what were the intermediate phases that the brain passed through in the transition from nonspeaking to speaking primates?

When it comes to emotions, though, we face a different problem. Contrary to the views of some humanists, I believe that emotions are anything but uniquely human traits and, in fact, that some emotional systems in the brain are essentially the same in many of the backboned creatures, including mammals, reptiles, and birds, and possibly amphibians and fishes as well. If this is true, and I'll try to convince you that it is, our first order of business is quite different from that of the evolutionary linguists. Rather than trying to figure out what is unique about human emotion, we need to examine how evolution stubbornly maintains emotional functions across species while changing many other brain functions and bodily traits.

If people had wings, William James would have posed his famous question about running away from the bear in terms of flying away. He would have asked whether fear is the result of flying away from danger or whether flying from danger causes us to be afraid. Stated this way, the question loses none of its meaning. Escaping from danger is something that all animals have to do to survive. Uniquely human traits, like the ability to compose poetry or solve differential equations, are irrelevant to what goes on when we are faced with a sudden and immediate threat to our existence. What is important is that the brain have a mechanism for detecting the danger and responding to it appropriately and quickly. The particular behavior that occurs is tailored to the species (running, flying, swimming), but the brain function underlying that response is the same—protection against the danger.[10] This is as true of a human animal as of a slimy reptile. And, as we will see, evolution has seen fit to pretty much leave well enough alone inside the brain when it comes to these functions.

Emotional Descent

The belief that at least some emotions might be shared by man and other creatures has been around for a long time, at least since Plato proclaimed that the passions are wild beasts trying to escape from the human body.[11] But an understanding of how and why aspects of mind and behavior might be commonly represented in humans and other species remained completely obscure until Charles Darwin conceived of the theory of evolution by natural selection in the last century.[12]

Darwin got his ideas by looking at life around him. He noted that children resemble their parents, but differ from them as well. And he was fascinated with the ability of breeders of domestic animals to build traits in offspring by carefully mixing and matching parents—cows could be made to produce more milk and horses to run faster by preselecting the parents. He reasoned that something similar might occur naturally. Armed with these observations, and others made on his famous voyage to the Galápagos Islands, Darwin proposed that, through heritability and variability, "descent with modification" occurs.

Stephen J. Gould tells us that Darwin did not use the term "evolution" to describe natural selection.[13] At the time, evolution had two other connotations, both of which were incompatible with Darwin's theory. One had to do with the notion that embryos grow from preformed homunculi enclosed in the egg and sperm (tiny preserved versions of Adam and Eve). The other was a vernacular usage that implied constant progress toward an ideal. Darwin felt that a so-called lower form of life, like an amoeba, could be as adapted to its environment as a human is to its—humans, in other words, are not necessarily closer to some evolutionary ideal than other animals. It was really Herbert Spencer, a contemporary of Darwin's, who transformed "descent with modification" into "evolution," the catchier term that we use today.[14]

In rough-and-ready terms, Darwin's theory of natural selection went something like this.[15] Those traits that were useful to the survival of a species in a particular environment became, over the long run, characteristic traits of the species. And, by the same token, the characteristic traits of current species exist because they contributed to the survival of distant ancestors. Because of limited food supplies, not all individuals that are born survive to the point of sexual maturity and procreate. The less fit get weeded out so that over time more and more of the better fit become parents and pass on their fitness to their offspring. But if the environment happens to change, and it does so constantly, then different traits become relevant to survival, and these eventually get selected for. Species that adapt in this way survive, whereas those that do not become extinct.

Darwin's theory is most often thought of as an explanation of how physical features of species evolved. However, he argued that mind and behavior are also shaped by natural selection. James Gould, a behavioral biologist, makes this point forcefully:

> Darwin's revolutionary insights into evolution . . . demonstrated for the first time the inextricable link between an animal's world and its behavior. His theory of natural selection made it possible to understand why animals are so well endowed with mysterious instincts—why a wasp, for example, gathers food she has never eaten to feed larvae she will never see. Natural selection, Darwin hypothesized, favors animals which leave the most offspring. Through countless generations the survivors of the unceasing struggle for a limited amount of food have to be ever more perfectly adapted to their worlds, both morphologically and behaviorally. . . . Carefully programmed behavior like that of the wasp must provide an enormous competitive advantage for animals.[16]

In *The Expression of the Emotions in Man and Animals,* Darwin proposed that "the chief expressive actions, exhibited by man and by the lower animals, are now innate or inherited,—that is, have not been learnt by the individual."[17] As evidence for emotional innateness, he noted the similarity of expressions both within and between species. In humans, Darwin was particularly impressed with the fact that the bodily expressions (especially of the face) occurring during emotions are similar in people around the world, regardless of racial origins or cultural heritage. He also pointed out that these same expressions are present in persons born blind, and thus lacking the opportunity to have learned the muscle movements from seeing them in others, and are also present in very young children, who also have had little opportunity to learn to express emotions by imitation.[18]

Darwin mustered instances of all sorts of bodily expressions that are similar in different species. Although the greatest similarities were found between closely related species, Darwin was able to identify some striking similarities, even within fairly dissimilar organisms. He pointed out how common it is for animals of all varieties, including humans, to urinate and defecate in the face of extreme danger. And many animals erect body hair in dangerous situations, presumably to make themselves look more vicious than they otherwise would. Piloerection, according to Darwin, is probably one of the most general of the emotional expressions, occurring in dogs, lions, hyenas, cows, pigs, antelopes, horses, cats, rodents, bats, to name a few.

Darwin suggested that goose bumps, a mild form of piloerection in humans, occur as a vestige of the more dramatic displays in our mammalian cousins. He points out that it is a remarkable fact that the thinly scattered hairs on the human body are erected in rage and terror, emotional states that cause body hair to stand on end in furry animals, where body piloerection has some purpose. But he noted that piloerection also occurs on the part of the human body that is well endowed with hair, the head, using Brutus' statement to the ghost of Caesar as evidence: "that mak'st my blood cold, and my hair stare."

Darwin gave many other examples of common emotional expression in different species. For example, he equated the snarl of an angry human with similar behaviors in other creatures. Again turning to literature for support, he quotes Dickens' description in *Oliver Twist* of a furious mob witnessing the capture of an atrocious murderer on the streets of London: "the people as jumping up one behind another, snarling with their teeth, and making at him like wild beasts." Darwin goes on to note that "Everyone who has had much to do with young children must have seen how naturally they take to biting, when in a passion. It seems as instinctive in them as in young crocodiles, who snap their little jaws as soon as they emerge from the egg." He also quotes from Dr. Maudsley, who specialized in human insanity and for whom the renowned Maudsley Hospital in London is named: "whence come 'the savage snarl, the destructive disposition, the obscene language, the wild howl, the offensive habits, displayed by some of the insane? Why should a human being, deprived of his reason, ever become so brutal in character, as some do, unless he has the brute nature within him?'" In response, Darwin says, "This question must, as it would appear, be answered in the affirmative."

For Darwin, an important function of emotional expressions is communication between individuals—they show others what particular emotional state one is in. Emission of vicious sounds and enlarging body parts (flashing of feathers, extension of fins or pointy spines, puffing up, and, as we have seen, erection of body hair), are used throughout the animal kingdom to dissuade an enemy from attacking. Sounds, smells, and various postures and displays of body parts or hidden colors serve as signals of sexual receptiveness as well. Sounds are also used to warn others that danger is near. While these signals are somewhat relevant to humans, in the passage below Darwin describes some emotional expressions that are particularly important to our species:

> The movements of expression in the face and body, whatever their origin may have been, are in themselves of much importance in our welfare. They serve as the first means of communication between the mother and her infant; she smiles approval, and thus encourages her child on the right path, or frowns disapproval. We readily perceive sympathy in others by their expression; our sufferings are thus mitigated and our pleasures increased; and mutual good feeling is thus strengthened. The movements of expression give vividness and energy to our spoken words. They reveal the thoughts and intentions of others more truly than do words, which may be falsified.

FIGURE 5-1
Commonality of Emotional Expression
in the Faces of Animals and People.

Some emotional expressions are similar in humans and other animals. These two drawings illustrate angry facial expressions in a chimpanzee and human. In both species an expression of anger often involves a direct gaze and a partly opened mouth with lips retracted vertically so that the teeth show. (Drawings, by Eric Stoelting, are reprinted with permission from S. Chevalier-Skolnikoff [1973], Facial expression of emotion in nonhuman primates. In P. Ekman, *Darwin and Facial Expression*. New York: Academic Press.)

A picture may be worth a thousand words, but bodily expressions are priceless commodities in the emotional marketplace.

Darwin argued that although emotional expressions can sometimes be muted by willpower, they are usually involuntary actions. He pointed out how easy it is to tell the difference between a real, involuntary smile and one that is feigned. And he gives us an example from his own life to illustrate how difficult it is to suppress an emotional reaction that has been elicited naturally: "I put my face close to the thick glass-plate in front of a puff-ader in the Zoological Gardens, with the firm determination of not starting back if the snake struck at me; but, as soon as the blow was struck, my resolution went for nothing, and I jumped a yard or two backwards with astonishing rapidity. My will and reason were powerless against the imagination of a danger which had never been experienced."

Within the general class of innate emotions, Darwin suggested that some have older evolutionary histories than others. He noted that fear and rage were expressed in our remote ancestors almost as they are today in humans. Suffering, as in grief or anxiety, though, he placed closer to human origins. Nevertheless, Darwin was well aware of the pitfalls of such ideas about the time of origin of different emotions and noted: "It is a curious, though perhaps an idle speculation, how early in the long line of our progenitors the various expressive movements, now exhibited by man, were successively acquired."

Basic Instinct

A number of modern theorists carry on Darwin's tradition in their emphasis on a set of basic, innate emotions. For many, basic emotions are defined by universal facial expressions that are similar across many different cultures. In Darwin's day, the universality of emotional expression across cultures was presumed from casual observation, but modern researchers have gone into remote areas of the world to firmly establish with scientific methods that at least some emotions have fairly universal modes of expression, especially in the face. On the basis of this kind of evidence, the late Sylvan Tomkins proposed the existence of eight basic emotions: surprise, interest, joy, rage, fear, disgust, shame, and anguish.[19] These were said to represent innate, patterned responses that are controlled by "hardwired" brain systems. A similar theory involving eight basic emotions has been proposed by Carroll Izard.[20] Paul Ekman has a shorter list, consisting of six basic emotions with universal facial expression: surprise, happiness, anger, fear, disgust and sadness.[21] Other theorists, like Robert Plutchik[22] and Nico Frijda,[23] do not rely exclusively on facial expressions, but instead argue for the primacy of more global action tendencies involving many body parts. Plutchik points out that as one goes down the evolutionary scale there are fewer and fewer facial expressions, but still lots of emotional expressions involving other bodily systems. Plutchik's emotions list overlaps with the others, but also diverges to some extent—it is similar to Ekman's, with the addition of acceptance, anticipation, and surprise. Philip Johnson-Laird and Keith Oatley approach the problem of basic emotions by looking at the kinds of words we have for talking about emotions.[24] They come up with a list of five that overlaps with Ekman's six, dropping surprise. Jaak Panksepp has taken a different approach, using the behavioral consequences of electrical stimulation of areas of the rat brain to reveal four basic emotional response patterns: panic, rage, expectancy, and fear.[25] Other theorists have other ways of identifying basic emotions and their lists also overlap and diverge from the ones already described.[26]

Most basic emotions theorists assume that there are also nonbasic emotions that are the result of blends or mixes of the more basic ones. Izard, for example, describes anxiety as the combination of fear and two additional emotions, which can be either guilt, interest, shame, anger, or distress. Plutchik has one of the better developed theories of emotion mixes. He has a circle of emotions, analogous to a circle of colors in which mixing of elementary colors gives new ones. Each basic emotion occupies a position on the circle. Blends of two basic emotions are called dyads. Blends involving adjacent emotions in the circle are first-order dyads, blends involving emotions that are separated by one other emotion are second-order dyads, and so on. Love, in this scheme, is a first-order dyad resulting from the blending of adjacent basic emotions joy and acceptance, whereas guilt is a second-order dyad involving joy and fear, which are separated by acceptance. The further away two basic emotions are, the less likely they are to mix. And if two distant emotions mix, conflict is likely. Fear and surprise are adjacent and readily blend to give rise to alarm, but joy and fear are separated by acceptance and their fusion is imperfect—the conflict that results is the source of the emotion guilt.

The mixing of basic emotions into higher order emotions is typically thought of as a cognitive operation. According to basic emotions theorists, some if not all of the biologically basic emotions are shared with lower animals, but the derived or nonbasic emotions tend to be more uniquely human. Since the derived emotions are constructed by cognitive operations, they could only be the same to the extent that two animals share the same cognitive capacities. And since it is in the area of cognition that humans are believed to differ most significantly from other mammals, nonbasic, cognitively constructed emotions are more likely than basic emotions to differ between humans and other species. Richard Lazarus, for example, proposes that pride, shame, and gratitude might be uniquely human emotions.[27]

Plutchik's 8 Basic Emotions	Some Psychosocially Derived Emotions
	Primary Dyads (mix of adjacent emotions) - joy + acceptance = friendliness - fear + surprise = alarm **Secondary Dyads** (mix of emotions, once removed - joy + fear = guilt - sadness + anger = sullenness **Tertiary Dyads** (mix of emotions, twice removed) - joy + surprise = delight - anticipation + fear = anxiety

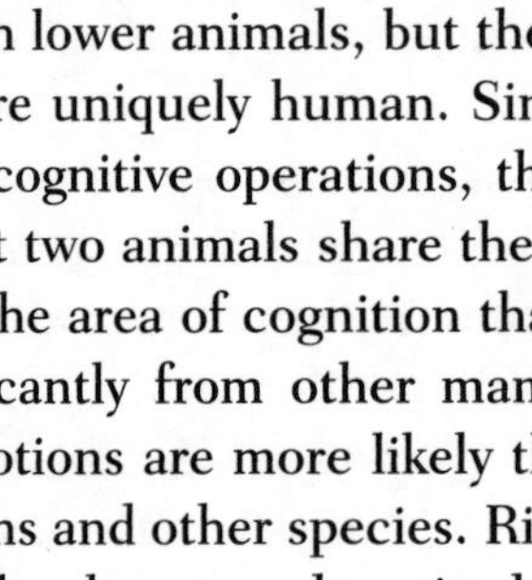

FIGURE 5-2
Plutchik's Theory of Basic and Derived Emotions.

(Based on figure 11.4 and table 11.3 in R. Plutchik [1980], *Emotion: A Psychoevolutionary Synthesis.* New York: Harper and Row.)

Being a Wild Pig

The idea of biologically primitive emotions has many supporters but has also had its detractors. One challenge comes from various forms of cognitive emotion theory that propose that specific emotions, even those that are described as basic emotions, are psychological, not biological, constructions. Emotions, in this view, are due to the internal representation and interpretation (appraisal) of situations, not to the mindless workings of biological hardware.

We saw many examples of cognitive views of emotion in Chapter 3. Here, however, I want to focus on the social constructivist approach, which is even further removed from the biology of emotion than most other cognitive approaches. These theorists argue that emotions are products of society, not biology.[28] Cognitive processes play an important role in these theories by providing the mechanism through which the social environment is represented and, on the basis of past experience and future expectations, interpreted. Emotional diversity across cultures is used as evidence in support of this position.

James Averill, a major proponent of social constructivism, describes a behavior pattern, called "being a wild pig," that is quite unusual by Western standards, but is common and even "normal" among the Gururumba, a horticultural people living in the highlands of New Zealand.[29] The behavior gets its name by analogy. There are no undomesticated pigs in this culture, but occasionally, and for unknown reasons, a domesticated one will go through a temporary condition in which it runs wild. But the pig can, with appropriate measures, be redomesticated and returned to the normal pig life among the villagers. And, in a similar vein, Gururumba people can act this way, becoming violent and aggressive and looting and stealing, but seldom causing harm or taking anything of importance, and eventually returning to routine life. In some instances, after several days of living in the forest, during which time the stolen objects are destroyed, the person returns to the village spontaneously with no memory of the experience and is never reminded of the event by the villagers. Others, though, have to be captured and treated like a wild pig—held over a smoking fire until the old self returns. The Gururumba believe that being a wild pig occurs when one is bitten by the ghost of someone who recently died. As a result, social controls on behavior are lost and primitive impulses are set free. According to Averill, being a wild pig is a social, not a biological or even an individual, condition. Westerners are prone to think of this as psychotic, abnormal behavior, but for the Gururumba it is instead a way of relieving stress and maintaining community mental health in the village. Averill uses "being a wild pig" to support his claim that "most standard emotional reactions are socially constructed or institutionalized patterns of response" rather than biologically determined events (one wonders, though, where the wild impulses come from).

Another example of an emotional condition that is not common in Western cultures is the state of mind called "amae" in Japan.[30] Amae has no literal translation in Indo-European languages. The condition it represents is believed by some to be a key to understanding important aspects of Japanese personality structure.[31] It roughly means to presume upon another's love or to indulge in another's kindness. The Japanese psychiatrist Doi calls amae a sense of helplessness and the desire to be loved, to be a passive love object.[32] He believes that amae also occurs in Westerners, but in a much more limited way. The Japanese frequently amaeru (the verb form) but seldom talk about it because it is a nonverbal condition and it would be inappropriate to point it out in another. According to Doi, "those who are close to each other—that is to say, who are privileged to merge with each other—do not need words to express their feelings. One surely would not feel merged with another (that is amae), if one had to verbalize the need to do so!" Doi says that Americans feel encouraged and reassured by such verbal exchanges, but the Japanese neither need it nor find it desirable.

Display Rules

Social constructivists can produce endless lists of all sorts of ways that emotions differ in different cultures or social situations.[33] Certain emotion words from islands in the South Pacific or other remote areas have no translation in English. And even amongst Western cultures, there are differences in emotion words.[34]

But these kinds of observations are not enough to take down the basic emotions view. Basic emotions theorists do not deny that some differences exist in the way emotions are labeled and even expressed between cultures, or even between individuals within a culture. They simply say that some emotions and their expressions are fairly constant in all people. The social constructivists can then counter with the fact that a given individual may express a basic emotion, like anger, differently in different situations—overt anger is more likely to be displayed at those below than those above one in a social hierarchy.

In an attempt to reconcile theories that emphasize the similarity of facial expression across cultures and those that emphasize differences, basic emotions theorist Paul Ekman proposed a distinction between universal emotional expressions (especially facial expressions), which are common to all cultures, and other bodily movements (emblems and illustrators, for example) that vary from culture to culture.[35] Emblems are movements with a specific verbal meaning, such as head nodding to signify yes or no, or shrugging to indicate that you don't know the answer to a question. Emblems could be expressed in words but are not. Illustrators are closely tied to the content and flow of speech. They punctuate speech, help fill in when words cannot be found, or help explain what is being said. In some cultures people "talk with their hands" more than in others. Ekman suggests that social constructivists may be focusing on learned cultural differences in emotional expression, while the basic emotions theorists have been focused on the unlearned, universal expressions that occur in the movement of facial muscles during the occurrence of basic (innate) emotions in all cultures.

Ekman does not claim that basic emotional expressions always look exactly the same. He points out that even universal facial expressions can be regulated by learning and culture. They can be interrupted, diminished, or amplified by learned factors, or even masked by other emotions.[36] He uses the term "display rules" to refer to the conventions, norms, and habits that people develop to manage their emotional expressions. Display rules specify who can show what emotion to whom and when and how much. In Western cultures, there is a grief hierarchy at funerals. As Mark Twain said, "Where a blood relation sobs, an intimate friend should choke up, a distant acquaintance should sigh, a stranger should merely fumble sympathetically with his handkerchief.[37] According to Ekman, if the secretary looks sadder than the wife, suspicions may be aroused. Ekman also suggests that display rules can be personalized and override cultural norms. Some people end up being stoics and show little emotion, even in situations where society allows emotions to flow freely. In Ekman's view, the concept of basic emotions accounts for the similarity of basic emotional expression across individuals and cultures and display rules take care of many of the differences.

Ekman performed a powerful test of his hypothesis.[38] Starting with the assumption that Westerners are more emotionally expressive than Orientals, he studied the facial expressions of Japanese and American subjects while they watched an emotion-arousing film. The subjects were tested in their native countries, and they watched the film while either sitting alone in a room or sitting in a room with an authoritative-looking experimenter in a white coat. Their faces were secretly recorded on videotape throughout. Later, facial expressions were coded by observers who were ignorant of what the subjects were watching. In the private viewing condition, there was a tremendous similarity in the emotions expressed at various points in the film by the Japanese and American subjects. But when the white-coated experimenter was present, the facial movements were no longer the same. The Japanese looked more polite and showed more smiling and less emotional diversity than the Americans. Interestingly, slow-motion analysis of the film revealed that the smiles and other polite facial expressions of the Japanese subjects were superimposed over brief, prior-occurring facial movements that were, according to Ekman, the basic emotions leaking through.

Display rules are learned as part of one's socialization and become so ingrained that, like the basic emotional expressions themselves, they occur automatically, which is to say without conscious participation. At the same time, an individual may sometimes deliberately choose to conceal emotions for a particular advantage in a specific situation. This, however, is a skill that is hard to master—we aren't all good poker players.

Emotional Responses: Parts or Wholes?

The combination of universal emotional expressions and display rules goes a long way toward accounting for individual and cross-cultural variation in the expression of basic emotions, but has not completely inoculated the idea of basic emotions against further challenge. Cognitive scientists Andrew Ortony and Terrance Turner have raised important questions about whether basic emotions can be defined by universal facial expressions, or any other means.[39] They asked why, if basic emotions are so basic, there is so much disagreement about what the basic ones are, and why emotions that are considered basic by some theorists (like interest and desire) are not even considered to be emotions by others. Ortony and Turner then go on to argue that perhaps it is not the emotions and their expressions that are so basic. Instead, they propose that there might be basic, maybe even innate, response components that can be utilized in the expression of emotions, but that are used in other nonemotional situations as well. They note, "emotion expressions are built up by drawing on a repertoire of biologically determined components, and . . . many emotions are often, but by no means always, associated with the same limited subset of such components." They point out that bodily expressions similar to those in an emotion can arise independent of emotions and that the expression typical of one emotion can appear during a different emotional state. Shivering can occur because you are cold or because you are afraid. Crying can occur in extreme happiness as well as sadness. Frowning occurs in anger, but also in frustration, and eyebrows are raised in anger, but also in any condition that requires that we carefully attend to the environment.

For Ortony and Turner, emotion involves higher cognitive processes (appraisals) that organize the various responses that are appropriate to the situation faced by the organism. They accept that component responses can be biologically determined, but place emotion itself in the world of psychological rather than biological determinism. Fear, in their view, is not a biological package that is unwrapped by danger. It is a psychologically constructed set of responses and experiences that are tailored to the particular dangerous situation. There are no emotional responses, there are just responses,

and these are put together on the spot when appraisals are made—
the particular set of responses that occurs depends on the particular
appraisal that occurs. As a result, the number of different emotions is
limited only by the number of different appraisals that one can make.
And because certain appraisals occur frequently and are often talked
about by people, they are easily and reliably labeled with precise
terms in most languages and this makes them seem basic (universal).

The reason that Ortony and Turner pushed for a difference between the innateness of emotional expressions and the innateness of
response components is simple. If there are no universal expressions
characteristic of certain emotions, then the evidence that some emotions, the so-called basic emotions, are biologically determined is
brought to its knees. And if emotions are not biologically determined,
then they must be psychologically determined. But Ortony and
Turner seem to make two unacceptable assumptions. First, just because an appraisal is mental does not mean that it is not also biological. In fact, appraisals play a biological role in some basic emotions
theories as the link between emotional stimuli and the characteristic
responses they produce. Second, the innateness of individual response components does not preclude the possibility that higher levels of expression are also innate. Some innate behavioral patterns are
known to involve hierarchically organized response components.[40]
For example, reproductive behavior is often brought on by the presence of hormones that act on certain parts of the brain. When an organism is in the right hormonal state, either mating or fighting can
occur, depending on whether a receptive female or a competitive
male happens to be around. And these behaviors, though innate, involve many complex levels of control. Mating, for example, may start
with a courtship dance, approach toward the partner, and ultimately
end in copulation. Each phase, itself, has a complex hierarchy of
events controlled by different levels of the nervous system, with the
lower levels controlling the most specific components (individual patterns of muscle contraction and relaxation) and higher levels of the
nervous system specifying more general aspects of behavior (the act
of copulation).

Ortony and Turner caused quite a stir in the world of basic emotions. They made it painfully clear that basic emotions theorists
could no longer continue to agree that basic emotions exist and at the

same time disagree about what the basic ones are. But now that the dust has settled, it seems that Ortony and Turner were probably too hard on the basic emotions view. Some of the differences between the basic emotions lists of different investigators have to do with the words used rather than with the emotions implied by the words.[41] For example, joy and happiness, basic emotions in different lists, are probably just different names for the same emotion. If we allow these kinds of translations, there turns out to be a good deal of overlap of the different lists: many if not most of the lists include some version of fear, anger, disgust, and joy. Most of the remaining disagreement is over the fringe cases, like interest, desire, and surprise. The basic emotions theorists are not as divergent as they appeared, and, as we will see, at least for some emotions, the evidence for an innate, biological organization is quite strong.

If It Ain't Broke . . .

As has been apparent since Darwin's time (and even before) different animals can act in very similar ways under similar circumstances. This is what led Darwin to propose that certain human emotions have their roots in our animal ancestors. But behavioral commonalities between species can occur at several different levels, and not all of them involve responses that look the same.[42] In other words, the gold standard of whether two animals are doing the same thing is not necessarily whether the two things look exactly the same—emotional commonalities between species might be even broader than conceived by Darwin.

In order for behavior to occur, muscles have to move. So the reason that facial expressions of particular emotions look the same in different people is because everyone contracts and relaxes facial muscles in roughly the same way when exposed to a stimulus that characteristically evokes that emotion. And to the extent that different species show similar kinds of expressions it is because they are contracting and relaxing the same or similar muscle groups—the muscle movements required to furrow the brow and expose the teeth in anger are similar in a human and a chimp. At the same time, the behaviors may be similar at some broader level, but not at the level of individual muscles. People run from danger on two legs, but many other land mammals tend to do so on all four: although quadrupeds use more muscles and different patterns of muscle coordination than bipeds, the function performed is the same—escape. Most important, even when the behaviors are very different, the function achieved may be the same. Plutchik puts this nicely: "although a deer may run from danger, a bird may fly from it, and a fish may swim from it, there is a functional equivalence to all the different patterns of behavior; namely, they all have the common function of separating an organism from a threat to its survival."[43] Obviously, running, flying, and swimming are different behaviors involving different muscles, but each achieves escape.

The implication of Plutchik's notion is that certain basic functions that are necessary for survival have been conserved throughout evolution. They have been modified as needed, but the changes have occurred against a fairly consistent background. In an influential treatise on mother-child bonding in humans, the psychoanalytic theorist John Bowlby makes a similar point:

> The basic structure of man's behavioral equipment resembles that of infrahuman species but has in the course of evolution undergone special modifications that permit the same ends to be reached by a much greater diversity of means. . . . The early form is not superseded: it is modified, elaborated, and augmented but it still determines the overall pattern. . . . Instinctive behavior in humans . . . is assumed to derive from some prototypes that are common to other animal species.[44]

I don't mean to minimize the importance of species differences. The things that distinguish one species from another are often things that allowed its ancestors to survive their particular struggle for existence and pass on their traits to their offspring. The kind of body an animal has obviously limits the kinds of behaviors in which the animal can engage. Nevertheless, evolutionary solutions to problems that are common to many species may have some underlying functional equivalence that cuts across the behavioral differences imposed by the uniqueness of body forms.

The obvious question that this discussion raises is, how could a functional equivalence of behavior be maintained across species, especially across species in which the way the function is expressed behaviorally is radically different? The short answer to this very complicated issue is that the brain systems involved in mediating the function are the same in different species.

We know that there is a great deal of similarity in brain organization across the various vertebrate species. All vertebrates have a hindbrain, midbrain, and forebrain, and within each of the three divisions, one can find all of the basic structures and major neural pathways in all animals.[45] At the same time there are obvious differences between the brains of widely different groups of animals. Species differences can involve any brain region or pathway, due to particular brain specializations required for certain species-specific adaptations or to random changes. However, as one follows brain evolution from fish, through amphibians and reptiles, to mammals, and ultimately to humans, the greatest changes appear to have taken place in the forebrain.[46] But evolution should not be thought of as an ascending scale. It is more like a branching tree.[47] The long process of human brain evolution has not just been a matter of making the forebrain bigger and bigger; it has also become more diversified.[48] For example, as we saw in Chapter 4, it was long thought that the neocortex was a mammalian specialization, one that did not exist in other classes of animals (the designation "neo" reflects the supposed evolutionary newness of this part of the brain). However, it is now known that all vertebrates have areas of the cortex that correspond with what is called the neocortex in mammals—these are just located in a different place in nonmammalian species (birds and reptiles, for example) than in mammals, which caused anatomists to misjudge what these regions are.[49] Nevertheless, there are areas of the human neocortex that are apparently not present in the brains of other animals.[50] In spite of this diversification, though, brain evolution is basically conservative, and certain systems, especially those that have been generally useful for survival and have been around for a long time, have been preserved in their basic structure and function.

Circuits in the brain, like all other body parts, are assembled during embryonic development by processes encoded in our genes. If different animals indeed have circuits that achieve some common

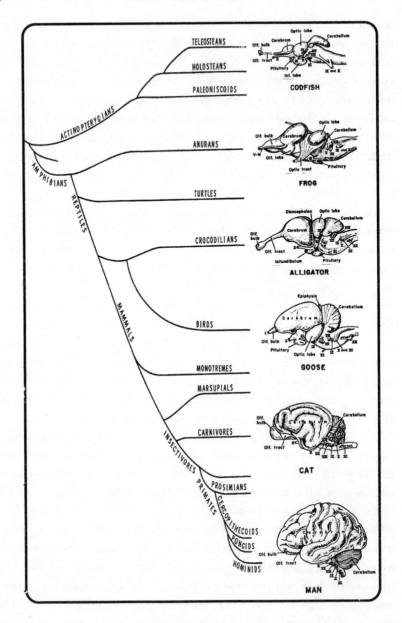

FIGURE 5-3
The Branching Tree of Brain Evolution.

(Modified from figure 5 of W. Hodos [1970], Evolutionary interpretation of neural and behavioral studies of living vertebrates. In F. O. Schmitt, ed., *The Neurosciences: Second Study Program.* New York: Rockefeller University Press. Used by permission of the Rockefeller University Press.)

function, but do it by controlling different behaviors, we would be led to the conclusion that the genetic code that controls the wiring of the functions in the brain during development is conserved across species in spite of the fact that the genetic code that constructs the body parts used to express those functions is different. Evolution, in other words, creates unique behavioral solutions to the problem of survival in different species, but it may do so by following a kind of "if it ain't broke don't fix it" rule for the underlying brain systems.

For now, I'm going ask you to take it on faith that the brain systems underlying certain emotional behaviors have been preserved throughout many levels of brain evolution. In the next chapter, though, I will present very strong evidence that this is true within the mammalian class, and also describe some hints that it may extend to existing reptiles and birds as well.

Throughout this discussion of the evolution of emotion, I've said nothing about what most people consider the most important, in fact, the defining feature of an emotion: the subjective feeling that comes with it. The reason for this is that I believe that the basic building blocks of emotions are neural systems that mediate behavioral interactions with the environment, particularly behaviors that take care of fundamental problems of survival.[51] And while all animals have some version of these survival systems in their brains, I believe that feelings can only occur when a survival system is present in a brain that also has the capacity for consciousness. To the extent that consciousness is a recent (in evolutionary time) development,[52] feelings came after responses in the emotional chicken-and-egg problem. I'm not going to say which animals are conscious (which ones have feelings) and which ones are not (which ones don't have feelings). But I will say that capacity to have feelings is directly tied to the capacity to be consciously aware of one's self and the relation of oneself to the rest of the world. We will return to these issues in Chapter 9. For now, I want to continue to pursue some ideas about the evolution of behaviors that are crucial to survival, or more precisely, some ideas about the evolution of the neural systems underlying these behaviors.

Specialized versus General-Purpose Neural Systems

Modern evolutionarily minded emotions theorists, like Ekman, argue that emotions deal with "fundamental life tasks."[53] A similar point is made by Johnson-Laird and Oatley, who say that each emotion "prompts us in a direction which in the course of evolution has done better than other solutions to recurring circumstances."[54] And Tooby and Cosmides argue that emotions involve situations that have occurred over and over throughout our evolutionary history (escaping from danger, finding food and mates) and cause us to appraise present events in terms of our ancestral past—that the structure of the past imposes an interpretive landscape on the present.[55]

In a sense, coming up with a list of the special adaptive behaviors that are crucial to survival would essentially be a list of basic emotions. I think starting with universal behavioral functions is a better way of producing a list of basic emotions than the more standard ways—facial expressions, emotion words in different languages, or conscious introspections. However, I'm not concerned with defining, from the start, what the different emotions are and I have no interest in producing yet another basic emotions list. Obviously, it is ultimately important to understand what all the biologically derived and socially constructed emotions are, and to determine where the line should be drawn between them. It is also important to draw the line between mental phenomena that are emotions and those that are not. However, for good reasons, efforts to identify what all of the emotions are frequently get bogged down in arguments over the fringe instances, as when Ortony and Turner took basic emotions theorists to task for their inability to agree about what the various basic emotions are, and especially for disagreeing about the fuzzy cases, like surprise, interest, and desire. I believe that once we've built up a core knowledge about the clear instances we will be in a better position to deal with the fuzzy ones, but we haven't reached that point yet.

To the extent that emotional responses evolved, they evolved for different reasons, and it seems obvious to me that there must be different brain systems to take care of these different kinds of functions. Lumping all of these together under the unitary concept of emotional behavior provides us with a convenient way of organizing things—for distinguishing behaviors that we call emotional (for example, those involved with fighting, feeding, sex, and social bonding) from those that reflect cognitive functions (like reasoning, abstract thinking, problem solving, and concept formation). However, the use of a label, like "emotional behavior," should not necessarily lead us to assume that all of the labeled functions are mediated by one system of the brain. Seeing and hearing are both sensory functions, but each has its own neural machinery.

I think that the most practical working hypothesis is that different classes of emotional behavior represent different kinds of functions that take care of different kinds of problems for the animal and have different brain systems devoted to them. If this is true, then different emotions should be studied as separate functional units.

At the neural level, each emotional unit can be thought of as consisting of a set of inputs, an appraisal mechanism, and a set of outputs. The appraisal mechanism is programmed by evolution to detect certain input or trigger stimuli that are relevant to the function of the network. We'll call these "natural triggers."[56] The sight of a predator is a good example. It is not uncommon for prey species to recognize predators the first time they see them. Evolution has programmed the prey brain so that certain features of the way the predator looks, sounds, or smells will be automatically appraised as being a source of danger. But the appraisal mechanism also has the capacity to learn about stimuli that tend to be associated with and predictive of the occurrence of natural triggers. These we'll call "learned triggers." The place where a predator was seen last, or the sound it made when it was charging toward the prey are good examples. When the appraisal mechanism receives trigger inputs of either type, it unleashes certain patterns of response that have tended to be useful in dealing with situations that have routinely activated the appraisal mechanism in ancestral animals. These networks evolved because they serve the function of connecting trigger stimuli with responses that are likely to succeed in keeping the organism alive. And because different kinds of problems of survival have different trigger stimuli and require different kinds of responses to deal with them, different neural systems are devoted to them.[57]

The particular functional unit that I have focused my research on is the fear system of the brain. In the next several chapters, we will look closely at the fear system, which is understood as well or better than other emotional systems. Once we see how this system is organized, we will be in a better position to consider the manner in which other emotions are organized in the brain, and how these relate to the fear system.

Why Fear?

I'm going to now lay out some of the reasons why I believe the fear system of the brain is a particularly good one to focus on as an anchoring point. However, I want to first be explicit about what I think the fear system is. The system is not, strictly speaking, a system that results in the experience of fear. It is a system that detects danger and produces responses that maximize the probability of surviving a dangerous situation in the most beneficial way. It is, in other words, a system of defensive behavior. As noted above, I believe that emotional behaviors, like defensive behaviors, evolved independent of, which is to say before, conscious feelings, and that we should not be too quick to assume that when an animal, other than a human one, is in danger it feels afraid. We should, in other words, take defensive behaviors at face value—they represent the operation of brain systems that have been programmed by evolution to deal with danger in routine ways. Although we can become conscious of the operation of the defense system, especially when it leads to behavioral expressions, the system operates independently of consciousness—it is part of what we called the emotional unconscious in the Chapter 3. Interactions between the defense system and consciousness underlie feelings of fear, but the defense system's function in life, or at least the function it evolved to achieve, is survival in the face of danger. Feelings of fear are a by-product of the evolution of two neural systems: one that mediates defensive behavior and one that creates consciousness. Either one alone is not enough to produce subjective fear. Feeling afraid can be very useful, but this is not the function programmed into the neural system of defense by evolution.

With the territory staked out in this way, let's now consider why the defensive system of the brain and its associated subjective emotion, fear, are attractive starting points for studying the emotional brain. I'll discuss three points below: fear is pervasive, fear is important in psychopathology, and fear is expressed similarly in man and many other animals. In the next chapter, another crucial point will be considered, namely that the neural basis of fear is similar in humans and other animals.

Fear Is Pervasive: William James once said that nothing marks the ascendancy of man from beast more clearly than the reduction of the conditions under which fear is evoked in humans.[58] By this, it would seem that James meant that man has managed to establish a less dangerous way of living. It is certainly true that in comparison to our primate ancestors, who lived in a world in which being someone's dinner was an ever-present possibility, humans have created a way of living in which the likelihood of encountering predators is greatly reduced. But not all dangers come in the form of bloodthirsty beasts. Snakes and tigers are rare in modern cities, except in zoos, where viewing dangerous animals in captivity reinforces our hope that life is safe. But in our quest to conquer nature we have created new forms of danger. Automobiles, airplanes, weapons, and nuclear energy give us a step up on the wild, but each is also a potential source of harm. We've traded in the dangers of a life amongst the wild things for other dangers that may, in the end, be far more harmful to our species than any natural predator. The dangers we face are not fewer or less significant than those of our animal ancestors, they're just different.

Even a casual analysis of the number of ways the concept of fear can be expressed in the English language reveals its importance in our lives: alarm, scare, worry, concern, misgiving, qualm, disquiet, uneasiness, wariness, nervousness, edginess, jitteriness, apprehension, anxiety, trepidation, fright, dread, anguish, panic, terror, horror, consternation, distress, unnerved, distraught, threatened, defensive.[59] The so-called ascent of man occurred in spite of the continued existence of fear rather than at its expense. As the renowned human ethologist Eibl-Eibesfeldt notes, "Perhaps man is one of the most fearful creatures, since added to the basic fear of predators and hostile conspecifics come intellectually based existential fears."[60] Indeed, for the existential philosophers (like Kierkegaard, Heidegger, and Sartre), dread, angst, and anguish are at the core of human existence.[61]

One can find evidence of fear lurking in the background of many kinds of emotions that on the surface might seem to be the antithesis of fear. Courage is the ability to overcome fear. Children learn to be moral to some extent by their fear of what will happen if they are not. Laws reflect our fear of social disorder and, by the same token, social order is maintained, however imperfectly, by fear of the consequences of breaking the rules. World peace is a desirable humanitarian goal, but in practice war is avoided, at least in part, because the weak fear the strong. These are bleak statements, hopefully overstatements, but even as partial truths they emphasize how deeply fear cuts into the mental fabric of persons and societies.

Fear Plays an Important Role in Psychopathology: While fear is a part of everyone's life, too much or inappropriate fear accounts for many common psychiatric problems. Anxiety, a brooding fear of what might happen, was at the core of Freud's psychoanalytic theory. Phobias are specific fears taken to extreme. Phobic objects (snakes, spiders, heights, water, open places, social situations) are often legitimately threatening, but not to the extent believed by the phobic person. Obsessive-compulsive disorder often involves extreme fear of something, like germs, and the patients will engage in compulsive rituals to avoid the feared object or event or to rid themselves of the fear object once it is encountered. Panic disorder involves the rapid onset of a host of physical symptoms and often the overwhelming fear that death is near. Post-traumatic stress disorder (PTSD), previously referred to as shell shock, often occurs in war veterans, who can be sent into intense distress by a stimulus that has some resemblance to events associated with battlefield trauma. Thunderclaps and the sound of a car backfiring are common examples. But PTSD extends to many other kinds of traumatic situations, including physical and sexual abuse. Fear is a core emotion in psychopathology.

Fear Is Expressed Similarly in Humans and Other Animals: It may not be the case that every form of emotional behavior has a long evolutionary history. Guilt and shame, for example, may be special human emotions.[62] Nevertheless, as we will see, human defensive behavior clearly seems to have a long evolutionary history. As a result, we can study fear responses in animals for the purpose of illuminating the mechanisms of human fear, including pathological fear. This is crucial, since for both ethical and practical reasons it is not possible to study brain mechanisms in much detail in humans.

All animals have to protect themselves from dangerous situations in order to survive, and there are only a limited number of strategies that animals can call upon to deal with danger. Isaac Marks, who has written extensively on fear, summarizes these as withdrawal (avoiding the danger or escape from it), immobility (freezing), defensive aggression (appearing to be dangerous and/or fighting back), or submission (appeasement).[63] The extent to which these strategies apply across the various vertebrates is striking.

Consider the following description of human defense by Caroline and Robert Blanchard, pioneers in fear research:

> If something unexpected occurs—a loud noise or sudden movement—people tend to respond immediately . . . stop what they are doing . . . orient toward the stimulus, and try to identify its potentiality for actual danger. This happens very quickly, in a reflex-like sequence in which action precedes any voluntary or consciously intentioned behavior. A poorly localizable or identifiable threat source, such as a sound in the night, may elicit an active immobility so profound that the frightened person can hardly speak or even breathe, i.e. freezing. However, if the danger source has been localized and an avenue for flight or concealment is plausible, the person will probably try to flee or hide. . . . Actual contact, particularly painful contact, with the threat source is also likely to elicit thrashing, biting, scratching, and other potentially damaging activities by the terrified person.[64]

Though anecdotal, the Blanchards' description goes a long way toward accounting for the way people behave when threatened. And different people tend to do roughly the same things in similar kinds of situations. This uniformity suggests that either we all learn to be fearful in the same way, or, more likely, that patterns of fear reactivity are genetically programmed into the human brain.

Research by the Blanchards and others has shown that the reaction pattern described above for a frightened human also occurs when rats are in danger.[65] For example, if a laboratory-reared rat (one that has never had the opportunity to see a cat or be threatened by one) is exposed to a cat, it stops what it is doing and turns toward the cat. Depending on whether the cat is close or far away and whether the two animals are in an enclosed or an open area, the rat will either freeze or try to escape. If trapped by the cat, the rat will vocalize and ultimately will attack the cat. This striking functional correspondence between human and rat fear responses holds for many mammals and other vertebrates: it is quite common to observe startle, orienting, then freezing or fleeing or attack, in the face of danger. We've already seen examples from Darwin about how hair erection is a common defense response in many animals, including people, and how it may be related to the flashing of feathers in birds and fin extensions in fish.

Not only are some general patterns of behavior similar in different animals, but so too are some of the underlying physiological changes that occur in dangerous or stressful situations. For example, it is well known that soldiers in battle fail to notice injuries that would, under less traumatic circumstances, be excruciatingly painful. Similarly, a rat, when exposed to a cat, will fail to notice painful heat applied to its tail.[66] The cat poses a greater overall threat than a wound to the tail, and pain suppression in the face of danger allows the organism to use its resources to deal with the most significant danger. In both humans and rats, stress-induced analgesia is a consequence of activation of the brain's natural opiate system.[67] When the brain detects danger, it also sends messages through the nerves of the autonomic nervous system to bodily organs and adjusts the activity of those organs to match the demands of the situation. Nerves reaching the gut, heart, blood vessels, and sweat and salivary glands give rise to the taut stomach, racing heart, high blood pressure, clammy hands and feet, and dry mouth that typify fear in humans. The cardiovascular responses associated with defensive behavior have been examined in birds, rats, rabbits, cats, dogs, monkeys, baboons, and people, to name a few of the better studied species, and the responses are controlled by similar kinds of brain networks and body chemistry in these different species.[68] Threatening stimuli also cause the pituitary gland to release adrenocorticotropic hormone (ACTH) that results in the release of a steroid hormone from the adrenal gland.[69] The adrenal hormone then travels back to the brain. Initially, these hormones help the body deal with the stress, but if the stress is prolonged the hormone can begin to have pathological consequences, interfering with cognitive functions and even causing brain damage.[70] This so-called stress response is ubiquitous amongst mammals, and also occurs in other vertebrates.[71] These various bodily responses are not random activities. They each play an important role in the emotional reaction and each functions similarly in diverse animal groups.

Nevertheless, it would be wrong to give the impression that all animals respond exactly the same in the face of danger. Obviously, they do not. Each animal is the product of its own evolutionary history. Within the general classes of defense reactions, much variation is possible. In fact, defense reactions should be thought of as constantly changing, dynamic solutions to the problem of survival. They are not static structures created in ancestral species and maintained unchanged. They change as the world in which they operate changes. For example, Richard Dawkins describes predators and prey as involved in evolutionary arms races, where a particular adaptation that makes a prey better at defending against a predator can lead to the selection of traits that then give the predator the edge up—the color of the prey may change so that it blends in better with the environment, and the predator may, in turn, evolve a more sensitive perceptual system for detecting the camouflaged prey.[72] But Dawkins also notes a certain imbalance in these arms races, what he calls the "life/dinner" principle. According to this notion, rabbits run faster than foxes because rabbits are running for their life but foxes are only running for their dinner. As a result, genetic mutations that make foxes run more slowly are more likely to survive in the gene pool than mutations that make rabbits run more slowly, since the penalty of slowness is more severe for rabbits than foxes—a fox may reproduce after being outrun by a rabbit, but no rabbit ever reproduced after being caught by a fox.

In spite of the fact that species can have their own special ways of responding to danger, commonality of functional patterns is the rule. In fact, what distinguishes fear reactions in humans and other animals is not so much the ways in which fear is expressed as the different kinds of trigger stimuli that activate the appraisal mechanism of the defensive system. Each animal has to be able to detect the particular things that are dangerous to it, but there is an evolutionary economy to using universal response strategies—withdrawal, immobility, aggression, submission—and universal physiological adjustments. Added cognitive power opens up the defensive hardware to new kinds of events, new learned triggers. Humans fear things that a rat could never conceptualize, but the human and rat body respond much the same to their special triggers.

The implications of this situation are enormous. For the purpose of understanding how fear is generated, it does not matter so much how we activate the system or whether we activate the system in a person or a rat. The system will respond in pretty much the same way using a limited set of given defense response strategies available to it. We can thus design experiments in rats (or other laboratory animals) for the purpose of understanding how the human fear system works.

Genetic Determinism and Emotional Freedom

All this talk about the evolution of emotional behavior is likely to make the imagination run wild with ideas about genetic determination of our emotions. After all, any characteristic that has evolved has done so because of the representation of that characteristic in the genes of the species. But I want to make clear two different implications of the genetics of emotional behavior.

On the one hand, there is the way genes maintain similar behavioral expressions of defense within a species and similar defensive functions across diverse species. This occurs, as I've argued, because the neural system of defense is conserved in evolution. As a result, all humans have the same general ways of expressing themselves when in danger, and these tend to be similar to the ways that other animals have for expressing themselves in the face of danger. This view of emotional genetics tries to find the common ground of emotional reactions across individuals and species—the stuff that particular emotional systems evolved to do.[73]

On the other hand, there is the question of how genes contribute to differences between individuals. Some people are good fighters, others are not. Some are adept in detecting dangers, others are oblivious to their surroundings. Differences between individuals in fearful behavior are due, at least in part, to genetic variation.

So far, I've emphasized the first implication—the way genes make emotional reactions similar amongst humans and between humans and other animals. But it is important to also consider in some detail the ways in which genes make us different from each other. We will then discuss whether, and if so to what extent, such differences predestine us to act in some particular way, again concentrating on the fear system.

Temperament runs through bloodlines. Some breeds of horses or dogs are jumpy, others complacent. These characteristics can sometimes be side effects of some other trait that was selected for, like running speed, but temperament can also be selected for itself. Indeed, selective breeding has been used to create strains of rats and mice that are particularly timid or courageous.[74]

For example, rats don't normally congregate in wide-open spaces. This makes a lot of sense evolutionarily—open places are unprotected from land and air predators and can be very dangerous for rodents. Those ancestral rodents that tended to hang out in an open area probably did not do so well in their struggle to survive, whereas those that hightailed it out to the nearest safe place did. Psychologists created an apparatus for testing this behavior—a large, well-lit circular arena called "the open field."[75] If you put your garden-variety rat in the center of an open field apparatus, it will make a beeline to the wall, which is the most protected place available. The rats also defecate—like people, rats can have the "$#!+" scared out of them. Defecation is controlled by the autonomic nervous system and the number of fecal pellets (poops) that are dropped is a reliable and measure of ANS activity. Defecation in the open field or other potentially dangerous situations has become a fairly standard measure of "fearfulness" in rodents.[76] But not all rats drop the same number of pellets in the open field, and the amount one rat drops tends to be fairly constant. If you divide a large group into those that drop more and fewer pellets in the open field, and then start breeding them on the basis of this selected trait, you can, in a few generations, create strains of timid and courageous rats—rats from the low pellet-dropping line act more courageous in the open field (they stay in the unprotected area longer) and in a variety of other tests. From this example, it is easy to imagine how personality traits might come to be part of a family, or even a culture. All you need is a few generations of inbreeding amongst a limited gene pool to begin to stabilize behaviorally significant characteristics.

In fact, considerable evidence shows that there is a genetic component to fear behavior in humans.[77] For example, identical twins (even those reared in separate homes) are far more similar in fearfulness than fraternal twins. This conclusion applies across many kinds of measurements, including tests of shyness, worry, fear of strangers, social introversion/extroversion, and others. Similarly, anxiety, phobic, and obsessive compulsive disorders tend to run in families and to be more likely to occur in both identical than in both fraternal twins.

The genetics of defensive behavior has been studied most extensively in bacteria.[78] Although not known as a particularly sophisticated organism from the psychological point of view, they do protect themselves from danger and there may be some biological lessons to be learned. Their defensive repertoire consists of moving away from substances assessed as harmful. The specific gene mutations controlling this behavior, which involves complex coding of chemical constituents in the immediate environment, have been identified. Similarly, much progress has been made in genetic analyses of fruit fly defensive behavior.[79] Through some ingenious experiments, Tim Tully has shown that these creatures can learn to avoid danger (electric shock) on the basis of stimulus cues (odors)—once shocked in the presence of a certain smell, they tend to avoid a chamber that has the smell. Using the modern tools of molecular biology and genetics, mutant flies have been created that are unable to use the smell cues to avoid the shock. They can smell just fine, they just can't link the smell with danger. It is admittedly a far leap from defensive responses in flies to humans, and at least a quantum leap from bacterial to human behavior. However, studies in these simple creatures may pave the way for future researchers to perform similar kinds of experiments in mammals, and these kinds of studies may shed light on the genetics of fear in humans. There is, after all, massive overlap in the genetic makeup of humans and chimpanzees, and a good deal of overlap in humans and other mammals as well.[80]

There's no denying that genes make each of us different from one another and explain at least part of the variability in the way different people act in dangerous and other situations. But we have to be very careful in interpreting differences in behavior between different people. As Richard Dawkins puts it, "If I am homozygous for a gene G, nothing save mutation can prevent my passing G on to all my children. So much is inexorable. But whether or not I, or my children, show the phenotypic effect normally associated with possession of G may depend very much on how we are brought up, what diet or education we experience, and what other genes we happen to possess."[81]

The bottom line is that our genes give us the raw materials out of which to build our emotions. They specify the kind of nervous system we will have, the kinds of mental processes in which it can engage, and the kinds of bodily functions it can control. But the exact way we act, think, and feel in a particular situation is determined by many other factors and is not predestined in our genes. Some, if not many, emotions do have a biological basis, but social, which is to say cognitive, factors are also crucially important. Nature and nurture are partners in our emotional life. The trick is to figure what their unique contributions are.

6

A FEW DEGREES
OF SEPARATION

ⷮⷮⷮ

"The BRAIN—is wider than the sky—."

Emily Dickinson, *The Poems of Emily Dickinson*[1]

ONLY A FEW NEURAL links separate any particular set of neurons in the brain from most others. As a result, it is sometimes said that figuring out connections between brain areas is a waste of time, since information reaching one area can eventually influence many. But this criticism is misplaced. By way of a small number of acquaintances, we are each potentially connected to everyone else in the world.[2] Yet, we only get around to meeting a small subset of the earth's population in our lives. Communication between people, like the flow of information between neurons, is selective.

But how does one go about figuring out the selective channels of information flow in the brain? There are billions of neurons, and each gives rise to one or more axons (nerve fibers that allow neurons to communicate with one another). The axons themselves branch, so that the number of synapses (the connection made by an axon from one neuron with another) is far greater than the number of neurons. And each neuron has multiple dendrites that receive thousands of synaptic contacts from many others. Can we ever hope to relate this intricate mesh of interconnected neural elements to emotion, a term that itself refers to an enormously complex set of phenomena?

The field of neuroscience has a vast arsenal of techniques for figuring out how the brain is organized—how it is wired together.

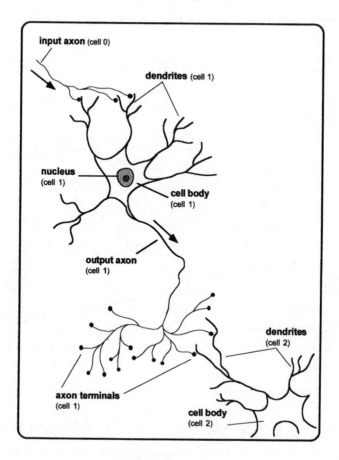

FIGURE 6-1
A Neuron.

Neurons (brain cells) have three parts: a cell body, an axon, and some den-drites. Typically, information from other neurons comes into a brain cell by way of the dendrites (but the cell body or axon can also receive inputs). Each cell receives inputs from many others. When a neuron receives enough inputs at the same time, it will fire an action potential (a wave of electrical charge) down the axon. Although a neuron usually has only one axon, it branches ex-tensively, allowing many other neurons to be influenced. When the action po-tential reaches the axon terminals, a chemical, called a neurotransmitter, is released. The neurotransmitter diffuses from the terminal to the dendrites of adjacent neurons and contributes to the firing of action potentials in these. The space between the axon terminal of one cell and its neighbor is called the synapse. For this reason, communication between neurons is referred to as synaptic transmission. (Based on figure 1 in B. Katz [1966], *Nerve, Muscle, and Synapse.* New York: McGraw-Hill.)

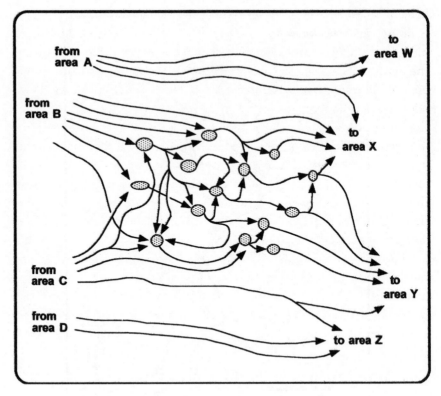

FIGURE 6-2
Neurons Are Connected in Complex but Systematic Ways.

Although the trillions of connections made by the billions of neurons in the
brain may seem to constitute a hopelessly complex web of relations, very sys-
tematic patterns of interactions exist between neurons in various brain areas.
The interconnected brain network shown in the center receives inputs from
areas B and C, but not from A or D, and gives rise to outputs that reach areas
X and Y, but not W or Z. Further, area C communicates with Y both directly
and by way of links in the central network. In real brains, these relations are
figured out by tracing axonal connections between areas, as illustrated in fig-
ure 6-8.

Though these techniques make important, even crucial, contributions to the effort to understand the emotional brain, they are not
enough. In order to figure out how emotional functions are mediated
by specific patterns of neural wiring, we also need good ways of
telling when the brain is in an emotional state. For this we depend on

behavioral tools, ways of determining, from what an animal or person is doing, that the brain is engaged in emotional activity. And if the picture of the emotional brain that I have been painting is accurate, the particular behavioral tools we need will be dictated by the kind of emotional function we are interested in understanding: the tools that allow us to reliably measure responses that depend upon the system that underlies fear behavior will probably not be very useful for studying aggressive or sexual behavior or mother-infant relations. Armed with a good behavioral task, together with the bag of tricks that modern brain science offers, we can go searching for the brain networks that mediate specific emotional functions and actually expect to find them. But without good behavioral tools, the effort to understand emotional networks is doomed.

Fortunately, there is an incredibly good task for studying fear mechanisms. It is called fear conditioning. Below I will explain what fear conditioning is and why it is so useful. I will then describe how, using fear conditioning, it has been possible to isolate, from the billions of neurons and trillions of connections, those that are important in fear behavior.

For Whom the Bell Tolls

If your neighbor's dog bites you, you will probably be wary every time you walk by his property. His house and yard, as well as sight and sound of the beast, have become emotional stimuli for you because of their association with the unpleasant event. This is fear conditioning in action. It turns meaningless stimuli into warning signs, cues that signal potentially dangerous situations on the basis of past experiences with similar situations.

In a typical fear conditioning experiment, the subject, say a rat, is placed in a small cage. A sound then comes on, followed by a brief, mild shock to the feet. After very few such pairings of the sound and the shock, the rat begins to act afraid when it hears the sound: it stops dead in its tracks and adopts the characteristic freezing posture—crouching down and remaining motionless, except for the rhythmic chest movements required for breathing. In addition, the rat's fur stands on end, its blood pressure and heart rate rise, and stress hormones are released into its bloodstream. These and other conditioned responses are expressed in essentially the same way in every rat, and also occur when a rat encounters its perennial arch-enemy, a cat, strongly suggesting that, as a result of fear conditioning, the sound activates the neural system that controls responses involved in dealing with predators and other natural dangers.

Fear conditioning is a variation on the procedure discovered by Ivan Pavlov around the turn of the century.[3] As everyone knows, the great Russian physiologist observed that his dogs salivated when a bell was rung if the sound of the bell had previously occurred while the dog had a juicy morsel of meat in its mouth. Pavlov proposed that the overlap in time of the meat in the mouth with the sound of the bell resulted in the creation of an association (a connection in the brain) between the two stimuli, such that the sound was able to substitute for the meat in the elicitation of salivation.

Pavlov abhorred psychological explanations of behavior and

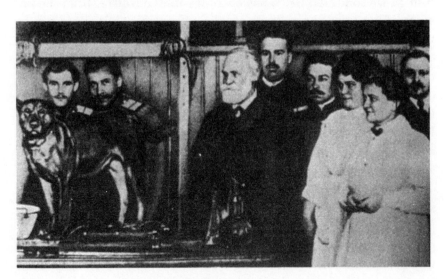

FIGURE 6-3
Pavlov and His Dog.

Photograph of I. P. Pavlov demonstrating classical conditioning to students and visitors at the Russian Army Medical Academy sometime around 1904. (Caption from figure on p. 177 of C. Blakemore and S. Greenfield [1987], *Mindwaves.* Oxford: Basil Blackwell.)

sought to account for the anticipatory salivation physiologically, without having to "resort to fantastic speculations as to the existence of any subjective state in the animal which may be conjectured on analogy with ourselves." He thus explicitly rejected the idea that salivation occurred because the hungry dogs began to think about the food when they heard the bell. In this way Pavlov, like William James (see Chapter 3), removed subjective emotional states from the chain of events leading to emotional behavior.

Pavlov called the meat an unconditioned stimulus (US), the bell a conditioned stimulus (CS), and the salivation elicited by the CS a conditioned response (CR). This terminology derives from the fact that the capacity of the bell to elicit salivation was conditional upon its relation to the meat, which elicited salivation naturally, which is to say, unconditionally. Applying these terms to the fear conditioning experiment described above, the tone was the CS, the shock was the US, and the behavioral and autonomic expressions were the CRs. And in the language used in the previous chapter to describe the stimuli that initiate emotional behaviors, a US is a *natural trigger* while a CS is a *learned trigger*.

Fear conditioning does not involve response learning. Although rats freeze when they are exposed to a tone after but not before conditioning, conditioning does not teach the rats how to freeze. Freezing is something that rats do naturally when they are exposed to danger. Laboratory-bred rats who have never seen a cat will freeze if they encounter one.[4] Freezing is a built-in response, an innate defense response, that can be activated by either *natural or learned triggers*.

Fear conditioning opens up channels of evolutionarily shaped responsivity to new environmental events, allowing novel stimuli that predict danger (like sounds made by an approaching predator or the place where a predator was seen) to gain control over tried-and-true ways of responding to danger. The danger predicted by these *learned trigger stimuli* can be real or imagined, concrete or abstract, allowing a great range of external (environmental) and internal (mental) conditions to serve as CSs.

Conditioned fear learning occurs quickly, and can occur after a single CS-US pairing. An animal in the wild does not have the opportunity for trial-and-error learning. Evolution has arranged things

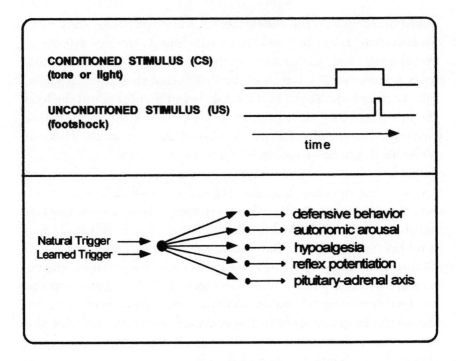

FIGURE 6-4
Fear Conditioning.

In fear conditioning an unconditioned stimulus (typically a brief, mild foot-shock) is delivered at the end of the conditioned stimulus (usually a tone or light). After a few pairings, the conditioned stimulus acquires the capacity to elicit a wide variety of bodily responses. Similar responses occur in the presence of natural dangers that are innately programmed into the brain. For example, in the presence of either a conditioned fear stimulus or a cat, rats will freeze and exhibit blood pressure and heart rate changes, alterations in pain responsivity, more sensitive reflexes, and elevation of stress hormones from the pituitary gland. Because rats do not require prior exposure to cats to exhibit these responses, the cat is a natural trigger *of defense responses for rats. And because the tone only elicits these responses after fear conditioning, it is a* learned trigger. *Similar patterns of defense responses occur in humans and other animals when exposed to fear triggers (natural and learned). Studies of nonhuman animals can thus illuminate important aspects of fear reactivity in humans.*

so that if you survive one encounter with a predator you can use your experience to help you survive in future situations. For example, if the last time a rabbit went to a certain watering hole it encountered a fox and barely escaped, it will probably either avoid that watering hole in the future or the next time it goes there it will approach the scene with trepidation, taking small cautious steps, searching the environment for any clue that might signal that a fox is near.[5] The watering hole and fox have been linked up in the rabbit's brain, and being near the watering hole puts the rabbit on the defensive.

Not only is fear conditioning quick, it is also very long lasting. In fact, there is little forgetting when it comes to conditioned fear. The passing of time is not enough to get rid of it.[6] Nevertheless, repeated exposure to the CS in the absence of the US can lead to "extinction." That is, the capacity of the CS to elicit the fear reaction is diminished by presentation of the CS over and over without the US. If our thirsty but fearful rabbit has only one watering hole to which it can go, and visits it day after day without again encountering a fox, it will eventually act as though it never met a fox there.

But extinction does not involve an elimination of the relation between the CS and US. Pavlov observed that a conditioned response could be completely extinguished on one day, and on the next day the CS was again effective in eliciting the response. He called this "spontaneous recovery."[7] Recovery of extinguished conditioned responses can also be induced. This has been nicely demonstrated in studies by Mark Bouton.[8] After rats received tone-shock pairings in one chamber, he put them in a new chamber and gave them the tone CS over and over until the conditioned fear responses were no longer elicited—the conditioned fear reaction was completely extinguished. He then showed that simply placing the animals back in the chamber where the CS and US were previously paired was enough to *renew* the conditioned fear response to the CS. Extinguished conditioned fear responses can also be *reinstated* by exposing the animals to the US or some other stressful event.[9] Spontaneous recovery, renewal, and reinstatement suggest that extinction does not eliminate the memory that the CS was once associated with danger but instead reduces the likelihood that the CS will elicit the fear response.

These findings in rats fit well with observations on humans with pathological fears (phobias).[10] As a result of psychotherapy, the fear of the phobic stimulus can be kept under control for many years. Then, after some stress or trauma, the fear reaction can return in full force. Like extinction, therapy does not erase the memory that ties fear reactions to trigger stimuli. Both processes simply prevent the stimuli from unleashing the fear reaction. I'll have much more to say about this in Chapter 8.

The indelibility of learned fear has an upside and a downside. It is obviously very useful for our brain to be able to retain records of those stimuli and situations that have been associated with danger in the past. But these potent memories, which are typically formed in traumatic circumstances, can also find their way into everyday life, intruding into situations in which they are not especially useful, and such intrusions can be quite disruptive to normal mental functioning. We'll consider traumatic memory again in Chapters 7 and 8.

Although most of the research on the neural basis of conditioned fear has been conducted in animals, fear conditioning procedures can be used in identical ways in humans.[11] Numerous studies of humans have conditioned autonomic nervous system responses, such as changes in heart rate or in sweat gland activity (so-called galvanic skin responses), by pairing tones or other neutral stimuli with mild shocks. Because conditioned fear responses are not dependent on verbal behavior and conscious awareness, they have often been used to study unconscious (subliminal) emotional processing in humans, as described in Chapter 3.

When a human is presented with a consciously perceptible CS that predicts the imminent delivery of a painful stimulus, he or she typically feels fearful or anxious during the CS.[12] We might therefore be inclined to say that the CS elicits a state of fear that then causes the responses. In fact, a number of psychologists and neuroscientists who study fear conditioning assume that "fear" connects the CS to the CR.[13] However, like Pavlov and James, I find it neither necessary nor desirable to insert a conscious state of fear into the chain of events connecting trigger stimuli to fear responses. Here are my reasons why. First, fear conditioning procedures can be used to couple defensive responses to neutral stimuli in worms, flies, and snails, as well as in fish, frogs, lizards, pigeons, rats, cats, dogs, monkeys, and people.[14] I doubt that all of these animals consciously experience fear in the presence of a CS that predicts danger. This is admittedly a slippery slope to slide down, and one that I'm going to delay detailed discussion on until Chapter 9. But if for the time being we assume I'm correct that we don't need conscious fear to explain fear responses in some species, then we don't need it to explain fear responses in humans.[15] Second, even in humans, the one species in which we can study conscious processes with some confidence, fear conditioning can be achieved without conscious awareness of the CS or the relation between the CS and US.[16] The conscious fear that can come with fear conditioning in a human is not a cause of the fear responses; it is one consequence (and not an obligatory one) of activating the defense system in a brain that also has consciousness.

One of the key aspects of fear conditioning that makes it so valuable as a tool for studying the brain mechanisms of fear is that the fear responses come to be coupled to a specific stimulus. This offers

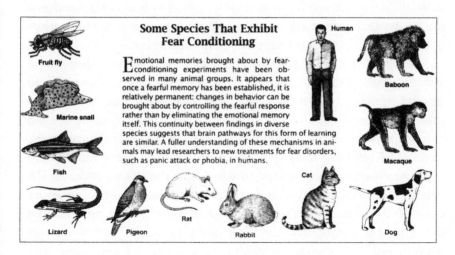

Some Species That Exhibit Fear Conditioning

Emotional memories brought about by fear-conditioning experiments have been observed in many animal groups. It appears that once a fearful memory has been established, it is relatively permanent: changes in behavior can be brought about by controlling the fearful response rather than by eliminating the emotional memory itself. This continuity between findings in diverse species suggests that brain pathways for this form of learning are similar. A fuller understanding of these mechanisms in animals may lead researchers to new treatments for fear disorders, such as panic attack or phobia, in humans.

FIGURE 6-5
Animals Throughout the Phyla Can Be Fear Conditioned.

Fear conditioning is an evolutionarily old solution to the problem of acquiring and storing information about harmful or potentially harmful stimuli and situations. It has been studied in several invertebrate species, and in a variety of vertebrates. Within the vertebrates, the behavioral expression of fear conditioning and its neural basis appear very similar in all species that have been examined in detail. (From J.E. LeDoux, Emotion, memory and the brain. *Scientific American* [June, 1994], vol 270, p.39. © 1994 by Scientific American Inc., all rights reserved.)

several important advantages. First, once the stimulus is established as a learned trigger of fear, it will lead to the expression of fear responses each time it occurs. The expression of the fear response is thus under the control of the experimenter, which is very convenient. Second, we can begin to build the emotional processing circuit on the shoulders of the known organization of the sensory system engaged by the CS. Since the sensory systems are understood better than other aspects of the brain, we can use these as a launching pad, tracing the fear processing circuit forward from them. Third, the CS can be a very simple sensory stimulus that is processed with minimal brain power, allowing us to bypass much of the cognitive machinery in the study of fear. We can, in other words, study how the brain appraises the danger implied by a stimulus without getting too bogged down in how the stimulus itself is processed. While it is possible to use either a simple tone or a spoken sentence as a CS, it will be much more difficult to trace the pathways involved in fear conditioning to the sentence, since the processing of the sentence is a much more complex, and less well understood, brain operation.

Fear conditioning is thus an excellent experimental technique for studying the control of fear or defense responses by the brain. It can be applied up and down the phyla. The stimuli involved can be specified and controlled, and the sensory system that processes the CS can be used as the starting point for tracing the pathways through the brain. The learning takes place very quickly and lasts indefinitely. Fear conditioning can be used to study how the brain processes the conditioned fear stimulus and controls defense responses that are coupled to them. It can also be used to examine the mechanisms through which emotional memories are established, stored, and retrieved, and, in humans, the mechanisms underlying conscious fear.

Fear conditioning is not the only way to study fear behavior[17] and it may not be a valid model of all of the many phenomena that are referred to by the term "fear."[18] Nevertheless, it is a quite powerful and versatile model of fear behavior and has been very effectively used to trace brain pathways. Fear conditioning may not tell us everything we need to know about fear, but it has been an excellent way to get started.

Measure for Measure

Once the meaning of a stimulus has been modified by fear conditioning, the next occurrence of the stimulus unleashes a whole host of bodily responses that prepare the organism to deal with the impending danger about which the stimulus warns. Any of these can be used to measure the effects of conditioning.

For example, when a conditioned fear stimulus occurs, the subject will typically stop all movement—it will freeze.[19] Many predators respond to movement[20] and withholding movement is often the best thing to do when danger is near.[21] Freezing can also be thought of as preparatory to rapid escape when the coast clears, or to defensive fighting if escape is not possible. Since the muscle contractions that underlie freezing require metabolic energy, blood has to be sent to those muscles. Indeed, the autonomic nervous system is strongly activated by a conditioned fear stimulus, producing a variety of cardiovascular and other visceral responses that help support the freezing response. These also help the body prepare for the escape or fighting responses that are likely to follow.[22] Additionally, stress hormones are released into the bloodstream to further help the body cope with the threatening situation.[23] Reactivity to pain is also suppressed, which is useful since the conditioned stimulus often announces a situation in which the probability of bodily harm is high.[24] And reflexes (like eyeblink or startle responses) are potentiated, allowing quicker, more efficient reactions to stimuli that normally elicit protective movements.[25]

These various responses are part of the body's overall adaptive reaction to danger and each has been used to examine the brain systems involved in conditioned fear responses. For example, David Cohen[26] has studied the brain pathways of fear conditioning in pigeons using heart rate responses, and Bruce Kapp,[27] Neil Schneidermann and Phil McCabe[28] and Don Powell[29] have used heart rate responses in rabbits. Michael Fanselow[30] has used freezing and pain suppression in rats as measures, while Michael Davis[31] has exploited the potentiation of reflexes by a fear eliciting conditioned stimulus, also in rats. Orville Smith[32] has studied fear conditioning in baboons, measuring a variety of cardiovascular responses in conjunction with measures of movement inhibition. And in my research on the brain mechanisms of fear conditioning, I've made simultaneous measurements of freezing and blood pressure responses in rats.[33]

The amazing fact is that it has not really mattered very much how conditioned fear has been measured, or what species has been studied, as all of the approaches have converged on a common set of brain structures and pathways that are important. Although there are some minor differences and controversies over some of the details, in broad outline there is remarkable consensus. This contrasts with studies of the neural basis of many other behaviors, where slight changes in the experimental procedure or the species can result in profound differences in the neural systems involved. Fear conditioning is so important that the brain does the job the same way no matter how we ask it to do it.

Highways and Byways

Imagine being in a unfamiliar land. You are handed a piece of paper on which the locations of a starting point and a destination are indi-

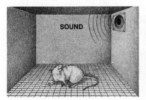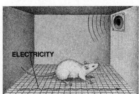

FIGURE 6-6
A Rat Undergoing Fear Conditioning.

The rat is first exposed to the sound alone. It orients toward the sound, but after several occurrences, the sound is ignored. Next, the sound and the brief, relatively mild shock occur together several times. Later, the sound, when presented alone, will elicit conditioned fear responses. The sound, by association with the shock, has become a learned trigger of fear responses. This is similar to what goes on in humans when they are exposed to dangers or trauma. The stimuli associated with the danger or trauma become learned triggers that unleash emotional reactions in us. Studies of fear conditioning in rats can thus reveal important aspects of the way human emotional (fear) learning occurs. (From J.E. LeDoux, Emotion, memory and the brain. *Scientific American* [June 1994], vol 270, p. 34. © 1994 by Scientific American Inc., all rights reserved.)

cated. There are lots of other points marked on the paper. There are also some lines between some of the points, indicating possible ways to get from one to another. But you are told that the lines between the points may or may not indicate real roads, and also that not all of the roads that exist between points are marked. Your job is to get in your car at the starting point and find the best way to the destination, and to make an accurate map along the way.

This is essentially the problem that we faced when we began to try to figure out how networks in the brain make it possible for a novel acoustic stimulus to come to elicit defensive responses as a result of fear conditioning. We knew the starting point (the ear and its connections into the brain) and the end point (the behavioral defense responses and their autonomic concomitants), but the points that linked the inputs and outputs in the brain were unclear. Many of the relevant connections in the brain had been demonstrated with older techniques that were prone to lead to false results—identifying nonexistent connections between two points or failing to find real ones.[34] Relatively little work on the neural basis of fear had used fear conditioning.[35] And while research on fear using techniques other than fear conditioning had suggested some ideas about which brain areas might be involved, it wasn't clear whether these were essential way stations, interesting detours, or just plain wrong turns.

Go with the Flow: Much of the earlier work on the emotional brain had started in the middle of the brain, not surprisingly, in the limbic system.[36] This work showed that lesions of limbic areas can interfere with some emotional behaviors, and that stimulation of limbic areas can elicit emotional responses. But these studies left unclear how the lesioned or stimulated area relates to the rest of the brain. Also, most of the earlier work used techniques that lacked a discrete eliciting stimulus and thus could not benefit from the advantages, described above, that a conditioned stimulus offers.

My approach was to let the natural flow of information through the brain be my guide.[37] In other words, I started at the beginning, at the point that the auditory-conditioned stimulus enters the brain, and tried to trace the pathways forward from this system toward the final destinations that control the conditioned fear responses. I thought that this strategy would be the best and most direct way of figuring out the road map of fear. In retrospect, this strategy worked pretty well.

I began by asking a simple question: which parts of the auditory system are required for auditory fear conditioning (fear conditioning tasks in which an auditory stimulus serves the CS)?[38] The auditory system, like other sensory systems, is organized such that the cortical component is the highest level; it is the culmination of a sequence of information processing steps that start with the peripheral sensory receptors, in this case, receptors located in the ear. I reasoned that damaging the ear would be uninteresting, since a deaf animal is obviously not going to be able to learn anything about a sound. So, instead, I started by damaging the highest part of the auditory pathway. If auditory cortex lesions interfered with fear conditioning, I would be able to conclude that the auditory stimulus had to go all the way through the system in order for conditioning to occur, and that the next step in the pathway should be an output connection of the auditory cortex. If, however, auditory cortex lesions did not disrupt conditioning, I would have to make lesions in lower stations to find the highest level that the auditory stimulus has to reach in order for conditioning to take place.

Damage to the auditory cortex, in fact, turned out to have no effect at all on the conditioning of either the freezing or the blood pressure responses. I then lesioned the next lower station, the auditory thalamus, and these lesions completely prevented fear conditioning. So did lesions of the next lower auditory station in the midbrain. On the basis of these studies I concluded that the auditory stimulus has to rise through the auditory pathway from the ear to the thalamus, but does not have to go the full distance to the auditory cortex. This presented me with a paradox.

Traditionally, the sensory processing structures below the cortex are viewed as slaves to the cortical master. Their job is to get the information to the cortex, where all of the interesting things are done to the stimulus, like assembling neural bits and pieces of the input into the perceptions of the external world that we experience. According to neuroanatomy textbooks, the auditory cortex was the main if not the only target of the auditory thalamus. Where, then, was the auditory stimulus going after it left the thalamus in its journey toward emotional reactivity, if not to the cortex?

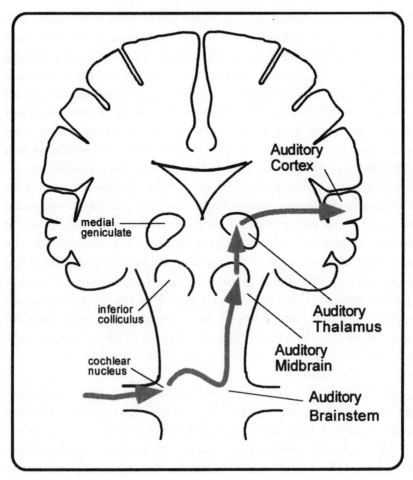

FIGURE 6-7
Auditory Processing Pathways.

*This is a highly simplified depiction of auditory pathways in the human brain.
A similar organization plan holds for other vertebrate species. Acoustic signals
in the environment are picked up by special receptors in the ear (not shown)
and transmitted into the brain by way of the auditory nerve (arrow at bottom
left), which terminates in the auditory brainstem nuclei (cochlear nucleus and
related regions). Axons from these regions then mostly cross over to the other
side of the brain and ascend to the inferior colliculus of the midbrain. Inferior
collicular axons then travel to the auditory thalamic relay nucleus, the medial
geniculate body, which provides the major inputs to the auditory cortex. The
auditory cortex is composed of a number of regions and subregions (not
shown).*

Through the Looking Glass: In order to get some reasonable ideas about where the signal might go to after the auditory thalamus, I took advantage of techniques for tracing pathways in the brain. To use these, you have to inject a small amount of a tracer substance in the brain area you are interested in. Tracers are chemicals that are absorbed by the cell bodies of neurons located in the injected area and shipped down the axon to the nerve terminals. Neurons are constantly moving molecules around inside them—many important things, like neurotransmitters, are manufactured in the cell body and then transported down the axon to the terminal region where they are used in communication across synapses. After the tracer enters the cell body, it can ride piggyback on these mobile substances until it reaches the terminal region of the axon, where it is deposited. The fate of the tracer can then be visualized by chemical reactions that "stain" those parts of the brain that contain the transported substance. These techniques make it possible to figure out where the neurons in one area send their fibers. Since information can only get from one area of the brain to another by way of fibers, knowing the fiber connections of an area tells us where information processed in an area is sent next.

So we injected a tracer into the auditory thalamus.[39] The substance injected sounds more like an ingredient of an exotic salad in a macrobiotic café than the chemical basis of a sophisticated neuroscience technique: wheat germ agglutinin conjugated horseradish peroxidase, or just WGA-HRP for short. The next day the brain was removed and sectioned, and the sections were stained by reacting them with a special chemical potion. We put the stained sections on slides and then looked at them with a microscope set up for dark-field optics, which involves shining indirect light onto the slide—this makes it easier to see the tracer reaction in the sections.

I'll never forget the first time I looked at WGA-HRP with dark-field optics. Bright orange particles formed streams and speckles against a dark blue-gray background. It was like looking into a strange world of inner space. It was incredibly beautiful and I stayed glued to the microscope for hours.

Once I got past the sheer beauty of the staining, I turned to the task at hand, which was to find out where, if anywhere, the auditory thalamus projected to besides the auditory cortex. I found four sub-

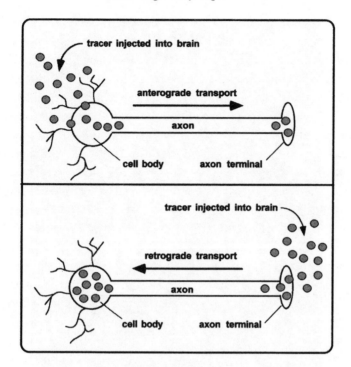

FIGURE 6-8
Tracing Pathways in the Brain with Axonal Transport.

In order to figure out whether neurons in two different brain regions are interconnected, tracers are injected into one of the regions. The tracer is then picked up by neurons that are bathed by the injection. Once the tracer is inside the neuron, it is transported through the axon. Some tracers are picked up by cell bodies and transported to axon terminals (anterograde transport), whereas other tracers are picked up by terminals and transported to cell bodies (retrograde transport).

cortical regions that contained heavy sprinkling with the tiny orange dots, suggesting that these regions receive projections from the auditory thalamus. This was surprising, given the well-received view that sensory areas of the thalamus project mainly, if not exclusively, to the cortex.

It seemed likely that one of the four labeled regions might be the crucial next step in the fear conditioning pathway—the place where the stimulus goes after the thalamus. So, I designed a lesion study that would interrupt the flow of information from the auditory thalamus to each of these regions.[40] Three of the lesions had absolutely no

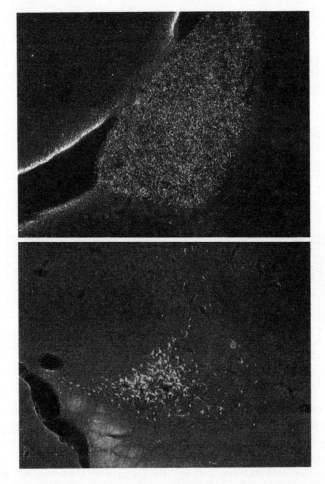

FIGURE 6-9
Examples of Anterograde and Retrograde Transport
in the Thalamo-Amygdala Pathway.

The top photograph shows anterograde labeling of terminals in the lateral amygdala after an injection of a tracer in the auditory thalamus. These terminals in the lateral amygdala thus originate from cell bodies in the auditory thalamus. Note the fine, punctate nature of anterograde terminal labeling. The bottom photograph shows cell bodies in the auditory thalamus that were retrogradely labeled by an injection of a tracer in the lateral nucleus of the amygdala. The labeled cells are the bright white structures that cluster together in a triangular region. The cells in the auditory thalamus thus send their axons to the lateral amygdala. Note the large size of the labeled cell bodies, as compared to the terminals above. The two images are black-and-white photographs of dark-field illuminated brain sections taken through a microscope.

effect. But disconnection of auditory thalamus from the fourth area—the amygdala—prevented conditioning from taking place.

Almond Joy: The amygdala is a small region in the forebrain, named by the early anatomists for its almond shape (amygdala is the Latin word for almond). It was one of the areas of the limbic system and had long been thought of as being important for various forms of emotional behavior—earlier studies of the Klüver-Bucy syndrome had pointed to it (see Chapter 4), as had electrical stimulation studies (see below).

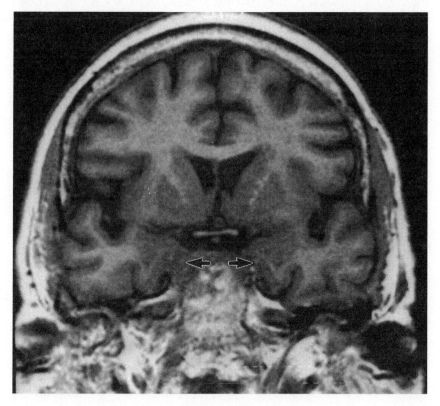

FIGURE 6-10
**Magnetic Resonance Imaging Scan Showing the Location
of the Amygdala in the Human Brain.**

The amygdala on each side of the brain is indicated by the arrows. (Image provided by E. A. Phelps of Yale University.)

The discovery of a pathway that could transmit information directly to the amygdala from the thalamus suggested how a conditioned fear stimulus could elicit fear responses without the aid of the cortex. The direct thalamic input to the amygdala simply allowed the cortex to be bypassed. The brain is indeed a complex mesh of connections, but anatomical findings were taking us on a delightful journey of discovery through this neuronal maze.

I wasn't really looking for the amygdala in my work. The dissection of the brain's pathways just took me there. But my studies, when they first started coming out, fit nicely with a set of findings that Bruce Kapp had obtained concerning a subregion of the amygdala—the central nucleus. Noting that the central nucleus has connections with the brain stem areas involved in the control of heart rate and other autonomic nervous system responses, he proposed that this region might be a link in the neural system through which the autonomic responses elicited by a conditioned fear stimulus are expressed. And when he lesioned the central nucleus in the rabbit, his hypothesis was confirmed—the lesions dramatically interfered with the conditioning of heart rate responses to a tone paired with shock.[41]

Kapp went on to show that stimulation of the central amygdala produced heart rate and other autonomic responses, strengthening his idea that the central nucleus was an important forebrain link in the control of autonomic responses by the brain stem. However, he also found that stimulation of the central nucleus elicited freezing responses, suggesting that the central amygdala might not just be involved in the control of autonomic responses, but might be part of a general-purpose defense response control network.

Indeed, subsequent research by several laboratories has shown that lesions of the central nucleus interfere with essentially every measure of conditioned fear, including freezing behavior, autonomic responses, suppression of pain, stress hormone release, and reflex potentiation.[42] It was also found that each of these responses are mediated by different outputs of the central nucleus.[43] For example, I demonstrated that lesions of different projections of the central nucleus separately interfered with freezing and blood pressure conditioned responses—lesions of one of the projections (the periaqueductal gray) interfered with freezing but not blood pressure responses, whereas lesions of another (the lateral hypothalamus) interfered with the blood pressure but not the freezing response.[44] And while lesions of a third projection (the bed nucleus of the stria terminalis) had no effect on either of these responses, other scientists later showed that lesions of this region interfere with the elicitation of stress hormones by the CS.[45]

Journey to the Center of the Amygdala: The studies of the central amygdala and its outputs seemed to clear up how the responses get expressed, but some mysteries still remained about how the stimulus reaches the central nucleus in its quest to gain control over the responses. Again using the WGA-HRP tracing techniques, I examined whether the auditory stimulus might be sent to the central amygdala directly from the auditory thalamus.[46]

I injected the tracer WGA-HRP into the central nucleus. This time, though, I was tracing connections in the reverse direction, from the area of termination of a pathway back to the cell bodies that give rise to it—the tracer does its piggyback ride in this direction as well. When I examined the sections under the microscope, I found bright orange cells containing the tracer in thalamic areas adjacent to the auditory thalamus but not the auditory thalamus itself. As a result, it seemed unlikely that an auditory stimulus is sent directly to the central nucleus in the process of controlling fear responses.

But when I made injections in another amygdala subregion, the lateral nucleus, there were orange cell bodies in the auditory thalamus.[47] And when I aimed injections for the region of the auditory thalamus that contained these labeled cells, I found the fine orange speckles characteristic of terminals in the lateral nucleus (see Figure 6-9). It seemed that the auditory stimulus might travel from the thalamus to the lateral nucleus of the amygdala. To test this hypothesis, I made lesions of the lateral nucleus. Like central amygdala lesions, these interfered with fear conditioning.[48]

On the basis of these lesion studies, together with the results of anatomical tracing experiments, the lateral nucleus came to be thought of as the region of the amygdala that receives the CS inputs in fear conditioning and the central nucleus as the interface with response control systems. The inputs and outputs had been mapped.

Still, an important set of linkages remained uncharted. If the CS inputs enter the amygdala by way of the lateral nucleus and the CR

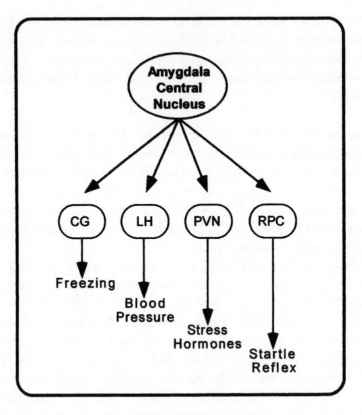

FIGURE 6-11
**Different Outputs of the Amygdala Control Different
Conditioned Fear Responses.**

In the presence of danger or stimuli that warn of danger, behavioral, auto-
nomic, and endocrine responses are expressed, and reflexes are modulated.
Each of these responses is controlled by a different set of outputs from the cen-
tral nucleus of the amygdala. Lesions of the central nucleus block the expres-
sion of all these responses, whereas lesions of the output pathways block only
individual responses. Selected examples of central amygdala outputs are
shown. Abbreviations: CG, central gray; LH, lateral hypothalamus; PVN, par-
aventricular hypothalamus (which receives inputs from the central amygdala
directly and by way of the bed nucleus of the stria terminalis); RPC, reticulo-
pontis caudalis.

outputs leave through the central nucleus, how does information received by the lateral nucleus reach the central nucleus? Although this
question has not yet been answered completely, anatomical findings
have provided us with some clues.[49] The lateral nucleus has some di-

rect projections to the central nucleus, and also can influence the central nucleus by way of projections to two other amygdala nuclei (the basal and accessory basal), each of which gives rise to strong projections to the central nucleus. There are thus several ways for information entering the lateral nucleus to reach the central nucleus, but exactly which is most crucial is not yet known.

The amygdala is composed of about a dozen or so subregions, and not all or even most are involved in fear conditioning. Only lesions that damage amygdala regions that are part of the fear conditioning circuitry should be expected to disrupt fear conditioning. The lateral and central nuclei are, without doubt, crucially involved, but the role of other amygdala regions is still under study.

The Low and the High Road: The fact that emotional learning can be mediated by pathways that bypass the neocortex is intriguing, for it suggests that emotional responses can occur without the involvement of the higher processing systems of the brain, systems believed to be involved in thinking, reasoning, and consciousness. But before we pursue this notion, we need to further consider the role of the auditory cortex in fear conditioning.

In the experiments described so far, a simple sound was paired with a shock. The auditory cortex is clearly not needed for this. But suppose the situation is somewhat more complex. Instead of just one tone paired with a shock, suppose the animal gets two similar tones, one paired with the shock and the other not, and has to learn to distinguish between them. Would the auditory cortex then be required? Neil Schneidermann, Phil McCabe, and their colleagues looked at this question in a study of heart rate conditioning in rabbits.[50] With enough training, the rabbits eventually only expressed heart rate responses to the sound that had been associated with the shock. And when the auditory cortex was lesioned, this capacity was lost. Interestingly, the auditory cortex lesions did not interfere with conditioning by blocking responses to the stimulus paired with the shock. Instead, the cortically lesioned animals responded to both stimuli as if they had each been paired with the shock.

These findings make sense given what we know about the neurons in the thalamus that project to the amygdala as opposed to those that provide the major inputs to the auditory cortex.[51] If you put an

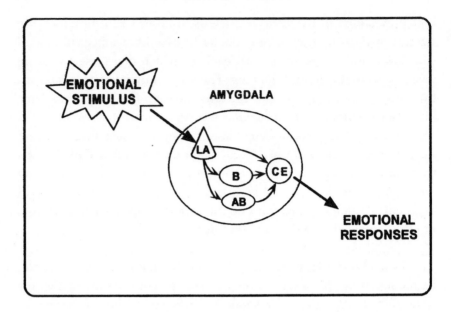

FIGURE 6-12
Organization of Information-Processing Pathways
in the Amygdala.

The lateral nucleus (LA) is the gateway into the amygdala. Stimuli from the outside world are transmitted to LA, which then processes the stimuli and distributes the results to other regions of the amygdala, including the basal (B), accessory basal (AB), and central nuclei (CE). The central nucleus is then the main connection with areas that control emotional responses. As shown in figure 6-11, different outputs of the central nucleus regulate the expression of different responses.

electrode in the brain, you can record the electrical activity of individual neurons in response to auditory stimulation. Neurons in the area of the thalamus that projects to the primary auditory cortex are narrowly tuned—they are very particular about what they will respond to. But cells in the thalamic areas that project to the amygdala are less picky—they respond to a much wider range of stimuli and are said to be broadly tuned. The Beatles and Rolling Stones (or, if you like, Oasis and the Cranberries) will sound the same to the amygdala by way of the thalamic projections but quite different by way of the cortical projections. So when two similar stimuli are used in a conditioning study, the thalamus will send the amygdala essentially the same information, regardless of which stimulus it is processing, but when the cortex processes the different stimuli it will send the amygdala different signals. If the cortex is damaged, the animal has only the direct thalamic pathway and thus the amygdala treats the two stimuli the same—both elicit conditioned fear.

The Quick and the Dead: Why should the brain be organized this way? Why should it have the lowly thalamic road when it also has the high cortical road?

Our only source of information about the brains of animals from long ago is the brains of their living descendants. Studies of living fish, amphibians, and reptiles suggest that sensory projections to rudimentary cortical areas were probably relatively weak compared to projections to subcortical regions in primordial animals.[52] In contemporary mammals, the thalamic projections to cortical pathways are far more elaborate and important channels of information processing. As a result, it is possible that in mammals the direct thalamic pathway to the amygdala is simply an evolutionary relic, the brain's version of an appendix. But I don't think this is the case. There's been ample time for the direct thalamo-amygdala pathways to have atrophied if they were not useful. But they have not. The fact that they have existed for millions and millions of years side by side with thalamo-cortical pathways suggests that they still serve some useful function. But what could that function be?

Although the thalamic system cannot make fine distinctions, it has an important advantage over the cortical input pathway to the amygdala. That advantage is time. In a rat it takes about twelve milliseconds (twelve one-thousandths of a second) for an acoustic stimulus to reach the amygdala through the thalamic pathway, and almost twice as long through the cortical pathway. The thalamic pathway is thus faster. It cannot tell the amygdala exactly what is there, but can provide a fast signal that warns that something dangerous may be there. It is a quick and dirty processing system.

Imagine walking in the woods. A crackling sound occurs. It goes straight to the amygdala through the thalamic pathway. The sound also goes from the thalamus to the cortex, which recognizes the sound to be a dry twig that snapped under the weight of your boot, or that of a rattlesnake shaking its tail. But by the time the cortex has

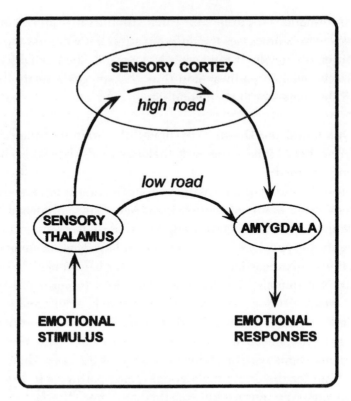

FIGURE 6-13
The Low and the High Roads to the Amygdala.

Information about external stimuli reaches the amygdala by way of direct path-ways from the thalamus (the low road) as well as by way of pathways from the thalamus to the cortex to the amygdala. The direct thalamo-amygdala path is a shorter and thus a faster transmission route than the pathway from the thala-mus through the cortex to the amygdala. However, because the direct pathway bypasses the cortex, it is unable to benefit from cortical processing. As a result, it can only provide the amygdala with a crude representation of the stimulus. It is thus a quick and dirty processing pathway. The direct pathway allows us to begin to respond to potentially dangerous stimuli before we fully know what the stimulus is. This can be very useful in dangerous situations. However, its utility requires that the cortical pathway be able to override the direct pathway. It is possible that the direct pathway is responsible for the control of emotional re-sponses that we don't understand. This may occur in all of us some of the time, but may be a predominant mode of functioning in individuals with certain emotional disorders (discussed in more detail in Chapter 8).

figured this out, the amygdala is already starting to defend against the snake. The information received from the thalamus is unfiltered and biased toward evoking responses. The cortex's job is to prevent the inappropriate response rather than to produce the appropriate one. Alternatively, suppose there is a slender curved shape on the path. The curvature and slenderness reach the amygdala from the thalamus, whereas only the cortex distinguishes a coiled up snake from a curved stick. If it is a snake, the amygdala is ahead of the game. From the point of view of survival, it is better to respond to potentially dangerous events as if they were in fact the real thing than to fail to respond. The cost of treating a stick as a snake is less, in the long run, than the cost of treating a snake as a stick.

So we can begin to see the outline of a fear reaction system. It involves parallel transmission to the amygdala from the sensory thalamus and sensory cortex. The subcortical pathways provide a crude image of the external world, whereas more detailed and accurate representations come from the cortex. While the pathway from the thalamus only involves one link, several links are required to activate the amygdala by way of the cortex. Since each link adds time, the thalamic pathway is faster. Interestingly, the thalamo-amygdala and cortico-amygdala pathways converge in the lateral nucleus of the amygdala. In all likelihood, normally both pathways transmit signals to the lateral nucleus, which appears to play a pivotal role in coordinating the sensory processes that constitute the conditioned fear stimulus. And once the information has reached the lateral nucleus it can be distributed through the internal amygdala pathways to the central nucleus, which then unleashes the full repertoire of defensive reactions. Although I have mainly discussed my own work, research by others (especially Michael Davis, Michael Fanselow, Norman Weinberger, and Bruce Kapp) has also contributed significantly to our understanding of the neural basis of fear conditioning.[53]

A Sea Horse for All Occasions: Consider another example. You are walking down the street and notice someone running toward you. The person, upon reaching you, hits you on the head and steals your wallet or purse. The next time someone is running toward you, chances are a set of standard fear responses will be set into play. You will probably freeze and prepare to defend yourself, your blood pressure and

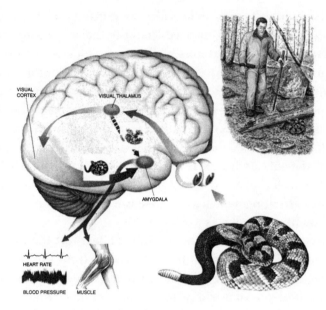

VISUAL CORTEX

VISUAL THALAMUS

AMYGDALA

HEART RATE

BLOOD PRESSURE   MUSCLE

FIGURE 6-14
Brain Pathways of Defense.

As the hiker walks through the woods, he abruptly encounters a snake coiled up behind a log on the path (upper right inset). The visual stimulus is first processed in the brain by the thalamus. Part of the thalamus passes crude, almost archetypal, information directly to the amygdala. This quick and dirty transmission allows the brain to start to respond to the possible danger signified by a thin, curved object, which could be a snake, or could be a stick or some other benign object. Meanwhile, the thalamus also sends visual information to the visual cortex (this part of the thalamus has a greater ability to encode the details of the stimulus than does the part that sends inputs to the amygdala). The visual cortex then goes about the business of creating a detailed and accurate representation of the stimulus. The outcome of cortical processing is then fed to the amygdala as well. Although the cortical pathway provides the amygdala with a more accurate representation than the direct pathway to the amygdala from the thalamus, it takes longer for the information to reach the amygdala by way of the cortex. In situations of danger, it is very useful to be able to respond quickly. The time saved by the amygdala in acting on the thalamic information, rather than waiting for the cortical input, may be the difference between life and death. It is better to have treated a stick as a snake than not to have responded to a possible snake. Most of what we know about these pathways has actually been learned by studies of the auditory as opposed to the visual system, but the same organizational principles seem to apply. (From J.E. LeDoux, Emotion, memory and the brain. Scientific American [June 1994], vol 270, p. 38. © 1994 by Scientific American Inc., all rights reserved.)

heart rate will rise, your palms and feet will sweat, stress hormones will begin to flow through your bloodstream, and so on. The sight of someone running toward you has become a conditioned fear stimulus. But suppose you later find yourself on the street where you were mugged. Although there is no one running toward you, your body may still be going through its defense motions. The reason for this is that not only did you get conditioned to the immediate stimulus directly associated with the trauma (the sight of the mugger running toward you), but also to the other stimuli that just happen to have been there. These made up the occasion or context in which the mugging took place, and like the sight of the mugger they too were conditioned by the traumatic experience.

Psychologists have studied contextual conditioning extensively. If you place a rat in a box and give it a few exposures to a mild shock in the presence of a tone, the rat will become conditioned to the tone, as we've already seen, but will also get conditioned to the box. So the next time the rat is placed in the box, the conditioned fear responses—freezing, autonomic and endocrine arousal, pain suppression, reflex potentiation—will occur, even in the absence of the tone. The context has become a CS.

In a contextual fear conditioning experiment, the context is made up of all of the stimuli present, other than the explicit CS. In other words, the CS is in the foreground—it is the most salient and predictive stimulus with respect to the shock. All other stimuli are in the background of the CS and constitute the context. The context is always there, but the CS only comes on sometimes. For this reason, it is often necessary to test the effects of a CS in a novel context, one that has not been associated with the shock, since fear responses elicited by the ever-present context can prevent the detection of responses that occur to the occasionally occurring CS.

In a sense contextual conditioning is incidental learning. During conditioning, the subject is paying attention to the most obvious stimulus (the tone CS) but the other stimuli get bought for the same purchase price. This is very useful from an evolutionary point of view. Our rabbit that escaped from the fox got conditioned not only to the stimuli that were immediately and directly associated with the arrival of the fox—its sight and smell and the sounds it made when attacking—but also to the place where the fox encounter took place—the watering hole and its surroundings. These extra stimuli are very useful in expanding the impact of conditioning beyond the most obvious and direct stimuli, allowing the organism to use even remotely related cues to avoid or escape from danger.

The interesting thing about a context is that it is not a particular stimulus but a collection of many. For some time it has been thought that the integration of individual stimuli into a context that no longer contains the individual elements is a function of the hippocampus.[54] Unlike the amygdala, the hippocampus does not get information from brain regions that process individual sensory stimuli, like lights and tones.[55] Instead, the sights and sounds of a place are pooled together before reaching the hippocampus, and one job of this brain region is to create a representation of the context that contains not individual stimuli but relations between stimuli.[56]

With this view of the hippocampus in mind, Russ Phillips and I, as well as Mike Fanselow and colleagues, examined whether the hippocampus might play a crucial role in the conditioning of fear responses to background contextual events.[57] In other words, we examined whether damage to the hippocampus might interfere with the conditioning of fear responses to the chamber in which tone-shock pairings occurred. Normal rats froze as soon as they were placed in the conditioning box. Rats with hippocampal lesions showed little freezing to the conditioning box. But as soon as the tone came on, the lesioned rats started freezing. The hippocampal lesion, in other words, selectively eliminated fear responses elicited by contextual stimuli without affecting fear responses elicited by a tone. The tone still worked because the tone could get to the amygdala directly. We reasoned that the hippocampal lesioned animals showed no fear responses to the box because they couldn't form the contextual representation and send it to the amygdala. Indeed, amygdala damage interfered with contextual conditioning just as it did with tone conditioning.[58]

A Hub in the Wheel of Fear: The amygdala is like the hub of a wheel. It receives low-level inputs from sensory-specific regions of the thalamus, higher level information from sensory-specific cortex, and still higher level (sensory independent) information about the general situation from the hippocampal formation. Through such

connections, the amygdala is able to process the emotional significance of individual stimuli as well as complex situations. The amygdala is, in essence, involved in the appraisal of emotional meaning. It
is where trigger stimuli do their triggering.

It is not unreasonable to suggest that by knowing what the different inputs to the amygdala are, and having some idea of what function those areas play in cognition, we can get some reasonable
hypotheses about what kinds of cognitive representations can arouse
fear responses. And by the same token, if we know how the brain
achieves some cognitive function, and we can determine how the
brain regions involved in that function are connected with the amygdala, we can come up with some plausible ideas about how fear might
be aroused by that kind of cognition.

It is easy to imagine how malfunctions of the amygdala and its
neural partners might lead to emotional disorders. If in some individuals (for genetic or acquired reasons) thalamic pathways are dominant or otherwise uncoupled from the cortical pathways, these
persons might form emotional memories on the basis of stimulus
events that do not coincide with their ongoing conscious perceptions
of the world mediated by the cortex. That is, because thalamic pathways to the amygdala exit the sensory system before conscious perceptions are created at the cortical level, the processing that occurs
through these subcortical pathways, which can only represent features and fragments of stimuli, does not necessarily coincide with the
perceptions occurring in the cortex. Such people would have very
poor insight into their emotions. At the same time, if the hippocampal system were uncoupled from the thalamic and cortical projections to the amygdala, we might have persons who express emotions
that are inappropriate to the immediate context, including possibly
the social context. These are purely speculative suggestions at this
point, but they are consistent with the facts now available.

Same as It Ever Was

Through studies of fear conditioning in rats, we have been able to
map out in great detail the brain mechanisms that underlie fear reactions. The reason we study fear in rats is obvious—we want to learn

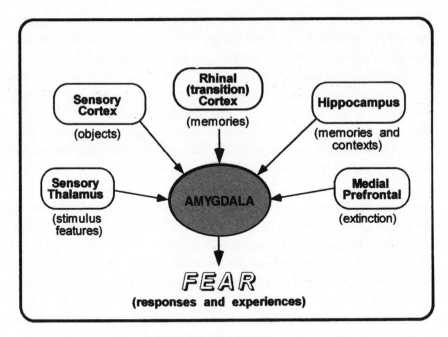

FIGURE 6-15
The Amygdala: Hub in the Wheel of Fear.

The amygdala receives inputs from a wide range of levels of cognitive processing. By way of inputs from sensory areas of the thalamus, the emotional functions of the amygdala can be triggered by low-level stimulus features, whereas inputs from cortical sensory processing systems (especially the late stages of processing in these systems) allow more complex aspects of stimulus processing (objects and events) to activate the amygdala. Inputs from the hippocampus play an important role in setting the emotional context. In addition, as we'll see in Chapter 7, the hippocampus and related areas of the cortex (including the rhinal or transitional cortical areas) are involved in the formation and retrieval of explicit memories, and inputs to the amygdala from these areas may allow emotions to be triggered by such memories. The medial prefrontal cortex has been implicated in the process known as extinction, whereby the ability of conditioned fear stimuli to elicit conditioned fear responses is weakened by repeated exposure to the conditioned stimulus without the unconditioned stimulus. Inputs to the amygdala from the medial prefrontal cortex appear to contribute to this process (see Chapter 8). By knowing which cortical areas project to the amygdala, and knowing the functions in which those areas participate, we can make predictions about how those functions might contribute to fear reactions. Anatomy can, in other words, illuminate psychology.

how human fear works. Less obvious, perhaps, is whether this is a reasonable approach. Can we really learn something about human fear by studying the brain of a rat? I believe we can.

Although no other creature has been studied as thoroughly with fear conditioning as the rat, and though no other technique has been used to study fear more extensively than fear conditioning, if we compile the evidence across species and experimental approaches we reach the inescapable conclusion that the basic brain mechanisms of fear are essentially the same through many levels of evolutionary development.

Let's start with our basic model of fear, fear conditioning. The effects of amygdala lesions on fear conditioning have been studied in birds, rats, rabbits, monkeys, and people using autonomic nervous system activity as the conditioned response. In each of these species, damage to the amygdala interferes with conditioned fear reactions—the CS fails to elicit the CR when the amygdala is damaged.

Pigeons are the only nonmammalian species in which the effects of amygdala lesions on fear conditioning have been examined. The similarity of the effects in pigeons and mammals means either that the amygdala was selected as a key component of the defense system of the vertebrate brain before birds and mammals separated from reptiles, or that the amygdala evolved to perform this function separately in the two post-reptilian lines. The best way to resolve this issue would be to know whether amygdala lesions interrupt fear conditioning in reptiles. Unfortunately, this experiment has not been performed. As a result, we need to turn to some other kind of evidence in search of an answer.

Another technique that has been used to map the brain pathways of fear or defensive behavior is brain stimulation. These techniques have been applied to reptiles as well as mammals and birds, and might thus be able to help us piece together an answer as to whether the amygdala has been involved in defense since at least the time when birds and mammals diverged from reptiles.

The first step we need to take, though, is to be certain that brain stimulation identifies the same pathways of fear reactivity that studies of fear conditioning have in the mammalian brain, where fear conditioning has been most clearly related to brain pathways. There is a long and interesting history to studies of brain stimulation in mammals, which we will only be able to touch on here.[59] Our main concern is whether stimulation of the amygdala, the heart and soul of the fear system revealed by fear conditioning studies, gives rise to defense responses in mammals. Clearly this occurs. It is well established that stimulation of the amygdala in anesthetized mammals elicits autonomic nervous system responses, and in awake mammals such stimulations elicit freezing, escape, and defensive attack responses, in addition to autonomic changes.[60] These kinds of studies have been performed in rats, cats, dogs, rabbits, and monkeys, all with similar results. Further, defense responses can be elicited from the central nucleus of the amygdala, the region by which the amygdala communicates with brain stem areas that control conditioned fear responses. And interruption of the pathways connecting the amygdala with these brain stem pathways interferes with the expression of the defense responses. Studies of fear conditioning and brain stimulation reveal similar output pathways in the expression of fear responses.

Let's now descend the phyletic tree and see what happens when we stimulate the amygdala of reptiles. It's tricky business to use living reptiles as examples of what reptiles might have been like when mammals diverged, as current reptiles themselves come from lines that have diverged from the ancestral lines. Nevertheless, since brain and behavior are not preserved in fossil records, this is the only way comparative studies of brain function can be conducted. Stimulation of the amygdala in lizards elicits the defensive behaviors these animals characteristically show when they are threatened by a predator, and lesions of the same regions reduce the expression of these behaviors in response to natural trigger stimuli.[61]

Now going up the branching evolutionary tree, we can consider the effects of stimulation of the human amygdala.[62] Such studies are performed in conjunction with brain surgery for otherwise untreatable epilepsy. Since the stimuli are delivered to the amygdala while the subjects are awake, it is possible to not only record expressive responses that are elicited, but also to ask the subjects to report on their experiences. Interestingly, the most common experience reported is a sense of foreboding danger, of fear. Fear is also the most commonly reported experience occurring in association with epileptic seizures, which are in essence spontaneous electrical stimulations that originate in the amygdala.

Recent studies of humans with amygdala damage also suggest that it plays a special role in fear. It is extremely rare to encounter patients with damage to only the amygdala, but it is not that rare to come across patients with damage that includes the amygdala. This is particularly common in patients who undergo surgery to remove epileptic regions of their temporal lobe. Kevin LaBar, Liz Phelps, and I conducted a study of fear conditioning in patients of this type.[63] Because we were studying humans rather than rats, we chose to use a very loud obnoxious noise as the US instead of electric shock. This worked just fine for conditioning autonomic nervous system responses to a softer, non-noxious sound in the control subjects. Importantly, we found that autonomic conditioned responses were reduced in the temporal lobe lesioned group. Interestingly, the patients consciously "knew" the relationship between the CS and US: when asked what went on in the experiment, they typically said, "Oh, there was a sound followed by this other really loud sound." This knowledge was not enough to transform the meaningless sound into a trigger stimulus. Although the lesions included areas other than the amygdala, we know from the animal studies that of all the areas included in the lesion, damage to the amygdala is the likely cause of the deficit in fear conditioning. This is a good example of why animal studies are so important. Without the animal studies the human experiment would be uninterpretable.

Although damage restricted to the human amygdala is very rare, Antonio Damasio and his colleagues at the University of Iowa have come across such a patient.[64] They have performed some extremely important and fascinating studies on her. For example, in one study they examined her ability to detect the emotional expression on faces. She was able to correctly identify most classes of expressions, except when the faces showed fear. And most importantly they have recently examined whether the capacity for fear conditioning is interfered with. Indeed, it was. Unlike the temporal lobe lesioned patients, this case unequivocally implicates the amygdala. Again, though, this study was inspired by the body of animal research that had already implicated the amygdala. If this study had been performed twenty years ago, before any of the animal conditioning studies had been done, we would have little understanding of the pathways through which the amygdala contributes to fear conditioning. In point of fact, though, the human studies might not have even been performed had the animal studies not set the stage for them—without the known effects of amygdala damage on conditioned fear in experimental animals, why would anyone consider doing such a study in humans with amygdala pathology?

The point of this discussion is to illustrate that the amygdala seems to do the same thing—take care of fear responses—in all species that have an amygdala. This is not the only function of the amygdala,[65] but it is certainly an important one. The function seems to have been established eons ago, probably at least since dinosaurs ruled the earth, and to have been maintained through diverse branches of evolutionary development. Defense against danger is perhaps an organism's number one priority and it appears that in the major groups of vertebrate animals that have been studied (reptiles, birds, and mammals) the brain performs this function using a common architectural plan.

The remarkable fact is that at the level of behavior, defense against danger is achieved in many different ways in different species, yet the amygdala's role is constant. It is this neural correspondence across species that no doubt allows diverse behaviors to achieve the same evolutionary function in different animals. This functional equivalence and neural correspondence applies to many vertebrate brains, including human brains. When it comes to detecting and responding to danger, the brain just hasn't changed much. In some ways we are emotional lizards.[66] I am quite confident in telling you that studies of fear reactions in rats tell us a great deal about how fear mechanisms work in our brains as well.

Beyond Evolution

By way of the amygdala and its input and output connections, the brain is programmed to detect dangers, both those that were routinely experienced by our ancestors and those learned about by each of us as individuals, and to produce protective responses that are most effective for our particular body type, and for the ancient environmental conditions under which the responses were selected.

Prepackaged responses have been shaped by evolution and occur automatically, or as Darwin pointed out, involuntarily.[67] They take place before the brain has had the chance to start thinking about what to do. Thinking takes time, but responding to danger often needs to occur quickly and without much mulling over the decision. Recall Darwin's encounter with the puff adder at the Zoological Gardens—the snake struck and Darwin recoiled back quick as a flash. If the snake had not been behind glass, Darwin's life would have been at the mercy of his involuntary responses—if they were quick enough, he would have survived; if they were too slow, he would have perished. He certainly had no time to decide whether or not to jump once the snake started to strike. And even though he had resolved not to jump, he could not stop himself.

While many animals get through life mostly on emotional automatic pilot, those animals that can readily switch from automatic pilot to willful control have a tremendous extra advantage. This advantage depends on the wedding of emotional and cognitive functions. So far we've emphasized the role of cognitive processes as a source of signals that can trigger prepackaged emotional reactions. But cognition also contributes to emotion by giving us the ability to make decisions about what kind of action should occur next, given the situation in which we find ourselves now. One of the reasons that cognition is so useful a part of the mental arsenal is that it allows this shift from *reaction* to *action*. The survival advantages that come from being able to make this shift may have been an important ingredient that shaped the evolutionary elaboration of cognition in mammals and the explosion of cognition in primates, especially in humans.

In responding first with its most-likely-to-succeed behavior, the brain buys time. This is not to say that the brain responds automatically first for the purpose of buying time. The automatic responses came first, in the evolutionary sense, and cannot exist for the purpose of serving responses that evolved later. Buying time is a fortunate by-product of the way information processing is constrained by brain organization.

Imagine that you are a small mammal, say a prairie dog. You come out of your burrow to look for dinner. You begin exploring around, and all of a sudden you spot a bobcat, which you know to be a serious enemy. You immediately stop all movement. Freezing is evolution's gift to you. You do it without having to weigh decisions. It just happens. The sight or sound of the bobcat goes straight to your amygdala and out comes the freezing response. If you had to make a deliberate decision about what to do, you would have to consider the likelihood of each possible choice succeeding or failing and could get so bogged down in decision making that you might be eaten before you made the choice. And if you started fidgeting around or pacing while trying to decide, you would surely attract the predator's attention and certainly decrease your likelihood of surviving. Freezing, of course, is not the only automatic response. But it is a fairly universal initial response to detection of danger throughout the animal kingdom (see Chapter 5). Automatic responses like freezing have the advantage of having been test-piloted through the ages; reasoned responses do not come with this kind of fine-tuning.

Presumably, evolution could work toward making cognition faster, so that thought could always precede action, eliminating involuntary action altogether from the behavioral repertoire. But this would be quite costly. There are many things that we are better off not having to think about, like putting one foot in front of the other when we walk, blinking when objects come near the eye, getting the glove to just the right spot to catch a fly ball, inserting the subject and verb in the correct place when we speak, responding quickly and appropriately to danger, and so forth. Behavioral and mental functions would slow down to a crawl if every response had to be preceded by a thought.

But no matter how useful automatic reactions are, they are only a quick fix, especially in humans. Eventually you take control. You make a plan and carry it out. This requires that your cognitive resources be directed to the emotional problem. You have to stop thinking about whatever you were thinking about before the danger occurred and start thinking about the danger you are facing (and already responding to automatically). Robert and Caroline Blanchard call this behavior "risk assessment."[68] This is something we do all the time. We're always sizing up situations and planning how to maximize our gains and minimize our losses. Surviving is not just something we do in the presence of a wild beast. Social situations are often survival encounters.

We don't really fully understand how the human brain sizes up a situation, comes up with a set of potential courses of action, predicts possible outcomes of different actions, assigns priorities to possible actions, and chooses a particular action, but these activities are unquestionably amongst the most sophisticated cognitive functions. They allow the crucial shift from reaction to action. From what we currently know, it seems likely that regions like the prefrontal cortex may be involved.[69] The prefrontal cortex is the part of the cerebral cortex that has expanded the most in primates, and it may not even exist in other mammals.[70] When this region is damaged in people, they have great difficulty in planning what to do.[71] So-called frontal lobe patients tend to do the same thing over and over again. They are glued to the present and unable to project themselves into the future. Some regions of the prefrontal cortex are linked with the amygdala, and together these regions, and possibly others, may play key roles in planning and executing emotional actions. We'll again consider the role of the prefrontal cortex in emotion when we turn to the topic of emotional consciousness in Chapter 9. Another brain region that may be involved is the basal ganglia, a collection of areas in the subcortical forebrain. These regions have long been implicated in controlling movement, and recent work has shown that interactions between the amygdala and the basal ganglia may be important in instrumental emotional behavior, which is essentially what I am calling emotional actions.[72]

Emotional plans are a wonderful addition to emotional automaticity. They allow us to be emotional *actors*, rather than just *reactors*. But the capacity to make this switch has a price. Once you start thinking, not only do you try to figure the best thing to do in the face of several possible next moves that a predator (including a social predator) is likely to make, you also think about what will happen if the plan fails. Bigger brains allow better plans, but for these you pay in the currency of anxiety, a topic that we'll return to in Chapter 8.

The appraisal theorist Lazarus has talked about emotional coping.[73] In the scheme presented here, emotional coping represents the cognitive planning of voluntary *actions* once we find ourselves in the midst of an involuntarily elicited emotional *reaction*. Evolutionary programming sets the emotional ball rolling, but from then on we are very much in the driver's seat. How effectively we deal with this responsibility is a matter of our genetic constitution, past experience, and cognitive creativity, to name but a few of the many factors that are important. And while we will need to understand all of these before we understand "emotion," it seems to me that the way to start understanding emotion is by elucidating the first step in the sequence—the elicitation of prepackaged emotional *reactions* by innate or learned trigger stimuli. We clearly need to go beyond evolution in order to understand emotion, but we should get past it by understanding its contribution rather than ignoring it. I think we have now done that, at least for the emotion fear, or at least for those aspects of the emotion fear that are captured by studies of fear conditioning.

7

REMEMBRANCE
OF EMOTIONS PAST

"Every man has reminiscences which he would not tell to everyone but only to his friends. He has other matters in his mind which he would not reveal even to his friends, but only to himself, and that in secret. But there are other things which a man is afraid to tell even to himself, and every decent man has a number of such things stored away in his mind."

Fyodor Dostoevsky, *Notes from the Underground*[1]

BICYCLING. SPEAKING ENGLISH. The Pledge of Allegiance. Multiplication by 7s. The rules of dominoes. Bowel control. A taste for spinach. Immense fear of snakes. Balancing when standing. The meaning of "halcyon days." The words to "Subterranean Homesick Blues." Anxiety associated with the sound of a dentist drill. The smell of banana pudding.

What do all of these have in common? They are each things I've learned and stored in my brain. Some I've learned to do, or learned to expect; others are remembered personal experiences; and still others are just rote facts.

For a long time, it was thought that there was one kind of learning system that would take care of all the learning the brain does. During the behaviorist reign, for example, it was assumed that psychologists could study any kind of learning in any kind of animal and find out how humans learn the things we learn. This logic was not only applied to those things that humans and animals both do, like finding food and avoiding danger, but also to things that humans do easily and animals do poorly if at all, like speaking.

It is now known that there are multiple memory systems in the brain, each devoted to different memory functions. The brain system that allowed me to learn to hit a baseball is different from the one that allows me to remember trying to hit the ball and failing, and this is different still from the system that made me tense and anxious when I stepped up to the plate after having been beaned the last time up. Though these are each forms of long-term memory (memory that lasts more than a few seconds), they are mediated by different neural networks. Different kinds of memory, like different kinds of emotions and different kinds of sensations, come out of different brain systems.

In this chapter we are going to be concerned with two learning systems that the brain uses to form memories about emotional experiences. The separate existence of these two kinds of memories in the brain is nicely illustrated by considering a famous case study in which one of these systems was damaged, but the other continued to function normally.

Is That a Pin in Your Hand or Are You Just Glad to See Me?

In the early part of this century, a French physician named Edouard Claparede examined a female patient who, as a result of brain damage, had seemingly lost all ability to create new memories.[2] Each time Claparede walked into the room he had to reintroduce himself to her, as she had no recollection of having seen him before. The memory problem was so severe that if Claparede left the room and returned a few minutes later, she wouldn't remember having seen him.

One day, he tried something new. He entered the room, and, as on every other day, he held out his hand to greet her. In typical fashion she shook his hand. But when their hands met, she quickly pulled hers back, for Claparede had concealed a tack in his palm and had pricked her with it. The next time he returned to the room to greet her, she still had no recognition of him, but she refused to shake his hand. She could not tell him why she would not shake hands with him, but she wouldn't do it.

Claparede had come to signify danger. He was no longer just a man, no longer just a doctor, but had become a stimulus with a specific emotional meaning. Although the patient did not have a conscious memory of the situation, subconsciously she learned that shaking Claparede's hand could cause her harm, and her brain used this stored information, this memory, to prevent the unpleasantness from occurring again.

These instances of memory sparing and loss were not easily interpreted in Claparede's time and until recently were thought of as reflecting the survival and breakdown of different aspects of one learning and memory system. But modern studies of the brain mechanisms of memory have given us a different view. It now seems that Claparede was seeing the operation of two different memory systems in his patient—one involved in forming memories of experiences and making those memories available for conscious recollection at some later time, and another operating outside of consciousness and controlling behavior without explicit awareness of the past learning.

Conscious recollection is the kind of memory that we have in mind when we use the term "memory" in everyday conversation: to remember is to be conscious of some past experience, and to have a memory problem (again, in everyday parlance) is to have difficulty with this ability. Scientists refer to conscious recollections as declarative or explicit memories.[3] Memories created this way can be brought to mind and described verbally. Sometimes we may have trouble dredging up the memory, but it is potentially available as a conscious memory. As a result of brain damage, Claparede's patient had a problem with this type of memory.

But the patient's ability to protect herself from a situation of potential danger by refusing to shake hands reflects a different kind of memory system. This system forms implicit or nondeclarative memories about dangerous or otherwise threatening situations. Memories of this type, as we saw in the last chapter, are created through the mechanisms of fear conditioning—because of its association with the painful pinprick, the sight of Claparede became a *learned trigger* of defensive behavior (a conditioned fear stimulus). We also saw that conditioned fear responses involve implicit or unconscious processes in two important senses: the learning that occurs does not depend on conscious awareness and, once the learning has taken place, the stimulus does not have to be consciously perceived in order to elicit the conditioned emotional responses. We may become aware that fear conditioning has taken place, but we do not have control over its occurrence or conscious access to its workings. Claparede's patient shows us something similar: as a result of brain damage, she had no conscious memory of the learning experience through which the conditioned fear stimulus implicitly acquired the capacity to protect her from being pricked again.

Through brain damage we can thus see the operation of an implicit emotional memory system in the absence of explicit conscious memory of the emotional learning experience. Normally, though, in the undamaged brain, explicit memory and implicit emotional memory systems are working at the same time, each forming their own special brand of memories. So if you met Claparede today and he was, after all these years, still up to his old tricks, you would form an explicit conscious memory of being pricked by the old codger, as well as an implicit or unconscious memory. We are going to call the implicit, fear-conditioned memory an "emotional memory" and the explicit declarative memory a "memory of an emotion." Having already explored how fear conditioning works, we will now examine the neural organization of the explicit or declarative memory system, and also take a look at interactions between this conscious memory network and the unconsciously functioning fear conditioning system.

Henry Mnemonic: The Life and Times of Case H.M.

Karl Lashley, the father of modern physiological psychology and one of the most influential brain researchers in the first half of the twentieth century, conducted an extensive series of investigations attempting to find the locus of memory in the rat brain.[4] His conclusion, that memory is not mediated by any particular neural system but is instead diffusely distributed in the brain, was widely accepted. By mid-century researchers had quit looking for the location of memory in the brain—it seemed that this was a fruitless and even a misguided quest. However, the tides began to shift when a young man suffering from an extreme case of epilepsy was operated on in Hartford, Connecticut, in 1953.[5]

Known to legions of brain scientists and psychologists as H.M.,[6] this patient has single-handedly, though unwittingly, shaped the course of research on the brain mechanisms of explicit (conscious) memory over the past forty years. At the time of the operation he was twenty-seven and had been experiencing convulsive epileptic attacks since sixteen. All attempts to control the seizures with medications available at the time had failed. Because of the severity and intractability of his epilepsy, H.M. was deemed an appropriate candidate for a radical, last-resort, experimental procedure in which the brain tissue containing the major sites or "foci" of the disease are removed. In his case, it was necessary to remove large regions of the temporal lobes on both sides of his brain.

Measured by the extent to which its medical goal was achieved, the surgery was a great success—the epileptic seizures came to be controllable by anticonvulsant medications. On the other hand, there was one unfortunate and unanticipated consequence. H.M. lost his memory. More specifically, he lost his capacity to form explicit, declarative, or conscious long-term memories. However, the distinction between explicit and implicit memories did not arise until much later, and in fact was based in part on the studies of H.M. So we will forsake the distinction for a while until we've considered H.M. and his problems in more detail.

H.M.'s memory disorder, his amnesia, has been studied and written about extensively over the years. Neal Cohen and Howard Eichenbaum, two leading memory researchers, recently summarized H.M.'s condition: "Now, nearly 40 years after his surgery, H.M. does not know his age or the current date; does not know where he is living; does not know the current status of his parents (who are long deceased); and does not know his own history. . . ."[7] And Larry Squire, another leader in the field, describes it this way: "Although his epileptic condition was markedly improved, he could accomplish little, if any, new learning. . . . His impairment in new learning is so pervasive and severe that he requires constant supervisory care. He does not learn the names or faces of those who see him regularly. Having aged since his surgery, he does not now recognize a photograph of himself."[8] But probably the most straightforward and telling characterization of H.M.'s condition appeared in the first publication that described his unfortunate state. William Scoville, the surgeon, and Brenda Milner, the psychologist who studied H.M. initially, noted that H.M. forgot the events of daily life as quickly as they occurred.[9]

One of the facts that was clear from Milner's studies was that H.M.'s memory problem had nothing to do with a loss of intellectual ability. H.M.'s IQ after the surgery was in the normal range, in fact on the high side of normal, and remained there over the years. The black holes of knowledge in his mind did not reflect some general breakdown in his ability to think and reason. He was not stupid. He simply couldn't remember.

In many ways, H.M.'s memory deficit was quite similar to the disorder in Claparede's patient. However, for two reasons, H.M. is a more important case for understanding memory. The first is that H.M. was extensively examined from the mid-1950s until only a few years ago. Probably no patient in the history of neurology has been studied in such detail and over such an extended period. Throughout, he was a willing and able subject, but in recent years, as age took its toll, he became less capable of participating in these studies. The result of all this work is that we know exactly which aspects of his memory were compromised. The second reason that H.M. has been so important for understanding memory is that we know the location of the damage in his brain. His lesion was the result of a precise surgical removal (rather than an accident of nature). The surgical record thus indicates where the damage is. It has also been possible to look inside his skull with modern brain imaging techniques and confirm the location of the damage. By combining this exacting neurological information about the locus of brain damage with the detailed information about which aspects of memory are disturbed and intact, researchers studying H.M. have obtained important insights into the way memory is organized in the brain.

The Long and the Short of It[10]

Today, it is widely accepted that memory can be divided into a short-term store, which lasts seconds, and a long-term one lasting from minutes to a lifetime.[11] What you are conscious of now is what is mometarily in your short-term memory (especially what is called working memory, a special kind of short-term memory that will be discussed in Chapter 9), and what goes into your short-term memory is what can go into your long-term memory.[12] This distinction had been around since the late nineteenth century, having been proposed (with different terms) by William James (who else?),[13] but the most conclusive evidence that short- and long-term memory are really different processes mediated by distinct brain systems probably came from Milner's early studies of H.M.

Although H.M. seemed to forget almost everything that happened to him (he was unable to form long-term memories), he could nevertheless hold on to information for a few seconds (he had short-term memory). For example, if he was shown a card with a picture on it and the card was put away, he could say what was on the card if he was asked immediately, but if a minute or so passed he was completely unable to say what he had seen, or even whether he had seen anything. From the results of many kinds of tests, it became clear that removal of regions of the temporal lobe in H.M. interfered with long- but not short-term memory, suggesting that the formation of long-term memories is mediated by the temporal lobe, but that short-term memory involves some other brain system.[14]

H.M. has also taught us that the brain system involved in forming new long-term memories is different from the one that stores old long-term memories. H.M. could remember events from his childhood and early adult life quite well. In fact, his memory of things before the operation was good, up to a couple of years prior to the surgery. Consequently, Milner pointed out that H.M. had a very severe anterograde amnesia (an inability to put new information into long-term memory) but only a mild retrograde amnesia (an inability to remember things that happened before the surgery). H.M.'s major deficit was thus one of depositing new learning into the long-term memory bank, rather than withdrawing information placed there earlier in life.

The findings from H.M. thus clearly distinguished short-term and long-term memory, and also suggested that long-term memory involves at least two stages, an initial one requiring the temporal lobe regions that were removed, and a later stage involving some other brain regions, most likely areas of the neocortex.[15] The temporal lobe is needed for forming long-term memories, but gradually, over years, memories become independent of this brain system. These are powerful concepts that remain central to our understanding of the brain mechanisms of memory.

In Search of a Model

The areas of the temporal lobe that were damaged in H.M. included major portions of the hippocampus and amygdala, and surrounding transitional areas. Some of these were areas that MacLean had identified as components of the limbic system, which, as we saw earlier, was supposed to constitute the emotional system of the brain. H.M. provided some of the first difficulties for the limbic system theory of emotion, suggesting that some regions of the limbic system are involved at least as much in cognitive functions (like memory) as in emotion.

Although several temporal lobe regions were damaged in H.M., the view emerged that damage to the hippocampus was primarily responsible for the memory disorder. Other patients were operated on, in addition to H.M., and when these were all considered together it seemed that the extent of the memory disorder was directly related to the amount of the hippocampus that had been removed. On the basis of these observations, the hippocampus emerged as the leading candidate brain region for the laying down of new memories. Surgeons now make every effort to leave the hippocampus and related brain regions intact, at least on one side of the brain, when operating on the temporal lobes so that devastating effects on memory can be prevented.

By the late 1950s, the task at hand for memory researchers seemed clear and straightforward: turn to studies of experimental animals to figure out how the hippocampus accomplishes its mnemonic job. In animal studies, memory is tested not by asking the subject whether he or she remembers, but by determining whether behavioral performance is affected by prior learning experiences. Countless studies of the effects of hippocampectomy (hippocampal removal) on memory were performed in a variety of animals. The results were inconsistent and disappointing. Lesions sometimes interfered with the ability of animals to remember what they learned, and sometimes did not. It seemed that either the human and nonhuman brain have different mechanisms of memory, or that the researchers had just not found the right way to test memory in animals.

But in the early 1970s David Gaffan, an Oxford psychologist, came up with a way of testing memory in monkeys that proved to be a reliable measure of hippocampal-dependent functions.[16] It was a task called delayed nonmatching to sample. The monkey was shown a stimulus, say a toy soldier. The stimulus was then removed. After a delay, two stimuli appeared, the toy soldier and a toy car of about the same size. The monkey could get a treat (like a raisin or Froot Loop) by picking the stimulus that had not appeared before (the stimulus that did not match the sample), which in this case was the car. If the sample (the soldier) was picked, no treat followed.

Having a sweet tooth, monkeys are very willing to play these kinds of games. Normal monkeys do fine, even at relatively long delays between the sample and the two test stimuli. Monkeys with hippocampal damage also perform reasonably well at short delays. But as the delay increases, they perform miserably—they respond randomly to the two stimuli, choosing the stimulus that matches the sample as often as the nonmatch.[17] This breakdown at the long delays cannot be due to a simple failure to learn the rule (pick the stimulus that does not match the sample). They learn the rule before the hippocampus is removed, so they already know it and just have to apply it to the stimuli that appear in a particular test. Most important, they use the rule well at short delays. The problem is really one of holding on to the memory of the sample long enough to choose the nonmatching item.

Delayed nonmatching to sample does not exactly resemble the kinds of tasks used to test memory in amnesic or normal humans.[18] Humans are given verbal instructions about how to perform the task, whereas animals are given weeks or months of behavioral training so that they can learn the rule. Humans are typically tested on verbal material or are required to give verbal responses even with nonverbal test stimuli. Animals always express their memory through behavioral performance. Humans are not given sweets every time they get an answer right. The important thing about delayed nonmatching to sam-

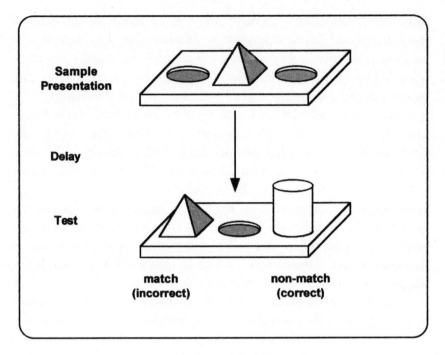

FIGURE 7-1
Delayed Nonmatching to Sample Procedure.

In this procedure, a monkey is shown a sample stimulus (in the center of the tray). After a delay, the sample is presented along with a novel stimulus. If the monkey picks the novel stimulus (the nonmatch) he will find a reward under it (peanut, Fruit Loop, or raisin). This procedure has been used extensively to study the role of the hippocampus and related cortical areas in memory processes in animals. (Based on an illustration provided by E. A. Murray of the National Institute of Mental Health.)

ple was thus not that it perfectly corresponded to the kinds of tests used to reveal memory problems in H.M. but that it proved to be a reliable means of revealing a hippocampal-dependent memory in animals. For this reason, delayed nonmatching to sample became the gold standard for modeling human temporal lobe amnesia in monkeys.

Delayed nonmatching to sample was also tried in studies of other species, particularly rats, and was found to be a good way of testing hippocampal-dependent memory in these animals as well.[19] But through studies of rats, other kinds of tasks were also discovered that reliably implicated the hippocampus. These mostly involved various forms of learning and memory that depend on the use of spatial cues. In one task, rats are tested in a maze in which different alleys radiate out from a central platform.[20] The rat is put in the center and has to choose one of the alleys. His job is to remember which alleys he's not gone down before. If he picks one of the previously unvisited alleys, he gets a treat. If he goes down a previously visited one, he gets nothing. The only way to solve this task is to use spatial cues, such as the location of an alley with respect to the location of other items in the room in which the maze is. In another task, rats are put into a tank containing milky water.[21] They are decent swimmers, but don't really care for it, and will swim to safety as soon as possible. Initially, there is a platform above the water. Once they've learned where it is, the platform is submerged just below the surface. The rats have to remember where the platform was and use spatial cues around the room to guide their swim to safety. Lesions of the hippocampus interfere with spatial memory in both the radial maze and the water maze.

By the late 1970s, the ducks seemed to be lining up. Studies of animals and humans were finally both pointing to the hippocampus as a key player in the game of memory. But then Mortimer Mishkin of the National Institute of Mental Health noted a problem with this neat and tidy story about the role of the hippocampus in memory and amnesia.[22] He pointed out that all of the patients, including H.M., who became amnesic as a result of temporal lobe lesions had damage to the amygdala as well as the hippocampus. Might the amygdala also be important? Mishkin tested this idea by examining the effects of combined lesions of the hippocampus and amygdala versus separate lesions of these two areas in monkeys. The findings seemed crystal clear. Damage to the amygdala and hippocampus together was more detrimental than damage to either alone on delayed nonmatching to sample. The idea that limbic areas, like the amygdala and hippocampus, are more involved in emotion than cognition was already challenged by the discovery that the hippocampus contributes to cognition (memory). The possibility that the amygdala was part of the memory system blurred this distinction between cognitive and emotional functions of limbic areas even more.

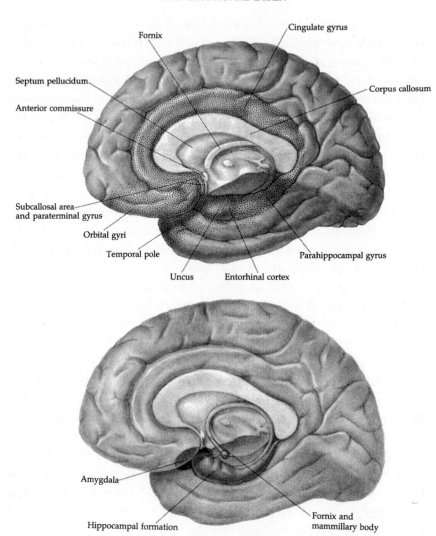

FIGURE 7-2
Location of the Hippocampus and Amygdala and Surrounding Cortical Areas.

The two diagrams show the medial or inside wall of the human cerebrum. The stippled area is the classic limbic lobe (see Chapter 4). The amygdala and hippocampus are found deep inside the medial part of the temporal lobe, underneath the uncus, entorhinal cortex, and parahippocampal gyrus (top). These cortical areas have been stripped away to show the location of the hippocampus and amygdala in the bottom illustration. (Reprinted from figures 15-1 and 15-2 in J. H. Martin [1989], *Neuroanatomy: Text and Atlas.* New York: Elsevier. Copyright © [1989] by Appleton and Lange.)

Other researchers, however, did not fully accept the view that the amygdala was part of the memory system and by the late 1980s the tide was shifting back toward the hippocampus as the core of the long-term memory system. Larry Squire, Stuart Zola-Morgan, and David Amaral of San Diego examined a patient with a severe memory disorder, not unlike H.M.'s.[23] Not too long afterward, the patient died, and the brain was made available for analysis. This patient turned out to have a pure hippocampal lesion. There was no detectable damage anywhere else. This selective lesion resulted from anoxia, a reduction in oxygen supply to the brain, which especially affects cells in the hippocampus. Amnesia, it seemed, could result from damage to only the hippocampus.

Why, then, did the combined hippocampal and amygdala lesion produce more of a deficit on delayed nonmatching to sample than the hippocampal lesions alone in monkeys? The San Diego team next took on this issue. They noted that in the process of removing the amygdala, surgeons often damage cortical areas that provide an important linkage between the neocortex and the hippocampus. Perhaps, Mishkin's effect was not due to amygdala damage but to an interruption of the flow of information back and forth between the neocortex and the hippocampus. The San Diego researchers figured out how to remove the amygdala without disturbing the cortical areas related to the hippocampus. This pure amygdala lesion had no effect on delayed nonmatching to sample.[24] Importantly, though, the pure amygdala lesion did produce the emotional concomitants of the Klüver-Bucy syndrome, especially reduced fear.[25] The role of the hippocampus in memory seemed rescued, and the burden of cognition was again lifted from the amygdala.

What, then, is the relative contribution of the hippocampus as opposed to those pesky cortical areas surrounding the amygdala and hippocampus? Mishkin and Betsy Murray showed that damage to the surrounding cortex also produces deficits in delayed nonmatching to sample; in fact, these lesions produced more of a deficit than the hippocampal damage.[26] On the basis of this finding, Murray and Mishkin questioned the premier role of the hippocampus in memory and argued instead that the surrounding cortex is particularly crucial. Other researchers, however, point out that this is too strong a conclusion to base solely on delayed nonmatching to sample, which may

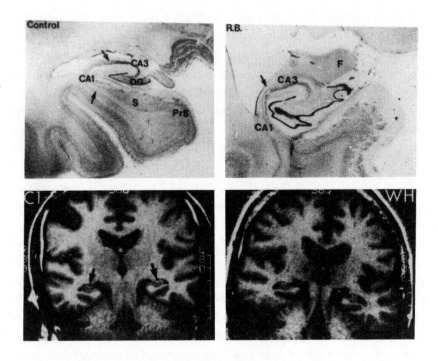

FIGURE 7-3
Magnetic Resonance Imaging Scan of the Normal
and Damaged Hippocampus.

Section through the hippocampus of a normal human (top left) and an am-
nesic patient (top right). The CA1 region of the hippocampus is indicated by
the arrow in the normal brain. In the amnesic patient the CA1 region is dam-
aged. Magnetic resonance scans of a normal human (bottom left) and an am-
nesic patient (bottom right). The hippocampal formation is greatly reduced in
the amnesic patient. (Top panels reprinted with permission from L. R. Squire
[1986], Mechanisms of Memory, *Science* 232, 1612–1619, © 1986 American Association for the Advancement of Science. Bottom panels reprinted with permission
from G. Press, D. G. Amaral, and L. R. Squire [1989], Hippocampal abnormalities
in amnesic patients revealed by high-resolution magnetic resonance imaging. *Nature*
341, p. 54, © Macmillan Magazines Ltd.)

not be the magic bullet that it has been made out to be.[27] After all,
there is pretty solid evidence that pure hippocampal damage in humans can lead to amnesia (recall the anoxia case above). Delayed
nonmatching to sample may be a better test of the function of the
surrounding cortex than of the hippocampus, which would suggest
that these two areas each contribute uniquely to memory.[28]

This debate over the details will no doubt continue. However, most researchers in the field are in agreement about the broad outline of how the temporal lobe memory system works.[29] Sensory processing areas of the cortex receive inputs about external events and create perceptual representations of the stimuli. These representations are then shuttled to the surrounding cortical regions, which, in turn, send further processed representations to the hippocampus. The hippocampus then communicates back with the surrounding regions, which communicate with the neocortex. The maintenance of the memory over the short run (a few years) requires that the temporal lobe memory system be intact, either because components of this system store the memory trace or because the trace is maintained by interactions between the temporal lobe system and the neocortex. Gradually, over years, the hippocampus relinquishes its control over the memory to the neocortex, where the memory appears to remain as long as it is a memory, which may be a lifetime.

This model of memory, which has emerged from studies of amnesic animals and humans, gives us a way of understanding the mental changes that take place over time in Alzheimer's disease.[30] The disease begins its attack on the brain in the temporal lobe, particularly in the hippocampus, thus explaining why forgetfulness is the first warning sign. But the disease eventually creeps into the neocortex, suggesting why, as the disease progresses, all aspects of memory (old and new) are compromised, along with a variety of other cortically dependent cognitive functions. Without years of research on amnesia in both humans and animals the cognitive dissolution that occurs as Alzheimer's disease spreads through the forebrain would not be so readily interpreted. And having these insights about how the disease is compromising the mind and brain in tandem may be one of the best aids in figuring out approaches to preventing, arresting, or reversing the cognitive meltdown that occurs.

Pockets of Memory

In the early days, H.M. failed to form new long-term memories in the vast majority of memory tasks that he was given.[31] It did not matter so much whether he was tested with words, pictures, or sounds, he

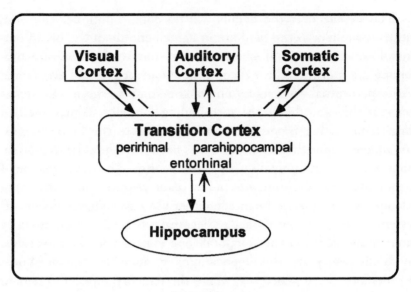

FIGURE 7-4
Cortical Inputs to the Hippocampus.

Each of the major sensory processing systems of the neocortex gives rise to projections to areas that are transitional between the neocortex and hippocampus (that is, the perirhinal and parahippocampal areas). These send their outputs to the entorhinal cortex. The entorhinal cortex then provides the main source of inputs to the hippocampal formation. The hippocampus projects back to the neocortex by way of the same pathways through the transitional cortex.

could not remember. His memory problem was, accordingly, described as a "global amnesia." The few odd things that he could retain seemed, at first, like isolated, unrelated snippets of memory. However, as more and more findings came in from different kinds of memory tests, it became clear that there were well-defined pockets of memory sparing in H.M. As a result of these discoveries, temporal lobe amnesia is no longer considered to be a global memory disorder affecting all forms of new learning. By figuring out what kinds of learning functions are spared and disrupted in amnesia, researchers have been able to characterize the contribution of the temporal lobe system to memory.

One of the first observations of spared learning resulted when Milner asked H.M. to try to copy a picture of a star while only watching a mirror reflection of his hand.[32] This required that he learn to control his hand on the basis of the abnormal (visually reversed) feedback coming to his brain about where his hand was in space. He did poorly the first time, but with practice he improved, and he retained the ability to express the improved performance over time. Suzanne Corkin of MIT then found that H.M. also improved with practice in another manual skill learning task—one in which he was required to keep a handheld stylus on a small dot that was spinning around on a turntable.[33] As with the mirror drawing task, the more times he did it the better he got. Interestingly, and importantly, on both manual skill learning tasks, he improved in spite of the fact that he had no conscious memory of the earlier experiences that led to the improved performance. These findings suggested that the learning and remembrance of manual skills might be mediated by some system other than the temporal lobe system.

Neal Cohen later examined whether spared skill learning ability in amnesia might extend to what is called cognitive skills, the ability to get better at doing mental tasks.[34] He showed that the ability of amnesics to read mirror images of words improved with practice (e.g., "egral" is the mirror image of "large"). He also showed that the patients could learn some complicated rule-based strategies required to solve certain mathematical problems or puzzles. One much discussed instance is a puzzle game called the Tower of Hanoi. To solve this problem, discs of different sizes have to be moved in a certain way between three pegs without ever letting a smaller peg be under a larger one. Even normal subjects have difficulty finding the "optimal" solution to the puzzle. However, with lots of practice, the amnesic patients, including H.M., were able to achieve this solution. As with the other learning tasks, they had no recollection of playing the game.

Research by Elizabeth Warrington and Larry Weiskrantz in England showed that "priming" is preserved in amnesic patients.[35] Like the other instances of spared learning and memory in amnesia, priming involves the demonstration of learning by the effects of prior experience on later behavioral performance rather than by the subject's knowledge of the prior learning. For example, in one version of priming, the subject is given a list of words. Later, if asked to recall the items that were on the list, amnesic patients perform miserably. However, if instead of being asked to recall the items they are given fragments of words and asked to complete them, like normal subjects they do better on the fragments that go with words in the study list than they do for fragments that have no match in the study list.

Weiskrantz and Warrington also showed that the classical conditioning of eyeblink responses is preserved in amnesia.[36] In this task, a tone is paired with an aversive stimulus (usually an air puff to the eye). After hundreds of trials, the tone elicits eyelid closure immediately before the onset of the air puff. This precisely timed response protects the delicate tissues of the eye from the air puff. Amnesic patients show normal eyeblink conditioning. This is not surprising given the fact that we now know from animal studies that eyeblink conditioning involves circuits in the brain stem and is unaffected by removal of all brain tissue above the midbrain.[37] The patients nevertheless later have no memory of having seen the conditioning apparatus.

The Multiplicity of Memory

What do all these spared learning and memory functions have in common, and how do they differ from the functions that are disrupted in temporal lobe amnesia? Cohen and Squire put all of the findings together and came up with an answer.[38] They proposed that damage to the temporal lobe memory system interferes with the ability to consciously recollect, but leaves intact the ability to learn certain skills. They called these two processes declarative and procedural memory. A similar dichotomy was offered by Daniel Schacter of Harvard, who distinguished between explicit and implicit memory.[39] Conscious awareness of the basis of performance occurs in explicit memory, but in implicit memory performance is guided by unconscious factors. Skill learning, priming, and classical conditioning are all examples of implicit or procedural learning. These are each intact in temporal lobe amnesia and involve brain areas other than the temporal lobe memory system. Other memory dichotomies have been proposed over the years,[40] but the distinction between conscious, explicit, declarative memory, on the one hand, and unconscious, implicit, procedural memory, on the other, has had the greatest impact on current thinking and will be emphasized here.

The distinction between explicit and implicit memory is dramatically illustrated by a study performed by Squire and his colleagues.[41] They showed that amnesics could be made to either succeed or fail a memory test, simply by changing the instructions—some instructions took the patients down the explicit memory path, which gave rise to failure, whereas other instructions led them on a successful stroll through implicit memory land. In all conditions the stimuli were the same, and only the memory instruction changed. The subjects were first given a list of words to study. Then a few minutes later, they received one of three sets of instructions: recall as many words as you can from the list; use the following cues to help you remember as many words on the list as you can; or, say the first word that comes to mind when you see the following cues. The cues in the latter two conditions were three-letter stems of words that had been on the list: MOT for MOTEL, ABS for ABSENT, INC for INCOME, and so on. Each stem could come from many other words: MOT could be from MOTHER or MOTLEY as well as MOTEL. Not surprisingly, the amnesics did poorly when they had to recall without any cues. They also did poorly when told to use the cues to help them remember the words. But they were as good as normal subjects when the instruction was to say the first word that comes to mind after seeing a cue. In the latter case, the cues were primes rather than recall aids. When performing the priming task, and thus using an implicit memory system, they functioned fine, but damage to the temporal lobe memory system prevented them from consciously recalling the items, even with the aid of cues. Howard Eichenbaum, in studies of rats, found something similar: depending on the instructions given to rats (through training experiences), he showed that it was possible to make a learning situation either dependent upon or independent of the hippocampus.[42]

Cohen and Squire were quick to point out that explicit, declarative memory is mediated by a single memory system, the temporal lobe memory system, but that there are multiple implicit or procedural memory systems. Thus, the brain system that mediates priming is different from the systems involved in skill learning or classical conditioning. Further, different forms of classical conditioning are also mediated by different neural systems—eyeblink conditioning by brain stem circuits and fear conditioning by the amygdala and its connections. The brain clearly has multiple memory systems, each devoted to different kinds of learning and memory functions.

In retrospect, the multiplicity of memory systems should have been apparent from the fact that it was so hard to find memory tasks that depend on the hippocampus in animals. Although a few such tasks were found, the vast majority of the memory tasks used to study animal memory are performed just fine in the absence of the hippocampus. If performance on some tasks depends on the hippocampus and performance on others does not, it must be the case that memory is not a unitary phenomenon and that different memory systems exist in the brain. But in the 1960s and 1970s, there wasn't a clear framework for understanding these variable effects. They led to confusion rather than clarity. The idea of multiple memory systems helped it all make sense.

So What Does the Hippocampus Represent?

We can get a pretty good idea about what makes the hippocampus so important for its brand of memory by examining the kinds of inputs that the hippocampus receives from the neocortex.[43] As we mentioned above, the major link between the hippocampus and the neocortex is the transition cortex (see Figure 7-4). This region receives inputs from the highest stages of neocortical processing in each of the major sensory modalities. So once a cortical sensory system has done all that it can do with a stimulus, say a sight or a sound, it ships the information to the transition region, where the different sensory modalities can be mixed together. This means that in the transition circuits we can begin to form representations of the world that are no longer just visual or auditory or olfactory, but that include all of these at once. We begin to leave the purely perceptual and enter the conceptual domain of the brain. The transition region then sends these conceptual representations to the hippocampus, where even more complex representations are created.

One of the first clues as to the way the hippocampus accomplishes its job came from a study performed in the early 1970s by

John O'Keefe at University College, London.[44] He found that cells in the hippocampus of a rat became very active when the rat moved into a certain part of a test chamber. The cells then became inactive when the rat moved elsewhere. He found lots of these cells, and each one became active in a different place. O'Keefe called these "place cells." The chamber was topless and rats could see out into the room. O'Keefe showed that the firing of the cells was controlled by the rat's sense of where it was in the room, for if the various cues around the room were removed, the firing patterns changed dramatically. Importantly, though, the place cells were not strictly responding to visual stimuli, since they maintained their "place fields" (the location where they became active) in complete darkness. O'Keefe and colleague Lynn Nadel published an influential book in 1978 called *The Hippocampus as a Cognitive Map* in which they proposed that the hippocampus forms sensory-independent spatial representations of the world.[45] One important function of these spatial representations, according to O'Keefe and Nadel, is to create a context in which to place memories. Context makes memories autobiographical, locating them in space and time, and this, they say, accounts for the role of the hippocampus in memory. They proposed an early multiple memory system account that distinguished a locale (spatial) memory system mediated by the hippocampus from several other systems mediated by other brain regions. O'Keefe and Nadel were mainly concerned with the locale system and made no attempt to identify the brain systems underlying the other forms of learning.

O'Keefe's observations, and the book with Nadel, created a whole industry devoted to understanding the role of the hippocampus in processing spatial cues. The demonstration of hippocampal-dependent memory in the radial maze[46] and the water maze[47] were direct outgrowths of the place cell findings and many experiments were conducted to figure out exactly how the hippocampus encodes space. In addition to O'Keefe's continued research,[48] particularly notable has been the work of Bruce McNaughton and Carol Barnes in Tucson,[49] the late David Olton in Baltimore,[50] Richard Morris in Edinburgh,[51] and Jim Ranck, John Kubie, and Bob Muller in Brooklyn.[52]

But not all investigators have accepted the idea that the hippocampus is a spatial machine. Howard Eichenbaum, for example, questions the role of the hippocampus in spatial processing per se, arguing that what the hippocampus is especially good at and important for is creating representations that involve the multiple cues at once, with space being a particular example of this rather than the primary instance of it.[53] Others, like Jerry Rudy and Rob Sutherland, have argued that the hippocampus creates representations that involve configurations (blends) of cues that transcend the individual stimuli making up the configuration.[54] This differs from Eichenbaum's hypothesis, which argues that the hippocampal representation involves the relation between individual cues rather than a representation in which the cues are fused into a newly synthesized configuration.

More work is needed to choose between spatial, configural, and relational hypotheses. The ultimate verdict will rest with the one that eventually explains how the sights, smells, and sounds of an experience, as well as the arrangement of all of the various stimuli and events in space and time, are represented in the hippocampus.

When Paul MacLean was putting forth his limbic system theory, he proposed that the hippocampus was an ideal place for emotion to reside. He suggested that because of its primitive, simple architecture, the hippocampus wouldn't be able to make fine distinctions between stimuli and would easily mix things up.[55] This, MacLean suggested, might account for the irrationality and confusion of our emotional life. But today, the pendulum has swung in the other direction. The hippocampus is thought to have an exquisite design that leads to sophisticated computational power[56] rather than a primitive organization that leads to confusion. The hippocampus has indeed come to be thought of as a key link in one of the most important cognitive systems of the brain, the temporal lobe memory system.

Tweedledee and Tweedledum: Emotional Memories and Memories of Emotions

Let's now explore the implications of the distinction between explicit and implicit memory for our understanding of how memories are formed in an emotional situation. Suppose you are driving down the road and have a terrible accident. The horn gets stuck on. You are in pain and are generally traumatized by the experience. Later, when you hear the sound of a horn, both the implicit and explicit memory systems are activated. The sound of the horn (or a neural representation of it), having become a conditioned fear stimulus, goes straight from the auditory system to the amygdala and implicitly elicits bodily responses that typically occur in situations of danger: muscle tension (a vestige of freezing), changes in blood pressure and heart rate, increased perspiration, and so on. The sound also travels through the cortex to the temporal lobe memory system, where explicit declarative memories are activated. You are reminded of the accident. You consciously remember where you were going and who you were with. You also remember how awful it was. But in the declarative memory system there is nothing different about the fact that you were with Bob and the fact that the accident was awful. Both are just facts, propositions that can be declared, about the experience. The particular fact that the accident was awful is not an emotional memory. It is a declarative memory about an emotional experience. It is mediated by the temporal lobe memory system and it has no emotional consequences itself. In order to have an aversive emotional memory, complete with the bodily experiences that come with an emotion, you have to activate an emotional memory system, for example, the implicit fear memory system involving the amygdala (see Figure 7-5).

There is a place, though, where explicit memories of emotional experiences and implicit emotional memories meet—in working memory and its creation of immediate conscious experience (working memory and consciousness will be discussed in Chapter 9). The sound of the horn, through the implicit emotional memory system, opens the floodgates of emotional arousal, turning on all the bodily responses associated with fear and defense. The fact that you are aroused becomes part of your current experience. This fact comes to rest side by side in consciousness with your explicit memory of the accident. Without the emotional arousal elicited through the implicit system, the conscious memory would be emotionally flat. But the co-representation in awareness of the conscious memory and the current emotional arousal give an emotional flavoring to the conscious memory. Actually, these two events (the past memory and the present arousal) are seamlessly fused as a unified conscious experience of the

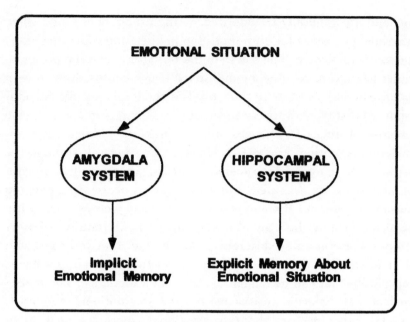

FIGURE 7-5

Brain Systems of Emotional Memory and Memory of Emotion.

It is now common to think of the brain as containing a variety of different memory systems. Conscious, declarative or explicit memory is mediated by the hippocampus and related cortical areas, whereas various unconscious or implicit forms of memory are mediated by different systems. One implicit memory system is an emotional (fear) memory system involving the amygdala and related areas. In traumatic situations, implicit and explicit systems function in parallel. Later, if you are exposed to stimuli that were present during the trauma, both systems will most likely be reactivated. Through the hippocampal system you will remember who you were with and what you were doing during the trauma, and will also remember, as a cold fact, that the situation was awful. Through the amygdala system the stimuli will cause your muscles to tense up, your blood pressure and heart rate to change, and hormones to be released, among other bodily and brain responses. Because these systems are activated by the same stimuli and are functioning at the same time, the two kinds of memories seem to be part of one unified memory function. Only by taking these systems apart, especially through studies of experimental animals but also through important studies of rare human cases, are we able to understand how memory systems are operating in parallel to give rise to independent memory functions.

moment. This unified experience of the past memory and the arousal can then potentially get converted into a new explicit long-term memory, one that will include the fact that you were emotionally aroused last time you remembered the accident. In this case the memory of the accident did not lead to the emotional arousal. The implicit arousal of emotion gave emotional coloration to the explicit memory (see Figure 7-6).

Nevertheless, we know from personal experience that conscious memories can make us tense and anxious, and we need to account for this as well. All that is needed for this to occur is a set of connections from the explicit memory system to the amygdala. There are in fact abundant connections from the hippocampus and the transition regions, as well as many other areas of the cortex, to the amygdala.

It is also possible that implicitly processed stimuli activate the amygdala without activating explicit memories or otherwise being represented in consciousness. As we saw in Chapters 2 and 3, unconscious processing of stimuli can occur either because the stimulus itself is unnoticed or because its implications are unnoticed. For example, suppose the accident described above happened long ago and your explicit memory system has since forgotten about many of the details, such as the fact that the horn had been stuck on. The sound of a horn now, many years later, is ignored by the explicit memory system. But if the emotional memory system has not forgotten, the sound of the horn, when it hits the amygdala, will trigger an emotional reaction. In a situation like this, you may find yourself in the throes of an emotional state that exists for reasons you do not quite understand. This condition of being emotionally aroused and not knowing why is all too common for most of us, and was, in fact, the key condition for which the Schachter-Singer theory of emotion tried to account. But in order for emotion to be aroused in this way, the implicit emotional memory system would have to be less forgetful than the explicit memory system. Two facts suggest that this may be the case. One is that the explicit memory system is notoriously forgetful and inaccurate (as we'll see below). The other is that conditioned fear responses exhibit little diminution with the passage of time. In fact, they often increase in their potency as time wears on, a phenomenon called "the incubation of fear."[57] It is possible to decrease the potency of a conditioned response by presenting the *learned trigger*, the CS,

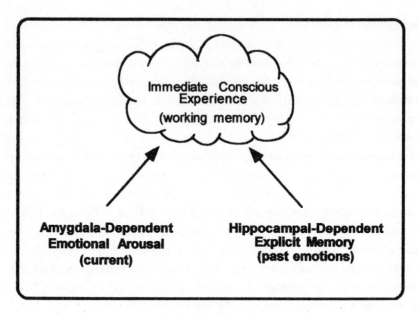

FIGURE 7-6
Intersection of Explicit Memory and Emotional Arousal
in Immediate Conscious Experience.

The outcome of activity in the explicit memory system of the hippocampus is a conscious awareness of stored knowledge or personal experiences. The outcome of activity in the amygdala is the expression of emotional (defensive) responses. But we also become conscious of the fact that we are emotionally aroused, allowing us to fuse, in consciousness, explicit memories of past situations with immediate emotional arousal. In this way, new explicit memories that are formed about past memories can be given emotional coloration as well.

over and over again without the US. However, so-called extinguished responses often recur on their own and even when they don't they can be brought back to life by stressful events.[58] Observations like these have led us to conclude that conditioned fear learning is particularly resilient, and in fact may represent an indelible form of learning. This conclusion has extremely important implications for understanding certain psychiatric conditions, as we'll see in the next chapter.

Infantile Amnesia

The idea of separate systems devoted to forming implicit emotional memories and explicit memories of emotions is relevant for understanding infantile amnesia, our inability to remember experiences from early childhood, roughly before age three. Infantile amnesia was first discussed by Freud, who noted that there had not been enough astonishment of the fact that by the time a child is two he can speak well and is at home with complicated mental situations, but if he is later told of some remark made during this time, he will have no memory of it.[59]

Lynn Nadel, together with Jake Jacobs, proposed that the key to infantile amnesia was the relatively prolonged period of maturation that the hippocampus goes through.[60] In order to be fully functional, a brain region has to grow its cells and get them connected with other cells in the various regions with which it communicates. It seems to take the hippocampus a bit longer than most other brain regions to get its act together. So Jacobs and Nadel proposed that we don't have explicit memories of early childhood because the system that forms them is not ready to do its job. Other brain systems, though, must be ready to do their learning and remembering sooner, since children learn lots of things during this amnesic time, even if they don't have conscious memories of the learning.

Jacobs and Nadel were particularly interested in the way that early trauma, though not remembered, might have lasting, detrimental influences on mental life. They proposed that the system that forms unconscious memories of traumatic events might mature before the hippocampus. They did not identify what this unconscious system for traumatic learning and memory was, but we now know, of course, that this system crucially involves the amygdala and its connections.

Although there is a dearth of biological research on the developmental maturation of the amygdala, behavioral studies suggest that the amygdala does indeed mature before the hippocampus. Jerry Rudy and his colleagues at the University of Colorado examined the age at which rats could learn hippocampal-dependent versus amygdala-dependent tasks.[61] They found that the amygdala task was acquired earlier in life than the hippocampal task. The amygdala appears to be functionally mature before the hippocampus.

The separate function and differential maturation of the amygdala has important implications for understanding psychopathological conditions. We'll explore these further in the next chapter.

Flashbulb Memories

Gary Larson, in *The Far Side,* has an illustration with a bunch of animals sitting around in a forest setting.[62] The caption reads something like this: all animals in the forest know where they were and who they were with when they heard the news that Bambi's mother had been shot. You probably recognize this as a takeoff on the phenomenon, characteristic of American baby-boomers and their parents, of being able to remember exactly what they were doing when they heard that President Kennedy had been shot. Psychologists describe this phenomenon as a "flashbulb memory," a memory that is made especially crisp and clear because of its emotional implications.[63] Recent findings, described below, by Jim McGaugh and his colleagues at the University of California at Irvine, together with the idea of separate systems for detecting the emotional implications of a situation and for representing emotional situations in explicit memory, help us understand the biological basis of flashbulb memories.

McGaugh's laboratory has long been concerned with the role of peripheral hormones, like adrenaline, in the solidification of memory processes.[64] His studies show that if rats are given a shot of adrenaline right after learning something, they show an enhanced memory of the learning situation. This suggests that if adrenaline is released naturally (from the adrenal gland) in some situation, that experience will be remembered especially well. Since emotional arousal usually results in the release of adrenaline, it might be expected (as suggested by the flashbulb idea) that the explicit conscious memory of emotional situations would be stronger than the explicit memory of nonemotional situations. It would also be expected that blockade of the effects of adrenaline would neutralize the memory-enhancing effects of emotional arousal.

McGaugh and Larry Cahill tested these hypotheses. They asked human subjects to read a story about a boy riding a bike. For some of the subjects, the boy takes a ride on his bike, goes home, and he and his mom drive to the hospital to pick up his dad, a doctor. For other subjects, the boy takes a ride on his bike, is hit by a car, and rushed to the hospital where his dad, a doctor, works. The words in the two stories are matched as closely as possible, with only the emotional implications manipulated. After reading the stories, and before being tested for recall, half the subjects in each group were given either a shot of placebo or a drug that blocks the effects of adrenaline. For the placebo-treated subjects, those that read the emotional story remembered many more details than those that read the mundane story. However, for the subjects receiving adrenaline blockade, there was no difference in the memory of the emotional and the nonemotional stories—both of these groups performed like the placebo group that read the nonemotional story. Adrenaline blockade, indeed, prevented the memory-enhancing effects of emotional arousal.

McGaugh has suggested some practical applications of this fascinating result. Rescue workers and soldiers in battle are often traumatized by the memories of the horrific scenes they witness. Perhaps it may be possible, immediately after the experience, to block the effects of adrenaline and spare them some anguish later.

But how does an emotional situation lead to the release of adrenaline in the first place? This, not surprisingly, takes us back to the amygdala. As we've repeatedly seen, when the amygdala detects an aversive emotional situation, it turns on all sorts of bodily systems, including the autonomic nervous system. The consequence of autonomic nervous system activation of the adrenal gland is the release of adrenaline into the bloodstream. The adrenaline then appears to influence the brain, although indirectly. This feedback (William James style) then interacts with systems that are also active at the time, such as the hippocampal system that is forming the explicit memory of the situation. Although the manner in which the feedback strengthens the explicit memory is not yet completely understood, it seems that the adrenaline somehow gets back to the brain and influences the functioning of the temporal lobe memory system, strengthening the memories being created there (see Figure 7-7).[65]

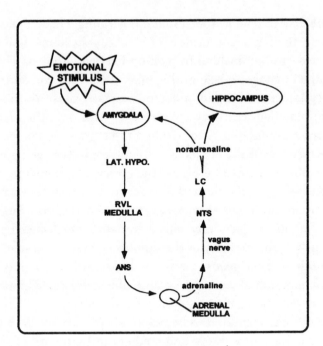

FIGURE 7-7
Modulation of Memory Circuits by Adrenaline.

Studies by McGaugh and colleagues have suggested that the hormone adrenaline, released during stress, stabilizes and strengthens memories. However, since adrenaline cannot normally enter the brain from the blood (adrenaline molecules are too big to cross the blood-brain barrier), the action must be indirect. The diagram shows how adrenaline might have its indirect actions on the brain. Stimuli associated with danger activate the amygdala. By way of pathways through the lateral hypothalamus (LAT. HYPO.) to the rostral ventral lateral (RVL) medulla, the autonomic nervous system (ANS) is aroused. One of the many target organs influenced by ANS arousal is the adrenal medulla. It releases adrenaline, which has widespread actions in the body. Of particular importance in memory modulation appears to be an effect on the vagus nerve, which terminates in the nucleus of the solitary tract (NTS) in the medulla. NTS then sends outputs to the locus coeruleus (LC), which releases noradrenaline in widespread areas of the forebrain, including the amygdala and hippocampus. By influencing amygdala and hippocampal functions, implicit emotional memories and explicit memories of emotion might be modulated.

Some Caveats

The idea that we remember best (or better) those things that are important to us—those things that elicit emotions in us—makes sense intuitively, and is also supported by quite a lot of research. However, there are some important qualifications to this notion that should be kept in mind.

Memory Is Selective: Not all aspects of an experience are remembered equally well, and the memory improvement produced by emotional arousal may affect some aspects more than others.[66] If you are robbed at gunpoint, you will probably later remember the robbery much better than other things that happened to you on the same day. Nevertheless, the vividness and accuracy of your memory of the details about the robbery may vary considerably. In general, the memory of things that are central to the episode (like the appearance of the gun) or that are particularly obvious (like the race and body style of the perpetrator) appear to be remembered better than more peripheral or more subtle details (hair and eye color, the presence or absence of facial hair, the model or color of the getaway car, etc.). Unfortunately, these extra details are often important in tracking down suspects and unequivocally identifying the perpetrator.

The exact details that are remembered probably depend on a variety of individualistic factors, not the least of which is what the victim was focused on at the time. If the victim paid more attention to the gun pointed at his face than to the face of the person pointing the gun, a reasonable thing to do under the circumstances, the appearance of the gun will be remembered better than the face of the perpetrator. An innocent bystander watching all of this may focus on different things, and may have very different explicit memories of the crime than the victim. Explicit memories are very closely related to what gets attended to during the experience.[67]

At the same time, implicit emotional memories may capture aspects of experiences that escape attention and awareness. As we saw in Chapter 3, autonomic responses have been useful in showing the presence of emotional memories that were not consciously encoded. It is conceivable that the physiological measurement of autonomic responses in a victim might be a more sensitive measure of the memory of a perpetrator than the victim's explicit memory. Polygraph tests, which involve measurements of autonomic nervous system function, though unreliable, are sometimes used as a means of getting a suspect's unconscious involuntary reactions to reveal guilt. A reverse polygraph test that probes the involuntary unconscious life of the victim could also be used, though the results of such tests would suffer from uncertainty as well.

Memories Are Imperfect Reconstructions of Experiences: Even though a memory of an emotional experience is strong and vivid, it is not necessarily accurate. Explicit memories, regardless of their emotional implications, are not carbon copies of the experiences that created them. They are reconstructions at the time of recall, and the state of the brain at the time of recall can influence the way in which the withdrawn memory is remembered. As Sir Frederic Bartlett demonstrated long ago, explicit memories involve simplifications, additions, elaborations, and rationalizations of learning experiences, as well as omissions of elements of the initial learning.[68] The memory, in short, occurs in the context of what Bartlett called a cognitive schema, which includes the expectations and biases of the person doing the remembering.[69]

The vulnerability of memory to modification by events that take place after the memory was formed has been documented in many studies and anecdotal reports. The writings of Elizabeth Loftus, a psychologist who specializes in memory malleability, and her colleagues provide lots of examples.[70] One involves Brigadier General Elliot Thorpe, who witnessed the bombing of Pearl Harbor. He described the event one way at the time of his retirement but had given a very different version in an earlier memoir, and both had many inconsistencies with facts established from other sources. Another example comes from the trial of Carl Gustav Christer Pettersson, accused of murdering the prime minister of Sweden, Olof Palme, while Mr. and Mrs. Palme were walking home from a movie.[71] The defense had a memory psychologist evaluate Mrs. Palme's testimony at different times after the murder. The psychologist was called as an expert witness and testified that Mrs. Palme's testimony had become more and more vivid and detailed as more time passed, suggesting that factors other than her experience of the crime influenced the way she remembered the incident. It was argued that she incorporated information from newspaper and television coverage into her memory. A third example comes from an experiment performed by a pioneer cognitive psychologist, Ulric Neisser, who examined people's memories of the explosion of the space shuttle *Challenger* at two times—the day after and several years later.[72] Most of the subjects said their memories of what they were doing when they heard the news were very good. Yet, in many instances, the memory at the later time was very different from the memory reported the day after. These various accounts do not question the vividness of memories established during emotionally arousing experiences, but they encourage a healthy suspicion of the accuracy of explicit memories, even explicit memories of emotional situations, when the details have important consequences.

Memory of Emotional Events May Also Be Poor: It is sometimes said that emotional events, especially traumatic ones, are accompanied by a selective amnesia for the experience, rather than an improved memory of it. Numerous anecdotal reports suggest that combat soldiers or victims of rape, incest, or other violent crimes can have very weak or nonexistent explicit memories of traumatic experiences. These observations are consistent with Freud's theory that unpleasant events are repressed, shunted out of consciousness.[73] The conditions that might lead to the loss of memory as opposed to the facilitation of memory are not understood, but may have something to do with the intensity and duration of the emotional trauma. We will return to this topic, and possible biological mechanisms through which amnesia for traumatic memory might occur, in the next chapter.

Moody Memories

Learning that takes place in one situation or state is generally remembered best when you are in the same situation or state.[74] If you learn a list of words while under the influence of marijuana, your memory of the list may be better when you are again "stoned" than when you are "straight." So-called state-dependent learning applies to lots of situations, not just drug states. Memory for words is better if subjects are tested in the room where the words were learned than if tested in a novel room. And memory for words is also better if the learning and the recall take place while the subject is in the same mood state. A corollary to this is the fact that we are more likely to have unpleasant memories when we are sad, and pleasant ones when happy. The so-called mood congruity of memory is amplified in depressed persons, who seem at times to only be capable of maudlin memories. The existence of separate systems for storing implicit emotional memories and explicit memories of emotions helps us understand how the content of memory is influenced by emotional states.

Many psychologists believe that memories are stored in associative networks, cognitive structures in which the various components of the memory are each separately represented and linked together.[75] In order for a memory to appear in consciousness, the associative network has to reach a certain level of activation, which occurs as a function of the number of components of the memory that are activated and the weight of each activated component. The weight of a component is the contribution that it makes to the overall memory in the network. Things that are essential aspects of a memory will have stronger weights than things that are less essential. The more cues that were present during learning that are also present during remembering, and the stronger the weights of the memory components that are activated by the cues present during remembering, the more likely it is that the memory will occur.

One of the components of an explicit memory of a past emotional experience will be the emotional implications of the experience. The presence of cues that activate this component will facilitate activation of the associative network. The relevant cues, in this case, will be cues from within the brain and body that signal that you are in the same emotional state as during the learning. These cues will occur because the stimuli that act on the explicit system also act on the implicit emotional memory system, causing the return of the emotional state you were in when the explicit memory system did its learning. The match between the current emotional state and the emotional state stored as part of the explicit memory facilitates the activation of the explicit memory. Co-activation of implicit emotional memory may

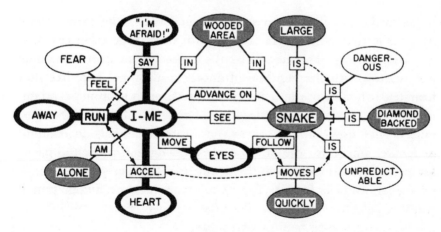

FIGURE 7-8
An Associative Memory Network for Fear.

In associative network models, memory is viewed as being stored as connections between nodes *of knowledge. The more extensively connected the nodes, the more easily retrieved and vivid the memory. The illustration shows a hypothetical associative network that might underlie a snake phobia. In this model, the phobia is maintained by propositional (verbal) information.* (From Figure 7.1 in P. Lang [1984], Cognition in emotion: concept and action. In C.E. Izard, J. Kagan, and R.B. Zajonc, eds., *Emotions, Cognition, and behavior.* New York: Cambridge University Press, © 1984 by Cambridge University Press. Reprinted with the permission of Cambridge University Press.)

thus help the explicit system during remembering as well as during learning.

Synaptic Muscle

So far we've looked at learning and memory from the neural system point of view. Now, it is time to peer deeper into the workings of the brain and take a look at how neurons and their synapses contribute to learning and memory functions.

It is widely believed that learning involves the strengthening of synaptic connections between neurons. From a purely structural point of view, synapses are minuscule spaces between neurons. More importantly, they are the tiny spaces formed by the adjoinment of two neurons at the points where those neurons exchange information.

Synapses, you'll recall, involve the contact of an axon terminal of one neuron with the dendrite of another. Electrical impulses flow from the cell body of the sending neuron through its axon to the terminal. The terminal then releases a chemical, called a neurotransmitter, that flows into the synaptic space and binds to receptor molecules (made for the purpose of receiving that particular transmitter substance) located on the dendrite of the receiving neuron. If enough transmitter binds to the receptors on the receiving neuron, it will "fire" electrical impulses down its axon, which will contribute to the firing of the next neuron, and so on.

In 1949, Donald Hebb, the great Canadian psychologist, proposed a way that learning might take place at the level of synapses.[76] Imagine two neurons, X and Y, that are anatomically interconnected but have a weak synaptic relation. That is, when X fires, Y could potentially fire but does not. However, if on some occasion Y is firing when the impulses from X reach Y, something happens between those two cells—a functional bond is created. As a result, the next time X fires, the likelihood that Y will also fire is increased. A connection between two cells that is strengthened in this way is now referred to a Hebbian synapse.[77] Perhaps nothing captures the essence of the Hebbian idea better than the oft-used slogan "cells that fire together wire together." Hebbian plasticity is shown in Figure 7-9.

For many years, Hebb's hypothesis was considered an interesting but ungrounded idea about how learning might take place. It was a hypothesis in need of a factual basis. In the early 1970s it got just the factual boost it needed to become everyone's favorite idea about how learning surely takes place. The boost came from a series of studies of hippocampal synaptic function carried out by Tim Bliss and Terje Lømo.[78]

It was known at the time that electrical stimulation of the pathway that connects the transition areas with the hippocampus elicits neural activity in the hippocampus. The activity can be measured as a neural response called a field potential, which reflects the overall synaptic response of the various hippocampal cells that are fired by the stimulus. Bliss and Lømo showed that the size of the field potential, and thus the magnitude of the synaptic response, could be in-

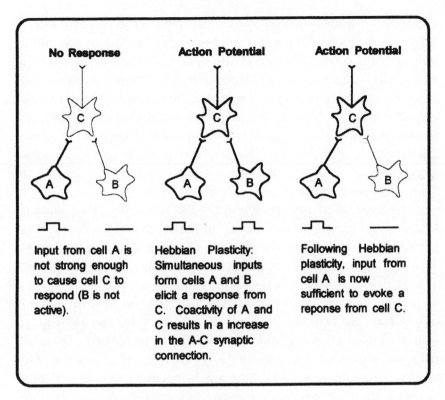

No Response

Action Potential

Action Potential

Input from cell A is not strong enough to cause cell C to respond (B is not active).

Hebbian Plasticity: Simultaneous inputs form cells A and B elicit a response from C. Coactivity of A and C results in a increase in the A-C synaptic connection.

Following Hebbian plasticity, input from cell A is now sufficient to evoke a reponse from cell C.

FIGURE 7-9
Hebbian Plasticity.

In 1949, Donald Hebb proposed that learning might involve changes in neural function brought about when two cells are active at the same time. To-day, so-called Hebbian plasticity is everyone's favorite idea about how learning and memory work at the level of individual cells in the brain. As the figure shows, Hebbian plasticity occurs between two cells (A and C) if they fire at the same time. In the illustration, A does not normally fire C but B does. So if B causes C to fire and A happens to fire at the same time, something occurs in the link between A and C such that A acquires the ability to fire C on its own. The exact nature of what occurs between A and C has been a mystery. However, recent work in neuroscience has identified a mechanism that makes Hebbian-like plasticity possible. This mechanism is called long-term potentiation (LTP) and involves glutamate and its receptors. LTP and glutamate receptor function are illustrated in figures 7-10 and 7-11, respectively.

creased by a simple manipulation. They zapped the pathway with a brief period of stimulation at a very high rate (one hundred stimulus pulses in a second). The size of the synaptic response elicited by a single pulse test stimulus was bigger after than before the intervening zap. The zap, in other words, increased the strength of the synaptic connection between the transition region and the hippocampus. And most importantly, the changes that were produced appeared to be enduring rather than fleeting. The production of changes in synaptic strength as a result of brief stimulations is usually referred to as "long-term potentiation" (LTP) (see Figure 7-10).

The fact that a brief episode in the life of a neuron can produce long-lasting changes in the behavior of that neuron immediately suggested that LTP might just be the stuff of which memories are made. This notion, considered somewhat fanciful at first, gained credence as later discoveries identified additional properties of LTP.

One of these is the specificity of LTP.[79] A given neuron receives inputs from many others. Neuron Z, for example, receives inputs from X, Y, and others. If induction of LTP by stimulating the X–Z pathway facilitated not only the X–Z synapses but also the Y–Z synapses, then there would not be much specificity to the phenomenon and its usefulness as a model of how memories are created through very specific learning experiences would be limited. But zapping the X–Z pathway changes the synaptic strength of this connection and leaves unaltered the strength of the Y–Z connection. LTP does not change the whole post-synaptic neuron, making it more sensitive to any input; it only changes the particular synapses on the post-synaptic neuron that were involved in the experience. Like learning, LTP is experience-specific.

Another important property of LTP is cooperativity.[80] In order for LTP to occur, a certain number of inputs to a cell have to be stimulated so that enough synapses are activated. If too few are stimulated, LTP does not result. Inputs, in other words, have to cooperate for LTP to occur.

A special version of cooperativity that is particularly important for drawing the connection between LTP and learning is associativity.[81] Again consider neuron Z that receives inputs from X and Y. If the X–Z and the Y–Z pathways are zapped at the same time, test stimuli applied to either pathway give a bigger synaptic response than if either

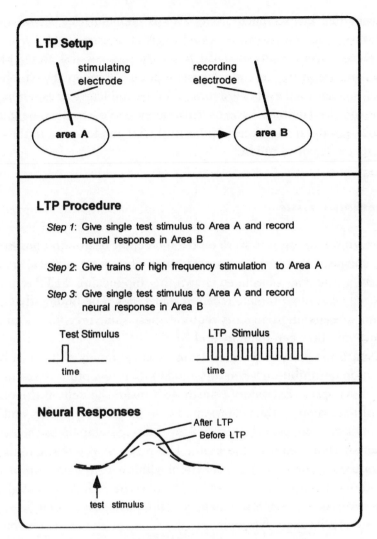

FIGURE 7-10
Long-Term Potentiation (LTP).

LTP involves a strengthening of the functional connection between two brain areas (areas A and B). Because connections between brain areas involve synapses, LTP is believed to involve an enhancement in transmission across synapses. LTP is induced in the laboratory by giving a burst of electrical stimuli to area A. As a result of this treatment, the neural response to a single test stimulus is amplified. Since the same stimulus gives a bigger response after the pathway has been treated with the burst, the burst enhances transmission in the pathway.

pathway had been zapped alone. This is cooperativity between two pathways. The two pathways are now linked or associated.

The associative property of LTP provides a key link to the Hebbian learning principle and suggests a potential means by which associations between events are formed in natural learning experiences. However, the Hebbian basis of learning gained even more weight as discoveries about the molecular basis of LTP and learning in the hippocampus began to roll in.

Mnemonic Glue

An enormous amount of work on the molecular basis of hippocampal LTP suggests that the neurotransmitter glutamate plays a crucial role. In particular, it has been shown that hippocampal LTP requires a special class of glutamate receptor molecules. The finding that hippocampal-dependent memory requires these same receptors is an important link between memory and LTP.

Neurotransmitters released from axon terminals either result in excitation or inhibition when they bind to their receptors on the other side of synapses. Excitatory transmitters make the cell on the other side of the synapse (the postsynaptic cell) more likely to fire, and inhibitory transmitters make it less likely to fire. Glutamate is the major excitatory transmitter in the brain. The primary way that glutamate transmission works is that packets of glutamate released from the axon terminal cross the synapse and bind to the AMPA class of glutamate receptors.[82] When this happens, the postsynaptic cell fires impulses down its axon. Normally, another class of glutamate receptors, NMDA receptors, are cooped up and glutamate reaching them has no effect.[83] But when the postsynaptic cell fires, the NMDA receptors become available to bind glutamate (see Figure 7-11).

The fact that NMDA receptors are only open to the public when the cell that possesses them has just fired allows the NMDA receptor to serve as a means for forming associations between stimuli. The NMDA receptor, in fact, seems to be the way the Hebbian rule (neurons that fire together wire together) is actually realized in the brain.

Imagine that impulses from one input pathway cause the release of glutamate, which binds to the postsynaptic neuron and causes the

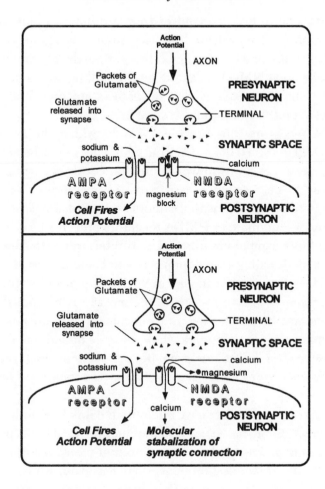

FIGURE 7-11
Glutamate Receptors.

When an action potential comes down the axon to the terminal area, it causes packets of glutamate to be released from the terminal of the presynaptic neuron. The released glutamate diffuses into the synaptic space and binds to AMPA and NMDA receptors on the dendrites of postsynaptic neurons. When glutamate binds to AMPA receptors, sodium and potassium flow into the postsynaptic neuron and help generate an action potential (above). Although NMDA receptors are normally blocked by magnesium, the magnesium block is removed by the action of glutamate at AMPA receptors. Calcium then flows into the cell below, resulting in a host of molecular changes that then strengthen and stabilize the connection between the pre- and postsynaptic neuron. (Illustration based on figure 1 in F.A. Edwards (1992), Potentially right on both sides. Current Opinion in Neurobiology *2: 299–401.)*

postsynaptic cell to fire. If impulses from a different input pathway cause glutamate to be released at synapses on the same cell, and these impulses arrive when the cell is firing, then the glutamate binds to the briefly open NMDA receptors on this cell (as well as to AMPA receptors). The net result is that an association or connection is formed between the two inputs.

NMDA receptors thus provide a way in which the associative property of LTP, the Hebbian learning principle, might be achieved, and, more generally, a way in which simultaneously occurring events might come to be associated as part of the memory of an experience.[84] It is thus significant that administration of drugs that block the binding of glutamate to NMDA receptors prevents LTP from occurring in hippocampal circuits and also interferes with hippocampal-dependent learning (for example, spatial learning in the water maze).[85] The exact manner in which NMDA receptors contribute to LTP and memory is currently one of the most heavily studied topics in neuroscience. Involved is the influx of calcium into the postsynaptic cell, which sets into motion a whole cascade of additional molecular steps that stabilize the synaptic connections and thus the enhanced synaptic response (see discussion of molecular blindness below).

A number of researchers have attempted to link LTP and memory more directly.[86] Some have shown that induction of LTP in a pathway affects learning processes that depend on that pathway. Others have found that natural learning influences the ease with which LTP occurs. And still others have found that during learning, changes similar to those occurring in LTP take place in pathways that mediate the learning.

While the correspondence between LTP and natural learning is becoming more and more compelling, the case for LTP being the basis of learning remains unproven. No study has actually shown that the changes induced by LTP actually account for learning. Many laboratories are working fast and furiously to convert the correlations between LTP and learning into a causal linkage. Many workers in the field believe that the causal connection is there and that it is just a matter of time until the appropriate way to demonstrate the relation is discovered.

The Molecular Blindness of Memory

Initially, LTP was believed to be mainly a hippocampal phenomenon. This certainly added fuel to the fiery attempts to develop animal models for studying the contribution of the hippocampus to memory. Now, it is known that LTP occurs in many brain regions and in many learning systems. Of special relevance to our concern here is the fact that LTP has been demonstrated in pathways that are involved in fear conditioning,[87] and that blockade of NMDA receptors in the amygdala prevents fear conditioning.[88]

NMDA-dependent synaptic plasticity may be a fairly universal way that the brain learns and stores information at the molecular level. While there are other forms of plasticity that do not depend on NMDA receptors (even in the hippocampus),[89] it nevertheless seems that NMDA-dependent plasticity is one of the major learning devices, and that the brain may in fact have a limited number of learning mechanisms that it uses in a variety of different situations.

If we look more closely at how memories are stabilized, the idea that fairly universal mechanisms are used to form different kinds of memories becomes even more compelling. Studies of species as different as snails, mice, and fruit flies have converged in their conclusions about the kinds of molecular events that convert learning experiences into long-term memories. Protein synthesis, which is controlled by genetic machinery located in the cell nucleus, seems to play a crucial role. If protein synthesis is blocked, long-term memories are not formed.[90] The long-term memory of an experience, in other words, may be maintained by proteins made in cells after learning has taken place. Proteins appear to be important because they make up genes, which control the manufacture of certain chemicals that are required for memory stabilization. Disruption of protein synthesis appears to interfere with the formation of most kinds of long-term memories in most kinds of animals. It also interferes with the long-term maintenance of LTP.[91]

One chemical that appears to be particularly important is cyclic AMP (cAMP). This substance takes over where neurotransmitters leave off. Neurotransmitters allow cells X and Y to communicate with Z; cAMP then helps Z remember that the firing of X and Y at Z occurred at the same time—that X and Y were associated. cAMP is involved in communication between different parts within a cell rather than between cells. The contribution of cAMP to memory was first shown in studies of snails by Eric Kandel, one of the leading researchers of the neurobiology of memory.[92] Kandel also showed that drugs that block the expression of cAMP disrupt hippocampal memory and LTP.[93] New genetic tools have been used to create animals that are incapable of making cAMP. Tim Tully has shown that fruit flies lacking this gene have amnesia for certain long-term memory tasks,[94] and Kandel and Alcino Silva[95] have each shown that genetically engineered mice that are unable to make cAMP have deficient hippocampal LTP and are unable to form new long-term memories in tasks that are dependent on the hippocampus. The mechanisms of memory stabilization appear to be remarkably similar across diverse species and diverse learning procedures. Although there may be more than one such mechanism, the number of them may be relatively small.

The idea that nature might use one or a few molecular mechanisms in many different learning networks in many different kinds of animals has a very important implication. Different forms of learning are not necessarily distinguishable at the level of molecular events, but instead obtain their unique properties by way of the circuits of which they are part. There may well be a universality, or a least a generality, of memory at the molecular level, but there is a multiplicity of memory at the systems level.

Claparede Redux

It should now be clear how it was possible for Claparede's patient to have formed an implicit memory of the pinprick without having an explicit conscious memory of the experience that led to the formation of the implicit memory. Most likely, her temporal lobe memory system was damaged. And, given that the implicit memory she formed involved fear conditioning, it also seems likely that her amygdala was alive and well. Admittedly, these are retrospective guesses since we have no idea where the lesion was in her brain. However, these guesses are based on forty years of research into the neural basis of memory, and even if for some unknown reason they are wrong in her

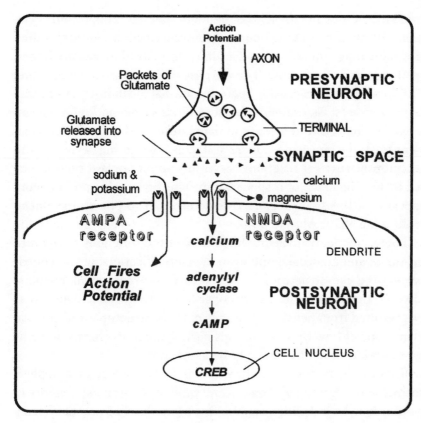

FIGURE 7-12
Molecular Stabilization of Synaptic Plasticity and Memory.

When glutamate binds to the NMDA receptors of a cell that has just fired an action potential, the magnesium block of the NMDA receptor is removed and calcium flows in. Calcium influx, in turn, activates adenylyl cyclase, which leads to an increase in cyclic AMP (cAMP); cAMP elevation then activates cAMP-inducible genes in the cell nucleus by way of the gene transcription factor, CREB. CREB induces proteins, such as synaptic effector proteins, that may contribute to the long-term maintenance of LTP, possibly by stabilizing changes in the structure of the postsynaptic dendrites. (Based on figure 7-12 above and figure 1 in M. Mayford, T. Abel, and E.R. Kandel [1995], Transgenic approaches to cognition. *Current Opinion in Neurobiology* 5:141–48.)

case (something we'll never know), they will surely turn out to often be correct predictions for future cases in which we can verify the locus of brain damage.

The multiplicity of memory at the systems level is what makes a

given kind of memory the kind of memory that it is. Hippocampal circuits, with their massive neocortical interconnections, are well suited
for establishing complex memories in which lots of events are bound
together in space and time. The purpose of these circuits, according
to Eichenbaum, is to provide representational flexibility.[96] No particular response is associated with these kinds of memories—they can
be used in many different ways in many different kinds of situations.
In contrast, the amygdala is more suited as a triggering device for the
execution of survival reactions. Stimulus situations are rigidly coupled to specific kinds of responses through the learning and memory
functions of this brain region. It is wired so as to preempt the need
for thinking about what to do.

These are clearly oversimplifications of the functions of the hippocampus and amygdala, and even oversimplifications of the contribution of these structures to declarative and emotional memory.
However, the simplifications are consistent with the conclusions that
have resulted from behavioral studies of these structures and capture
at least part of how these structures participate in the forms of memory with which each has come to be associated.

If looked at microscopically, which is to say molecularly, implicit
(unconscious) emotional memory and explicit (conscious) memory of
emotion may be indistinguishable. But at the level of neural systems
and their functions, these are clearly unique operations of the brain.
Although we know much more at this point about the separate operation of these two systems, we are beginning to also see how they interact. And these interactions are at the core of what gives emotional
qualities to memories of emotions past.

8

WHERE THE WILD
THINGS ARE

"A phobia, like a psychoanalytic theory, is a story about where the wild things are."

Adam Phillips, *On Kissing, Tickling, and Being Bored: Psychoanalytic Essays on the Unexamined Life*[1]

IN 1793, REVOLUTION WAS in the air in Paris. But the French Revolution about which we are concerned here took place, not in the streets, but in mental asylums. Philippe Pinel had the radical opinion that the mentally ill were not hopeless wild animals that should be incarcerated and tortured, but were people who should be treated with decency and respect. When the Revolution's prison commissioner heard of Pinel's plans to rehabilitate the insane, he asked, "Are you not yourself mad to free these beasts?" Pinel responded, "I am convinced that the *people* are not incurable if they can have air and liberty." Some of the "beasts" recovered under Pinel's guidance. One became his bodyguard.[2]

By 1800 Pinel had become one of the most influential physicians in Paris and he was called upon by the Revolution's Society of Observers of Man to evaluate a truly wild beast, a boy around eleven years old, who, a few months earlier, had been captured in a small village in southern France. As recounted by Roger Shattuck, author of a fascinating book about the Wild Boy of Aveyron, the incident went like this:

Before dawn on January 9, 1800, a remarkable creature came out of the woods near the village of Saint-Sernin in southern France. No one expected him. No one recognized him. He was human in bodily form and walked erect. Everything else about him suggested an animal. He was naked except for the tatters of a shirt and showed no modesty, no awareness of himself as a human person related in any way to the people who had captured him. He could not speak and made only weird, meaningless cries.[3]

In spite of his prior successes, Pinel felt that rehabilitation was not possible in the case of the Wild Boy. According to Shattuck, Pinel seems not to have seriously pondered whether the boy's condition was due to "organic" or "functional" causes, a distinction that Pinel commonly made in other cases. Such an analysis might have led to a more informed decision about whether the boy was curable. If the problem was organic, say due to brain damage, then his wild state might indeed be untreatable. But if life's circumstances—the lack of nurturing care during his early childhood, the absence of social stimulation, his stressful, traumatic existence in a hostile environment—were the causes, some cure might have been possible. As Shattuck notes, we will never know the answer.

So-called functional disorders are indeed more likely to be treatable than those related to organic causes. However, the distinction between organic and functional maladies needs to be made cautiously, and should in no way imply that some mental disorders are attacks on the brain and others on the mind. As Shakespeare said, the brain is the soul's dwelling place.[4] Mental disorders, like mental order, reflect the workings of the brain.

Actually, Shakespeare's phrase was the soul's *frail* dwelling place, which speaks to the thinness of the line between mental health and illness. We all experience sadness and worry from time to time. But when these become excessive and inappropriate to the circumstances, we slide from normal to pathological emotions.

In this chapter we are going to be especially concerned with the pathological emotions called anxiety disorders. These are among the most common forms of mental illness.[5] I will argue they involve the fear system of the brain, and that the progress we've made in understanding how the fear system normally works also helps us understand what goes wrong in anxiety disorders. I'll propose that anxiety disorders come about when the fear system breaks loose from the cortical controls that usually keep our primitive impulses—the wild things in us—at bay.

A Brief History of Mental Illness

The diagnosis of mental disorders has its roots in the work of Emil Kraepelin in the late nineteenth century. He distinguished schizophrenia from manic-depression by showing that these illnesses take different courses. Freud, Kraepelin's contemporary, was more concerned with neuroses than with psychotic conditions like schizophrenia and emphasized intrapsychic conflict and the resulting anxiety as the cause. According to psychiatrist Peter Kramer, by mid-century American psychiatrists had outdone Freud.[6] They had adopted the spectrum model of mental illness, which assumed that all forms of psychopathology are secondary to anxiety.[7] Neurosis was, in the typical Freudian view, the result of a partially successful defense against anxiety that was accompanied by symptom formation. But under the spectrum model even psychosis came to be viewed as the result of anxiety, such excess anxiety that the ego crumbled and regressed. Mental health and mental illness were distinguished by the degree of anxiety present, and the same treatment, the reduction of inner conflict via psychotherapy, was applicable to all ailments.

The tides have since shifted. Mental health professionals now have a dazzling array of diagnostic categories available to them. All one has to do to see how radically things have changed is to thumb through the diagnostic bible, the American Psychiatric Association's *Diagnostic and Statistical Manual of Mental Disorders* (DSM), first published in 1980, now in its fourth edition.[8] There are a host of phobias, different kinds of panic attacks, a variety of mood and thought disorders, somatization disorders, antisocial personality conditions, numerous forms of substance abuse, and other conditions. In addition, there are overlaps, such as panic with agoraphobia (fear of open or crowded places), or manic-depression with cocaine dependence, and so on.

In spite of this diagnostic diversity, it is clear that some categories of mental illness occur more than others. The U.S. Public Health

Service counts and classifies the prevalence of different forms of mental disorders.[9] In 1994, about 51 million Americans eighteen years and older had some form of diagnosed mental illness, with about 11 million of those involving substance abuse. Of the remaining 40 million, more than half were accounted for by the category of anxiety disorders, and somewhat less than half by mood disorders (especially depression), with schizophrenia and assorted other conditions accounting for the rest.

The high proportion of mental disorders that involve anxiety does not vindicate the spectrum theory, for treating depression or schizophrenia as anxiety is probably not going to get you as far as treating them uniquely. However, it does emphasize the importance of understanding the nature of anxiety and its various manifestations. Fortunately, the understanding of the fear system that has been achieved can help us explain how anxiety disorders arise, and may also help us figure out how to treat them and possibly prevent their occurrence.

Fear and Loathing in Anxiety

Anxiety and fear are closely related. Both are reactions to harmful or potentially harmful situations. Anxiety is usually distinguished from fear by the lack of an external stimulus that elicits the reaction—anxiety comes from within us, fear from the outside world. The sight of a snake elicits fear, but the remembrance of some unpleasant experience with a snake or the anticipation that you may encounter a snake are conditions of anxiety. Anxiety has also been described as unresolved fear.[10] Fear, according to this view, is related to the behavioral acts of escape and avoidance in threatening situations, and when these actions are thwarted, fear becomes anxiety.

Fear and anxiety are normal reactions to dangers (real or imagined) and are not themselves pathological conditions. When fear and anxiety are more recurrent and persistent than what is reasonable under the circumstances, and when they impede normal life, then a fear/anxiety disorder exists.[11]

Conditions that reflect anxiety and its defenses (conversion, repression, displacement)[12] were called neuroses by Freud. Today, the field of psychiatry is less devoutly Freudian than it once was and the term "neurosis" is deemphasized in DSM to avoid the implication that symptoms of anxiety necessarily reflect Freudian defense mechanisms.[13] Consequently, while DSM "anxiety disorders" include conditions that Freud called anxiety neuroses, more contemporary diagnoses appear as well.[14] The full complement of DSM anxiety disorders are: panic, phobias, post-traumatic stress disorder, obsessive-compulsive disorder, and generalized anxiety.

The characteristic features of these disorders are intense feelings of anxiety and avoidance of situations that are likely to bring on these feelings.[15] *Phobias* are fears of specific stimuli or situations that are in excess of the actual threat posed. Exposure to the phobic object or situation reliably elicits a profound state of anxiety. The person will go to great lengths to avoid the object or situation. *Panic* attacks involve discrete periods of intense anxiety and discomfort. The afflicted person often feels like he or she is suffocating. Unlike phobias, the attacks are often unpredictable and frequently not related to any particular external stimulus or situation. Sometimes panic is accompanied by agoraphobia. In severe cases, avoidance of such situations can lead to a sheltered existence. *Post-traumatic stress disorder* (PTSD) involves severe anxiety elicited by stimuli that were present during some extreme trauma or that are somehow related to stimuli that occurred during the trauma. It is common in war veterans but also occurs in victims of severe physical or sexual abuse or natural disasters. Situations or even thoughts that are likely to remind the person of the trauma are avoided. *Obsessive-compulsive disorder* involves intrusive, repetitive, and persistent thoughts and/or repetitive behaviors that are performed in a very precise way in response to obsessive thoughts. The compulsive behaviors are meant to neutralize anxiety, but the behaviors are either not well connected to the situation or are excessive responses to the situation that they are intended to neutralize. *Generalized anxiety,* also known as free-floating anxiety, involves excessive worry about unrelated things for a long period of time.

DSM outlines symptoms and situational factors that allow skilled clinicians to distinguish the various anxiety disorders. However, Arne Öhman, a leader in the study of human fear and anxiety, has recently argued that, "when comparing the physiological responses seen in phobics exposed to their feared objects with those seen in PTSD patients exposed to relevant traumatic scenes for the disorder, and with physiological responses during panic attacks, one is much more struck by the similarities than by the differences."[16] He goes on to argue that panic, phobic fear, and PTSD reflect the "activation of one and the same underlying anxiety response." This is essentially the case that I will make. However, I state the idea in terms of brain systems rather than symptoms: anxiety disorders reflect the operation of the fear system of the brain. Öhman leaves generalized anxiety out of his grouping because it involves a stable personality trait rather than discrete episodes of anxiety, a distinction that is often referred to as one between trait and state anxiety. However, generalized anxiety most likely involves the same underlying brain system (at least partly) as the other anxiety disorders.

Little Albert Meets Little Hans

Anxiety disorders can arise at any time, but most often appear in early adult life. Why does this happen? How does the brain go from a state in which it is not especially anxious to one in which it is pathologically worried or exhibiting neurotic behaviors that keep the worry in check?

Most theorists from Freud onward have assumed that clinically debilitating anxiety is the result of traumatic learning experiences that create unpleasant memories. Breuer and Freud,[17] in the famous case of Anna O., for example, argued that "hysterics suffer mainly from reminiscences," or as Matthew Erdelyi puts it, "traumatic memories which they have expunged from consciousness."[18] Since fear conditioning is the *sine qua non* of traumatic learning, it should come as no surprise that fear conditioning has been proposed to be involved in the genesis of pathogenic anxiety. Though long considered controversial and incomplete, as we will see, new findings have made it seem more likely, and even quite plausible, that fear conditioning contributes significantly to anxiety disorders.[19]

The conditioning theory of anxiety arose in the 1920s, a time when psychologists were beginning to explain most aspects of behavior in terms of learning experiences, and particularly in terms of Pavlov's conditioned reflexes.[20] John Watson, the father of behaviorism, claimed to have conditioned an animal phobia in an eleven-month-old boy, Little Albert, by making a loud clanging sound while the boy was happily playing with a rat.[21] Thereafter, the boy avoided playing with the rat and cried when he was near it. To explain this finding, Watson proposed that certain stimuli (loud noises, painful stimuli, sudden loss of physical support) are innately capable of eliciting fear reactions. When these unconditioned stimuli occur, other stimuli that happen to be present acquire the capacity to elicit conditioned fear. According to Watson, neuroses arise as a result of these traumatic learning situations and then persist and influence behavior throughout life.[22]

Watson's theory of anxiety, as well as his behaviorist view of psychology, was based on Pavlovian conditioned reflex learning. But by the 1930s, another form of learning, called instrumental conditioning, had come to be of equal importance to behaviorists.[23] In instrumental conditioning, an arbitrary response (like pressing a bar or making a turn in a maze) is learned if it is reinforced, which means it is either followed by the presentation of a reward or the omission of a punishment. The response is learned because it is reinforced, and thereafter is performed in order to get the reward or avoid the punishment. While Pavlovian conditioning involves the transfer of meaning from an emotionally arousing to a neutral stimulus, in instrumental conditioning the association is between an emotionally arousing stimulus and neutral response.

Behaviorism and psychoanalysis were radically different approaches, but both sought to understand why we act the way we do. O. Hobart Mowrer, a leading behaviorist, saw value in both approaches and set out in the 1940s to translate Freud's theory of anxiety neurosis into the language of learning theory.[24] Using the principles of Pavlovian and instrumental conditioning, Mowrer hoped to solve what he called the "neurotic paradox": "a normal sensible man, or even a beast to the limits of his intelligence, will weigh and balance the consequences of his acts. . . . If the net effect is unfavorable, the action producing it will be inhibited, abandoned. In neurosis, however, one sees actions which have predominantly unfavorable consequences, yet they persist over a period of months, years, or a lifetime."[25]

Anxiety, according to Mowrer, motivates us to deal with traumatic events in advance of their occurrence. And because anxiety reduction brings about relief or security, it is a powerful reinforcer of instrumental behaviors (arbitrary responses that are learned because they satisfy some need or accomplish some goal). Responses that reduce anxiety are thus learned and maintained.

Mowrer felt that anxiety is initially learned much like Watson had suggested—stimuli that are present during painful or traumatic stimulation acquire the capacity to elicit anxiety. Because anxiety is uncomfortable, when the stimuli that elicit it are present the anxious person will be motivated to change the circumstances, to remove himself from where the anxiety-causing stimuli are, and to avoid such situations in the future. The reduction in anxiety that these responses produce then reinforces the behaviors and perpetuate their performance. This is often useful, but sometimes it leads to neurotic symptoms.

Consider a real-life example. A man is mugged in an elevator. From that day on, he becomes afraid of riding in elevators. He avoids them as much as possible. He consults a therapist, who tries to reassure him that it is highly unlikely that he will be mugged again in an elevator, especially if he rides at busy times. But the reassurance is not helpful. The man must get to his office on the thirteenth floor. This makes him anxious. In spite of the inconvenience that it causes him, each day he takes the stairs. The reduction in anxiety that results from taking the stairs, according to Mowrer's theory, maintains the neurotic behavior of taking the stairs.

Mowrer, like existentialist philosophers, saw anxiety as an important part of human existence, as fundamental to what is special about humans, but also as a clue to our frailty:

> By and large, behavior that reduces anxiety also operates to lessen the danger that it presages. An antelope that scents a panther is likely not only to feel less uneasy (anxious) if it moves out of the range of the odor of the panther but also likely to be in fact somewhat safer. A primitive village that is threatened by marauding men or beasts sleeps better after it has surrounded itself with a deep moat or a sturdy stockade. And a modern mother is made emotionally more comfortable after her child has been properly vaccinated against a dreaded disease. This capacity to be made uncomfortable

by the mere prospect of traumatic experiences, in advance of their actual occurrence (or reoccurrence), and to be motivated thereby to take realistic precautions against them, is unquestionably a tremendously important and useful psychological mechanism, and the fact that the forward-looking, anxiety-arousing propensity of the human mind is more highly developed than it is in lower animals probably accounts for many of man's unique accomplishments. But it also accounts for some of his most conspicuous failures.[26]

Mowrer paved the way for a behavioral interpretation of Freud, but this pursuit was most successfully implemented by another behavioral psychologist, Neal Miller.[27] Miller had been attempting to work out in detail how fear might serve as a drive, like hunger or sex, an internal signal that motivates one to act in a way that reduces the drive. Just as a hungry animal looks for food, a fearful one tries to get away from the stimuli that arouse fear. He trained rats to avoid being shocked by jumping over a hurdle that separated two compartments whenever a buzzer sounded.[28] The first phase involved fear conditioning: the buzzer came on and the rats were shocked. Then, through random actions, they learned that if they jumped over the hurdle during the buzzer, they could avoid getting shocked. Once the rat figured this out, it would jump every time it heard the buzzer, even if the shock was turned off. The shock was no longer present and was thus no longer the motivator. The avoidance response seemed, as Mowrer had suggested, to be maintained by the anticipation of shock, by the fear elicited by the warning signal. But to prove that fear was the motivator, Miller changed the rules on the rat. Previously, when the rat jumped over the hurdle, the buzzer went off, and turning the buzzer off seemed to be sufficient reinforcement to keep the rat jumping. But now the buzzer stayed on when the rat jumped and would only go off if the rat pressed a lever. And once this was learned Miller changed the game again, forcing the rat to learn still another response to turn the buzzer off. While the initial response was learned because it allowed the rat to avoid the shock, the subsequent ones were never associated with the shock. They were reinforced by the fact that they turned off the sound. According to Miller, the findings showed that fear is a drive, an internal energizer of behavior, and that behaviors that reduce fear are reinforced and thereby become habitual ways of acting (note, however, that "fear" is an internal bodily signal, like hunger, and does not necessarily refer to subjective, consciously experienced fear in this theory).

Miller felt that this new view of fear as a drive was the key to a truly scientific approach to psychoanalytic principles. Together with John Dollard, a trained analyst, Miller attempted to account for unconscious neurotic conflict and its expression as symptoms in terms of the principles of animal learning.[29] Just as a rat could learn any response that allowed it to escape from or avoid an anxiety-provoking situation, humans learn all sorts of instrumental responses that allow them to escape or avoid anxiety and guilt caused by neurotic conflict.[30] As Dollard and Miller put it:

> the symptoms of the neurotic are the most obvious aspects of his problem. These are what the patient is familiar with and feels he should be rid of. The phobias, inhibitions, avoidances, compulsions, rationalizations, and psychosomatic symptoms of the neurotic are experienced as a nuisance by him and by all who have to deal with him. . . . When a successful symptom occurs it is reinforced because it reduces neurotic misery. The symptom is thus learned as a habit.[31]

Conditioned fear theories of anxiety took a different turn in the early 1960s. In contrast to the tradition of Mowrer and Miller, who saw Freud as scientifically imprecise but on the right track, the new theorists had little patience with the psychoanalytic view of anxiety and its emphasis on unresolved and unconscious conflict. Joseph Wolpe was one of these. He reinterpreted Freud's famous phobic case, Little Hans,[32] in terms of simple Pavlovian conditioning.[33] Hans, a five-year-old boy, became afraid of horses one day while witnessing a frightening event in which a horse fell down. Freud's view was that the horse phobia was an unresolved Oedipal conflict—Hans' fear of being castrated by his father for desiring his mother was displaced to horses. The trauma of witnessing the horse falling was the occasion that allowed the phobia to cover for the underlying conflict. But Wolpe saw it differently. Like all good conditioning theorists, he argued that a neutral stimulus, like a horse, that occurs in the presence of a trauma will acquire the capacity to elicit fear reactions, and that phobias are nothing more than fear (anxiety) that has been conditioned to some otherwise meaningless event. In making his case,

Wolpe severely criticized Freud's selective use of information that confirmed his theory and his selective disregard for information that went against it. For example, Hans himself supposedly said that he "got the nonsense" when he saw the horse fall down, and his father, in support of this view, said the anxiety broke out immediately after the incident. Freud dismissed these surface explanations, but Wolpe took them at face value. For Wolpe, Little Hans was just like Little Albert. The conditioning theory had come full circle.

The distinction between Watson's and Wolpe's purely Pavlovian approach and Mowrer's and Miller's psychoanalytic translations is more than just one of the language used to describe how anxiety arises. It also impacts importantly on the issue of how anxiety should be treated. Freudians, and their behavioral protégés, saw the goal of therapy as the resolution of unconscious conflict. The other school, typified by Wolpe, had no use for unconscious explanations and saw neurotic symptoms as nothing more and nothing less than conditioned responses. In the words of Stanley Rachman and Hans Eysenck, two other leaders in this movement, "Get rid of the symptom . . . and you have eliminated the neurosis."[34]

In spite of many important differences, there is a common theme that runs through psychoanalytic and the various conditioning theories—anxiety is the result of traumatic learning experiences. Since traumatic learning involves (at least in part) fear conditioning, it is possible that similar brain mechanisms contribute to pathogenic anxiety in humans and conditioned fear in animals. If so, findings from easily performed animal experiments could be used to understand how anxiety is learned, unlearned, and controlled in humans. However, before we can accept this rather strong, and some would say controversial, conclusion, we need to consider some additional ideas about the relation of fear conditioning to anxiety disorders, and some additional facts about the organization and function of the fear system of the brain.

Ready to Fear

In the early 1970s, Martin Seligman, an experimental psychologist who had been studying conditioned fear in animals, pointed out some striking differences between human anxiety and laboratory conditioned fear.[35] Especially important to Seligman was the fact that avoidance conditioning extinguishes quickly if the animal is prevented from making the avoidance response and alternative solutions for escape or avoidance are not provided. Recall that Miller's rats kept jumping over the hurdle when the buzzer sounded even when the shock was turned off. They never had the chance to find out that the shock was off because they kept jumping. But Seligman's point is that if the hurdle is replaced with a wall, thus preventing the avoidance response, the rat soon learns that the buzzer is no longer followed by a shock and begins to ignore the buzzer. If the wall is now removed and the hurdle returned, jumping no longer occurs in response to the buzzer. Forcing the rat to see that the buzzer doesn't lead to danger extinguishes the fear and this leads to the extinction of the neurotic avoidance response. In contrast, telling an acrophobic that no one has ever accidentally fallen off the Empire State Building and that he will be just fine if he goes to the top, or forcing him to go up there to prove the point, does not help, and can even make the fear of heights worse rather than better. Human phobias seem more resistant to extinction, and more irrational, than conditioned fears in animals.

The key to this difference, in Seligman's view, is the fact that while laboratory experiments use arbitrary, meaningless stimuli (flashing lights or buzzers), phobias tend to involve specific classes of highly meaningful objects or situations (insects, snakes, heights). He argued that perhaps we are prepared by evolution to learn about certain things more easily than others, and that these biologically driven instances of learning are especially potent and long lasting. Phobias, in this light, reflect our evolutionary preparation to learn about danger and to retain the learned information especially strongly.

In a relatively stable environment, it is generally a good bet that the dangers a species faces will change slowly. As a result, having a ready-made means of rapidly learning about things that were dangerous to one's ancestors, and theirs, is in general useful. But since our environment is very different from the one in which early humans lived, our genetic preparation to learn about ancestral dangers can get us into trouble, as when it causes us to develop fears of things that are not particularly dangerous in our world.

With the notion of preparedness, Seligman injected a dose of biological realism into the plain vanilla conditioning theory that Watson and later behaviorists popularized. Ironically, the phenomenon of preparedness may have played a seminal role in Watson's conditioning of Little Albert. Several later studies failed to reproduce Watson's findings[36] and these results have often been used as ammunition against fear conditioning theories of anxiety. But Seligman notes that in choosing a furry animal as the conditioned stimulus, Watson may have unwittingly used a prepared stimulus, and the failure of the later studies may well be because they used inanimate, meaningless stimuli.

Preparedness theory quickly received strong support from studies by Susan Mineka.[37] It had long been thought that monkeys have an inherited fear of snakes, so that the first time a monkey saw a snake it would act afraid and protect itself. However, Mineka showed that laboratory-reared monkeys are in fact not afraid on the first exposure to a snake. Most of the earlier work had involved testing of the young monkeys in the presence of their mothers. If the young monkey is shown the snake when separated from its mother, it doesn't act afraid. It appears that the infant learns to be afraid of the snakes by seeing its mother acting afraid. The young monkeys did not learn about nonfrightening things in this way, suggesting that there is something special about biologically relevant stimuli that makes them susceptible to rapid and potent observational learning. Humans learn many things by observing others in social situations and it has been proposed that anxiety, especially pathological anxiety, is sometimes or even often learned by social observation.[38]

In recent years, preparedness theory has been championed by Öhman.[39] Öhman believes that evolution has equipped contemporary humans with a propensity to associate fear with situations that threatened the survival of our ancestors. To the extent that this propensity evolved, it must be based in our genes, and genetic variation must therefore exist. As a result, although humans are in general prepared to acquire fears of ancestral dangers easily, some individuals must be more prepared than others to acquire specific fears. These super-prepared humans are, he proposes, vulnerable to phobias.

Öhman has subjected preparedness theory to stringent tests. He started with the assumption that snakes and insects are common objects of phobias and are likely to be prime examples of prepared stimuli, whereas flowers are not common phobic objects. He then used these fear-relevant (prepared) and fear-irrelevant stimuli in conditioning studies in humans. In support of preparedness theory, he found that conditioned fear (measured by autonomic nervous system responses) was more resistant to extinction with fear-relevant than with fear-irrelevant stimuli. Further, when modern fear-relevant stimuli (guns and knives) were used, no evidence for resistance to extinction was found, suggesting that evolution has not yet had enough time to build these dangers in. He also showed that phobics respond to a greater degree when they see stimuli relevant to their own phobia than when they see other fear-relevant stimuli—snake phobics gave bigger conditioned responses to snake pictures than to spider pictures and spider phobics did the reverse. This is consistent with his contention that phobics are super-prepared genetically to respond to the objects of their phobia. Finally, using special procedures to prevent conditioned stimuli from being consciously perceived, he was able to produce the prepared conditioning in the absence of awareness of the conditioned stimuli. This shows that phobias can be learned and expressed independently of consciousness, which may be related to their seemingly irrational nature.

Preparedness theory goes a long way toward dealing with some of the shortcomings of the traditional fear conditioning theories of anxiety, particularly the fact that in anxiety disorders fear doesn't extinguish easily and is especially irrational. Nevertheless, important aspects of phobias and other anxiety disorders remained unexplained. People become anxious about objects and situations that are not evolutionarily prepared—like fear of cars or elevators. Anxiety disorders can and often do exist in the absence of a memory of a traumatic experience, suggesting that maybe traumatic conditioning is not so important. And sometimes a clear trauma precedes the onset of an anxiety disorder, but the trauma is unrelated to the disorder (for example, the death of one's mother preceding the development of a fear of heights)—this doesn't make sense if the anxiety was conditioned by the trauma. However, our understanding of the brain mechanisms of conditioned fear, together with new observations about the effects of stress on the brain, give us additional clues that help fill these gaps.

New Twists on Anxiety: Clues from the Brain

In further pursuing the nature of anxiety disorders, we'll draw upon the notion, developed in the previous chapter, of multiple memory systems. In particular, we'll examine some of the implications of the idea that during a traumatic learning situation, conscious memories are laid down by a system involving the hippocampus and related cortical areas, and unconscious memories established by fear conditioning mechanisms operating through an amygdala-based system. These two systems operate in parallel and store different kinds of information relevant to the experience. And when stimuli that were present during the initial trauma are later encountered, each system can potentially retrieve its memories. In the case of the amygdala system, retrieval results in expression of bodily responses that prepare for danger, and in the case of the hippocampal system, conscious remembrances occur.

It is very helpful to keep the workings of the declarative system separate from other memory systems when considering how anxiety disorders might arise and be maintained. This point was made by Jake Jacobs and Lynn Nadel in a 1985 article that greatly influenced my thinking about the effects of stress on the fear system.[40]

Stress-Induced Loss and Recovery of Traumatic Memories: The fact that some clinically anxious persons do not recall any particular traumatic event that might be the cause of their anxiety has been an especially sharp thorn in the side of conditioning theories. In contrast, the main competition, Freud's psychoanalytic theory, assumes that anxiety will only result when traumatic memories are dispatched to the unconscious corners of the mind. Not wanting to call upon anything so mysterious and scientifically unfounded as repression, conditioning theorists have struggled with instances where there is no memory of an instigating trauma. Either no trauma, and thus no conditioning, occurred, or the trauma occurred but is not remembered. Both possibilities leave conditioning theorists with something to explain.

A possible solution to this puzzle has emerged from recent work showing that stressful events can cause malfunctions in the hippocampus. This suggests that at least in some instances the failure to recall an instigating trauma may be due to a stress-induced breakdown in hippocampal memory function.[41] In order to understand how and why this occurs, we need to explore the biological effects of stress.

When people or other animals are exposed to a stressful situation, the adrenal gland secretes a steroid hormone into the bloodstream.[42] Adrenal steroids play an important role in helping the body mobilize its energy resources to deal with the stressful situation. As we saw in Chapter 6, the amygdala is critically involved in the control of the release of adrenal steroids. When the amygdala detects danger, it sends messages to the hypothalamus, which in turn sends messages to the pituitary gland, and the result is the release of a hormone called ACTH. ACTH flows through the blood to the adrenal gland to cause the release of steroid hormone. In addition to reaching target sites in the body, the steroid hormone flows through the blood into the brain, where it binds to receptors in the hippocampus, amygdala, prefrontal cortex, and other regions. Because the adrenal and pituitary secretions are reliably elicited by stressful events, they are called stress hormones.

It has been recognized for some time that the hippocampal steroid receptors are part of a control system that helps regulate how much adrenal steroid hormone is released.[43] When the hormone binds to receptors in the hippocampus, messages are sent to the hypothalamus to tell it to tell the pituitary and adrenal glands to slow down the release. In the face of stress, the amygdala keeps saying "release" and the hippocampus keeps saying "slow down." Through multiple cycles through these loops the concentration of the stress hormones in the blood is delicately matched to the demands of the stressful situation.

If stress persists too long, the hippocampus begins to falter in its ability to control the release of the stress hormones, and to perform its routine functions. Stressed rats are unable to learn and remember how to perform behavioral tasks that depend on the hippocampus.[44] For example, they fail to learn the location of the safe platform in the water maze task described in the last chapter. Stress also interferes with the ability to induce long-term potentiation in the hippocampus,[45] which probably explains why the memory failure occurs. Im-

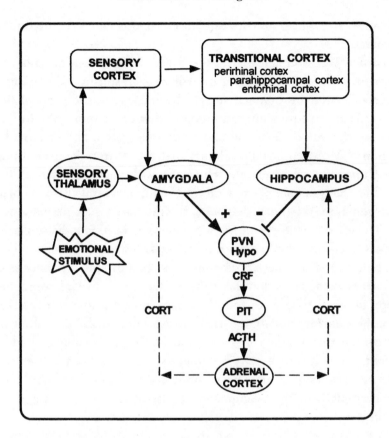

FIGURE 8-1
Stress Pathways.

Stimuli associated with danger activate the amygdala. By way of pathways from the amygdala to the paraventricular nucleus of the hypothalamus (PVN Hypo), corticotrophin-releasing factor (CRF) is sent to the pituitary gland, which, in turn, releases adrenocorticotropic hormone (ACTH) into the blood-stream. ACTH then acts on the adrenal cortex, causing it to release steroid hormones (CORT) into the bloodstream. CORT freely travels from the blood into the brain, where it binds to specialized receptors on neurons in regions of the hippocampus and amygdala, as well as other regions. Through the hippocampus, CORT inhibits the further release of CRF from the PVN. However, as long as the emotional stimulus is present, the amygdala will attempt to cause PVN to release CRF. The balance between the excitatory inputs (+) from the amygdala and the inhibitory inputs (-) from the hippocampus to PVN determines how much CRF, ACTH, and ultimately CORT will be released.

portantly, stress also impairs explicit conscious memory functions in humans.[46]

Bruce McEwen, a leader in the study of the biology of stress, has shown that severe but temporary stress can result in a shriveling up of dendrites in the hippocampus.[47] Dendrites are the parts of neurons that receive incoming inputs and that are responsible, in large part, for the initial phases of long-term potentiation and memory formation.[48] McEwen has also shown that if the stress is discontinued these changes are reversible. However, with prolonged stress, irreversible changes take place. Cells in the hippocampus actually begin to degenerate. When this happens, the memory loss is permanent.

The effects of stress on the hippocampus were first discovered by Robert Sapolsky, who had been studying the effects of social stress on the behavior of monkeys.[49] The monkeys had lived in a colony as social subordinates to a dominant male. Over several years, some died. Upon autopsy, they were found to have stomach ulcers, consistent with their having lived under stress. Most dramatically, though, it was discovered that marked degeneration of the hippocampus had occurred. There was little sign of damage to any other part of the brain. This basic finding has now been confirmed in a number of situations. For example, the hippocampus is degenerated in mice living under social stress.[50]

Recent studies have shown that the human hippocampus too is vulnerable to stress.[51] In survivors of trauma, like victims of repeated childhood abuse or Vietnam veterans with post-traumatic stress disorder, the hippocampus is shrunken. These same persons exhibit significant deficits in memory ability, without any loss in IQ or other cognitive functions. Stressful life events can alter the human hippocampus and its memory functions.

It seems clear that adrenal steroids account for these physical changes in the hippocampus and in the memory problems that result.[52] For example, there is a condition called Cushing's disease in which tumors develop in the adrenal gland and excess steroid hormone is secreted. These persons have long been known to have memory problems. Recent studies have also shown that the hippocampus is shrunken in this disease. Also, if rats or humans are injected with high levels of steroids, mimicking the effects of severe stress, hippocampal cell death and memory problems result. And if rats are

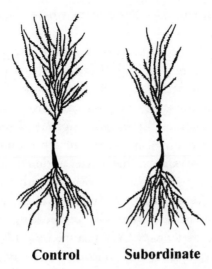

Control   Subordinate

FIGURE 8-2
Dendrites Shriveled by Social Stress.

Neurons are shown from unstressed (control) and stressed (subordinate) tree shrews, a mammalian species related to early primate evolution. The stress in this experiment involved exposing subordinate males to a dominant male. Repeated social stress of this type reduced the branching and length of dendrites. Compare the top half of the cell from the unstressed control and from the stressed subordinate. (Reprinted from A.M. Magarinos, B.S. McEwen, G. Flugge, and E. Fuchs [1996], Chronic psychosocial stress causes apical dendritic atophy of hippocampal CA3 pyramidal neurons in subordinate tree shrews. *Journal of Neuroscience* 16 (3534–40.)

given drugs that block the effects of steroids, they are made immune to the effects of stress on the hippocampus and on memory.

There's one more relationship between stress and memory that's worth pointing out. One of the consequences of excess life stress is depression, and depressed persons sometimes have poor memory. It is quite possible that the memory disturbances that occur in depression are closely tied up with the effects of stress on the hippocampus.

Sometimes stress helps in the formation of explicit memories, making them stronger (recall the flashbulb hypothesis), but it can also devastate explicit memory. We now have a plausible explanation for this paradox. Memory is likely to be enhanced by mild stress, due to the facilitatory effects of adrenaline (Chapter 7), but may be interfered with if the stress is sufficiently intense and prolonged to raise the level of adrenal steroids to the point where the hippocampus is adversely affected.

Most of the evidence for adverse effects of stress on memory has come from rather severe conditions in which the stress continued for days. A key issue is whether a single, unrepeated traumatic experience, such as being mugged or raped, can raise steroid levels sufficiently to adversely affect the hippocampus and produce a loss of memory for the incident. Although there are no definitive answers yet, recent studies have shown that a brief period of stress can disrupt spatial memory in rats and interfere with the induction of long-term potentiation in the hippocampus.[53] And both of these effects are prevented if the adrenal gland is removed, implicating adrenal steroids.

Now comes the tricky part. Let's assume that it is indeed possible for a temporary period of trauma to lead to an amnesia for the experience. Can one then later recover a memory of these events? Although we can identify in a general sense the kinds of conditions under which recovery is possible or impossible, we can't say whether it occurred in a particular instance. For example, if the hippocampus was completely shut down by the stress to the point where it had no capacity to form a memory during the event,[54] then it will be impossible through any means to dredge up a conscious memory of the event. If no such memory was formed, then no such memory can be retrieved or recovered. On the other hand, if the hippocampus was only partially affected by the trauma, it may have participated in the formation of a weak and fragmented memory. In such a situation, it may be possible to mentally reconstruct aspects of the experience. Such memories will by necessity involve "filling in the blanks," and the accuracy of the memory will be a function of how much filling in was done and how critical the filled-in parts were to the essence of the memory.

Explicit, conscious memories, as I emphasized in the last chapter, are reconstructions that blend information stored in long-term memory with one's current frame of mind. Even memories that are formed with a perfectly well-functioning hippocampus are easily distorted by experiences that occur between the formation of the memory and its retrieval. This has been demonstrated in numerous experiments by Elizabeth Loftus and her colleagues.[55] Particularly important are their studies showing how easy it is to induce a false memory by controlling events that happen after the memory is established, or to create from scratch a memory of an experience that never happened. The subjects in these studies fully believe their memories, but because they have occurred in controlled laboratory experiments it is possible to show that the memory is fabricated. At the same time, there are also carefully controlled laboratory studies showing that information that was initially processed consciously and stored, but later forgotten, can be brought back, a phenomenon called hypermesia that we looked at in Chapter 3.[56]

The only thing that is clear about memory recovery in real life is that there is no way for outsiders to definitely determine whether a particular memory is real or fabricated in the absence of solid corroborating evidence (fabrication does not imply that the person is lying, only that the memory is false). There are surely victims of horrible incidents who have lost their memory of the event, and there may be some who can later piece together a memory of what happened. However, distinguishing between fabricated and real memories simply on the basis of self-knowledge can be tricky. Salvador Dali once said, "The difference between false memories and true ones is the same as for jewels: it is always the false ones that look the most real, the most brilliant."[57] Whether he was right might be debated, but as we saw earlier (Chapters 2 and 3), introspective knowledge of thought processes provides a highly inaccurate window into the mind, even in mundane (nontraumatic) situations. Things are likely to be even worse when confusion abounds, as it must during and following trauma. The waters of memory recovery are treacherous and should be walked through very carefully.

As far as is known, stress does not interfere with the workings of the amygdala, and, as we'll see below, stress may even enhance amygdala functions. It is thus completely possible that one might have poor conscious memory of a traumatic experience, but at the same time form very powerful implicit, unconscious emotional memories through amygdala-mediated fear conditioning. And because of other effects of stress to be described below, these potent unconscious fears can become very resistant to extinction. They can, in other words, become unconscious sources of intense anxiety that potentially exert their opaque and perverse influences throughout life. However, there is no way for these powerful implicit memories to then be converted into explicit memories. Again, if a conscious memory wasn't formed, it can't be recovered.

That Freud was correct in his belief that aspects of traumatic experiences are sometimes stored in memory systems that are not directly accessible from consciousness seems clear. Less certain is whether repression (in the Freudian sense) is involved. The failure to remember traumatic events may sometimes be due to a stress-induced shutdown of the hippocampus, although this remains to be proven. In light of this, though, there is nothing particularly devastating to the conditioning theory of anxiety about the fact that the traumatic origin of the anxiety is not always remembered. Of course, repression of unpleasant experience may well be a real phenomenon, one that we still don't understand scientifically. And some anxiety disorders may develop without an initial trauma. Nevertheless, we at least have a possible mechanism that might account for some aspects of these disorders in easily understood biological terms.

Amplification of Emotional Memory by Irrelevant Stressors: There is a flip side to the debilitating effects of intense stress on explicit conscious memory of trauma. The same amount of stress that can lead to an amnesia for a trauma may amplify implicit or unconscious memories that are formed during the traumatic event.

For example, recent studies have shown that if rats are given injections of adrenal steroids at levels that mimic very severe stress, there is a dramatic decrease in the amount of a certain chemical, called corticotropin-releasing factor (CRF), in the part of the hypothalamus that controls the release of the stress hormone, ACTH, from the pituitary gland.[58] CRF is in fact the neurotransmitter that stimulates ACTH release. The decrease in CRF in this pathway reflects the negative feedback control over stress hormones by the hippocampus—once the blood level of adrenal steroids reaches a certain level, the hippocampus tells the hypothalamus to slow down the secretions. And when the steroid level reaches a critical point, the hippocampal circuits begin to falter. In stark contrast, there is a dramatic increase in CRF in the central nucleus of the amygdala under the same conditions—as blood levels of steroids increase, the amygdala may keep getting more and more active. The bottom line is that the effects of stress on the amygdala seem very different from the effects on the hippocampal-hypothalamic circuit.

On the basis of these observations, Keith Corodimas, Jay Schulkin, and I predicted that during intense stress the learning and memory processes mediated by the amygdala might be facilitated and we examined the effects of stress hormone overload on conditioned fear behavior.[59] In line with the prediction, we found that the strength of learned fear was increased in the steroid-treated rats relative to other rats that didn't have the steroids. Although this result is somewhat preliminary, studies using other forms of Pavlovian conditioning have also found that stress enhances conditioned responses.[60]

If indeed the hippocampus is impaired and the amygdala facilitated by stress, it would suggest the possibility that stress shifts us into a mode of operation in which we react to danger rather than think about it. It's not clear whether this is a specific adaptation or whether we're just lucky that when the higher functions break down our fallback position is one in which we can let evolution do the thinking for us.

The finding that stress hormones can amplify conditioned fear responses has an important implication for our understanding of anxiety disorders, and in particular for understanding why these sometimes seem to occur or get worse after unrelated stressful events.[61] During stress, weak conditioned fear responses may become stronger. The responses could be weak either because they were weakly conditioned, or because they were previously extinguished or were otherwise treated into remission. Either way, their strength might be increased by stress. For example, a snake phobic might be in remission for years but upon the death of his spouse the phobia returns. Alternatively, a mild fear of heights, one that causes few problems in everyday life, might be converted into a pathological fear under the amplifying influences of stress. The stress is unrelated to the disorder that develops and is instead a condition that lowers the threshold for an anxiety disorder, making the individual vulnerable to anxiety, but not dictating the nature of the disorder that will emerge. The latter is probably determined by the kinds of fears and other vulnerabilities that the person has lurking inside.

**Brain Malfunctions Can Make Unprepared Learning Resistant
to Extinction:** Neurotic fears are notoriously difficult to shake. This
is the bane of a therapist's professional existence, but also his or her
bread and butter. While preparedness provides one way out of this
dilemma, there is another. Fear responses conditioned to arbitrary
tones or lights in rats can be made highly resistant to extinction if
certain cortical areas that project to the amygdala are damaged. This
suggests that these areas of the cortex may be malfunctioning in
some cases of pathogenic anxiety, allowing ordinary stimuli to be conditioned by the amygdala in a way that resists extinction.

Several years ago we were examining the effects of damage to visual areas of the cortex on the ability of rats to be conditioned to visual stimuli.[62] The lesioned rats learned just fine, supporting our
contention that there are subcortical pathways that take sensory information to the amygdala during conditioning. But when we tried to
extinguish the fear responses in these animals, something unusual
happened. We couldn't do it. Normal rats, after several days of seeing
the light without the shock, stopped acting afraid in the presence of
the light. But the rats with lesions of the visual cortex were like Energizer batteries—they just kept going and going and going.

We never thought that the visual cortex was the seat of extinction.
Instead, we proposed that the visual cortex might be a necessary link
between the visual world and other higher order cortical areas that
are necessary for extinction. One area that seemed like a possible reg-
ulator of extinction was the medial prefrontal cortex. This area receives signals from the sensory regions of the cortex and from the
amygdala, and sends connections back to the amygdala, as well as to
many of the areas to which the amygdala projects.[63] The medial prefrontal cortex is thus nicely situated to be able to regulate the outputs
of the amygdala on the basis of events in the outside world as well as
on the basis of the amygdala's interpretation of those events. When
Maria Morgan made lesions of this region, rats continued to act fearful in the presence of a conditioned fear stimulus long after rats without lesions of this area had stopped acting afraid.[64]

The amygdala of the cortically lesioned rat, like the neurotic human, stubbornly expresses its fear memories in the face of information showing that the stimulus is no longer associated with danger.
Extinction appears to involve the cortical regulation over the amyg-

dala, and even unprepared conditioned fear can be resistant to extinction when the amygdala is freed from these cortical controls.

One of the hallmarks of frontal lobe damage in humans is perseveration, the inability to stop doing something once it is no longer appropriate.[65] For example, when frontal lobe patients are performing a task in which a rule must be followed, they have great difficulty in changing their behavior when the rule is switched. In a standard version of this test, the patient is given a stack of cards, each with one or more colored symbols on it. The patient's job is to figure out, on the basis of feedback about whether each response is correct, which kind of cue (color, shape, or number) is the current solution. Once they get going on a principle (like shape) they can do the task fine. But if all of a sudden the principle shifts (say, to color), they keep following the old rule. Sometimes they even know what they should do, but can't make their behavior match their knowledge. They are rigid and inflexible, and perseverate in their ways, even when it is obvious that the behavior is not appropriate to the situation. This seems to characterize their behavior in real life as well.

Although perseveration is usually thought of as a cognitive or thought disorder, it seems that our findings about fear extinction in rats with prefrontal lesions might reflect the same kind of difficulty, but in the domain of emotion. In fact, we used the expression "emotional perseveration" to describe the failure of our rats to extinguish conditioned fear responses.[66] While cognitive perseveration is produced by damage to the lateral areas of the prefrontal cortex, emotional perseveration resulted from damage to a small part of the medial prefrontal region.[67] The lateral and medial prefrontal areas may perform the same operation, adapting behavior to changing conditions, with the involvement in cognitive or emotional functions determined by the areas with which the prefrontal region works in conjunction. The medial cortex, in other words, engages in response switching behavior because it is part of the prefrontal cortex, and it engages in response switching guided by emotional information because it is connected with the amygdala. Edmund Rolls has proposed a similar role for the medial prefrontal cortex in emotion on the basis of studies in which he has recorded from neurons in this region while monkeys performed tasks where the reinforcer (reward or punishment) associated with certain responses changed frequently.[68] Other ideas about the contribution of prefrontal cortex to emotion have been proposed as well, and the work of Antonio Damasio is particularly notable.[69] Some of these ideas will be considered in the next chapter on emotional consciousness.

The prefrontal cortex, like the hippocampus, may be altered by stress. Recent research has shown that the prefrontal cortex, like the hippocampus, offers a counterforce that keeps too much of the stress hormones from being released.[70] Since prolonged stress results in a breakdown in this negative feedback control function, it may be the case that both the prefrontal cortex and hippocampus are adversely affected. A stress-induced shutdown of the prefrontal cortex might release the brakes on the amygdala, making new learning stronger and more resistant to extinction, and possibly allowing previously extinguished conditioned fears to be expressed anew.

Just because clinical fear is difficult to extinguish does not mean that it involves a different brain system from the one that mediates extinguishable conditioned fears in animals. Differences in the ease of extinction of conditioned fear in laboratory experiments and in anxious persons are more likely to reflect differences in the way the fear system works in normal and anxious brains rather than differences in the system used by the brain to learn conditioned fear and clinical anxiety. This doesn't mean that anxious persons, like our rats, are walking around with holes in their prefrontal cortex. There are many subtle ways in which disruptions in electrical and chemical functions can adversely affect a brain region, with lesions being just an extreme example of this.

Gone but Not Forgotten—The Indelibility of Emotional Memory: Our finding that when the medial prefrontal cortex is damaged routine fear conditioning becomes resistant to extinction has another important implication. It also suggests that extinction prevents the expression of conditioned fear responses but does not erase the implicit memories that underlie these responses.[71] Extinction, in other words, involves the cortical control over the amygdala's output rather than a wiping clean of the amygdala's memory slate.

The idea that extinction does not involve the erasure of emotional memories but instead prevents their expression is consistent with a number of findings about conditioned responses.[72] Pavlov, for example, found that extinguished responses would, with simply the passage of time, *spontaneously recover*. It is also known that if a rat is conditioned by pairing a tone and shock in one box, and the fear response elicited by the tone is completely extinguished in another box, the conditioned response elicited by the tone will be *renewed* if the rat is returned to the original training box. An extinguished response can also be *reinstated* by giving the rat an exposure to the US or, importantly, to other forms of stressful stimulation. Stress, in other words, can bring back extinguished, or perhaps weakly established but unextinguished, conditioned responses.[73] Each of these examples, like our lesion study, demonstrates that emotional memories are not erased by extinction but are simply held in check. Extinguished memories, like Lazarus, can be called back to life.

I recently had a scientific "ah ha" experience, one of those rare, wonderful moments when a new set of findings from the lab suddenly makes you see something puzzling in a new, crystal clear way. The studies involved recordings of electrical activity of the amygdala before and after fear conditioning by Greg Quirk, Chris Repa, and me.[74] We found dramatic increases in electrical responses elicited by the tone CS after conditioning, and these increases were reversed by extinction. However, because we were recording from multiple individual neurons at the same time, we were also able to look at the activity relationships between the cells. Conditioning increased the functional interactions between neurons so that the likelihood that two cells would fire at the same time dramatically increased. These interactions were seen both in the response to the stimulus and in the spontaneous firing of the cells when nothing in particular was going on. What was most interesting was that in some of the cells, these functional interactions were not reversed by extinction. Conditioning appears to have created what Donald Hebb called "cell assemblies,"[75] and some of these seemed to be resistant to extinction. Although the tone was no longer causing the cells to fire (they had extinguished), the functional interactions between the cells, as seen in their spontaneous firings, remained. It is as if these functional couplings are holding the memory even at a time when the external triggers of the memory (for example, phobic stimuli) are no longer effective in activating the memory and its associated behaviors (for example, phobic responses). Although highly speculative at this point, the observations suggest clues as to how memories can live in the brain at a time when they are not accessible by external stimuli (Figure 8-3). All that it would take to reactivate those memories would be a change in the strength of the input to the cell assembly. This may be something that stress can accomplish.

Unconscious fear memories established through the amygdala appear to be indelibly burned into the brain. They are probably with us for life. This is often very useful, especially in a stable, unchanging world, since we don't want to have to learn about the same kinds of dangers over and over again. But the downside is that sometimes the things that are imprinted in the amygdala's circuits are maladaptive. In these instances, we pay dearly for the incredible efficiencies of the fear system.

Psychiatrist Roger Pitman has astutely noted that findings from studies of fear conditioning in rats have important implications for how anxiety is treated.[76] The classic treatment, based on Mowrer's and Miller's theory, was to force the patient to be exposed to the anxiety-causing stimuli without allowing any avoidance or escape behavior and thereby try to extinguish the anxiety that the stimuli elicit. But in light of the indelibility of the amygdala's hold on traumatic memories, he suggests a bleaker, though perhaps more realistic, assessment. We may not be able to get rid of the implicit memories that underlie anxiety disorders. If this is the case, the best we can hope for is to exercise control over them.

The Fear System and Specific Anxiety Disorders

Until fairly recently, the various anxiety disorders were not distinguished and were not treated differently.[77] Panic and PTSD, for example, did not appear in the DSM until 1980. And although phobias have long been associated with neuroses, they were typically thought of as neurotic symptoms rather than a particular kind of anxiety disorder. With the emergence of clear diagnostic distinctions between different anxiety disorders, disorder-specific fear conditioning theories have been proposed. Below, I'll attempt to buttress disorder-specific theories of phobias, PTSD, and panic with findings about the brain mechanisms of fear conditioning.[78]

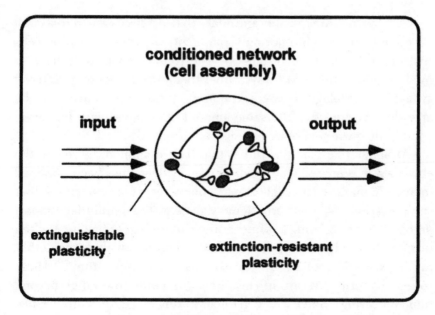

FIGURE 8-3
Creation of Extinction-Resistant Learning in the Brain.

Recent studies have recorded neural activity in the amygdala during conditioning and extinction. After conditioning, the response of individual cells to the conditioned stimulus is increased (the same input produces a bigger output). In addition, individual cells develop stronger interconnections so that when one fires the others also fire. These interconnected neurons are called a cell assembly. While the response of individual cells to the conditioned stimulus diminishes during extinction, in some cases the conditioned interconnections persist. These cell assemblies within the amygdala, or between the amygdala and cortical areas, may constitute an important aspect of the long-term, extinction-resistant, implicit memory created by fear conditioning.

Phobic Fears: Contemporary ideas about phobias continue to be centered around the notion of preparedness. Normally, the strength of conditioning is determined mainly (though not exclusively) by how traumatic the unconditioned stimulus is. But in prepared fear conditioning, the CS also contributes some of the emotional impact. As a result, given two conditioned stimuli, one biologically prepared to be conditioned to danger and the other not, the same unconditioned stimulus should support the establishment of a stronger conditioned response for the prepared stimulus. How might that work in the brain?

Perhaps neurons in the amygdala that process prepared stimuli have some prewired but normally impotent connections to other cells that control emotional responses. The trauma might only have to mildly massage these pathways rather than create from scratch novel synaptic assemblages between the input and output neurons of the amygdala. In this way, the same amount of trauma might buy more conditioning when prepared stimuli are involved.

Although there are no studies that have examined the role of the amygdala in prepared fear conditioning, evidence has been obtained indicating that the amygdala is particularly responsive to stimuli that serve as species-specific emotional signals, with stimuli that support prepared learning being a prime example of these. For instance, when rats are exposed to a cat, they give off calls, sounds that warn other rats to stay clear of where the sounds are coming from.[79] These sounds, it turns out, are in the ultrasonic range (the range beyond human hearing). Since cats can't hear in this range, the calls are like secret encrypted messages that pass undetected through enemy lines. In recent experiments, Fabio Bordi and I found some neurons in the rat amygdala that responded especially briskly to ultrasounds similar to the warning calls.[80] The rat amygdala may be evolutionarily prepared to respond to these sounds and to learn about them. In fact, the amygdala of all creatures may be prepared to respond to species-relevant cues.[81] For example, faces are important emotional signals in the lives of primates, and neurons in the monkey amygdala respond briskly to the sight of monkey faces.[82]

As we saw in Chapter 6, information about external stimuli reaches the amygdala from two pathways, one subcortical, the other cortical. The subcortical pathway is shorter and faster but imprecise, and the cortical pathway has the opposite attributes. And as we saw in Chapter 7, learning and memory appear to involve the potentiation of synaptic transmission in these pathways. In the normal brain the potentiation probably occurs in both pathways, which work together in the conditioning and expression of fear responses to external stimuli. But suppose, because of genetic predisposition or past experiences, phobic learning were to involve the subcortical pathway to a greater extent than the cortical pathway, especially for prepared stimuli. This might explain why phobias generalize broadly—as Öhman has pointed out, phobics can sometimes lose track of what they are afraid of when fear generalizes.[83] The subcortical pathway, not being very capable of making fine distinctions, may produce learning that more freely spreads to other stimuli. And this pathway, being subcortical, would also presumably be particularly difficult to gain conscious, cortical control over. Interestingly, the high-frequency sounds that turned on amygdala cells so effectively did so through the quick and dirty subcortical pathways.

Although amygdala-mediated fear conditioning is a form of implicit learning (regardless of the input pathways involved), phobics are consciously afraid of their phobic stimuli. This means that they also have an explicit conscious memory, formed through their temporal lobe memory system, that reminds them that they are afraid of snakes, heights, or whatever. This memory might be established during the initial traumatic learning situation, but some phobics do not recall such a learning experience, possibly because of a stress-induced memory loss. In such instances, the conscious memory of being phobically afraid could be established in later experiences with the phobic object. When the object is encountered, the amygdala will unconsciously detect the stimulus and produce the bodily expression of fear. Upon becoming aware of this bodily response, the person attributes (à la Schachter and Singer) the arousal to the most likely object and forms the memory that they are afraid of objects of that type. In the case of standard phobic objects (snakes, spiders, heights), these phobic attributions are probably facilitated by the fact that the person knows that people are often afraid of these things. Once this explicit memory is created, its retrieval into consciousness becomes a potent stimulus that is itself capable of activating the amygdala and producing anxiety by way of connections from cortical areas (including the hippocampus) to the amygdala. Even if one does not have a conscious memory of the initial learning, there is likely to be an awareness of the phobic condition stored in explicit memory.

Not everyone exposed to a traumatic event develops a phobia. Some people's brains, because of their genetic makeup or past experiences, must be predisposed to react to traumatic learning experiences in this particular way. In these people, the amygdala may be supersensitive to some class of prepared stimuli or the amygdala may have other alterations that make fear conditioning especially potent. On the other hand, as we've seen, changes in the frontal lobe may predispose some people to develop fears that resist extinction, even when unprepared stimuli are involved.

Traumatic Stress: PTSD was once known as shell shock, battle fatigue, or war neurosis, because it was most commonly diagnosed in war veterans.[84] Although it occurs in victims of many kinds of trauma, the following quotation from a Vietnam veteran illustrates the phenomenon:

> I can't get the memories out of my mind! The images come flooding back in vivid detail, triggered by the most inconsequential things, like a door slamming or the smell of stir-fried pork. Last night I went to bed, was having a good sleep for a change. Then . . . there was a bolt of crackling thunder. I awoke instantly, frozen in fear. I am right back in Vietnam. . . . My hands are freezing, yet sweat pours from my entire body. I feel each hair on the back of my neck standing on end. I can't catch my breath and my heart is pounding. . . . The next clap of thunder makes me jump so much that I fall to the floor. . . . [85]

The similarity between disorders of this type and laboratory-conditioned fear has not escaped the notice of psychiatrists. Conditioned fear was in fact proposed as the explanation of war neuroses in veterans of World War I.[86] Two of the most noted contemporary psychiatrists who study PTSD are Dennis Charney of Yale and Roger Pitman of Harvard, both of whom champion the notion that fear conditioning is involved in the disorder.[87]

The difference between a fear conditioning theory of phobia and PTSD is one of where the conditioning process gets its strength. In the case of prepared phobic learning, the conditioned stimulus makes the learning especially strong. The unconditioned stimulus is typically unpleasant and may even be painful, but is not necessarily extraordinary. However, in the case of PTSD, the conditioned stimulus events are less notable than the unconditioned stimulus. PTSD, in fact, is defined in DMS-III-R as involving a trauma that is far outside the realm of experiences in ordinary life.

Once we assume that the trauma in PTSD is an extraordinary event, an especially potent US, a fairly standard view of the way the amygdala mediates conditioned fear provides a plausible account of this disorder. Admittedly, we don't know exactly what combination of factors come together to make up the horrendous US at the neuronal level, but we can easily imagine that such a neural condition exists, one that bombards the amygdala with electrical and chemical signals that are particularly potent as reinforcers of Pavlovian conditioning. These powerful reinforcing stimuli are then linked synaptically with the sounds, sights, and smells of the battle, which also reach the amygdala. Later, the occurrence of these same conditioned stimuli, or stimuli related to them, elicit profound fear responses by reactivating these powerfully potentiated amygdala circuits.

Conditioned stimuli activate the amygdala unconsciously, but at the same time reach the temporal lobe memory system and can lead to the recall of the initial trauma or to the recall of recent episodes in which the initial trauma is relieved. These conscious memories, together with the awareness of now being in a state of strong emotional arousal (due to the unconscious activation of fear responses through the amygdala), then gives rise to conscious anxiety and worry. These cognitions about the emotional arousal, in turn, flow from the neocortex and hippocampus to further arouse the amygdala. And the bodily expression of the amygdala's responses keeps the cortex aware that emotional arousal is ongoing, and further facilitates the anxious thoughts and memories. The brain enters into a vicious cycle of emotional and cognitive excitement and, like a runaway train, just keeps picking up speed.

It is possible that in PTSD, as proposed for phobic learning, the direct projections to the amygdala from subcortical sensory processing regions are involved. If this were so, it would explain why the attacks are so impulsive and uncontrollable, and tend to generalize so readily (from gunshots to lightning to slamming doors). As we've seen, the subcortical pathways are quick and dirty transmission routes. They turn the amygdala on and start emotional reactions before the cortex has a chance to figure out what it is that is being reacted to. And since these pathways are not very capable of distinguishing between stimuli, generalization readily occurs (a slamming door may indeed not sound very different from a gunshot to this circuit). Perhaps trauma, for some reasons (genetic or experiential) in some persons, biases the brain in such a way that the thalamic pathways to the amygdala predominate over the cortical ones, allowing these low-level processing networks to take the lead in the learning and storage of information. Later exposure to stimuli that even remotely resemble those occurring during the trauma would then pass, like greased lightning, over the potentiated pathways to the amygdala, unleashing the fear reaction. Quite possibly, it is harder for one to gain conscious willful control over these subcortical pathways. At the same time, because conscious memories are formed during anxiety attacks, the bodily sensations associated with those attacks, when recognized consciously, become potent elicitors or at least facilitators of anxiety. Next, we'll see just how bodily sensations can drive anxiety in panic disorders, which often occur in conjunction with PTSD.

Panic: Panic attacks are the most commonly diagnosed anxiety disorder.[88] They are similar to phobic and PTSD reactions in the sense that the patient suffers from strong emotional arousal, including intense activation of the sympathetic nervous system. However, while phobic and PTSD responses occur in the presence of external stimuli, panic attack appears to be more related to internal stimuli.[89] And because panic involves internal events, it is especially difficult for the person to avoid the stimuli that bring it on. Panic patients thus differ in this respect from patients with PTSD and phobia, who engage in extensive avoidance behavior.[90]

A panic attack can be induced by having the patient hyperventilate or inhale a gaseous mixture rich in carbon dioxide, or giving the patient an intravenous injection of sodium lactate.[91] These procedures give rise to internal signals (bodily sensations) similar to those that are typically present during a naturally occurring attack. Panic can also be induced by the provision of false feedback about the rate at which the heart is beating, making the patient believe that heightened bodily arousal is occurring when it is not.[92] The belief that panic is occurring may be an important link in the chain of events that tie together the occurrence of bodily sensations and full-blown panic.

There are a number of theories of why panic occurs, including biological explanations (e.g., supersensitivity to carbon dioxide) and psychological ones (e.g., a history of childhood separation anxiety).[93] I will make no attempt to review or evaluate the various theories here. My aim instead is to discuss one theory, the conditioning theory, and to consider how it might be implemented in the brains of panic patients.

One common view is that artificial panic induction procedures lead to bodily sensations that then serve as conditioned stimuli.[94] Having experienced panic before, the patient learns the warning signs. When these internal signals occur (even when artificially induced) the patient feels that panic is starting.[95] This cognitive appraisal of bodily sensations then drives the system into panic. Induced panic, and presumably natural panic, by this way of thinking, is a conditioned response to internal stimuli that occurred during past panic attacks. It has even been argued that these internal sensations might be prepared stimuli, thus further linking panic and phobia and their underlying mechanism.[96] Support for the preparedness of such internal stimuli comes from Donald Klein's theory that panic represents the activation of an evolutionarily old suffocation alarm system.[97]

The most complete conditioning theory of panic has been developed by Wolpe.[98] He has argued that the first panic attack is the result of experiencing the consequences of hyperventilation, which increases the carbon dioxide in the lungs and blood and results in a variety of unpleasant bodily sensations (dizziness, racing heart, the feeling of suffocation). The hyperventilation can arise for a variety of reasons. Certain drugs like cocaine, amphetamine, or LSD, or exposure to toxic chemicals in the workplace, can be the cause. However, according to Wolpe, most often panic occurs in persons who are particularly anxious and worried and who have been under a lot of stress. One study cited by Wolpe found that severe marital conflict occurred during the year before the first panic attack in 84 percent of the patients surveyed, emphasizing again that cognitive factors can lift anxiety over the threshold.

According to Wolpe, the cause of the first panic is not important. It can be organic or psychological. Regardless, once panic occurs, the stimuli that happen to be present at the time will become conditioned fear stimuli. But unlike typical fear conditioning situations, the critical stimuli are internal rather than external. For example, an elevation of blood pressure that occurs in response to hyperventilation might become a conditioned fear stimulus. If blood pressure happens to increase for some other reason, such as talking to a superior or being in some other socially tense situation, the noxious sensations previously elicited by hyperventilation, having been conditioned to increases in blood pressure levels, are now brought on. These sensations are then noticed and interpreted as indicative of the onset of a panic attack. In contrast, the CS (elevation of blood pressure) is not easily noticed (high blood pressure is in fact sometimes called the "silent killer"), and the panic appears to be spontaneous. External stimuli can also become conditioned panic stimuli. If the first panic occurred in a car, then being in cars may make it more likely that panic will occur there. Nevertheless, in Wolpe's model, the internal stimuli play the leading role.

Let's now consider the sequence of events by which the amygdala might participate in conditioned panic. There are neurons in the lower brain stem that are very sensitive to changes in blood level of carbon dioxide.[99] The amygdala, it turns out, receives inputs from the neurons in this region.[100] The amygdala also receives information about the status of the internal organs—the rate at which the heart is beating, the level of blood pressure, and other vital statistics from the inner core of the body.[101] By integrating these internal signals about the state of bodily organs (the conditioned stimuli) with information about the level of carbon dioxide in the blood (the unconditioned stimulus), the amygdala could form synaptic linkages between the co-occurring events, allowing the internal signals to substitute for the carbon dioxide effects in producing a profound activation of the sympathetic nervous system through the outputs of the amygdala. Once the sympathetic nervous system is activated in this way, the person becomes aware of the bodily arousal and is reminded, through explicit memory, that the symptoms being experienced tend to occur in panic attacks, suggesting that one might be starting. These conscious memories and thoughts about the possibility of panic might, then, by way of projections to the amygdala from the hippocampus and neocortex, lead to further and continued activation of the sympathetic nervous system, and to the build-up of a full-blown panic attack. Alternatively, in the case of false feedback about the status of heart rate or other bodily functions, the chain of events probably starts with cortical cognitions (for example, the belief that the heart is beating fast), which then serve as retrieval cues for explicit memories of past experiences in which fast heart beating occurred (past panic attacks).

These conscious thoughts and explicit memories, again by way of connections from neocortical areas and the hippocampus to the amygdala, then trigger the amygdala and its sympathetic outflow as before.

These neuro-scenarios, of course, are hypothetical, as there has not been any research on the role of the amygdala in panic. However, while the contribution of these circuits to human panic disorder is hypothetical, the circuits and their functions are real and it is quite conceivable that they might contribute to panic in the way described.

Bad Habits and Anxious Thoughts

The avoidance responses that so typify anxiety disorders fall somewhere between what I described earlier as innate emotional *reactions* and voluntary emotional *actions*. Avoidance responses are instrumental responses that are learned because they are reinforced. They are then performed habitually, which is to say automatically, when the appropriate stimuli occur. But unlike innate responses, avoidance responses are more or less arbitrarily related to danger. Innate emotional reactions occur when the amygdala is turned on (by innate or learned triggers) because the response is hardwired to the amygdala. In contrast, for avoidance, the brain has learned some response that can be performed in the presence of a learned trigger that short-circuits the innate response. For example, initially rats freeze when they hear a sound that predicts a shock. With time, they may learn to jump up at just the right moment during the sound to avoid the shock, or to jump over a barrier during the sound, or to turn a wheel to inactivate the shock. These responses, once learned, prevent emotional arousal. They are performed automatically, without conscious decision. They become habits, ways of automatically responding to stimuli that routinely warn of danger. Like conditioned fear responses, they are performed automatically, but they are learned rather than innate responses.

Emotional habits can be very useful. If you find out that going to a certain water hole is likely to put you face to face with a bloodthirsty predator, then the best thing to do is to avoid going there. But if you stop going to water holes because you become anxious whenever you begin to look for water, or you start drinking less water than you need to maintain your health whenever you do get around to drinking, then your avoidance response has become detrimental to routine life. You have an anxiety disorder.

The automatic nature of emotional habits can be extremely useful, allowing you to avoid routine dangers without having to give them much thought. However, when emotional habits become anxiety disorders, then the rigid unextinguishable learning that typifies avoidance behavior becomes a liability.

Many of the leading drugs for treating anxiety have been developed because of their efficiency in reducing avoidance behavior in animals. For example, if a rat is shocked when it steps off a platform in a test chamber, it will remain on the platform when it is placed in the chamber the next day. However, if the rat gets a shot of Valium just before being placed on the platform on the second day, it will be much more likely to step off the platform to figure out if the danger still exists. In other words, the rat is less fearful, less anxious, about the situation when it receives the drug.

As Mowrer and Miller proposed, avoidance learning is usually thought of as taking place in two stages. First, fear conditioning occurs. Then, a response is learned because it supposedly reduces the learned fear. We know that the amygdala is required for the fear conditioning part, but the brain mechanisms involved in the instrumental avoidance response are less clearly understood. It seems that structures like the basal ganglia, frontal cortex, and hippocampus may be involved.[102] There is controversy as to just where in the brain drugs like Valium have their anxiety-reducing effects.[103] In fact, however, they probably act in a number of places.

Let's consider how a drug like Valium might work in the amygdala. Valium belongs to the class of drugs known as benzodiazepines. These drugs have natural receptors in the brain. When you take Valium, it binds to the benzodiazepine receptors all over the brain. These receptors do a very specific thing. They facilitate the effects of the inhibitory neurotransmitter, GABA. So you basically increase inhibition in a variety of brain areas. In some brain regions, this will not have any consequence for anxiety because that region is not involved in that function. Basically, if a brain region is involved in anxiety, whatever it does during anxiety-provoking situations, it will probably do less of it in the presence of Valium. For example, the lateral nucleus is the sensory-input region of the amygdala. The increase of inhibition in this region will raise the threshold for anxiety. Stimuli that would normally elicit fearful responses through the amygdala no longer do so (see Figure 8-4). Jeffrey Gray has proposed that the antianxiety drugs work through the hippocampus (albeit indirectly).[104] This may be true as well, reducing the ability of explicit memories to make us anxious and afraid.

The brain circuits of avoidance are far less clear than the circuits of fear conditioning. Avoidance is more complex: it involves fear conditioning plus instrumental learning. Also, there are many ways in which avoidance conditioning studies can be performed and a great variety of responses can be conditioned this way. Avoidance responses are arbitrary. Anything that reduces the exposure to fear-eliciting events can be an avoidance response. These factors make the brain systems of avoidance more difficult to track down. However, now that we have a good handle on the brain mechanisms involved in the first phase of avoidance learning (the fear conditioning phase), we can more wisely approach the second phase.

Psychotherapy: Just Another Way to Rewire the Brain

Freud's psychoanalytic theory and the various conditioning theories all assume that anxiety is the result of traumatic learning experiences that foster the establishment of anxiety-producing long-term memories. In this sense, psychoanalytic and conditioning theories have drawn similar conclusions about the origins of anxiety. However, the two kinds of theories lead to different therapeutic approaches. Psychoanalysis seeks to help make the patient conscious of the origins of inner conflict, whereas behavior therapy, the name given to therapies inspired by conditioning theories, tries to rid the person of the symptoms of anxiety, often through various forms of extinction therapy. There is a good deal of debate about the best treatment strategy: psychoanalysis, behavioral therapy, or most recently cognitive therapy.[105] However, extinction therapies, either alone or in combination with other approaches, are commonly recommended for many anxiety disorders.[106]

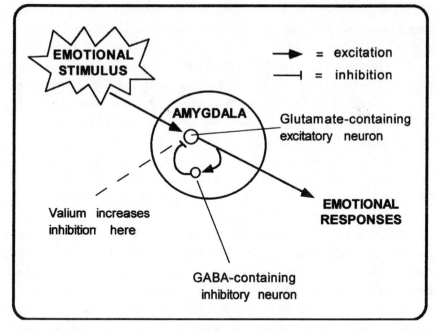

FIGURE 8-4
One Way Valium Might Reduce Fear and Anxiety.

Valium and some other antianxiety drugs act by increasing the ability of inhibitory neurons to prevent excitatory transmission. When we are under the influence of Valium, external emotional stimuli (as well as thoughts) are less capable of producing emotional responses, in part (perhaps) because of an action on GABA inhibitory neurons in the amygdala.

The prototypical extinction therapy pioneered by Wolpe starts off with relaxation training.[107] Once the patient learns to feel comfortable in the therapeutic setting, he or she is asked to produce emotional images, starting with less frightening images and working toward more frightening ones. This is called systematic desensitization. The desensitization can then move from images to real objects and situations that cause anxiety, again starting with the least and moving toward the more frightening. Erdelyi interpreted systematic desensitization in the language of conditioning: present the CS in degrees until the conditioned emotional responses drop out.[108] The CS comes to be associated with a new US, safety, and the new conditioned response is no response. Erdelyi suggests that the standard techniques of psychoanalytic cathartic therapy (hypnotic induction, lying on a couch, trust in the therapist, image production) may accomplish the same thing as Wolpian therapy: extinction of the learned emotional reaction.

Figuring out the brain mechanisms of extinction is obviously going to be an important part of understanding how therapy works. As we've seen, extinction appears to involve interactions between the medial prefrontal cortex and the amygdala. And work by Michael Davis has shown that extinction occurs through the same kind of synaptic mechanism that conditioning does: NMDA-dependent synaptic plasticity in the amygdala.[109] When NMDA receptors are blocked, it may be that the amygdala can't learn what the prefrontal cortex is trying to teach it—to inhibit a particular emotional memory.

These observations give us a different kind of understanding of therapy. Therapy is just another way of creating synaptic potentiation in brain pathways that control the amygdala. The amygdala's emotional memories, as we've seen, are indelibly burned into its circuits. The best we can hope to do is to regulate their expression. And the way we do this is by getting the cortex to control the amygdala.

Behavior (extinction) therapy and psychoanalysis have the same goal—help the person with their problem. In both cases, the effects may be achieved by helping the cortex gain control over the amygdala. However, the neural roads taken may be different. Extinction therapy may take place through a form of implicit learning involving the prefrontal-amygdala circuit, whereas psychoanalysis, with emphasis on conscious insight and conscious appraisals, may involve the control of the amygdala by explicit knowledge through the temporal lobe memory system and other cortical areas involved in conscious awareness (see Chapter 9). Interestingly, it is well known that the connections from the cortical areas to the amygdala are far weaker than the connections from the amygdala to the cortex.[110] This may explain why it is so easy for emotional information to invade our conscious thoughts, but so hard for us to gain conscious control over our emotions. Psychoanalysis may be such a prolonged process because of this asymmetry in connections between the cortex and amygdala.

(No) *Thanks for the Memories*

The ability to rapidly form memories of stimuli associated with danger, to hold on to them for long periods of time (perhaps eternally), and use them automatically when similar situations occur in the future is one of the brain's most powerful and efficient learning and memory functions. But this incredible luxury is costly. We sometimes, perhaps all too often, develop fears and anxieties about things that we would just as well not have. What is so useful about being afraid of heights or elevators or certain foods or means of travel? While there are risks associated with each of these things, the chances of them causing harm are usually relatively small. We have more fears than we need, and it seems that our utterly efficient fear conditioning system, combined with an extremely powerful ability to think about our fears and an inability to control them, is probably at fault. As we'll see in the next chapter, though, there is some hope that the future evolution of the human brain will take care of this imbalance.

9

ONCE MORE,
WITH FEELINGS

൙

"Men believe themselves to be free, simply because they are conscious of their actions, and unconscious of the causes whereby those actions are determined."

Baruch Spinoza, *Ethics*[1]

"How small the cosmos . . . how paltry and puny in comparison to human consciousness, to a single individual recollection. . . ."

Vladimir Nabokov, *Speak, Memory*[2]

THE PICTURE OF EMOTION I've painted so far is largely one of automaticity. I've shown how our brains are programmed by evolution to respond in certain ways to significant situations. Significance can be signaled by information built into the brain by evolution or by memories established through past experiences. In either case, though, the initial responses elicited by significant stimuli are automatic and require neither conscious awareness of the stimulus nor conscious control of the responses.

This scenario, you may say, is fine for the control of the bodily responses. But these are not the essence of an emotion. They occur during an emotion, but an emotion is something else, something more. An emotion is a subjective experience, a passionate invasion of consciousness, a feeling.

I've spent most of this book trying to show that much of what the brain does during an emotion occurs outside of conscious awareness.

It's now time to give consciousness its due. It's time to see what role consciousness has in emotion, and what role emotion has in consciousness. It's time to look at emotion once again, this time with feelings as part of the picture.[3]

A Simple Idea

My idea about the nature of conscious emotional experiences, emotional feelings, is incredibly simple. It is that a subjective emotional experience, like the feeling of being afraid, results when we become consciously aware that an emotion system of the brain, like the defense system, is active. In order for this to occur, we need at least two things. We need a defense system and we need to have the capacity to be consciously aware of its activity. The upside of this line of thought is that once we understand consciousness we will also understand subjective emotional experiences. The downside is that in order to understand subjective emotional experiences, we've got to figure out consciousness.

To my way of thinking, then, emotional experience is not really a problem about emotion. It is, instead, a problem about how conscious experiences occur. Because the scientific study of emotions has mostly been about conscious emotional experiences,[4] scientists who study emotions have set things up so that they will not understand emotions until they've understood the mind-body problem, the problem of how consciousness comes out of brains, arguably the most difficult problem there is and ever was.[5]

The field got this way at the beginning, when William James brought up the business with the bear. He started with a question about why the sight of a bear makes us run away (the stimulus-to-response problem in emotion) but ended up with a question about why we feel afraid when we see the bear (the stimulus-to-feeling problem in emotion). Ever since, the study of emotion has been focused on where conscious feelings come from.[6]

All areas of psychology have had to deal with consciousness. Perception and memory, for example, also involve conscious experiences. To perceive an apple is to be aware that an apple is there, and to remember something about an apple is to be aware of that particular thing about an apple. The difficulty of scientifically understanding the conscious content that occurs during perception, memory, or emotion is what led to the behaviorist movement in psychology.[7] And the success of the cognitive movement as an alternative to behaviorism was largely due to the fact that it could deal with the mind in terms of processes that occur unconsciously, and thus without having to first solve the problem of how conscious content is created. But because emotion was left out of the cognitive revolution,[8] it somehow did not reap the benefits that come from thinking of minds in terms of unconscious processes rather than in terms of conscious content. The study of emotion is, as a result, still focused on where subjective feelings come from rather than on the unconscious processes that sometimes do and sometimes do not give rise to those conscious states.

By treating emotions as unconscious processes that can sometimes give rise to conscious content, we lift the burden of the mind-body problem from the shoulders of emotion researchers and allow them to get on with the problem of figuring out how the brain does its unconscious emotional business. But we also see how conscious emotional experiences are probably created. They are probably created the same way that other conscious experiences are—by the establishment of a conscious representation of the workings of underlying processing systems.[9] Although much remains unknown about how conscious representations come about, recent studies have begun to provide important clues.

Short Stuff

There have been many ideas about what consciousness is and isn't.[10] While you could hardly say that there is a consensus on this topic, many of the theories that have been proposed in recent years are built around the concept of working memory.[11]

Remember this number: 783445. Now close your eyes and repeat it, and then count backward from 99 to 91 by 2s and try repeating the number again. Chances are you can't. The reason for this is that thinking occurs in a mental workspace that has a limited capacity. When you started using the workspace to do the subtraction problem you bumped the stored number out. This workspace is called working memory, a temporary storage mechanism that allows several pieces of information to be held in mind at the same time and compared, contrasted, and otherwise interrelated.[12]

Working memory is pretty much what used to just be called short-term memory. However, the term working memory implies not just a temporary storage system but an active processing mechanism used in thinking and reasoning.

Much of our understanding of working memory is owed to the pioneering work of Alan Baddeley in the early 1970s.[13] It was known from a famous study performed by one of the pioneers of cognitive psychology, George Miller, that short-term memory has a capacity limit of about seven pieces of information.[14] Baddeley reasoned that if he had subjects actively remember six things, like six digits, they should have trouble performing, at the same time, other tasks that require temporary storage since the mental workspace would be mostly used up. To test this, he had his subjects rehearse the digits out loud while, at the same time, reading sentences and pressing buttons to verify whether the sentence referred to something true or false. Baddeley found that sentence comprehension was greatly slowed down, but to his surprise the subjects could still do it to some extent.

Baddeley's experiment led him to reformulate the notion of short-term memory. He replaced the generic notion of short-term memory with the concept of working memory, which, he suggested, consists of a general-purpose temporary storage system utilized in all active thinking processes and several specialized temporary storage systems that are only called into play when specific kinds of information have to be held on to.

Borrowing a term from computer technology, memory researchers sometimes refer to temporary storage mechanisms as buffers. It is now believed that a number of specialized buffers exist. For example, each sensory system has one or more temporary buffers. These aid in perception, allowing the system to compare what it is seeing or hearing now to what it saw or heard a moment ago. There are also temporary buffers associated with aspects of language use (these help you keep the first part of a sentence in mind until you've heard the last part so that the whole thing can be understood). The specialized memory buffers work in parallel, independent of one another.

The general-purpose system consists of a *workspace,* where information from the specialized buffers can be held on to temporarily, and a set of so-called *executive* functions that control operations performed on this information. The executive functions take care of the overall coordination of the activities of working memory, such as determining which specialized systems should be attended to at the moment and shuffling information in and out of the workspace from these and other systems.

Although only a limited amount of information can be held in the general workspace at any one time, any kind of information can be held on to. As a result, different kinds of information can be interrelated in working memory (the way something looks, sounds, and smells can be associated with its name in working memory). And thanks to "chunking," another of George Miller's many insights into the cognitive mind, the capacity limit of working memory (about seven pieces of information) can be overcome to some degree: we can remember seven of just about anything (letters, words, or ideas), so that the amount of information actually represented by the seven pieces of information can be enormous (think of all that is implied by the names of seven countries).[15]

The stuff in working memory is the stuff we are currently thinking about or paying attention to. But working memory is not a pure product of the here and now. It also depends on what we know and what kinds of experiences we've had in the past. In other words, it depends on long-term memory. In order to be aware that you are looking at a basketball, it is not enough for the basketball to be represented as a purely visual pattern (a round, orange object with thin black lines around it) by your visual system. The pattern has to also have grabbed the attention of the working memory executive. This means that the pattern is what is being held in the visual short-term memory buffer and that the visual buffer, as opposed to the auditory or other buffers, is the one with which the executive is working. But neither is this enough. Only when the visual pattern is matched with information in long-term memory (stored facts about and stored past experiences with similar objects) does the visual stimulus become recognized as a basketball. But in addition to being important in figuring out the meaning of information being picked up by lower level specialized systems, stored knowledge also influences the workings of the lower level systems. For example, once memories having to do with basketballs are activated and made available to working memory, the operation of the specialized processors becomes biased toward detecting and picking up on external information that is relevant to basketballs. This influence of memory on perception is an example of what cognitive scientists sometimes call top-down processing, which contrasts with the build-up of perceptions from sensory processing, known as bottom-up processing.

Working memory, in short, sits at the crossroads of bottom-up and top-down processing systems and makes high-level thinking and reasoning possible. Stephen Kosslyn, a leading cognitive scientist, puts it this way:

> Working memory . . . corresponds to the activated information in long-term memories, the information in short-term memories, and the decision processes that manage which information is activated in the long-term memories and retained in the short-term memories. . . . This kind of working memory system is necessary for a wide range of tasks, such as performing mental arithmetic, reading, problem solving and . . . reasoning in general. All of these tasks require not only some form of temporary storage, but also an interplay between information that is stored temporarily and a larger body of stored knowledge.[16]

The Here and the Now in the Brain

How, then, does working memory work in the brain? Studies conducted in the 1930s by C.F. Jacobsen provide the foundation for our understanding of this problem.[17] He trained monkeys using something called the delayed response task. The monkey sat in a chair and watched the experimenter put a raisin under one of two objects that were side by side. A curtain was then lowered for a certain amount of time (the delay) and then the monkey was allowed to choose. In order to get the raisin, the monkey had to remember not which object the raisin was under but whether the raisin was under the left or the right object. Correct performance, in other words, required that the monkey hold in mind the spatial location of the raisin during the delay period (during which the playing field was hidden from view). At very short delays (a few seconds), normal monkeys did quite well, and performance got predictably worse as the delay increased (from seconds to minutes). However, monkeys with damage to the prefrontal cortex performed poorly, even at the short delays. On the basis of this and research that followed, the prefrontal cortex has come to be thought of as playing a role in temporary memory processes, processes that we now refer to as working memory.

In the last chapter, we examined the role of the *medial* prefrontal cortex in the extinction of emotional memory. In contrast, it is the *lat-*

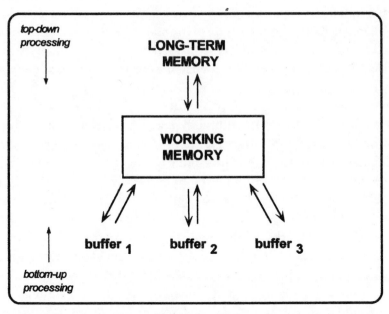

FIGURE 9-1
Relation of Specialized Short-Term Buffers, Long-Term Explicit Memory, and Working Memory.

Stimuli processed in different specialized systems (such as sensory, spatial, or language systems) can be held simultaneously in short-term buffers. The various short-term buffers provide potential inputs to working memory, which can deal most effectively with only one of the buffers at a time. Working memory integrates information received from short-term buffers with long-term memories that are also activated.

eral prefrontal cortex that has most often been implicated in working memory. The lateral prefrontal cortex is believed to exist only in primates and is considerably larger in humans than in other primates.[18] It is not surprising that one of the most sophisticated cognitive functions of the brain should involve this region.

In recent years, the role of the lateral prefrontal cortex in working memory has been studied extensively by the laboratories of Joaquin Fuster at UCLA and Pat Goldman-Rakic at Yale.[19] Both researchers have recorded the electrical activity of lateral prefrontal neurons while monkeys performed delayed response tasks and other tests requiring short-term storage. They have shown that cells in this region become particularly active during the delay periods. It is likely that these cells are actively involved in holding on to the information during the delay.

The contribution of the lateral prefrontal cortex to working memory is still being explored. However, considerable evidence suggests that the lateral prefrontal cortex is involved in the executive or general-purpose aspects of working memory. For example, damage to this region in humans interferes with working memory regardless of the kind of stimulus information involved.[20] Further, brain imaging studies in humans have shown that a variety of different kinds of working memory tasks result in the activation of the lateral prefrontal cortex.[21] In one recent study, for example, subjects were required to perform a verbal and a visual task either one at a time or at the same time.[22] The results showed that the lateral prefrontal cortex was activated when the two tasks were performed together, thus taxing the executive functions of working memory, but not when the tasks were performed separately.

The lateral prefrontal cortex is ideally suited to perform these general-purpose working memory functions. It has connections with the various sensory systems (like the visual and auditory systems) and other neocortical systems that perform specialized temporary storage functions (like spatial and verbal storage) and is also connected with the hippocampus and other cortical areas involved in long-term memory.[23] In addition, it has connections with areas of the cortex involved in movement control, allowing decisions made by the executive to be turned into voluntarily performed actions.[24] Recent studies have begun to show how the lateral prefrontal cortex interacts with some of these areas. Best understood are interactions with temporary storage buffers in the visual cortex.

Cortical visual processing begins in the primary visual area located in the occipital lobe (the rear-most part of the cortex). This area receives visual information from the visual thalamus, processes it, and then distributes its outputs to a variety of other cortical regions. Although the cortical visual system is enormously complex,[25] the neural pathways responsible for two aspects of visual processing are fairly well understood. These involve the determination of "what" a stimulus is and "where" it is located.[26] The "what" pathway involves a processing stream that travels from the primary visual cortex to the temporal lobe and the "where" pathway goes from the primary cortex to the parietal lobe.

Goldman-Rakic and colleagues recorded from cells in the parietal lobe "where" pathway during short-term memory tests requiring the temporary remembrance of the spatial location of visual stimuli. They found that cells there, like cells in the lateral prefrontal cortex, were active, suggesting that they were keeping track of the location, during the delay.[27] The parietal and frontal regions in question are anatomically interconnected—the parietal area sends axons to the prefrontal region and the prefrontal region sends axons back to the parietal area. These findings suggest that the parietal lobe visual area works with the lateral prefrontal cortex to maintain information about the spatial location of visual stimuli in working memory. Similarly, Robert Desimone found evidence for reciprocal interactions between the visual areas of the temporal lobe (the "what" pathway) and the lateral prefrontal cortex in studies involving the recognition of whether a particular object had been seen recently.[28]

The maintenance of visual information in working memory thus appears to crucially depend on interactions between the lateral prefrontal region and specialized areas of the visual cortex.[29] The pathway from the specialized visual areas tell the prefrontal cortex "what" is out there and "where" it is located (bottom-up processing). The prefrontal cortex, by way of pathways back to the visual areas, primes the visual system to attend to those objects and spatial locations that are being processed in working memory (top-down processing). As we've seen, these kinds of top-down influences on sensory processing

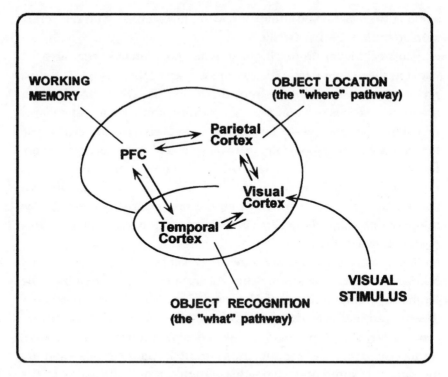

FIGURE 9-2
**Relation of the "What" and "Where" Visual Pathways
to Working Memory.**

Visual information, received by the visual cortex, is distributed to cortical areas that perform specialized visual processing functions. Two well-studied specialized functions are those involved in object recognition (mediated by the "what" pathway) and object location (mediated by the "where" pathway). These specialized visual pathways provide inputs to the prefrontal cortex (PFC), which plays a crucial role in working memory. The specialized systems also receive inputs back from the prefrontal cortex, allowing the information content of working memory to influence further processing of incoming information. Leftward-going arrows represent bottom-up processing and rightward-going ones top-down processing.

are believed to be important aspects of the executive control functions of working memory.

Recent studies, especially by Goldman-Rakic and associates, have raised questions about the role of the prefrontal cortex as a general-purpose working memory processor.[30] For example, they have found that different parts of the lateral prefrontal cortex participate in working memory when animals have to determine "what" a visual stimulus is as opposed to "where" it is located, suggesting that different parts of the prefrontal cortex are specialized for different kinds of working memory tasks. While these findings show that parts of the prefrontal cortex participate uniquely in different short-term memory tasks, they do not rule out the existence of a general-purpose workspace and a set of executive functions that coordinate the activity of the specialized systems, especially since the tasks studied did not tax the capacity of working memory in a way that would reveal a limited-capacity system.[31] Studies that have taxed the system, like the imaging studies in humans described above, suggest that neurons in the lateral prefrontal cortex are part of a general-purpose working memory network. At the same time, it is possible, given Goldman-Rakic's findings, that the general-purpose aspects of working memory are not localized to a single place in the lateral prefrontal cortex but instead are distributed over the region. That this may occur is suggested by the fact that some cells in the specialized areas of the lateral prefrontal cortex participate in multiple working memory tasks.[32]

There is also evidence that the general-purpose functions of working memory involve areas other than the lateral prefrontal cortex. For example, imaging studies in humans have shown that another area of the frontal lobe, the anterior cingulate cortex, is also activated by working memory and related cognitive tasks.[33] Like the lateral prefrontal cortex, the anterior cingulate region receives inputs from the various specialized sensory buffers, and the anterior cingulate and the lateral prefrontal cortex are anatomically interconnected.[34] Moreover, both regions are part of what has been called the frontal lobe attentional network, a cognitive system involved in selective attention, mental resource allocation, decision making processes, and voluntary movement control.[35] It is tempting to think of the general-purpose aspects of working memory as involving neurons in the lateral prefrontal and anterior cingulate regions working together. Earlier (Chapter 4) we saw that the cingulate cortex was once considered the seat of the soul (consciousness). Given the new work implicating the cingulate region in working memory, the older idea may not be so far off the mark.

One other area of the prefrontal cortex, the orbital region, located on the underneath side of the frontal lobe, has emerged as important as well. Damage to this region in animals interferes with short-term memory about reward information, about what is good and bad at the moment,[36] and cells in this region are sensitive to whether a stimulus has just led to a reward or punishment.[37] Humans with orbital frontal damage become oblivious to social and emotional cues and some exhibit sociopathic behavior.[38] This area receives inputs from sensory processing systems (including their temporary buffers) and is also intimately connected with the amygdala and the anterior cingulate region. The orbital cortex provides a link through which emotional processing by the amygdala might be related in working memory to information being processed in sensory or other regions of the neocortex. We'll have more to say about this later.

There is still much to be learned about working memory and its neural basis. It is not clear, for example, whether both the temporary workspace and the executive functions are actually located in the frontal cortex. It is possible that the prefrontal areas do not store anything but instead just control the activity of other regions, allowing the activity in some areas to rise above the threshold for consciousness and inhibiting the activity of the others.[39] In spite of the fact that we still have much to learn, the researchers in this area have made considerable progress on this very tough, and very important, problem.

The Platform of Awareness

Tennessee Williams said, "Life is all memory except for the one present moment that goes by you so quick you hardly catch it going."[40] What Williams didn't realize is that even the immediate present involves memory—what we know about the one present moment is basically what is in our working memory. Working memory allows us to know that the "here and now" is "here" and is happening "now." This insight underlies the notion, adopted by a number of contemporary cognitive scientists, that consciousness is the awareness of what is in working memory. ◂

For example, Stephen Kosslyn argues that to be aware of something, that something must be in working memory.[41] John Kihlstrom

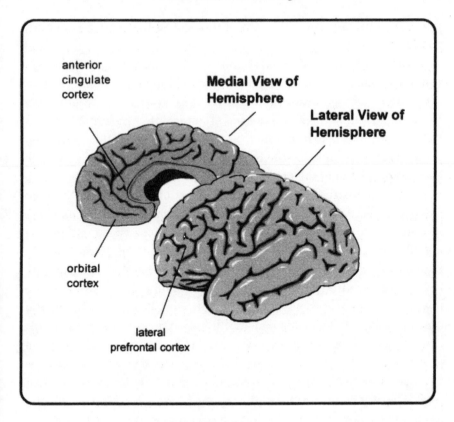

FIGURE 9-3
Frontal Cortex Areas Involved in Aspects of Working Memory.

Some areas of the frontal lobe that have been implicated in working memory functions include the lateral prefrontal cortex and the orbital and anterior cingulate cortex.

proposes that a link must be made between the mental representation of an event and a mental representation of the "self" as the agent or experiencer in order for us to be conscious of that event. These integrated episodic representations, according to Kihlstrom, reside in working memory.[42] Philip Johnson-Laird notes that the contents of working memory are what we are conscious of at the moment.[43] Bernard Baars, in an influential book called A *Cognitive Theory of Consciousness*, treats "consciousness as a kind of momentary working memory."[44] And several contemporary theories equate consciousness with focused attention, which is achieved through an executive or supervisory function similar to that proposed in the working memory theories.[45]

The conscious and unconscious aspects of thought are sometimes described in terms of serial and parallel functions. Consciousness seems to do things serially, more or less one at a time,[46] whereas the unconscious mind, being composed of many different systems, seems to work more or less in parallel. Some cognitive scientists have suggested that consciousness involves a limited-capacity serial processor that sits at the top of the cognitive hierarchy above a variety of special-purpose processors that are organized in parallel (some, like Stephen Kosslyn and Daniel Dennett, have even suggested that consciousness is a virtual serial processor—a parallel processor that emulates or acts like a serial one).[47] Serial processors create representations by manipulating symbols,[48] and we are only conscious of information that is represented symbolically.[49] Information processing by the lower level parallel processors occurs subsymbolically,[50] in codes that are not decipherable consciously. Philip Johnson-Laird puts it this way: since consciousness "is at the top, its instructions can specify a goal in explicitly symbolic terms, such as to get up and walk. It does not need to send detailed instructions about how to contract muscles. These will be formulated in progressively finer detail by the processors at lower levels. . . . It [consciousness] receives the results of computations from the lower processors, but again in a high-level and explicitly symbolic form."[51] This reasoning yields an explanation for why we are conscious of the outcome of mental computations but not of the computations themselves and how we can produce behaviors without knowing how individual muscles are controlled. In other words, the consciousness processor works at the symbolic level, which yields introspectively accessible content, but the parallel processors work subsymbolically and their operations are not directly accessible from consciousness.[52] And since not all subsymbolic processors necessarily feed into the consciousness processor, some subsymbolic processing remains inacessible.

Working memory is the limited-capacity serial processor that creates and manipulates symbolic representations. It is where the integrated monitoring and control of various lower level specialized processors takes place. Working memory is, in other words, a crucial part of the system that gives rise to consciousness.

The advantage of a working memory concept of consciousness over many other formulations is that it allows the problem to be posed in a concrete fashion. Concreteness for the sake of concreteness would not be so good, but in this case it seems to buy us something. As working memory, consciousness can be thought of in terms of a computational system, a system that creates representations by performing computations, by processing information. Viewed in computational terms, consciousness can be explored both psychologically and neurologically, and its underlying processes can even be modeled using computer simulations.

However, it is not clear that consciousness is computable. Johnson-Laird reminds us that a computer simulation of the weather is not the same thing as rain or sunshine.[53] Working memory theories, in dealing with consciousness in terms of processes rather than as content, try to explain what kinds of computational functions might be responsible for and underlie conscious experiences but they do not explain what it is like to have those experiences.[54] These theories provide an account of the way human minds work, in a general sense, rather than an account of what a particular experience is like in a particular mind. They can suggest how a representation might be created in working memory but not what it is like to be aware of that representation. They suggest how decision processes in working memory might lead to movement but not what it is like to actually decide to move. In other words, working memory is likely to be an important, and possibly an essential, aspect of consciousness. It is in fact likely to be the platform on which a conscious experience stands. But consciousness, especially its phenomenal or subjective nature, is not completely explained by the computational processes that underlie working memory, at least not in a way that anyone presently comprehends.[55]

Figuring out the exact nature of consciousness and the mechanisms by which it emerges out of collections of neurons is truly an important problem. Many questions remain to be answered about how working memory is mediated by the brain and how consciousness relates to the working memory system and/or other brain systems. However, it is not necessary for emotions researchers to solve these problems, nor is it necessary for us to wait for the solutions before studying how emotions work. Emotion researchers need to figure out how emotional information gets represented in working memory. The rest of the problem, figuring out how the contents of working memory become consciously experienced and how these subjective phenomena emerge from the brain, belongs on the shoulders of all mind scientists. Emotions researchers certainly have a lot to contribute to the study of consciousness, but figuring out consciousness is not their job, or at least theirs alone. Although this may seem obvious, the study of emotion has been so focused on the problem of emotional consciousness that the basic underlying emotional mechanisms have often been given short shrift.

The Emotional Present

I admit that I've passed the emotional consciousness buck. I've redefined the problem of emotional feelings as the problem of how emotional information comes to be represented in working memory. This won't make you happy if you want to know exactly what a feeling is or if you want to know how something as intangible as a feeling could be part of something so tangible as a brain. It won't, in other words, solve the mind-body problem. However, as important as solving the mind-body problem would be, it's not the only problem worth solving. And figuring out the mind-body problem wouldn't tell us what's unique about those states of mind we call emotions, nor would it explain why different emotions feel the way they do. Neither would it tell us what goes wrong in emotional disorders or suggest ways of treating or curing them. In order to understand what an emotion is and how particular emotional feelings come about we've got to understand the way the specialized emotion systems operate and determine how their activity gets represented in working memory.

Some might say I'm taking a big chance. I'm resting our understanding of our feelings, our most private and intimate states of mind, on the possibility that working memory is the key to consciousness. But really what I'm doing is using working memory as an "in principle" way of explaining feelings. I'm saying that feelings come about when the activity of specialized emotion systems gets represented in the system that gives rise to consciousness, and I'm using working memory as a fairly widely accepted version of how the latter might come about.

We've gone into great detail as to how one specialized emotion system, the defense system, works. So let's now see how the activity of this system might come to be represented in working memory and thereby give rise to the feeling we know as fear.

From Conscious Appraisals to Emotions: You encounter a rabbit while walking along a path in the woods. Light reflected from the rabbit is picked up by your eyes. The signals are then transmitted through the visual system to your visual thalamus, and then to your visual cortex, where a sensory representation of the rabbit is created and held in a short-term visual object buffer. Connections from the visual cortex to the cortical long-term memory networks activate relevant memories (facts about rabbits stored in memory as well as memories about past experiences you may have had with rabbits). By way of connections between the long-term memory networks and the working memory system, activated long-term memories are integrated with the sensory representation of the stimulus in working memory, allowing you to be consciously aware that the object you are looking at is a rabbit.

A few strides later down the path, there is a snake coiled up next to a log. Your eyes also pick up on this stimulus. Conscious representations are created in the same way as for the rabbit—by the integration in working memory of short-term visual representations with information from long-term memory. However, in the case of the snake, in addition to being aware of the kind of animal you are looking at, long-term memory also informs you that this kind of animal can be dangerous and that you might be in danger.

According to cognitive appraisal theories, the processes described so far would constitute your assessment of the situation and should be enough to account for the "fear" that you are feeling as a result of encountering the snake. The difference between the working memory representation of the rabbit and the snake is that the latter includes information about the snake being dangerous. But these cognitive representations and appraisals in working memory are not enough to turn the experience into a full-blown emotional experience. Davy Crockett, you may remember, said his love for his wife was so hot that it mighty nigh burst his boilers. There is nothing equivalent to boiler bursting going on here. Something else is needed to turn cognitive appraisals into emotions, to turn experiences into emotional experiences. That something, of course, is the activation of the system built by evolution to deal with dangers. That system, as we've seen, crucially involves the amygdala.

Many but not all people who encounter a snake in a situation such as the one described will have a full-blown emotional reaction that includes bodily responses and emotional feelings.[56] This will only occur if the visual representation of the snake triggers the amygdala. A whole host of output pathways will then be activated. Activation of these outputs is what makes the encounter with the snake an emotional experience, and the absence of activation is what prevents the encounter with the rabbit from being one.[57]

What is it about the activation of amygdala outputs that converts an experience into an emotional experience? To understand this we need to consider some of the various consequences of turning on amygdala outputs. These outputs provide the basic ingredients that, when mixed together in working memory with short-term sensory representations and the long-term memories activated by these sensory representations, create an emotional experience.

Ingredient 1: Direct Amygdala Influences on the Cortex: The amygdala has projections to many cortical areas.[58] In fact, as we've alredy seen, the projections of the amygdala to the cortex are considerably greater than the projections from the cortex to the amygdala (see Figure 9-4). In addition to projecting back to cortical sensory areas from which it receives inputs, the amygdala also projects to some sensory processing areas from which it does not receive inputs. For example, in order for a visual stimulus to reach the amygdala by way of the cortex, the stimulus has to go through the primary cortex, to a secondary region, and then to a third cortical area in the temporal lobe (which does the short-term buffering of visual object information). This third area then projects to the amygdala. The amygdala projects back to this area, but also to the other two earlier visual processing regions. As a result, once the amygdala is activated, it is able to influence the cortical areas that are processing the stimuli that are activating it (see Figure 9-4). This might be very important in directing attention to emotionally relevant stimuli by keeping the short-term object buffer focused on the stimuli to which the amygdala is assigning significance. The amygdala also has an impressive set of connections with long-term memory networks involving the hippocampal system and areas of the cortex that interact with the hippocampus in long-lasting information storage. These pathways may contribute to the activation of long-term memories relevant to the emotional implications of immediately present stimuli. Although the amygdala has relatively meager connections with the lateral prefrontal cortex, it sends rather strong connections to the anterior cingulate cortex, one of the other partners in the frontal lobe working memory executive circuitry. It also sends connections to the orbital cortex, another player in working memory that may be especially involved in working memories about rewards and punishments. By way of these connections with specialized short-term buffers, long-term memory networks, and the networks of the frontal lobe, the amygdala can influence the information content of working memory (Figure 9-5). There is obviously a good deal of redundancy built into this system, making it possible for the conscious awareness of amygdala activity to come about in several ways.

In sum, connections from the amygdala to the cortex allow the defense networks of the amygdala to influence attention, perception, and memory in situations where we are facing danger. At the same time, though, these kinds of connections would seem to be inadequate in completely explaining why a perception, memory, or thought about an emotional event should "feel" different from one about a nonemotional event. They provide working memory with information about whether something good or bad is present, but are insufficient for producing the feelings that come from the awareness that something good or bad is present. For this we need other connections as well.

Ingredient 2: Amygdala-Triggered Arousal: In addition to the direct influences of the amygdala on the cortex, there are a number of indirect channels through which the effects of amygdala activation can impact on cortical processing. An extremely important set of such connections involves the arousal systems of the brain.

It has long been believed that the difference between being

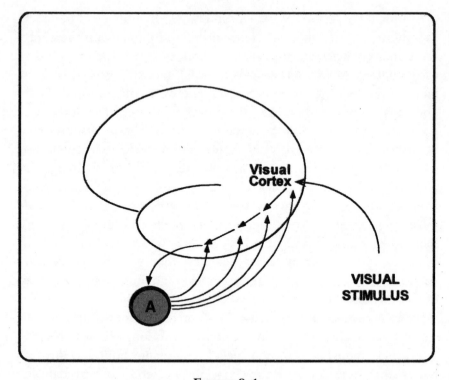

FIGURE 9-4

**The Amygdala's Influence on Sensory Areas of Cortex Is Greater
Than the Influence of the Same Areas on the Amygdala.**

*The amygdala receives inputs from the latest stages of cortical processing
within the sensory systems, but projects back to all stages of cortical processing,
even the earliest. An example from the visual system is shown.*

awake and alert, on the one hand, and drowsy or asleep on the other
is related to the arousal level of the cortex.[59] When you are alert and
paying attention to something important, your cortex is aroused.
When you are drowsy and not focusing on anything, the cortex is in
the unaroused state. During sleep, the cortex is in the unaroused
state, except during dream sleep when it is highly aroused. In dream
sleep, in fact, the cortex is in a state of arousal that is very similar to
the alert waking state, except that it has no access to external stimuli
and only processes internal events.[60]

Cortical arousal can be easily detected by putting electrodes on
the scalp of a human. These electrodes pick up the electrical activity

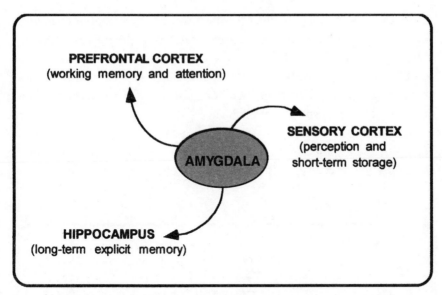

FIGURE 9-5
Some Cortical Outputs of the Amygdala and Their Function.

Areas of the amygdala project to a wide variety of cortical areas. Included are projections to all stages of cortical sensory processing (see figure 9-4), to prefrontal cortex, and to the hippocampus and related cortical areas. Through these projections, the amygdala can influence ongoing perceptions, mental imagery, attention, short-term memory, working memory, and long-term memory, as well as the various higher-order thought processes that these make possible.

of cortical cells through the skull. This electroencephalogram or EEG is slow and rhythmic when the cortex is not aroused and fast and out of sync (desynchronized) during arousal.

When arousal occurs, cells in the cortex, and in the thalamic regions that supply the cortex with its major inputs, become more sensitive.[61] They go from a state in which they tend to fire action potentials at a very slow rate and more or less in synchrony to a state in which they are generally out of sync but with some cells being driven especially strongly by incoming stimuli.

While much of the cortex is potentially hypersensitive to inputs during arousal, the systems that are processing information are able to make the most use of this effect. For example, if arousal is triggered by the sight of a snake, the neurons that are actively involved in processing the snake, retrieving long-term memories about snakes, and creating working memory representations of the snake are going to be especially affected by arousal. Other neurons are inactive at this point and don't reap the benefits. In this way, a very specific information-processing result is achieved by a very nonspecific mechanism (Figure 9-6). This is a wonderful trick.

A number of different systems appear to contribute to arousal. Four of these are located in regions of the brain stem. Each has a specific chemical identity, which means the cells in each contain differ-

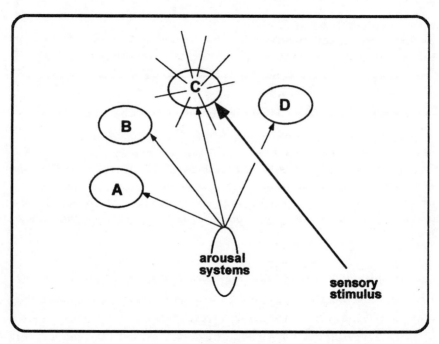

FIGURE 9-6
How Nonspecific Arousal Achieves a Specific Effect.

Arousal systems act in nonspecific ways throughout the forebrain. One of their main contributions is to make cells more sensitive to incoming signals. Those cells that are processing stimuli during arousal will be especially affected. In this way, very specific effects are achieved by nonspecific arousal. In the example shown, arousal systems potentially influence areas A, B, C, and D. However, the effects of arousal are greatest in area C, which is processing a stimulus. Other areas are inactive during arousal and thus do not reap the benefits of arousal.

ent neurotransmitters that are released by their axon terminals when the cells are activated. One group makes acetylcholine (ACh), another noradrenaline, another dopamine, and another serotonin. A fifth group, also containing ACh, is located in the forebrain, near the amygdala. The axons of each of these cell groups terminate in widespread areas of the forebrain. In the presence of novel or otherwise significant stimuli the axon terminals release their neurotransmitters and "arouse" cortical cells, making them especially receptive to incoming signals.

Arousal is important in all mental functions. It contributes significantly to attention, perception, memory, emotion, and problem solving. Without arousal, we fail to notice what is going on—we don't attend to the details. But too much arousal is not good either. If you are overaroused you become tense and anxious and unproductive. You need to have just the right level of activation to perform optimally.[62]

Emotional reactions are typically accompanied by intense cortical arousal. Certain emotion theories around mid-century proposed that emotions represent one end of an arousal continuum that spans from being completely unconscious (in a coma), to asleep, to awake but drowsy, to alert, to emotionally aroused. This high level of arousal is, in part, the explanation for why it is hard to concentrate on other things and work efficiently when you are in an emotional state. Arousal helps lock you into the emotional state you are in. This can be very useful (you don't want to get distracted when you are in danger), but can also be an annoyance (once the fear system is turned on, it's hard to turn it off—this is the nature of anxiety).

Although each of the arousal systems probably contributes to arousal in the presence of stimuli that are dangerous or that warn of danger, it appears that interactions between the amygdala and the nearby ACh-containing system in the forebrain are particularly important.[63] This ACh-containing system is called the nucleus basalis. Damage to the amygdala or to the nucleus basalis prevents stimuli that warn of danger, like conditioned fear stimuli, from eliciting arousal. Moreover, stimulation of the amygdala or the nucleus basalis elicits cortical arousal artificially. And administration of drugs that block the actions of ACh in the cortex prevents these effects on arousal of conditioned stimuli, amygdala stimulation, or nucleus basalis stimulation from occurring. Together, these and other findings suggest that when the amygdala detects danger it activates the nucleus basalis, which then releases ACh throughout the cortex. The amygdala also interacts with the other arousal systems located in the brain stem, and the overall effect of amygdala activation on arousal certainly involves these as well.[64]

Although there are a number of different ways that the nucleus basalis cells can be turned on, the way they are turned on by a dangerous stimulus is through the activity of the amygdala.[65] Other kinds of emotional networks most likely have their own ways of interacting with the arousal systems and altering cortical processing.

Arousal occurs to any novel stimulus that we encounter and not just to emotional stimuli. The difference is that a novel but insignificant stimulus will elicit a temporary state of arousal that dissipates almost immediately but arousal is prolonged in the presence of emotional stimuli. If you are face-to-face with a predator it is crucial that you not lose interest in what is going on or be distracted by some other event. While this seems so obvious as to be silly, it is only so because the brain does it so effortlessly.

Why is arousal perpetuated to emotional but not to other stimuli? Again, the answer probably has to do with the involvement of the amygdala. The arousal elicited by a novel stimulus does not require the amygdala. Instead, it is mediated by direct inputs from sensory systems to arousal networks.[66] These kinds of arousal effects quickly habituate. If the stimulus is meaningful, say dangerous, then the amygdala is brought into the act and it also activates arousal systems. This adds impetus to keep arousal going. The continued presence of the stimulus and its continued interpretation by the amygdala as dangerous continues to drive arousal systems, and these systems, in turn, keep cortical networks that are processing the stimulus in a state of hypersensitivity. The amygdala, it should be noted, is also the recipient of arousal system axons, so that amygdala activation of arousal systems also helps keep the amygdala aroused. These are self-perpetuating, vicious cycles of emotional reactivity. Arousal locks you into whatever emotional state you are in when arousal occurs, unless something else occurs that is significant enough and arousing enough to shift the focus of arousal.

The information content provided by arousal systems is weak. The cortex is unable to discern that danger (as opposed to some other emotional condition) exists from the pattern of neural messages it receives from arousal systems. Arousal systems simply say that something important is going on. The combination of nonspecific cortical arousal and specific information provided by direct projections from the amygdala to the cortex allows the establishment of a working memory that says that something important is going on and that it involves the fear system of the brain. These representations converge in working memory with the representations from specialized short-term memory buffers and with representations from long-term memory triggered by current stimuli and by amygdala processing. The continued driving of the amygdala by the dangerous stimulus keeps the arousal systems active, which keeps the amygdala and cortical networks actively engaged in the situation as well. Cognitive inference and decision making processes controlled by the working memory executive become actively focused on the emotionally arousing situation, trying to figure out what is going on and what should be done about it. All other inputs that are vying for the attention of working memory are blocked out.

We now have many of the basic ingredients for a complete emotional experience. But one more is needed.

Ingredient 3: Bodily Feedback: As we've seen in earlier chapters, activation of the amygdala results in the automatic activation of networks that control the expression of a variety of responses: species-specific behaviors (freezing, fleeing, fighting, facial expressions), autonomic nervous system (ANS) responses (changes in blood pressure and heart rate, piloerection, sweating), and hormonal responses (release of stress hormones, like adrenaline and adrenal steroids, as well as a host of peptides, into the bloodstream). The ANS and hormonal responses can be considered together as visceral responses—responses of the internal organs and glands (the viscera). When these behavioral and visceral responses are expressed, they create signals in the body that return to the brain.

The opportunities for bodily feedback during emotional reactions to influence information processing by the brain and the way we consciously feel are enormous. Nevertheless, much debate has occurred over whether feedback has any effect on emotional experience and if so how much (see Chapter 3). William James, you'll recall, is the father of the feedback theory. He argued that we do not cry because we are sad or run from danger because we are afraid, but instead we are sad because we cry and are afraid because we run. James was attacked by Cannon, who argued that feedback, especially from the viscera, would be too slow and undifferentiated to determine what emotion you are feeling at the moment. Let's ignore the fact that James included somatic as well as visceral feedback in his theory for now and just consider the validity of Cannon's claims about the viscera.

In Cannon's day, the visceral systems were indeed thought to respond uniformly in all situations. However, we now know that the ANS, which controls the viscera, has the ability to respond selectively, so that visceral organs can be activated in different ways in different situations. Recent studies show, for example, that different emotions (anger, fear, disgust, sadness, happiness, surprise) can be distinguished to some extent on the basis of different autonomic nervous system responses (like skin temperature and heart rate).[67]

The main hormone that was thought to be important for emotional experience in Cannon's time was adrenaline, which is under the control of the ANS and thus was thought to respond uniformly in different situations. However, we now know that there are steroid and peptide hormones that are released by body organs during emotional arousal and that travel in the blood to the brain. It is conceivable that activation of different emotional systems in the brain results in different patterns of hormone release from body organs, which in turn would produce different patterns of chemical feedback to the brain that could have unique effects in different emotions.

Regardless of their specificity, though, visceral responses have relatively slow actions, too slow in fact to be the factor that determines what emotion you experience in a given moment. At a minimum, it takes a second or two for signals to travel from the brain to the viscera and then for the viscera to respond and for the signals created by these responses to return to the brain. For some systems the delay is even longer. It's not so much the travel time from the brain to the organs by way of nerve pathways that's slow, it's the response time of the organs themselves. Visceral organs are made up of what is called "smooth muscle," which responds much more slowly than the striated muscles that move our skeleton during behavioral acts. Also, for hormonal responses the travel time in the blood to the brain can be slow, and for some hormones (like adrenal steroids) the effects on the brain can require the synthesis of new proteins and can take hours to be achieved.

On the other hand, emotional states are dynamic. For example, fear can turn into anger or disgust or relief as an emotional episode unfolds, and it is possible that visceral feedback contributes to these emotional changes over time. While arousal is nonspecific and tends to lock you into the state you are in when the arousal occurs, unique patterns of visceral, especially chemical, feedback have the potential for altering which brain systems are active and thus may contribute to transitions from one emotion to another within a given emotional event.

So Cannon was on target about the inability of visceral responses to determine emotional feelings, but more because of their slow time course than their lack of specificity. At the same time, though, Cannon's critique was somewhat inappropriate given that James had argued for the importance of somatic as well as visceral feedback. And the somatic system clearly has the requisite speed and specificity to contribute to emotional experiences (it takes much less than a second for your striated muscles to respond to a stimulus and for the sensations from these responses to reach your cortex). This point was noted many years ago by Sylvan Tomkins and was the basis of his facial feedback theory of emotion,[68] which has been taken up and pursued in recent years by Carroll Izard.[69]

While most contemporary ideas about somatic feedback and emotional experience have been about feedback from facial expressions, a recent theory by Antonio Damasio, the somatic marker hypothesis, calls upon the entire pattern of somatic and visceral feedback from the body.[70] Damasio proposes that such information underlies "gut feelings" and plays a crucial role in our emotional experiences and decision making processes.

When all the interactions between the various systems are taken together, the possibilities for the generation of emotion-specific patterns of feedback are staggering. This is especially true when considered from the point of view of what would be necessary to scientifically document the existence of these patterns, or, even more difficult, to prove that feedback is not important.

One approach to this problem has been to study emotional feelings in persons who have spinal cord injuries, in whom the flow of information from the brain to the body and from the body back to the brain is, to a great degree, interrupted. An early study claimed that patients with the most severe damage had a dulling of the intensity of emotional feelings and a reduction in the range of emotions experienced, lending support to the idea that feedback plays an important role.[71] Later studies suggest that the first study was flawed and that when the experiment is done properly no deficits in emotional feelings result.[72] However, spinal cord injury does not completely interrupt information flow between the brain and body. For example, spinal cord injury can spare the vagus nerve, which transmits much information from the visceral organs to the brain, and it also fails to interfere with the flow of hormones and peptides from the brain to the body and from the body to the brain. And, of course, the nerves controlling facial movements and sending sensations from facial movements back to the brain are intact, since these go directly between the brain and face without going through the spinal cord. Failure to find a dulling of emotional experiences, or a restriction of the range of emotional experiences, in these patients does not really prove anything.[73]

There is one remaining argument against a contribution of feedback to emotion that needs to be considered. Although somatic responses, like facial or somatic muscle movements, have the requisite speed and specificity to contribute to emotional feelings, it has been argued that these cannot do the trick either. The same response (like running) can occur during different emotions (running to obtain food or to escape from danger) and diametrically opposed responses can occur during the same emotion (we can run or freeze in fear). While these comments are obviously true, it is important to remember that bodily feedback occurs in a biological context. Bodily feedback, when detected by the brain, is recorded by the systems that produced the responses in the first place. Although we may run both to get food and to escape from danger, the feedback from the somatic and visceral responses that return to the brain will interact with different systems in these two instances. The feedback from running from danger will find the food-seeking system idle but the defense system active. The same pattern of feedback can have unique contributions when it interacts with specific brain systems.

William James said that he found it impossible to imagine an emotional experience occurring in the absence of the bodily responses that accompany it—he didn't believe in disembodied emotions.[74] I have to agree for several reasons. First of all, it seems from personal experience that emotions work this way. Most of us feel our emotions in our body, which is why we have such expressions as "an aching heart" and a "gut-wrenching" experience. While personal experience is not a good way to prove anything (we've seen the perils of introspection as scientific data), there's nothing wrong with using it as a takeoff point for a more penetrating analysis. Second, the evidence against feedback playing a role is weak—the spinal cord studies are inconclusive at best. Third, there is plenty of feedback available during emotional responses, and quite a bit of it is fast enough and specific enough to play a role in subjective experiences. Fourth, studies by Paul Ekman and by Robert Zajonc have shown that feedback is indeed used.[75] For example, Ekman had subjects move certain facial muscles. Unbeknownst to the subjects, they were being made to exhibit the facial expressions characteristic of different emotions. They then had to answer some questions about their mood. It turns out that the way the subjects felt was significantly influenced by whether they had been wearing positive or negative emotion expressions. Putting on a happy face may not be such a bad idea when you are feeling blue.

It's hard to believe that after all these years we actually still don't have a clear and definitive understanding of the role of body states in emotions. However, I'm placing my bets in favor of feedback playing a role. Emotional systems evolved as ways of matching bodily responses with the demands being made by the environment, and I can't see many ways that a full-blooded emotional feeling could exist without a body attached to the brain that is trying to have the feeling.

There is one way, though, that should be mentioned. It involves what Damasio calls "as if" loops. In certain situations, it may be possible to imagine what bodily feedback would feel like if it occurred. This "as if" feedback then becomes cognitively represented in working memory and can influence feelings and decisions. We saw evidence that this could occur in Chapter 3 when we considered a study by Valins. He gave subjects false feedback about their heart rate. Their belief that their heart rate was changing was enough to make them feel as though they were emotionally aroused and that they liked certain pictures more than others. This kind of situation, obviously, could only exist in a brain that had experienced real feedback many times so that the way feedback feels and works could be imagined and used to actually influence subjective experiences. This reinforces, rather than questions, the role of body states in emotional feelings.

Feelings: The Bare Essentials

We now have all the ingredients of an emotional feeling, all the things needed to turn an emotional reaction into a conscious emotional experience. We've got a specialized emotion system that receives sensory inputs and produces behavioral, autonomic, and hormonal responses. We've got cortical sensory buffers that hold on to information about the currently present stimuli. We've got a working memory executive that keeps track of the short-term buffers, retrieves information from long-term memory, and interprets the contents of the short-term buffers in terms of activated long-term memories. We also have cortical arousal. And finally, we have bodily feedback—somatic and visceral information that returns to the brain during an act of emotional responding. When all of these systems function together a conscious emotional experience is inevitable. When some components are present and others lacking, emotional experiences may still occur, depending on what's there and what's not. Let's see what's dispensable and indispensable for the emotion fear.

- You *can't* have a conscious emotional feeling of being afraid without aspects of the emotional experience being represented in working memory. Working memory is the gateway to subjective experiences, emotional and nonemotional ones, and is indispensable in the creation of a conscious emotional feeling.

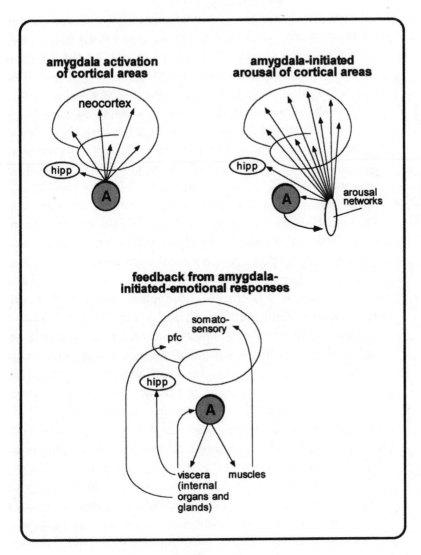

FIGURE 9-7
Some *Neural* Ingredients of a Conscious Emotional Experience.

Conscious emotional experiences are made up of a number of ingredients. Some of the factors that contribute are illustrated, including direct inputs from the amygdala to cortical areas (sensory and higher-order processing regions), inputs from the amygdala to nonspecific arousal systems and from these to widespread areas of the forebrain (cortical and subcortical areas), and feedback to the amygdala and cortical areas from the bodily expression of emotion. Note that the bodily expressions (visceral and muscular) are themselves controlled by the amygdala. A, amygdala; hipp, hippocampus; pfc, prefrontal cortex.

- You *can't* have a complete feeling of fear without the activation of the amygdala. In the presence of a fear-arousing stimulus, and the absence of amygdala activation (for example, if your amygdala were damaged), you might use your cognitive powers to conclude that in situations like this you usually feel "fearful," but the fearful feelings would be lacking because of the importance of amygdala inputs to working memory, of amygdala-triggered arousal, and of amygdala-mediated bodily responses that produce feedback. Cognitive mechanisms, like "as-if" loops, might compensate to some extent, but they can't fully.[76]

- You *can't* have a sustained feeling of fear without the activation of arousal systems. These play an essential role in keeping conscious attention directed toward the emotional situation, and without their involvement emotional states would be fleeting. You might be temporarily aroused but your emotion would dissipate as soon as it occurred. Although all novel stimuli activate arousal systems, particularly important to the persistence of emotional responses and emotional feelings is the activation of arousal systems by the amygdala. Amygdala-triggered arousal not only arouses the cortex but also arouses the amygdala, causing the latter to continue to activate the arousal systems, creating the vicious cycles of emotional arousal.

- You *can't* have a sustained emotional experience without feedback from the body or without at least long-term memories that allow the creation of "as-if" feedback. But even "as-if" feedback has to be taught by real-life feedback. The body is crucial to an emotional experience, either because it provides sensations that make an emotion feel a certain way right now or because it once provided the sensations that created memories of what specific emotions felt like in the past.

- You probably *can* have an emotional feeling without the direct projections to the cortex from the amygdala. These help working memory know which specialized emotion system is active, but this can be figured out indirectly. Nevertheless, the emotion will be different in the absence of this input than in its presence.

- You *can* have an emotional feeling without being conscious of the eliciting stimulus—without the actual eliciting stimulus being represented in a short-term cortical buffer and held in working memory. As we saw in Chapter 3, stimuli that are not noticed, or that are noticed but their implications aren't, can unconsciously trigger emotional behaviors and visceral responses. In such situations, the stimulus content of working memory will be amplified by the arousal and feedback that result, causing you to attribute the arousal and bodily feelings to the stimuli that are present in working memory. However, because the stimuli in working memory did not trigger the amygdala, the situation will be misdiagnosed (recall Schachter and Singer's subjects who were artificially aroused and who misattributed their arousal to their surroundings). And if there is nothing particular occupying working memory, you will be in a situation where your feelings are not understood. If emotions are triggered by stimuli that are processed unconsciously, you will not be able to later reflect back on those experiences and explain why they occurred with any degree of accuracy. Contrary to the primary supposition of cognitive appraisal theories, the core of an emotion is not an introspectively accessible conscious representation. Feelings do involve conscious content, but we don't necessarily have conscious access to the processes that produce the content. And even when we do have introspective access, the conscious content is not likely to be what triggered the emotional responses in the first place. The emotional responses and the conscious content are both products of specialized emotion systems that operate unconsciously.

What's Different About Thoughts and Feelings?

Conscious emotional feelings and conscious thoughts are in some sense very similar. They both involve the symbolic representation in working memory of subsymbolic processes carried out by systems that work unconsciously. The difference between them is not due to the system that does the consciousness part but instead is due to two other factors. One is that emotional feelings and mere thoughts are generated by different subsymbolic systems. The other is that emotional feelings involve many more brain systems than thoughts.

When we are in the throes of emotion, it is because something important, perhaps life threatening, is occurring, and much of the brain's resources are brought to bear on the problem. Emotions create a flurry of activity all devoted to one goal. Thoughts, unless they trigger emotional systems, don't do this. We can daydream while doing other things, like reading or eating, and go back and forth between the daydream and the other activities. But when faced with danger or other challenging emotional situations, we don't have time to kill nor do we have spare mental resources. The whole self gets absorbed in the emotion. As Klaus Scherer has argued, emotions cause a mobilization and synchronization of the brain's activities.[77]

Do Fish Have Feelings Too?

Philosophers have something called "the problem of other minds." In simple terms, it is the difficulty, if not the impossibility, of proving that anyone, other than oneself, is conscious. This is an onerous problem that applies both to the minds of other humans and other animals. We are somewhat better off in the case of other humans than other animals though. Depending on how strict we are (philosophically), we can usually convince ourselves that most other humans have emotional feelings and other conscious states of mind because we can talk to them and compare notes about our mental experiences with them—this is one of the beauties of having natural language. We may not be completely justified philosophically in our conclusion that other people are conscious, but from a practical point of view it is useful to live our lives in violation of philosophical certainty and treat others as if they are conscious. Fortunately, though, there is another reason to adopt the belief that other humans are conscious. Since all humans have pretty much the same kind of brain architecture we can assume that, barring pathological conditions, the same general kinds of functions come out of all human brains—if I'm conscious and you have the same kind of brain that I do, then you are probably conscious as well. This kind of reasoning holds for brain functions that we know something about (like perception and memory), so we might reasonably expect it to also hold for conscious awareness.

But no matter how firm or flimsy the arguments about consciousness in other humans are, when it comes to making the leap to the minds of other animals, we are on considerably shakier ground. Our ability to hold conversations with other animals is somewhere between not at all and not much.[78] And while our brain is, in many ways, incredibly similar to the brains of other creatures (this is what makes much of brain research possible), it also differs in some important ways. The human brain, most especially the cerebral cortex, is much larger than it should be, given our body size.[79] This alone would give us reason to be cautious about attributing consciousness to other animals. However, there are other facts to take into account. First, as we've seen, the part of the human cortex that has increased in size the most is the prefrontal cortex,[80] which is the part of the brain that has been implicated in working memory, the gateway to consciousness. Some brain scientists believe that this part of the cortex doesn't even exist except in primates.[81] And there is behavioral evidence that only the higher primates, in whom the prefrontal cortex is especially well developed, are self-aware, as determined by their ability to recognize themselves in a mirror.[82] Second, natural language only exists in the human brain.[83] Although the exact nature of the brain specialization involved in making language possible is not fully understood, something changed with the evolution of the human brain to make language happen. Not surprisingly, the development of language has often been said to be the key to human consciousness.[84] Clearly, the human brain is sufficiently different from the brains of other animals to give us reasons for being very cautious about attributing consciousness beyond our species. As a result, the arguments that allow us to say with some degree of confidence that other humans have conscious states do not allow us to insert consciousness into the mental life of most other animals.

My idea about consciousness in other animals is this. Consciousness is something that happened after the cortex expanded in mammals. It requires the capacity to relate several things at once (for example, the way a stimulus looks, memories of past experiences with that stimulus or related stimuli, a conception of the self as the experiencer).[85] A brain that cannot form these relations, due to the absence of a cortical system that can put all of the information together at the same time, cannot be conscious. Consciousness, so defined, is undoubtedly present in humans. To the extent that other animals have the capacity to hold and manipulate information in a generalized mental workspace, they probably also have the potential capacity to be conscious. This formulation allows the possibility that some other mammals, especially (but not exclusively) some other primates, are conscious. However, in humans, the presence of natural language alters the brain significantly. Often we categorize and label our experiences in linguistic terms, and store the experiences in ways that can be accessed linguistically. Whatever consciousness exists outside of humans is likely to be very different from the kind of consciousness that we have.

The bottom line is this. Human consciousness is the way it is because of the way our brain is. Other animals may also be conscious in their own special way due to the way their brains are. And still others are probably not conscious at all, again due to the kinds of brains they have. At the same time, though, consciousness is neither the prerequisite to nor the same thing as the capacity to think and reason. An animal can solve lots of problems without being overtly conscious of what it is doing and why it is doing it. Obviously, consciousness elevates thinking to a new level, but it isn't the same thing as thinking.

Emotional feelings result when we become consciously aware that an emotion system of the brain is active. Any organism that has consciousness also has feelings. However, feelings will be different in a brain that can classify the world linguistically and categorize experiences in words than in a brain that cannot. The difference between fear, anxiety, terror, apprehension, and the like would not be possible without language. At the same time, none of these words would have any point if it were not for the existence of an underlying emotion system that generates the brain states and bodily expressions to which these words apply. Emotions evolved not as conscious feelings, linguistically differentiated or otherwise, but as brain states and bodily responses. The brain states and bodily responses are the fundamental facts of an emotion, and the conscious feelings are the frills that have added icing to the emotional cake.

Qué Será Será

Where is evolution taking our brain? While it is true that whatever will be will be, we have the opportunity to take a peek at what evolution is up to. It's not that evolution is forward thinking. It only has hindsight.[86] However, we *are* evolution in progress and we can see what sorts of changes might be happening in our brain by looking at trends in brain evolution across related species.

As things now stand, the amygdala has a greater influence on the cortex than the cortex has on the amygdala, allowing emotional arousal to dominate and control thinking. Throughout the mammals, pathways from the amygdala to the cortex overshadow the pathways from the cortex to the amygdala. Although thoughts can easily trigger emotions (by activating the amygdala), we are not very effective at willfully turning off emotions (by deactivating the amygdala). Telling yourself that you should not be anxious or depressed does not help much.

At the same time, it is apparent that the cortical connections with the amygdala are far greater in primates than in other mammals. This suggests the possibility that as these connections continue to expand, the cortex might gain more and more control over the amygdala, possibly allowing future humans to be better able to control their emotions.

Yet, there is another possibility. The increased connectivity between the amygdala and cortex involves fibers going from the cortex to the amygdala as well as from the amygdala to the cortex. If these nerve pathways strike a balance, it is possible that the struggle between thought and emotion may ultimately be resolved not by the dominance of emotional centers by cortical cognitions, but by a more harmonious integration of reason and passion. With increased connectivity between the cortex and amygdala, cognition and emotion might begin to work together rather than separately.

Oscar Wilde once said, "It is because Humanity has never known where it was going that it has been able to find its way."[87] But wouldn't it be wonderful if we did understand where our emotions were taking us from moment to moment, day to day, and year to year, and why? If the trends toward cognitive-emotional connectivity in the brain are any indication, our brains may, in fact, be moving in this direction.

NOTES

CHAPTER 1: WHAT'S LOVE GOT TO DO WITH IT?

1. Dreiser (1900).
2. The study of emotions in brain science has gone through cycles. We'll review this history in detail in Chapter 4. For now, I'll just note that neuroscientists have, in recent decades, been much more interested in the intellectual or cognitive aspects of the mind than in emotions. However, this is starting to change. Although there are still relatively few neuroscientists who claim *emotions* as their main interest, emotional functions of the brain are becoming more popular as research topics. There are several reasons for this shift. One has to do with the recognition that the mind is more than cognition, so that the focus on cognitive processes by neuroscientists only reveals part of the mind. Another is the realization that the subjective states of awareness that accompany emotions are just part of the overall emotion process, and that much can be learned by studying how the brain processes stimuli and controls objectively measured responses in emotional situations. Since stimulus processing and response control can be studied in animals, but subjective awareness cannot, a focus on processing and responses has facilitated research. These notions are developed further in Chapters 2 and 3.
3. Gazzaniga, Bogen, and Sperry (1962); Gazzaniga, Bogen, and Sperry (1965); Gazzaniga (1970).
4. Bogen and Vogel (1962).
5. D. Wilson, et al (1977).
6. Our research on the Dartmouth patients between 1974 and 1978 is summarized in Gazzaniga and LeDoux (1978).
7. Gazzaniga (1972).

8. Studies of this patient are described in Gazzaniga and LeDoux (1978).
9. See Davidson (1992); Heilman and Satz (1983); Gainotti (1972).
10. A similar point was made by E. Duffy in the 1940s [Duffy (1941)]. However, while Duffy wished to do away with talk about emotion, I want to understand what emotions are. The key is the use of the plural rather than the singular. I don't think that there is anything called "emotion" but I do believe that there are lots of "emotions."

CHAPTER 2: SOULS ON ICE

1. This quote was seen on the wall behind the counter at Kim's Underground Video in Greenwich Village in Manhattan.
2. Melville (1930).
3. Bangs (1978).
4. Theories of emotion will be discussed in this chapter and Chapter 3.
5. Fehr and Russell (1984).
6. Plato, *Phaedo,* cited in Flew (1964).
7. Gardner (1987).
8. Watson (1929); Skinner (1938).
9. Actually, psychology, as a field of science, did not exist until the late nineteenth century, when it emerged in Germany as the experimental study of consciousness [see Boring (1950)]. Before that, mental phenomena were the business of philosophers. And following Descartes' proclamation, "I think therefore I am," mind and consciousness came to be equated in Western philosophical discussions, a trend that was inherited by scientific psychology when it emerged. For a translation of some of Descartes' key writings, see Smith (1958). For a summary of the importance of Descartes' views in forcing the modern equation of mind as consciousness, see Rorty (1979). According to Rorty, mind and consciousness were not such interchangeable ideas before Descartes introduced the notion of an all-knowing soul (consciousness), that had no unknowable (unconscious) aspects. If it wasn't knowable (available to conscious) it wasn't mental. In this way, certain things that we consider mental today (like sensations and some aspects of emotions) were demoted to physical states by Descartes.
10. Ryle (1949).
11. The following summary is based on Gardner (1987).
12. Putnam (1960).
13. Rorty (1979).
14. Lashley (1950b).
15. Neisser (1976); Gardner (1987); Kihlstrom (1987).

16. For example, an abacus is a computer made of sticks and stones. It does calculations using an algorithm or program that is built into its design. For some problems, it is as effective as (and in some instances more practical than) an electronic computer.

17. Kihlstrom (1987).

18. Freud (1925). For a reinterpretation of Freudian concepts in terms of cognitive science, see Erdelyi (1985).

19. Erdelyi (1985).

20. These are sometimes called preperceptual or preattentive processes. For example, in visual perception, the determination of the intensity of light reflecting from different parts of a stimulus or the direction of movement of a stimulus occur preconsciously. For a discussion of these processes, see Marr (1982); Ullman (1984).

21. Kosslyn and Koenig (1992); Kosslyn (1983); Kosslyn (1980). For a challenge to Kosslyn's theory, see Pylyshyn (1984).

22. Pinker (1994).

23. Nisbett and Wilson (1977).

24. However, not everyone agrees with the strong claims made by Nisbett and Wilson. For example, following Nisbett and Wilson's study, Ericcson and Simon (1984) attempted to identify whether there might be some kinds of conscious introspections that could be trusted. After an exhaustive study, they concluded that verbal reports about the state of one's mind can be used reliably to indicate the outcome of a decision (whether one thing is bigger than another, whether you like or dislike something, or whether you plan to do something) but that such reports are less reliable about the processes leading up to a decision, especially if there is some delay between the occurrence of the process and the report. They emphasized that information in short-term memory is most accessible, allowing for accurate descriptions of processes as they occur or shortly thereafter, but once information decays from or is displaced from short-term memory, accessibility can decline. Some say that since the events that cause a behavior or mental state typically occur right before the behavior or state, we typically have conscious access to causes because the causal events are still in short-term memory, a view sometimes known as folk psychology [see Goldman (1993); Churchland (1984); Arnold (1960); Johnson-Laird and Oatley (1992); Oatley and Duncan (1994)]. However, in my mind, this view is problematic in at least three respects. First, it assumes that all of the stimuli that have significant mental effects occupy short-term memory and thus are noticed and appreciated. As we will see in the next chapter, some things are not noticed but still influence us, and other things are fully noticed

but their significance is processed implicitly and not consciously appreciated. This latter point means that stimuli that are consciously perceived can have important unconscious effects, influencing our emotions, goals, and attitudes without our being aware that they are being influenced. Second, it assumes that the stimuli that provoke behavior are what cause it, which is not necessarily the case. Innocuous events can set us off if we are in a bad mood. The mood, more than the eliciting stimulus, is the cause in such situations. Third, it assumes that we can correctly identify from the many stimuli that were available the exact ones that actually elicited the response. Obviously, we are often correct, otherwise life would be chaotic and impossible (incidentally, the chaotic and impossible life of persons suffering from mental illness may represent a breakdown in these mechanisms, either the introspective one, the attribution one, or the balance between them). But whether we are correct about causes because we have introspective access to causal events or because we are very good at attributing cause on the basis of noticing correlations is less clear. Regardless, even if we wholly accept the Ericsson and Simon view, that some aspects of cognition can be characterized on the basis of introspective verbal reports, there remains room for much of the cognitive mind to operate below the tip of the iceberg. For a discussion of some additional issues, see Bowers and Meichenbaum (1984); Miller and Gazzaniga (1984); Marcel and Bisiach (1988). Also, see the June 1992 issue of *American Psychologist*, which has numerous articles on this topic.

25. Gazzaniga and LeDoux (1978).
26. For summary, see Gazzaniga (1970).
27. These ideas are elaborated on and expanded in Gazzaniga (1985); Gazzaniga (1988); LeDoux (1985).
28. I am grateful to several people for their discussions with me about unconscious processing, including Daniel Schacter, Matthew Erdelyi, John Bargh, and John Kihlstrom. From their comments, and from my own reading of the literature, several methodological problems that plague studies of unconscious processing of stimuli are apparent. One is that much of the work has involved subliminal perception or masking, both of which involve very brief stimulus exposures. This limits the amount of information that can be presented at one time and also limits the amount of cognitive resources that can be dedicated to the processing task. It is likely that the limits of the unconscious found through such studies reflect, at least to some extent, methodological limitations rather than the real limits of unconscious processing. Another problem with the arguments against the existence of a sophisti-

cated cognitive unconscious is the fact that most of the work has used verbal stimuli (words, sentences) to test processing limits. These are the currency of the systems that are involved in conscious processing, which is an evolutionarily new system. Unconscious processing, on the other hand, is the stock-in-trade of evolutionarily old systems that are likely to be more readily studied with nonverbal measures. Indeed, some of the strongest evidence for unconscious processing comes from studies using pictorial rather than verbal stimuli. These studies will be examined in Chapter 3. Another methodological problem is that of drawing the line between conscious and unconscious processing. Several recent attempts to use more sophisticated analytic techniques to draw the line have been made. Included is work by Merikle, Jacoby, Erdelyi, Bargh, and Kihlstrom (citations below). Each of these concludes that the cognitive unconscious can process significant meanings. Also, as indicated in the text, stimuli that are consciously processed can also be processed by unconscious systems, which may in fact do different things with them; and stimuli that are noticed and attended to can have important unconscious influences because it is their activation of unconscious meanings that is most important, not their physical features. These ideas are elaborated on further in the next chapter. A sampling of citations include: Merikle (1992); Kihlstrom, Barnhardt, and Tataryn (1992); Erdelyi (1992); Bargh (1992); Bargh (1990); Jacoby et al (1992).

29. Bowers (1984); Bowers and Meichenbaum (1984); Bargh (1992); Bargh (1990); Jacoby et al (1992).
30. Posner (1990); Anderson (1990); Kosslyn and Koenig (1992); Gardner (1987).
31. The mind-body problem, the problem of how the mind relates to the brain and the rest of the body, is a deeply troubling philosophical problem. It has always been a thorn in the side of psychology. For a nice summary of the issues involved see Churchland (1984). For a summary of the early impact on psychology, see Boring (1950). The mind-body problem and its relation to cognitive science is discussed in Gardner (1987). Another discussion of the mind-body problem that I like is in Jackendoff (1987).
32. As I was finalizing this book there was a very exciting chess match going on in Philadelphia between grand master Gary Kasparov and a computer. The computer gave Kasparov a run for his money.
33. Gardner (1987).
34. Neisser (1967).
35. Fodor (1975).

36. Von Eckardt (1993).
37. Russell (1905).
38. Fodor (1975).
39. The history of artificial intelligence is nicely summarized in Gardner (1987).
40. The following summary of the work of Johnson-Laird and Kahnemann and Tversky is based on a description in Gardner (1987).
41. Johnson-Laird (1988).
42. Kahneman, Slovic, and Tversky (1982).
43. Frank (1988).
44. Tooby and Cosmides (1990).
45. Goleman (1995).
46. Aristotle (1941); de Sousa (1980); Solomon (1993).
47. Damasio (1994).
48. Dyer (1987); Scherer (1993b); Frijda and Swagerman (1987); Sloman (1987); Grossberg (1982); Armony et al (1995).
49. Johnson-Laird (1988).
50. Simon (1967).
51. Abelson (1963).
52. Miller and Johnson-Laird (1976).
53. Newell, Rosenblum, and Laird (1989).
54. Hilgard (1980).
55. Churchland and Sejnowski (1990).
56. We'll discuss the bodily responses in emotions in Chapters 3–6.
57. James (1884).

CHAPTER 3: BLOOD, SWEAT, AND TEARS

1. Crockett (1845).
2. James (1884).
3. Ibid.
4. Cannon (1929).
5. To be fair, though, it is important to note that James proposed that the whole body response in an emotion determines the feedback, not just the ANS response.
6. Modern research on bodily responses suggests that there may be more specificity than proposed by Cannon [see Ekman et al (1983); Levenson (1992); Cacioppo et al (1993)].
7. Watson (1929); Watson and Rayner (1920); Skinner (1938); Duffy (1941); Lindsley (1951).
8. Ryle (1949).

9. Schachter and Singer (1962).

10. Valins (1966).

11. Frijda (1986); Plutchik (1980).

12. Aristotle (1941); Spinoza (1955); Descartes (1958).

13. Arnold (1960).

14. Lazarus (1966).

15. Lazarus (1991).

16. See Frijda (1993); Scherer (1993a); Lazarus (1991); C.A. Smith and P.C. Ellsworth (1985); Ortony and Turner (1990).

17. C.A. Smith and P.C. Ellsworth (1985).

18. See Frijda (1993); Scherer (1988).

19. Zajonc (1980).

20. Bornstein (1992).

21. The New Look in psychology got going as a result of studies by Jerry Bruner [Bruner and Postman (1947)]. It quickly faded, was revived by an article by M. Erdelyi in the mid-1970s [Erdelyi (1974)], slipped away again, but has returned for a third time [Greenwald (1992)].

22. Psychology and psychoanalysis, though both seek to understand mind and behavior, take very different approaches.

23. Erdelyi (1974).

24. The irony is that verbal reports are mainly useful as a means of knowing what a subject is consciously aware of. In adopting verbal reports, behaviorists were befriending the very concept that behaviorism sought to do away with—consciousness.

25. McGinnies (1949); Dixon (1971).

26. Lazarus and McCleary (1951).

27. Loftus and Klinger (1992).

28. Moore (1988).

29. Packard (1957).

30. Eagly and Chaiken (1993).

31. Eriksen (1960).

32. For discussion, see Bowers (1984); Bowers and Meichenbaum (1984).

33. Erdelyi (1974); Erdelyi (1985).

34. Dixon (1971); Dixon (1981); Wolitsky and Wachtel (1973); Erdelyi (1985); Erdelyi (1992); Ionescu and Erdelyi (1992); Greenwald (1992).

35. Merikle (1992); Kihlstrom, Barnhardt, and Tataryn (1992a); Erdelyi (1992); Bargh (1992); Bargh (1990); Jacoby et al (1992); Murphy and Zajonc (1993).

36. Bornstein (1992).

37. Ibid.

38. Murphy and Zajonc (1993).

39. This discussion of the Pöetzl effect is based on Ionescu and Erdelyi (1992).
40. Erdelyi (1985); Erdelyi (1992); Ionescu and Erdelyi (1992).
41. Bowers (1984); Bowers and Meichenbaum (1984).
42. Shevrin et al (1992); also see Shevrin (1992).
43. Bargh (1992); Bargh (1990).
44. Jacoby et al (1992).
45. Bargh (1992).
46. Merikle (1992); Kihlstrom, Barnhardt, and Tataryn (1992b); Erdelyi (1992); Bargh (1992); Bargh (1990); Jacoby et al (1992).
47. Nevertheless, the relevance of unconscious emotional processing for everyday life needs to be carefully considered. I will describe two of the main arguments against the relevance of unconscious processing and attempt to refute both. Both accept that unconscious processing can exist in the laboratory but question whether it is very meaningful in life. The first argument is that life does not work the way unconscious processing tasks (subliminal perception, masking, or shadowing) do since we normally have the opportunity to look at or listen to the stimuli we encounter. However, life may be more like these experiments than it seems. After all, at any one moment there are more stimuli available than can be registered by the limited-capacity serial-processing system that gives rise to conscious content (see Chapter 9). Stimuli that are not noticed can be implicitly perceived and implicitly remembered by unconscious processing systems that chug away outside of awareness (see Chapter 2). At the same time, as we saw in the present chapter, stimuli that are fully perceptible, and even stimuli that are fully perceived and consciously registered, can enter the brain and their implicit meanings can activate goals, attitudes, and emotions without our being aware of these influences. The second argument against the relevance of unconscious processing says that while it may happen during everyday life, it is a fairly unsophisticated form of processing, being limited to physical stimulus features rather than to concepts [for this argument, see: Greenwald (1992); Bruner (1992); Hirst (1994)]. There are three rebuttals to this. The first is that there is in fact evidence for the unconscious processing of conceptual meanings as well as physical features [see Murphy and Zajonc (1993); Öhman (1992); Kihlstrom, Barnhardt, and Tataryn (1992)]. It has been admittedly more difficult to demonstrate unconscious conceptual priming, but it seems to exist. Second, we may not have a very accurate picture of the sophistication of unconscious processing. Most of the work done so far has used verbal stimuli to analyze conceptual processing, but the unconscious mind

may work more fluently in nonverbal modalities (as we'll discuss at the end of this chapter). We will probably not gain an accurate picture of how the more basic unconscious systems work as long as most work on unconscious processing is done using verbal stimuli. Third, some of the best evidence for unconscious processing comes from studies of emotional processing, which is particularly resistant to verbalization. Finally, even if it were true that unconscious perception is limited to stimulus features, as opposed to higher order concepts, there would be important implications for the unconscious emotional processing. As we have seen, primitive physical features of a person, like the color of their skin or the intonation of their voice, are sufficient to unconsciously activate emotions, attitudes, goals, and intentions.

48. Damasio (1994).
49. Arnold (1960); Johnson-Laird and Oatley (1992); Oatley and Duncan (1994); Goldman (1993).
50. S.J. Gould (1977).
51. Hebb (1946).
52. Rorty (1980).
53. Frijda (1993).
54. Scherer (1943a).
55. Bowers (1984).
56. Lazarus (1991).
57. Scherer (1943a).
58. Ericsson and Simon (1984); Nisbett and Wilson (1977); Bowers and Meichenbaum (1984); Miller and Gazzaniga (1984). Also, see Chapter 2 and footnote 24 in Chapter 2 for some discussion of these issues.
59. Erdelyi (1992).
60. Zajonc (1984); Lazarus (1984); Kleinginna and Kleinginna (1985); Leventhal and Scherer (1987).
61. Dyer (1987); K.R. Scherer (1993b); Frijda and Swagerman (1987); Sloman (1987); Grossberg (1982); Armony et al (1995).
62. Some AI proponents assume that emotional feelings and other states of consicousness could be programnmed into a computer if we could just get the right algorithm. For example, see: Newell (1980); Minsky (1985); Sloman and Croucher (1981). For a rebuttal to the notion that computers might have feelings or other conscious states, see Searle (1984).
63. Messick (1963), p. 317.
64. Kelley (1963), p. 222.
65. Ibid.

CHAPTER 4: THE HOLY GRAIL

1. Paraphrased from my memory of a line from a Woody Allen film.
2. MacLean (1949); MacLean (1952).
3. Boring (1950).
4. It is widely believed that Gall was the father of phrenology, but it turns out, according to Mark Rosenzweig [Rosenzweig (1996)], that Gall called his theory "organology" and it was his followers who popularized this view and turned it into "phrenology."
5. See Boring (1950).
6. However, there is still a modern antilocalizationist movement. John (1972) and Freeman (1994) are proponents.
7. Blindness due to cortical damage is called "cortical blindness." However, people who are cortically blind still have some rudimentary visual perception that operates outside of consciousness. Thus, they can reach toward a stimulus in front of them, but claim not to see it. For more information, see Weiskrantz (1988).
8. Van Essen (1985); Ungerleider and Mishkin (1982).
9. Although it is possible for the functions of a cortical area to be taken over by neighboring tissue if that area is damaged in early life, once the function has developed, such replacements do not normally occur.
10. Darwin (1859).
11. For a history of early studies using stimulation and ablation, see Boring (1950).
12. For a history of early neurological studies of humans, see Plum and Volpe (1987).
13. Animal experiments can yield very detailed information and can be used to elucidate the basic neural systems underlying psychological functions. Human findings have traditionally been based on accidents of nature rather than careful experiments. However, new imaging techniques, which allow the visualization of brain activity from outside the brain, are offering new ways of performing detailed studies of human brain function (some applications of imaging are described in Chapter 9). Nevertheless, the findings from such studies represent correlations between brain activity and psychological states and do not show that the brain activity is responsible for the state. Imaging studies often depend on a solid understanding of basic brain processes from studies of animals to help interpret the findings.
14. Summarized in LeDoux (1987).
15. Kaada (1960); Kaada (1967).

16. Head (1921) proposed that the cortex inhibits subcortical areas.
17. Bard (1929); Cannon (1929).
18. See Cannon (1929).
19. Cannon (1929).
20. Papez (1937).
21. Peffiefer (1955).
22. Herrick (1933).
23. Broca (1978).
24. Papez (1937).
25. Descartes (1958).
26. Papez (1937).
27. Klüver and Bucy (1937); Klüver and Bucy (1939).
28. Klüver and Bucy (1937).
29. Weiskrantz (1956); Downer (1961); Horel, Keating, and Misantone (1975); Jones and Mishkin (1972); Aggleton and Mishkin (1986); Rolls (1992b); Ono and Nishijo (1992); Gaffan (1992).
30. MacLean (1949); MacLean (1952).
31. MacLean (1949).
32. MacLean (1949).
33. Ibid.
34. Ibid.
35. Ibid.
36. MacLean (1952).
37. MacLean (1970); MacLean (1990).
38. MacLean (1970).
39. Other contemporary theories with evolutionary perspectives include: Plutchik (1993); Ekman (1992a); Izard (1992a).
40. Historical facts can be found in: Nauta and Karten (1970); Karten and Shimizu (1991); Northcutt and Kaas (1995).
41. Nauta and Karten (1970); Karten and Shimizu (1991); Northcutt and Kaas (1995).
42. Karten and Shimizu (1991); Northcutt and Kaas (1995); Ebbesson (1980); Swanson (1983).
43. Brodal (1982); Swanson (1983); LeDoux (1991).
44. An important exception is the role of the hippocampus in negative feedback control of stress responses, as described in Chapter 8.
45. Others have also proposed getting rid of the limbic system: Brodal (1982); Kotter and Meyer (1992).

CHAPTER 5: THE WAY WE WERE

1. Leonardo da Vinci (1939).
2. Dawkins (1982).
3. Quoted by Dawkins (1982).
4. Dawkins (1982).
5. Pinker (1995).
6. Fodor (1983); Gazzaniga (1988).
7. Nottebohm, Kasparian, Pandazis (1981); Krebs (1990); Sherry, Jacobs, and Gaulin (1992); Sengelaub (1989); Purves, White, and Andrews (1994); Geschwind and Levitsky (1968); Galaburda et al (1987). These references were taken from Finlay and Darlington (1995).
8. Finlay and Darlington (1995).
9. Pinker (1994).
10. This point is nicely made by Plutchik (1980) and will be considered in more detail later.
11. Plato, *Phaedo,* cited in Flew (1964).
12. Darwin (1859).
13. S.J. Gould (1977).
14. Cited by S.J. Gould (1977).
15. Simpson (1953); J.M. Smith (1958); Ayala and Valentine (1979); J.L. Gould (1982).
16. J.L. Gould (1982).
17. Darwin (1872). All references to Darwin below are from this source, unless otherwise indicated.
18. Summarized by Plutchik (1980).
19. Tomkins (1962).
20. Izard (1977); Izard (1992a).
21. Ekman (1984).
22. Plutchik (1980).
23. Frijda (1986).
24. Johnson-Laird and Oatley (1992).
25. Panksepp (1982).
26. Arnold (1960); Fehr and Russell (1984); J.A. Gray (1982).
27. C.A. Smith and R.S. Lazarus (1990).
28. Harré (1986).
29. Averill (1980). Averill's account of the Gururumba is based on research conducted by Newman [P.L. Newman (1960)].
30. Morsbach and Tyler (1986).
31. Ibid.
32. Doi (1973).

33. Heelas (1986); Davitz (1969); Geertz (1959).
34. Wierzbicka (1994).
35. Ekman (1980).
36. Ibid.
37. Twain (1962).
38. Ekman (1980).
39. Ortony and Turner (1990).
40. Gallistel (1980).
41. Ekman (1992a); Izard (1992a).
42. Plutchik (1980).
43. Ibid.
44. Bowlby (1969).
45. Shepherd (1983).
46. Nauta and Karten (1970).
47. S.J. Gould (1977); Pinker (1994).
48. Preuss (1995); Reep (1984); Uylings and van Eden (1990).
49. Nauta and Karten (1970); Karten and Shimizu (1991); Northcutt and Kaas (1995).
50. Preuss (1995); Geschwind (1965).
51. For example, protection from danger, finding food and shelter and suitable mates, and the like.
52. For example, see Jaynes (1976).
53. Ekman (1992a).
54. Johnson-Laird and Oatley (1992).
55. Tooby and Cosmedies (1990).
56. Natural triggers are what ethologists call sign stimuli. These elicit behavioral and/or physiological responses innately. They are also similar to unconditioned stimuli, which elicit responses innately as well (see Chapter 6).
57. Examples include sexual partner recognition or food detection networks.
58. James (1890).
59. Marks (1987).
60. Eibl-Eibesfeldt and Sutterlin (1990).
61. Kierkegaard (1844); Sartre (1943); Heidegger (1927).
62. Lazarus (1991).
63. Marks (1987).
64. D.C. Blanchard and R.J. Blanchard (1989).
65. D.C. Blanchard and R.J. Blanchard (1988); R.J. Blanchard and D.C. Blanchard (1989).

66. Bolles and Fanselow (1980); Watkins and Mayer (1982); Helmstetter (1992).
67. Bolles and Fanselow (1980); Watkins and Mayer (1982); Helmstetter (1992).
68. Among vertebrates, the organizational plan of autonomic nervous system function is similar from amphibians through mammals, including man [Shepherd (1983)].
69. Jacobson and Sapolsky (1991).
70. This will be discussed in some detail in Chapter 8.
71. The neuroendocrine systems, like most other neural systems, is similarly organized in different species. For examples, see: Shepherd (1983); J.A. Gray (1987); McEwen and Sapolsky (1995).
72. Dawkins (1982).
73. This is similar to the approach of ethologists, who look at the invariant, evolutionarily prescribed aspects of behavior, and of evolutionary psychologists, who tend to emphasize evolution's effects on the mind. For a summary of ethological approaches, see J.L. Gould (1982). For an example of the evolutionary psychology approach, see Tooby and Cosmedies (1990).
74. This work is summarized in: J.A. Gray (1987).
75. Wilcock and Broadhurst (1967).
76. See J.A. Gray (1987); Marks (1987).
77. Marks (1987); Kagan and Snidman (1991).
78. J.L. Gould (1982).
79. Tully (1991).
80. Sibley and Ahlquist (1984).
81. Dawkins (1982).

CHAPTER 6: A FEW DEGREES OF SEPARATION

1. Dickinson (1955).
2. This title is based on the popular play and film *Six Degrees of Separation* by John Guare (1990).
3. Pavlov (1927).
4. D.C. Blanchard and R.J. Blanchard (1972).
5. R.J. Blanchard et al (1993); D.C. Blanchard and R.J. Blanchard (1988).
6. Campeau, Liang, and Davis (1990); Gleitman and Holmes (1967).
7. Pavlov (1927).
8. Bouton (1994); Bouton and D. Swartzentruber (1991).
9. Campbell and Jaynes (1966).

10. Jacobs and Nadel (1985); Marks (1987).

11. Hodes, Cook, and Lang (1985); Hugdahl (1995); Öhman (1992).

12. However, whether fear is experienced is not crucial, since the system is an implicit or unconscious learning system, the processing of which may or may not reach consciousness. Explicit and implicit learning systems will be discussed in Chapter 7.

13. McAllister and McAllister (1971); Brown, Kalish, and Farber (1951); Davis, Hitchcock, and Rosen (1987).

14. For some examples see Carew, Hawkins, and Kandel (1983); Tully (1991); D. H. Cohen (1980); Schneiderman et al (1974); Bolles and Fanselow (1980); Smith et al (1980); Öhman (1992).

15. This is called Occam's razor, or the law of parsimony, and it dictates that we not call upon a complex explanation or process when a simpler one will do. The recent revival of anthropocentric thinking about animal minds [see McDonald (1995); Masson and McCarthy (1995)] intentionally violates this law, which I think is a mistake. If you can't prove consciousness in a particular creature, then you shouldn't use consciousness as an explanation of its behavior.

16. This has always been controversial. However, recent studies by Öhman have shown that conditioning can occur in the absence of conscious awareness of the conditioned stimulus and its relation to the unconditioned stimulus. He uses "backwards masking," which allows the CS to enter the brain but not to enter consciousness [Öhman (1992)].

17. Other ways to study fear include the use of electical brain stimulation to directly elicit fear responses or the use of avoidance conditioning procedures [see LeDoux (1995)].

18. It is possible that some aspects of fear, like fear of failing or fear of being afraid, are not easily modeled by fear conditioning.

19. Freezing occurs in many species in response to sudden danger [Marks (1987)] but has been studied as a conditioned response mostly in rats.

20. Von Uexkull (1934).

21. Archer (1979).

22. Cannon (1929); Hilton (1979); Mancia and Zanchetti (1981).

23. Mason (1968); van de Kar et al (1991).

24. Bolles and Fanselow (1980); Watkins and Mayer (1982); Helmstetter (1992).

25. Brown, Kalish, and Farber (1951); Davis (1992b); Weisz, Harden, and Xiang (1992).

26. D.H. Cohen (1980).

27. Kapp et al (1992).

28. McCabe et al (1992).

29. Powell and Levine-Bryce (1989).
30. Fanselow (1994).
31. Davis (1992).
32. O.A. Smith et al (1980).
33. LeDoux (1994), (1995).
34. Most of the older data was based on the placement of a lesion in a brain area. The area then degenerated and the nerve fibers that originated there would in turn degenerate. By using special stains, the degenerating fibers could then be seen. However, because fibers passing through but not originating in the lesioned area were also damaged, it was possible to get false results. Although newer techniques using tracer chemicals also have this problem to some extent (since the tracer can be taken up by passing axons in some cases), it is much less of a problem than with the older techniques.
35. Studies by Cohen in the pigeon and Kapp in rabbits, however, had used fear conditioning to identify brain mechanisms of fear learning and were important stimuli to me when I was starting to design my early experiments [D.H. Cohen (1980); B.S. Kapp et al (1979)].
36. For a review of studies of the role of limbic areas in fear behavior and other emotional and memory functions, see Isaacson (1982).
37. Many of the lesion and tracing studies described were conducted in the Neurobiology Laboratory at Cornell University Medical College in Manhattan. Don Reis was the director of the lab, and a collaborator. The main collaborator on the anatomical work was David Ruggerio and Claudia Farb. A number of researchers worked on the behavioral studies, including Akira Sakaguchi, Jiro Iwata, and Piera Cicchetti.
38. LeDoux, Sakaguchi, and Reis (1984).
39. Ibid.
40. LeDoux et al (1986).
41. Kapp's work was seminal in starting this field. In 1979 he published the first study showing the lesions of the central nucleus of the amygdala disrupt fear conditioning. Later studies used stimulation, tracing, and unit recording techniques to show without a doubt that the central amygdala was an important structure in fear conditioning [summarized in Kapp, Pascoe, and Bixler (1984)].
42. The effects of central nucleus of the amygdala lesions are summarized in Kapp et al (1990); Davis (1992); LeDoux (1993); LeDoux (1995).
43. Kapp et al (1990); Davis (1992); LeDoux (1993); LeDoux (1995).
44. LeDoux et al (1988).
45. T.S. Gray et al (1993).
46. LeDoux, Farb, and Ruggiero (1990).

47. Ibid.
48. LeDoux et al (1990).
49. Price, Russchen, and Amaral (1987); Amaral et al (1992); Savander et al (1995); Pitkänen et al (1995).
50. Jarrell et al (1987).
51. For discussion of processing differences between auditory thalamus and cortex in fear conditioning, see Weinberger (1995); Bordi and LeDoux (1994a); Bordi and LeDoux (1994b).
52. Nauta and Karten (1970); Northcutt and Kaas (1995).
53. Kapp et al (1992); Davis et al (1992); Fanselow (1994) Weinberger (1995). For an alternative interpretation of the role of the thalamic pathway, see Campeau and Davis (1995). For a rebuttal of their interpretation see Corodimas and LeDoux (1995).
54. O'Keefe and Nadel (1978); Nadel and Willner (1980); Eichenbaum and Otto (1992); Sutherland and Rudy (1989).
55. Amaral (1987); Van Hoesen (1982).
56. O'Keefe and Nadel (1978); Nadel and Willner (1980); Eichenbaum and Otto (1992); Sutherland and Rudy (1989).
57. Phillips and LeDoux (1992); Kim and Fanselow (1992); Maren and Fanselow (1996).
58. Other researchers who have studied contextual fear conditioning include R.J. Blanchard, D.C. Blanchard, and R.A. Fial (1970) and Selden et al (1991).
59. LeDoux (1987); Bandler, Carrive, and Zhang (1991); Kaada (1967).
60. For review see LeDoux (1987). Although there are some situational and species differences in defense response expression, the amygdala is still involved in defense response control.
61. Greenberg, Scott, and Crews (1984); Tarr (1977).
62. Gloor, Olivier, and Quesney (1981); Halgren (1992).
63. LaBar et al (1995).
64. Bechara et al (1995); Adolphs et al (1995); Hamann et al (1995).
65. Aggleton (1992).
66. This brash statement applies to the bodily reaction to danger and not to the cognitive representation of danger or the conscious experience of fear in dangerous situations.
67. Darwin (1872).
68. D.C. Blanchard and R.J. Blanchard (1988).
69. Fuster (1989); Goldman-Rakic (1992).
70. Preuss (1995); Povinelli and Preuss (1995).
71. Luria (1966); Fuster (1989); Nauta (1971); Damasio (1994); Stuss (1991); Milner (1964).

72. Everitt and Robbins (1992); Hiroi and White (1991).
73. Lazarus (1966); Lazarus (1991).

CHAPTER 7: REMEMBRANCE OF EMOTIONS PAST

1. Dostoyevsky (1864), quoted in Erdelyi (1985).
2. Claparede (1911).
3. Declarative memory and explicit memory are both terms that are used to distinguish conscious recollection from memories that are based on unconscious processes. The two terms, however, come from somewhat different kinds of research. Declarative memory came out of research aimed at understanding the function of the temporal lobe memory system, which we'll have much to say about. In contrast, explicit memory came out of research on the psychology of memory more than the neural basis of memory. Here, the two terms will be used interchangeably to refer to conscious memory and to distinguish memory that involves conscious recollection from memory that is based on unconscious processes, as conscious memory is now clearly established to be a function of the temporal lobe memory system.
4. Lashley (1950a). In this book, Lashley concluded that memory was not localized to any one system of the brain. This conclusion has turned out to be completely wrong. How did one of the most careful researchers in the history of brain science make such a big mistake? Lashley, like most researchers of his day, assumed that any task that measured a change in behavior at some point in time as a result of some earlier experience was as good as any other task in measuring memory. He chose to use various maze learning tasks in his quest to find memory in the brain. We now know that these mazes can be solved in many different ways—a blind animal, for example, can use touch or smell cues. The fact that the maze problems had multiple solutions meant that multiple memory systems were engaged in the learning. As a result, no one brain lesion would interfere with performance. Lashley was thus led to the false conclusion that memory is widely distributed because he used behavioral tasks that called into play multiple memory systems located in different brain regions. We now interpret this in terms of the existence of multiple memory systems in the brain.
5. Scoville and Milner (1957).
6. It is usual in studies of patients to refer to them by their initials in order to protect their identity. It is fairly commonly known, though, that H.M.'s first name was Henry.
7. N.J. Cohen and H. Eichenbaum (1993).

8. Squire (1987).
9. Scoville and Milner (1957).
10. This section is based on descriptions of H.M. found in several publications: Scoville and Milner (1957); Squire (1987); N.J. Cohen and H. Eichenbaum (1993).
11. There is also an intermediate store that has been discovered through studies in which drugs are used to interfere with storage and through studies of animals lacking certain chemicals in their nervous systems.
12. There are patients in whom aspects of short-term memory (STM) are interfered with (they perform poorly on the digit span test, a measure of STM) but they can form long-term memories of other things. However, STM is itself modular and it is unlikely that you could have a long-term memory of some stimulus that you failed to have an STM of.
13. James (1890). James distinguished primary versus secondary memory, which roughly correspond to what we have in mind when we talk about short- and long-term memory today, although there are some subtle differences in the concepts.
14. As we will see in Chapter 9, short-term memory is now often thought of as a working memory system and is believed to involve the prefrontal cortex. For a discussion of the role of the prefrontal cortex in temporary memory processes, see Fuster (1989); Goldman-Rakic (1993).
15. Squire, Knowlton, and Musen (1993); Teyler and DiScenna (1986); McClelland et al (1995).
16. Gaffan (1974).
17. Zola-Morgan and Squire (1993); Murray (1992); Mishkin (1982).
18. Iversen (1976); N.J. Cohen and H. Eichenbaum (1993).
19. N.J. Cohen and H. Eichenbaum (1993).
20. Olton, Becker, and Handleman (1979).
21. Morris (1984); Morris et al (1982).
22. Mishkin (1978).
23. Zola-Morgan, Squire, and Amaral (1986).
24. Zola-Morgan, Squire, and Amaral (1989).
25. Zola-Morgan et al (1991).
26. Meunier et al (1993); Murray (1992).
27. Squire, Knowlton, and Musen (1993); Zola-Morgan and Squire (1993); Eichenbaum, Otto, and Cohen (1994); N.J. Cohen and H. Eichenbaum (1993).
28. Eichenbaum, Otto, and Cohen (1994).
29. Zola-Morgan and Squire (1993); N.J. Cohen and H. Eichenbaum (1993); McClelland, McNaughton, and O'Reilly (1995); Murray (1992).

30. DeLeon et al (1989); Parasuramna and Martin (1994).
31. Milner (1962).
32. Milner (1965).
33. Corkin (1968).
34. N.J. Cohen (1980); N.J. Cohen and L. Squire (1980); N.J. Cohen and S. Corkin (1981).
35. Warrington and Weiskrantz (1973).
36. Weiskrantz and Warrington (1979).
37. Steinmetz and Thompson (1991).
38. N.J. Cohen and L. Squire (1980); Squire and Cohen (1984); Squire, Cohen, and Nadel (1984).
39. Schacter and Graf (1986).
40. Tulving (1983); O'Keefe and Nadel (1978); Olton, Becker, and Handleman (1979); Mishkin, Malamut, and Bachevalier (1984).
41. Graff, Squire, and Mandler (1984).
42. Cohen and Eichenbaum (1993).
43. Amaral (1987).
44. O'Keefe (1976).
45. O'Keefe and Nadel (1978).
46. Olton, Becker, and Handleman (1979).
47. Morris et al (1982).
48. O'Keefe (1993).
49. McNaughton and Barnes (1990); Barnes et al (1995); Wilson and Mc-Naughton (1994).
50. Olton, Becker, and Handleman (1979).
51. Morris (1984); Morris et al (1982).
52. Kubie, Muller, and Bostock (1990); Kubie and Ranck (1983); Muller, Ranck, and Taube (1996).
53. Eichenbaum, Otto, and Cohen (1994).
54. Rudy and Sutherland (1992).
55. MacLean (1949; 1952).
56. McClelland, McNaughton, and O'Reilly (1995); Gluck and Myers (1995).
57. Eysenck (1979).
58. Jacobs and Nadel (1985).
59. Freud (1966).
60. Jacobs and Nadel (1985).
61. Rudy and Morledge (1994).
62. I became aware of this Gary Larson cartoon by attending lectures on memory by J. McGaugh, who often shows a slide of the drawing.
63. R. Brown and J. Kulik (1977); Christianson (1989).

64. McGaugh et al (1995); Cahill et al (1994); McGaugh et al (1993); McGaugh (1990).

65. Adrenaline doesn't actually get into the brain directly under normal circumstances and McGaugh believes that it has its effects by way of the vagus nerve, which then influences several brain systems, including the amygdala and hippocampus indirectly. Although McGaugh emphasizes action in the amygdala, it would seem that the hippocampus may also be affected, since explicit memory strength is altered. This could be a parallel effect on the hippocampus and amygdala. Also, it is possible that the amygdala is more important in his animal learning studies and the hippocampus in the human studies because of differences in the tasks used. Alternatively, it is possible that the effects are on the amygdala, which then influences the hippocampus. Paul Gold (1992) has a somewhat different view of the effects of adrenaline on memory. His work suggests that adrenaline releases glucose into the blood. Blood-borne glucose readily gets into the brain and serves as a source of energy for neurons in areas like the hippocampus. This increase in hippocampal energy resources might then help strengthen memories being created through the temporal lobe memory system.

66. Christianson (1992b).

67. Ibid.

68. Bartlett (1932).

69. Erdelyi (1985).

70. Loftus (1993); Loftus and Hoffman (1989).

71. Christianson (1992a).

72. Neisser and Harsch (1992).

73. Freud (1966).

74. Bower (1992).

75. Bower, 1992; Lang, 1984.

76. Hebb (1949).

77. Brown et al (1989); Cotman, Monaghan, and Ganong (1988).

78. Bliss and Lømo (1973).

79. Cotman et al (1988); Nicoll and Malenka (1995); Madison et al (1991); Lynch (1986); Staübli (1995); McNaughton and Barnes (1990).

80. Cotman et al (1988); Nicoll and Malenka (1995); Madison et al (1991); Staübli (1995); McNaughton and Barnes (1990).

81. Cotman et al (1988); Nicoll and Malenka (1995); Madison et al (1991); Lynch (1986); Staübli (1995); McNaughton and Barnes (1990).

82. AMPA and NMDA are the two major classes of glutamate receptors [Collingridge and Lester (1989); Cotman et al (1988)].

83. Collingridge and Lester (1989); Cotman et al (1988).

84. Bliss and Collingridge (1993); Brown et al (1988); Cotman et al (1988); Staübli (1995); Lynch (1986); McNaughton and Barnes (1990).
85. Morris et al (1986); but see Saucier and Cain (1996); Bannerman et al (1996).
86. Skelton et al (1987); Berger (1984); Laroche et al (1995); Barnes (1995); Staübli (1995); Rogan and LeDoux (1995); Barnes et al (1995); Dudai (1995).
87. Clugnet and LeDoux (1990); Rogan and LeDoux (1995); Chapman et al (1990).
88. Miserendino et al (1990); Fanselow and Kim (1994).
89. Nicoll and Malenka (1995); Staübli (1995).
90. Squire and Davis (1975); Rose (1995); Rosenzweig (1996).
91. Kandel (1989); Lisman (1995).
92. Kandel and Schwartz (1982).
93. Frey, Huang, and Kandel (1993).
94. Yin et al (1994).
95. Mayford, Abel, and Kandel (1995); Bourtchouladze et al (1994).
96. Eichenbaum and Otto (1992).

CHAPTER 8: WHERE THE WILD THINGS ARE

1. Phillips (1993).
2. Wilson (1968).
3. Shattuck (1980).
4. Shakespeare, quoted in Grey Walter (1953).
5. Manderscheid and Sonnenschein (1994).
6. This paragraph is based on Kramer (1993).
7. Klein (1981).
8. *Diagnostic and statistical manual of mental disorders* (1994).
9. Manderscheid and Sonnenschein (1994).
10. Öhman (1992); Epstein (1972).
11. Öhman (1992); Lader and Marks (1973).
12. Zuckerman (1991).
13. Ibid.
14. Freud included dysthymia and somatoform disorders under anxiety. DSM IV includes dysthymia with depressive illness under mood disorders and has a separate classification for somatoform disorders.
15. The following brief descriptions of anxiety disorders are taken from the longer DSM IV descriptions.
16. Öhman (1992).

17. Breuer and Freud, quoted in Erdelyi (1985).
18. Erdelyi (1985).
19. It's not necessary for a fear conditioning interpretation of anxiety to be correct in order to make the point I want to make here—that anxiety disorders reflect the operation of the fear system of the brain. However, since the most thorough understanding of the fear system has come from studies of fear conditioning, my job is made much easier if I can piggyback on fear conditioning explanations of anxiety. As the following discussion will, I hope, show, the conditioning theory is in fact plausible.
20. This history is summarized in Chapter 2.
21. Watson and Rayner (1920).
22. Waton's position is summarized by Eysenck (1979).
23. Thorndike (1913); Skinner (1938); Hull (1943); Tolman (1932).
24. Mowrer (1939).
25. Ibid.
26. Ibid.
27. N.E. Miller (1948).
28. This experiment was described by Hall and Lindzey (1957).
29. Dollard and Miller (1950).
30. This point was made by Hall and Lindzey (1957).
31. Dollard and Miller (1950).
32. Freud (1909).
33. Wolpe and Rachman (1960).
34. Eysenck and Rachman (1965).
35. Seligman (1971).
36. Reviewed by Seligman (1971).
37. Mineka et al (1984).
38. Bandura (1969).
39. Öhman (1992).
40. Jacobs and Nadel (1985).
41. Ibid.
42. For a summary of the adrenal steroid response to stress, see: J. A. Gray (1987); McEwen and Sapolsky (1995).
43. Jacobson and Sapolsky (1991).
44. Diamond and Rose (1994); Diamond and Rose (1993); Diamond et al (1994); Luine (1994).
45. Shors et al (1990); Pavlides, Watanabe, and McEwen (1993); Diamond et al (1994); Diamond and Rose (1994).
46. McNally et al (1995); Bremner et al (1993); Newcomer et al (1994); Wolkowitz, Reuss, and Weingartner (1990); McEwen and Sapolsky (1995).

47. McEwen (1992).
48. Bekkers and Stevens (1989); Coss and Perkel (1985); Koch, Zador, and Brown (1992).
49. Sapolsky (1990); Uno et al (1989).
50. McKittrick et al (1995); Blanchard et al (1995).
51. Bremner et al (1995).
52. McEwen and Sapolsky (1995).
53. Diamond and Rose (1994); Diamond et al (1993); Diamond et al (1994); Luine (1994).
54. It is important to point out that damage to the hippocampus can result in a retrograde amnesia as well as an anterograde one. This is important since it takes time for the steroids to build up and have their effect. So even though the hippocampus may participate in the initial phases of memory formation while the trauma is just beginning, and it may take a while for the steroids to build up. Once the hippocampus is interfered with, the effects can act to prevent the solidification of the memories that happened at the beginning of the trauma as well.
55. Loftus and Hoffman (1989); Loftus et al (1989); Loftus (1993).
56. Erdelyi (1984).
57. Dali (1948).
58. Makino, Gold, and Schulkin (1994); Swanson and Simmons (1989).
59. Corodimas et al (1994).
60. Servatius and Shors (1994).
61. Jacobs and Nadel (1985).
62. LeDoux, Romanski, and Xagoraris (1989).
63. Amaral et al (1992).
64. Morgan, Romanski, and LeDoux (1993).
65. Luria (1966); Fuster (1989); Nauta (1971); Damasio (1994); Stuss (1991); Petrides (1994); Stuss (1991); Shimamura (1995); Milner (1964).
66. Morgan, Romanski, and LeDoux (1993).
67. Morgan and LeDoux (1995).
68. Thorpe, Rolls, and Maddison (1983); Rolls (1985); Rolls (1992b).
69. Damasio (1994); Stuss (1991); Luria (1966); Fuster (1989); Nauta (1971).
70. Diorio, Viau, and Meaney (1993).
71. LeDoux, Romanski, and Xagoraris (1989).
72. Bouton and Peck (1989); Bouton and Swartzentruber (1991); Bouton (1994).
73. Jacobs and Nadel (1985).
74. Quirk, Repa, and LeDoux (1995).

75. Hebb (1949).
76. Shalev, Rogel-Fuchs, and Pitman (1992).
77. Kramer (1993).
78. I will have relatively little to say about generalized anxiety and obsessive compulsive disorder. For a theory of general anxiety, see J.A. Gray (1982). And for a critique of his theory, especially of the fact that the theory does not include a major role for the amygdala in anxiety, see LeDoux (1993). For the record, though, it should be noted that Neil McNaughton and Gray are currently working on a revision of *The Neuropsychology of Anxiety,* based on the large body of work that has emerged since 1982, which will give the amygdala a more prominent role.
79. Blanchard et al (1991).
80. Bordi and LeDoux (1992).
81. Of course, genetic preparation to respond to certain stimuli and past learning about stimuli that are important to the species probably both contribute.
82. Rolls (1992a); Allman and Brothers (1994).
83. Öhman (1992).
84. Charney et al (1993); Kolb (1987).
85. Charney et al (1993).
86. Kolb (1987).
87. Charney et al (1993); Shalev, Rogel-Fuchs, and Pitman (1992).
88. *Diagnostic and statistical manual of mental disorders* (1987).
89. *Diagnostic and statistical manual of mental disorders* (1987); Öhman (1992).
90. *Diagnostic and statistical manual of mental disorders* (1987).
91. Margraf, Ehlers, and Roth (1986b); Margraf, Ehlers, and Roth (1986a); Klein (1993).
92. Ehlers and Margraf (1987).
93. Ackerman and Sachar (1974); Margraf, Ehlers, and Roth (1986b); Wolpe (1988).
94. Ackerman and Sachar (1974); Margraf, Ehlers, and Roth (1986b); Wolpe (1988).
95. Margraf, Ehlers, and Roth (1986a).
96. Ibid.
97. Klein (1993).
98. Wolpe (1988).
99. Benarroch et al (1986); Ruggiero et al (1991).
100. Ruggiero et al (1991).
101. Cechetto and Calaresu (1984).

102. J.A. Gray (1982); J.A. Gray (1987); Sarter and Markowitsch (1985); LeDoux (1993); Isaacson (1982).
103. J.A. Gray (1982); Nagy, Zambo, and Decsi (1979).
104. J.A. Gray (1982).
105. Cognitive therapy attempts to eliminate pathological emotions by changing appraisals and thoughts. Some representative cognitive approaches to phobias and other anxiety disorders are: Lang (1979); Lang (1993); Koa and Kozak (1986); Beck and Emery (1985).
106. Reid (1989).
107. Summarized by Erdelyi (1985).
108. Erdelyi (1985).
109. Falls, Miserendino, and Davis (1992).
110. Amaral et al (1992).

CHAPTER 9: ONCE MORE, WITH FEELINGS

1. Spinoza (1955).
2. Nabokov (1966).
3. Feelings constitute the subjective experiences we know our emotions by and are the hallmark of an emotion from the point of view of the person experiencing the feeling. Not all feelings are emotions, but all conscious emotional experiences are feelings. This point is nicely made by Damasio (1994).
4. There are some scientists who have studied aspects of emotions other than their conscious properties, but these have been in the minority and often they too have in the end been mostly concerned with the conscious aspects. Some theorists who have included unconscious processes include: Izard (1992b); Zajonc (1980); Ekman (1980); Mandler (1975); Mandler (1992).
5. Churchland (1984); Boring (1950); Gardner (1987); Jackendoff (1987); Rorty (1979); Searle (1992); Eccles (1990); Picton and Stuss (1994); Chalmers (1996); Humphrey (1992).
6. There are of course exceptions. See note 4 above.
7. See Chapter 2.
8. See Chapters 2 and 3.
9. This statement raises as many questions as it answers, and it certainly does not solve the problem of how conscious emotional experiences occur in the brain. However, it does two other things that are important. First, it provides a way of conceptualizing what an emotional experience is. Second, it shows that we are no worse off in under-

standing where conscious emotions come from than we are in understanding where conscious perceptions or memories come from. The latter is a crucial realization, for it puts the emotion on a par with other aspects of the mind as a scientific topic for the first time since the dawn of behaviorism.

10. Some recent discussions of consciousness include: Dennett (1991); Johnson-Laird (1988); Minsky (1985); Penrose (1989); Humphrey (1992); Gazzaniga (1992); Shallice (1988); Kinsbourne (1988); Churchland (1988); Posner and Snyder (1975); Shiffrin and Schneider (1977); Baars (1988); Kosslyn and Koenig (1992); Mandler (1988); Norman and Shallice (1980); Churchland (1984); Jackendoff (1987); Rorty (1979); Searle (1992); Eccles (1990); Picton and Stuss (1994); Harnad (1982); Hirst (1994); Chalmers (1996); Velams (1991); Dennett and Kinsbourne (1992); Crick (1995); Sperry (1969); Maccel and Bisiach (1988); Crick and Koch (1992); Edelman (1989).

11. A number of contemporary theories assume that the contents of working memory are what we are conscious of (some of these are described below in the text). The working memory theories are varied but all assume the existence of some executive, or supervisory, mechanism involved in the focusing of attention, such that the thing you are attending to is what working memory works on. I'm going to embrace the working memory theory of consciousness, not because I believe that it completely explains consciousness, but because I believe that it gives us a framework for illustrating how feelings are created. I'm going to describe a feeling as the representation of the activity of an emotional processing system in working memory. This framework can be easily transported to some other framework if the working memory theory proves to be inadequate.

12. Baddeley (1982).

13. Baddeley and Hitch (1974); Baddeley (1992).

14. Miller (1956).

15. Baars (1988).

16. Kosslyn and Koenig (1992).

17. Jacobsen and Nissen (1937).

18. Preuss (1995).

19. Fuster (1989); Goldman-Rakic (1987); Goldman-Rakic (1993); Wilson, Scalaidhe, and Goldman-Rakic (1993).

20. Petrides (1994); Fuster (1989).

21. Petrides et al (1993); Jonides et al (1993); Grasby et al (1993); Schwartz et al (1995).

22. D'Esposito et al (1995).

23. Fuster (1989); Goldman-Rakic (1987); Reep (1984); Uylings and van Eden (1990).
24. Fuster (1989); Goldman-Rakic (1987).
25. Van Essen (1985).
26. Ungerleider and Mishkin (1982); Ungerleider and Haxby (1994).
27. Goldman-Rakic (1988).
28. Desimone et al (1995).
29. This simple story involving specialized short-term buffers in the sensory systems and a general-purpose working memory mechanism in the prefrontal cortex is somewhat more complicated than the way I have presented it. The prefrontal cortex itself seems to have regions that are specialized, at least to some degree, for specific kinds of working memory functions. Such findings, however, do not discredit the notion that the prefrontal cortex is involved in the general-purpose or executive aspects of working memory since only some cells in these areas play specialized roles. Interactions between the general-purpose cells in different areas may coordinate the overall activity of working memory. It is thus possible that the executive functions of the prefrontal cortex might be mediated by cells that are distributed across the different prefrontal subsystems rather than by cells that are collected together in one region.
30. F.A.W. Wilson, S.P.O Scalaidhe, and P.S. Goldman-Rakic (1993).
31. The studies have examined one kind of memory at a time rather than putting different kinds of memory in competition.
32. Petrides (1994).
33. D'Esposito et al (1995); Corbetta et al (1991); Posner and Petersen (1990).
34. Goldman-Rakic (1988); J.M. Fuster (1989).
35. Posner (1992).
36. Gaffan, Murray, and Fabre-Thorpe (1993).
37. Thorpe, Rolls, and Maddison (1983); Rolls (1992b); Ono and Nishijo (1992).
38. Damasio (1994).
39. Kosslyn and Koenig (1992); Shimamura (1995).
40. Williams (1964).
41. Kosslyn and Koenig (1992).
42. Kihlstrom (1987).
43. Johnson-Laird (1988).
44. Baars (1988).
45. Shallice (1988); Posner and Snyder (1975); Shiffrin and Schneider (1977); Norman and Shallice (1980).

46. However, under some conditions, consciousness can be divided: Hirst et al (1980); Kihlstrom (1984).

47. Summarized by Dennett (1991).

48. Newell, Rosenbloom, and Laird (1989); Newell and Simon (1972).

49. Johnson-Laird (1988).

50. Smolensky (1990); Rumelhart et al (1988).

51. Johnson-Laird (1988).

52. That symbolic architecture is the basis of consciousness is somewhat counterintuitive since cognitive science was founded on the symbol manipulation approach, but has mostly been about unconscious processes. However, we are not aware of the processes by which symbols are manipulated, but only of the outcome of the manipulations. Symbol manipulation may be the architecture of consciousness, but there is still something missing between symbolic representation and conscious awareness. And that is the big question about consciousness.

53. Johnson-Laird (1988).

54. Tom Nagel's discussion of what it is like to be a bat is relevant here: Nagel (1974).

55. For a discussion of the difference between phenomenal consciousness and access consciousness, see Jackendoff (1987); N. Block (1995).

56. Right now, we are concerned with what happens if a snake is a potent emotional stimulus for you rather than with the manner in which emotional potency is created (emotional learning in neutral and evolutionarily prepared situations was discussed in earlier chapters).

57. But if you have, in your past, experienced rabbits in association with some trauma or stress, then the rabbit too could serve as a trigger stimulus that would turn on the amygdala and its outputs.

58. Amaral et al (1992).

59. Moruzzi and Magoun (1949).

60. Hobson and Steriade (1986); McCormick and Bal (1994).

61. This applies to arousal occurring during waking states. Arousal also occurs during sleep, especially dream or REM sleep. In this case the cortex becomes insensitive in external inputs and is focused instead on internal stimuli [Hobson and Steriade (1986); McCormick and Bal (1994)].

62. This is generally known as the Yerkes-Dodson law in psychology.

63. Kapp et al (1992); Weinberger (1995).

64. Amygdala interactions with brainstem arousal systems is described in LeDoux (1995); Gallagher and Holland (1994).

65. Kapp et al (1992).

66. It appears in fact that the cortex arouses itself since sensory stimuli first go to the cortex and are then sent back to the brain stem and these inputs trigger the arousal system, which then arouses the cortex [Lindsley (1951)].
67. Ekman, Levenson, and Friesen (1983); R.W. Levenson (1992).
68. Tomkins (1962).
69. Izard (1971); Izard (1992a).
70. Damasio (1994).
71. Hohmann (1966).
72. B. Bermond, B. Nieuwenhuyse, L. Fasotti, and J. Schuerman (1991).
73. Also, the patients were not tested during emotional experiences but were asked to recall past emotions. This approach, as we saw in Chapters 2 and 3, is plagued with problems.
74. James (1890).
75. Ekman (1992b); Ekman (1993); Adelman and Zajonc (1989).
76. There are now several patients with amygdala damage. [Adolphs et al (1995); Bechara et al (1995); Young et al (1995).] However, these people have a congenital disorder. Whenever the brain is damaged in early life, there are numerous compensatory mechanisms. For example, if the visual cortex is damaged, the auditory cortex can take on some visual functions. We have to be very cautious in using negative findings in patients with developmental disorders to infer what normally goes on in the brain.
77. Scherer (1993a); Leventhal and Scherer (1987); Scherer (1984).
78. Pinker (1994).
79. Jerison (1973).
80. Preuss (1995); Reep (1984); Uylings and van Eden (1990).
81. Preuss (1995); Povinelli and Preuss (1995).
82. Gallup (1991).
83. Pinker (1994).
84. The relation between language and consciousness is complex and controversial. Some propose that all thought (and our consciousness of our thoughts) takes place in a propositional mode, a language of thought, whereas others argue that thought can occur in nonpropositional, say pictorial or visual, terms. My view is that while language is not a necessary precursor to consciousness, the presence of language (or at least the cognitive capacities that make language possible) allows a unique kind of awareness in humans. This does not mean that one must be able to speak or understand speech in order to be conscious. Deaf and dumb individuals, for example, are no less conscious than the rest of us. They have the cognitive capacities that make language, and linguistically

based thought, possible. They simply cannot use those capacities to understand speech or produce it themselves.

85. Kihlstrom (1987); LeDoux (1989).
86. Dawkins (1982).
87. Wilde (1909).

BIBLIOGRAPHY

Abelson, R. P. (1963). Computer simulation of "hot" cognition. In *Computer simulation of personality*, S. S. Tomkins and S. Messick, eds. (New York: Wiley).

Ackerman, S., and Sachar, E. (1974). The lactate theory of anxiety: A review and reevaluation. *Psychosomatic Medicine 36*, 69–81.

Adelman, P. K., and Zajonc, R. B. (1989). Facial efference and the experience of emotion. *Annual Review of Psychology 40*, 249-80.

Adolphs, R., Tranel, D., Damasio, H., and Damasio, A. R. (1995). Fear and the human amygdala. *Journal of Neuroscience 15*, 5879–91

Aggleton, J. P. (1992). *The amygdala: Neurobiological aspects of emotion, memory, and mental dysfunction* (New York: Wiley-Liss).

Aggleton, J. P., and Mishkin, M. (1986). The amygdala: Sensory gateway to the emotions. In *Emotion: Theory, research and experience* (Vol. 3), R. Plutchik and H. Kellerman, eds. (Orlando: Academic Press), pp. 281–99.

Allman, J., and Brothers, L. (1994). Faces, fear and the amygdala. *Nature 372*, 613–14.

Amaral, D. G. (1987). Memory: Anatomical organization of candidate brain regions. In *Handbook of Physiology. Section 1: The Nervous System. Vol. 5: Higher Functions of the Brain*, F. Plum, ed. (Bethesda, MD: American Physiological Society), pp. 211–94.

Amaral, D. G., Price, J. L., Pitkänen, A., and Carmichael, S. T. (1992). Anatomical organization of the primate amygdaloid complex. In *The amygdala: Neurobiological aspects of emotion, memory, and mental dysfunction*, J. P. Aggleton, ed. (New York: Wiley-Liss), pp. 1–66.

Anderson, J. R. (1990). *Cognitive psychology and its implications*, 3rd edition (New York: Freeman).

Archer, J. (1979). Behavioral aspects of fear. In *Fear in animals and man*, W. Sluckin, ed. (New York: Van Nostrand Reinhold).

Aristotle (1941). In *The basic works of Aristotle*, R. McKeon, ed. (New York: Random House).

Armony, J.L., Servan-Schreiber, D., Cohen, J.D., and LeDoux, J.E. (1995). An anatomically constrained neural network model of fear conditioning. *Behavioral Neuroscience 109*, 246–57.

Arnold, M. B. (1960). *Emotion and personality* (New York: Columbia University Press).

Averill, J. (1980). Emotion and anxiety: Sociocultural, biological, and psychological determinants. In *Explaining emotions*, A. O. Rorty, ed. (Berkeley: University of California Press).

Ayala, E. J., and Valentine, J. W. (1979). *Evolving*. Benjamin Cummings.

Baars, B. J. (1988). *A cognitive theory of consciousness* (New York: Cambridge University Press).

Baddeley, A. (1982). *Your memory: A user's guide* (New York: Macmillan).

Baddeley, A. (1992). Working memory. *Science 255*, 556–59.

Baddeley, A., and Hitch, G. J. (1974). Working memory. In *The psychology of learning and motivation*, vol. 8, G. Bower, ed. (New York: Academic Press).

Bandler, R., Carrive, P., and Zhang, S. P. (1991). Integration of somatic and autonomic reactions within the midbrain periaqueductal grey: Viscerotopic, somatotopic and functional organization. *Progress in Brain Research 87*, 269–305.

Bandura, A. (1969). *Principles of behavior modification* (New York: Holt).

Bangs, L. (1978). *Gig* (New York: Gig Enterprises).

Bannerman D. M., Good, M. A., Butcher, S. P., Ramsay, M., and Morris, R. G. M. (1995). Distinct components of spatial learning revealed by prior training and NMDA receptor blockade. *Nature 378*, 182–86.

Bard, P. (1929). The central representation of the sympathetic system: As indicated by certain physiological observations. *Archives of Neurology and Psychiatry 22*, 230–46.

Bargh, J. A. (1990). Auto-motives: Preconscious determinants of social interaction. In *Handbook of motivation and cognition*, T. Higgins and R. M. Sorrentino, eds., pp. 93–130 (New York: Guilford).

Bargh, J. A. (1992). Being unaware of the stimulus vs. unaware of its interpretation: Why subliminality per se does matter to social psychology. In *Perception without awareness*, R. Bornstein and T. Pittman, eds. (New York: Guilford).

Barnes, C. A. (1995). Involvement of LTP in memory: Are we "searching under the streetlight?" *Neuron 15,* 751–54.

Barnes, C. A., Erickson, C. A., Davis, S., and McNaughton, B. L. (1995). Hippocampal synaptic enhancement as a basis for learning and memory: A selected review of current evidence from behaving animals. In *Brain and memory: Modulation and mediation of neuroplasticity,* J. L. McGaugh, N. M. Weinberger, and G. Lynch, eds. (New York: Oxford University Press), pp. 259–76.

Bartlett, F. C. (1932). *Remembering* (Cambridge: Cambridge University Press).

Bechara, A., Tranel, D., Damasio, H., Adolphs, R., Rockland, C., and Damasio, A. R. (1995). Double dissociation of conditioning and declarative knowledge relative to the amygdala and hippocampus in humans. *Science 269,* 1115–18.

Beck, A. T., and Emery, G. (1985). *Anxiety disorders and phobias: A cognitive perspective* (New York: Basic Books).

Bekkers, J. M., and Stevens, C. F. (1989). NMDA and non-NMDA receptors are co-localized at individual excitatory synapses in cultured rat hippocampus. *Nature 341,* 230–33.

Benarroch, E. E., Granata, A. R., Ruggiero, D. A., Park, D. H., and Reis, D. J. (1986). Neurons of C1 area mediate cardiovascular responses initiated from ventral medullary surface. *American Physiological Society,* R932–R945.

Berger, T. W. (1984). Long-term potentiation of hippocampal synaptic transmission affects rate of behavioral learning. *Science 224,* 627–29.

Bermond, B., and Nieuwenhuyse, B., Fasotti, L. and Schuerman, J. (1995). Spinal cord lesions, peripheral feedback, and intensities of emotional feelings. *Cognition and Emotion 5,* 201–20.

Blanchard, C., Spencer, R. L., Weiss, S. M., Blanchard, R., McEwen, B. S., and Sakai, R. (1995). Visible burrow system as a model of chronic social stress. *Behavioral Neuroendocrinology 20,* 117–39.

Blanchard, D. C., and Blanchard, R. J. (1972). Innate and conditioned reactions to threat in rats with amygdaloid lesions. *Journal of Comparative Physiological Psychology 81,* 281–90.

Blanchard, D. C., and Blanchard, R. J. (1988). Ethoexperimental approaches to the biology of emotion. *Annual Review of Psychology 39,* 43–68

Blanchard, D. C., and Blanchard, R. J. (1989). Experimental animal models of aggression: what do they say about human behaviour? In *Human aggression: Naturalistic approaches,* J. Archer and K. Browne, eds. (New York: Routledge), pp. 94–121.

Blanchard, R. J., and Blanchard, D. C. (1989). Antipredator defensive behaviors in a visible burrow system. *Journal of Comparative Psychology* 103, 70–82.

Blanchard, R. J., Blanchard, D. C., and Fial, R. A. (1970). Hippocampal lesions in rats and their effect on activity, avoidance, and aggression. *Journal of Comparative Physiological Psychology 71(1)*, 92–102.

Blanchard, R. J., Weiss, S., Agullana, R., Flores, T., and Blanchard, D. C. (1991). Antipredator ultrasounds: Sex differences and drug effects. *Neuroscience Abstracts 17.*

Blanchard, R. J., Yudko, E. B., Rodgers, R. J., and Blanchard, D. C. (1993). Defense system psychopharmacology: An ethological approach to the pharmacology of fear and anxiety. *Behavioural Brain Research 58,* 155–66.

Bliss, T. V. P., and Collingridge, G. L. (1993). A synaptic model of memory: Long-term potentiation in the hippocampus. *Nature 361,* 31–39.

Bliss, T. V. P., and Lomo, T. (1973). Long-lasting potentiation of synaptic transmission in the dentate area of the anaesthetized rabbit following stimulation of the perforant path. *Journal of Physiology 232,* 331–56.

Block, N. (1995). On a confusion about a function of consciousness. *Behavioral and Brain Sciences 18,* 227–87.

Bogen, J. E., and Vogel, P. J. (1962). Cerebral commissurotomy: A case report. *Bulletin of the Los Angeles Neurological Society 27,* 169.

Bolles, R. C., and Fanselow, M. S. (1980). A perceptual-defensive-recuperative model of fear and pain. *Behavioral and Brain Sciences 3,* 291–323.

Bordi, F., and LeDoux, J. (1992). Sensory tuning beyond the sensory system: An initial analysis of auditory properties of neurons in the lateral amygdaloid nucleus and qverlying areas of the striatum. *Journal of Neuroscience 12 (7),* 2493–2503.

Bordi, F., and LeDoux, J. E. (1994a). Response properties of single units in areas of rat auditory thalamus that project to the amygdala. I: Acoustic discharge patterns and frequency receptive fields. *Experimental Brain Research 98,* 261–74.

Bordi, F., and LeDoux, J. E. (1994b). Response properties of single units in areas of rat auditory thalamus that project to the amygdala. II: Cells receiving convergent auditory and somatosensory inputs and cells antidromically activated by amygdala stimulation. *Experimental Brain Research 98,* 275–86.

Boring, E. G. (1950). *A history of experimental psychology* (New York: Appleton-Century-Crofts).

Bornstein, R. F. (1992). Subliminal mere exposure effects. In *Perception without awareness: Cognitive, clinical, and social perspectives*, R. F. Bornstein and T. S. Pittman, eds. (New York: Guilford), pp. 191–210.

Bourtchouladze, R., Frengeulli, B., Blendy, J., Cioffi, D., Schutz, G., and Silva, A. J. (1994). Deficient long-term memory in mice with a targeted mutation of the cAMP-responsive element binding protein. *Cell 79*, 59–68.

Bouton, M. E. (1994). Conditioning, remembering, and forgetting. *Journal of Experimental Psychology: Animal Behavior Processes 20*, 219–31.

Bouton, M. E., and Peck, C. A. (1989). Context effects on conditioning, extinction, and reinstatement in an appetitive conditioning preparation. *Animal Learning and Behavior 17*, 188–98.

Bouton, M. E., and Swartzentruber, D. (1991). Sources of relapse after extinction in Pavlovian and instrumental learning. *Clinical Psychology Review 11*, 123–40.

Bower, G. (1992). How might emotions affect learning? In *Handbook of emotion and memory: Research and theory*, S.-A. Christianson, ed. (Hillsdale, NJ: Erlbaum).

Bowers, K. S. (1984). On being unconsciously influenced and informed. In *The unconscious reconsidered*, K. S. Bowers and D. Meichenbaum, eds. (New York: Wiley) 227–72.

Bowers, K. S., and Meichenbaum, D. (1984). *The unconscious reconsidered* (New York: Wiley).

Bowlby, J. (1969). *Attachment and Loss: Vol. 1, Attachment* (New York: Basic Books).

Bremner, J. D., Randall, T., Scott, T. M., Brunen, R. A., Seibyl, J. P., Southwick, S. M., Delaney, R. C., McCarthy, G., Charney, D. S., and Innis, R. B. (1995). MRI-based measurement of hippocampal volume in patients with combat-related PTSD. *American Journal of Psychiatry 152*, 973–81.

Bremner, J. D., Scott, T. M., Delaney, R. C., Southwick, S. M., Mason, J. W., Johnson, C. R., Innis, R. B., McCarthy, G., and Charney, D. S. (1993). Deficits in short-term memory in posttraumatic stress disorder. *American Journal of Psychiatry 150*, 1015–19.

Broca, P. (1978). Anatomie comparée des circonvolutions cérébrales. Le grand lobe limbique et la scissure limbique dans le série des mammifères. *Revue Anthropologique, Ser. 21 21*, 385–498.

Brodal, A. (1982). *Neurological anatomy* (New York: Oxford University Press).

Brown, J. S., Kalish, H. I., and Farber, I. E. (1951). Conditioned fear as revealed by magnitude of startle response to an auditory stimulus. *Journal of Experimental Psychology 41*, 317–28.

Brown, R., and Kulik, J. (1977). Flashbulb memories. *Cognition* 5, 73–99.

Brown, T. H., Chapman, P. F., Kairiss, E. W., and Keenan, C. L. (1988). Long-term synaptic potentiation. *Science* 242, 724–28.

Brown, T. H., Ganong, A. H., Kairiss, E. W., Keenan, C. L., and Kelso, S. R. (1989). Long-term potentiation in two synaptic systems of the hippocampal brain slice. In *Neural models of plasticity,* J. H. Byrne and W. O. Berry, eds. (San Diego: Academic Press), pp. 266–306.

Bruner, J. (1992). Another look at New Look 1. *American Psychologist* 47, 780–83.

Bruner, J. S., and Postman, L. (1947). Emotional selectivity in perception and reaction. *Journal of Personality* 16, 60–77.

Cacioppo, J. T., Klein, D. J., Berntson, G. G., and Hatfield, E. (1993). The psychophysiology of emotion. In *Handbook of emotions,* M. Lewis and J. M. Haviland, eds. (New York: Guilford), pp. 119–42.

Cahill, L., Prins, B., Weber, M., and McGaugh, J. L. (1994). Beta-adrenergic activation and memory for emotional events. *Nature* 371, 702–4.

Campbell, B. A., and Jaynes, J. (1966). Reinstatement. *Psychological Review* 73, 478–80.

Campeau, S. and Davis, M. (1995). Involvement of subcortical and cortical afferents to the lateral nucleus of the amygdala in fear conditioning measured with fear-potentiated startle in rats trained concurrently with auditory and visual conditioned stimuli. *Journal of Neuroscience* 15, 2312–27.

Campeau, S., Liang, K. C., and Davis, M. (1990). Long-term retention of fear-potentiated startle following a short training session. *Animal Learning and Behavior* 18(4), 462–68.

Cannon, W. B. (1929). *Bodily changes in pain, hunger, fear, and rage,* vol. 2 (New York: Appleton).

Carew, T. J., Hawkins, R. D., and Kandel, E. R. (1983). Differential classical conditioning of a defensive withdrawal reflex in Aplysia californica. *Science* 219, 397–400.

Cechetto, D. F., and Calaresu, F. R. (1984). Units in the amygdala responding to activation of carotid baro- and chemoreceptors. *American Journal of Physiology* 246, R832–R836.

Chalmers, D. (1996). The Conscious Mind (New York: Oxford).

Chapman, P. F., Kairiss, E. W., Keenan, C. L., and Brown, T. H. (1990). Long-term synaptic potentiation in the amygdala. *Synapse* 6, 271–278.

Charney, D. S., Deutch, A. V., Krystal, J. H., Southwick, A. M., and Davis, M. (1993). Psychobiologic mechanisms of posttraumatic stress disorder. *Archives of General Psychiatry* 50, 295–305.

Christianson, S.-A. (1989). Flashbulb memories: Special, but not so special. *Memory and Cognition 17*, 435–43

Christianson, S.-A. (1992a). Eyewitness memory for stressful events: Methodological quandaries and ethical dilemmas. In *Handbook of emotion and memory: Research and theory,* S.-A. Christianson, ed. (Hillsdale, NJ: Erlbaum).

Christianson, S.-A. (1992b). Remembering emotional events: Potential mechanisms. In *Handbook of emotion and memory: Research and theory,* S.-A. Christianson, ed. (Hillsdale, NJ: Erlbaum).

Churchland, P. (1984). *Matter and consciousness* (Cambridge: MIT Press).

Churchland, P. (1988). Reduction and the neurobiological basis of consciousness. In *Consciousness in contemporary science,* A. Marcel and E. Bisiach, eds. (Oxford: Clarendon Press).

Churchland, P. S., and Sejnowski, T. J. (1990). In *Neural connections, mental computation,* L. Nadel, L. Cooper, P. Culicover, and M. Harnish, eds. (Cambridge: MIT Press).

Claparede, E. (1911). Recognition and "me-ness." In *Organization and pathology of thought* (1951), D. Rapaport, ed. (New York: Columbia University Press), pp. 58–75.

Clugnet, M. C., and LeDoux, J. E. (1990). Synaptic plasticity in fear conditioning circuits: Induction of LTP in the lateral nucleus of the amygdala by stimulation of the medial geniculate body. *Journal of Neuroscience 10,* 2818–24.

Cohen, D. H. (1980). The functional neuroanatomy of a conditioned response. In *Neural mechanisms of goal-directed behavior and learning,* R. F. Thompson, L. H. Hicks, and B. Shvyrkov, eds. (New York: Academic Press), pp. 283–302.

Cohen, N. J. (1980). *Neuropsychological evidence for a distinction between procedural and declarative knowledge in human memory and amnesia* (San Diego: University of California Press).

Cohen, N. J., and Corkin, S. (1981). The amnestic patient H.M.: Learning and retention of cognitive skills. *Society for Neuroscience Abstracts 7,* 517–18.

Cohen, N. J., and Eichenbaum, H. (1993). *Memory, amnesia, and the hippocampal system* (Cambridge: MIT Press).

Cohen, N. J., and Squire, L. (1980). Preserved learning and retention of pattern-analyzing skill in amnesia: Dissociation of knowing how and knowing that. *Science 210,* 207–9.

Collingridge, G. L., and Lester, R. A. J. (1989). Excitatory amino acid receptors in the vertebrate central nervous system. *Pharmacological Reviews 40,* 143–210.

Corbetta, M., Miezin, F. M., Dobmeyer, S., Shulman, G. L., and Petersen, S. E. (1991). Selective and divided attention during visual discriminations of shape, color, and speed: Functional anatomy by positron emission tomography. *Journal of Neuroscience 11*, 2383–2402.

Corkin, S. (1968). Acquisition of motor skill after bilateral medial temporal lobe excision. *Neuropsychologia 6*, 255–65.

Corodimas, K. P. and LeDoux, J. E. (1995) Disruptive effects of posttraining perihinal cortex lesions on conditioned fear: Contributions of contextual cues. *Behavioral Neuroscience 109*, 613–19.

Corodimas, K. P., LeDoux J. E., Gold, P. W., and Schulkin, J. (1994). Corticosterone potentiation of learned fear. *Annals of the New York Academy of Sciences 746*, 392–93.

Coss, R. G., and Perkel, D. H. (1985). The function of dendritic spines: A review of theoretical issues. *Behavioral and Neural Biology 44*, 151–85.

Cotman, C. W., Monaghan, D. T., and Ganong, A. H. (1988). Excitatory amino acid neurotransmission: NMDA receptors and Hebb-type synaptic plasticity. *Annual Review of Neuroscience 11*, 61–80.

Crick, F. (1994). *The Astonishing Hypothesis* (New York: Scribners).

Crick, F. and Koch, C. (1990). Toward a neurobiological theory of consciousness. *The Neurosciences 2*, 263–75.

Crockett, D. (1845). *A narrative of the life of David Crockett* (New York: Nafis & Cornish).

Dali, S. (1976). *The secret life of Salvador Dali* (London: Vision Press).

Damasio, A. (1994). *Descarte's error: Emotion, reason, and the human brain* (New York: Grosset/Putnam).

Darwin, C. (1859). *The origin of species by means of natural selection; Or, the preservation of favored races in the struggle for life* (New York: Collier).

Darwin, C. (1872). *The expression of the emotions in man and animals* (Chicago: University of Chicago Press, 1965).

Davidson, R. (1992). Emotion and affective style: Hemispheric substrates. *Psychological Science 3*, 39–43.

Davis, M. (1992a). The role of amygdala in conditioned fear. In *The amygdala: Neurobiological aspects of emotion, memory, and mental dysfunction*, J. P. Aggleton, ed. (New York: Wiley-Liss), pp. 255–306.

Davis, M. (1992b). The role of the amygdala in fear-potentiated startle: Implications for animal models of anxiety. *Trends in Pharmacological Science 13*, 35–41.

Davis, M., Hitchcock, J. M., and Rosen, J. B. (1987). Anxiety and the amygdala: pharmacological and anatomical analysis of the fear-potentiated startle paradigm. In *The psychology of learning and motivation*, Vol. 21, G. H. Bower, ed. (San Diego: Academic Press), pp. 263–305.

Davitz, H. J. (1969). *The language of emotion* (London: Academic Press).

Dawkins, R. (1982). *The extended phenotype: The gene as the unit of selection* (San Francisco: Freeman).

DeLeon, M. J., George, A. E., Stylopoulos, L. A., Smith, G., and Miller, D. C. (1989). Early marker for Alzheimer's disease: The atrophic hippocampus. *Lancet* September 16, 672–73.

Dennett, D. C. (1991). *Consciousness explained* (Boston: Little, Brown).

Dennett, D. C. and Kinsbourne, M. (1992). Time and the observer: The where and when of consciousness in the brain. *Behavioral and Brain Sciences, 15,* 183–247.

Descartes, R. (1958). *Philosophical writings*, N. K. Smith, ed. (New York: Modern Library).

Desimone, R., Miller, E. K., Chelazzi, L., and Lueschow, A. (1995). Multiple memory systems in the visual cortex. In *The cognitive neurosciences*, M. S. Gazzaniga, ed. (Cambridge: MIT Press), pp. 475–86.

de Sousa, R. (1980). The rationality of emotions. In *Explaining emotions*, A. O. Rorty, ed. (Berkeley: University of California Press).

D'Esposito, M., Detre, J., Alsop, D., Shin, R., Atlas, S., and Grossman, M. (1995). The neural basis of the central executive system of working memory. *Nature* 378, 279–81.

Diagnostic and statistical manual of mental disorders (1994), 4th edition (Washington, D.C.: American Psychiatric Association).

Diamond, D. M. and Rose, G. M. (1993). Psychological stress interferes with working, but not reference, spatial memory. *Society for Neuroscience Abstracts 19,* 366.

Diamond, D. M., Fleshner, M. and Rose, G. M. (1994). Psychological stress repeatedly blocks hippocampal primed burst potentiation in behaving rats. *Behavioural Brain Research 62,* 1–9.

Diamond, D. M., Branch, B. J., Rose, G. M., and Tocco, G. (1994). Stress effects on memory and AMPA receptors are abolished by adrenalectomy. *Society for Neuroscience Abstracts 20,* 1215.

Diamond, D. M., and Rose, G. (1994). Stress impairs LTP and hippocampal-dependent memory. *Annals of the New York Academy of Sciences* 746, 411–14.

Dickinson, E. (1955). The brain (#632). In T. H. Johnson (ed.) *The Poems of Emily Dickinson* (Cambridge, MA: Belknap).

Diorio, D., Viau, V., and Meaney, M. J. (1993). The role of the medial prefrontal cortex (cingulate gyrus) in the regulation of hypothalamic-pituitary-adrenal responses to stress. *Journal of Neuroscience 13,* 3839–47.

Dixon, N. F. (1971). *Subliminal perception: The nature of controversy* (London: McGraw-Hill).

Dixon, N. F. (1981). *Preconscious processing* (New York: Wiley).

Doi, T. (1973). *The anatomy of dependence* (Tokyo: Kodansha International).

Dollard, J. C., and Miller, N. E.,(1950). *Personality and psychotherapy* (New York: McGraw-Hill).

Dostoyevsky, F. (1864). *Notes from the underground* (New York: Dell).

Downer, J. D. C. (1961). Changes in visual gnostic function and emotional behavior following unilateral temporal lobe damage in the "split-brain" monkey. *Nature 191,* 50–51.

Dreiser, T. (1900). *Sister Carrie* (New York: Doubleday).

Dudai, Y. (1995). On the relevance of long-term potentiation to learning and memory. In J. L. McGaugh, N. M. Weinberger, and G. Lynch, ed. *Brain and memory: Modulation and mediation of neuroplasticity.* (New York: Oxford University Press).

Duffy, E. (1941). An explanation of "emotional" phenomena without the use of the concept "emotion." *Journal of General Psychology 25,* 283–93.

Dyer, M. G. (1987). Emotions and their computations: Three computer models. *Cognition and Emotion 1,* 323–47.

Eagly, A., and Chaiken, S. (1993). *The psychology of attitudes* (Fort Worth: Harcourt Brace Jovanovich).

Ebbesson, S. O. E. (1980). The parcellation theory and its relation to interspecific variability in brain organization, evolutionary and ontogenetic development, and neural plasticity. *Cell and Tissue Research 213,* 179–212.

Eccles, J. C. (1990). A unitary hypothesis of mind-brain interaction in the cerebral cortex. *Proceedings of the Royal Society of London 240,* 433–51.

Edelman, G. (1989). *The Remembered Present: A Biological Theory of Consciousness* (New York: Basic Books).

Edmunds, M. (1974). *Defence in animals: A survey of anti-predator defences* (New York: Longman).

Ehlers, A., and Margraf, J. (1987). Anxiety induced by false heart rate feedback in patients with panic disorder. *Behaviour Research and Therapy 26,* 1–11.

Eibl-Eibesfeldt, I., and Sutterlin, C. (1990). Fear, defence and aggression in animals and man: Some ethological perspectives. In *Fear and defense,* P. F. Brain, S. Parmigiani, R. Blanchard, and D. Mainardi, eds. (London: Harwood), pp. 381–408.

Eichenbaum, H., and Otto, T. (1992). The hippocampus: What does it do? *Behavioral and Neural Biology 57,* 2–36.

Eichenbaum, H., Otto, T., and Cohen, N. J. (1994). Two functional components of the hippocampal memory system. *Behavioral and Brain Sciences 17*, 449–518.

Ekman, P. (1980). Biological and cultural contributions to body and facial movement in the expression of emotions. In *Explaining emotions*, A. O. Rorty, ed. (Berkeley: University of California Press).

Ekman, P. (1984). Expression and nature of emotion. In *Approaches to emotion*, K. Scherer and P. Ekman, eds. (Hillsdale, NJ: Erlbaum), pp. 319–43.

Ekman, P. (1992a). An argument for basic emotions. *Cognition and Emotion 6*, 169–200.

Ekman, P. (1992b). Facial expressions of emotion: New findings, new questions. *Psychological Science 3*, 34–38.

Ekman, P. (1993). Facial expression and emotion. *American Psychologist 48*.

Ekman, P., Levenson, R. W., and Friesen, W. V. (1983). Autonomic nervous system activity distinguishes among emotions. *Science 221*, 1208–10.

Epstein, S. (1972). The nature of anxiety with emphasis upon its relationship to expectancy. In *Anxiety: Current trends in theory and research*, C. D. Speilberger, ed. (New York: Academic Press).

Erdelyi, M. H. (1974). A new look at the new look: Perceptual defense and vigilance. *Psychological Review 81*, 1–25.

Erdelyi, M. H. (1984). The recovery of unconscious (inaccessible) memories: Laboratory studies of hypermnesia. In *The psychology of learning and motivation: Advances in research and theory*, G. Bower, ed. (New York: Academic Press), pp. 95–127.

Erdelyi, M. (1985). *Psychoanalysis: Freud's cognitive psychology* (New York: Freeman).

Erdelyi, M. H. (1992). Psychodynamics and the unconscious. *American Psychologist 47*, 784–87.

Ericcson, K. A., and Simon, H. (1984). *Protocol analysis: Verbal reports as data* (Cambridge: MIT Press).

Eriksen, C. W. (1960). Discrimination and learning without awareness: A methodological survey and evaluation. *Psychological Review 67*, 279–300.

Everitt, B. J. and Robbins, T. W. (1942). Amygdala—ventral striatal interactions and reward related processes. In J. Aggleton (ed.) *The Amygdala: Neurobiological Aspects of Emotion, Memory and Mental Dysfunction* (New York: Wiley-Liss).

Eysenck, H. J. (1979). The conditioning model of neurosis. *Behavioral and Brain Sciences 2*, 155–99.

Eysenck, H. J., and Rachman, S. (1965). *The causes and cures of neuroses* (San Diego: Knapp).

Falls, W. A., Miserendino, M. J. D., and Davis, M. (1992). Extinction of fear-potentiated startle: Blockade by infusion of an NMDA antagonist into the amygdala. *Journal of Neuroscience 12(3)*, 854–63.

Fanselow, M. S. (1994). Neural organization of the defensive behavior system responsible for fear. *Psychonomic Bulletin and Review 1*, 429–38.

Fanselow, M. S., and Kim, J. J. (1994). Acquisition of contextual Pavlovian fear conditioning is blocked by application of an NMDA receptor antagonist DL-2-amino-5-phosphonovaleric acid to the basolateral amygdala. *Behavioral Neuroscience 108*, 210–12.

Fehr, F. S., and Russell, J. A. (1984). Concept of emotion viewed from a prototype perspective. *Journal of Experimental Psychology, General 113*, 464–86.

Finlay, B., and Darlington, R. (1995). Linked regularities in the development and evolution of mammalian brains. *Science*, 1578–84.

Flew, A. (1964). *Body, mind and death* (New York: Macmillan).

Fodor, J. (1975). *The language of thought* (Cambridge: Harvard University Press).

Fodor, J. (1983). *The modularity of mind* (Cambridge: MIT Press).

Frank, R. H. (1988). *Passions within reason: The strategic role of the emotions* (New York: Norton).

Freeman, W. J. (1994). Role of chaotic dynamics in neural plasticity. *Progress in Brain Research 102*, 319–33.

Freud, S. (1909). The analysis of a phobia in a five-year-old boy. In *Collected papers* (London: Hogarth).

Freud, S. (1925). The unconscious. In *Collected papers* (London: Hogarth).

Freud, S. (1966). *Introductory lectures on psychoanalysis*, Standard Edition, J. Strachey, ed. (New York: Norton).

Frey, U., Huang, Y.-Y., and Kandel, E. R. (1993). Effects of cAMP simulate a late stage of LTP in hippocampal CA1 neurons. *Science 260*, 1661–64.

Frijda, N. (1986). *The emotions* (Cambridge: Cambridge University Press).

Frijda, N. H. (1993). The place of appraisal in emotion. *Cognition and Emotion 7*, 357–88.

Frijda, N., and Swagerman, J. (1987). Can computers feel? Theory and design of an emotional system. *Cognition and Emotion 1*, 235–57.

Fuster, J. M. (1989). *The prefrontal cortex* (New York: Raven).

Gaffan, D. (1974). Recognition impaired and association intact in the memory of monkeys after transection of the fornix. *Journal of Comparative and Physiological Psychology 86*, 1100–1109.

Gaffan, D. (1992). Amygdala and the memory of reward. In *The amygdala: Neurobiological aspects of emotion, memory, and mental dysfunction*, J. P. Aggleton, ed. (New York: Wiley-Liss), pp. 471–83.

Gaffan, D., Murray, E. A., and Fabre-Thorpe, M. (1993). Interaction of the amygdala with the frontal lobe in reward memory. *European Journal of Neuroscience 5*, 968–75.

Gainotti, G. (1972). Emotional behavior and hemispheric side of the lesion. *Cortex 8*, 41–55.

Galaburda, A. M., Corsiglia, J., Rosen, G. D., and Sherman, G. F. (1987). Planum temporale asymmetry, reappraisal since Geschwind and Levitsky. *Neuropsychologia 25*, 853–68.

Gallagher, M., and Holland, P. (1994). The amygdala complex. Proceedings of the National Academy of Sciences, U.S.A. 91, 11, 771–76.

Gallistel, R. (1980). *The organization of action: A new synthesis* (Hillsdale, NJ: Erlbaum).

Gallup, G. (1991). Toward a comparative psychology of self-awareness: Species limitations and cognitive consequences. In *The self: Interdisciplinary approaches*, J. Strauss and G. R. Goethals, eds. (New York: Springer).

Gardner, H. (1987). *The mind's new science: A history of the cognitive revolution* (New York: Basic Books).

Gazzaniga, M. S. (1970). *The bisected brain* (New York: Appleton-Century-Crofts).

Gazzaniga, M. S. (1972). One brain—two minds. *American Scientist 60*, 311–17.

Gazzaniga, M. S. (1985). *The social brain* (New York: Basic Books).

Gazzaniga, M. S. (1988). Brain modularity: Towards a philosophy of conscious experience. In *Consciousness in contemporary science*, A. J. Marcel and E. Bisiach, eds. (Oxford: Clarendon Press).

Gazzaniga, M. S. (1992). *Nature's mind* (New York: Basic Books).

Gazzaniga, M. S., Bogen, J. E., and Sperry, R. W. (1962). Some functional effects of sectioning the cerebral commissures in man. *Proceedings of the National Academy of Sciences USA 48*, 1765–69.

Gazzaniga, M. S., Bogen, J. E., and Sperry, R. W. (1965). Cerebral commissurotomy in man: Minor hemisphere dominance for certain visuo-spatial functions. *Journal of Neurosurgery 23*, 394–99.

Gazzaniga, M. S., and LeDoux, J. E. (1978). *The Integrated Mind* (New York: Plenum).

Geertz, H. (1959). The vocabulary of emotion. *Psychiatry 22*, 225–37.

Geschwind, N. (1965). The disconnexion syndromes in animals and man. I. *Brain 88*, 237–94.

Geschwind, N., and Levitsky, W. (1968). Human brain: Left-right asymmetries in temporal speech region. *Science 161*, 186–87.

Gleitman, H., and Holmes, P. A. (1967). Retention of incompletely learned CER in rats. *Psychonomic Science 7*, 19–20.

Gloor, P., Olivier, A., and Quesney, L. F. (1981). The role of the amygdala in the expression of psychic phenomena in temporal lobe seizures. In *The amygdaloid complex*, Y. Ben-Ari, ed. (New York: Elsevier/North-Holland Biomedical Press), pp. 489–98.

Gluck, M. A., and Myers, C. E. (1995). Representation and association in memory: A neurocomputational view of hippocampal function. *Current Directions in Psychological Science 4*, 23–29.

Gold, P. E. (1992). Modulation of memory processing: enhancement of memory in rodents and humans. In L. R. Squire and N. Butters *Neuropsychology of Memory* (New York: Guilford), 402–14.

Goldman, A. I. (1993). The psychology of folk psychology. *Behavioral and Brain Sciences 16*, 15–28.

Goldman-Rakic, P. S. (1988). Topography of cognition: Parallel distributed networks in primate association cortex. *Annual Review of Neuroscience 11*, 137–56.

Goldman-Rakic, P. S. (1987). Circuitry of primate prefrontal cortex and regulation of behavior by representational memory. In *Handbook of physiology. Section 1: The nervous system. Vol. 5: Higher Functions of the Brain*, F. Plum, ed. (Bethesda, MD: American Physiological Society, pp. 373–417.

Goldman-Rakic, P. S. (1993). Working memory and the mind. In *Mind and brain: Readings from Scientific American magazine*, W. H. Freeman, ed. (New York: Freeman), pp. 66–77.

Goleman, D. (1995). *Emotional intelligence* (New York: Bantam).

Gould, J. L. (1982). *Ethology: The mechanisms and evolution of behavior* (New York: Norton).

Gould, S. J. (1977). *Ever since Darwin: Reflections in natural history* (New York: Norton).

Graff, P., Squire, L. R., and Mandler, G. (1984). The information that amnesic patients do not forget. *Journal of Experimental Psychology: Learning, Memory and Cognition 10*, 16–178.

Grasby, P. M., Firth, C. D., Friston, K. J., Bench, C., Frackowiak, R. S. J., and Dolan, R. J. (1993). Functional mapping of brain areas implicated in auditory-verbal memory function. *Brain 116*, 1–20.

Gray, J. A. (1982). *The neuropsychology of anxiety* (New York: Oxford University Press).

Gray, J. A. (1987). *The psychology of fear and stress*, Vol. 2 (New York: Cambridge University Press).

Gray, T. S., Piechowski, R. A., Yracheta, J. M., Rittenhouse, P. A., Betha, C. L., and van der Kar, L. D. (1993). Ibotenic acid lesions in the bed nucleus of the stria terminalis attenuate conditioned stress induced increases in prolactin, ACTH, and corticosterone. *Neuroendocrinology 57*, 517–24.

Greenberg, N., Scott, M., and Crews, D. (1984). Role of the amygdala in the reproductive and aggressive behavior of the lizard. *Physiology and Behavior 32*, 147–51.

Greenwald, A. G. (1992). New look 3: Unconscious cognition reclaimed. *American Psychologist 47*, 766–79.

Grey Walter, W. (1953). *The living brain* (New York: Norton).

Grossberg, S. (1982). A psychophysiological theory of reinforcement, drive, motivation and attention. *Journal of Theoretical Biology 1*, 286–369.

Guare, J. (1990). *Six degrees of separation* (New York: Random House).

Halgren, E. (1992). Emotional neurophysiology of the amygdala within the context of human cognition. In *The amygdala: Neurobiological aspects of emotion, memory, and mental dysfunction*, J. Aggleton, ed. (New York: Wiley-Liss), pp. 191–228.

Hall, C. S., and Lindzey, G. (1957). *Theories of personality* (New York: Wiley).

Hamann, S. B., Stefanacci, L., Squire, L., Adolphs, R., Tranel, D., Damasio, H., Damasio, A. (1996). Recognizing facial emotion. *Nature 379*, 497.

Harnad, S. (1982). Consciousness: An afterthought. *Cognition and Brain Theory 5*, 29–47.

Harré, R. (1986). *The social construction of emotions* (New York: Blackwell).

Head, H. (1921). Release function in the nervous system. *Proceedings of the Royal Society of London: Biology 92B*, 184–87.

Hebb, D. O. (1946). Emotion in man and animal: An analysis of the intuitive processes of recognition. *Psychological Review 53*, 88–106.

Hebb, D. O. (1949). *The organization of behavior* (New York: Wiley).

Heelas, P. (1986). Emotion talk across cultures. In *The social construction of emotions*, R. Harré, ed. (New York: Blackwell).

Heidegger, M. (1927). *Being and time* (New York: SUNY Press).

Heilman, K. and Satz, P., eds. (1983). *Neuropsychology of Human Emotion*. (New York: Guilford Press).

Helmstetter, F. (1992). The amygdala is essential for the expression of conditioned hypoalgesia. *Behavioral Neuroscience 106*, 518–28.

Herrick, C. J. (1933). The functions of the olfactory parts of the cerebral cortex. *Proceedings of the National Academy of Sciences USA 19*, 7–14.

Hilgard, E. R. (1980). The trilogy of mind: Cognition, affection, and conation. *Journal of the History of the Behavioral Sciences 16*, 107–17.

Hilton, S. M. (1979). The defense reaction as a paradigm for cardiovascular control. In *Integrative functions of the autonomnic nervous system*, C. M. Brooks, K. Koizuni, and A. Sato, eds. (Tokyo: University of Tokyo Press), pp. 443–49.

Hirst, W. (1994). Cognitive aspects of consciousness. In *The cognitive neurosciences*, M. S. Gazzaniga, ed. (Cambridge: MIT Press).

Hirst, W., Spelke, E. S., Reaves, C. C., Charack, G., and Neisser, U. (1980). Dividing attention without alternation or automaticity. *Journal of Experimental Psychology, General 109*, 98–117.

Hobson, J. A., and Steriade, M. (1986). Neuronal basis of behavioral state control. In Handbook of Physiology. Section 1: The Nervous System. Vol. 4: *Intrinsic Regulatory Systems of the Brain*. V. B. Mountcastle, ed. (Bethesda, MD: American Physiological Society), pp. 701–823.

Hodes, R. L., Cook, E. W., and Lang, P. J. (1985). Individual differences in autonomic response: Conditioned association or conditioned fear? *Psychophysiology 22*, 545–60.

Hohmann, G. W. (1966). Some effects of spinal cord lesions on experienced emotional feelings. *Psychophysiology 3*.

Horel, J. A., Keating, E. G., and Misantone, L. J. (1975). Partial Kluver-Bucy syndrome produced by destroying temporal neocortex or amygdala. *Brain Research 94*, 347–59.

Hugdahl, K., (1995). Psychophysiology: The Mind-Body Perspective (Cambridge: Harvard University Press).

Hull, C. L. (1943). *Principles of behavior* (New York: Appleton-Century-Crofts).

Humphrey, N. (1992). *A history of the mind* (New York: Simon & Schuster).

Ionescu, M. D., and Erdelyi, M. H. (1992). The direct recovery of subliminal stimuli. In *Perception without awareness: Cognitive, clinical, and social perspectives*, R. F. Bornstein and T. S. Pittman, eds. (New York: Guilford), pp. 143–69.

Isaacson, R. L. (1982). The limbic system (New York: Plenum).

Iversen, S. (1976). Do temporal lobe lesions produce amnesia in animals? *International Review of Neurobiology 19*, 1–49.

Izard, C. E. (1971). *The face of emotion* (New York: Appleton-Century-Crofts).

Izard, C. E. (1977). *Human emotions* (New York: Plenum).

Izard, C. E. (1992a). Basic emotions, relations among emotions, and emotion-cognition relations. *Psychological Review 99*, 561–65.

Izard, C. E. (1992b). Four systems for emotion activation: Cognitive and noncognitive. *Psychological Review 100,* 68–90.

Jackendoff, R. (1987). *Consciousness and the computational mind* (Cambridge: Bradford Books, MIT Press).

Jacobs, W. J., and Nadel, L. (1985). Stress-induced recovery of fears and phobias. *Psychological Review 92,* 512–31.

Jacobsen, C. F., and Nissen, H. W. (1937). Studies of cerebral function in primates: IV. The effects of frontal lobe lesions on the delayed alternation habit in monkeys. *Journal of Comparative and Physiological Psychology 23,* 101–12.

Jacobson, L., and Sapolsky, R. (1991). The role of the hippocampus in feedback regulation of the hypothalamic-pituitary-adrenocortical axis. *Endocrine Reviews 12(2),* 118–34.

Jacoby, L. L., Toth, J. P., Lindsay, D. S., and Debner, J. A. (1992). Lectures for a layperson: Methods for revealing unconscious processes. In *Perception without awareness: Cognitive, clinical, and social perspectives,* R. F. Bornstein and T. S. Pittman, eds. (New York: Guilford), pp. 81–120.

James, W. (1884). What is an emotion? *Mind 9,* 188–205.

James, W. (1890). *Principles of psychology* (New York: Holt).

Jarrell, T. W., Gentile, C. G., Romanski, L. M., McCabe, P. M., and Schneiderman, N. (1987). Involvement of cortical and thalamic auditory regions in retention of differential bradycardia conditioning to acoustic conditioned stimuli in rabbits. *Brain Research 412,* 285–94.

Jaynes, J. (1976). *The origin of consciousness in the breakdown of the bicameral mind* (Boston: Houghton Mifflin).

Jerison, H. (1973). *Evolution of brain and intelligence* (New York: Academic Press).

John, E. R. (1972). Switchboard versus statistical theories of learning. *Science 177,* 850–64.

Johnson-Laird, P. N. (1988). *The computer and the mind: An introduction to cognitive science* (Cambridge: Harvard University Press).

Johnson-Laird, P. N., and Oatley, K. (1992). Basic emotions, rationality, and folk theory. *Cognition and Emotion 6,* 201–23.

Jones, B., and Mishkin, M. (1972). Limbic lesions and the problem of stimulus-reinforcement associations. *Experimental Neurology 36,* 362–77.

Jonides, J., Smith, E. E., Keoppe, R. A., Awh, E., Minoshima, S., and Mintun, M. A. (1993). Spatial working memory humans as revealed by PET. *Nature 363,* 623–25.

Kaada, B. R. (1960). Cingulate, posterior orbital, anterior insular and temporal pole cortex. In *Handbook of physiology. Section 1, Vol. 2: Neuro-*

physiology, J. Field, H. J. Magoun and V. E. Hall, eds. (Washington, D.C.: American Physiological Society), pp. 1345–72.

Kaada, B. R. (1967). Brain mechanisms related to aggressive behavior. In *Aggression and defense—Neural mechanisms and social patterns,* C. Clemente and D. B. Lindsley, eds. (Berkeley: University of California Press), pp. 95–133.

Kagan, J. and Snidman, N. (1991). Infant predictors of inhibited and uninhibited profiles. *Psychological Science 2,* 40–43.

Kahneman, D., Slovic, P., and Tversky, A. (1982). *Judgement under uncertainty: Heuristics and biases* (Cambridge: Cambridge University Press).

Kandel, E., and Schwartz, J. (1982). Molecular biology of an elementary form of learning: Modulation of transmitter release by cAMP. *Science 218,* 433–43.

Kandel, E. R. (1989). Genes, nerve cells, and the remembrance of things past. *Journal of Neuropsychiatry,* 103–25.

Kapp, B. S., Whalen, P. J., Supple, W. F., and Pascoe, J. P. (1992). Amygdaloid contributions to conditioned arousal and sensory information processing. In *The amygdala: Neurobiological aspects of emotion, memory, and mental dysfunction,* J. P. Aggleton, ed. (New York: Wiley-Liss).

Kapp, B. S., Frysinger, R. C., Gallagher, M., and Haselton, J. (1979). Amygdala central nucleus lesions: Effect on heart rate conditioning in the rabbit. *Physiology and Behavior 23,* 1109–17.

Kapp, B. S., Pascoe, J. P., and Bixler, M. A. (1984). The amygdala: A neuroanatomical systems approach to its contributions to aversive conditioning. In *Neuropsychology of memory,* N. Buttlers and L. R. Squire, eds. (New York: Guilford), pp. 473–88.

Kapp, B. S., Wilson, A., Pascoe, J., Supple, W., and Whalen, P. J. (1990). A neuroanatomical systems analysis of conditioned bradycardia in the rabbit. In *Learning and computational neuroscience: Foundations of adaptive networks.,* M. Gabriel and J. Moore, eds. (Cambridge: MIT Press), pp. 53–90.

Karten, H. J., and Shimizu, T. (1991). Are visual hierarchies in the brains of the beholders? Constancy and variability in the visual system of birds and mammals. In *The changing visual system,* P. Bagnoli and W. Hodos, eds. (New York: Plenum), pp. 51–59.

Keating, G. E., Kormann, L. A., and Horel, J. A. (1970). The behavioral effects of stimulating and ablating the reptilian amygdala (Caiman sklerops). *Physiology and Behavior 5,* 55–59.

Kelley, G. A. (1963). Discussion: Aldous, the personable computer. In *Computer simulation of personality: Frontier of psychological theory,* S. S. Tomkins and S. Messick, eds. (New York: Wiley).

Kierkegaard, S. (1844). *The concept of dread* (Princeton: Princeton University Press).

Kihlstrom, J. F. (1984). Conscious, subconscious, unconscious: A cognitive perspective. In *The unconscious reconsidered*, K. S. Bowers and D. Meichenbaum, eds. (New York: Wiley), pp. 149–211.

Kihlstrom, J. F. (1987). The cognitive unconscious. *Science 237*, 1445–52.

Kihlstrom, J. F., Barnhardt, T. M., and Tataryn, D. J. (1992a). Implicit perception. In *Perception without awareness: Cognitive, clinical, and social perspectives*, R. F. Bornstein and T. S. Pittman, eds. (New York: Guilford), pp. 17–54.

Kihlstrom, J. F., Barnhardt, T. M., and Tatryn, D. J. (1992b); The psychological unconscious: Found, lost, regained. *American Psychologist 47*, 788–91.

Kim, J. J., and Fanselow, M. S. (1992). Modality-specific retrograde amnesia of fear. *Science 256*, 675–77.

Kinsbourne, M. (1988). Integrated field theory of consciousness. In *Consciousness in contemporary science*, A. Marcel and E. Bisiach, eds. (Oxford: Oxford University Press).

Klein, D. (1981). Anxiety reconceptualized. In *New research and changing concepts*, D. Klein and J. Rabkin, eds. (New York: Raven).

Klein, D. F. (1993). False suffocation alarms, spontaneous panics, and related conditions: An integrative hypothesis. *Archives of General Psychiatry 50*, 306–17.

Kleinginna, P. R., and Kleinginna, A. M. (1985). Cognition and affect: A reply to Lazarus and Zajonc. *American Psychologist 40*, 470–71.

Klüver, H., and Bucy, P. C. (1939). Preliminary analysis of functions of the temporal lobes in monkeys. *Archives of Neurology and Psychiatry 42*, 979–1000.

Klüver, H., and Bucy, P. C. (1937). "Psychic blindness" and other symptoms following bilateral temporal lobectomy in rhesus monkeys. *American Journal of Physiology 119*, 352–53.

Koa, E. B., and Kozak, E. J. (1986). Emotional processing of fear: Exposure to corrective information. *Psychological Bulletin 99*, 20–35.

Koch, C., Zador, A., and Brown, T. H. (1992). Dendritic spines: Convergence of theory and experiment. *Science 256*, 973–74.

Kolb, L. C. (1987). A neuropsychological hypothesis explaining post-traumatic stress disorders. *American Journal of Psychiatry 144*, 989–995.

Kosslyn, S. M. (1980). *Image and mind* (Cambridge: Harvard University Press).

Kosslyn, S. M. (1983). *Ghosts in the mind's machine* (New York: Norton).

Kosslyn, S. M., and Koenig, O. (1992). *Wet mind: The new cognitive neuroscience* (New York: Macmillan).

Kotter, R., and Meyer, N. (1992). The limbic system: a review of its empirical foundation. *Behavioural Brain Research 52,* 105–27.

Kramer, P. (1993). *Listening to Prozac* (New York: Viking).

Krebs, J. R. (1990). Food-storage birds: Adaptive specialization in brain and behavior? *Philosophical Transactions of the Royal Society. London. Series B: Biological Sciences 329,* 153–60.

Kubie, J., and Ranck, J. (1983). Sensory-behavioral correlates of individual hippocampal neurons in three situations: Space and context. In *The neurobiology of the hippocampus,* W. Seifert, ed. (New York: Academic Press).

Kubie, J. L., Muller, R. U., and Bostock, E. (1990). Spatial firing properties of hippocampal theta cells. *Journal of Neuroscience 10(4),* 1110–23.

LaBar, K. S., LeDoux, J. E., Spencer, D. D., and Phelps, E. A. (1995). Impaired fear conditioning following unilateral temporal lobectomy in humans. *Journal of Neuroscience 15,* 6846–55.

Lader, M., and Marks, I. (1973). *Clinical anxiety* (London: Heinemann).

Lang, P. (1979). A bioinformational theory of emotional imagery. *Psychophysiology 16,* 495–512.

Lang, P. (1993). The network model of emotion: Motivational concerns. In *Advances in social cognition,* R. S. Wyer and T. K. Srull, eds. (Hillsdale, NJ: Erlbaum), pp. 109–33.

Laroche, S., Doyere, V., Redini-Del Negro, C., and Burette, F. (1995). Neural mechanisms of associative memory: Role of long-term potentiation. In *Brain and memory: Modulation and mediation of neuroplasticity,* J. L. McGaugh, N. M. Weinberger, and G. Lynch, eds. (New York: Oxford University Press), pp. 277–302.

Lashley, K. S. (1950a). In search of the engram. *Symposia of the Society for Experimental Biology IV,* 454–82.

Lashley, K. (1950b). The problem of serial order in behavior. In *Cerebral mechanisms in behavior,* L. A. Jeffers, ed. (New York: Wiley).

Lazarus, R. S. (1966). Psychological stress and the coping process (New York: McGraw Hill).

Lazarus, R. S. (1984). On the primacy of cognition. *American Psychologist,* 39, 124–29.

Lazarus, R. S. (1991). Cognition and motivation in emotion. *American Psychologist 46(4),* 352–67.

Lazarus, R., and McCleary, R. (1951). Autonomic discrimination without awareness: A study of subception. *Psychological Review 58,* 113–22.

LeDoux, J. E. (1985). Brain, mind, and language. In *Brain and mind*, D. A. Oakley, ed. (London: Methuen).

LeDoux, J. E. (1987). Emotion. In *Handbook of Physiology. Section 1: The Nervous System. Vol. 5; Higher Functions of the Brain*, F. Plum, ed. (Bethesda, MD: American Physiological Society), pp. 419–60.

LeDoux, J. E. (1989). Cognitive-emotional interactions in the brain. *Cognition and Emotion* 3, 267–289.

LeDoux, J. E. (1991). Emotion and the limbic system concept. *Concepts in Neuroscience* 2, 169–99.

LeDoux, J. E. (1993). Emotional memory systems in the brain. *Behavioural Brain Research* 58, 69–79.

LeDoux, J. E. (1994). Emotion, memory and the brain. *Scientific American* 270, 32–39.

LeDoux, J. E. (1995). Emotion: Clues from the brain. *Annual Review of Psychology* 46, 209–35.

LeDoux, J. E., Cicchetti, P., Xagoraris, A., and Romanski, L. M. (1990). The lateral amygdaloid nucleus: Sensory interface of the amygdala in fear conditioning. *Journal of Neuroscience* 10, 1062–69.

LeDoux, J. E., Farb, C. F., and Ruggiero, D. A. (1990). Topographic organization of neurons in the acoustic thalamus that project to the amygdala. *Journal of Neuroscience* 10, 1043–54.

LeDoux, J. E., Iwata, J., Cicchetti, P., and Reis, D. J. (1988). Different projections of the central amygdaloid nucleus mediate autonomic and behavioral correlates of conditioned fear. *Journal of Neuroscience* 8, 2517–29.

LeDoux, J. E., Romanski, L. M., and Xagoraris, A. E. (1989). Indelibility of subcortical emotional memories. *Journal of Cognitive Neuroscience* l, 238–43.

LeDoux, J. E., Sakaguchi, A., Iwata, J., and Reis, D. J. (1986). Interruption of projections from the medial geniculate body to an archi-neostriatal field disrupts the classical conditioning of emotional responses to acoustic stimuli in the rat. *Neuroscience* 17, 615–27.

LeDoux, J. E., Sakaguchi, A., and Reis, D. J. (1984). Subcortical efferent projections of the medial geniculate nucleus mediate emotional responses conditioned by acoustic stimuli. *Journal of Neuroscience* 4(3), 683–98.

Leonardo da Vinci (1939). *The notebooks of Leonardo da Vinci*. (New York: Reynal & Hitchcock).

Levenson, R. W. (1992). Autonomic nervous system differences among emotions. *Psychological Science* 3, 23–27.

Leventhal, H., and Scherer, K. (1987). The relationship of emotion to cognition: A functional approach to a semantic controversy. *Cognition and Emotion 1*, 3–28.

Lindsley, D. B. (1951). Emotions. In *Handbook of Experimental Psychology*, S. S. Stevens, ed. (New York: Wiley), pp. 473–516.

Lisman, J. (1995). What does the nucleus know about memories? *Journal of NIH Research 7*, 43–46.

Loftus, E. (1993). The reality of repressed memories. *American Psychologist 48*, 518–37.

Loftus, E. F., Donders, K., Hoffman, H. G., and Schooler, J. W. (1989). Creating new memories that are quickly accessed and confidently held. *Memory and Cognition 17*, 607–16.

Loftus, E. F., and Hoffman, H. G. (1989). Misinformation and memory: The creation of new memories. *Journal of Experimental Psychology: General 118*, 100–104.

Loftus, E. F., and Klinger, M. R. (1992). Is the unconscious smart or dumb? *American Psychologist 47*, 761–65.

Luine, V. N. (1994). Steroid hormone influences on spatial memory. *Annals of the New York Academy of Sciences 743*, 201–11.

Luria, A. (1966). Higher cortical functions in man (New York: Basic Books).

Lynch, G. (1986). *Synapses, circuits, and the beginnings of memory* (Cambridge: MIT Press).

MacLean, P. D. (1949). Psychosomatic disease and the "visceral brain": recent developments bearing on the Papez theory of emotion. *Psychosomatic Medicine 11*, 338–53.

MacLean, P. D. (1952). Some psychiatric implications of physiological studies on frontotemporal portion of limbic system (visceral brain). *Electroencephalography and Clinical Neurophysiology 4*, 407–18.

MacLean, P. D. (1970). The triune brain, emotion and scientific bias. In *The neurosciences: Second study program*, F. O. Schmitt, ed. (New York: Rockefeller University Press), pp. 336–49.

MacLean, P. D. (1990). *The triune brain in evolution: Role in paleocerebral functions* (New York: Plenum).

Madison, D. V., Malenka, R. C., and Nicoll, R. A. (1991). Mechanisms underlying long-term potentiation of synaptic transmission. *Annual Review of Neuroscience 14*, 379–97.

Makino, S., Gold, P. W., and Schulkin, J. (1994). Corticosterone effects on corticotropin-releasing hormone mRNA in the central nucleus of the amygdala and the parvocellular region of the paraventricular nucleus of the hypothalamus. *Brain Research 640*, 105–12.

Mancia, G., and Zanchetti, A. (1981). Hypothalamic control of autonomic functions. In *Handbook of the hypothalamus Vol. 3: Behavioral studies of the hypothalamus*, P. J. Morgane and J. Panksepp, eds. (New York: Marcel Dekker), pp. 147–202.

Manderscheid, R. W., and Sonnenschein, M. A. (1994). *Mental health, United States 1994* (Rockville, MD: U.S. Department of Public Health and Human Services).

Mandler, G. (1975). *Mind and emotion* (New York: Wiley).

Mandler, G. (1988). Memory: Conscious and unconscious. In *Memory: Interdisciplinary approaches*, P. R. Solomon, G. R. Goethals, C. M. Kelly, and B. R. Stephens, eds. (New York: Springer).

Mandler, G. (1992). Memory, arousal, and mood. In *Handbook of emotion and memory: Research and theory*, S.-A. Christianson, ed. (Hillsdale, NJ: Erlbaum).

Marcel, A. J., and Bisiach, E. (1988). *Consciousness in contemporary science* (Oxford: Clarendon Press).

Margraf, J., Ehlers, A., and Roth, W. T. (1986a). Biological models of panic disorder and agoraphobia—a review. *Behaviour Research and Therapy* 24, 553–67.

Margraf, J., Ehlers, A., and Roth, W. T. (1986b). Sodium lactate infusions and panic attacks: A review and critique. *Psychosomatic Medicine* 48, 23– 51.

Marks, I. (1987). *Fears, phobias, and rituals: Panic, anxiety and their disorders* (New York: Oxford University Press).

Marr, D. (1982). *Vision: A computational investigation into the human representation and processing of visual information* (San Francisco: Freeman).

Mason, J. W. (1968). A review of psychoendocrine research on the sympathetic-adrenal medullary system. *Psychosomatic Medicine* 30, 631–53.

Masson, J. M., and McCarthy, S. (1995). *When elephants weep: The emotional lives of animals* (New York: Delacorte).

Mayford, M., Abel, T., and Kandel, E. R. (1995). Transgenic approaches to cognition. *Current Opinions in Neurobiology* 5, 141–48.

McAllister, W. R., and McAllister, D. E. (1971). Behavioral measurement of conditioned fear. In *Aversive conditioning and learning*, F. R. Brush, ed. (New York: Academic Press), pp. 105–79.

McCabe, P. M., Schneiderman, N., Jarrell, T. W., Gentile, C. G., Teich, A. H., Winters, R. W., and Liskowsky, D. R. (1992). Central pathways involved in differential classical conditioning of heart rate responses. In *Learning and memory: The behavioral and biological substrates*, I. Gormenzano, E.A., ed. (Hillsdale, NJ: Erlbaum), pp. 321–46.

McClelland, J. L., McNaughton, B. L., and O'Reilly, R. C. (1995). Why there are complementary learning systems in the hippocampus and neocortex: Insights from the successes and failures of connectionist models of learning and memory. *Psychological Review 102*, 419–57.

McCormick, D. A., and Bal, T. (1994). Sensory gating mechanisms of the thalamus. *Current Opinion in Neurobiology 4*, 550–56.

McDonald, K. A. (1995). Scientists rethink anthropomorphism. *The Chronicle of Higher Education*, February 24, 1995.

McEwen, B. S. (1992). Paradoxical effects of adrenal steroids on the brain: Protection versus degeneration. *Biological Psychiatry 31*, 177–99.

McEwen, B., and Sapolsky, R. (1995). Stress and cognitive functioning. *Current Opinion in Neurobiology 5*, 205–16.

McGaugh, J. L. (1990). Significance and remembrance: The role of neuromodulatory systems. *Psychological Science 1*, 15–25.

McGaugh, J. L., Cahill, L., Parent, M. B., Mesches, M. H., Coleman-Mesches, K., and Salinas, J. A. (1995). Involvement of the amygdala in the regulation of memory storage. In *Plasticity in the central nervous system: Learning and memory*, J. L. McGaugh, F. Bermudez-Rattoni, and R. A. Prado-Alcala, eds. (Hillsdale, NJ: Erlbaum).

McGaugh, J. L., Introini-Collison, I. B., Cahill, L. F., Castellano, C., Dalmaz, C., Parent, M. B., and Williams, C. L. (1993). Neuromodulatory systems and memory storage: Role of the amygdala. *Behavioural Brain Research 58*, 81–90.

McGinnies, E. (1949). Emotionality and perceptual defense. *Psychological Review 56*, 244–51.

McKittrick, C., Blanchard, C., Blanchard, R., McEwen, B. S., and Sakai, R. (1995). Serotonin receptor binding in a colony model of chronic social stress. *Biological Psychiatry 37*, 383–93.

McNally, R. J., Lasko, N. B., Macklin, M. L., and Pitman, R. K. (1995). Autobiographical memory disturbance in combat-related posttraumatic stress disorder. *Behavior Research and Therapy 33*, 619–30.

McNaughton, B. L., and Barnes, C. A. (1990). From cooperative synaptic enhancement to associative memory: Bridging the abyss. *Seminars in the Neurosciences 2*, 403–16.

Melville, H. (1930). *Moby-Dick* (New York: Penguin).

Merikle, P. M. (1992). Perception without awareness. *American Psychologist 47*, 792–95.

Messick, S. (1963). Computer models and personality theory. In *Computer simulation of personality: Frontier of psychological theory*, S. S. Tomkins and S. Mesnick, eds. (New York: Wiley), 305–17.

Meunier, M., Bachevalier, J., Mishkin, M., and Murray, E. A. (1993). Effects on visual recognition of combined and separate ablations of the entorhinal and perirhinal cortex in rhesus monkeys. *Journal of Neuroscience 13*, 5418–32.

Miller, G. (1956). The magical number seven, plus or minus two: Some limits on our capacity for processing information. *Psychological Review 63*, 81–97.

Miller, G. A., and Gazzaniga, M. S. (1984). The cognitive sciences. In *Handbook of cognitive neuroscience*, M. S. Gazzaniga, ed. (New York: Plenum).

Miller, G. A., and Johnson-Laird, P. (1976). *Language and perception* (Cambridge: Cambridge University Press).

Miller, N. E. (1948). Studies of fear as an acquirable drive: I. Fear as motivation and fear reduction as reinforcement in the learning of new responses. *Journal of Experimental Psychology 38*, 89–101.

Milner, B. (1962). Les troubles de la mémoire accompagnant des lésions hippocampiques bilaterales. In *Physiologie de l'hippocampe*, P. Plassouant, ed. (Paris: Centre de la Recherche Scientifique).

Milner, B. (1964). Some effects of frontal lobectomy in man. In J. M. Warren and K. Akert, eds. *The Frontal Granular Cortex and Behavior.* (New York: McGraw-Hill), pp. 313–34.

Milner, B. (1965). Memory disturbances after bilateral hippocampal lesions in man. In *Cognitive processes and brain*, P. M. Milner and S. E. Glickman, eds. (Princeton: Van Nostrand).

Mineka, S., Davidson, M., Cook, M. and Keir, R. (1984). Observational conditioning of snake fear in rhesus monkeys. *Journal of Abnormal Psychology 93*, 355–72.

Minsky, M. (1985). *The society of mind* (New York: Touchstone Books/Simon & Schuster).

Miserendino, M. J. D., Sananes, C. B., Melia, K. R., and Davis, M. (1990). Blocking of acquisition but not expression of conditioned fear-potentiated startle by NMDA antagonists in the amygdala. *Nature 345*, 716–18.

Mishkin, M. (1978). Memory in monkeys severely impaired by combined but not separate removal amygdala and hippocampus. *Nature 273*, 297–98.

Mishkin, M. (1982). A memory system in the monkey. *Philosophical Transactions of the Royal Society, London, Series B: Biological Sciences. 298*, 85–95.

Mishkin, M., Malamut, B., and Bachevalier, J. (1984). Memories and habits: Two neural systems. In *The neurobiology of learning and memory*, J. L. McGaugh, G. Lynch, and N. M. Weinberger, eds. (New York: Guilford).

Moore, T. E. (1988). The case against subliminal manipulation. *Psychology and Marketing* 5, 297–316.

Morgan, M., and LeDoux, J. E. (1995). Differential contribution of dorsal and ventral medial prefrontal cortex to the acquisition and extinction of conditioned fear. *Behavioral Neuroscience* 109, 681–88.

Morgan, M. A., Romanski, L. M., and LeDoux, J. E. (1993). Extinction of emotional learning: Contribution of medial prefrontal cortex. *Neuroscience Letters* 163, 109–13.

Morris, R. G. M. (1984). Development of a water-maze procedure for studying spatial learning in the rat. *Journal of Neuroscience Methods* 11, 47–60.

Morris, R. G. M., Anderson, E., Lynch, G. S., and Baudry, M. (1986). Selective impairment of learning and blockade of long-term potentiation by and N-methyl-D-asparate receptor antagonist, AP5. *Nature* 319, 774–76.

Morris, R. G. M., Garrard, P., Rawlins, J. N. P., and O'Keefe, J. (1982). Place navigation impaired in rats with hippocampal lesions. *Nature* 273, 297–98.

Morsbach, H., and Tyler, W. J. (1986). A Japanese emotion: Amae. In *The social construction of emotions*, R. Harré, ed. (New York: Blackwell).

Moruzzi, G., and Magoun, H. W. (1949). Brain stem reticular formation and activation of the EEG. *Electroencephalography and Clinical Neurophysiology* 1, 455–73.

Mowrer, O. H. (1939). A stimulus-response analysis of anxiety and its role as a reinforcing agent. *Psychological Review* 46, 553–65.

Muller, R., Ranck, J., and Taube, J. (1996). Head direction cells: Properties and functional significance. *Current Opinion in Neurobiology* (in press).

Murphy, S., and Zajonc, R. (1993). Affect, cognition, and awareness: Affective priming with suboptimal and optimal stimuli. *Journal of Personality and Social Psychology* 64, 723–39.

Murray, E. A. (1992). Medial temporal lobe structures contributing to recognition memory: The amygdaloid complex versus the rhinal cortex. In J. P. Aggleton, ed. *The Amygdala: Neurobiological Aspects of Emotion, Memory, and Mental Dysfunction.* (New York: Wiley-Liss, Inc.).

Nabokov, V. (1966). Speak, memory: An autobiography revisited (New York: Putnam).

Nadel, L., and Willner, J. (1980). Context and conditioning: A place for space. *Physiological Psychology* 8, 218–28.

Nagel, T. (1974). What is it like to be a bat? *Philosophical Review* 83, 4435–50.

Nagy, J., Zambo, K., and Decsi, L. (1979). Anti-anxiety action of diazepam after intraamygdaloid application in the rat. *Neuropharmacology 18*, 573–76.

Nauta, W. J. H. (1971). The problem of the frontal lobe: A reinterpretation. *Journal of Psychiatric Research 8*, 167–87.

Nauta, W. J. H., and Karten, H. J. (1970). A general profile of the vertebrate brain, with sidelights on the ancestry of cerebral cortex. In *The neurosciences: Second study program*, F. O. Schmitt, ed. (New York: Rockefeller University Press), pp. 7–26.

Neisser, U. (1976). *Cognition and reality* (San Francisco: Freeman).

Neisser, U. (1967). *Cognitive psychology* (New York: Appleton-Century-Crofts).

Neisser, U., and Harsch, N. (1992). Phantom flashbulbs: False recollections of hearing the news about *Challenger*. In *Affect and accuracy in recall: Studies of "flashbulb" memories*, E. Winograd and U. Neisser, eds. (New York: Cambridge University Press).

Newcomer, J. W., Craft, S., Hershey, T., Askins, K., and Bardgett, M. E. (1994). Glucocorticoid-induced impairment in declarative memory performance in adult humans. *Journal of Neuroscience 14*, 2047–53.

Newell, A. (1980). Physical symbol systems. *Cognition 4*, 135–43.

Newell, A., Rosenbloom, P. S., and Laird, J. E. (1989). Symbolic architecture for cognition. In *Foundations of cognitive science*, M. Posner, ed. (Cambridge: MIT Press).

Newell, A., and Simon, H. (1972). *Human problem solving* (Boston: Little, Brown).

Newman, P. L. (1960). "Wild man" behavior in a New Guinea highlands community. *American Anthropologist 66*, 1–19.

Nicoll, R. A., and Malenka, R. C. (1995). Contrasting properties of two forms of long-term potentiation in the hippocampus. *Nature 377*, 115–18.

Nisbett, R. E., and Wilson, T. D. (1977). Telling more than we can know: Verbal reports on mental processes. *Psychological Review 84*, 231–59.

Norman, D. A., and Shallice, T. (1980). Attention to action: Willed and automatic control of behavior. In *Consciousness and self-regulation*, R. J. Davidson, G. E. Schwartz, and D. Shapiro, eds. (New York: Plenum).

Northcutt, R. G., and Kaas, J. H. (1995). The emergence and evolution of mammalian neocortex. *Trends in Neuroscience 18*, 373–79.

Nottebohm, F., Kasparian, S., and Pandazis, C. (1981). Brain space for a learned task. *Brain Research 213*, 99–109.

Oatley, K., and Duncan, E. (1994). The experience of emotions in everyday life. *Cognition and Emotion 8*, 369–81.

Öhman, A. (1992). Fear and anxiety as emotional phenomena: Clinical, phenomenological, evolutionary perspectives, and information-processing mechanisms. In *Handbook of the emotions,* M. Lewis and J. M. Haviland, eds. (New York: Guilford), pp. 511–36.

O'Keefe, J. (1976). Place units in the hippocampus of the freely moving rat. *Experimental Neurology 51,* 78–109.

O'Keefe, J. (1993). Hippocampus, theta, and spatial memory. *Current Opinion in Neurobiology 3,* 917–24.

O'Keefe, J., and Nadel, L. (1978). *The hippocampus as a cognitive map* (Oxford: Clarendon Press).

Olton, D., Becker, J. T., and Handleman, G. E. (1979). Hippocampus, space and memory. *Behavioral and Brain Sciences 2,* 313–65.

Ono, T., and Nishijo, H. (1992). Neurophysiological basis of the Klüver-Bucy syndrome: Responses of monkey amygdaloid neurons to biologically significant objects. In *The amygdala: Neurobiological aspects of emotion, memory, and mental dysfunction,* J. P. Aggleton, ed. (New York: Wiley-Liss), pp. 167–90.

Ortony, A., and Turner, T. J. (1990). What's basic about basic emotions? *Psychological Review 97,* 315–31.

Packard, V. (1957). *The hidden persuaders* (New York: D. M. McKay).

Panksepp, J. (1982). Toward a general psychobiological theory of emotions. *Behavioral and Brain Sciences 5,* 407–67.

Papez, J. W. (1937). A proposed mechanism of emotion. *Archives of Neurology and Psychiatry 79,* 217–24.

Parasuramna, R., and Martin, A. (1994). Cognition in Alzheimer's disease. *Current Opinion in Neurobiology 4,* 237–44.

Pavlides, C., Watanabe, Y., and McEwen, B. S. (1993). Effects of glucocorticoids on hippocampal long-term potentiation. *Hippocampus 3,* 183–192.

Pavlov, I. P. (1927). *Conditioned reflexes* (New York: Dover).

Peffiefer, J. (1955). *The human brain* (New York: Harper & Row).

Penrose, R. (1989). *The emperor's new mind: Concerning computers, minds, and the laws of physics* (New York: Penguin).

Peterson E. (1980). Behavioral studies of telencephalic function in reptiles. In: Ebbesson S. O. E., ed. *Comparative Neurology of the Telencephalon* (New York: Plenum Press), pp. 343–88.

Petrides, M. (1994). Frontal lobes and behaviour. *Current Opinion in Neurobiology 4,* 207–11.

Petrides, M., Alivsatos, B., Meyer, E., and Evans, A. C. (1993). Functional activation of the human frontal cortex during the performance of verbal working memory tasks. *Proceedings of the National Academy of Sciences USA 90*, 878–82.

Phillips, A. (1993). *On kissing, tickling, and being bored: Psychoanalytic essays on the unexamined life* (Cambridge: Harvard University Press).

Phillips, R. G., and LeDoux, J. E. (1992). Differential contribution of amygdala and hippocampus to cued and contextual fear conditioning. *Behavioral Neuroscience 106*, 274–85.

Picton, T. W., and Stuss, D. T. (1994). Neurobiology of conscious experience. *Current Opinion in Neurobiology 4*, 256–65.

Pinker, S. (1994). *The language instinct: How the mind creates language* (New York: Morrow).

Pinker, S. (1995). Language is a human instinct. In *The third culture*, J. Brockman, ed. (New York: Simon & Schuster).

Pitkänen, A., Stefanacci, L., Farb, C. R., Go, C.-G., LeDoux, J. E., and Amaral, D. G. (1995). Intrinsic connections of the rat amygdaloid complex: Projections originating in the lateral nucleus. *Journal of Comparative Neurology 356*, 288–310.

Plum, F., and Volpe, B. T. (1987). Neuroscience and higher brain function: From myth to public responsibility. In *Handbook of physiology. Section 1: The nervous system, Vol. 5: Higher Functions of the Brain*, F. Plum, ed. (Bethesda, MD: American Physiological Society).

Plutchik, R. (1980). Emotion: A psychoevolutionary synthesis (New York: Harper & Row).

Plutchik, R. (1993). Emotions and their vicissitudes: Emotions and psychopathology. In *Handbook of emotions*, M. Lewis and J. M. Haviland, eds. (New York: Guilford), pp. 53–65.

Posner, M. I. (1990). *Foundations of cognitive science* (Cambridge: MIT Press).

Posner, M. (1992). Attention as a cognitive and neural system. *Current Directions in Psychological Science 1*, 11–14.

Posner, M., and Petersen, S. (1990). The attention system of the human brain. *Annual Review of Neuroscience 13*, 25–42.

Posner, M., and Snyder, C. (1975). Facilitation and inhibition in the processing of signals. In *Attention and performance V*, P. Rabbitt and S. Domic, eds. (London: Academic Press).

Povinelli, D. J., and Preuss, T. M. (1995). Theory of mind: Evolutionary history of a cognitive specialization. *Trends in Neuroscience 18*, 418–24.

Powell, D. A., and Levine-Bryce, D. (1989). A comparison of two model systems of associative learning: Heart rate and eyeblink conditioning in the rabbit. *Psychophysiology 25*, 672–82.

Preuss, T. M. (1995). Do rats have prefrontal cortex? The Rose-Woolsey-Akert program reconsidered. *Journal of Cognitive Neuroscience 7*, 1–24.

Price, J. L., Russchen, F. T., and Amaral, D. G. (1987). The limbic region. II: The amygdaloid complex. In *Handbook of Chemical Neuroanatomy. Vol. 5: Integrated Systems of the CNS, Part 1*, A. Bjorklund, T. Hokfelt, and L. W. Swanson, eds. (Amsterdam: Elsevier), pp. 279–388.

Purves, D., White, L. E., and Andrews, T. J. (1994). Manual asymmetry and handedness. *Proceedings of the National Academy of Sciences USA 91*, 5030–32.

Putnam, H. (1960). Minds and machines. In *Dimensions of mind*, S. Hook, ed. (New York: Collier).

Pylyshyn, Z. (1984). *Computation and cognition: Toward a foundation for cognitive science* (Cambridge, MA: Bradford Books, MIT Press).

Quirk, G. J., Repa, J. C., and LeDoux, J. E. (1995). Fear conditioning enhances auditory short-latency responses of single units in the lateral nucleus of the amygdala: Simultaneous multichannel recordings in freely behaving rats. *Neuron 15*, 1029–39.

Reep, R. (1984). Relationship between prefrontal and limbic cortex: A comparative anatomical review. *Brain, Behavior and Evolution 25*, 5–80.

Reid, W. H. (1989). *The treatment of psychiatric disorders: Revised for the DSM-III-R* (New York: Brunner/Mazel).

Rogan, M. T., and LeDoux, J. E. (1995). LTP is accompanied by commensurate enhancement of auditory-evoked responses in a fear conditioning circuit. *Neuron 15*, 127–36.

Rolls, E. T. (1985). Connections, functions and dysfunctions of limbic structures, the prefrontal cortex, and hypothalamus. In *The scientific basis of clinical neurology*, M. Swash and C. Kennard, eds. (London: Churchill Livingstone), pp. 201–13.

Rolls, E. T. (1992a). Neurophysiological mechanisms underlying face processing within and beyond the temporal cortical visual areas. *Philosophical Transactions of the Royal Society, London, Series B, Biological Sciences 335*, 11–21.

Rolls, E. T. (1992b). Neurophysiology and functions of the primate amygdala. In *The amygdala: Neurobiological aspects of emotion, memory, and mental dysfunction*, J. P. Aggleton, ed. (New York: Wiley-Liss), pp. 143–65.

Rose, S. P. R. (1995). Glycoproteins and memory formation. *Behavioural Brain Research 66*, 73–78.

Rorty, A. O. (1980). Explaining emotions. In *Explaining emotions*, A. O. Rorty, ed. (Berkeley: University of California Press).

Rorty, R. (1979). *Philosophy and the mirror of nature* (Princeton: Princeton University Press).

Rosenzweig, M. (1996). Aspects of the search for neural mechanisms of memory. *Annual Review of Psychology 47,* 1–32.

Rudy, J. W., and Morledge, P. (1994). Ontogeny of contextual fear conditioning in rats: Implications for consolidation, infantile amnesia, and hippocampal system function. *Behavioral Neuroscience 108,* 227–34.

Rudy, J. W., and Sutherland, R. J. (1992). Configural and elemental associations and the memory coherence problem. *Journal of Cognitive Neuroscience 4(3),* 208–16.

Ruggiero, D. A., Gomez, R. E., Cravo, S. L., Mtui, E., Anwar, M., and Reis, D. J. (1991). The rostral ventrolateral medulla: Anatomical substrates of cardiopulmonary integration. In *Cardiorespiratory and motor coordination,* H.-P. Koepchen and T. Huopaniemi, eds. (New York: Springer), pp. 89–102.

Rumelhart, D. E. and McClelland, J. E. (1988). *Parallel Distributed Processing: Explorations in the Microstructure of Cognition.* (Cambridge: Bradford Books, MIT Press).

Russell, B. (1905). On denoting. *Mind 14,* 479–93.

Ryle, G. (1949). *The concept of mind* (New York: Barnes & Noble).

Sapolsky, R. M. (1990). Stress in the wild. *Scientific American 262,* 116–23.

Sarter, M. F., and Markowitsch, H. J. (1985). Involvement of the amygdala in learning and memory: A critical review, with emphasis on anatomical relations. *Behavioral Neuroscience 99,* 342–80.

Sartre, J.-P. (1943). *Being and nothingness* (New York: Philosophical Library).

Saucier, D. and Cain, D. P. (1995). Spatial learning without NMDA receptor-dependent long-term potentiation. *Nature 378,* 186–89.

Savander, V., Go, C. G., LeDoux, J. E., and Pitkänen, A. (1995). Intrinsic connections of the rat amygdaloid complex: Projections originating in the basal nucleus. *Journal of Comparative Neurology 361,* 345–68.

Schachter, S., and Singer, J. E. (1962). Cognitive, social, and physiological determinants of emotional state. *Psychological Review 69,* 379–99.

Schacter, D. L., and Graf, P. (1986). Effects of elaborative processing on implicit and explicit memory for new associations. *Journal of Experimental Psychology: Learning, Memory, and Cognition 12(3),* 432–44.

Scherer, K. R. (1984). On the nature and function of emotion: A component process approach. In *Approaches to emotion,* K. R. Scherer and P. Ekman, eds. (Hillsdale, NJ: Erlbaum), pp. 293–317.

Scherer, K. R. (1988). Criteria for emotion-antecedent appraisal: A review. In *Cognitive perspectives on emotion and motivation,* V. Hamilton, G. H.

Bower, and N. H. Frijda, eds. (Norwell, MA: Kluwer Academic Publishers), pp. 89–126.

Scherer, K. R. (1993a). Neuroscience projections to current debates in emotion psychology. *Cognition and Emotion* 7, 1–41.

Scherer, K. R. (1993b). Studying the emotion-antecedent appraisal process: An expert system approach. *Cognition and Emotion* 7, 325–55.

Schneiderman, N., Francis, J., Sampson, L. D., and Schwaber, J. S. (1974). CNS integration of learned cardiovascular behavior. In *Limbic and autonomic nervous system research*, L. V. DiCara, ed. (New York: Plenum), pp. 277–309.

Schwartz, B. E., Halgren, E., Fuster, J. M., Simpkins, E., Gee, M., and Mandelkern, M. (1995). Cortical metabolic activation in humans during a visual memory task. *Cerebral Cortex* 5.

Scoville, W. B., and Milner, B. (1957). Loss of recent memory after bilateral hippocampal lesions. *Journal of Neurology and Psychiatry* 20, 11–21.

Searle, J. (1984). *Minds, brains, science* (Cambridge: Harvard University Press).

Searle, J. (1992). *The rediscovery of the mind* (Cambridge: MIT Press).

Selden, N. R. W., Everitt, B. J., Jarrard, L. E., and Robbins, T. W. (1991). Complementary roles for the amygdala and hippocampus in aversive conditioning to explicit and contextual cues. *Neuroscience* 42(2), 335–50.

Seligman, M. E. P. (1971). Phobias and Preparedness. *Behavior Therapy* 2, 307–20.

Sengelaub, D. R. (1989). Cell generation, migration, death and growth in neural systems mediating social behavior. In *Advances in Comparative and Environmental Physiology 3: Molecular and Cellular Basis of Social Behavior in Vertebrates*, J. Balthazart, ed. (New York: Springer), pp. 239–67.

Servatius, R. J., and Shors, T. J. (1994). Exposure to inescapable stress persistently facilitates associative and nonassociative learning in rats. *Behavioral Neuroscience* 108, 1101–06.

Shalev, A. Y., Rogel-Fuchs, Y., and Pitman, R. K. (1992). Conditioned fear and psychological trauma. *Biological Psychiatry* 31, 863–65.

Shallice, T. (1988). Information processing models of consciousness. In *Consciousness in contemporary science*, A. Marcel and E. Bisiach, eds. (Oxford: Clarendon Press).

Shattuck, R. (1980). *The forbidden experiment* (New York: Farrar, Straus & Giroux).

Shepherd, G. (1983). *Neurobiology* (New York: Oxford University Press).

Sherry, D. F., Jacobs, L. F., and Gaulin, S. J. C. (1992). Spatial memory and adaptive specialization of the hippocampus. *Trends in Neuroscience 15,* 298–303.

Shevrin, H. (1992). Subliminal perception, memory, and consciousness: Cognitive and dynamic perspectives. In *Perception without awareness: Cognitive, clinical, and social perspectives,* R. F. Bornstein and T. S. Pittman, eds. (New York: Guilford), pp. 123–42.

Shevrin, H., Williams, W. J., Marshall, R. E., Hertel, R. K., Bond, J. A., and Brakel, L. A. (1992). Event-related potential indicators of the dynamic unconscious. *Consciousness and Cognition 1,* 340–66.

Shiffrin, M., and Schneider, W. (1977). Controlled and automatic human information processing: II. Perceptual learning, automatic attending, and a general theory. *Psychological Review 84,* 127–90.

Shimamura, A. (1995). Memory and frontal lobe function. In *The cognitive neurosciences,* M. S. Gazzaniga, ed. (Cambridge: MIT Press).

Shors, T. J., Foy, M. R., Levine, S., and Thompson, R. F. (1990). Unpredictable and uncontrollable stress impairs neuronal plasticity in the rat hippocampus. *Brain Research Bulletin 24,* 663–67.

Sibley, C. G., and Ahlquist, J. E. (1984). The phylogeny of the hominoid primates, as indicated by DNA-DNA hybridization. *Journal of Molecular Evolution 20,* 2–15.

Simon, H. A. (1967). Motivational and emotional controls of cognition. *Psychological Review 74,* 29–39.

Simpson, G. G. (1953). *The major features of evolution* (New York: Columbia University Press).

Simpson, G. G. (1967). *The meaning of evolution,* revised edition (New Haven: Yale University Press).

Skelton, R. W., Scarth, A. S., Wilkie, D. M., Miller, J. J., and Philips, G. (1987). Long-term increases in dentate granule cell responsivity accompany operant conditioning. *Journal of Neuroscience 7,* 3081–3087.

Skinner, B. F. (1938). *The behavior of organisms: An experimental analysis* (New York: Appleton-Century-Crofts).

Sloman, A. (1987). Motives, mechanisms and emotions. *Cognition and Emotion.* 1:217–33.

Sloman, A., and Croucher, M. (1981). Why robots will have emotions. In *Seventh Proceedings of the International Joint Conference on Artificial Intelligence* (Vancouver, British Columbia), pp. 197–202.

Smith, C. A., and Ellsworth, P. C. (1985). Patterns of cognitive appraisal in emotion. *Journal of Personality and Social Psychology 56,* 339–53.

Smith, C. A., and Lazarus, R. S. (1990). Emotion and adaptation. In *Handbook of personality: Theory and research*, L. A. Pervin, ed. (New York: Guilford), pp. 609–37.

Smith, J. M. (1958). *The theory of evolution* (Middlesex, England: Penguin).

Smith, O. A., Astley, C. A., Devito, J. L., Stein, J. M., and Walsh, R. E. (1980). Functional analysis of hypothalamic control of the cardiovascular responses accompanying emotional behavior. *Federation Proceedings* 39(8), 2487–94.

Smolensky, P. (1990). Connectionist modeling: Neural computation/mental connections. In *Neural connections, mental computation*, L. Nadel, L. Cooper, P. Culicover, and M. Harnish, eds. (Cambridge: MIT Press).

Solomon, R. C. (1993). The philosophy of emotions. In *Handbook of emotions*, M. Lewis and J. Haviland, eds. (New York: Guilford).

Sperry, R. W. (1969). A modified concept of consciousness. *Psychological Review* 76, 532–36.

Spinoza, B. (1955). *Works of Spinoza* (New York: Dover).

Squire, L. (1987). *Memory and the brain* (New York: Oxford University Press).

Squire, L. R., and Cohen, N. J. (1984). Human memory and amnesia. In *Neurobiology of learning and memory*, G. Lynch, J. L. McGaugh, and N. M. Weinberger, eds. (New York: Guilford).

Squire, L. R., Cohen, N. J., and Nadel, L. (1984). The medial temporal region and memory consolidation: A new hypothesis. In *Memory consolidation*, H. Eingartner and E. Parker, eds. (Hillsdale, NJ: Erlbaum).

Squire, L. R., and Davis, H. P. (1975). Cerebral protein synthesis inhibition and discrimination training: Effects of extent and duration of inhibition. *Behavioral Biology* 13, 49–57.

Squire, L. R., Knowlton, B., and Musen, G. (1993). The structure and organization of memory. *Annual Review of Psychology*, 44, 453–95.

Staübli, U. V. (1995). Parallel properties of long-term potentiation and memory. In *Brain and memory: Modulation and mediation of neuroplasticity*, J. L. McGaugh, N. M. Weinberger, and G. Lynch, eds. (New York: Oxford University Press), pp. 303–18.

Steinmetz, J. E., and Thompson, R. F. (1991). Brain substrates of aversive classical conditioning. In *Neurobiology of learning, emotion and affect*, J. I. Madden, ed. (New York: Raven), pp. 97–120.

Stuss, D. T. (1991). Self, awareness, and the frontal lobes: A neuropsychological perspective. In *The self: Interdisciplinary approaches*, J. Strauss and G. R. Goethals, eds. (New York: Springer).

Sutherland, R. J., and Rudy, J. W. (1989). Configural association theory: The role of the hippocampal formation in learning, memory, and amnesia. *Psychobiology* 17, 129–44.

Swanson, L. W. (1983). The hippocampus and the concept of the limbic system. In *Neurobiology of the hippocampus*, W. Seifert, ed. (London: Academic Press), pp. 3–19

Swanson, L. W. and Simmons, D. M. (1989). Differential steroid hormone and neural influences on peptide mRNA levels in CRH cells of the paraventricular nucleus: A hybridization histochemical study in the rat. *Journal of Comparative Neurology 285*, 413–35

Swartz, B. E., Halgren, E., Fuster, J. M., Simpkins, E., Gee, M., and Mandelkern, M. (1995). Cortical metabolic activation in humans during a visual memory task. *Cerebral Cortex 5*, 205–14.

Tarr, R. S. (1977). Role of the amygdala in the intraspecies aggressive behavior of the iguanid lizard. *Physiology and Behavior 18*, 1153–58.

Teyler, T. J., and DiScenna, P. (1986). The hippocampal memory indexing theory. *Behavioral Neuroscience 100*, 147–54.

Thorndike, E. L. (1913). *The psychology of learning* (New York: Teachers College Press).

Thorpe, S. J., Rolls, E. T., and Maddison, S. (1983). The orbitofrontal cortex: Neuronal activity in the behaving monkey. *Experimental Brain Research 49*, 93–115.

Tolman, E. C. (1932). *Purposive behavior* (New York: Appleton-Century-Crofts).

Tomkins, S. S. (1962). Affect, imagery, consciousness (New York: Springer).

Tooby, J., and Cosmides, L. (1990). The past explains the present: Emotional adaptations and the structure of ancestral environments. *Ethological Sociobiology 11*, 375–424.

Tully, T. (1991). Genetic dissection of learning and memory in drosophila melanogaster. In *Neurobiology of learning, emotion and affect*, J. I. Madden, ed. (New York: Raven), pp. 29–66.

Tulving, E. (1983). *Elements of episodic memory* (New York: Oxford University Press).

Twain, M. (1962). *Letters from the earth: "From an unfinished burlesque of books on etiquette." Part 1, "At the funeral,"* B. DeVoto, ed. (New York: Harper and Row).

Ullman, S. (1984). Early processing of visual information. In *Handbook of cognitive neuroscience*, M. S. Gazzaniga, ed. (New York: Plenum).

Ungerleider, L. G., and Haxby, J. (1994). What and where in the human brain. *Current Opinion in Neurobiology 4*, 157–65.

Ungerleider, L. G., and Mishkin, M. (1982). Two cortical visual systems. In *Analysis of visual behavior*, D. J. Ingle, M. A. Goodale, and R. J. W. Mansfield, eds. (Cambridge: MIT Press), pp. 549–86.

Uno, H., Ross, T., Else, J., Suleman, M., and Sapolsky, R. (1989). Hippocampal damage associated with prolonged and fatal stress in primates. *Journal of Neuroscience 9*, 1705–11.

Uylings, H. B. M., and van Eden, C. G. (1990). Qualitative and quantitative comparison of the prefrontal cortex in rat and in primates, including humans. *Progress in Brain Research 85*, 31–62.

Valins, S. (1966). Cognitive effects of false heart-rate feedback. *Journal of Personality and Social Psychology 4*, 400–408.

van de Kar, L. D., Piechowski, R. A., Rittenhouse, P. A., and Gray, T. S. (1991). Amygdaloid lesions: Differential effect on conditioned stress and immobilization-induced increases in corticosterone and renin secretion. *Neuroendocrinology 54*, 89–95.

Van Essen, D. C. (1985). Functional organization of primate visual cortex. In *Cerebral cortex*, A. Peters and E. G. Jones, eds. (New York: Plenum), pp. 259–328.

Van Hoesen, G. W. (1982). The parahippocampal gyrus: New observations regarding its cortical connections in the monkey. *Trends in Neuroscience 5*, 345–50.

Velams, M. (1991). Is human information processing conscious? *Behavioral and Brain Sciences 14*, 651–726.

von Eckardt, B. (1993). *What is cognitive science?* (Cambridge: MIT Press).

von Uexkull, J. (1934). A stroll through the world of animals and man. In *Instinctive behavior: The development of a modern concept*, C. H. Chiller, ed. (London: Methuen).

Walter, W. G. (1953). *The living brain* (New York: Norton).

Warrington, E., and Weiskrantz, L. (1973). The effect of prior learning on subsequent retention in amnesic patients. *Neuropsychologia 20*, 233–48.

Watkins, L. R., and Mayer, D. J. (1982). Organization of endogenous opiate and nonopiate pain control systems. *Science 216*, 1185–92.

Watson, J. B. (1929). *Behaviorism* (New York: Norton).

Watson, J. B., and Rayner, R. (1920). Conditioned emotional reactions. *Journal of Experimental Psychology 3*, 1–14.

Weinberger, N. M. (1995). Retuning the brain by fear conditioning. In *The cognitive neurosciences*, M. S. Gazzaniga, ed. (Cambridge: MIT Press), pp. 1071–90.

Weiskrantz, L. (1956). Behavioral changes associated with ablation of the amygdaloid complex in monkeys. *Journal of Comparative Physiological Psychology 49*, 381–91.

Weiskrantz, L. (1988). Some contributions of neuropsychology of vision and memory to the problem of consciousness. In *Consciousness in contemporary science,* A. Marcel and E. Bisiach, eds. (Oxford: Clarendon Press).

Weiskrantz, L., and Warrington, E. (1979). Conditioning in amnesic patients. *Neuropsychologia 17,* 187–94

Weisz, D. J., Harden, D. G., and Xiang, Z. (1992). Effects of amygdala lesions on reflex facilitation and conditioned response acquisition during nictitating membrane response conditioning in rabbit. *Behavioral Neuroscience 106,* 262–73.

Wierzbicka, A. (1994). Emotion, language and cultural scripts. In S. Kitayama and H. R. Marcus, *Emotion and Culture* (Washington: American Psychological Association).

Wilcock, J., and Broadhurst, P. L. (1967). Strain differences in emotionality: Open-field and conditioned avoidance behavior in the rat. *Journal of Comparative Physiological Psychology 63,* 335–38.

Wilde, O. (1909). Gilbert. *Intentions* (New York: Lamb Publishing).

Williams, T. (1964). *The milk train doesn't stop here anymore* (Norfolk, CT: New Directions).

Wilson, D., Reeves, A., Gazzaniga, M. S., and Culver, C. (1977). Cerebral commissurotomy for the control of intractable epilepsy. *Neurology 27,* 708–15.

Wilson, F. A. W., O Scalaidhe, S. P., and Goldman-Rakic, P. S. (1993). Dissociation of object and spatial processing domains in primate prefrontal cortex. *Science 260,* 1955–58.

Wilson, M. A., and McNaughton, B. L. (1994). Reactivation of hippocampal ensemble memories during sleep. *Science 265,* 676–79.

Wilson, J. R. (1968). *The mind* (New York: Time-Life Books, Life Science Library).

Wolitsky, D. L., and Wachtel, P. L. (1973). *Personality and perception.* In B. B. Wolman (ed.) *Handbook of General Psychology* (Englewood, NJ: Prentice-Hall), pp. 826–57.

Wolkowitz, O., Reuss, V., and Weingartner, H. (1990). Cognitive effects of corticosteroids. *American Journal of Psychiatry 147,* 1297–1303.

Wolpe, J. (1988). Panic disorder: A product of classical conditioning. *Behavior Research and Therapy 26,* 441–50.

Wolpe, J., and Rachman, S. (1960). Psychoanalytic evidence: A critique of Freud's case of Little Hans. *Journal of Nervous and Mental Disease 130,* 198–220.

Yin, J. C. P., Wallach, J. S., Del Vecchio, M., Wilder, E. L., Zhou, H., Quinn, W. G., and Tully, T. (1994). Induction of a dominant-negative CREB transgene specifically blocks long-term memory in drosophila. *Cell 79*, 49–58.

Young, A. W., Aggleton, J. P., Hellawell, D. J., Johnson, M., Broks, P., and Hanley, J. R. (1995). Face processing impairments after amygdalotomy. *Brain 118*, 15–24.

Zajonc, R. (1980). Feeling and thinking: Preferences need no inferences. *American Psychologist 35*, 151–75.

Zajonc, R. B. (1984). On the primacy of affect. *American Psychologist 39*, 117–23.

Zola-Morgan, S., and Squire, L. R. (1993). Neuroanatomy of memory. *Annual Review of Neuroscience 16*, 547–63.

Zola-Morgan, S., Squire, L. R., Alvarez-Royo, P., and Clower, R. P. (1991). Independence of memory functions and emotional behavior: separate contributions of the hippocampal formation and the amygdala. *Hippocampus 1*, 207–20.

Zola-Morgan, S., Squire, L. R., and Amaral, D. G. (1986). Human amnesia and the medial temporal region: Enduring memory impairment following a bilateral lesion limited to field CA1 of the hippocampus. *Journal of Neuroscience 6(10)*, 2950–67.

Zola-Morgan, S., Squire, L. R., and Amaral, D. G. (1989). Lesions of the amygdala that spare adjacent cortical regions do not impair memory or exacerbate the impairment following lesions of the hippocampal formation. *Journal of Neuroscience 9*, 1922–36.

Zuckerman, M. (1991). *Psychobiology of personality* (Cambridge: Cambridge University Press).

INDEX

COSMO GORDON LANG

Sir William Orpen.

THE ARCHBISHOP OF YORK

COSMO GORDON LANG

by

J. G. LOCKHART

Author of *Viscount Halifax*, *Cecil Rhodes*, etc.

HODDER AND STOUGHTON LIMITED

FIRST PRINTED SEPTEMBER 1949

Made and Printed in Great Britain for
HODDER AND STOUGHTON LTD., London
by T. and A. CONSTABLE LTD., Printers, Edinburgh

INTRODUCTION

"IT is probably useless," Archbishop Lang wrote in 1929, " for any man who has held a post of great public importance to say that he wishes no biography to be published after his death. That was the wish, for example, of Archbishop Temple (Frederick Temple), and two volumes of memoirs by seven friends were the result. In my own case I have certainly little desire for any 'Life.' For one thing, the materials are too scanty. There is little beyond the record of Church affairs; but what makes a 'Life' worth reading is not detail of this kind, but revelation of the man's mind, purpose, character. Where will any biographer find this in my case? A few sermons and speeches, not the most important and effective, have been printed and published: a few have been written. But the great bulk have no record or exist only in imperfect newspaper reports or my own illegible notes. The ceaseless pressure of public work which has always afflicted me, the extraordinary increase in the correspondence of every Bishop, and the use of shorthand writers and the typing machine have prevented me from having any correspondence which dealt with large questions of thought or policy, still more any correspondence which revealed my own inner life. I have never had any correspondents to whom I was wont to write freely and fully. And I have always—perhaps wrongly—been very reserved about all the inner life which is really what makes a man. True, I have written long accounts, for my own remembrance and for recalling, for example, those moments when that inner life has been emancipated from the pressure of work—many in the little chapel at Ballure which I call 'the Cell' and several happy and blessed Holy Weeks at Cuddesdon; and it is in these moments that I feel I have lived my real life—at least what I hope is my real life. I must suppose that anyone into whose hands my private papers may fall might wish to make some use of these notes, but they are largely too intimate to be put before a public gaze and are too illegible to be deciphered."

He adds that for the benefit of his biographer, whom he declares more than once that he sincerely pities, he has begun to "jot down" in moments of leisure, such as occur during convalescence, some account of his life, and in particular of periods and episodes known only to himself. As the years passed those jottings increased. They filled many notebooks and ran into scores of thousands of words. They are necessarily, as the Archbishop meant them to be, the hard core of this book, and any considerable quoted passages not otherwise assigned are taken from them. Some may think I should have included more of Lang's own words, even possibly have let them stand unbuttressed, or perhaps supported by a few explanatory notes. There were several reasons against doing this. One was that the result would have been not a Life but an autobiography, which is a very different thing. Another was that the jottings are of uneven literary quality. Often he wrote so fully and with such care that the result could be printed as it stands. On the other hand, the notes are sometimes little more than the jottings he professed them to be; big gaps in his life are left unfilled; and occasionally more is written about an episode than, in a longer retrospect, its importance warrants. So, while I have drawn very freely on this autobiographical material, I have omitted much which the Archbishop evidently thought should be included and have supplemented from other sources the information he prepared. To this extent, however, I have complied with his expressed wishes. I have not attempted a "record of Church affairs," but have rather tried to reveal "the man's mind, purpose, character."

The other sources used are certain papers of his own on special subjects, like the death of King George V and the Abdication of King Edward VIII; the notebook diaries he kept at Ballure (to which he has alluded), almost but happily not quite undecipherable; and a large collection of letters, mostly of a personal interest, which he left to his literary executor. These I have further supplemented with letters, memoranda and recollections which a large number of people, whose kindness I gratefully acknowledge, have placed at my disposal.

My first and largest debt is to the Dean of Westminster, Dr. Don, who is the Archbishop's literary executor and was undoubtedly the man he would himself have chosen to be his biographer. Unfortunately the weight of ecclesiastical duty made it impossible for the Dean to undertake this task; but he has spared neither time nor trouble to make my work easier and without his help the book could hardly have been written.

I am also deeply in the debt of the Archbishop of York, the Bishop of Chichester, the Bishop of Winchester, the Bishop of Pretoria, Bishop

Norman Lang, Canon J. A. Douglas, the Archdeacon of Canterbury, the Rev. E. K. Talbot, the late Canon Crawley, Mrs. Crawley, the Rev. Lumley Green-Wilkinson, the Rev. C. S. Donald, Mrs. Macdonald of Largie, Mrs. Lionel Ford and the Rev. Ian White-Thomson. They have given me valuable, indeed indispensable, help in a great variety of ways. The Archbishop of York, the Bishop of Chichester, the Bishop of Winchester and the Rev. E. K. Talbot, besides providing me with their personal recollections, have read, with comment and correction, several of the chapters; and I should add that, like everyone else who has written about anyone concerned in the ecclesiastical history of the first thirty years of this century, I must make grateful acknowledgment to Dr. Bell's remarkable Life of Archbishop Davidson. The Bishop of Pretoria placed at my disposal all his letters from Archbishop Lang, who wrote to him almost weekly over a period of more than thirty-five years. Bishop Norman Lang also let me use his large collection of his brother's letters and was most helpful on family history. Canon Douglas contributed a long paper, which probably he is the only living person qualified to write, on the Archbishop's work for Reunion. The Archdeacon of Canterbury, Canon and Mrs. Crawley, the Rev. Lumley Green-Wilkinson, the Rev. C. S. Donald and Mrs. Lionel Ford have all supplied me with memoranda and correspondence. Mrs Macdonald of Largie very kindly invited me to Ballure, so that I was able to see something, on the ground and under her guidance, of the Archbishop's much-loved Highland home.

These were my principal creditors; but I must also acknowledge an especial indebtedness to many other people who have sent me memoranda or letters or both: Mr. P. K. Lang and the Very Rev. Dr. Marshall Lang, brothers of the Archbishop; Mrs. J. M. Mitchell for a paper written by her father, the late Canon Tupper-Carey; the Master of the Temple for material about the early days; Canon J. G. Simpson, who had known and corresponded with the Archbishop ever since they were both Ordinands at Cuddesdon, and sent me his recollections and many letters; Dr. C. C. J. Webb for an estimate of the Archbishop's services as Dean of Divinity at Magdalen; the Bishop of Brechin for some memories of the Archbishop's visits to Cuddesdon; Sir Dougal Malcolm for his invaluable assistance over the chapter on All Souls; Mrs. Lancashire, for allowing me to print her account of the Mallard Feast of 1901; Lord Macmillan for information about the Archbishop's work as a Trustee of the British Museum and in other connexions; Lord Quickswood for an appreciation of his oratory; Mr. Guy O. Grenier, who for many years collected press cuttings referring to the Archbishop and sent me these from Ceylon; and Mr. Clifford Witting, who compiled the index.

These are only some of the numerous people whose ample assistance has enabled this book to be written. Many more, some of whom have asked that no acknowledgment should be made, have been extremely kind in lending me letters and helping me in various ways. I hope they will accept a general and most grateful recognition of what they have done.

While the book owes much of any interest it may have to those, mentioned and unmentioned, who have contributed so largely in so many forms, I could hardly have written it at all, and would certainly have taken much longer to write it, had it not been for the generous hospitality of Colonel Edmondstoune Cranstoun of Corehouse and the late Miss Edmondstoune Cranstoun, and of Major and Mrs. Hope of Luffness, under whose respective roofs by far the greater part of the work was done.

J. G. LOCKHART.

COREHOUSE, LANARK, SCOTLAND.
August 1948.

CONTENTS

ILLUSTRATIONS

ILLUSTRATIONS

Chapter I

FORBEARS

IN 1864 the Parish Minister of Fyvie, Aberdeenshire, was John Marshall
Lang, a promising young man who had come there five years earlier
from the city of Aberdeen. He was of good Scottish stock, stemming
back on one side to a certain David Marshall, a surgeon in the Royal
Navy in the early years of the eighteenth century. When David left the
Service, he settled down on a property at Neilsland, in Lanarkshire. He
and his wife, Anna Weir, had one son, also David, who in turn had
another son, John, grandfather of the Minister of Fyvie. This John
Marshall married Elizabeth Stobie, of Luscar in Fife, a property which
had been in the Stobie family since the reign of Charles II. A Stobie
fought at Bothwell Brig (on the Covenanting side), and there is an
intricate and not entirely convincing connexion with the Woodrows,
ancestors of Woodrow Wilson, President of the United States.

John and Elizabeth Marshall had one child, a daughter, Anna by
name, who was born in 1807 and married Gavin Lang, Minister of the
Parish of Glassford, a windswept village between Hamilton and Strathaven
in the Middle Ward of Lanarkshire. Of the Langs nothing seems to
be known, beyond the solitary fact that Gavin's father was a West India
merchant.

Genealogies are dry dead stuff until they are brought to life by
persons, places or events, and with Gavin and Anna the story of the
Langs may be said to have really begun. The little Manse at Glassford,
with its nine acres of glebe and an accompanying stipend of about five
pounds a week, was a quarter of a mile from the village, in country so
open that when the wind blew hard from the west, a whiff of the open
sea would be carried from the Ayrshire coast, many miles away. The
village was a simple and happy community. The men were mostly
hand-loom weavers, great players of quoits in summer and curling in
winter; and the women were careful housewives who came to church
on Sunday with their Bibles wrapped up in their handkerchiefs. At
about nine each evening the passer-by would hear the "sough" of psalms
behind the lighted cottage windows, and Communion Sunday was the
great day in the Calendar.

Here in 1834 John Marshall Lang was born, fourth of a future family of eleven children. Many years afterwards he recorded some memories of his parents. "My father," he wrote, "was a parish minister of the old school, a simple, straight, conscientious pastor, who tended his flock in his own way, and who had no ambitions beyond those of serving his parish, and maintaining the use and wont of the Church of Scotland." "If he was not loved," the son added, "he was greatly respected by his parishioners." At least it would seem that the Year of Disruption (1843) passed with hardly more than a rippling of the quiet waters, and although thereafter some of Mr. Lang's parishioners stole off on Sunday morning to the new Free Kirk at Strathaven, there was none of the bitterness found elsewhere and no rival rose up in Glassford to challenge the Establishment.

The Minister's wife was a more forceful character than her husband : she was to have a grandson who was said to take after her both in his face and in his ways. "She was a remarkable woman," her son wrote of her. "Her early home had been a beautiful place (Neilsland) in the neighbourhood of Hamilton, then a most pleasant locality,[1] a place that to her children was the dearest spot on earth. The environment of the young girl was that of a country house a century ago, where lairds assembled whose potations were sometimes long and deep. . . . Notwithstanding all her work and the anxiety of her household, my mother was the most sprightly of hostesses, her talk full of ripple and radiance, quick in jest and repartee, a sweet singer of 'auld Scotch sangs,' with a saving sense of humour and an indefinable charm of manner."

A manse in those days had to be an elastic and hospitable house, and Glassford followed the rule. At Christmas as many as eighteen people might be crowded under its roof, and of Mrs. Lang it was said that "if Satan himself rang the bell she would meet him with a smile and a welcome." A barrel of meal stood in the kitchen, and there was a plate of broth, a bowl of milk, and some oatcake for any hungry man or woman who came to the Minister's door.

The fourth son was to become the Very Rev. John Marshall Lang, a minister like his father, and a man of distinction in the Kirk. At one time he was regarded with mild suspicion by some of his more old-fashioned colleagues on account of his supposed "High Church" opinions and practices. As early as his first charge, at the East Church of Aberdeen,

---

[1] Evidently the coal had not yet been found.

he persuaded his congregation to stand instead of sitting "for praise," on the ground that if standing was right for the choir it was also right for the congregation; and stand they did until the Presbytery of Aberdeen intervened, censured the Minister, and forbade the innovation. "We were told to sit down and we obeyed," was the Minister's rueful comment. But if he bowed to authority, he retained his opinions, and at Anderston in Glasgow and at Morningside in the suburbs of Edinburgh he introduced changes which to-day would appear quite usual but in those times were thought heterodox and dangerous. At Morningside he even built an apse with an altar in the centre and shifted the pulpit to one side.

In 1873, when he moved to the famous Barony Kirk of Glasgow, the reforms became still more drastic. He succeeded Norman Macleod, the noted preacher, writer and philanthropist, whose sermons were much commended by Queen Victoria. Lang considered the "Auld Kirk" in which Macleod had won his fame and found it wanting. It was a square ugly building, surrounded by galleries, "with a lofty pulpit flanked by steep stairs up which the Beadle panted to deposit 'the Book' before service began." So Lang, during his ministry, collected about £28,000, acquired a site close by the existing building, and raised a successor to the "Auld Kirk." This was pure Gothic, a style at that time strange to the Church of Scotland, of sandstone, with tall pillars, chancel and nave. A chapel, provided by the Minister's sister, Mrs. Cunliffe, in memory of her husband, contained the first fresco painting of Our Lord yet seen in that Church. Such things smacked of prelacy if not of popery. The Minister went further. He abolished pew rents, held daily services, observed Holy Week, and had the Psalms chanted. No doubt a good many grey heads were shaken, and it says much for the tact, the talents and the persistence of the Minister that he was allowed to prevail in his practices. The murmurs soon died away, and as many as two thousand people would come to the church on Sunday evenings to hear him preach. Both in the pulpit and on the platform—and especially on the platform—he spoke with eloquence and power, and sometimes with an intensity that completely carried away his hearers. He gave one of his most moving addresses when presenting to the General Assembly a Report on the religious condition of Scotland. At the close, writes his son Norman, "members of the Assembly and listeners in the galleries all rose in a body waving hats, handkerchiefs and umbrellas, with applause lasting many minutes. . . ."

Or there is the tribute of another son:

My father was a man of fine presence. He had a noble courtesy of manner: towards the other sex it tended to become a rather elaborate old-world courtliness. Towards children it was full of a delightful blend of condescension and understanding and fun, which always put them at their ease and attracted them to him. Towards working folk and the poor it combined sympathy and kindly humour with respect. I shall always think of him as a great gentleman. He was not a scholar, not a theologian, but in spite of hard public and pastoral work he read widely and eagerly. He was a very powerful preacher, with a real gift of eloquent speech and a fervour which was commended by his fine voice and presence. I suppose he might be described as a liberal Evangelical, but he was never a party man, and he had great sympathy with movements such as the Scottish Church Society for promoting the seemliness and liturgical order of public worship. Indeed, in his earlier days he had been regarded as a dangerous innovator.... He was too busy with his labours in Glasgow to have much time for the business of the General Assembly; but he took a leading part in its debates, was Chairman of a very important Commission on the Religious Life of the people, and in due course (in 1893) was Moderator—and a Moderator of great dignity.

It was a surprise to many—not least to himself—when, in 1900, on the nomination of his friend Lord Balfour of Burleigh, then Secretary for Scotland, he was appointed Principal of Aberdeen University. I suppose it was the last instance of the appointment of distinguished ministers to these chief academic posts; and there were some who thought then that the day for such appointments was past and that this post ought to have been given to some eminent scholar. But no one could doubt that he was a success. His dignity and eloquence made him a worthy representative of the University; his urbanity and experience of affairs made him a good chairman; and his personality had a strong influence on the sometimes turbulent students. Above all, he was a man of deep, unaffected, undemonstrative piety, whose religion was the inspiration of his life.

In 1859 he married Hannah Keith, daughter of Dr. Peter Hay Keith, Minister of the Collegiate Church of Hamilton. Langs and Keiths were not merely near neighbours: they had a common heritage in the Kirk, of which so many of them were or would be ministers, and in Lanarkshire,

4

the home of their forbears. The Keiths even share with the Langs their elusive claim to kinship with Woodrow Wilson; indeed their right is the clearer, for the President's maternal great-grandmother seems to have been a great-grand-aunt of Hannah's father—a relationship which a Scot at any rate will readily recognise, although an Englishman might shrink from attempting too close a definition of the kinship. Hannah herself was a lively pretty girl, with a strong sense of humour and "a pithy downrightness of speech." She was a devoted wife and mother, never allowing the press of parish work to bring disorder to the house, nor the toil of looking after a husband and seven children to keep her from her part in the work of the parish.

While Marshall Lang was in his first charge at Aberdeen his health suffered from overwork, and this explains the move in 1859 for six happy, healthy years to the small country parish of Fyvie. The place is famed for the castle, with its curse, attributed to Thomas the Rhymer himself, its "stanes three," which have brought no luck to its owners, its hidden chamber and its hauntings; the laird in those days being Colonel William Cosmo Gordon, of the family of the Marquis of Aberdeen. To a "sunny howe" in the village close by Lang brought his young wife, and in it their first three sons, Gavin, Patrick and Cosmo, were born.

Chapter II

BIRTH AND BOYHOOD

"**P**UIR wee lamb, it'll be a mercy if the Lord takes him." So the nurse mournfully observed when, on Hallowe'en, 1864, a third child was born to the Langs. The comment implies a puling infant, with nothing about him to suggest that he would grow up to unusually good health and a long life; or indeed that he would survive those first doubtful weeks and an epidemic of whooping-cough which was presently to carry away an elder brother, Gavin. But survive he did, and in due course was baptised by a neighbouring minister, Dr. Gray. He was named Cosmo Gordon, after the Laird of Fyvie, Cosmo recalling an eighteenth-century connexion of the Gordons with the family of the Medici in Florence. The Laird was also "William," and this name, too, the minister mistakenly or absent-mindedly bestowed on the infant, who, however, abandoned it soon after he was of an age to abandon anything. It continued to be used on official documents and formal occasions, as when he was ordained deacon and priest, or received an honorary degree, but for all ordinary purposes it vanished.

Some two months after Cosmo's birth the family moved to Glasgow, where Mr. Lang had charge of a new church in the Anderston district of the Barony Parish. Cosmo was too young to remember anything of the house at 4 Hillhead Gardens, which became the Manse.

> My earliest recollection is . . . of the isle of Arran. It is of being chased, in the arms of my nurse, by a bull; and I have even now a vivid remembrance of a white gate reached for safety by a panting woman. My next clear recollection is more pathetic: the sands of St. Andrews and my nurse after the manner of her tribe, at least in those days, ducking me mercilessly in the sea. Choking and breathless I could stand this tyranny no longer. With a wild "will to freedom" I tore myself from her grasp and naked as I was ran for dear liberty along the sands. . . .

In 1868 there was another move, to Morningside near Edinburgh, "at that time a quaint country village, with villas and quiet lanes, and no houses beyond it."

The real scene of my childhood was the garden of the Bank House,

6

Morningside. . . . I suppose it was quite a small garden, but it was my world, from the age of four to nine. It was my *own* world, where my imagination for once had its unclouded day. It was a world of "make-believe." Lessons there were, even for a while at an old dame's school: brothers there were, three of them. Sometimes I made the younger, next to me, the unwilling and mystified vassal to my dreams. But the world I remember is the garden—the trees behind which robber-knights were stalked and slain; the earth under a shrub where on a cold day unknown to all I sat, self-stripped, indulging in all the pathos of a beggar-child; the bundle of sticks on which I stood enduring the fancied flames as a Christian martyr; the great black roaring cat, who was to me the Devil walking about seeking whom he might devour—I can see him now, stealthy and sinister, creeping along the wall—at whom I threw every missile of fervent and pious wrath. In all that world I reigned supreme, fancy free. . . . These were the years, never to be repeated, when I was master of my own realm, the glorious realm of imagination, the "land of make-believe." . . . Of course there will be pains as well as pleasure in the kingdom of an imaginative child. How well I remember, during many nights after my mother had been reading the *Pilgrim's Progress*, watching in terror Apollyon's face on the wall, rolling his fiery tongue!

Or again, a little later, when I suppose I was eight or perhaps nine. It was at Ardrishaig on Loch Fyne and my young eyes saw the sun setting in the west. I became convinced that some great adventure or discovery was awaiting me there. I must at all costs go and find it. It was the call of the unknown, of the Ideal World. I set off, walked and ran for miles along the banks of the Crinan Canal, which led westwards. I became tired and hungry, and still the thrill I was seeking never came. Weary and disillusioned, I sank down on the bank. There the realities of life—the pursuers and the punishments—overtook me and I learned the bitter lesson of life, that ideals must ever be sought but never found.

In 1873, when Cosmo was nine, Mr. Lang returned to Glasgow, on his appointment to the historic Barony Church itself. The family's home was at 5 Woodlands Terrace, a large house on high ground, near the valley of the Kelvin, with a view from the upper windows of the hills of Dumbarton and Renfrew. But there was no garden in which children could play without contention. For more children had arrived or were

7

to come—Douglas in 1866, Marshall in 1868, Hannah (the only girl) in 1870, Norman in 1875 and David in 1878. The absence of a garden cramped the vigorous spirits of a family ultimately of seven, and this contraction led, I fear, to a good deal of quarrelling, which never meant then or since any breach of unity, but was certainly unlovely.

Cosmo and Patrick probably hunted together as a rule; but if near in age, they were widely different in temperament, a visiting lawyer (with some injustice to Patrick) once dubbing them "Cosmos and Chaos." Presently Cosmo was sent to the Park School,

one of those admirable day schools for which Scotland is or was famous, under D. W. F. Collier, whose school-books of the time were widely used, a good-looking, genial, cultured, gentlemanly man, with white hair and a ruddy complexion. But I was never greatly interested in its proceedings or ambitious to excel. The only prize which I used to get was for an essay in English literature—one, I remember, on Coleridge's *Ancient Mariner*. I played football, but only intermittently.

He had other, more exciting interests. His fantasies had changed, become perhaps more mundane, but were as real as anything he had found in the garden at Morningside. "Indeed, when I was twelve and thirteen, my life was in a sense more full, important and responsible than it has ever been since." Those were the great days of Disraeli's Government, of the Turkish crisis and, ultimately, of Peace with Honour. Cosmo therefore was in public life, even more, in the Government, for "I filled the posts first of Foreign Secretary and then of Prime Minister of the country."

It was an anxious time. The Russo-Turkish War broke out, and as Secretary for Foreign Affairs my mind was kept busy, and as Prime Minister I attended the Congress of Berlin. My speeches and despatches were written out in large notebooks which I had constant difficulty in concealing; and the speeches before listening Senates were delivered either on long walks or in fields or in my bedroom. . . . When afterwards I knew the first Lord Goschen very well and he was most kind to me, it sometimes amused me to remember that I had sent him to Constantinople with my instructions and was concerned with him in the Treaty of San Stefano! I can see myself now on a rainy day, sitting in a corner and inditing despatches to Constantinople and St. Petersburg. . . .

To these days belongs a fragment that has survived the years—no less than an imaginary entry in *Who's Who*,[1] so correct in form that up to a point it might almost be taken as a genuine extract. The early years of "William Cosmo Gordon Lange" (sic) were faithfully recorded. Then, at fourteen, he goes to Glasgow University (a likely forecast), where he graduated as a Master of Arts. He went up to Cambridge, was called to the Scottish Bar, and "his business at the Bar being not at first remunerative, he turned to literature, where he has achieved a marvellous success as novelist, poet, historian." Success at the Bar followed, he married "the younger daughter of the Earl of Kintore," and went into politics as a Conservative. "At once, he was a marked man." In 1902 he was Under-Secretary for Foreign Affairs, and since in 1903 Lord Salisbury was conveniently ill, Mr "Lange" was in virtual control of foreign policy. Other high offices followed and finally in 1912 he became Earl of Norham and Prime Minister. Appended is the record of his marriage and its results—eight fine children, including an eldest son who became "Viscount Claverton" and a daughter Emily, who married the Duke of Richmond and Gordon; and a mention of his residences—a country seat in Norfolk, another in Wiltshire, and a third in Argyll. So the record ran, certainly not lacking in ambition and confidence, but not quite so wild a surmise as it would have seemed to any of the brothers who had looked over his shoulder.

That at any rate was how the world shaped itself to the handsome, dreaming boy, who had already shown, in childish essay and crude ballad, a gift of expression beyond his age. From the meagre records of these years two facts emerge of some significance for the future. The first is the presence of the Kirk in the background and in the bones of the boy's family and forbears. His father and both his grandfathers were ministers; their life and his (for a time) was the life of the Manse. The second is a habit of fantasy more persistent than is usual even with children of his age. His imagined world was almost, if not quite, as real as the one in which he lived; his day-dreams were blended with his hopes and ambitions; they were not fragmentary episodes, but were built up piece by piece into a consistent career. Nor—it is a fair conjecture—in all the coming years did he ever entirely lose either the Kirk or the habit of getting outside his surroundings and, as it were, of superimposing a picture of what might be on life as it actually was.

[1] Appendix I.

9

Chapter III

GLASGOW UNIVERSITY

IN 1878, at the age of fourteen, Cosmo left Dr. Collier's school and entered the University of Glasgow. "Arrayed in a red gown flapping about his knees, with a black mortar-board set primly on his head," one of his brothers recalls, he left the house morning by morning with Patrick, to attend classes and lectures which began at the early hour of eight. In those days the University was a land of giants. Sir Richard Jebb, one of the greatest Greek scholars not only of his time but of all time; Edward Caird, pupil of Jowett, future Master of Balliol and leading philosopher of his day; John Nichol, better as a teacher than as a poet; Sir William Thomson, afterwards Lord Kelvin, scientist and inventor; and George Ramsay, the genial and gifted Latinist and Professor of Humanities—here was a galaxy of talent. But the teaching was hardly equal to the talent.

> I fear I made little use of the first years. Latin . . . and Greek had as their Professors the bluff and genial George Ramsay and the refined and shy and sensitive Richard Jebb. But the large classes were not fitted for teaching and only those already well-taught could catch inspiration from the Professors. I never recovered from bad teaching at school and from the absorbing preoccupation with the affairs of State; and alas! I have remained through life a very poor "scholar." . . . I can never attempt to read Latin or Greek aloud without, like Agag, walking delicately and fearing . . . that I am about to be found out.

The giants, like the prophets, were not always accorded honour in their own country, or rather in their own classes. Afterwards Cosmo was to remember

> the indignities which a refined scholar like Jebb and a world-renowned scientist like Sir William Thomson (Lord Kelvin) suffered at the hands of the Scottish boors who formed a large part of their classes. In the case of Jebb, what he must have suffered was the atmosphere of an ignorance and indifference, natural enough in boys and men who knew little more than the elements of the Greek language, and

of incapacity to appreciate his own exquisite scholarship. Even they, however, could sometimes appreciate his quiet wit. Once the class of old Veitch, the Professor of Logic and Rhetoric inhabiting the room above Jebb's, stamped on the floor with their feet in applauding one of the Professor's well-known periods, so vigorously that some of the plaster of the ceiling fell on Jebb's platform. "I fear," he said drily, "that my premises cannot support my colleague's conclusions."

Jebb, at least, could look after himself with the "Scottish boors," painful as he might sometimes find them. He had a quick temper and has been described as "striking terror into the hearts of any students."

But the case of Thomson was more pathetic, or rather more scandalous. I suppose he was the worst conceivable teacher of the elements of a subject to ignorant pupils. He could not adjust his mind to theirs. He was at home with logarithms, but kept an assistant at his side to do simple sums. When genuinely excited himself with pure scientific joy over some experiments, he would be interrupted by some vulgar noise from the back benches. I remember once he was making some experiments in sound. It involved the use of a series of little trumpets. He blew them with all the delight of a child. Suddenly a shower of pennies was thrown from the back benches, as if he were a street performer. His face changed, as if he had been struck, and became pale with impotent indignation. How he was able to endure these constant indignities for more than a quarter of a century I can never understand. Seeing that he once remarked to me about an answer I was suddenly called to give, "Now, really, I don't think I have ever heard anything so foolish," it may be supposed that I was a poor pupil. Indeed the whole realm of physics and mathematics was to me, then and always, unintelligible.

He found it indeed not only unintelligible, but almost intolerably tedious; and one day at home, when he was grappling with some mathematical problem, he yawned so widely that his jaws were locked. They remained immovable and Cosmo speechless until a doctor came in and put him right.

Much more congenial than any mathematical study were the lectures on literature from John Nichol, "in his own desultory way a fine teacher";

but of all the giants of those days in Glasgow Caird had most to give the boy, and gave it in full measure.

My mind . . . found its first real awakening through the lectures of Edward Caird . . . on Philosophy, moral and metaphysical. Then suddenly it leapt into life. I found myself in a new country, exciting and delightful, and yet one in which from the first I felt myself at home, an eager citizen of it. Caird's lectures, delivered with all the earnestness of a preacher, were partly historical, a criticism of philosophers and their systems, partly expository of his own position, that of a discriminating but fervent Hegelian. I recall the intellectual thrill when he introduced me to the great men of the Republic of Philosophy, one after another, Plato and Aristotle, Descartes with his "*Cogito ergo sum*," Berkeley and Hume, Hamilton and Reid, the mighty Kant and the wonderful Spinoza, and above all the Master, at once acclaimed by me as mine—Hegel. Of course, the introductions led only to a very slight and superficial acquaintance. But to hold any converse with those mighty men made a new and exciting epoch in my life. For the time, like the universe (as I was taught), I "existed" only in and for thought. I smile now as I think of the boy of sixteen deep in Hutchison Stirling's *Secret of Hegel*; and when within a year [1] I made for the first time the acquaintance of English public school boys at Balliol, it seemed to me that they belonged not only geographically but intellectually to another country. It took me some time to learn the language and habits of theirs, and though I soon became perhaps too easily accustomed to them, I always felt that I had moved about in a world which they had not begun to realise. For Caird's class did not merely introduce me to the great masters of thought. It made me think. I almost feel as if I *thought* more constantly and steadily at sixteen than I have ever done since. It was a proud moment when, on receiving back from the Professor one of my essays, I saw that he had written on it: "This essay shows signs of remarkable speculative ability"; and these essays gave me, by the votes of the class, the second place for the year, after a keen contest for the first. . . .

Indeed, it was this intellectual awakening that led to the first real awakening of the spirit. I remember one experience, strange perhaps in a mere boy, which might be classed with the experience of sudden conversions. I was standing, full of thought, in Kelvingrove Park,

[1] Rather more than a year. He went to Balliol in 1882, just before he was eighteen.

12

when suddenly I cried aloud—if anyone had heard he must have thought the boy was mad: "The Universe is one and its Unity and Ultimate Reality is God!" Easy words, no doubt, but they were the quick and real expression of an overwhelming sense that then and there I had got behind phenomena to Reality and found that Reality was God.

I have never wholly lost that sense. This half-intellectual, half-spiritual "conversion" has been as abiding as, perhaps more abiding than, such experiences usually are. From that moment it lay at the root of all my religious life and thought.

I have just [1] been reading the *Autobiography* of my friend Lord Haldane. He too, another Scottish boy, had drunk early these waters of philosophy—drunk more deeply far; but I used to tell him that my draught was at least earlier in life even than his. I was sixteen and he was seventeen when we first "found ourselves" in philosophic study and thought. The "outlook," as he calls it, which was thus gained sufficed him for his religious life. In my case, it was rather a foundation on which later religious convictions and experiences were based. But in my case, as in his, these early studies liberated us from the bondage of the claims of mere physical science, which lay so heavy on the mind of the late nineteenth-century generation. I think I may add that even I, whose later religious development was in some ways so different, have always, like him, regarded any attempts, however authoritative, to formulate beliefs in God as necessarily only "symbols," to express truths which transcend definition. Yet some of those "symbols," though never exhaustive of the truth behind and beyond them, may give "sufficient light for us in the dark to rise by." Of course, always in the background were the influences, habits, atmosphere of a Christian home, where the Christian faith was commended by the lives of my elders. But certainly it was the study of philosophy, however superficial, which, so to say, brought its background into consciousness and gave it new meaning. I discovered the other day a long paper, almost a treatise, written when I was sixteen, which endeavoured to state the main Christian position in terms of Hegelian thought, as Caird was wont to present it, and I am bound to say that, in spite of many juvenile exaggerations and much untested philosophy, it surprised me by its range and vigour. It was not wholly "puerile."

[1] This was written in 1929.

13

Looking back on those days he felt that this intense preoccupation with philosophy and day-dreams made his life "rather solitary." He had no intimate friendships, few real interests outside his books and his thoughts. "Perhaps to these early habits is due the fact that I have never found it easy to exchange deeper thoughts, even with the many friends of later days." But the preoccupation, he protests, did not turn him into a "moody youth" or a prig. He had no particular affection or aptitude for games, but was an active member of the Dialectic Society, the debating club of the University, where he spoke as a Conservative of the Left, what would later have been dubbed a Tory Democrat, with Lord Beaconsfield as the star he would follow.

His academic career, too, was full of promise, for after a little less than four years at the University he had passed all his examinations for the degree of Master of Arts and had won two prizes, the Gartmore Medal for an essay on Politics and the Henderson Prize for an essay on Church History. He also won prizes in class, for which, according to the custom of the University, he was elected by the votes of his fellows. Once, when he had been voted the prize for Logic, he was obliged to appear with the other students, some two hundred in number, before Sir William Thomson, in the class of Natural History and Science. When all were seated, the Professor called on Mr. Lang to answer some searching questions. "Tell me as briefly as possible," he said in his high voice, "what are the movements of a curler when he plays his stone." Cosmo pondered for a moment and then answered the question entirely to his own satisfaction and to that of his companions. Whereupon Sir William declared his explanation hopelessly "illogical," a verdict which was received with jeers and cheers by those who had just voted Lang their chief logician.

Behind these interests and activities was his life at home. The Barony Church was a large undertaking, with its twenty-one elders, its thirteen hundred schoolchildren, its guilds, its Bible Classes, its numerous organisations, and all the coming and going and business of the parish. The Minister's days were well filled and much of his supposed leisure was perforce given to preparation of the sermons which drew a great congregation Sunday after Sunday to hear him. He had little enough time to spare for his growing family; and in addition his aloofness, his reticence, and a deep-seated reserve seem to have built barriers between him and them, and more especially between him and Cosmo. If there was no lack of affection, there was equally no intimacy. The father was less a presence in the family circle than a Voice in the Study, especially on a Saturday morning, when the other occupants of the house were hushed and awed and the sermon for Sunday was being rehearsed, phrase by phrase and word by word. It is true that he tried to keep Saturday afternoon free for a walk with his wife and family, but in this he was not always successful. Only the two months' annual holiday brought a break in the routine,

when we migrated to houses, often farmhouses, in the country. All the associations with home which have for me any remembrances of pleasure are bound up with these holidays. They were often spent in different places in the beautiful island of Arran. Other holidays were spent in Wigtownshire, the hill country of Lanarkshire, in Argyllshire and other parts of the Highlands. . . . There life was real, vivid, delightful. There, too, my father was set free from all his sermons and public duties, which in Glasgow more or less completely withdrew him from companionship with his children, and my mother from her household cares; and they entered fully and heartily into our play and plans. During the long summer days (except when I was busy with affairs of State!) we bathed and rowed and took endless walks and climbed the mountains. In the evenings and on wet days my father would read aloud the novels of Scott and Dickens and other stories. That is why Scotland to us means not the cities but the seas, the lochs, the glens, the mountains. All of later holiday sojourn for the last thirty-five years in my beloved West Argyll has only kept ever deep and fresh the spirit of the Highlands which I drank in during the days of boyhood. This, year after year, has sustained the enthusiastic, romantic, perhaps sentimental Highlander who lives within my breast. To this day there are no sounds that so immediately stir my deepest and most abiding memories and emotions as the plash of the waves on a Western sea or the call of the curlew on the hills. And often I hear them behind the voices of Bishops in debate or the endless speeches in the Church Assembly. They seem like the songs of Zion in a strange land, and "in my dreams I see the Hebrides."[1]

Those early holidays were an enduring memory, with all their little incidents and activities. In 1875 and 1876 the younger boys produced a family paper, *The Blackwater Magazine*, with Patrick as editor and

[1] " And we in dreams behold the Hebrides " (Galt).

Cosmo as "chief author," and blood-and-thunder stuff that Scott and Dickens would not have written but may possibly have inspired, and that doubtless the whole party enjoyed.

But the enchanted days soon ended, the magic faded, and back in grey, foggy Glasgow the Minister returned to his old aloofness and his family to their wonted awe. "I don't feel that to the end any of us reached that sort of ready and free companionship which often, especially in England, brings fathers and sons close together." Yet, looking back, Cosmo preferred the reverence he felt for his father to the "casual and jaunty familiarity" of a later generation.

My mother's personality, though even more distinctive and decided, was of another type. She was in mind and speech practical, down-right, frank and forcible. In a double sense her temper was quick—quick to rise and equally quick to subside. My father accustomed himself with a patient smile to let pass the hasty words which spoke out the first impression and to wait for those which spoke out the second. The surface waters were easily ruffled, the deeper currents of the real character remained undisturbed. I think I inherit from her a foolish readiness to be irritated by the small surface annoyances, mishaps, provocations of life, while deeper, more important matters, which seem to vex the souls of others, leave me calm. She had many attached friends who relished her frank outspoken ways because they knew the inner truth and loyalty of her life. We, her children, though sometimes checked and, so to say, put off by this quickness of temper and speech, never failed to feel her unswerving love and care. She was a wonderful manager, and I cannot imagine how she was able to provide unfailingly for her large family out of comparatively scanty resources. It must have been a long labour, but it was a labour of love, ungrudgingly offered. Perhaps we missed the gentle and wise sympathy with which a mother draws out the confidence of her children. But I shall always be thankful that I had a mother who loved us intensely and toiled for us, but never spoiled us, and whose love was "without dissimulation" or sentimentality. The discipline was bracing and we knew that its source was love. The basis of her strong character was a deep and steadfast Christian faith. Every day, before addressing herself to its practical business, she would meditate quietly over the texts of her *Daily Light*.

She was nearer to the children than their father could ever be.

THE VERY REV. JOHN MARSHALL LANG, D.D.

HANNAH LANG

Although she was strict with them, and could be stern, she had an infectious laugh and a sense of humour which perhaps had as much to do with their discipline as any homily. Though all had their fair share of her, Cosmo was probably nearest and dearest, the prime source of her pride and anxiety. "Your mother worships Cosmo," a friend of the family observed. Cosmo understood her so well; and later on, when sometimes she fell into an amusing kind of fractiousness about nothing in particular, he it was who would quell the sudden little squalls by some turn of humour which left his mother laughing at herself.

There were frequent visits to the grandmothers at Bothwell and Hamilton, to old Mrs. Lang, the singer of "auld Scotch sangs," who presided over a generous tea-table at which the youngest of the company was always given the charge of asking a blessing, or to old Mrs. Keith, who had a cheerful and beautiful home which she loved to fill with her grandchildren. They were "both, in their different ways, remarkable women."

I have little recollection of their husbands, only as to one, of a hand coming from a white bed laid upon my child-head, and as to the other, of a rather irritable old gentleman out of whose way it was wise to keep. The two grandmothers had a great place in my early life, if only because the Christmas holidays were always spent with them. My father's mother was a woman of outstanding ability of mind and fervour of piety. Though as I remember her she was always more or less an invalid, in the extent and power of her influence she was a true "Mother in Israel." Even as a boy I felt the moving power of her prayers; in long and eloquent letters she used to pour out her longings for my young soul; yet all this fervour was saved from oppressiveness by her rich sense of humour and width of sympathy and interests. She was a woman of the same quality as wonderful old Mrs. Haldane.[1] . . .

My mother's mother was a woman of singular beauty of face, great strength of character, and a piety as fervent as my other grandmother's, though perhaps of a rather narrower Evangelical type. In her house was a complete edition of Scott's novels, and holiday after holiday I devoured them. I think I must have read almost all of them before I was fourteen, and still I never spend a holiday without taking one or other of them with me. It was fitting that I should have

---

[1] Mrs. Haldane of Cloan, mother of Viscount Haldane.

learned to know and love Sir Walter in her house, for as a girl in Ayrshire she and her sisters used to feign colds in order to be able to stay indoors to read the Waverleys as they came out; and she used to tell me of the thrill with which more than once she saw "the Sheriff" at her father's table, when the knowledge that this bluff and kindly guest was himself the Wizard was still supposed to be a secret.

Chapter IV

OVER THE BORDER

IN 1881, when not yet seventeen, Cosmo crossed the Border for the first time. He stayed in London and, in the company of his cousin, Richard Cunliffe, visited Paris—an even greater adventure for a boy of his age. Some of the letters he wrote home describing his experiences and impressions have survived.

He surveyed Paris with mixed feelings. It shocked and yet attracted him. Perhaps he was still too young, a little too close to the Manse, and too deeply rooted in young Toryism to take its flavour. "To think," he exclaimed after a visit to Versailles, "of its being the property of some measly Republicans. Bah! All over it they have carved their sham and disgusting false motto, '*Liberté, Egalité, Fraternité.*'" Nor did he care for the look of the people he saw in the streets of the capital. "I notice here how much *paint* the fashionable ladies seem to use on their faces." The French manners disgusted him, their "politeness" was overrated, a myth. The Bourse "appalled me," and as for the Continental Sunday, an Auld Licht could not have spoken more forcefully. He attended Mass at Notre Dame—"Tell it not in Gath (Bothwell), publish it not in Askalon (Hamilton)" [1]—and reported that the vestments "would cause the Vicar of St. Albans [2] to be filled with righteous envy." Yet with all its shortcomings Paris had a charm which did not quite elude him. "It seemed as if Eternal youth had chosen this City of Beauty as his dwelling-place . . . and yet the nation is weak and sinful." He was very young and very Scots, and his head was full of Hegel.

Probably London, where he stayed at Highbury with his uncle, David Marshall Lang, was a more rewarding experience. He wrote home enthusiastically, relating all that he had seen and heard. The Tower was a little disappointing; not so the top of the Monument, with its vista of steeples. He visited Westminster Abbey, where he spent five enthralling hours—there was "something infinite about the Abbey" and he could hardly tear himself away.

[1] No doubt an allusion to the grandmothers. Mrs. Lang lived in Bothwell, and Mrs. Keith in Hamilton.
[2] The Rev. A. H. Mackonochie, who at that time was having trouble with the ecclesiastical authorities. It ended in 1882 with his resignation.

I went to St. Paul's to hear the great Liddon. There was a large crowd. I got squeezed into the south transept. I was myself spellbound by the voice, rising up into this vast dome. But there was immediately in front of me a typical English lower middle-class family—father, mother, son and daughter. They were not spellbound; indeed they fidgeted and looked about; and papa said to mamma: "What's it all about?" That evening I went, again alone, to Spurgeon's Tabernacle. The mighty Puritan was in possession of his platform, sometimes colloquial, even vulgar some might think, sometimes breaking out into bursts of fervid eloquence. Strangely enough, the same family as at St. Paul's was in front of me. It was they who were spellbound now. As the long sermon ended, papa said to mamma, "Ah, that's the stuff for me!"

On this visit he made his first acquaintance with the Church of England, though not with the Anglican Communion. The Langs had no prejudice against Episcopacy, and sometimes at Christmas in Glasgow Mrs. Lang would take the children to "St. Mary's Cathedral" [1] for services she thought more appropriate to the day than were those of the Kirk. The Church of England, now encountered, at once attracted him; but "all the same," he wrote, "while I am in Scotland at least, I will never become an Episcopalian, for constitutional reasons." There was a day in the Royal Academy and another in Richmond Park—"a most beautiful place. It made me think at once that it must have been the forest in which Rosalind and Orlando made love, Jaques made speeches, and Touchstone made jokes"; while Windsor Castle, also seen, "far exceeded my anticipations."

He "*must* go to Hughenden," and was only waiting for a fine day. But before the fine day came, his idol of many years, Lord Beaconsfield, had died.

I went on a solitary pilgrimage to Hughenden Church on the day after his funeral. [2] There, by the way, I had a rather curious experience. I found myself in the church among a small group of people. They were conducted to a sort of vault under the church, on one side of it. With the ingenuous audacity of youth I went with them and saw the

---

[1] Probably St. Mary's, Renfield Street, the predecessor of the present Cathedral. In those days there was no Episcopalian Cathedral.

[2] In this memory may have played a trick, for Beaconsfield was buried on April 26th and Cosmo's pilgrimage seems to have been in the first days of May.

graves of my leader, his wife and Mr. Brydges Williams. I think it was a party of his own friends.

A little later he had a sight of the dead man's great rival.

I had gone by myself to the Chapel Royal at St. James's Palace. It was more crowded on Sundays then than now. As I had no card of admission, I was bidden to stand aside till the service began. Somewhat later, Mr. and Mrs. Gladstone arrived. I was then allowed to pass in and, as I happened to follow Mr. and Mrs. G. immediately, I suppose the verger thought I was a young G. Anyhow, I found myself in the same pew with the great man. The sermon, I remember, was preached by Bishop Jackson of London, commending the newly formed Bishop of London's Fund. The great man became drowsy. When the Bishop referred to the claims of the Fund on persons of great responsibility, Mrs. G. poked her lord with her umbrella and whispered: "William, you ought to be listening to this," and the fiery eyes opened on the preacher and the hand went up behind his ear.

Cosmo was taken for a first visit to the House of Commons, but confessed in after years that his only recollections were of a severe attack of nose-bleeding, brought on by his excitement, just as he was starting off, and of his feeling, as he looked round him—"Shall I ever be a member here?" His letters tell a little more, for he was lucky enough to be in the House for the debate on the Land Bill and to hear speeches from Gladstone, Hartington and Chamberlain.

There was also the theatre, hitherto a forbidden territory. Might he go and see *Othello*? Irving and Booth were playing and, after all, Shakespeare was different. "Now don't be alarmed . . . sooner than go to a modern comedy I would cut off my head." There spoke the Manse again. The answer is unrecorded, but must have been favourable, for Cosmo went, to his ample gratification, so entering a world that would mean much to him a little later. But at the time he was still embedded in family life, and with all the excitements of this first major excursion, his thoughts were constantly returning to Glasgow. "Have you made up your mind about Summer quarters?" he wrote from London. "Remember—boat, bathing, and no snobbishness—three indispensable conditions." At the time he asked for little more.

Chapter V

BALLIOL

A LITTLE later in the same year (1881) Cosmo crossed the Border again.

I went up to Cambridge to stay with a Scottish friend who had gone to Trinity. It was my first sight of an English University. I was fascinated—by the beauty, the history, the comradeship. King's College Chapel simply carried off my head and my heart. On emerging from it, without, of course, consulting anybody or even thinking of any prosaic details of ways and means, I went straight to the porter's lodge and asked him: "Whom must I see to become a member of this College?" The good porter was obviously unaccustomed to such a question from a stray youth: not thus do English boys enter Oxford or Cambridge; but he told me to go to Mr. George Prothero and pointed to his rooms. I went at once. Prothero was then, I think, Senior Tutor of King's . . . I was a very young Scot, unknown, unintroduced. I repeated my question. He was more taken aback even than the porter. But he was very indulgent and kind and gave me all information. Then and there I determined to join a college which possessed such a chapel. When I recrossed the Border and told my parents they were naturally surprised; and I am surprised now to think of their readiness to accept my ambition, for my father had a large family and not more than £800 or £900 a year! But sure enough, in the following January (1882), the ingenuous youth returned to King's for the entrance examination. The snow was on the ground and the "backs" were robed in white. I always remember my first quarters in an English College. They were the rooms of a Fellow and Tutor, Cook, on the ground floor on the right of the main building. I easily passed the examination.

"We have admitted you to the College on the results of your exam^n.," wrote Prothero. "Your essay was very good but almost illegible; your mathematics appear to have been shaky; you should work them up before October, as it is very important you should pass the whole of the Littlego, including the Additional Subjects, before the end of your first term. . . .

"You really should try to improve your handwriting. I had great difficulty in making out much that you wrote, and this fault will stand in your way considerably if you do not mend it."

As the correspondents of over sixty years will testify, he never did mend it.

I left accepted for matriculation and hopeful of a scholarship in the following October. But when I discovered that if, in those days, I intended to read for a Tripos, I would have to pass what I think were called "Additional Subjects," involving much mathematics, I turned away, faithless to my first enthusiasm, from the prospect of wading to the Moral Sciences or History Tripos through weary bogs of my hated mathematics.

When in 1920 he went to Cambridge to receive the honorary degree of LL.D., he was able to twit his hosts that he had got it without any mathematics, to puzzle them by claiming (improperly) to be a Kingsman, and finally to console them and himself with the reminder that

> 'Tis better to have loved and lost
> Than never to have loved at all.

Fleeting as his visits had been, they gave him a glimpse of Oscar Browning, then at the beginning of his long reign.

He made me come twice to his rooms, once for a sort of musical party, repeated Prothero's encouragement, and made me feel happy and at ease. In later days, when with all the world I heard stories of "O. B.'s" cults of the great, I set against them this wholly spontaneous kindness to a young and obscure Scot.

He had entered on this Cambridge venture entirely upon his own initiative, without consulting anyone; and later he would say that King's had turned his life to an English University and away from the Scots Bar, hitherto his projected pathway into politics. "I always keep for King's its own place in my heart."

It will be recalled that "the Earl of Norham" in his youthful days had gone to Cambridge, so that the plan may nevertheless have been at the back of Cosmo's mind, even if he were unconscious of its presence. Now that mathematics had ruled Cambridge out, there remained another place—from his point of view, only one other place. Again without consulting anyone he took the first necessary steps, and when October came it was not to Cambridge and King's that he went, but to Oxford and Balliol.

He chose Balliol for his College because Caird recommended it, and also possibly for its traditional connexion with Glasgow University. But he was no Snell Exhibitioner. He was a commoner, son of a minister with a big parish, a large family, and "not more than £800 or £900 a year." How could it be done? How was it done? The problem was no new one in Scotland, which has always counted education as something above price. Years later, when the old life lay long behind him, Cosmo was to speak at a dinner of the London Society of Sons of the Scottish Manse. He began, Lord Macmillan recalls, by chaffing the company on the presence in their midst of a prelate, and more, of an archprelate. Then, obviously moved himself, he moved his hearers by suggesting that

> there is not one of us here who has not in his heart a vision of a Scottish Manse, perhaps in some remote parish of the Highlands, a hardy and happy home, where a revered father and mother sacrificed everything to give to their sons the nurture and the admonition, the inspiration and the education to fit them to attain to a worthy station in life and to render good service in their day and generation.

His own career at Balliol had made two very old demands on one Scottish household—self-sacrifice from the parents and thrift from the son. Both were met, and with some "generous help" from Cosmo's maternal grandmother, Mrs. Keith, the venture was possible.

On a damp, misty morning early in October, 1882, a rather forlorn and very obscure young Scot arrived in Oxford and took up his abode in small lodgings in New Inn Hill Street as a commoner of Balliol. . . . Encouraged by my experience at King's, I hoped I might conceivably get a History Scholarship later. When I arrived, I knew literally no one in the College, or indeed at Oxford, except, I think, James Dodd, afterwards Permanent Secretary for Scotland, at Lincoln; and in Balliol I had an introduction to a Snell Exhibitioner, George Saunders, afterwards well known as the correspondent of the *Times* at Berlin and of another paper at Paris. I can't imagine anyone going up to an Oxford College more lonely. Soon through

Saunders I made some acquaintances, among the first the jovial Hepburn Miller, afterwards one of the Law Professors at Edinburgh, a son of Judge Lord Craigmillar. At first I was rather melancholy, and to this day the road to the Castle on dim October afternoons always brings back my feelings then.

His letters to his mother, which she kept till her death, tell something of his life. At the outset Oxford and Oxford men disappointed him a little. "After a fortnight's existence as an out-College freshman . . . I must say that with one or two good exceptions I have rarely heard conversation that could be called intellectual." English boys, fresh from their public schools, seemed immature to a young Hegelian from Glasgow University. Possibly, too, he was missing the family circle. "You seem to think," he wrote to his mother on October 29th, "I can never have any qualms of home-sickness. Well, perhaps I'm not so sentimental as some people . . . but do you think it possible that a youth who has been in the midst of home-life, living alone in a little sitting-room in the top regions of a strange house, surrounded by no familiar faces or scenes, his only intercourse with comparative strangers—that such a one should not at times . . . feel that curious sensation which is produced by the memories of home?"

Happily the "curious sensation" did not live very long. He began to make friends, even with his fellow-lodger, who tried him with unseasonable flute-playing and proved on acquaintance to be infected with "High Churchism." "I could not convince him on the irreconcilability of some of his points, such as the Divine appointment of Episcopal Orders." He started to row, enduring good-humouredly much abuse from his coach, until on doctor's advice he gave up his place in the boat. He heard one Scott Holland [1] preach, "a coming man, I believe; has a loud, strong voice and a good 'English' style of preaching. He is very like a mediaeval monk." He joined the Carlyle Society and moved a resolution against Women's Rights. He made his maiden speech at the Oxford Union—on the decay of the Conservative Party. Oxford, as is her wont and in her way, was making him her own.

The great Jowett was the Master of Balliol.

Jowett, "the Jowler," as we used to call him, was still the most conspicuous personality in Oxford. For part of my time he was Vice-Chancellor; and then all men and things in Oxford knew

---

[1] Canon Henry Scott Holland.

"little Benjamin" to be "their ruler." It is easy to describe his appearance—the little figure with its black swallow-tail coat and white shirt-front and "choker," the ruddy chubby face with its rather fretful mouth "like a cherub out of condition," the chirpy voice. But how difficult to describe either his character or his influence!

What he was to his friends is written in all the chronicles of his generation. I can only write of him as we knew him in my time in College. The days of his real influence were over, for those were the days when he was tutor. Few of us knew him well or saw much of him; but every man in College knew very definitely that he was *there*. However withdrawn, his personality was potent. Of course, we all circulated the stories about him and added our own. (Shortly before his death he asked his friend, Raper of Trinity, to tell him these Jowett stories. "I told them all," the Master said drily, "of Jenkyns (a former Master) except one—and that's not true.") But in his presence the boldest was cowed or at least constrained, and he had a genius and a reputation for snubbing which kept the nerves quick. I well remember my first evening in his house. We were a small company of freshmen invited to "take wine" with the Master. The ceremony, which took place after dinner in Hall, was sitting round the Master's table in his dining-room, sipping light claret and eating preserved cherries. We were all so shy that, as often happened, our *gaucherie* irritated the Master and he gave up any effort to talk. Result—very soon a deadlock in the conversation. The silence was oppressive. At last, a scholar from Christ's Hospital, accustomed to independence in the London streets, boldly broke it. "Master," he said, "I like the painting in the Chapel awfully." The Master looked at him and said in his direst, crispest tone: "Don't say 'awfully.' This isn't a girls' school; and it isn't paint: it's alabaster." It was really cruel. The luckless adventurer in the conversation, who had meant to help us all out of an intolerable situation, flushed as if a whip had struck his face and from that moment became an Ishmael in the College, his hand against every man of authority.

But the Master did not mean to be cruel. In truth—and this is the real explanation of many similar situations—he was himself really a shy man in the sense of being acutely self-conscious; and it was irritation with himself far more than irritation with the poor scholar that accounted for his sharp retort. The two things that brought his snubbing into action were awkwardness and pretentiousness. I remember an instance of the latter which provoked the most telling snub I ever heard, deadly because of its icy restraint. We were reading an essay. One man, thinking himself clever, read out from his essay a preposterous phrase—"every social reformer from Jesus Christ to Charles Bradlaugh." The Master, as was his wont, was walking round the table. He stopped, fixed the man with a scornful eye, and said, "Read that again." The wretched phrase was repeated. Twice over the Master insisted, "Read it again." By that time it was fairly rubbed in and even the author looked ashamed of it. Then the Master said with cutting quietness: "Not good. Go on." It is impossible to convey in words the effectiveness of the snub. Anything pompous, artificial, pretentious or crudely conventional stirred his irritability. What he liked was sincerity and reality.

The Master had a reputation for snobbery as well as snubbing, for paying marked attention to men of what is called "good family." The truth is that when he knew that a man, by virtue of his mere position, was bound to have some influence for good or evil, the Master felt bound to help him to make it for good. And he was right. No doubt, also, he took special notice of men of brains, the Asquiths of each generation. But there too his object was to do what he could to make brains effective for good. And again he was right. But he was often just as ready to help men who were poor and obscure. I know of one man, shy, very poor, an orphan, helping to maintain brothers and sisters, gifted indeed but almost unknown in the College, to whom the Master was a real father in kindness and help.

What did I owe him? It is difficult to say. I think mainly a sense of honesty and reality in the use of words. I remember his saying to me, after I had read an essay full, no doubt, of early untested metaphysical phrases: "You forget that words are not always ideas, nor are ideas always realities." He made you wish to think clearly and write and speak simply, a very salutary bit of education both of mind and character. Once he had been a very real influence in the religious life of his time, but in my day that time had largely passed. At least such influence never reached me. His sermons in Chapel excited my curiosity rather than impressed either my mind or my spirit. Two sermons I remember. One began with the text: "Man shall not live by bread alone but by every word that proceedeth out of the mouth . . ." Then he stopped, and quietly resumed : "I propose to-day to omit the familiar and profound concluding words of this text and to address to you some remarks on Conversation." And very good and shrewd remarks they were. The other sermon was one on Prayer, but I only remember his caustic illustrations of the wrong kinds of prayer—"from the prayer of the man who says, 'O Lord, please give me that appointment for which I am so eminently fitted,' to the prayer of the beggar who says, 'O Lord, please give me eighteen pence.'" . . .

I think that in these later years of his life it was either to older people, men of affairs or literature, or, as so often happened to reserved men, to women that he opened himself out, rather than to undergraduates. He felt more at his ease with them, because they were more at ease with him. And there were many who owed to him, even in his old age, advice which cleared their minds in difficulties and strengthened their characters.

Though I had no intimate relations with him, he was always very kind to me. . . .

In the opinion of Mrs. Lang, he was too kind. "It quite pains me to think," she wrote rather later, "how 'the Master' leads you *away from* instead of *into* this highest life." She was especially distressed that Cosmo should have dined with him on Sunday and hoped her son would be preserved from his hurtful influence.

In front of him, during that first term, loomed a formidable hurdle. He had determined to sit for the Brakenbury Scholarship, which was, and is, the Blue Ribbon of history scholarship at any University of the British Isles. It was his first serious test and he approached it without very much confidence. The competition threatened to be severe. There were Mallet,[1] reputed one of the most brilliant men of his year; Adkins,[2] who had been third the previous year; Nichol, son of the Professor of Literature at Glasgow; and other candidates of promise. He was very conscious of temerity in challenging such a company. However, he persisted. "I had given up every hope," he wrote to his mother, "more than a sickly belief in a far-off possibility." When the result came out, he was sitting by himself reading *John Inglesant*. Presently a band of friends came whooping into the room. He had won

[1] Sir Charles Mallet, M.P.
[2] Sir William Ryland Adkins, M.P., Recorder of Birmingham.

the Brakenbury. Next morning he wrote gaily to his grandmother, Mrs. Lang:

I thought you might like to hear how I had got on in the scholarship exam. The results were published last night; and alas! in the Brakenbury Competition fourteen or so good men have received a crushing disappointment. The successful candidate is a young Scotch freshman—from Glasgow University, I think. The result, he says, is a complete surprise to himself; though others declare that they expected it all along. Happy man! His name, I think, is C. G. Lang: I wonder if he is any relation of your grandson of that name. If he is, let me congratulate you for him. The competition seems to have been very close: there were a number of very formidable men in— young Nichol, the Glasgow Professor's son, among them; and I believe two exhibitions will be given also to the second and third— Adkins and Mallet, clever both of them and disappointed.

Dropping that interesting third person, my dear Granny, I may say that my surprise exceeds my rejoicing almost, at the result. I had quite settled that I could not get it; but it is otherwise—let us rejoice together. The position of a scholar at Balliol (no mean honour, let me assure you, though *I* say it), the advantages it brings—these are great factors in my enjoyment; but not the least factor is the relief it will give to the good old people at Hamilton. Perhaps it was to their remembering me in my exam. in the best of all ways that I owe my success, such as it is.

Apart from every other advantage, the scholarship brought much-needed relief to the family finances. The frequent references to money difficulties in the early letters recur at the rarest intervals after the winning of the Brakenbury. Yet money was not his father's chief concern. "I am sure," he wrote on hearing the news, "that you will take your victory in the right manner—not getting elated over it, but feeling all the more humble." More than once he exhorts his son to read the 121st Psalm.[1]

This success was accompanied by an absurd failure. I was ploughed in "Smalls" and had the satisfaction of knowing that Gladstone had suffered the same fate. My failure was in arithmetic, and neither then nor ever after have I been able to do anything with sums. My brain still reels before the simplest exercises of addition, subtraction or multiplication. I share Walter Scott's Pet Marjorie's opinion of

---

[1] "I will lift up mine eyes unto the hills . . ."

them. With the help of a coach I struggled through next term and the discreditable episode was forgotten.

In January he moved into College, to first-floor rooms on the north-west corner of the Garden Quad. As winner of the Brakenbury he was now something of a marked man, and in these more favourable quarters he made a number of new friends:—Hubert Chitty, afterwards Bursar of Winchester, "then a great football player, known by all his friends as 'the Crawler,'" "Tab" Brassey, afterwards Lord Brassey; Anthony Hope Hawkins, better known as Anthony Hope, author of *The Prisoner of Zenda*; J. A. Spender, editor of the *Westminster Gazette* in the days of its glory; and many others.

Among the more senior men was a group called "The Passionate Pilgrims," surrounded with a literary halo—J. W. Mackail, Henry Beeching, and Bowyer Nichols, who had just brought out a volume of verse, *Love in Idleness*. We were all then more or less in the school of Rossetti and Burne-Jones. . . .

Two years senior to me was Francis Pember, our show-under-graduate, so to say, scholar, prolific prize-winner and admirable athlete, afterwards my dear friend as Warden of All Souls, and Edward Grey, afterwards the great Foreign Secretary, then an idle, handsome man who did little, but who even then, we all knew, might do anything. I have often recalled what I used to describe as his first introduction to public life. The Master . . . used as part of his policy to invite chosen undergraduates to meet the big folk of the world who were staying with him. On one occasion his guest was Bob Lowe, Lord Sherbrooke. Grey and I were the undergraduates honoured by an invitation to meet him. We went in together. The Master, in his crispest tone, introduced the future Foreign Secretary thus: "Lord Sherbrooke, let me introduce a young man, the bearer of an honoured name to which at present he is doing little credit—Sir Edward Grey." I remember Grey's frank laugh as he said: "Not a very flattering introduction, but I fear only too well deserved." The Master was quite deliberate. It was his way of saying: "Here is your proper company, and this is all you are doing to prepare yourself for it." Yet he had another, gentler, and equally character-istic way of dealing with Grey, as he (Grey) himself told me. For his idleness he was sent down for a term. During its course he was surprised to get an invitation from the Master to spend a week-end as the Master's guest, an original treatment of a man sent down in disgrace. The time passed, the Master said little to Grey, and there was a large company. At last, on the Monday morning, just as Grey was leaving for the train, the Master put his hand lightly on his shoulder and said: "You *will* read, won't you?" These five words, said Grey afterwards, were worth more than many exhortations.

Among other guests of the Master I remember meeting Robert Browning, looking more like a prosperous business man than a poet, exchanging sallies and compliments with Miss Sellars of Edinburgh; and Henry Irving. To him I did a good turn. Little thought was given in the Master's house to the comfort of smokers; so I had the cheek to invite Irving and his manager, Bram Stoker,[1] to my rooms, where till early in the morning he told stories in a singularly un-dramatic way.

In a letter to his mother he describes Browning as "a bald little old gentleman, with a tasty little white beard, and blue eyes half keen and half mild, and a good Roman profile." His manner was like that of "a good half-pay officer, with his venerable tales of men and things." The friends multiplied, but in Oxford, as in Glasgow and after-wards, there was no uninhibited intimacy. As he himself said, he did not find it easy "to exchange deeper thoughts." At Oxford he was admired and well liked, even if his friends, according to the late Lord Charnwood, laughed at him a little. Consciously, but in the kindliest way, "they made it their mission to humanise this young portent from the learned and rugged north, and I was a near enough spectator to have now a strong opinion that they did it very well."

I shall always regard it as a signal proof of the generosity, the frank-ness, the open-mindedness, the absence of any snobbery in Oxford life that it so fully opened out its friendship to the lonely young Scot of 1882. I came up with no introductions, I had no social position, I had no wealth—in spite of all sorts of social distractions I like to think that I never spent more than £200 a year and that I left without a penny of debt—I had no athletic eminence, nothing but a place among the forwards of the College Rugby XV which I filled with more energy than distinction. Yet the doors were opened wide.

The old life at Glasgow was receding—but not very much as yet. Holidays were still spent with the family, or at any rate with one or

---

[1] Author of *Dracula.*

other of the younger members. Bishop Norman Lang recalls a journey in Cosmo's company to Sligachan in Skye, where he, aged fourteen, was taken to climb Scuir-nan-Gillean, a formidable ascent which the inexperienced should never attempt without a guide. Cosmo knew little or nothing about climbing, and when he and his brother reached the Pinnacles on the east side of the mountain, they stuck, unable to go either up or down and hanging above a precipice by their fingers and toes. Fortunately, just as they were at the end of their strength, a guide with another party heard their cries and got them off with the help of a rope. Cosmo, his brother reported, was outwardly calm, but afterwards confessed that he was in a blue funk and did not feel at all ready to die.

Cosmo wrote home with the greatest regularity and affection and made a point of attending chapel every morning. "I am so *very* pleased," his mother wrote, "to hear that you have *never* missed morning chapel, though I needn't say, I am sure, that doesn't come in place of your private prayers." A few days later he had to confess with distress that he had overslept and spoilt his record.

"I am a little afraid," his mother wrote again, "your Sundays are a little more *secular* than I would like." He was breakfasting and lunching out and spending the evening in "young men's rooms."

It is easy perhaps to smile at her fears and her dislike of habits that seem harmless to-day; easier certainly than it is to assess the value of such a standard of life and conduct as Cosmo received from his parents and his early environment, or of the prayers that followed him, then and always, wherever he went and whatever he did. He at least was conscious to the end of his life that however far he had travelled from his father and mother and the life of the Manse, they had given him something beyond any price a man could pay.

C. G. LANG AT OXFORD

CUDDESDON PARISH CHURCH

Chapter VI

OXFORD

THE new term threw Cosmo headlong into the life of the Oxford Clubs. He was a member of the Brakenbury and the Devorguilla at Balliol, and was shortly to join Vincent's and the Canning and to be a founder of the Oxford University Dramatic Society. He had already spoken at the Union, and in February (1883) made his name there with a speech on the disestablishment of the Church of Scotland. "At one bound I seemed to have leapt into fame." Bruce Williamson of Balliol, afterwards historian to the Inner Temple, had moved the resolution in favour of disestablishment. "This stirred the ancestral blood in my veins and I found myself delivering a fervent oration."

"It seems probable," reported the *Oxford Magazine*, "that at last the Union Society may congratulate itself on the possession of an orator who is something more than a mere debater. The young gentleman who opposed the motion last Thursday in favour of the disestablishment of the Scottish Church spoke with such fire and intensity of conviction that the House was fairly carried away, and accorded him a hearty ovation which was thoroughly deserved.

"It is the general opinion that no more eloquent speech has been heard in the Union during the last three years."

Anthony Hope Hawkins was in the Chair, Charles Mallet (Cosmo's rival for the Brakenbury) was Secretary, and although the audience was not large, when the comparatively unknown freshman from Balliol sat down he was given round upon round of applause. The great ones then got together in some excitement and agreed, in Mallet's words, that a new Demosthenes had risen among them. "I have been told, what is very likely true, that never in my later life have I made a better speech." At any rate its fame and his ran through the University and remained in the memories of those present. Nor can it have happened before or be likely to happen again that a future Archbishop of Canterbury should achieve his first great oratorical success with a speech in defence of the establishment of the Church of Scotland.

Lord Robert Cecil,[1] a contemporary at University College, who missed this occasion, doubts if in all his subsequent career Lang "surpassed his speeches as an undergraduate". They were, he went on to say, "addressed not to the emotions but to the reason. He had the power of delivering an admirably phrased and closely knit argument in such a form that even the impatient and rather frivolous youth of Oxford listened intently."

Speaking of a later debate, another friend, Tupper-Carey,[2] pays an even more enthusiastic tribute to Cosmo's oratory: "I can see him now, standing at the table, with his chest thrown out, his head thrown back, pouring out a torrent of words to the assembled undergraduates. I was enthralled; I had never heard anything like it in my life."

He had, to an unusual degree, the gift of thinking upon his feet and of clothing the resulting thought in apt words and well-constructed sentences, such as come to others only after much preparation, if at all. Once he had to take an essay to a tutor, but had been pressed for time and the essay was unwritten. So he sat, with a blank sheet of paper in front of him, ostensibly reading and in fact improvising. All went well until presently the tutor stopped him and asked him to repeat a sentence. Cosmo hesitated, apparently uncertain of the passage indicated, was told to hand over the essay, and of course there was nothing to see.

The speech on disestablishment naturally had its successors, in which Cosmo took the Conservative side against Anthony Hawkins, the leader of the Liberals; and at the end of that summer term he was elected President of the Union, without any opposition, an outstanding tribute to the fame he had won in debate. This spread beyond the bounds of Oxford, for in 1885, when he was barely twenty-one, he was actually invited to stand for Tredegar in the Conservative interest.

Nearly as significant as any triumph at the Union was his part in the Canning Club, the senior Conservative society at the University, which had lately flourished exceedingly under the secretaryship of George Nathaniel Curzon. It met, and still meets, in the rooms of its members, who listen to a paper from one of their number, drink the toast of "Church and King," and then have a discussion. Cosmo, in his second year, was chosen Secretary of the Club, which at that time included among its members the Duke of Newcastle, Earl Ferrers, Sir Drummond Chaplin and the Bishop of Argyll and the Isles, all, of course, in their

---

[1] Now Viscount Cecil of Chelwood.
[2] Canon A. D. Tupper-Carey.

undergraduate days. Lord Cecil, another member, says that Cosmo's progressive opinions were not always appreciated by the sterner Tories, but his ability was unquestioned. Tupper-Carey, also a member and the not uncritical friend of a lifetime, pays a compliment that has the suspicion of a double edge.

> He dominated us all by his eloquence. When he had delivered his address, we all felt that nothing more was to be said. None of us was able to stand up against him except Ferard, afterwards Rector of the Academy at Edinburgh. In a little thin voice he used to prick holes in what we thought was an unanswerable argument, and in a few minutes we saw the whole bubble collapse, to our intense relief.

But the general feeling in Oxford, Tupper-Carey adds, was that Lang was already fitted to be either Prime Minister or Archbishop of Canterbury.

Tupper-Carey was already one of Cosmo's closest friends, although there was not then, and still less was there later, a "marriage of true minds" or a match of temperament and character. "Tupper," as his friends all called him, was at this time a lively attractive young man, fresh from Eton, and was to become a great parish priest. He could get at once on the easiest terms with every sort of person, from the "drunks" of Leeds and Lowestoft to the millionaires of Monte Carlo. "If you don't love your people," Dolling once said, "you can do nothing with them. If you do, you can do anything." "Tupper" could do anything. Mercurial, overflowing with high spirits, irrepressible, he was everybody's friend and had a smile and a word for every passer-by in the streets of his parish. On the other hand, there was not much common ground between "Tupper" and bishops, still less between him and archbishops. Probably, too, being what he was, he could neither appreciate nor understand the intellectual fastidiousness and reserves of others, and in after years his ebullience would often irritate his friend; but Lang had and retained an affection for him, a respect for his human quality and his pastoral zeal; and when "Tupper" died, he wrote a short account of his life and work.

Cosmo already showed himself an admirable Chairman. Lord Cecil recalls a stormy meeting at the Union, when for some reason the President was absent. The House got so out of hand that at length Cosmo, as an ex-President, was summoned to take the Chair. He did so, and in a very short time quiet was restored.

His connexion with the Oxford University Dramatic Society, founded after the Philothespians had fallen into disfavour, was less spectacular, but shows the distance he had travelled since the days when he had asked for permission to go to *Othello*.

I was one of the founders, with Arthur Bourchier, James Adderley, Alan McKinnon and others. . . . It fell to me to open the first performance—Henry IV (First Part)—by reciting a prologue written by George Curzon, a rather dull and bombastic composition.

It was, the *Times* reported, "fairly delivered by Mr. C. G. Lang, made up as a doctor of divinity, though for what reason he was so attired was scarcely apparent to the house." Mr. Gilbert Coleridge has supplied the reason: it was "to give a due solemnity to the occasion." Many years afterwards Cosmo took the Chair at a dinner of old members of the O.U.D.S. and delighted the company by his recollections of incidents of the early days. He spoke in particular of this first performance, recalling how Gilbert Coleridge had borrowed Arthur Bourchier's dress clothes in order to increase his girth in the part of Falstaff.

The Clubs multiplied, and with them the friends—among others, F. Huth Jackson,[1] a future Director of the Bank of England, Henry Bowlby, afterwards of Eton and Lancing, Godfrey Bradby, Howard Pease, of the well-known North Country family, and Lionel Craufurd, afterwards Bishop of Stafford. At Oxford, friends and Clubs are old enemies of work, and Cosmo, like many others before and after him, no doubt found a difficulty in honouring an early resolution to work eight or nine hours a day. He was reading for "Greats," "where the combination of ancient literature, philosophy and history seemed to me then, as it seems still, to be the noblest basis of general culture ever conceived." As he was conscious of defective scholarship, he did not try for Honours in Classical Moderations, but took a Pass and went straight into his Finals. His tutor was Dr. Ritchie,[2] a Fellow of Jesus, "a thoughtful, friendly, rather mild and uninspiring teacher." He attended lectures on Roman History by Strachan Davidson,[3] later Master of Balliol, who "discussed our essays in every kind of posture and through wreaths of tobacco smoke"; and on Plato by "that fascinating

[1] The Rt. Hon. Frederick Huth Jackson.
[2] David George Ritchie.
[3] J. L. Strachan Davidson, Master from 1907-16.

and guileless thinker," Robert Louis Nettleship,[1] who taught by asking questions rather than by answering them. Everybody, except Cosmo himself, expected he would get a First. Although in 1884 he had tried and just failed to win the Stanhope, he had had a career of almost un-broken success and a First seemed to be its natural climax and crown. But it was not to be; and the postcard to Scotland from the College porter was "short, devastating"—"Sir, you have got a Second."

Dr. Ritchie was surprised and could only conclude that his papers were not up to the standard of his prepared essays.

"I consider (them)," he wrote, "the very ablest I have heard during my six years of teaching. If I may point to any fault, it was a certain too great *uniformity* of treatment which I have noticed among others who have come fresh from the influence of Professor Caird."

"It was long," Cosmo wrote, "before life smiled again," but in the following year (1885) he had a chance to repair his damaged reputation. He sat for the Honour School of Modern History, and this time he took no chances.

I set myself to work hard. Lodgings in St. Giles, where my companions were Godfrey Bradby and Howard Pease, were less distracting than my delightful rooms in College—"the Cottage," by the Hall on the ground floor—and for most of the year I kept to a steady daily seven or eight hours' average of work. My tutor was the rugged, original, forceful A. L. Smith (afterwards Master), the "Smuggins" of many men's grateful memories, and I took essays to Arthur Johnson at All Souls, and thus began a friendship ripened at All Souls and lasting for over forty years. In the Summer Term, I remember, I used to work till five, and then some of us used to row down to Sandford, bathe in the "Casher," have a light meal in the town, get back about 8.30; and then I worked again till midnight.

At his *viva voce* the examiner asked him with a smile what he thought about the character of Queen Elizabeth, but dismissed him almost before he had begun to answer; and he got a very good First. "The consciousness that the strength came from above will keep you *humble*," his father wrote. "May you never lose the humility and simplicity which are signs of the really blessed character."

With the pride of the parents in the successes of their son went a

---

[1] Fellow of Corpus Christi.

constant anxiety, which appears in all their letters, lest the successes should spoil him. Worldly triumphs were all very well, but there was something that mattered more. To their prayers and affectionate exhortations were added those of the grandmothers, and especially of old Mrs. Lang: that God might "hold up his goings in Thy path that his footsteps slip not." She was becoming an old woman, she declared, and her chief pleasure was in "thinking of her grandchildren," particularly perhaps of her "own beloved Cosmo."

On October 31st, 1885, he had come of age.

"I can't say," he wrote to his mother, "I feel much more developed now that I have ceased to be an infant, but no doubt the feeling will come. Yet as a matter of fact I feel much more juvenile now than I did four years ago, when I suffered from the disease of consumption of the brain by premature metaphysics.

"Yet in another sense I think I may say I feel more manly, less consumed by windy speculation, though possibly more consumed by equally windy self-conceit, and with a better eye to the practicalities of an active life. My friends tell me—and I am more or less conscious of it—that my character is Janus-like, double-faced, on one side metaphysical and even at times dreamy, on the other 'eminently practical,' possessing 'rigorous common sense' to an amount approaching dullness. The latter side, I rejoice, is rapidly coming to the front. The silly little boy who used to make the Morningside garden a battleground or a slum, himself a Napoleon or a street arab, who at a later stage used to fill 'straw paper' with incongruous epics, sonnets, heroics and hymns, all more excellent for intention than performance; the priggish 'halflin'' who slouched up to Glasgow College and smugged indoors over volumes of Hegel, which he foolishly thought he liked, and over religioso-philosophical effusions which he innocently imagined solutions of the universe—this interesting young person now becomes a man, respectable, worldly, rigorous and practical, still with a dash of the precocious prig.

"More seriously, I do recognise the wonderful tenderness of the Hand that has hitherto laid out the path before me, smoothing away difficulties and yet warning too in season. I like the fable of the little boy who trusted to the Great Hands.

"Of course a coming of age is a time for resolutions, and, like most people, I have made a good stock. Whether I shall dispose of them with profit to Time, with whom all our life is a bargaining, I cannot tell. My best wish for myself is that as I wish my manhood to express my principles, so I hope that more and more these principles may become *mine*, the Perfect Man. And I am sure my parents translate the wish into their prayer."

The day passed without celebration—"rain outside, reading within, humble meals and a philosophical pipe, with the company of two quiet souls."

Rather earlier a new and serious interest had come into his life. In the late autumn of 1883 Samuel Barnett,[1] Vicar of St. Jude's, Whitechapel, preached at St. Mary's on the claims of the poor upon Oxford, and the quiet, restrained tone of the preacher struck answering chords in Cosmo, who was among the congregation. The sermon was followed by a meeting in the rooms of Sidney Ball,[2] a Fellow of St. John's, when Barnett read a paper on University Settlements. For audience Arthur Acland[3] had brought the members of a small society of which he was the ruling spirit, known to its members as the Inner Circle and to outsiders as the "Upper Suckles." Cosmo does not appear to have belonged to it and was presumably taken by one of the members as a guest.

We who heard the paper decided that we must act upon it. It was soon determined that a University Settlement would be a fitting memorial to Arthur Toynbee, a lecturer at Balliol, whose self-sacrificing life of effort to bring Oxford's ideals to working men had just been prematurely closed. He had died shortly after I came up, but I remember being greatly impressed by his beautiful face as I saw it in Chapel. So began Toynbee Hall in Whitechapel. The two first undergraduate secretaries were Michael Sadler of Trinity (afterwards Master of University) and Lang of Balliol; and the first meeting of undergraduates on behalf of the Hall was held in my rooms. Thereafter I used to address meetings in College Halls and rooms to spread interest in the cause. To give reality to these speeches I paid my first visit to the East End, staying at 3 Hooper Square, Whitechapel, a house which had partially suggested a University Settlement. . . . This new interest took up much—too much—of my time; and I fear a very characteristic remark of the Master's proved

---

[1] The Rev. Samuel Augustus Barnett, Warden and afterwards President of Toynbee Hall. Died in 1913.
[2] Afterwards President of the College.
[3] Apparently the Rt. Hon. Sir Arthur Acland, Bt., M.P.

to be too well justified. It was at Collections, the ceremony at which at end of term we were brought before the Master's judgment seat. "Mr. Lang," he said drily, "you are making a great mistake. You forget that your business here is not to reform the East End of London, but to get a First Class in the School of Literae Humaniores."

It was the social rather than the religious side of the venture that attracted him; and when, a little later, Oxford House was projected, Cosmo actually wrote an article against the introduction of the "denominational spirit" into a social movement. His own religious position was as yet "very indefinite."

If it was not wholly negative, this was due mainly, I suppose, to the influence of home traditions. I attended Chapel regularly and I think that once or twice I received the Holy Communion there. As I had been admitted to Communion in the Church of Scotland, and as I was wholly ignorant of English ecclesiastical affairs, it did not ever occur to me that my being unconfirmed was any obstacle. But otherwise interest in religion was largely speculative and impersonal. I think I was very slack and intermittent in any habit of personal prayer. I used sometimes to attend the University sermon at St. Mary's and the special sermons for undergraduates just instituted . . . ; but I think the main motive was curiosity—to see what leading Anglican preachers were like and to hear what they had to say. . . . In my case I dare say it was partly due to an inherited interest in ministers and sermons. But I don't remember any of their discourses having made any impression. Of course, there were in my own and other men's rooms endless discussions on religious subjects, as on every subject under the sun, and I fancy that again, through hereditary influences, I would usually talk on the side of belief, but it was not till I had left Oxford that I cared enough positively and personally about religion even to be troubled by serious and searching doubt.

As yet no thought that he might become a priest had so much as entered his mind. It may be that he was still too full of the coming career. This would continue to conform, with some necessary variations, to that imagined programme he had made for himself when he was twelve or thirteen years old. It was true that he had gone to Oxford and not to Cambridge; and that thereafter the English and not the Scottish Bar was to be his destination; but in outline he was keeping to the plan. So it would go on. He would write, practise at the Bar, enter the House of Commons, take office. The earldom, the premiership and the titled bride were moving measurably nearer.

His time at Oxford was drawing to a close; but one ambition remained, a Fellowship at All Souls, which, apart from the unequalled prestige it carried, would be a valuable aid during his first unrewarding years as a briefless barrister. In February 1884 he had dined at All Souls —"a unique experience," which he described at length in his letters home. He sat for the Fellowship in October 1886. "I have done about as badly at All Souls as I could have done . . ." he wrote in depressed mood to his mother. "I *know* that I now for this year have no chance." He was "dull, stale and confused." His forebodings were justified; he failed, and a few days later was writing again to his mother: "I am far more sorry for you and father than for myself. . . . But—there is always next year; and even though it may never be granted to me to reach the chief end of my Oxford ambition, is it not the Divine Hand that is leading? If it is in a hard path, that is only because I need discipline."

Years afterwards he asserted that his lack of scholarship, due to poor early training in Glasgow, was responsible for this setback, as well as for his failure to get a First in Greats.

"There is always next year." But next year there was no election at All Souls, and Cosmo had to wait longer and endure the pangs of exile before he was allowed to enter the Promised Land.

Chapter VII

YEARS OF UNCERTAINTY

DAVID WYLIE, in Sir James Barrie's play, *What Every Woman Knows*, declares: "There are few more impressive sights in the world than a Scotsman on the make." By this Barrie meant nothing derogatory, rather a tribute to his own countrymen, in whose early careers there is often an element of planning and concentration less commonly found among the English. Lang's early life had at least the appearance of conforming with Barrie's *dictum*. His course had gone very much according to plan or pattern. He had had his "downs" as well as his "ups." He had won the Brakenbury, been President of the Union, got a First in History; on the other hand, he had also taken a Second in Greats and failed in his first assault on All Souls. But if it were possible to plot his career like a temperature chart, the general movement would have been up and the gradient steep. He came down in 1886 with a remarkable reputation. It may safely be presumed that if anyone then at Oxford had been asked to give the names of the three or four coming men of the time, Lang would have been in the list.

But the curtain was going up on a new Act, which began inevitably with a deflation. The small boy who has become a whale among other small boys finds himself a minnow when he goes to his public school. Five years later, a Prefect and Captain of the Cricket Eleven, he moves on to Oxford or Cambridge and discovers that he is again nobody. Three years pass, and in an aroma of creditable achievements he leaves the University, to find that in London a great many people hardly know the difference between a First and a Second Class and have never even heard of the Union; and that in most professions a Blue is not a negotiable asset. He has to start all over again, just as in one of those juvenile games, played with dice, an unlucky throw will send a player back to the beginning.

This was to be Lang's experience when he had finished his time at Oxford.

I wonder if there is any descent comparable in its dismal completeness to that of a young god from the Oxford Olympus, full of ambition, but without money or influence, to the stark realities and overwhelming loneliness of London. At Oxford, it seemed but a short step from the Union or the Canning Club to at least the first rung in the ladder of a political career. But arrival in London disclosed a dark chasm. I had no income of my own, and I dared not now draw any longer upon my father's. I betook myself to humble lodgings near Connaught Square; and there the change from Oxford life and hopes stood naked and without disguise.

He spent the summer of 1887 in Germany, with the idea that a proficiency in modern languages would help him in his next attempt at a Fellowship. He went to Göttingen, attending lectures at the University and mixing with the students. He lodged with "an old widow lady, poor as a Church mouse and proud as Lucifer of her lineage."

She knew no English (except to speak of "a half past cup of tea") and at first I knew no German; but we soon became great friends. She lived with an idle son, who had been wounded in the 1870 war with France. They were constantly quarrelling, especially at meals, and my few German words were unequal to the task of keeping the peace. He hated the English, and after my second visit he decamped with a comely Frau, the wife of a friend. . . .

I saw a good deal of student life, had long walks with one or two students in the Forest, and was invited to some of the beer-drinking evenings of their Corps and Clubs; and I sometimes frequented the place where, with the connivance of the police, their duels took place. As to the "Kneipes," they were to me amazing and somewhat disgusting performances. The amount of beer drunk was incredible —a man would consume 12 litres and think little of it. They were protected by getting physically sick before they could get drunk. It was an astonishing thing to see a Professor of European reputation retiring, after the manner of the Romans at a banquet, to get rid of some of his beer and then returning to drink more.

As to the duelling, no doubt in many ways it was a sorry affair, a poor substitute for the athletic contests at Oxford or Cambridge. Selected members of one Corps would offer a purely nominal and conventional insult to selected members of another, and the duels would result. But I am bound to say that it seemed to me a very real, if misplaced, trial of nerve as well as of skill to stand up against your adversary with the chance at any moment of having your nose split. Of course, the vital parts are carefully protected: you must

play your sword only with the wrist and you must keep your wrist
at a certain level; and a surgeon stands by to stop the fight if the
wound is serious or the bleeding excessive. Yet even so, I repeat,
it is a test of nerve. There are, or at least were, duels of a more serious
kind, fought for other than conventional insults. In my short time
at Göttingen there were two deaths from real sword fights.

Lang himself came unpleasantly near being involved in one of these
childish and sanguinary affairs.

One of my familiar acquaintances at Göttingen was an American
tutor in "pure mathematics" at an American University, who was
taking a special course of study at the University. He became
"betrothed" to a girl of the town, daughter of one of the innumerable
State officials. All was certainly in order according to social conventions. She was a beautiful and very charming girl. One evening
he and I were walking with her in Maavedel's Garden, the open-air
garden where at that time many of the Corps of Students sat at their
tables drinking beer. As we approached the table of one of the most
swagger Corps—even now I shall not mention its name—we noticed
that our approach seemed to cause immediate excitement. The
President of the Corps rose and, as we came up, advanced and suddenly, though not violently, struck the girl on the face. It appeared
that she was the toast of the Corps, and they were indignant at her
choice of an Englishman, as they thought my American friend was.
Having delivered this gross insult, he said (or in words to this effect):
"Now, *gnädiges Fräulein*, we shall see whether you will find in
your Englishman the honour you would find in a Prussian."
He then turned to her betrothed and said: "Sir, I am ready to
offer you any satisfaction: choose your weapon, your place, and
your time."
To my consternation—I am bound to confess—another student
addressed *me*, saying that as I was the Englishman's friend, he was
ready to meet me also. Of course, we were furious at their behaviour
to this innocent girl, but what was to be done? We knew that this
was a crack fighting Corps, that these men were experts in the
business, and that to gratify them would be to run the certain risk of
being badly, it might be even fatally, wounded.
After a hurried consultation in English, we decided on a course
of bluff; and the young lady afterwards entreated us not to notice

their insult. So we said we would communicate with them, and a formal exchange of cards followed. When we got home we sent a letter to the President and his second telling them that the weapon with which *we* of our race were accustomed to deal with men who insulted offenceless women was the horsewhip, and that if they liked to come to a named place at a named hour, we would be ready to apply it to them. The reply, of course, was that we were plainly men who did not know what honour was, and that Fräulein —— would doubtless take note of our cowardice. But there the episode ended, except that for some time we were apt to hear sneers muttered as we passed members of this famous Corps. Certainly the episode revealed a strange perversion of the claims of honour. Whether my friend and I came out of it well I must leave others to judge.

All the students, however, were not of this swashbuckling temper. Lang struck up acquaintance with several who were "genial, kindly, thoughtful"; and many of the people he met outside the University were "full of amiability and hospitality, and often of a very simple but real culture." With their help and encouragement he was "soon able to talk a sort of German which was described as *tapfer* (courageous)." Afterwards he looked back with genuine pleasure to his five months at Göttingen; and when, in the following summer, he revisited his former haunts, he was once more delighted to see "the excellent old Frau," to walk in the woods, and to listen to the singing of the peasants.

One day I heard two really admirable female voices sounding in duet through the wood, and then saw through the darkening branches two lively maidens walking hand in hand and singing. It was the sort of scene that brings back the old romantic life of the German Wälde.

He also went to Munich, where he discovered that

every man, woman and child . . . reckoned by the average drinks 485 litres of beer—i.e. about 800 pints—every year.

But since in his wanderings he saw only three drunk men, he wondered why we could not "have such beer for our working-men in England." The royal palace, with its pomp and circumstance, affronted him, for what, after all, were the Wittelsbachs compared with the older royal houses of Europe? Henry Bowlby was with him on this second visit, "the best companion a man could wish." They went together to see the sights and to hear "The Ring," but sometimes Lang would slip away by himself for a walk in the "English Garden," when he was troubled by gloomy thoughts and brooding speculations. For the future was indeed uncertain. Presently Bowlby returned home, to a fiancée, a job at Eton, and a private income of five hundred a year. "Lucky chap!" ruefully commented Lang, who had neither fiancée, nor job, nor private income.

He also visited Switzerland that summer with George Goschen,[1] who was ill for most of the time they were there. They stayed in the Engadine.

I remember in one of our hotels a formidable Victorian lady of high degree and strong Evangelical principles, who was travelling with her two very agreeable daughters. I once asked them whether they had read a certain novel. "Oh no," they demurely replied, "you see, Mamma does not allow us to read novels." "Well," I said, "that subject may be dismissed." "No," said one of them as demurely, "not quite; for, if we may tell you a secret, we promised Mamma that *we* would not read novels, but our maid reads them to us."

The mother of these ingenuous damsels delighted Lang with the information: "I have a nephew, such a noble young man, a clergyman who works in that dreadful East End of London; and he tells me of the dreadful things the people say about the aristocracy and Our Lord."

After the first visit to Germany Lang had to settle down to his new life in London, and the chill of the change from Oxford struck him like the blast of a winter wind. The return "marks the darkest and most depressing stage of my life," he wrote.

He had already been entered at the Inner Temple and eaten some of his dinners, but could not afford the fee he would have to pay to be a barrister's pupil and read in Chambers. He had somehow to enlarge his resources and, as All Souls was offering no Fellowship that autumn— "the fates seem to be against me at present"—he decided to compete for a University Prize Essay on the subject of Thomas Cromwell, Earl of Essex. He worked away at it in the Reading-room of the British Museum; and in after years, when he became Chairman of the Trustees of the Museum, he would recall "those rather dreary days when I sat with the strange and motley crowd of readers." Another disappointment followed. The Essay was nearing completion when he discovered that,

[1] The 2nd Viscount Goschen, Governor of Madras 1924-29.

owing to a change in the date for sending it in, he was too late to compete. Rather than waste the work he had done, he then resolved to turn the Essay into a book. Ill fortune, however, still followed him. One day he went out of his lodgings at 10 Portsea Place, Connaught Square, leaving the unfinished manuscript behind, and the little general servant, who was cleaning the room, took it for waste-paper and threw it on the fire. Lang was hardly consoled for the loss by the reflexion that he and Thomas Carlyle were fellow-sufferers.

Meanwhile the parents in Glasgow were becoming a little anxious about him. Without fully appreciating the circumstances, they thought it was time he settled down seriously to take his Bar examinations and serve his apprenticeship. With the support of the Brakenbury no longer behind him, his financial situation was most precarious; and on Woodlands Terrace "holidays" abroad sounded suspiciously like a waste of time and money he could ill afford. The necessity of explaining to the parents that he was not frittering away the hours unprofitably was an irksome addition to the other discouraging circumstances of his life in London. However,

Some relief in this time of depression came from a special experiment. . . . Still nursing political ambitions, I wanted to get alongside working men in their real thoughts and interests, as my Tory Democratic ideas convinced me that no party could be either useful or successful which did not understand and sympathise with them. Moreover, I was quite genuinely eager, with the memory and example of Arnold Toynbee before me and the teaching of Samuel Barnett, to share with them some of the gifts which Oxford had bestowed on me. Accordingly I arranged with the Oxford University Extension Delegacy to give a series of lectures on history, literature and economics to workers in the North of England. . . . These were the days when, under the influence of men at Cambridge like James Stuart and of men at Oxford like Hudson Shaw and Michael Sadler, the University Extension movement had all the glow of a young enthusiasm. It was really in spirit a true apostolate of University ideals among the people. My lectures and classes were almost all arranged through the Education Committees of the Co-operative Societies. In those early days these Committees had a far wider and fuller conception of education than they seem to have now. I had a round of centres across the industrial North in places like Bolton, Rochdale,

47

Wallsend, and not least the little Co-operative Wholesale Fustian Manufacturing Society at Hebden Bridge.

I really enjoyed my time: there was then such a real, often pathetic desire in the breasts of these working men to learn, to reach out to a wider life. There was then little of the later economic or political bias or class consciousness. I often stayed in their own homes, sharing their simple but delightfully courteous hospitality. It was especially at Hebden Bridge that I made some lasting friendships, and I remember now with real affection old Joe Craven, the chairman, Joseph Greenwood, the manager, and Leonard Stocks, the secretary of the little Corporation enterprise. They presented me with a complete suit of brown fustian, made by them, which I often wore. It was at Hebden Bridge that I made the acquaintance of a weaver-scholar, whom I have often taken as my text in speaking about Adult Education all over the country. I had begun some lectures on Browning—a sign that these were Victorian days! I told my working people that they would not make much of him unless they possessed some keys to open his treasures. I gave them one: "Ay, but a man's reach should exceed his grasp, or what's a heaven for?" After the class my friend walked with me very silent to the station. We walked still silent along the platform. Then he said: "Tell me that key again: I haven't got it yet." I repeated the words. After another length of the platform he said: "Tell it again," and I did so. Then the train came in and he said: "I haven't got it yet." Next week he met me with a radiant face: "I've got it now." You see how determined he was to grip things for himself—the right stuff for a scholar. From that day he devoted his leisure to the reading of English literature. Some years later he died, worn out by hard work and hard study, but not before he had written for one of the Quarterlies an essay on Milton, which some good writers declared to be a most original and interesting study of the great Puritan. He was a type of many others.

Here is another episode of those days—the first appearance among these simple, earnest working folk of the New Woman. She came in the charming person of Miss Beatrice Potter, afterwards Mrs. Sidney Webb. She was then engaged in compiling her history of the Co-operative movement. She had asked to be allowed to come to the Hebden Bridge Society. She came. I was there. We met in Joseph Greenwood's house. The wives considered that it was only proper that they should be with their husbands and they sat silent in their best beaded gowns. All went well till Miss Potter asked if she might smoke—an innocent request nowadays. But the ladies were obviously greatly shocked and became suspicious. I had arranged to take a long walk with the men next day to Haworth Moor, the home of the Brontës. Miss Potter said she would like to come. The ladies were now all the more convinced that they must be at hand to protect their lords. We started, an odd-looking party. But the good women, in their long dresses and elastic-sided boots, wholly unaccustomed to walk further than the distance between their homes and shop or chapel, soon gave up. They intimated to the New Woman that they must return. "I'm so sorry," said she. with engaging frankness, "but I'm going on." Then one guardian of the proprieties turned to another and said grimly: "The impident huzzy!"

These experiences refreshed and encouraged him, and afterwards he would say that he had learned far more from his new friends than they could have learned from him. In order to augment his slender income a little more, he also undertook some lectures outside the University Extension Courses and made his first ventures in journalism. He wrote reviews for the *Guardian*, the leading Church newspaper of the day, and found himself putting Lecky right about the history of England in the eighteenth century and correcting the Duke of Argyll's version of the economic history of Scotland. James Greenwood was then the editor of the *St. James's Gazette*, and to him too some articles went.

I once wrote a series of papers on Scottish life and character and sent them to him. He asked me to come and see him. He said he liked the papers and would have taken them, but for a strange coincidence. He had just accepted a series of papers on precisely the same subject from a writer who called himself Gavin Ogilvie. It was then the *nom de plume* of James Barrie. I think his papers were the *Auld Licht Idylls*.

Yet despite this little disappointment, things were looking up. Some of his Oxford friends were now in London and would take him away for a few hours from his books and gloomy thoughts. He paid a visit to Hatfield, presumably on the invitation of Lord Robert Cecil, and went to an evening party at the Foreign Office, where his eyes were

D   49

dazzled by the reigning beauties. He began to find his way about London and to learn its charm.

I shall always maintain that modern London can show nothing to compare with Hyde Park in the height of the season—the Victorias with their great ladies and splendid horses and, dashing through the midst of them, the fairy carriage of "the Princess," the centre of all admiring eyes, then in the height of her charm and beauty. Once, when I was talking to Arthur Balfour and Asquith at Grillions Club, I asked what in their judgment was something in those late Victorian days which would never be seen again and which nothing could replace. And it so happened that all three of us came to the same conclusion—Hyde Park on a summer afternoon in the season.

He did not, however, allow the attractions of Hyde Park on an afternoon in the season to lure him from his old allegiance to the East End. He went occasionally to Toynbee Hall, gave a few lectures, and visited the clubs for boys; but he found that in spite of his admiration for the Barnetts and their work, he got a little weary of some of the rather "superior" persons who frequented the Hall.

In contrast, I began to find the atmosphere at the Oxford House under Jimmy Adderley more congenial. It seemed to me less strained and self-conscious. The residents and visitors seemed to have less sense that they were, no doubt quite disinterestedly, studying problems or testing theories. At the Oxford House they were, rather, loyally accepting something old and tried and sure and bringing it as a gospel, a good gift, to the people. This seemed to give them a greater simplicity and cheerfulness. I was still quite detached from the Church; but I think this difference gave me my first insight into the truth that, while I thought the Church would cramp, it might in fact liberate, at least so far as social work was concerned. But this was only dimly conceived. I was indeed persuaded by Adderley to give some addresses on religion to working men. One was, with the assurance characteristic of the independent layman, called "Commonsense Christianity." . . . They were just the sort of thing I am always hearing from my good lay friends, who say they want Christianity without dogmas or creeds. I can at least understand them, for I was once myself one of these. All the same, Adderley seemed to find some merit in these talks, as he astounded me by asking whether I would not conduct a sort of Layman's Mission in

Bethnal Green! That was enough. I registered a vow that never again in my life would I be such a humbug as to give a religious address. I fear this is among my broken vows!

I had another check to my casual enterprises in East London. I was asked to speak for Oxford House at the annual meeting on its behalf at Oxford. The other speaker, if you please, was Temple, then Bishop of London. He spoke with force and fire and made a fine appeal for self-sacrifice. Then, to my consternation, he wound up by saying: "But why should I speak longer? I am to be followed by a young layman of Oxford House, who is doing what I've been talking about." I was dumbfounded, and could scarcely bring myself to begin my speech. Here was I, a casual layman who only varied an ordinary London layman's life by an occasional visit to the East End, posing as an example of Christian self-sacrifice! By myself, at least, I was pitifully found out, and in mere honesty determined, "No more of this for me."

He had a gnawing sense of his own insecurity and uncertainty. Ever since he went to Oxford, a strong tide had swept him along; but now he was in slack water.

It was the time, I suppose, which comes to all men of twenty-two or thereabouts, who have read or thought at all, and who are not absorbed in pleasure or business, when the ultimate problems of life begin to stir uneasy questions. Among them was the problem of God, intellectually very difficult, morally apt to be postponed, but always hovering in the background of the mind. Add to this that I had not yet found my environment and had nothing to which to adjust my inner life. And the frost of disillusionment had bitten the spring flowers rather badly. Small wonder that then life seemed rather drab and difficult. . . .

It was then, or shortly after, that I happened by chance to read these words from St. John's Gospel: "I am the light of the world: he that followeth me shall not walk in darkness, but shall have the light of life." I remember saying to myself: "I must trust the Man Who spoke those words and try my best to follow Him."

We should perhaps discount a little from his tale of gloom. A strong sense of the dramatic disposed him, quite unconsciously, to accentuate his contrasts. His black had to be very black, in order that the white which followed should stand out more clearly. In the garden at Morning-

side the "beggar-child" was never very far from Napoleon winning his battles; nor afterwards the schoolboy in Glasgow from the Earl of Norham governing an Empire. He liked, especially in retrospect, to emphasise the startling changes in a career sufficiently remarkable to need no emphasis. This same sense of drama possibly led him also, in all sincerity, to represent himself as more aloof from religion and its problems than he actually was in his Oxford days. For the purpose of the contrast the future Prince of the Church should rightly begin as a Gallio, caring for none of these things, or at least taking only a detached and impersonal interest in them. But his letters at the time tell a rather different story; nor do some rough notes of his own, written apparently in 1898, quite sustain the contrast.

Early training and a sort of innate, perhaps hereditary respect for the Church kept up some good decorous habits such as Church-going. I used to go pretty regularly to the Temple Church and occasionally to St. Paul's. I don't remember any sermon that impressed me, except, oddly enough, one of Wilson, the then headmaster of Clifton, at St. Paul's. I was struck by the manliness of it. Liddon never appealed to anything in me but admiration for his voice and the structure of his sermons. But Holland first began to set new thoughts moving. Of Vaughan's discourses at the Temple I remember nothing except that I used to think them very much out of touch with modern life and thought. Ainger's reading and the music attracted me much more. I can remember staying once or twice to Communion there. . . . I used to say my prayers, in a hurried perfunctory sort of way; but I fear not seldom they were forgotten, after some yielding to the temptations of youth deliberately left unsaid. Thank God I never "went wrong" in the moral sense; though I must confess that I played sometimes with those external temptations which our Christian London flaunts in the face of its young men, with such force and persistence that I believe nothing but the grace of God can keep a young fellow straight. . . . I had a liking for sermons as such. . . . I never read the Bible, except that once I remember sitting up to read Isaiah through. . . . Yet there was always a curious interest in religious things and persons, and a strong *intellectual* belief in the main Christian doctrines. Of the Church's Sacraments I knew absolutely nothing; but the ordinary sceptical difficulties of the average layman, which were quite familiar to me in books and conversations, never gripped me. The arguments did not impress; and I knew that if I only would live for my better self I must be a Christian. I suppose that sort of conviction must have been stronger than I can now remember. . . . I believe I sometimes said to my friends that "If I were only good enough I would be a parson to-morrow."

In the autumn of 1887 he turned at last to the Bar. Jowett had commended him as a promising prospective pupil to J. A. Hamilton.[1] The latter, when approached, excused himself on the grounds of insufficient work, but sent him on to W. S. Robson,[2] who had a good general practice and agreed to take Lang into his Chambers.

Robson was not a learned lawyer, but he had a singularly quick brain and great agility of argument. We became very good friends. His vehement radicalism was an admirable stimulus and corrective to my liberal Conservatism; and likewise he dabbled in metaphysics. When work was urgent, we had many good talks over a chop and a pint of champagne in the old Cock Tavern. His Chambers were a nest of radical politicians, like Corrie Grant and E. J. C. Morton, already in the House and burning with indignation at the Irish policy of "bloody Balfour." There was only one other pupil, a pleasant debonnair man of the world, who played at his work; so I had my fill of pleadings and papers. I don't know whether I was of any use to Robson, but the work was full of intellectual zest and interest. I migrated from my first obscure lodgings to share rooms in Palace Chambers, Westminster, now offices, then one of the first of service flats, with my friend Fritz (F. Huth Jackson), afterwards Director of the Bank of England and a Privy Councillor.

Here he was joined by his brother Patrick, who had just come back from South India and had started to work in the City.

In 1910, soon after Lang had become Archbishop of York, he visited South Shields, where Robson was fighting a seat for the Liberals in the General Election; and both Liberals and Conservatives agreed to cancel their meetings on a particular evening, so that they might support the Archbishop on his platform. In the course of his speech, thanking the candidates for this courtesy, Lang said: "I used to be Mr. Robson's ——

---

[1] Afterwards Lord Sumner.
[2] He later became Lord Robson, a Lord of Appeal in Ordinary, after being successively Solicitor-General and Attorney-General.

devil. And now," he added, drawing himself up to his full height, "I am his Archbishop!"

In October 1888 Lang had his second try for a Fellowship at All Souls, again with no great expectation of success. His reading had been much interrupted and his performance in the examination left him depressed. He was spending a week-end with Mr. Sydney Buxton [1] at Fox Warren in Surrey, when he got a telegram from his friend George Talbot. He had been elected. For a moment, he wrote to his mother, he "thought . . . it must be a hoax"; and then, after spending, he told Buxton, the happiest night of his life, he travelled on Sunday to Oxford on the happiest journey. The clouds at last had lifted; a new tide had gripped his drifting ship.

"I had now an income assured for seven years, a position of my own, and an abode once again in my beloved Oxford."

[1] Sydney Charles Buxton, afterwards 1st Earl of Buxton, High Commissioner and Governor-General of South Africa. Died in 1934.

Chapter VIII

ALL SOULS

FROM 1888, when Lang became a Fellow of All Souls, until his death in 1945, the College counted for so much to him that, without apology for anticipating events, this chapter will be given to a connexion which covered more than two-thirds of his life. He had a tag, as he called it, which he was fond of reproducing on what he deemed to be appropriate occasions:

Balliol was my mother, to whom I am bound by ties of filial gratitude;

All Souls is my wife, who gave me a home and most generously received me back after a temporary residence with

Magdalen, my very beautiful mistress, for whom during three years I forsook my wife!

He would sometimes add that since receiving his wife's forgiveness for this lapse their conjugal felicity had been unbroken.

All Souls College was founded by Archbishop Chichele in 1438 and differs from the other Oxford Colleges in not professing to be an educational institution for undergraduates. It was in part purpose, though not in name, a Chantry, in which prayers were to be offered for the repose of the soul of the Founder, of King Henry VI, of his father and uncle, and of those who had fallen in the French Wars. A further intention of the Founder was that the Fellows should be trained to "serve God in Church and State," a forecast of a function which in later days All Souls was faithfully to fulfil, so that it is, as it were, a link between the academic world of Oxford and the world of affairs outside. This second purpose may possibly have been the reason why the College escaped the rough attentions of the Reformers and the predatory hands of more than one monarch. Happily it did survive, to be, through its Fellowships, a sort of *corps d'élite* for the University, a unique combination of professors, teaching and research Fellows, and prize and non-resident Fellows. A Fellowship at All Souls became the highest academic prize that Oxford could offer and, apart from the credit it conveyed by association with a long roll of distinguished men, in 1888 it provided every newly elected Prize Fellow with an income of two hundred a year for seven years.[1] He could subsequently be re-elected for further periods of seven years, with an emolument of fifty pounds a year; and this re-election was customary, provided he had remained unmarried and had shown a proper devotion to the College.

Lang relinquished his Prize Fellowship in 1893, when he was appointed Dean of Divinity at Magdalen, but was re-elected on going to Portsea in 1896 and continued to be re-elected until in 1929 he became Archbishop of Canterbury and *ex officio* Visitor of the College. In 1942, when he resigned the Archbishopric, he was elected an Honorary Fellow, and so remained till his death.

In all this time Lang found in All Souls a place of unfailing refreshment and relaxation. Sir Dougal Malcolm,[2] who was himself elected a Fellow in 1899, has been kind enough to contribute some memories of Lang and his relations with the College:

> My recollection of him in those far-off days is of a restlessly energetic and very hard-worked man, for whom the College was a place of occasional and welcome rest and refuge. That indeed, save for the years of Visitorship, it was for him all his life. But he did not give an impression of weariness when he came there. On the contrary, he was alert in the College business and a leader of its merrymaking.

Much of the merrymaking was connected with a Mallard or Wild Drake, about whose origin there are many legends. According to the most popular tradition, when the foundations of the College were laid, a mallard of portentous size was discovered in a drain, and from this alleged event has sprung a ceremonial which has endured till the present day. There is an office—not to be found in any Statute or By-law of the College—of Lord Mallard, a master of revels or rather, perhaps, an Abbot of Misrule.

> It was my glory to hold that office in the College for some thirty years. It is, indeed, a strange office. The holder of it is not appointed: he *becomes*: he takes his place by the informal assent of the College. . . . Thus, when Sir Thomas Raleigh[3] went to India, I acted in his

---

[1] The conditions have been changed and the value of the Fellowship has since been raised to £350 a year for two years, and £400 a year for five years thereafter, if the holder is engaged on teaching or research.

[2] Sir Dougal Orme Malcolm, K.C.M.G., Fellow of All Souls and President of the British South Africa Company.

[3] Sir Thomas Raleigh, Member of the Council of India 1909-13. Died in 1920.

place, and when he returned and was unwilling to continue, I *became* Lord Mallard, and succeeded to the office and retained it ever after.

One of the Lord Mallard's duties is to sing the Song of the Mallard at the All Souls Day Gaudy and at the annual Bursar's Dinner. The Song is a doggerel dating back to the seventeenth century, or possibly to an earlier age. It was, Lang wrote, "a song like Melchizedek, without known origin, but the dear and odd expression of the College spirit from unknown times." For the benefit of those who may be interested a version of the words is printed in an Appendix.[1] Lang sang this strange ditty at every Gaudy from 1898 till 1928, even in the years after he had ceased to carry out the duties of Lord Mallard, and thereafter occasionally and by special request until his death. He sang it for the last time at the Gaudy of 1945, a few weeks before he died. But much earlier, after he had become Archbishop of York, he had felt "with excessive prudery" that he could no longer with propriety discharge the duties of Lord Mallard, and accordingly appointed first the late Professor W. P. Ker,[2] and later, on Ker's death, Sir Dougal Malcolm, to serve as his deputies.

Lang left his own account of the most notable occasion in his tenure of the office.

The most outstanding and historic duty of the Lord Mallard is to take charge of the Mallard Feast, once frequent and disorderly, and now restricted to the opening year of each century. I prize the memory that it fell to me in January 1900 [1901] to do this great thing. Little is known of what happened in 1800 [1801], except that Reginald Heber recorded that he observed the strange performance from Brasenose College. But there is a full record of what happened in 1900 [1901], kept by the Warden. Suffice it here to say that I was carried in a chair by four stalwart Fellows—Wilbraham,[3] Gwyer,[4] Steel-Maitland[5] and Fossie Cunliffe,[6] I think they were—for nearly two hours after midnight round the quadrangles and roofs of the College, with a dead mallard borne in front on a long pole (which I still possess), singing the Mallard Song all the time, preceded by the seniors—such grave and reverend persons as Warden Anson,[7]

[1] Appendix II.
[2] Professor of Poetry. Died in 1920.
[3] Sir Philip W. Baker-Wilbraham, First Church Estates Commissioner.
[4] Sir Maurice L. Gwyer, K.C.B., K.C.S.I., later Chief Justice of India.
[5] The Rt. Hon. Sir Arthur Steel-Maitland, M.P., Minister of Labour 1924-29. Died in 1935.
[6] Sir Foster Cunliffe, Bt. Killed in 1916.
[7] The Rt. Hon. Sir William Anson, M.P., Warden of All Souls 1881-1914. Died in 1914.

Dicey,[1] Holland [2] and the like—and followed by the juniors, all of them carrying staves and torches, a scene unimaginable in any place in the world except Oxford, or there in any society except All Souls. The whole strange ceremony had been kept secret; only late workers in the night can have heard the unusual sound, though it is said that Provost McGrath of Queen's muttered in his sleep: "I must send the Torpid down for this noise." [3]

Subsequently a medal, the work of John Tweed the sculptor, was struck to commemorate the celebration. On one side is a picture of Lang as Lord Mallard, dressed (prematurely) in the robes of a bishop, and on the other a picture of him being borne on his chair.

Such elaborate junketing may sound a little odd to anyone unconnected with All Souls, or at any rate with Oxford. But presumably, if Homer may be excused an occasional nod, a Fellow of All Souls may be allowed, once in a hundred years, to play the fool.

Lang adds that at the dinner a cable was sent to George Curzon, then Viceroy of India and an enthusiastic Quondam Fellow. It consisted of the one word "Swapping," from the chorus of the song; and very soon, from Government House, Calcutta, came the reply, in two words— "It was."

In the past the Mallard Feast had often been attended by revels and rites more unseemly than those of 1901, and even than those which in January 1801 Bishop Heber observed from his attic window. One or two of these old customs did not meet with the approval of the Lord Mallard of 1901.

Some changes I made from the ceremony of 1800 [1801]. I thought it unseemly that surplices should be worn and we contented ourselves with black gowns. There seemed something approaching irreverence in the notion of making the junior Fellows eat of the mallard's flesh and drink its blood so as to be incorporated into the spirit of All Souls. Instead of this I had a small silver mallard made and filled with wine, which the juniors drank. But when the bird was burned in the small hours in a bonfire, some of them could not be restrained from eating portions of his charred flesh.

[1] Professor A. V. Dicey, Vinerian Professor of English Law. Died in 1922.
[2] Thomas Erskine Holland, Professor of International Law and Diplomacy. Died in 1926.
[3] Mrs. Lancashire, daughter of Professor Holland, was an unauthorised observer of this frolic and, by the kind permission of the present Warden of All Souls, I am able to reproduce her account in an Appendix (III).

Sir Douglas Malcolm describes Lang as

> most admirably equipped for his office by his gracious cheery person-
> ality, by his clear pure tenor voice, and by that marvellous facility
> in oratory of any kind which, in so many different fields, distinguished
> him throughout his life.

He goes on to say :

> Lang's vocalism was not confined to the Song of the Mallard. There
> were many other songs with which he would delight the company
> on All Souls Gaudy Nights. There was one in particular supposed
> to be addressed by one old Peninsular War veteran to another,
> recalling the battles of that long struggle. It was known as "Dost
> thou remember?"[1] and, as given by Lang, touched a note of real
> pathos. The ex-Warden of All Souls has drawn my attention to
> the fact that the words and music of this song are to be found in a
> mid-nineteenth century novel entitled *The Starling*[2] about the Presby-
> terian folk of a tiny lowland Scottish town. (This was long before
> "Thrums" was heard of.) I have never seen them anywhere else.

Sir Charles Grant Robertson[3] and Sir Charles Oman[4] were others
who have given their sense of Lang's value to the College. "It was All
Souls that knew Lang," Grant Robertson wrote. It was a man "that
the larger world scarcely guessed at and in which all were equals and
friends." He was at his best in that congenial atmosphere. Though not
himself a scholar, he had a profound respect for learning in all its forms,
yet "could chaff professors and other men of erudition with a subtle
and delicious sauciness." He had formed very definite views about the
part All Souls should play in the life of the University, and at the College
meetings, which he never failed to attend, would intervene with invariable good sense and effect. Oman, too, in *Memories of Victorian
Oxford*, emphasises the excellence of his company, especially at the February Bursar's Dinner, when, after the singing of the Mallard, every
Fellow would be asked in turn to give a song. The results were of uncertain merit, but Lang, Oman says, had the best voice in the College,

---

[1]   " Dost thou remember, O my comrade hoary,
          The Days we fought and conquered side by side ? "
[2] By Norman Macleod, who preceded Lang's father at the Barony Church.
[3] Sir Charles Grant Robertson, Principal of Birmingham University 1920-38. Died
in 1946.
[4] Sir Charles Oman, M.P. for Oxford University and Chichele Professor of Modern
History.

his favourite contributions, besides "Dost thou remember?", being Jacobite melodies. After the singing the Fellows would adjourn to the smoking-room to talk or play whist, and at midnight sat down to an oyster supper in Hall. This last item was dropped from the programme during the war of 1914-1918 and was never revived.

Lang, too, left a few memories of his happy association with the College.

Wherever I was living I used to come up to my rooms for the College meetings and Gaudies three times a year, and often at other times. I cannot describe what a delight and relief it was to pass into this family life, with its old and new friends year after year, a family life in which we were all on equal terms and there was no respect of persons. I remember a great occasion when Mr. Gladstone, escaping for once from Mrs. G., spent most of a week in College as our Honorary Fellow. I think it was in my first year and I had to address him, and of course addressed him, as "Mr. Gladstone." The old man smiled and said, "Gladstone here, please." That was, of course, a counsel of perfection; but he entered delightfully into the life of the College. He indulged in the most Tory sentiments and in many reminiscences of his days at Christ Church. We asked him once what he thought was the most conspicuous difference between the undergraduates of his day and those of 1890. "I have no hesitation in replying," he said in his full tones. "It is the difference in dress. In my time we were so careful of our dress in walking in the High that some of my friends used to wear trousers in which they never sat down lest they should be creased. Now I observe undergraduates in the High with no trousers at all, their legs naked from above the knees." . . .

I shall never forget his reading the lessons in the Chapel. By a happy *Sors Liturgica* the Lessons for the day were from the Book of Revelation. His deep, melodious voice revelled in the sounding phrases, and the old man seemed himself to see the prophetic visions. The words "And I saw a great white horse" are inseparably linked in my memory with the G.O.M. But this is by the way; and a charming account of the visit was written by my friend Charles Fletcher [1] and published by Blackwell of Oxford.

To me the centre of the College and its life has always been the Chapel. It is there that old friends who have passed from us live—

[1] C. R. L. Fletcher, historian and Fellow of Magdalen. Died in 1934.

such as Henry Wakeman,[1] John Doyle,[2] Algy Whitmore,[3] Tom Raleigh, Robert Mowbray,[4] the immortal W. P. Ker, Edgeworth,[5] and not least dear old Arthur Johnson,[6] our Chaplain for some fifty years, whose reading of the Service with the rising and falling of his voice remains an imperishable memory. I at least am ever faithful to the original purpose of Chichele's College—to make remembrance of the souls of the departed.

Indeed, All Souls was more to him than an academic home. When he spoke of the College as his "wife," he was uttering no idle jest; for there, as in no other place on earth, he found that family life which in one form he had lost and in the other form he was never to have. So in 1929, when he became Visitor, he was able to write:

No words of mine can express the love I bear to the College, the gratitude of which my heart is full, or the sorrow with which I must now pass from the frequent residence in the College, with all its easy intimacy, into the remote dignity of its Visitor. . . . My Fellowship there, as I have said, meant that I never really left Oxford: it remained for all these years one of my homes and the centre of an abiding interest and love.

[1] Henry Offley Wakeman, Bursar of All Souls. **Died in 1899.**
[2] John A. Doyle, historian. **Died in 1907.**
[3] Charles Algernon Whitmore, M.P. **Died in 1908.**
[4] Sir Robert Mowbray, Bt., M.P. **Died in 1916.**
[5] F. Y. Edgeworth, Emeritus Professor of Political Economy. **Died in 1926.**
[6] Arthur Johnson, also of University College. **Died in 1927.**

Chapter IX

"WHY SHOULDN'T *YOU* BE ORDAINED?"

"IN the springtime of 1889 all was outwardly bright and promising. However ill at ease I may still have been in such inward life as there was, things seemed to be shaping well. I had my Fellowship and I had its income, to which occasional lectures and articles added. I had many friends. I liked my work in Chambers. It must have been fairly well done : I say this merely to explain what was to come. Robson always said I was bound to have succeeded. I learned later that when he took silk one of his best clients, a solicitor in large practice, who gave Robson a great deal of work, came to his clerk and asked for my address, saying that he wished to give me some of the work he had given to Robson. I was about to be called, with the intention of going on in Robson's Chambers as his 'devil.' There was then no sense of failure or disappointment, but rather a sense of reasonable hope and confidence.

"In this mood I went for a short spring holiday to stay with my lively young friend of the Union and Canning Club, Darrell Tupper-Carey, at his home in Wiltshire. One evening we were returning from a long ride on the Downs. He was intending to take Holy Orders, but naturally he was troubled by last doubts and difficulties. I expended my eloquence as a layman in trying to persuade him to go forward. Then suddenly—I can see the scene now—as the horses were walking down the slope in the setting sun, a question unbidden, wholly irrelevant to anything that had previously entered my thoughts, shot itself into my mind—'After all, why shouldn't *you* be ordained?'

"I laughed inwardly at this foolish question and dismissed it. But next morning it returned. It kept obtruding itself in the train on my way back to London. It haunted me when I returned to Robson's Chambers. All my efforts to silence it seemed only to make it more insistent. It began, so to say, to look out at me from the briefs and pleadings on the table. 'After all, why shouldn't *you* be ordained?'

"This went on for some weeks. At last I felt that I must deal seriously with this intrusive and persistent thing. For, of course, it was mere foolishness. Why on earth *should* I be ordained? It was clean contrary to my set ambitions. Nothing had occurred to change them, much, rather, to encourage them. I had had no sort of religious experience to justify the question. My attitude to the Christian religion was much what it had been at Oxford—respectful, resentful of the ordinary modes of attack on philosophic grounds, but in practice casual and intermittent. I was not much of a churchgoer in London. Sometimes I went to the Temple Church, but Vaughan's sermons affected me less than Ainger's reading. Occasionally I went to St. Paul's, and I remember being impressed, and that but for the time, by only two sermons—one by Wilson, then Headmaster of Clifton, for its honesty; the other one on an Easter Day by one Scott Holland (afterwards my dearest friend and spiritual counsellor), who had just become Canon, which made me think, 'Here's a man with something to say to *me*.' I knew no clergyman in London except Barnett. At Oxford, chiefly from curiosity, I had got an introduction to Charles Gore, then beginning the Pusey House. I remember his taking me a walk to the Cherwell meadows and my pounding him with objections to the High Church position, and I have been told that he returned to say that he had been talking to an intelligent man who seemed incapable of grasping Catholic principles! Certainly no man was ever less under ecclesiastical influence. And I fear, in spite of those ill-starred East End addresses, my prayers were few and formal.

"How, then, could I explain this absurdly insistent question? Was it an emergence from the subconscious life or some trace of heredity? But why should this emerge *now*? Was it some belated effect of the first post-Oxford depression? But why should this become active when the reasons for depression had gone? Was it, as it were, some germ which I had unknowingly caught in the East End, some unthought-out impression that after all only the spirit of Christianity could heal social evils, or that human personality was a nobler care than legal disputes? Perhaps, to some extent; for I remember the effect of walking home from his club with an East End boy. His talk, so frank and confidential, made the papers in Chambers next day seem strangely remote from human interest. Was it the prattle of this boy that injected the germ? Surely not.

"I could find no real reason behind the persistent question. Yet it *did* persist, and with growing force. 'After all, why shouldn't *you* be ordained?' As I could not get rid of it myself, I thought I had better get some help from others to get rid of it. I made Robert Cecil my confidant, the only one of my friends whom I cared to trouble about it. I was rather surprised and a little disconcerted when he said: 'Well,

I've always thought that you would make a better parson than lawyer'; and he added, what I think he would still say, that the pursuit of politics was a far poorer thing than the witness to religion. He advised me to see some wise clergyman who might help to rid me of my burden. I mentioned Scott Holland on the strength of that Easter sermon. He gave me a letter of introduction. But I could not bring myself to use it. For I was persuaded the whole thing was some odd obsession.

"At last, as I could *not* get rid of it and it was really disturbing my work, I was driven to pray about it. The result was only to increase its pressure; and more than this, to persuade me that a pressure more real and deep than itself was moving through it. Up and down the struggle went; until I knew that in my inmost self I was really saying, 'Yes, after all, I believe that I ought to be ordained.'

"Then I resolved to see Scott Holland. I bade him tell me what signs a perplexed man ought to have of any real vocation to Holy Orders. When he mentioned 'a love of souls' I could not understand his language. I think he was as much perplexed as I was, and no light came.

"It so happened that I had arranged to go and see a man who had attracted me at Oxford House—Freddy Sewell, long since in his early promise transferred to service in the Unseen World. He was at Cuddesdon College. I knew nothing of the place, but some instinct made me think : 'Perhaps I may get some light there.'

"I went to All Souls as usual for the week-end and on the Sunday walked over to Cuddesdon with Henry Wakeman of All Souls. It was a beautiful early summer day. I said nothing of what was in my mind to Sewell and watched the young men with a critical scrutiny. I liked the look of them, but plainly they were not 'my sort.' I went to the Parish Church for evensong. The whole scene is indelibly impressed on my memory. I sat in the second pew from the pulpit, then on the north side. I paid little attention to the service and less to the sermon, preached, I don't know about what, by the curate. But I had a strong sense that something was about to happen. I was not in the least excited; there was no sort of nervous tension; I had only prayed in a rather weary way during the service in some such manner as this—'I can't go on with this strange struggle. End it, O God, one way or another. If there *is* anything real, anything of Thy will, in this question, help me to answer it.' Then suddenly, while the unheeded sermon went on, I was gripped by a clear conviction. It had all the strength of a masterful inward voice. 'You are wanted. You are called. You must obey.'

"I knew at once that the thing was settled. The burden of the long struggle dropped. My mind was free. I don't want to write emotionally, but it is only recording fact to say that a wave of such peace and indeed joy as I had never known before filled my whole being. In the Chapel later, at Compline, it seemed to flow out in happy worship. I said nothing to anyone. But when, having missed the train at Wheatley, Wakeman and I (with J. A. R. Marriott,[1] who had joined us) set out to walk back to Oxford over Shotover Hill in the moonlight, I felt like a man who had been suddenly set free from chains; and I really could have shouted for joy. Little did my companions realise what was passing in my mind as we ran down the hill with the lights of Oxford twinkling beneath us. That night in my rooms at All Souls I prayed as I had never prayed in my life before. But all my prayers had the one refrain: 'I obey and I am free.' Later the words came to my mind: 'I will run the way of Thy Commandments when Thou hast set my heart at liberty.'

"I have set all this down simply as a record of experience. I dare say the pathologist or the psychologist could easily explain it away as an 'obsession' or a 'complex' or a nervous excitement thereby induced, with a consequent reaction of relief when it had gone, or the emergence under this excitement of subconscious impressions. And of course these things may have had their place. No experience, I suppose, is sudden without some previous inward preparation. All I know is that the experience itself was more real than any other in my inward life and more abiding. If there be a personal God, if He is ever concerned with or speaks to the individual spirit, He then and thus spoke to me. I have staked my life on this, and though the remembrance of it brings not only trust, but also, when I think of my sins and unworthiness, rebuke and humiliation, I dare not doubt its truth.

"Other decisions followed swiftly after. I resolved to stay on at All Souls and begin my reading of theology. I wrote to Robson to explain that my place in his Chambers would know me no more. He was greatly surprised, but most kind and sympathetic. I asked the Principal of Cuddesdon to take me in the ensuing August, as I thought this would be a test to show whether I could really carry on this new venture. I suppose others as well as Robson were equally surprised. Certainly my father was, and I think a little disappointed. I remember George Brodrick, Warden of Merton, who used to be very kind to me

[1] Sir John Marriott, M.P. for Oxford City and York, Fellow of Worcester. Died in 1945.

as a budding politician, saying after his manner: 'My dear fellow, when I heard that you proposed to be ordained I felt that between you and me there was a great gulf fixed; but when I heard that you were going to Cuddesdon, I realised that it was impassable.'

"As I had not been confirmed, Henry Wakeman wrote to that most beautiful, sane and cheerful of saints, Edward King, the Bishop of Lincoln, asking him to confirm me. I went to Lincoln in a mood of unwonted shyness and nervousness. This mood was not relieved when I arrived. There was an Ordinands' Retreat going on and I was ushered straight into the room where the Bishop was supping with his Ordinands, and someone was reading to them in their silence. I had never seen men in cassocks before and I felt desperately like a fish out of water. But when I took my place beside him, the dear old Bishop seemed to discern my discomfort of mind and, putting his hand on my thigh, whispered to me: 'They're not half as good as they look and I'm the naughtiest of them all.' Next morning, very early, he confirmed me in his Chapel and I made my Communion immediately after and returned to All Souls, at last a full member of the Church of England.

"The next step was formally to sever my connexion with the Bar. I had passed all the examinations and was down to be called at the next calling day. Naturally I hesitated, but finally on the very day I telegraphed that my name must be removed. And so the tie was cut. It was not without some heart-searching and pain. But what brought pain was not so much severance from the Bar as severance from the hopes of a political career to which the Bar was to lead. Indeed, some fifteen years passed before I could trust myself to visit the House of Commons. I was afraid that old wounds would bleed anew.

"Then came inevitably hesitations and difficulties about the obligations, intellectual and spiritual, of the new venture. I knew little or nothing about Anglican theology, and had only the vaguest notions about the principles or prejudices which determined ecclesiastical parties. For a long time I had known that if I were ever to identify myself with the Anglican Church it would be on its Catholic side. Why else would any such step be worth while, for with all that's best on the evangelical side I had been familiar from childhood? And such philosophic reading as I had had inclined me in the same direction. Yet now, as ever since, the remembrance of my home, of the currents of concerted life and thought which had flowed through it, made it impossible to accept the rigorous and exclusive aspects of Catholicism. There were indeed times when the more fundamental question thrust itself forward: 'If you are to be ordained to the priesthood, are you sure it ought to be priesthood in the Anglican Church and not priesthood in the Roman Church?'

"Here I may recall a very vivid dream in which these questions took shape and which for a time vaguely troubled me. With the inconsequence of dreams I was at Exeter station, possessed of a first-class ticket to London, and a warm rug, waiting for the London express and pleasurably anticipating a comfortable journey. When the train drew up and I was slipping into my first-class carriage, a hand was laid on my shoulder from behind and a voice of singular sweetness and yet decisiveness said: 'I think you must turn and come third-class with me.' I looked round and saw a figure holding a cloak before its face. I could not but obey the voice. I followed the figure into a third-class carriage. It sat down in front of me, withdrew the cloak from its face, and disclosed the features of—John Henry, Cardinal Newman! Moral—leave the security and comfort of the Anglican Establishment and face the strangeness and ascetic discipline of Rome. No man, I suppose, who has had to think out his religious position for himself, and who is by temperament inclined to the Catholic position, can ever have failed to feel the immense attractiveness of that august and world-wide communion. But a liberal bent of mind and the evangelical strain in my blood prevented me from yielding to it. I soon came to be convinced that the Anglican Church, *if true to its ideal*, stands for a truer, higher, more spiritual Catholicism than Rome. I must emphasise 'if true to its ideal,' for then and ever since I have felt here a difference from many at least who have been born and bred in the Church of England. It is not to that Church *as it is* at any particular time or in any particular place that my loyalty is given, but to that Church in its ideal, *as it might be*, as I believe it is meant to be, as it is capable of becoming. And after all, it is to the ideal of any institution—the State, marriage, political party—that ultimate loyalty is due and right.

"The purely intellectual difficulties which beset the Christian faith had already been met. As I have said before, such philosophic foundation as I had been able to build stood secure against their assault, though never against a full understanding of their force or a deep sympathy with those whom they assail. But it was difficult to find scope for a liberal bent of mind in the Tractarian tradition; and to me, as to many others then, a great and timely help towards reaching a liberal Catholicism came with the publication of the essays in the volume called *Lux Mundi*.

"On the intellectual side, therefore, I was ready to go forward towards Anglican ordination, but what of the spiritual side? It was there that I felt myself most lacking, for plainly it is only as protecting, vindicating, interpreting reality of spiritual experience that intellectual apprehension has any value. And here what had I but vague aspirations, imperfect prayers, and the memory of a strange summons? Hence I went to Cuddesdon College, partly to test myself, partly because it had been the scene of that summons, chiefly because I hoped I might there learn something of the spiritual life of the Church. Here only the most humble and guarded language is fitting, for this is holy ground. But it would show a mere lack of gratitude—gratitude which I cannot fully acknowledge or bestow—if I did not record that under God the life at Cuddesdon did fulfil my need and my hope. There, assuredly, I at least *learned* what that spiritual life was, learned for the first time what inward communion with God in Christ meant in actual experience. Would to God I had been true to what I learned, followed it, and completed it."

It is a temptation to leave the story as Lang himself has told it, without comment or addition, for on so private a matter a man is surely his own best witness. Yet it must be remembered that Lang wrote his account in 1929, and although the events of those spring weeks must often have been in his mind, and more and more as he grew older, after forty years time plays tricks with the memory. Most people have had the experience of being positive that something long past had happened in a particular way, only to be faced with irrefragable proof that it had happened otherwise, or of being quite sure of the geography of a particular spot, seen many years before, only to discover, on revisiting it, that it was so different as to be almost unrecognisable. To the normal tricks of time in blurring or distorting the memory must be added Lang's tendency, already observed, to give to the events of his life a dramatic form beyond their actual content; so that his testimony, though offered with confidence and in the utmost sincerity, cannot necessarily be accepted as final.

In these circumstances the letters he wrote at the time have an especial value. They leave out much that he has recorded; they add some facts that he had apparently forgotten; they give something of the background of his life during those weeks of decision; and in the main, although not entirely, they confirm his later narrative.

The relevance of what he wrote in 1889 and of what he wrote, in retrospect and after much reflexion, forty years later, cannot be questioned. Nor are the opinions of those who knew him best, both at the time and afterwards, entirely valueless. He took few into his confidence, either then or ever, and none completely. Even his father and mother were unaware of the crisis through which their son was passing, of the momentous choice he was about to make, until he stood on the threshold of decision. Yet it is helpful to learn what they thought about it all, on the strength of what they knew of him and what he told them. To all this ancillary evidence should be added some rough notes possibly compiled by Lang in 1898, and if so antedating his other record by thirty years.

Tupper-Carey, who rode with Lang on that afternoon in the early spring of 1889, had a perfect recollection of the occasion and the talk, which turned, as Lang has said, on whether or not "Tupper" himself should take Orders. As they walked their horses along the edge of the chalk downs above Ebberbourne, "Tupper" never suspected that his friend had begun to ask himself the same question; he had no hint of what was happening until, on the day before Lang was due to be called to the Bar, he walked into "Tupper's" rooms at Oxford.

"What do you think I am going to do?" he asked.

"You are going to be married," said "Tupper," whose own thoughts had begun to stray in that direction.

"No, I am going to take Orders."

Lang has told how in the weeks that followed that ride on the Downs, always between him and his books or his briefs the same question kept thrusting itself forward: "Why shouldn't *you* be ordained?"

At last the debate upset my work. The question stared at me from the blue foolscap on which I was drawing pleadings; it lurked in the pages of briefs; it met me in the Courts; it encountered me in the underground railway; it followed me down the Embankment to Chambers; it went to bed with me at night; it rose with me in the morning.

On April 30th he wrote at last to his father, feeling it "somewhat selfish" to trouble him when he was so preoccupied with the new church. But this was "a question of a change in my whole scheme of life." He had had for some years "a vague uneasiness," which had lately resolved itself into a feeling that "my true vocation is after all to

69

serve as a clergyman in the Church." He realised that he would be putting behind him the allurements of political life, to which the Bar was to have been the key. But were politics so desirable and was success at the Bar so sure? Those were "the lower grounds of my present state of mind . . . but you will believe me when I say simply that I kept down the feeling for the Church because I did not think I was in any way worthy of the holy office." At least he was ready to give up his political ambitions and fight against his besetting sins. And he believed "in all humility that I have some talents given to me by God which I can use for the good of others." He was, however, still bothered by a sense of his unfitness. "The thought forces itself upon me—'Have you enough— shall I call it?—*spiritual stock* with which to begin?' Candidly I say, 'No.'" But he had the hope that by honest effort this would come in time. He had not yet decided; but if he should choose the Bar, his name must go in the next day and he would be called ten days later; so time was short. He wrote at great length and begged for his father's counsel and help.

Four days later he had his answer. His father was indeed surprised. Except for a hint dropped once to Mrs. Lang, neither of the parents had had an inkling of this new idea. Why had his son left it till so late an hour, when his training was finished and he was about to be called? "My feeling is that, unless there is a bias so strong that you must accept it as God's bidding, a bias to the Holy Ministry which means a positive antipathy to any prospect opened up by the Bar—all your discipline and all your training for many years should be accepted as marking the way along which to do your part in the world." If he had that bias and antipathy, "then one can only say Amen." But let him consider well. He had spoken of the uncertainties of political life, but what was the prospect of the Church of England, with the case of the Bishop of Lincoln pending and Disestablishment in the offing? Of course, if his mind were really made up, there was no more to be said, save to remind him that while "there is no calling in which one's life is more distinctly associated with things Highest and Holiest," it was a vocation that "separates or should separate him from the ordinary ambitions of men and shuts him off to a consecrated life." He had to admit a feeling of personal disappointment. He had entered too completely into his son's plans for himself not to be distressed by the thought of casting them aside. But such a feeling did not really signify. "What you think, prayerfully and solemnly, you ought to do—you must do—we will accept." "Your mother sends her love. She has read over what I have written and concurs."

When we recall the sacrifices which father and mother had made to enable their son to receive the education necessary for a legal and political career, their forbearance, when his letter dropped like a bomb on the breakfast-table of the Manse, must be judged remarkable; the more so that it was not his father's Church in which he would minister and that they were being rushed headlong into offering advice which would anyhow probably be too late to affect the decision either way.

Lang replied at once. He still felt the fascination of the old ambitions, but this that had come to him was something stronger. He had tried to put the life he had once hoped for in the most favourable light, "and still and still the feeling that I can leave it all has been, I may almost say, welling up in renewing strength."

"I have not," he went on, "perhaps realised to myself or conveyed to you how long this desire to enter the Church has been present with me, pushed aside by the rapidity and heedlessness of daily life, and yet asserting itself again and again at special periods. So it is in no way a new idea."

At least it was not as new as Lang's later account suggests. He was deeply sorry for his father's disappointment. "But, my dear father, is it nothing to me to give up the dreams of my youth? They are still there, bright and engaging as ever, spite of passing cold and freezing blasts of the real world. I have of course lived in them far more than you, and may I not, let me repeat, feel justified by being able calmly to watch them fade and vanish? I know they will come back again. I know that that will be one of the great temptations and dangers of my new life." But God would help him to overcome the temptation. Meanwhile his purpose had hardened and he had telegraphed to the authorities of the Inner Temple to ask them to withdraw his name from the list of those who were to be called. Much had happened since he had received his father's letter. On the Saturday he had been to see Scott Holland and together they had discussed his difficulties. Scott Holland had been "most sympathetic and helpful," but dubious of his vocation. Then he had gone to Oxford and on Sunday morning had received the Sacrament, asking for God's guidance and getting, "more than on any other occasion, a real sense of God moving in my heart." In the afternoon, against Scott Holland's advice, he had walked over to Cuddesdon for the evening service at the parish church. There "I felt that the request was in some measure answered and that I *could* not go back to the old life."

> I did feel, as we rose to sing "Lead, Kindly Light" and the first strains of the beautiful hymn wandered down the aisle, that the light of God *was* leading and that I must follow.

The notes tell a little more of his experience.

> Then we went to Evensong at the Parish Church. How well I remember the scene, the summer sun, the peace and shade of the old church, the white surplices of the students in the Sanctuary! I sat alone in the little seat immediately below where the pulpit used to be. The service passed, and the sermon. I only remember a curious feeling: "When is the answer to be given to me?" That it was coming, that it was inevitable, I could not doubt. "It" seemed then as ever strangely impersonal. The sermon closed, the hymn was given out. It was "Lead, Kindly Light." I knew that the answer had come. It fell upon me and I yielded. "So long Thy power hath blest me, sure it still will lead me on." The long debate was over, the grip had tightened; I had long ceased to resist, now I accepted. When the hymn was over I was on my knees, praying as I had never prayed before. When I left the Church I was already a candidate for Holy Orders.

"Why should not *you* be ordained?" It was no longer an intermittent but insistent whisper: it was a Voice thundering in his ear. It was no longer a question: it was a command; and he had walked back to Oxford over Shotover Hill with his mind at peace.

In his notes Lang added details of the walk. He and Wakeman and Marriott had missed the last train at Wheatley, so they set off to walk, or rather to trot, to Oxford in the dark. They laughed and talked, walked and ran, and neither Wakeman nor Marriott, Lang supposed, had an idea of what had just happened to him. "As for me, I could have run for miles that night."

But Marriott at any rate had a sense of some strange event. Many years afterwards he wrote in *The Memories of Four-score Years*:

> One Sunday in May 1889 I had gone over to Cuddesdon to spend the day with my old friend Bishop Stubbs.[1] Lang had gone out the same day with Henry Offley Wakeman, like himself a Fellow of All

[1] The Rt. Rev. William Stubbs, Bishop of Oxford.

Souls, to spend the day at the college for ordinands. After Compline at the college the three of us set out to walk back to Oxford—some six miles away—over Shotover. It was a truly heavenly night; the sky was unclouded; the soft air was fragrant with May blossom; to the exquisite song of the nightingales we tarried again and again to listen. It was striking midnight as we crossed Magdalen Bridge, said good-night, and went our several ways. We had talked little: somehow I felt a sense of solemnity which has never left me.

Had something happened to my old friend then just about to be called to the Bar? I did not know; but very soon afterwards we learned that Lang had decided to abandon a career which would assuredly have led him either to 10 Downing Street or to the Woolsack, and to seek Holy Orders in the Church of England.

A long time afterwards Marriott met Lang, then Archbishop of York, staying at Lockinge for the week-end. On Sunday afternoon they went for a long walk together on the Downs. Marriott continues:

I asked him tentatively, "Do you remember another Sunday when we walked home together from Cuddesdon?"

"Am I ever likely to forget it?" he replied, very seriously.

"May I tell you what my own feelings were that night?"

"Do," he said.

Then I made my confession: "I felt somehow that I had been in the presence of one who had been on the Mount of Transfiguration."

"That," he said, "was exactly where I had been: that day was the turning point of my life."

So Lang always regarded that evening at Cuddesdon. Did he have, as he firmly believed, a genuine spiritual experience, God's direct answer to his prayers? Or, as he himself hints, would a pathologist or psychologist explain it all as the reaction of an overwrought and naturally emotional temperament to the circumstances of time and place, an evening of early summer in an old church and the moving strains of Newman's hymn? The two answers do not exclude each other, for God works His Will in His own way, taking account of and using the human instrument. People will answer the question according to predisposition, but perhaps the opinion which Lang gave on page 65 is as near to the truth as we are likely to get.

It was settled, and he removed his name finally from the list of those who were to be called to the Bar in a few days' time. He had made his decision and already his mind was beginning to form an idea of the place he would occupy in the Church of England.

I should wish to take my stand with those who have incorporated many of the best elements in the High Church ideal with the teaching of men like Maurice and Kingsley.

"The mention of Kingsley," he wrote in some notes on his time in London, "is the mention of the only personality which had so far got a hold of such religious life as I had. I remember reading his life in the dingy little lodgings. . . . Well, that book spoke to me as no living voice ever had, and I remember distinctly closing it with the feeling that had I been good enough I should have liked to take Orders and witness to the Kingsley ideal of Christianity."

He expanded his thoughts in letters to his mother a little later in the month. He had been reading Liddon's Bampton Lectures and Gore's book on the Church and the Ministry, the first with admiration, the second with misgivings. He found Gore's doctrine of strict Apostolic Succession very difficult to accept. "Even if logically and historically sound in itself, the theory cannot be so much as safely stated without the widest qualifications." It should be a source of quiet confidence to the Church of England in her own historical and doctrinal position, "not a blast of war against all outside it." Nothing counted beside the supreme fact that "Jesus Christ, the Son of God, died and reigns."

He had met Gore, walked and talked with him. "He is a really fine man . . . and it is easy to see how the whole fabric of his inner life is based upon two things—the Real Presence of Our Lord in the Eucharist and the Apostolic Succession. And they undoubtedly give him and his like an immense strength and confidence."

His ecclesiastical views apparently were causing his mother some distress, for presently he was writing: "You are evidently in great fear at my gradual High Churching. Very terrible, isn't it? But I am not yet so shaven as to be an ideal member of the true fold. There are one or two tough and shaggy hairs which are likely to prove obstinate." There was, once more, the Apostolic Succession. While he accepted it, he believed that a Church possessing it might still err and the error be "so serious as almost to justify, at least to excuse, historical breaks from her." The seceding bodies, although lacking the Apostolic Succession, could nevertheless be channels of God's grace; but the separation should be temporary and their work transitional. One day they should seek readmittance to a Church which had purified itself. So much he conceded to the Kirk.

His mother had also been shocked by his ready acceptance of the Real Presence, but the truth was that "we Scots are so steeped in anti-Roman suspicions that we don't see the true force of words." What he meant by "Real" was quite different from what she thought he meant. Finally, "Don't be alarmed about people influencing me. I only wish I were a little more open to influence. My fault is over-self-confidence, a tendency to stand too much on my own legs."

Indeed, at this stage he owed little to any man's influence, something perhaps to Scott Holland, but far more to his own mind and temperament, modified by early doses of Hegel and the upbringing of the Manse. Catholic faith and order attracted him, both theologically and emotionally. It satisfied his historical sense and brought a dignity and seemliness to worship. But its more extreme adherents never failed to irritate him. Some of them seemed to set far too much store on trifles, to the neglect of essentials, to be more concerned with ecclesiastical millinery than with the truths it was intended to symbolise; others were too distrustful of intellectual exploration; and few of them were sufficiently conscious of the social duty of the Church or of its evangelical mission. So he launched his ship neither on the turbulent torrent, whose rapids the ritualists were shooting, at some peril to themselves; nor on the narrow but placid stream which Liddon and the lawful successors of Pusey and the Tractarians were carefully navigating. He chose, rather, a third arm of the river, that of Liberal Catholicism, where he would be in the company of Gore, Scott Holland, and those who, a little later, were to be the comrades of *Lux Mundi*. He would not always agree with them, nor they with him, but he was and remained nearer to them than to any other body in the Church.

All this time he was writing to his mother of his doubts and difficulties. He needed confidants and so far he had told no one of his intentions, except Robert Cecil, Bowlby (the companion of his journey to Germany), and Scott Holland. The last had put tests to him and now was apparently satisfied that he had a vocation. But to make quite sure, before committing himself finally, he should spend a short time in "the hot *smelling* dismalness of Bethnal Green, at the Oxford House."

Then Robson had to be told, not a task to which he looked forward. Robson would be overcome with surprise and do his best to dissuade him. "Like so many of his gown, he thinks the Church only a sort of moral grandmother, best tended by meek and pious nonentities." In the end Robson proved more sympathetic than Lang had dared to hope.

At the end of May he went down to Barking in Essex to visit Hensley Henson,[1] whose acquaintance he had made at All Souls and Oxford House. "He is exceedingly young—his only experience was as head of Oxford House—but of a fiery and contagious energy and most eloquent. He came six months ago to a parish *dead*—250 a good congregation in the church; and now, when he preaches, every seat is filled—1100!" He had, Lang admitted, an "unruly tongue" and a "power of denunciation and sarcasm; but if these don't spoil him, he will become a great cleric." And a little later: "He is *by no means* the extreme High Churchman you think, but in many ways what people call 'broad.'"

Henson had the attractive notion of establishing a kind of outpost of All Souls at Barking and asked Lang to come as his curate when he had finished his training. Lang was not sure that this would be wise. They were too much of an age, too "familiar," and he felt that his first vicar should be someone who could treat him with authority. In the end he sent Henson a reluctant refusal.

Where was I to begin my work? . . . The urge was strong to get among the people and to share with them that Gospel of the Revelation of God in Christ which had now laid hold on my loyalty. I knew no clergy working in populous parishes, but Edward Talbot had just left the Wardenship of Keble College to be Vicar of Leeds. I remembered my days and lectures among the artisans of Yorkshire. I did not know him well, but I had stayed with him at Keble for that humiliating meeting on behalf of Oxford House already recorded.[2] So I ventured to write to him and ask whether he had a place for me on his staff.

"It will be a great favour and, I think, a great boon to me," he told his mother. A few days later Talbot replied: "Your letter has refreshed my heart as few things could. . . . I cannot hesitate a moment now to answer it. There shall be a place for you." Lang could go to Leeds as soon as he was ordained. "I certainly feel that much the best thing I can do is to work under such strong and *sagacious* leadership as Dr. Talbot's, in a great parish like Leeds."

[1] The Rt. Rev. H. H. Henson, Bishop of Durham 1920-39.   [2] See page 51.

Meanwhile, in spite of all these hard decisions, his ordinary life went on, divided between London and Oxford. He was dining out and meeting people, with much of his old enjoyment and interest.

On Friday I rowed—or rather helped to row—a party down the river, among them Mrs. Humphry Ward of *Robert Elsmere* fame and her husband. She is a sedate, rather sad-looking woman of middle age, with thoughtful eyes and a broad forehead, a Jewish nose and a not at all humorous mouth. No affectation and quiet, like a lady; in fact I was rather pleased, but not fascinated.

On June 16th he told his mother of his Confirmation at Lincoln, whose Bishop, Edward King, had just been cited to appear before the Archbishop of Canterbury on a charge of unlawful practices and rites.

I was very glad of the opportunity of seeing and making the acquaintance of the Bishop. Not of course (to calm your suspicious mind) because I look upon him as our new Apostle and Martyr—not at all—but because he is himself one of the most saintly and delightful of men. Also I knew that *he* would not, as many would, hurry over a single Confirmation as a merely formal proceeding; but that he would regard it as no less a spiritual reality because there was only one candidate. . . . I had an hour's talk with the Bishop. He is certainly a beautiful old man. As an agnostic friend once said to me of him, "He at least has the Divine light in his eyes." He was very kind and free in his manner and talk; and one saw that beneath what many think his outward obstinacy is a really wonderful fund of sympathy and tolerance. It would do many good to hear the kindly and indeed brotherly way in which he spoke of dissenters.

He arranged to confirm me in the chapel at half-past seven next morning, before his usual morning Celebration. Accordingly, at that hour the little service took place in the old chapel, which had served Bishops from St. Hugh downwards. No one was there but myself and the chaplains as witnesses. As if to show how real and solemn even he deemed the service, he wore the full gorgeous dress of an "Apostolical Bishop." His address, too, was very careful, suggestive and full. . . . And so he laid his hands upon me. It was impossible not to feel that it was a very solemn ceremony, leaving behind it also increased means of helpfulness, increased responsibility for the ordering of life. The Holy Communion shortly afterwards in the same chapel was a fitting end.

Next week he was in London, saying good-bye to Robson and to Palace Chambers, "the scene of many ambitions never to be fulfilled, of many sins to be wiped out, I trust, by a lifetime of higher service, of some depression, of more hopes, still possibly to be realised in fuller measure, of a strange mixed training, through which, may I without hypocrisy believe?, God was leading me in secret to this unthought-of end." On one of his evenings he went by himself to see Irving and Ellen Terry in *Macbeth*—"One of the finest things I ever saw"—and recalled a recent talk he had had with Canon Barnett of Whitechapel. He had asked Barnett what theology he should read, and the Canon had replied, "Browning and Shakespeare"—"in a way an absurd answer, but with a good kernel of truth, assuredly as to Shakespeare."

He had arranged to take his training at Cuddesdon. Where else would he go? But first he had a short holiday in Jersey, much needed "after the turbulence of this change and the anxiety of making so momentous a decision."

The version of the letters, of his friends, and of his rough notes differs, as will have been seen, very little in essentials from the account he himself wrote forty years afterwards. The change of mind and heart was not quite so sudden as, looking back, he thought it to have been. He had had a "vague uneasiness" for some years before he took his fateful ride with "Tupper." The idea that his true vocation was the priesthood was in the background of his thoughts, in his subconsciousness. For a long time, perhaps, it had been piling up, like a heap of explosives only waiting for a spark to touch them off. So it is with many; and some tiny, unrehearsed incident is the spark which releases all the power of an unsuspected charge.

Chapter X

CUDDESDON

THE choice of Cuddesdon was inevitable. Apart from an intimate association with Lang's recent spiritual crisis, it was close to Oxford and All Souls; and the tradition of men like Liddon and Edward King was a magnet to any prospective ordinand who was attracted by the faith and practice of the Oxford Movement. So, on a day late in August 1889, he and "Tupper" went there together.

"After dining with him (Lang) at All Souls," wrote "Tupper," "we drove out in a hansom to Cuddesdon, where he was deferentially received by the Principal. Although he was a Fellow of All Souls, and was on the eve of becoming a barrister, and might have been an M.P., yet he settled down quite happily among his fellow-students, who were all younger than himself."

Originally Lang had meant to stay for only one term and then to continue his theological reading at All Souls. He did not see himself happy for long in the juvenile and unfamiliar company at Cuddesdon, so plainly not his "sort," as he had observed on his first visit; "but gradually I found in most of them gifts of spirit which I lacked." Two of the students he mentions by name—F. W. Douglass, afterwards of the Oxford Mission to Calcutta, and Thomas Cook, who was to be Bishop of Lewes and died in 1928. "Nor can I forget the beautiful face and mind and spirit of Robert Ottley, the Vice-Principal." After Ottley's marriage the friendship, for some unexplained reason, flagged and finally failed, to Lang's lasting regret. "Ottley, the 'Vice,' I knew as an intimate friend: Ottley, the Canon of Christ Church, I never knew at all."

There gradually came the sense of a new comradeship at once spiritual and human, a taste, as it were, of what the Fellowship of the Church might be. And more and more completely the place itself in the beauty of the Oxfordshire country, the view of the Chilterns across the wide plain, wound its spell around me. . . . When I recall these things, I think with surprise of the wise men who belittle or indeed actively criticise a theological college such as Cuddesdon. For me at least the spirit of "the seminary" was unknown. The Principal, good, quiet, shrewd Ducat, left me much to myself. I read in my own way and was not expected to attend lectures.

Canon Ducat was a kindly little man, a Tractarian of the School of Pusey and Liddon, steering his ship with its human freight a trifle nervously between the Scylla of Biblical criticism, where stood the beckoning and formidable figure of Charles Gore, and the Charybdis of Rome, whither two of his most promising ordinands, thereafter to be known as Dom Chapman and Dom Bede Camm, had lately been drawn.

As might be expected, the events of the previous weeks had not only agitated the placid pool of the family circle at Woodlands Terrace, but had sent a few ripples into the wider waters of the Barony. Some of the parishioners were disposed to treat it almost as a scandal that the Minister's son not only should have apostatised from the Church of his upbringing, but was even touching the dangerous playthings of the Oxford Movement. Lang's family shared the qualms about Cuddesdon. It is true that his father, after those first hesitations, does not seem to have offered any further counsel. If he wrote, the letters no longer exist.

Though always loyal to his own Church, he had many sympathies with the Church of England. When I told him of my intention to be ordained in that Church, he was in no way displeased, though he was, I think, a little disappointed that I had turned from other ambitions, and sometimes, though very quietly and gently, troubled by some of the consequences which my new life brought with it. There was never any kind of breach between us.

Lang kept his old regard for the Church of Scotland, which he had once defended so eloquently in a speech to the Oxford Union. He had a particular esteem for the ministers of the Church. Years after he had left it he wrote:

With all my experience of English ecclesiastics, I am bound to say that I have not met among them many men of the personal dignity, impressiveness, elevation of tone and manner, which I associate with the great Scottish ministers whom I can remember in my youth.

The Minister, though "gently troubled," may have kept silence; but Mrs. Lang appears to have conveyed to her son the misgivings felt by her and some of her friends in the congregation. Their chief dislike was of ritualism, but on this Lang was quite unrepentant. Side by side with the supreme truths of which the Church was the repository, details of rites "were really too small to worry about." If some people were helped in their worship by these suspected practices, provided no wide doctrine of the Church was contradicted, "why in heaven's name shouldn't they be let alone?" That remained very much his attitude to such questions all his life, to the equal disappointment of those who upheld and those who challenged Catholic ceremonial. In the same letter Lang commented with amusement on Patrick's conviction that his younger brother had changed all his plans because "he had fallen in love and wished to marry."

He still wrote to his mother every week, but his path and that of his family, which had begun to diverge in his first days at Oxford, were drawing further and further apart. Until 1886 Lang had always taken his holidays with them; after that year he had his own separate plans. The days when he had demanded "boat, bathing, and no snobbishness" were indeed over. His friends and his interests were no longer theirs; and while there was never any estrangement and no single year marks the change in relationship, they came to mean less and less in his life, and he in theirs. Patrick was to be a banker, to stand for Parliament, and to serve his country in the Ministries of Reconstruction and Munitions. Douglas made his home in South Africa, where eventually he became Public Accountant and Auditor in Johannesburg. Marshall was to be a minister, and in time Moderator of the Church of Scotland, like his father before him. Norman, following his brother's example, was to enter the Church of England, to be Bishop Suffragan of Leicester and later Assistant Bishop of Peterborough, a career which brought him closer to his brother than were the other members of the family. David, the youngest, was an invalid all his life and never left the family circle. Hannah, the only sister, in the family tradition married the Rev. Robert Barclay, Minister of the West Kirk, Greenock.

In the coming years they would see their brother from time to time, visit him and stay with him, but rather as guests than as members of the same family. With his mother alone the old relationship endured until the day of her death. If the others henceforth have little place in the story, it is because they had, it must be owned, little place in his life.

He had engaged himself for the autumn of 1889 to deliver some lectures in Cornwall; and after viewing the prospect with dread, he rather enjoyed the tour. At Redruth he had tea with a curate, discovering some of the less attractive features of clerical life and an argument for the celibacy of the clergy. He was lecturing on the very diverse

F

subjects of the Tudors and Tennyson, and once again found his most repaying audiences among working men. He made time between lectures to see a little of the country, and a visit to Land's End, with the Atlantic breaking thunderously on the cliffs, left him reflecting, "I can feel what a poor, sorry fool I am, for all this brave show of words."

November saw him back at Cuddesdon; for he had decided to continue his reading there and not, as he had first intended, at All Souls. His letters to his mother begin to be largely about the books he has been reading: the Life of F. D. Maurice (not for the first time), as an antidote to too much doctrine; the Prophecies of Isaiah; the First Epistle to the Corinthians, which set him wondering "whether to admire St. Paul more as a saint or as a gentleman!" Finally there was *Lux Mundi*, which had just appeared. His father must get it at once. "It marks—especially Gore's essay on Inspiration—the absorption of the best 'Broad Church' thought with 'High Church.' To me it is a specially interesting book."

In December he preached his first sermon. "When I was at the Temple I used to think with characteristic presumption that I might have been a 'great hand' at preaching. *Now* I am so humiliated by my want of knowledge and, above all, of personal experience that I feel as if I could not and *dared* not say anything."

But Cuddesdon had a lighter side too. He played football, with vigour but without much proficiency. The irrepressible "Tupper," who was taking his training in a spirit of devotion tempered by gaiety, was one of his most frequent companions. In later years Lang would tell how "Tupper" once asked Mrs. Stubbs from the Bishop's Palace to tea. She had never been inside the College and, like the ladies of the Barony, regarded it with fear and suspicion. As "Tupper" took her round, they came across a collection of doormats in a passage. "These," he whispered conspiratorially to his horrified guest, "are the hair shirts for the students, for use in Lent."

"Tupper" too was to go after ordination to the Parish Church at Leeds; and he and Lang made a preliminary reconnaissance in company, staying with the Talbots and arranging to set up house together. "It's strange how our lives, otherwise utterly dissimilar, are running," commented Lang. But his greatest friend at Cuddesdon was Thomas Cook. "I am, I suspect, at bottom a naturally solitary person, who has somewhere, rather hard to reach, a strong craving for particular affection." Thomas Cook was one of the very few who ever penetrated to this hidden spot.

Mr. Harold Anson, afterwards Master of the Temple, joined the College in the autumn and has some recollections of Lang.

He lived in lodgings between the College and the Church, and we did not see a great deal of him. He gave one a feeling of reserve, and some of his fellow-students stood somewhat in awe of him. His chief friends were A. D. Tupper-Carey . . . Kenneth Mackenzie, afterwards Bishop of Argyll and the Isles, F. W. Douglass, now of the Oxford Mission to Calcutta, and Cook, afterwards Bishop of Lewes. A few of us sat at a small table for meals, which gained the unhappy name of the "Scorners'" Table, perhaps because we were apt to jibe at some of the ritual excesses of some of our fellow-students and at a few minor regulations of the College which we thought irksome and unnecessary.

I remember Lang's indignation when the Principal gave out in a lecture that marriage with a deceased wife's sister must be utterly condemned because of the Old Testament prohibition and the tradition of the Church. Lang asked for a debate on the subject and suggested to me that I should act as solicitor and he as Counsel. An open debate on Church prohibitions was something rather new and rather shocking to the Principal. When the hour came, the Principal laid down the law to which we were expected to conform. Then Lang rose up and "wiped the floor," demolishing mercilessly the Principal's argument and carrying all the students with him. I think the Principal, proud as he was of Lang, felt that this was a scene which must not occur again.

We always recognised that Lang was far away ahead of us all. We each had to read a sermon to the staff and students in church. This was an awesome undertaking, and we went through the ordeal with fear and trembling; but when Lang's turn came, he spoke with entire self-assurance and without a note. We called him the Lord High Cosmopolitan. . . .

I always found him most friendly, but he never let one get inside his intellectual and emotional defences. I think the highly charged but entirely sincere religious corporate life was something quite new to him, and all his life he looked back to it as a turning point.

In early April he spent his first Holy Week and Easter as an Anglican. It was, he reported, "a spiritual dissipation" of services, culminating, as midnight struck on Easter Eve, with "the sudden burst of long-suppressed jubilation—'Jesus Christ is risen to-day, Alleluia,' followed by the beautiful old Nocturne for Easter Eve and then by the Hallelujah Chorus on the organ; while the bells of the Church outside were ringing a peal of joy." "God did enable me during the past week," he wrote, "to get a little further into the secret of the Christian mystery and to realise a little more fully what the Passion and Resurrection of Our Lord mean, not only in the history of the world, but in the history of the individual soul." He ended with a lament: "It made me quite sad on Easter Sunday to think how feeble and beggarly was the welcome of my native country to the Risen King."

A more mundane incident is related by "Tupper." It was the custom for the students to give up smoking during Lent, and he recalled seeing Lang enter the Chapel at midnight with a face as white as a sheet, having just had his first pipe after the Lenten abstinence.

He was to be ordained on Trinity Sunday by the Bishop of Oxford. His opinions were settling and taking shape. "More and more I become convinced that the way of viewing the Christian Faith which is wanted in our time is one that shall combine that firm sacramental teaching which was the kernel of the Oxford Movement with the candour, freedom and breadth of view which marked Maurice, Kingsley and Robertson of Brighton." *Lux Mundi*, with all its imperfections and despite the shadow of Liddon's disapproval, pointed the way.

As for himself, as the day drew near, to his doubts of his own spiritual adequacy was added a fear that he might turn into the "spiky" and dogmatic type of young clergyman he had always disliked. "One of the Cecils and young Peel came out to see me the other day, to examine how far I had degenerated into the mere cleric, or worse still, the Cuddesdon cleric. I think their report was favourable." "I hope," he wrote a little later, "the coat won't wholly parsonise me."

On the Tuesday before Whitsunday he went into retreat. "If it isn't *real* to me," he wrote of his coming Ordination, ". . . then God help me. Life will henceforth be an intolerable imposture." But real it would be, he trusted, for God's Kindly Light had been leading him, from Glasgow to Oxford, from Oxford to London, from London to Cuddesdon, and so to this moment. "Surely everywhere are the signs of His pardon and guidance."

He was ordained by the Bishop of Oxford (on the title of his Fellowship at All Souls) at half-past ten on the morning of Trinity Sunday, in Cuddesdon Parish Church. "It is over," he wrote to his father and mother, neither of whom could be present. "I am a deacon in the Church of Christ, dedicated to His service for life." He had been moved, "even to tears," when he had entered the church in procession to the strains of Bright's Ordination hymn, and when presently the hands were laid on his head and he heard the solemn words of commission. He never forgot the awe and joy of the occasion. He read the Gospel at the service, of which neither then nor later would he write or speak much.

I suppose we Scotsmen are men of such strong emotions that we are compelled to keep them under strict restraint. Suffice it to say that on that day restraint was impossible, and a tide of overwhelming emotions rose. Little wonder, surely, if only because this Church was the very place where that unexpected summons had come and where I had learned the best and deepest secrets of life.

Among his papers, after his death, a scrap of writing was found on which he had jotted down the prayers he would use and the resolutions he would make on that Trinity Sunday.

O Love, I give myself to Thee,
Thine ever, only Thine to be.

This day I consecrate all that I have or hope to be to Thy service——all that I have been I lay at the foot of Thy Cross. O Crucified Lord! forgive the sins of my past life; fold me within the embrace of Thy all-prevailing sacrifice; purify me by Thy Passion; raise me by Thy perfect submission. Son of Man, hallow all my emotions and affections; gather them to Thyself and make them strong only for Thy service, enduring through Thy Presence. Eternal Word, sanctify my thoughts; make them free with the freedom of Thy Spirit. Son of God, consecrate my will to Thyself; unite it with Thine; and so fill me with Thine own abundant life. King of Glory, my Lord and Master, take my whole being, redeem it by Thy Blood; engird it with Thy power; use it in Thy service; and draw it ever closer to Thyself. From this day forth, O Master, take my life and let it be ever, only, all for Thee.

Attached is a list of his resolutions.

1. To be more strict in self-examination, that sense of sin and of dependence on Christ may be deepened.
2. To rise daily at latest at 7 a.m. and to spend at least half an hour before breakfast in prayer and meditation.
3. To spend at least ½ (? hour) every day in studying the Bible.

Sins to be specially guarded against.

Self-conceit and jealousy, with self-consciousness. (Illegible words)—careless use of time.

Ambitions.

1. To found at some time, if God will, an Order of the Cross, lay and clerical, to combine for prayer and communion and *active* warfare against evil, spe[cially] drunkenness, impurity and infidelity.
2. To have influence over men and esp[ecially] young men.
3. To promote the Unity of the Church in Great Britain.

So his time at Cuddesdon ended, but not, so long as he lived, his association with the College. Like All Souls and later Ballure, but differently, Cuddesdon was a place to which, year after year, he would return as to a home.

I look back to that year at Cuddesdon not only as the happiest I had ever spent, but as one which brought to me things without which all my after life would have been a weary and perhaps a barren toil. . . . However pitiful the lapses of life have been, it was at Cuddesdon that I discovered, as a quiet inward joy such as nothing in the world can give, the sense of a Divine Companionship in thought and prayer.

After he had become Archbishop, when other claims upon him allowed, he would spend Holy Week at Cuddesdon.

"The Parish Church of Cuddesdon is the true Mecca of my religion," he wrote, "the most sacred spot on earth to me."

Chapter XI

LEEDS

LANG'S next port, after Cuddesdon, was Leeds; but it was nearly All Souls again. Just before Ordination, the Warden offered him the post of Chaplain and Domestic Bursar for one year. Lang was much tempted, since the position would give him the opportunity he needed of filling up the gaps in his reading. In the end, however, he refused. To go back to All Souls would be too much of a return on his tracks and he wanted to be "up and doing." So to Leeds he went.

Once, when he was reading for the Bar, a speech-making journey had taken him through the city.

The train stopped just under the tower of what I came to know and love as the old Parish Church. Below the railway embankment was a group of dirty hovels. I said to myself, "There's a church and I suppose some poor devil of a parson is working in this slum." Then I saw a figure in a black coat and top-hat [1] moving through the slum; and I said, "And there goes the poor devil himself!" I little thought that within some eighteen months I would myself be the parson in that very place.

The Parish Church at Leeds has a noble tradition dating back to 1837 and Dr. Hook's famous ministry, in which the garnered fruits of the Tractarians were brought to a great industrial city. In Hook's day new churches and schools were founded; old churches were rebuilt; missions were launched. A city which for generations had been dominated by Nonconformity became a stronghold of the Church of England, and the Parish Church, the centre and powerhouse of these activities, had almost the status of a cathedral. Thither in 1888 went Edward Stuart Talbot, after eighteen years as Warden of Keble.

He was a reverent disciple of the great Tractarians, but he had learnt from his master (whom *longo intervallo* I would also humbly call my own), Richard Church, Dean of St. Paul's, to combine this reverence

---

[1] A note is added: " It was then a point of honour that curates of the Parish Church should wear top-hats and long frock-coats, as a badge of aristocracy, to distinguish them from the more common or garden curates in the city."

with a larger outlook; and he had been one of that brilliant company of Oxford Churchmen—such as Gore, Holland, Illingworth, Francis Paget, Aubrey Moore—whose spirit of liberal Catholicism had been expressed in the volume *Lux Mundi*. Indeed, so wide were his sympathies that it used to be said at Leeds that if you wanted to be a really intimate friend of the Vicar you had better profess to be agnostic! No man was ever a more devoted "Catholic" in the best sense of the term: no man was ever less of the mere ecclesiastic. His sermons were rather over the heads of the average Leeds man or woman and sometimes suffered . . . from lack of compression. But to those who had ears to hear they always stimulated both mind and spirit; and often he would emerge from the tangle of his thoughts into some clear, ringing phrase. It was perhaps in the Chapter of the huge Leeds Deanery, containing some forty clergy, and in private conversation that his noble spirit and large mind had most influence. For he was one of the comparatively few men I have known whose mere personality was itself a potent influence for good.

Lang liked to tell a story, subsequently printed in Lady Stephenson's *Edward Stuart Talbot*, illustrating how slowly but surely the new Vicar gained his hold on Leeds.

Just before I left I was talking to a typical, downright, good-hearted, self-made business man, who kept his Yorkshire speech. "I can't mak' nowt o' that Vicar. He's a good man, right enoof, and a clever, I suppose, but he's too 'oomble for the likes of uz: we want a strong man i' Leeds."

I merely said, "Wait a year or two and you'll change your mind."

Returning to Leeds just before the Vicar's departure as Bishop of Rochester, I met my friend again. He had no recollection, though I had, of our own previous conversation. But he said: "Nay, it's a bad business is this o' t'owd Vicar goin'. He's gotten a hold o' this place, sure enoof. He's taught *me* summat I never thowt, that it's the 'oomble man that's strong."

Mrs. Talbot was a Lyttelton by birth.

She was then . . . in what for anyone else would have been called a full age, just delightful, so bright and fresh and keen, flavouring real goodness with a charming spice of *diablerie* (I can find no other word). I always used to say that she at least managed to make the best of both worlds.

I can't resist telling the story of the day when a representative of the Leeds ladies—a very earnest woman—brought her the present she had chosen on her leaving Leeds. I think the ladies were surprised by her choice: it was a set of diamonds. But the earnest woman who brought the gift looked even more surprised when Mrs. Talbot held the diamonds up before the light and slowly said, with eyes sparkling like the diamonds themselves: "O diamonds, diamonds! I think I could sell my soul for diamonds." Her many friends will recognise how well these spontaneous words expressed that frankness and unconventionality which was one of her many charms; yet how they travestied her real depth of faith and goodness. It must be difficult for younger folk who have known her only when she has suffered from the deafness which she has borne with such gallantry,[1] to realise that in the days of her prime she was the life and soul of any talk that was going on, hopping from point to point like a bright and cheerful bird among the twigs of a tree. She made the Vicarage a place of light and life. It was to me a delightful home.

Lang was nearly twenty-six when he went to Leeds. He and "Tupper" had taken a small but comfortable house in Brunswick Place, just outside the parish, where they lived together for three months, until "Tupper" married. Lang was best man at the wedding and later joined the "Tuppers" in the Tirol, where they were spending their honeymoon. "Tupper" gave him a warm welcome and characteristically asked him to look after the bride for a day or two while he went climbing!

On returning to Leeds, Lang had to find fresh quarters.

With the ardour of youth I had at once set my heart on living in the midst of the poor folk who surrounded the Parish Church. One who had as a layman enthused about University Settlements could scarcely as a parson be content to live elsewhere. Simpson[2] and an elder curate known as Father Marks promised to join me. The other curates were very sniffy about our project, but the Vicar smiled upon our zeal. The difficulty was to get any sort of house in what was then a very derelict quarter of Leeds. At last an old public-house, which had been deprived of its licence, was secured. It was placed most conveniently, just beside the church, at the end of old Church

---

[1] She died in 1939.
[2] Canon J. G. Simpson, Canon and Precentor of St. Paul's Cathedral, 1911-1928, Dean of Peterborough, 1928-1942.

Row. But other conveniences besides that of site there were none. The public bar-room (retaining the bar) became our refectory, the more private bar-parlour with its stone floor became at first my study. My bedroom, which was never carpeted, was over one of the single rooms which abounded in that district, where tramp-folk lodged at sixpence a night. I used often to be disturbed by the oaths and screams of quarrelsome couples below. I once found in that room in utter squalor a man who had been a boy at Eton. "I was then, I've been ever since, a drifter," so he said, "and I've drifted down to this." After a year I migrated to another small house next door— so small that it had been condemned as a dwelling-house—a ground-floor room which could just hold a writing-table, a small bookcase and two chairs, which was my study, an upper room for bedroom (uncarpeted), containing an iron bedstead (on which I slept even at Bishopthorpe!), a small wash-stand, a chair and a tin bath. There was no bathroom in either house. This bedroom was so low that I could just stand upright within it and no more. This was my home for nearly three years, and I found it quite sufficient.

Sufficient it may have been : luxurious it certainly was not. Once, when Lang was away, "Tupper" had the misfortune to sleep in his bed and reported the night the most uncomfortable he had ever spent. The bed had only a blanket and sheet over a chain mattress. The chains ate into poor "Tupper's" bones ; the wind whistled through the ill-fitting boards ; and in the end, to get any sleep at all, he took the blanket off the bed and spent the rest of the night on the floor.

When Lang was Archbishop of York, he had to make a speech on Housing. He surprised his audience by remarking that once on a time he had lived most comfortably in a condemned tenement.

A few days later he received the following letter :

The Committee of the Ananias and Sapphira Club present their compliments to the Archbishop of York and beg to inform him that he has been elected an honorary member of the Club by virtue of the services rendered to the Club by the following extract.

An enclosed cutting from a newspaper gave the Archbishop's remarks.

To this old "pub" came with me Marks and Simpson and Charles Tyler, whom later, when he married, we called "Demas," as he had forsaken us, having loved this present world, and his new house we called Thessalonica. He was succeeded by a cheery Mullins from South Africa.

At first we were served by an ex-soldier and his wife. We had advertised for a couple without "encumbrances" in the way of children. Ere long the lady became unwell and we suffered much in consequence. But we were too innocent to divine the reason. One day I met Heygate, the Clerk in Orders (as the second Senior Curate was called), and on my approach he was convulsed by laughter and gasped congratulations on the birth of a baby at the Clergy House! For many days and from many quarters we received tender enquiries as to the welfare of the Clergy House baby. As soon as possible the parents and their "encumbrance" were removed, and we ran no such risks again. We were a very happy and merry party, and so successful was our pioneer experiment that after I left Leeds the present commodious Clergy House was built, almost in the same place.

The staff of the Parish Church was indeed "a very happy and merry party."

There was Wynne Healey (afterwards in my episcopal district in London as Vicar of St. Olave's, Woodberry Down), a bachelor of bachelors, a clerical Corney Grain, an accomplished artist alike in musical sketch and cookery, who disciplined our young enthusiasms by caustic criticism, yet who really loved his work and won much love in return.

There was "Rat" Heygate, the "Clerk in Orders," a most devoted parish priest, and there was Simpson, "the Prophet" as we called him, whom we tried to tame, and who combined prophetic zeal with a boisterous humour. His sermons even then reached a high level, both of thought and rhetoric, in the best sense of that often misused word. There was Tupper-Carey, then as ever since "Tupper," our Peter Pan who could never grow up, unconventional and lovable, at home in public-houses and yet devout with an almost French fervour, a really heroic worker among the poor. There was "Father" Marks, blending an earnest seriousness with a sly humour.

Happy as Lang was in their companionship, he yet felt that something was lacking.

"It sometimes makes me sad," he wrote to the Vicar towards the end of his time in Leeds, "to reflect that among all my fellow-curates there is hardly one, with the exception of that dear boy 'Tupper,' with whom I can exchange any thought that bears on one's own inner life. I hate *blabbing* about such things; but the want of such talk *occasionally* does give a *degree* of loneliness to one's life which seems strange in one of outward fellowship."

The craving continually recurred throughout his life, undiminished by a regretful awareness that the fault was not wholly with his companions.

They too were conscious of this aloofness. Canon Simpson, "the Prophet," recalls him as a friendly, even an affectionate, colleague, who dispensed nicknames to the other curates and "ragged" them in a good-tempered way. "But we hardly ventured to return the compliment. . . . His relationship with us was rather that of the friendly young don than of the fellow-undergraduate." Canon Simpson repeats the remark of a Dundee lady who heard Lang preach in Edinburgh: "Mr. Lang seems to me one of those Scotsmen who never allow you to see their minds in undress. His ideas are presented to you ready-made in the shop window."

Then there was the Vicar himself, who won at once and ever retained Lang's warm affection and respect.

Certainly contact with his personality was the richest gift he gave to me and—in greater or less measure—to all his curates. He knew then little or nothing of parish work; he was there a learner like ourselves. But, what was of infinitely greater value, we felt that in his presence all our little meannesses and faults were rebuked, all our rash and ready judgments sifted, all our best ideals both disciplined and quickened. I can't well express what I owed then, and have owed ever since, to his mind, his spirit, his example. I only wish I had proved more worthy of them.

Lang was in and out of the Vicarage constantly. A man would never know whom he would find there. There was a sprinkling of young Talbots and Lytteltons about. There would be some of the men who counted in the life of Leeds; there would be friends from Oxford and London, dons, scientists, or politicians like Arthur Balfour, an occasional visitor at Easter, with whom Lang walked and talked. "Through the gate of the Vicarage," Lang recalled, "there was a new intercourse between the grit of Leeds and the grace of the outside world."

His visits there were not, of course, simply social. Once a week two or three of the curates were summoned to the Vicarage at seven-thirty in the morning to read with Dr. Talbot for an hour, usually from "the Fathers," over a cup of coffee. Lang remarks that the curates endured the walk of two miles uphill from the Clergy House to the Vicarage at seven in the morning in the cause of sustaining the tradition of sound learning among the English clergy.

"To be in the Vicar's presence, once you knew him," Lang wrote to his mother when he was leaving Leeds, "was at once an inspiration and a rebuke. God bless the ramshackle old creature,[1] one of the best of His sons on earth."

Dr. Talbot returned the regard in full measure. "Tupper" has it that Lang "was consulted on matters of policy by the Vicar far more than the senior curate"; and according to Canon Topham, then curate at an adjacent church, Dr. Talbot was heard to say at luncheon that "Lang will some day be Archbishop of Canterbury."

His talent for preaching was at once recognised—though two of his earliest sermons were ruined by unhappy circumstances.

I shall never forget my first sermon. It was delivered on my very first Sunday in Leeds at a neighbouring half-country parish church, where the parson was ill and I was sent to take his place. There was a tiny congregation. Half-way through my discourse there suddenly rose a roar as of a bull of Bashan. An immense man was seized with an apoplectic fit. The children who were near the door rushed out in terror and would not return. Two or three men in the choir tried to carry the poor man out, but he thrust out his great legs, like weaver's beams, and smashed the seats. By this time hardly any congregation was left and only three or four nerve-wracked survivors heard the end of my discourse.

Afterwards he told his mother that he had had to endure much chaff from his clerical colleagues on the catastrophic result of his first sermon. Then there was the occasion when he made his *début* at the Men's Service.

It was at the Parish Church. I was in the full flood of youthful eloquence when an old, tall, white-haired man rose and said aloud: "Yoong man, stow that: I've heard it all before; aw'm for home." And he strode out.

---

[1] Dr. Talbot was not yet fifty !

Even in his first year he had his share of preaching at the Parish Church, despite a rule which excluded deacons from the pulpit.

Certainly it was a great inspiration to speak at the Sunday evening service, then, I hope still, thronged by people from every part of Leeds. I expect that all preachers would say, as I can, that their first sermons excited them more than any others later in life. I began then the habit I kept at St. Mary's, Oxford, at Portsea, and at St. Paul's, of preaching consecutive courses. I remember one, in my last Lent at Leeds, on "the Church," when to a congregation which crowded even the chancel steps (familiar to all lovers of "t'owd Church") I poured out the ardour of a new-found enthusiasm.

Father Talbot,[1] who was one of the boys at the Vicarage in those days at Leeds, writes:

I cannot say I can remember any sermon of his in those early days. But I do remember very well the effect of his preaching on the huge congregations that at that time filled the Parish Church. He could hold them to a rapt attention. Rich were the cadences of his voice, and shapely was the form of his sentences; but it was the glow of a *feu sacré* upon the lips of one who had so recently staked much on his convictions that was the really penetrating feature of his preaching. I expect that he never attained to a higher standard of effectiveness than in those years at Leeds and Portsea.

Canon Simpson, "the Prophet," thought him "even greater on the platform than in the pulpit." He was a brilliant example of φρόνησις (wisdom in action), as distinguished from σοφία (wisdom in thought), a bishop already in all but actual attainment, and very far from the ordinary English conception of a Scots preacher.

Lang stood erect in the pulpit, his head slightly thrown back, his arms rarely moving except to turn a page, his utterance calm and even, never rising or falling. The inward glow was discernible in melting eye and deep melodious voice, but the fire did not blaze forth in passionate speech.

Or there is the contemporary description in the reputed words of an old Yorkshireman: "What's this young man you've sent us, with eyes like a hawk's and a voice like a bell?"

His effectiveness at Leeds is beyond question; and it may be, as he

[1] The Rev. E. K. Talbot, Community of the Resurrection.

himself and Father Talbot suggest, that what later he gained in facility and experience, he lost in freshness and fire. When he was Bishop of Stepney he came back to preach at the Leeds Parish Church; and as he came out after his sermon, one of the girls he had known in the old days stopped him and said: "Nay, but ye preached better than that when ye were nobbut a curate."

So swiftly did his reputation grow that, although still a deacon,[1] he was invited to the Minster by the Dean of York. Unfortunately the Dean (A. P. Purey-Cust [2]) had not realised Lang's ecclesiastical status, and when told that he was only a deacon, was greatly disturbed.

"I fear," he said, "it is against all the rules for a deacon to preach in the Minster."

Lang at once offered to withdraw.

"No, no," said the Dean, "that won't do." A Quondam Fellow of All Souls himself, a perfect solution had occurred to him. Lang should preach, not as a deacon, but as a Fellow of All Souls; and through this odd hole in the regulations Lang climbed for the first time into the pulpit of the Minster.

As time went on, he was asked to preach outside the diocese. In November 1892 he was at Westminster Abbey and, as he wrote to his mother, could not help recalling his visit there at the age of sixteen, when he had looked at the statues of the statesmen and wondered if one day his own statue would be among them.

Besides the services, the visiting, the Missions, and all the routine of the Parish Church, other work crowded in on him. On the death of the Principal of the Clergy School, now vanished but then high in reputation, for two terms he took charge as acting Principal, an unusual post for a curate who was still a deacon. He still gave occasional lectures, mostly for the University Extension Delegacy, and, entering the columns of the local press, contributed to the *Leeds Mercury* and the *Yorkshire Post*. His journalistic enterprises did not win the unmixed favour of all his colleagues, and one evening Simpson posted on the board of the Clergy House what purported to be a message from the editor of the *Leeds Mercury* inviting Lang to write a leading article on the Boxing Kangaroo!

In 1891, when the Parish Church kept its jubilee, Lang was almost

---

[1] He was ordained priest at St. Mary's, Reading, on May 24th, 1891, but left no account of the ceremony either in his letters or in his autobiographical notes.

[2] Dean of York from 1880 to 1916, when he died.

inevitably charged with the compilation of a commemorative volume, which duly appeared under the title of *Church and Town for Fifty Years*. Although in literary merit far excelling other works of the kind, unguarded references to previous vicars still alive were the cause of some offence.

But, as he looked back on those days at Leeds, the memories that held and moved him most were of the humble people among whom he had worked. Of them he wrote at length.

My district was the Kirkgate and the courts opening out from it, including the dirty slum on which I had looked down from the train. To this later was added the Marsh Lane district, the most squalid part of Leeds. . . . I never saw anything worse, or indeed as bad, in East London. A few of my folk were decent artisans and small shop-keepers, more were casual labourers, most were the denizens of common lodging-houses or single rooms let out for the night. I don't think I exaggerate when I say that my first flock contained 2000 human (?) beings whose homes were either rooms let at sixpence a night or a corner in a lodging-house kitchen. I wonder where they all went when these squalid hovels were at last swept away. Some of them, especially the women in the Marsh Lane courts, were worse than beasts, for beasts are not degraded. I seem to see now their unkempt hair, their tattered clothes, their bleared eyes looking out at me with sullen suspicion. Many of them were the lowest class of prostitutes, but indeed, to put it bluntly, the unashamed promiscuousness of living made even the ordinary brothel respectable in comparison. . . .

I often had to interfere . . . with fierce fights. I found that it was generally possible to separate men, but never women, if they had once had their hands in each other's hair ! Once that stage had been reached, they would fall on each other anywhere until they had had it out.

There were indeed lighter experiences which a sense of humour made even enjoyable. There was, for example, one lodging-house which was the chosen home of the ladies and gentlemen who traded on the compassion of passers-by. At first they resented my coming among them, but when, rightly or wrongly, I promised I would never divulge their secrets, I was made free of their company. There I would see the blind man who had lost his sight in a colliery disaster going cheerfully to his locker and cooking his dinner with open eyes; the sailor who had lost his leg at the bombardment of Alexandria unstrapping it and letting it down; the soldier who had lost his arm in the service of his King and Country releasing it to put his potatoes on the fire.

There was another lodging-house frequented by street musicians, and we used to have wonderful concerts of trumpets, whistles, concertinas, and sentimental ballads round the kitchen fire. To act among such people as a minister of religion demanded more faith than courage, for in a dull, listless way they were ready enough to listen to such simple religious words as they could understand. I used often to speak in the lodging-houses of Him who had been born in that lodging-house at Bethlehem, and to try in their foetid single rooms to arouse the sense of shame or the spirit of hope. But there was little chance of any seed getting into, much less growing in, such a soil. It was, of course, hopeless to think of getting them inside a church. What would the "Cathedral service" in the Parish Church mean to them? And I had no sort of Mission room available. I remember succeeding in persuading a few of the more decent to attend the service of a Parochial Mission conducted with much fervour by E. J. Gough (afterwards Vicar of Newcastle). Only one of them, an anaemic, emotional youth, filled in a "resolution card" with my assistance; and next day I found he was using it for begging purposes! Most of them were really not human enough to get within the zone of religion; and how could they be human in such an environment?

Yet even there signs of a true humanity would sometimes break through the squalor. I have elsewhere told a tale of one of these poor wretched girls in a Marsh Lane court. She took pity on a young country lad far advanced in consumption, who had drifted into Leeds and, failing through illness to get employment and fearing the workhouse, had drifted down to Marsh Lane. She fed him with the rewards of her shame; she tended, protected, nursed him without reward. When he was dying, she fetched me, telling me that he had been bred a Christian and ought to die like one. When I buried him, in heavy rain, I saw her standing afar off. I met her as we left the cemetery and asked her why she had not come nearer, and then she said passionately, with tears in her eyes, "I wasn't going to let my black soul spoil his white one as it was passing." . . .

I have always said that the two places where I learned hope for humanity were the slums of Leeds and the prison at Portsmouth. . . .

There was one section . . . in whom I took a special interest—the street boys, sellers of matches and newspapers, who then abounded in the streets of Leeds, many of them parentless and homeless, living even at the age of eleven or twelve a lodging-house life. I took, at my own charges, helped ultimately by some friends in Leeds, a shop in Kirkgate with a dwelling-house over it, and converted it into a home for eight or ten of them. I got a good-hearted artisan and his cheerful wife to act as caretakers and parents of the Home. It was a queer, irresponsible, yet in many ways attractive family. In spite of all my care I don't think any of them came to much good. The tricks and shifts and fascinations of the street were too much for my good advice or my efforts to get them into regular jobs. Once, after a sermon on Christian hopefulness, to test its sincerity I made the quixotic resolve that I would stick to the next waif who came into the Home, *whatever happened*, till he was twenty-one. Next day my testing case arrived—a little bright homeless lad. I kept my resolve. I got him work, in due course I got him apprenticed to a trade. I was rewarded by much affection, but by nothing else. Long before the age of twenty-one was reached I knew my experiment was a failure. It is not enough to give chances: there must be the will to use them. . . .

In the midst of all these rather derelict folk one unfailing delight was the children; and, like Bishop Andrewes, I blessed God for "the sweetening of the world by infants." For some time I used to have an open party once a week for any of them who liked to come, in a large parochial room which I was allowed to use—little, tattered, dirty, charming guests, we had great fun, of a very boisterous and to me rather exhausting sort.

Afterwards Lang was thankful for these experiences at the beginning of his ministry. They took him into a world of which later he would see little and were good for him in other ways. "Visiting in the Leeds alleys," he wrote to his mother, "knocks a deal of false pride out of me."

He was also given the charge of what was known as the "A Division," a Sunday afternoon meeting of young men in the twenties and thirties. About eighty to a hundred of them, mostly from the families of superior artisans or shopkeepers, would assemble every Sunday. At first they were inclined to be suspicious of the new curate, and when he asked why they were shy of him, one of them replied : "Well, d'ye think ye can size oop any man in six months ?" With some of them he kept in touch all his life, and forty years later, when he was Archbishop of Canterbury, they would make an annual excursion to Lambeth to see him.

Another of his organisations was the Leeds Parish Church Club. The members were keen footballers and it fell to Lang to follow them round on their fixtures. Later, when he was at Magdalen, he invited a dozen of them to spend some days with him at Oxford. It was Eights Week and, running along the towpath with the boats, they caught the prevailing excitement. But as they had not mastered the names of the competing colleges, they were driven to substitute those of the football teams of Yorkshire, so that the air was rent with shouts of "Well rowed, Pudsa !"—"Well rowed, Stanningla !"—"Well rowed, Parish Church !"

Lang was keenly interested in industrial questions—a legacy from the old days of political ambitions and from his admiration for Maurice and Kingsley. He sometimes spoke at trade union meetings, and once, when there was trouble in the engineering trade, he and his colleagues of the Clergy House invited Tom Mann, a leader of the men, to stay with them. Mann was then a fiery young idealist, at the outset of his chequered career, and talked seriously to Lang of taking Orders. Lang asked Sir James Kitson,[1] the leader of the employers, to meet him, and over a late supper in the Clergy House they had a long and friendly talk which, Lang believed, was helpful towards a settlement of the dispute.

Possibly as a result of this encounter, Kitson became a friend, and at dinner at his house one night Lang met John Morley, who took him apart and questioned him closely about the attitude of young Oxford men towards religion.

The Leeds Infirmary, of which Lang was a chaplain, brought him into yet another circle, and he had two wards which he visited regularly. He did not limit his ministry to the patients, and one Advent gave a course of addresses to the medical staff and students on the intellectual bases of the Christian Faith. Among his hearers was a Junior House Surgeon, "a red-haired, disputatious but most agreeable young Irishman named Moynihan." [2] Lang did not flatter himself that he had made much impression in that quarter, but in after years, when Moynihan

[1] M.P. for Colne Valley 1892-1907, and afterwards Lord Airedale. Died in 1911.
[2] B. G. A. Moynihan : afterwards Lord Moynihan. Died in 1936.

was one of the most famous surgeons of the day, he vowed he had never forgotten those Advent talks. He also told Lang that after listening to him he had made a bet that the young curate would some day be Archbishop of Canterbury.

Father Talbot gives an idea of the impact of Lang upon those who knew him in those days at Leeds.

> He was a striking figure, with clear-cut features, eyes that had a remarkable way of kindling to his thought as he spoke, strongly marked eyebrows, and abundant dark hair. Vitality of mind and body were very evident. I remember his leading us boys as "hare" in a paper-chase and running us off our legs. There was something immediately arresting about his voice; whether in public speech or in conversation, it had a beauty and fulness of tone which, combined with dignity of utterance and a mastery of balanced language, invested even the commonplace with importance. But what captivated a youngster was the dramatic cast of his mind and conversation: he made one feel that life was rich with romantic possibilities. Always a brilliant *raconteur*, he excited a boy's imagination. This was specially true in regard to religion, which he charged with this dramatic quality; so that he aroused the sense of it being the greatest adventure in the world. He had an extraordinary power of stimulating one's aspiration and the loftiness of one's ambitions. By the generous expectations of you which he seemed to entertain, you were almost flattered into thinking yourself a finer fellow than was actually the case. And you were encouraged to hope that there was a big part for you to fill in an immensely exciting play. I think that he thought of himself in this dramatic fashion, and that he rarely lost "the sense of theatre." Events took on a new significance as they passed through the experience of one endowed with an unusually sensitive self-awareness; especially since he had, for the communication of that experience, so rich and vivid a medium of expression.

The years Lang spent at Leeds were among the happiest in his life. He worked tremendously hard, under a chief he loved and admired. He was accorded great freedom and given responsibilities beyond his years. He discovered his own gifts as a preacher. He made a host of friends, many of whom remained attached to him all his life. Best of all, he formed acquaintance at first hand with some of the most pressing of the Church's problems. And he was young and could not but know that he had lived up to and indeed surpassed every expectation of success that his friends had formed. Men were already beginning confidently to prophesy for him a distinguished career in the Church.

At the beginning of June 1893, when he was on a visit to All Souls, the President of Magdalen,[1] without preliminary warning, offered him the post of Dean of Divinity in that College. Lang was torn by doubts and hesitations. He had meant to spend at least another year in Leeds. There were the Clubs and the boys, whom he would be deserting. There was Dr. Talbot himself, whose wise and kindly counsel had counted for so much—how would he regard such a defection? On the other hand, the offer was most attractive. He would be in some sort of charge of young men, many of whom would pass on to positions of responsibility, all of whom were at a formative age. He would have time for reading—or so he then thought; and Magdalen, after all, was Magdalen.

His uncertainties were not diminished by a second offer which followed closely upon the first, and a third upon the heels of the second. The familiar little figure of Benjamin Jowett appeared at All Souls with the proposal that Lang should succeed Canon W. H. Fremantle as Fellow and Theological Tutor at Balliol.

I felt greatly honoured. I have often remembered and quoted some words he said in describing what my duties would be. The last sentence is an epitome of wisdom for pastoral work, and indeed for life: "You will try to make young men as good as young men can be made. *Don't expect too much and don't attempt too little.*" . . . I frankly told the Master what I felt—that my theological position was rather different from his, and that I had such respect for him that I could not bear to take any line against his views in his own College. He surprised me by saying: "I know this. It is just why I am asking you to come. My friends and I had our work to do in Oxford. I think it was worth doing. But it is largely done; and there are some things we don't seem to be able to do, and which I want done. We don't seem able now to inspire the young men. *We may have truth—* I think we have—*but we have no fire!*" It was said very simply, quietly, rather pathetically. . . . I was greatly touched; and though I could not accept his offer, I like to think that the old Master made it, and that this was in his mind on the last time I spoke to him before he passed away.

[1] Sir Herbert Warren, K.C.V.O., President of Magdalen 1885-1928. Died in 1930.

Sir William Anson and Gore, with whom he discussed the suggestion, were decidedly against it and perhaps determined his answer. They thought that, in spite of what Jowett had said, the position would be too difficult owing to the "theological incompatibility" of Master and Tutor. Yet it was, as Lang wrote to his mother, "most significant of the change of tone in modern Oxford that Jowett, the old chief of the extreme Broad Church Liberals, should even think of a man of my views to take on the religious supervision of Balliol College." But he felt that all the time he would, as it were, be looking over his shoulder.

The other invitation was from Ernest Wilberforce, Bishop of New-castle. Would Lang be Vicar of Newcastle and of the Cathedral Church? Once more Lang was tempted. He had been present at a Sunday evening service in the Cathedral and been deeply impressed both by the Vicar and the congregation. But at twenty-nine, with only three years in Orders behind him, he did not feel fitted for so responsible a charge. So this too he refused.

That left the tug-of-war between Leeds and Magdalen, and possibly the sympathetic though regretful attitude of Dr. Talbot decided the issue. Lang could still hardly bear the thought of leaving Leeds and, above all, the boys with and for whom he had worked so hard. "I feel like a cur with his tail between his legs," he told his mother. But in October he went, enduring all the harrowing incidents of departure, the goodbyes and the gifts. The young men bade him an affectionate farewell, presenting him with an engraving of Holman Hunt's "May Morning on Magdalen Tower." He travelled to Oxford with a black dog of depression on his shoulder. "I never knew," he wrote, "how dear dirty old Leeds had wound her way into my heart until she thus made beautiful Oxford seem painful in my eyes."

Chapter XII

MAGDALEN

L ANG, it will be recalled, was fond of alluding to Magdalen as his beautiful mistress, for whom during three years he deserted his lawful and loving wife, All Souls. This innocuous infidelity, which caused him some regret at the time, came about because, on accepting a Fellowship at Magdalen, he was compelled to become a Quondam Fellow of All Souls.

The post of Dean of Divinity, which Lang now filled, was intended to be a pastorate, and its occupant received licence and institution from the Bishop of Winchester as Visitor and Ordinary of the College. Lang was therefore able with perfect truth to tell his father that he too was now a parish minister.

His new office also carried the charge of the Choir and of the services in the Chapel. The Choir, of course, is famous, and all the artist in Lang reacted rapturously to his association with it.

The Magdalen Choir was then at the height of its fame. Sir John Stainer and Sir Walter Parratt had been succeeded by Varley Roberts. "The Doctor," as he was always called, was a great character, a bluff, outspoken, irascible, warm-hearted Yorkshireman. He was not— except in his own opinion, which he held with a naïveté which disarmed criticism—a great composer; but he was a very good organist and accompanist and a prince of choir-trainers. He devoted himself to his choir with whole-hearted enthusiasm, and certainly in his time it reached a very high standard. He resented any attempt to make the music congregational, except at the hymn on Sunday evening. I have a vivid memory of one characteristic scene. A good elderly Bishop (I think it was Bishop Hobhouse) was present at a weekday service. Proud of his voice, he began to join lustily in the Psalms. Suddenly the organ stopped. I looked up and saw the full red face of "The Doctor" glaring down from the organ-screen, indignant at this intrusion. The Bishop happened also to look up, and when their eyes met, "The Doctor" raised his fist and shook it at the Bishop. I felt sure there would be some row after the service was over. So I waited in the ante-chapel. Out came the Bishop from the Chapel: down came "The Doctor" from the organ loft. They met.

"How dare you spoil the chanting of the Psalms!" spluttered "The Doctor."

"And how dare you, sir, interrupt my joining in the worship of the House of God!" replied the offended Bishop.

"This isn't a House of God," blurted out "The Doctor," "it is a private Chapel."

So far as the spoiling of the service goes, "The Doctor" was right, for the acoustics of the Chapel are so wonderfully and delicately balanced that any voice outside the Choir itself strikes a jarring note and breaks the harmony. It was for this reason that I caused certain words which were sometimes criticised to be put on the cards of admission to the Chapel:

"Visitors are requested to join in the service silently."

It was a constant delight to join day after day during term, and twice a day, in this offering of beautiful sound; and it was also a great education in the noble heritage of the music of the English Church.

But his chief work was with the undergraduates. "To make Christ a more living force in this College—" he told his mother, "that is my duty."

I made up my mind from the first to get into easy and friendly relations with them all. And they made this very easy. Almost all of them were delightfully frank, natural and accessible. I think they came to look on me as something different from the official don. It was quite natural for me to call most of them, at least the leading men of the College, by their Christian names or by the nicknames by which they were known in College. Perhaps I saw too much of the leading men and too little of the more quiet and shy sort, especially among the "demies" or scholars, though I had many friends among them also. But I thought it important to be on these easy and friendly terms with the men who had most influence on the College life and tone, and so far as was possible to share their life with them. I did not in any way obtrude religion; but human relations made it often easy and natural to speak some word of advice or of reminder of the higher things. And I think they all knew and felt what I stood for in the College life. Some undergraduates tried to live a definitely Christian life—as, e.g., Willie Holland, afterwards so well known for his work in India, then as always most bright and cheerful, but at that time inclined through the influence of old Webb-Peploe to keep apart from the average "unconverted" crowd; and this group, of course, I tried to help as much as I could. The great body of the men were just healthy, happy, straightforward public school boys, taking life merrily as it came, sometimes noisy and uncontrolled, but fundamentally sound and good. There were, of course, a few, but very few rotters. There were occasional outbreaks of intemperance, especially at the Sunday evening "After Common Rooms," but they only reached the stage of noise and excessive hilarity.

Lang formed some of his longest and happiest friendships among these young men. There was Stafford Crawley,[1] who was to be his chaplain at Amen Court, his vicar at Bishopthorpe, and his lifelong friend. An older man was Jack Talbot, nephew of the Vicar of Leeds. There were the Leveson Gower brothers, Freddy,[2] who was to be Lang's curate at Portsea, and "Shrimp," [3] a "quaint, irresponsible, delightful creature." Geoffrey Robinson, to be better known as Geoffrey Dawson, a later editor of the *Times* for many years, was "a ruddy-faced boy from Eton, who concealed his steady reading behind a very eager College life." "Bal" (Balcarres) [4] was another friend, "who took me once over to Holland and Flanders, to see the pictures there, and gave me some lessons in the appreciation of art." Among many others whom Lang mentions were "two very special friends." Henry Wynyard Kaye, who died just after the war of 1914-1918, was "a singularly forcible, high-minded character, who always exercised a decisive influence wherever he was." The other was John Moreton Macdonald.

From these Magdalen days onward, until in 1921 I stood with his wife at his bedside as he passed away, he was one of my dearest and closest friends. A visit to him in the spring of 1894 at his Highland place, Largie Castle, in Kintyre, Argyll, led to my association with that lovely country.[5] . . . Ronald—or, as he was then called in his own family, John—was a very remarkable man. Had it not been for his deafness, which increased with years, he might have taken a leading place in Scottish affairs. His *History of France* in three volumes

---

[1] The Rev. A. S. Crawley, afterwards Canon of Windsor. Died 1948.
[2] The Rev. F. A. G. Leveson Gower.
[3] H. D. G. Leveson Gower, the well-known cricketer.
[4] The Earl of Crawford and Balcarres. Died in 1940.
[5] See Chapter XVII.

remains as a token of his intellectual ability. But it was in the region of character and of the spirit that he reached real distinction. A man among men, keen on sport, a lover of trees, an intrepid sailor, in his spirit he always stood apart: there he was "far ben." I always knew, and a little book of MS. prayers which he left, a copy of which I treasure, made it plain, that he lived in constant remembrance of the eternal, spiritual world, in a communion with God, never obtruded, rather concealed, but very real. When he died after a sudden attack of illness at Ballure, where he and his wife were staying with me, I knew that he was, to use his own phrase, "at home in his father's house." I cannot but think that my friendship with him and with his wife, and my home in the West Highlands which this friendship brought, were the richest gifts which Magdalen gave me.

The Leveson Gower brothers wrote of Lang's time at Magdalen in the *Oxford Magazine*.

"I still have very vivid recollections of the then Dean of Divinity—Cosmo, as the undergraduates always called him," wrote Mr. H. D. G. Leveson Gower. "He at once became 'one of us'; for while he always upheld the dignity of his office, he was still at heart an undergraduate. I can see him now, when, after some rag had taken place in College—and some of us had gone too far—not lecturing us, but making us feel how stupid we had been. 'What children you are! Don't be so silly again.' It was just the way he said things that made him so human; and we knew it. . . . On many occasions I wanted advice on how to act: Cosmo never failed me."

His brother spoke of Lang's "strong personality, his beautiful voice, and his natural goodness, stripped of any form of sanctimoniousness, which . . . created in fact a great spiritual force in the whole of Oxford."

Or there is the opinion of Dr. C. C. J. Webb, one of the younger members of the Senior Common Room. "I think," he writes, "those of us who had most to do with the undergraduates fully recognised how great an asset his (Lang's) influence over them was." Dr. Webb adds: "He certainly appeared to get on best with the socially prominent undergraduates . . . though it would have been very unfair to suggest that he neglected men of humble origin."

Lang's relations with the Senior Common Room were not quite so easy. By comparison, he found its atmosphere "stiff, self-conscious and restrained." The Fellows on their side thought that Lang was insufficiently interested in learning, and that sermons in which the undergraduates were warned against setting too high a value on intellectual success were both superfluous and inappropriate. According to Dr. Webb, he declared at one time he had been so out of temper with his colleagues that he deserted the high table and dined with the undergraduates.

But I had many good friends among the dons, notably Charles Fletcher,[1] the Tutor in history, quaint, original, sometimes eccentric, always lovable; and his friendship has grown with the years ever since. Charles Fletcher was indeed a character, so unique that I cannot but insert here an anecdote illustrating the strength of his prejudices and the warmth and generosity of his friendship. At a College meeting (of the Fellows) I innocently suggested that it would be more fitting that the Choirmen should disclose below their surplices cassocks rather than trousers. One of the Senior Fellows, a good Nonconformist, declared that this would be the thin end of the wedge, which would entirely alter the character of the Services and introduce Papistical ritual—what Fletcher called "Puseyism." Fletcher rose to say with deep emotion that he agreed with this view, that he could not bear to think of the Chapel becoming a Puseyite shrine, but that as the proposal was made by the present Dean of Divinity he must vote for it. Then he sat down with his head between his hands. It was a really costly sacrifice offered on the altar of friendship. . . .

Fletcher was convinced that there was a secret society among the English clergy sworn to Romanise the Church. He believed that they must have some secret sign of their own, like the Freemasons, and he was eager to discover it. One day I met two Oxford clerical dons whom he suspected to be likewise members of the conspiracy. They each said, "Is Charles Fletcher mad? He has just come up to me and whispered 'E.P.' in my ear, added, 'I've found you out,' and vanished." Later he went through the same performance with me. I laughed and asked him to give evidence of his discovery. He produced a copy of the *Guardian* and showed the "E.P." occurring frequently in the advertisements for curates. He was rather upset when I told him that this merely meant that the Eastward Position in celebrating the Holy Communion was the custom of that particular

---

[1] Fellow of All Souls and Magdalen. Died in 1934.

church. But I doubt whether he believed me. I expect he thought it was only another instance of a Puseyite *suppressio veri* !

A fellow-guest with Lang and Fletcher at Largie, the home of the Moreton Macdonalds, recalls how one morning the former, after celebrating Holy Communion in the Castle chapel, appeared at breakfast in his cassock. The sight so enraged Fletcher that he caught hold of the cassock and dragged its wearer half round the breakfast-table. Lang was not noticeably amused, but fortunately porridge and cold grouse proved a sufficient sedative for outraged feelings.

The President, T. Herbert Warren, always gave Lang the most generous support. His own position was not too easy, as he too had his critics in the Senior Common Room; but his devotion to the College was beyond a doubt and gradually overcame the opposition.

Lang's regard for him is possibly reflected in an absurd dream he was fond of telling. He thought he was leaning on a stile, looking over open country, when suddenly Mr. Gladstone appeared, mounted and furious, and after accusing him of having insulted Mrs. Gladstone, charged at him with levelled lance. Just as Lang thought that all was lost, the President of Magdalen came up and said, "Mr. Lang is a gentleman of blameless character." Whereupon the G.O.M. bowed and withdrew. The only probable part of this highly improbable affair is the characteristic statement attributed to Sir Herbert (then Mr.) Warren.

Any idea Lang may have had of a peaceful academic life, with much leisure for thought and reading, was speedily dispelled. He had worked very hard at Leeds: he worked, if anything, harder at Magdalen. He gave much of his time to the choristers, who were constantly in and out of his rooms, talking to him or sprawling on the floor and being told stories. One of these tales, continued by urgent request in one sitting after another, Lang wrote out during a holiday in the Highlands. He showed it to Charles Fletcher, who insisted that he must publish it, and on Lang consenting, prevailed on Smith, Elder & Co. to take it. The book appeared under the title of *The Young Clanroy*; its success was only moderate; and it was never reprinted. It is a romantic story of the "Forty-Five," and while hardly meriting the comparisons, which have been drawn, with the works of R. L. Stevenson and John Buchan, it has a stirring plot and, in the Highlands, an admirably depicted background. The scenes of action lack something of the nervous energy of the masters of that kind of literature, and the love episodes are stilted and rather unreal. (But so sometimes were Sir Walter's.) Afterwards Lang was just a little ashamed of this solitary essay in fiction. But if the jaded palate of the reading public remained untickled, the boys themselves thoroughly enjoyed the stories. And he not only brought the Highlands to them in this fashion: he also brought the boys to the Highlands, for twice he took parties of them to his new summer home in Argyll.

Besides the choristers there was the Chapel to be served and there was the flock, who would come and sit in his rooms and talk till the small hours. They called him Cosmo and treated him very much as one of themselves, after a fashion much more usual in these days than it was in those. Dr. Webb recalls a party he gave to Scottish undergraduates on his birthday, which was also Hallowe'en. They bobbed for apples, and Lang, as on a much earlier occasion in Glasgow, dislocated his jaw; while the doctor who was summoned was so exhausted by the labour of putting the jaw back in place that he himself fainted and had to be revived with brandy. It may be assumed, however, that this misadventure was not in Lang's mind when he wrote to his mother: "It is not the preaching that tires: it is the strain of *men*." He hardly ever had an evening alone; and the reading he had promised himself was never done, or even begun.

I shall never cease to regret this failure. No such opportunity has ever come again, and I have always deplored my lack of a basis of real theological learning. It is useless to complain: one has not wholly the ordering of one's life. But this lack of real knowledge of the habit of concentrated study and thought, of the discipline of mind and memory, have made much of my work slight and superficial, and remains as one of the many reasons which force me to realise how ill-equipped I am for the great offices which have come to me. It is pathetic to remember that I had intended at Oxford to write a book on the mind of St. Paul and had actually entered into contract with Rivingtons for its publication. But I could never make any headway with it and had finally to ask the publishers to release me.

But this lament referred to his life after he had taken on another onerous task. He had just finished his first year at Magdalen when the charge of the University Church of St. Mary's fell vacant. It was offered to Lang, and he, after some hesitation, accepted it. St. Mary's had fallen on evil days. The congregation had dwindled to a handful and the evening sermons for undergraduates had been abandoned. Yet it was the church where Keble had preached the famous sermon which has been recognised as the starting-point of the Oxford Movement, the church that had known Newman in his Anglican prime. Lang was equally attracted by the past glory and the future possibilities. He persuaded a reluctant College to alter its by-laws to enable him to double his duties, and was duly instituted as Vicar by Bishop Stubbs.

I was bidden to Cuddesdon Palace to be instituted, and the ceremony took place in the study. Only the Bishop and I were present. "Well, young man"—so he greeted me—"you're becoming an important person: this is a big work before you." After I had made the usual declarations and oaths he said, "Kneel down," and he read over me the form of institution and then said, "Let us pray." But no prayer came. I waited, kneeling. Still no prayer. Still I waited in some embarrassment. Then suddenly he said, "Get up," and as I rose he grasped my hand and said impulsively: "I couldn't find words: I felt it all too much. God bless you. God bless you. Goodbye."

The parish was insignificant, and so was the income, but the services, despite the aid of a curate, were a heavy tax on an already overburdened man. On Sundays he had to flit rapidly from the College Chapel to St. Mary's and back again, sometimes preaching three sermons in the day. The congregation gradually grew, and when he had been Vicar of St. Mary's for two years he was able to tell his mother that the communicants on Easter Day had multiplied tenfold.

He revived the services on Sunday evenings, choosing his preachers with the utmost care and filling the church with undergraduates as in the best of the old days.

The most vivid memory I have of these sermons is that of one delivered by Robert Dolling. I had great difficulty in persuading him to come: he protested that he was quite unfit to preach at a University. But he yielded and came. He took as his subject the cripple at the Gate Beautiful of the Temple. He began with some admirable remarks on art and the culture of beauty, which were evidently meant to lead up to the duty of those who enjoyed the beauty of Oxford to bring some of its influences to the poor. But I could see that Dolling was having heavy weather, reading from a MS. and obviously ill at ease. Suddenly he stopped, shut up the MS., looked round on the faces of the young men, and then said: "I can't go on with this. It has been written for me by a friend better able than I am to speak to University men. But it isn't my own stuff; and when I see you all here I must just say what is in my heart in my own way." Then he poured forth an impassioned plea for brotherliness towards the poor and outcast, and closed with a long, fervent, and very moving extempore prayer. That was Dolling all over.

To this Lang appended the story of a remarkable and disconcerting coincidence.

The Judge of Assizes was wont to go to St. Mary's before the opening of the Assizes for a service and sermon. On one occasion I was invited to preach the Assize sermon. The Judge was the famous Sir Henry Hawkins. It was the custom for the Vicar to meet the Judge and to escort him to his seat, and for the preacher immediately to mount the pulpit and begin his discourse. In my case the Vicar and the preacher were the same person. As Vicar I duly met the Judge on his arrival. He came in the old-fashioned elaborate Judge's coach. There was a crowd of urchins on the pavement to see the sight. As the Judge alighted his wig caught the top of the coach and was lifted up, disclosing a head as round and bald as a marble. The urchins at once burst out laughing. When the wig was readjusted, I escorted the Judge to his seat and then immediately as preacher began my sermon. The text—incredible as it may seem—was 2 Kings ii, 23 : "As he was going up by the way, there came forth little children out of the city, and mocked him, and said unto him, Go up, thou bald head; go up, thou bald head." I could not change the text: the discourse was on the decay of reverence. I wondered whether the Judge would think that I had given out the text on the spur of the moment. But at the close of the service he said to me with a dry smile, as I escorted him back to his coach: "A very excellent sermon—on a very apposite text."

Lang was profoundly conscious of the traditions of St. Mary's.

The thought of John Henry Newman was seldom absent from me, whether I was celebrating at his altar or preaching from the pulpit from which he spoke. There were very few traditions about him among the parishioners. But one old lady remembered him vividly and said to me—and I thought it very significant: "He used to wear a very shabby surplice, but when he read the lessons he seemed to be in Heaven."

Lang was anxious to make the great east window a memorial of the Oxford Movement, but left before he could carry out his plan. Some improvements he did effect, and one change which was not an improvement. He began the restoration of the tower and spire, which has since been successfully completed, and concealed with blue hangings some extremely unsightly panels in the choir, until such time as they could be removed. Unhappily he also used part of the fine old Jacobean altar rails to make a Litany desk, an act which Dr. Webb describes as "a vandalism"—a verdict with which Lang himself was later disposed to concur.

The work at St. Mary's brought him into touch with the men of other Colleges than Magdalen. There are indeed early indications of a new conception of the Vicar of St. Mary's as "an *ex-officio* pastor of all undergraduates," and it may have been with this idea that Lang addressed meetings in the different Colleges and helped to found a University Church Union.

All this, it may well be believed, left him little time for reading, or for concentrated thought, but an occasional letter to his mother or to his old Vicar shows that he was not allowing his mind to be altogether submerged by the waves of work. His opinion continued to develop very much along the lines he had already chosen.

"I have just read Church's *Life and Letters*," he wrote to Dr. Talbot. "It has been to me rebuke of all I know to be worst, vindication of what I hope to be best, in myself. . . . I envy you many things, but I envy none more than your friendship with the Dean. So far as is permitted by our very careful Mother, I hereby profess the cultus of St. Richard of St. Paul's! He and his character—above all, his point of view—appeal to me, *fetch* me, more than those of any Churchman. Newman did once; but somehow that spell has not held out. I think I date the beginning of its wane from reading the autobiography of Isaac Williams. He will always fascinate: at one time he might have commanded. Dr. Pusey—'outgone, outgone' altogether. I feel the awe. I reverence the moral whiteness and serenity as one reverences a snow cliff. But he is apart. Sometimes I do not feel that even if I were as good as I might be, the goodness thus given to *me* by God would quite translate itself in Pusey's language. And Dr. Liddon—well, you know how one feels about some houses or churches—'the design admirable, the scheme of the architecture perfect, but I could never feel *at home* there.' There is, I confess, in Liddon—it comes out in his remarks in Dr. Pusey's Life more than in his sermons—a hardness, a rigidity of dogmatic outline, which somewhat repel one. . . . These are all men I reverence, and in comparison with whom I feel myself to be a mere chatterer. I only say these things to help the expression of the gratitude and stimulus which I find when I come to the point of view of Dr. Church. . . . It is so large and calm and trustful, so utterly different from that—may I use the word ?—'cocksureness,' that atmosphere of the little Catholic books of doctrine, which is really cutting off the followers of the Oxford Movement from the best life and thought of the country. I always feel that one half of my mind on the great questions of religion is a big — ? — and it is a great help to know that a saint of the Church had that mark about him too."

He was to put much the same point a little differently in a letter he wrote in 1896 to Mr. Harold Anson :

There will always be the Platonist and the Aristotelian among Christian temperaments—the one ending with a decisive full stop, the other with a stop, and then always a little wistful point of interrogation. And this last comes, so I feel it, not from real *doubt*, but from a more acute susceptibility to the Mystery of Things.

In spite of the myriad claims of Oxford on his time, he managed an occasional escape from it and them. In February 1894 he preached his first sermon at St. Paul's—"it was strange to find oneself in that historic pulpit." Next month he was at Salisbury, to take the Three Hours Service on Good Friday. John Wordsworth, the Bishop, preached in the evening on "tasting death," and Lang was much moved by the thought that at the very moment the Bishop's wife, who was everything to him, was "dying in terrible pain of one of the worst forms of cancer." That summer he spent a week-end at Hatfield, where Archbishop Benson was among the guests. Lang had a long walk in the Park with Lord Salisbury and Dr. Talbot. They discussed religious education, on which the Conservative leader took a characteristically pessimistic view. Lang was not impressed by his attitude. "There is, with all his goodness, too much of the pride of intellect about him."

At the end of December 1895, Mr. A. J. Balfour, the new First Lord of the Treasury, whose acquaintance Lang had made at Leeds, wrote to offer him the parish church of Portsea, whose Vicar, Canon Edgar Jacob, had just been appointed Bishop of Newcastle. The parish covered the greater part of Portsmouth and carried the charge of about forty thousand people, a noble church and a large staff of curates. Lang at once went down to Portsea to survey the ground.

It did not at first attract me. True, the great church, built largely through the generosity of W. H. Smith, was most impressive, but my heart sank at the sight of Fratton Road—afterwards so familiar— and the long monotonous rows of artisan houses. I came back to Magdalen very uncertain in mind. Then I remember standing in the Cloisters and looking through them on the Chapel and the incomparable tower, and contrasting this beauty with what I had seen of Portsmouth. I thought of Oxford and the spell it has always laid upon me, then of my work among the men and at St. Mary's and the possibility of a better adjustment of their claims. And I said, "No. I can't leave this Oxford."

Apart from the wrench of leaving Oxford and Magdalen, there was a financial difficulty. Afterwards Lang used to say that the real value of the benefice of Portsea was minus nine hundred pounds a year, and he had no private means at all. He retired to the solitude of Land's End to think the matter over, and after much prayer and an "interior monition" wrote to Balfour on January 3rd, 1895, to decline the offer.

The new term began, the weeks went by, and presently Lang heard from Lord Hugh Cecil,[1] Balfour's cousin, that no appointment had been made to Portsea : man after man had been approached and had refused it, usually on the ground of finance.

The thought of this great parish and work going a-begging in this way troubled my conscience. I felt, "Here am I, without anyone depending on me. Someone must run risks, why should not I ?" I asked Hugh Cecil to sound Mr. Balfour as to whether after all these failures he might think of renewing his offer to me. The offer came immediately ; and this time, though sorely against all my inclinations and desires, I felt bound to accept. Almost all my friends deplored my decision : curiously enough, the only one who applauded it was the great George Curzon. It made me very unhappy, for I could not bear leaving these lads, and the beauty of Magdalen had gone very deeply into my heart.

[1] Now Lord Quickswood, Provost of Eton 1936-1944.

There was another complication of which the autobiographical notes give the barest of hints. The letters show that for some time Lang had felt the strain of the double work at Magdalen and St. Mary's was becoming intolerable. "In spite of all efforts I came gradually to the conclusion that either St. Mary's or Magdalen must be dropped." He could not bear to leave Magdalen, and "the difficulty of leaving St. Mary's and yet staying on in Oxford seemed very great." The only other solution was to give up both and leave Oxford altogether. A further "interior monition," reversing the judgment of its predecessor, made up his mind for him, and "with much doubt and trembling" he accepted Portsea. "I can't tell you," he wrote to his mother, "how bitter the thought of leaving is. . . . My very heart was in Magdalen, its young men, its Choir, its incomparable beauty. I *love* the place, and it is a veritable rending of heartstrings even to think of leaving it. And instead of it, a great waste of streets and houses."

Chapter XIII

PORTSEA

PORTSEA was to give Lang his solitary experience of the charge of a parish; that is, excluding his half-serious claim in connexion with the pastorate of Magdalen. But the work of a parish priest was a subject that always fascinated him; he gave much thought to it, and towards the end of his life, in the little memoir he wrote of his friend "Tupper," set down his reflexions, which are both interesting and revealing.

The parish priest, he says, must "at least be very human." He must be a man of God, but also "a man among his fellow-men," whom he must be able to "meet, appreciate, even enjoy." In his relations with them he must neither, as Jowett had once said, expect too much nor attempt too little. He must make "tolerant allowance for differences of temperament and circumstance," and never cease seeking for the Divine image among the lowest and apparently degraded. He has, of course, a duty to teach, and to build up those committed to him to be fitting members of Christ's Body. He must be an evangelist, not by spasmodical and sensational effort, but by quiet and steady work. And even if he finds the ideal is beyond his power to fulfil, he must never let it vanish from his sight.

Lang was now thirty-one. When Jacob went to Portsea, the parish church was a small dull building, served by a vicar and one curate.

> The Vicar, a worthy old Low-Churchman, was content with a minimum of duty; the curate was almost wholly employed in marrying or burying the parishioners. The parish church meant—could mean—little or nothing to the people. When Jacob left, there was a noble parish church capable of holding 2000 people, four mission churches, a company of ten curates, and a large and devoted flock; and the Church was an undoubted power in the parish and the city.

Jacob did in Portsea very much what Hook had done in Leeds, and the most striking memorial of his work was the church he built. He was, Lang said, "one of the most unself-conscious egoists I have ever known." To him the rebuilding of his church was the absorbing interest of his life; and it never occurred to him that anyone he met might not be equally concerned with his plans.

One day, travelling from Portsmouth to London and finding in his carriage an amiable elderly gentleman, he immediately and volubly expounded his great ideal of building a noble church to reach, impress and elevate the mass of people in his parish. His companion listened with patience and interest to all this eloquence, and when they reached Waterloo Station he said: "I have been much interested in your scheme, and if you would like to communicate with me further, here is my card. It will show you that I am specially interested in Portsmouth." It was the card of W. H. Smith, First Lord of the Admiralty. Needless to say, he did receive further communications from the Vicar of Portsea. The immediate result was a cheque for some thousands; from time to time as the scheme progressed, other and larger cheques arrived; until finally W. H. Smith had given over £30,000 of the £40,000 which enabled the church to be built.

The building is far from perfect architecturally. The nave is out of all proportion to the tower at one end and the choir at the other, and, while its size and dignity are impressive, dwarfs the Sanctuary. However, when filled, it holds 2000 people, every one of them within range of the eye and voice of the preacher.

In 1896 Portsea had a growing population of about 40,000. It was the mother parish of the greater part of Portsmouth, excluding the old town but including a wilderness of sprawling suburb. The people were mostly naval men and their families, dockyard workers and artisans. If comparatively lucky, they lived in neat but monotonous little houses, lining streets which seemed to have neither a beginning nor an end. If unlucky, they were herded in squalid and overcrowded slums.

The parish was divided into five districts, each with its own mission church and organisations and served by at least two curates. The clergy lived a communal life in the Vicarage, a house of moderate size in a large field. Under Lang the number of curates grew. At one time they were as many as sixteen and they were never less than fourteen, some sleeping in houses outside, but nearly all meeting in the Vicarage for meals. Lang began by doubting whether some of the staff he found there would quite suit him. They were good fellows, but, as he had thought at first of the young ordinands at Cuddesdon, not "my sort." Some of them were older than he was, and Jacob seems to have fostered a kind of muscular Christianity which could be a little trying.

On Sunday evenings the old Vicar, by way of finding and giving relief after a strenuous day, encouraged the supper to become a rag. Black coats were exchanged for college blazers; missiles of bread were thrown across the table; occasionally, I was told, the Vicar found himself put under the table. This might be all very well for an elderly Vicar, letting himself go; but an instinct told me it would not do in the case of a Vicar younger than some of his companions. So at once the *mot d'ordre* was given—the Sunday rag was to cease. Whatever the company may have said of it among themselves, it was obeyed. But it was once put to the test. One of them—I won't say who—older, I think, than myself, threw some bread across the table. I said quietly: "That is not allowed." Shortly after, the offence was repeated. I said: "So-and-So, since you can't behave at table, leave the room." Would he? If not, where was I? But, strange to say, he went. The principle of authority was established and the old rag vanished.

While most of Jacob's staff stayed on, there were a few changes and additions. Lang brought in some of his young men from Magdalen, including Freddy Leveson Gower, for whom he had an especial affection. His own brother Norman, lately ordained, joined him; and another promising youngster was Cyril Garbett, afterwards Bishop of South-wark and Winchester, and since 1942 Archbishop of York. No stipend for a senior was more than £130 a year, or for a junior more than £100; and some of the men were volunteers, getting nothing except their "keep."

There may not have been much high thinking, but there certainly was plain living. I fancy many of my companions could tell woeful tales of Friday codfish and of cold mutton, and of the monotonous sequence of the fare. There was no bathroom: each of us had his cold tub in the morning in his own room. The more cynical of them might say on looking back that it was no wonder that the Vicar lived on the profits he made as a lodging-house keeper. Certainly that was true. Practically the whole income went in paying these exiguous stipends; and my only means of existence were this small profit and the fifty pounds a year I received from my Fellowship at All Souls, to which most generously that beloved College had re-elected me when I left Magdalen.

"They were all," Lang wrote of his curates, "what is called 'public school' and University men. Almost all had been trained at Cuddesdon or at Wells." The tradition of muscular Christianity was maintained by a clerical cricket Eleven who were no mean adversaries. Once on the Portsmouth Ground they defeated the Channel Fleet; and another match they drew with the Shropshires, then the crack cricketing Regiment of the Army. At work or at play they turned out a good team. "No leader of a parish ever had a more lively, eager, hard-working and loyal band of comrades."

The curates, on their side, respected him a lot and feared him a little. Lang, probably purposely, kept his relations with them on a formal footing. They called him "Sir," and when they wanted to see him about anything, made appointments as though they were parishioners. Among themselves they sometimes laughed at his little ways, the diplomatic guns which he laid with such care and his unconcealed taste for the society of the important. They thought that he was too often absent from the parish on outside work of different kinds, and that his intention to climb to the top of the ladder was too plain even to be questioned. But such criticisms as they sometimes voiced among themselves were hushed by their admiration for his remarkable powers of oratory and administration. Even when most conscious of his human weaknesses, they never doubted his greatness. They were even a little alarmed by it. His persuasiveness, when he was set upon something, was almost irresistible; and whether he was sweeping a man into Orders or arranging some detail in the parish, they felt a battle with him was lost before it was fairly begun.

The Vicarage had another inmate to whom Lang pays a passing tribute.

This was James, the only dog I ever possessed or ever will possess. He was an Aberdeen terrier, of a good pedigree. He came with me from Magdalen. He threw himself with zest into parish life. He was most regular at the Vicarage prayers. His special delight was to accompany me when I gave Communion to sick persons, and his behaviour on these occasions was most devout. He was wont to retire under the bed in the sick-room for his own devotions. I sent him to Cuddesdon for a term, and he returned more than ever addicted to pious practices. Unfortunately, when I had made an oratory at the Vicarage, and he presented himself, as had been his wont, for prayers, I had to tell him that he must not enter. When he looked "Why?" I was rash enough to quote from the Book of Revelation, "Without are dogs." He gave a grunt of protest. Soon after, the first chapter of Revelation was the appointed second lesson on a Sunday evening. I went to the lectern in church to read it. Suddenly there came from the distant porch a short, sharp bark. The verger told me that James entered during the Magnificat, and that when I said, "Here beginneth the first chapter of the Book of Revelation," he emitted his bark of protest, to show, of course, what he thought of that book; and that having given his testimony he quietly retired. I have never heard of any other dog who knew the Church Calendar! This was the end of James's Church life. Deprived of Church privileges, it seemed, by the Holy Scriptures, he took to evil ways. He would vanish for days and return from these orgies "smelling 'orrid" and with bloodshot eyes. As he was no longer fit company in a Vicarage, I banished him to the country, to Norfolk, and there, alas! he ended his days as a victorious fighter and poacher. No wonder that, with this sad record, I have never undertaken the responsibility of another dog.

Lang arrived in Portsea early in June. On his first Sunday he read himself in, "making some comments on the Thirty-Nine Articles—poor things," as he told his mother. That afternoon he catechised over 1500 children and in the evening preached to a huge congregation. After the long interregnum plenty of work awaited the new Vicar, and at the same time he wanted to plan his policy. After a quick look round he decided that his predecessor had had a firm hold on the loyalty of the middle-aged, but that—in his later years at any rate—the young men had almost entirely eluded him. Here, for a start, was work very much to Lang's taste. While he thought that there was "a general want of depth and devotion in the atmosphere," he acknowledged that he had inherited from Jacob "great heartiness, much sincerity, and a strong sense that people and parson must work together." The churchmanship was not the kind to which he was accustomed. Jacob's church, it used to be said, had made a Churchman of him, but not, evidently, a High Churchman, for the services were conducted with a minimum of ceremony. Lang decided at once that while on the points that mattered he must stand firm, on what he regarded as the non-essential he would be tolerant, patient, and "quietly teach."

When I was appointed, rumours spread in the parish that the new Vicar was a dangerous High Churchman and Ritualist. While I was still at Magdalen I received a document signed by the churchwardens (these good friends were afterwards very repentant) and a host of parishioners revealing these suspicions and remonstrating against any changes in the services. As they had never even seen me, I confess I was annoyed, and my reply to the churchwardens was that I had read no other name than theirs and had destroyed the document! The first meeting of a sort of Church Council revealed how general were these suspicions. I think I dispelled most of them, though I made no secret of my position. There was one change against which they were adamant. The candles on the altar must not be lit! I told them plainly that in my teaching I must simply teach what I believed, but that in my ritual I would always be considerate towards the congregation. Result: the candles were not lit, and I never had a word of protest about my teaching.

But misgivings abounded in the town. One letter to a newspaper contained the statement that "the new Vicar was not ashamed to practise celibacy openly in the street"—a delightful phrase, afterwards shamelessly stolen by John Buchan in one of his novels. It so delighted me that I caused enquiries to be made and found it meant that I often crossed the road from the Vicarage to the Church in my cassock! The Protestants in the town, voiced by a good but fanatical incumbent called Lindsay Young, were always sniping; but there was never a breath of trouble in the church itself.

Afterwards Lang used to say that while he had been in many churches in many places, he had never known such an opportunity for the preacher as was offered by the congregation at Portsea. Normally he preached twice every Sunday, morning and evening, generally in consecutive courses, on the Gospels, the Epistles, the Prophets, the Creeds, the Sacraments, the Beatitudes, or the doctrine and history of the Church. That he should have combined a high and even standard of homiletics with so lavish an output is evidence both of his untiring industry and of his fertility of mind.

For preaching was only one of his duties. There were the manifold clubs and organisations of the parish, all of which required and received his attention. There was, as at Magdalen, the "strain of men." On one day, he told his mother, he had had thirty-five private interviews of twenty minutes each. At first at least, he found his new parishioners a little strange, without the forthrightness of Leeds or the youthful spirits of Magdalen. "They are not to me an easy or congenial folk," he wrote to one of his "boys" at Leeds. "I miss the freedom and frankness of the North." A new but agreeable duty was added by Magdalen which, with complimentary intention, transferred its College Mission from Shoreditch to a poor and squalid quarter of Portsea. Lang was delighted to have this link with the College.

He was also a chaplain to the local prison, going there every Saturday morning and at other times to visit special cases. He did not grudge a moment he spent on this work, which he always claimed had enlarged his knowledge of and faith in human nature. He has left a couple of stories of his prison experiences.

He was a young rascal from Southampton, aged about sixteen, always in trouble with the police, sent to prison again and again— these were the pre-Borstal days. In prison he was usually so ill-behaved that he had to suffer the punishment which the prison system in its wisdom imposed, that the only book he was permitted to read was the Bible. But the sharp-witted rascal read it hard. I wondered what he made of it. So once I found him reading the first part of Isaiah. I asked him what he thought of it. His reply surprised me: it showed he had discerned the real place of Isaiah as a national leader more truly than nine-tenths of regular Bible readers. "Well," he said, "I'd like to 'ave 'eard 'this 'ere chap on the Town 'All steps." Another time he was reading Ecclesiastes and this was his shrewd comment: "'E'd seen a deal o' life, the ole bloke 'as wrote that." But most surprising was what he once said. It was this: "When I read them names like Nebuchadnezzar, Chedorlaomer, Nebuzaradan, Belteshazzar and the like, I shut me eyes and I seem to see great shapes movin' before me." Great shapes—symbols of the great empires rising and falling in that old world; and this guttersnipe had the imagination to see them.

The other story showed how hard it was for a "criminal" to change his way of life.

There was a young housebreaker and pickpocket whom, as he had a long sentence, I saw very often. He was a really charming creature, good to look at, most frank and friendly. He had been born and had lived among "criminals" in the notorious region of Old Street. He had never intermingled with any other class. He had no inherited instincts of right and wrong. Once when I asked him if he never felt that it was wrong to pick people's pockets, he said that sometimes he thought it was odd to think what others probably thought of him. That was his nearest approach to conscience. He delighted in the exercise of his art of house-breaking and pocket-picking, and seemed to think it had been worth while to spend all but three in his last eight or nine years in prison, if only to enjoy his adventures. I once asked him to give a display of his skill. He placed me against the wall of his cell and said: "Suppose, sir, you're at Victoria Station looking at a time-table." Then he paced rapidly up and down the cell, constantly brushing against me as he passed. "That is the crowd," he said. Then, after a few minutes, he said, "Now look," and when I turned he showed me with a triumphant grin my purse, which he had extracted from my trousers pocket. . . .

Well, as the months passed and I had my weekly talks with him, he made it plain that he really wished to give up his old ways and companions. There was no sort of humbug about him. When his long sentence and my instruction were over, and he was at liberty, with his full desire I baptised him. But what was to be done with him? He had no education; he could scarcely read or write; but he was most intelligent. But he had one skilled craft in which he delighted for its own sake. Thus when I found him work as a labourer in a market garden, he was soon utterly bored. Then one of his former "pals" found him out and came to Portsmouth to win him back. Torn between memories and pleasures of his old life and the desires and weariness of the new, he came to see me and brought his "pal," a flashy young gentleman, overdressed and self-assured, evidently a prosperous thief. I sat between them at my table. I told my friend he must choose between us—the old life and its pleasures and the new life with its sacrifices and a new vision of what human life was meant to be. After a long pause he blurted out, with his face between his hands: "I want to go your way, sir, I do indeed; but"—and here sobs broke out—"I can't, I can't!" And he rose and flung himself out of the room with his rather perplexed "pal." I never saw him again. I only heard that after a month or two he had been sentenced to prison again—elsewhere.

But prison work was only a small part—perhaps smaller than in recollection it appeared to be—of Lang's work at Portsea.

"I always felt that he was greatest as a preacher and teacher," the Archbishop of York (a curate and afterwards himself Vicar of Portsea) wrote. "It is almost impossible to exaggerate the influence he exercised throughout the whole town by his Sunday sermons and the Men's Conferences. I have never heard such fine preaching; in the morning he usually preached for twenty minutes, in the evening for half an hour or more. He held the congregation literally spellbound. In the evening the church was packed, and before the doors were open often there was a small crowd waiting outside. The courses were occasionally very long: I think a course on Isaiah must have lasted about eighteen months, though he broke into this as occasion required for special sermons.

"The Men's Conference held in the afternoon was also very remarkable. He gave them of his best, though most of those who attended did not either belong to the Church or have any connexion with organised religion. On weekdays he had a very large Bible Class of women, attended possibly by two or three hundred; and in addition he gave full and careful teaching at his Confirmation Classes —there were twelve or fourteen of these, and they had to be attended by the junior members of the staff.

"He had great influence in the town, and on one occasion, on the eve of a Parliamentary election, possibly turned the scale: the Conservative candidate had accepted all the demands of the brewers, and Lang in his sermon made a vigorous protest, which was supposed to have affected—and probably did affect—a considerable number of votes.

"He was not a good visitor, and the ordinary parochial visitation he left to his curates. But there were special people over whom he took very great trouble. I remember one sick man whom he visited week after week over a long period of time."

Jacob had left a gap in his network of buildings and organisations. There was no large central institute or hall where meetings could be held. Lang sacrificed a part of the Vicarage field for a site and chose Sir Reginald Blomfield, who had built the church, as his architect. With some generous help from Lord Hambleden, son of the church's first benefactor, he then put up a large and convenient building which soon became so indispensable that no one could ever understand how the parish had once got on without it. Here, among other functions, was held the Men's Conference on every Sunday afternoon of spring, autumn and winter. Doctors, lawyers, sailors and dockyard workers would turn up from every quarter of Portsmouth, the average figure of attendance being about three hundred. Lang would open with an address on some such subject as the evidences of religion, and afterwards the audience might ask questions or make speeches. Although Lang owns that the Conference was a heaven-sent opportunity for every crank and bore in the city, he believed that it did them good, and their hearers no harm, to blow off steam in this way.

One afternoon I silenced an earnest and violent speaker by a cheap though very effective score, which was loudly applauded. I felt rather ashamed of it, and next Sunday, seeing the good man present, I told him that I wished to apologise to him for that cheap score and for the applause it won but did not deserve. He rose and said: "Well, sir, I've been at scores of debates, but I've never met the like of that; and if that's Christianity, it's the best proof of your religion that I've come across."

The Conference became very popular, and when Lang left, the members gave him a complete set of the *Dictionary of National Biography*.

Then there was the Royal Navy, with which Lang now became closely acquainted, and across the water, at Osborne, was the old Queen, very near the end of her long reign, but as keenly interested as ever in all that was happening. Lang's account of his visits to her and of his first associations with the Royal Family appears in the following chapter. In 1897 she kept her Diamond Jubilee. Lang went up to London and stayed with the Erskines for the day of the Service at St. Paul's—"*One felt the Empire*," he wrote—and then hurried back to Portsmouth for the local celebrations. He had filled the Vicarage with friends, to see the naval review, and there was a big Service of Thanksgiving at the church.

Two more years slipped by—almost imperceptibly in the routine and rush of work—and the South African War broke out, bringing new duties and in particular a seat on a Government Committee appointed to report on the overlapping of War Funds.

Lang did not have many dealings with his Bishop (Dr. Randall Davidson), and those he had were pleasant. Just after his appointment he had his first recorded meeting with the colleague of so many years and reported him "most kind, a charming mixture of Father and Brother in God, full of good advice and encouragement." Presently the Bishop was involved in the unhappy controversy with Fr. Dolling, of St. Agatha's, Landport, which ended in Dolling's departure from a notable ministry. Lang kept out of the dispute, the only judgment he passes on it being that "a circumspect Scot and an impulsive Irishman did not find it easy to understand each other." He had a profound admiration for Dolling as a parish priest, but if pressed, would probably have ventured the opinion that he might have shown a more accommodating spirit. Lang had his own difficulties with the "Protestant underworld," his chief antagonist being Mr. Lindsay Young, who once created a violent scene in the presence of the Bishop during a crowded meeting in the Town Hall on Church Extension.

Lang has left an account of another interruption of a rather different kind, when he was saved from acute embarrassment by the presence of mind and self-sacrificing spirit of the Superintendent of the Sunday School, Mr. G. Hellyer, an ex-Chief Petty Officer of the Navy.

One of the customary joint services of children from the whole parish was being held in the parish church. The church was crammed full of children, over 2000. Just as, during a hymn, I was leaving my place in the choir to enter the pulpit for my address, I saw a strange figure proceeding up the centre aisle. It was a woman, middle-aged, fantastically attired, prancing along like Madge Wild-fire (in *The Heart of Midlothian*) with smiles and mincing steps. The children were amazed. Just as I reached the chancel steps, I heard the good Hellyer asking her, "What do you want?" and her most disconcerting reply, "I want to kiss that man," pointing to me! What was I to do? If I retreated, I was sure she would follow me. If I advanced, she might embrace me before all the children. A most embarrassing moment! Suddenly Hellyer, with a broad smile on his quaint face, said to her: "Won't I do instead?" She smiled at him and said: "Well, I think you will." At once, with great gallantry, he gave her his arm and conducted her down the church while the hymn was closing. In the porch he gallantly kept his covenant; the lady retired, satisfied; and I was saved. In the vestry afterwards I thanked Hellyer for his self-sacrifice. He smiled and said: "Well, my New Year's resolution was, 'Try when you can to lubricate'; so that was my chance to do a little lubricating."

For most of his time at Portsea Lang was, it seemed, doing the work of two men. His industry and energy were without bounds, and he was young enough to burn his candle at both ends without harm to his health. His daily programme was so crowded that on any day it appeared impossible to insert a single extra engagement. Yet he was always ready to take on a new job, to accept an invitation to preach or to sit on a committee. Occasionally he even found time for a little amusement. He was fond of sailing, and when he could, which was not often, would race in the Solent with naval friends like Sir Michael Culme-Seymour, the Naval Commander-in-Chief, and "Rosy" Wemyss, afterwards Lord Wester-Wemyss.

> At the start the latter would always ask for a dispensation for any language he might use during the existence of the race, and at the finish I had to tell him that he had far exceeded my dispensation.

Lang stayed at Portsea for five years, and long afterwards could still see himself "standing on the big platform-like pulpit looking down on the great congregation, or walking swiftly along that ugly Fratton Road." His time there was by no means unhappy, even when contrasted with the vanished delights of Magdalen; and he was probably conscious that experience of the kind Portsea offered was essential to the career which stretched before him. For by now he knew most surely—had he ever doubted?—that he was destined for high office in the Church. One morning he and some members of the staff were discussing episcopal signatures, and Lang, catching up a piece of paper and writing 'Cosmo Cantuar' on it, asked, "How does this look?"

Such incidents should not be taken too seriously: they were the sort of story people were beginning to tell about Lang. That the idea of an exalted place in the Church was not entirely strange to him, at any rate in his lighter moments, is implied by a jesting letter he wrote in 1893 to "the Prophet," Canon Simpson, his colleague at Leeds, in which he subscribed himself "C. G. Cantuar." Yet while he cannot have been without some expectation of coming promotion, he was undoubtedly surprised when, one morning in March 1901, a telegram arrived from Sir Schomberg Macdonnell, Lord Salisbury's private secretary. "Announcement of your appointment," he read, "will be in the Press on Monday." In reply to a mystified telegram from Lang, the puzzle was solved. Lord Salisbury had written to offer him the appointment of Suffragan Bishop of Stepney and Canon of St. Paul's, in succession to Dr. Winnington

Ingram, who had just been translated to the See of London. Unfortunately Lord Salisbury had addressed his letter to Langport,[1] and after many days it was returned to him through the Dead Letter Office, "adorned with the stamps of many vain experiments." Lord Salisbury had then confessed himself at the end of his resources, and so remained until the telegram of enquiry reached him.

Lang learned that the idea had originated with the new Bishop of London, who had especially asked that Lang might follow him in Stepney. The incident sheds an interesting light on the casual way in which Lord Salisbury conducted his official correspondence. Lang was also a little piqued by the readiness with which the Prime Minister assumed that the offer would be accepted. Macdonnell's telegram did not ask Lang if he consented: it told him that the appointment was about to be announced. In fact, he probably never thought seriously of refusing it; although he went through the form of consulting his Bishop, who said, "I'm afraid you must go." It would be painful to leave his friends in Portsea and, as he wrote to his mother, "doubly hard to follow Ingram, who has been the idol of the East End." But any doubts he had were on the surface: deep down in him he was conscious of powers that only awaited to be released. Now this opportunity had come: he was only thirty-seven and he was to be a Bishop. Yet with all his innate confidence, the prospect awed as well as attracted him, for it was no light duty he was undertaking. "I must have some quiet time," he wrote to his mother, "to prepare for an event so unspeakably solemn as consecration to the office of a Bishop in the Church of God."

[1] He was probably thinking of Landport, the district of Portsmouth in which Portsea Vicarage lay, and the name of the Vicar changed it in his mind to Langport.

Chapter XIV

QUEEN VICTORIA AND THE ROYAL FAMILY

THE Vicar of Portsea had a Royal neighbour at Osborne in the Isle of Wight, where Queen Victoria was in the last years of her long reign. One day in January 1898 Lang received a letter from Lady Mallet, one of the Queen's Ladies-in-Waiting, conveying to him a command to preach in the chapel at Osborne on the following Sunday. He obeyed, of course, and subsequently the invitation was repeated—"Indeed I think I went twice every year until she died"; when, having been appointed one of the Queen's chaplains, he had a part in the funeral arrangements. The association with the Royal Family, which began in these days, lasted for as long as he lived.

Lang left very full notes of his visits to Osborne. In fact, he wrote two separate versions of them. The first account is in the form of a diary and was written while he was at Portsea; the date of the second is 1943. Both are supplemented by some very long descriptive letters to his mother, which probably served as one of the sources of the second account. For reasons of space it is clearly impossible, even if it were desirable, to reproduce all this material, which almost make a book by themselves; so, with much abbreviation, a collated account, drawing on all three sources, is offered here. So much is indicated as necessary because, whatever view may be taken by others, Lang set a high value on these experiences. "I shall ever," he wrote, "regard these visits to the great Queen as among the highest privileges of my life."

The first invitation—in January 1898—was to dine with the Household on Saturday night and to preach the next morning. Lang had been warned by the Bishop of Winchester that he might be asked to stay for Sunday night too and have dinner with the Queen. This extended invitation was usual, but was by no means a matter of course; no doubt it depended on the Royal opinion of the sermon preached in the morning. Lang, however, took no chances and arrived at Osborne with knee breeches and silk stockings.

In other respects he was so ill-equipped for the visit that he had to borrow freely from his curates—a tall hat from one, an umbrella from another, and a robes-bag from a third.

On Saturday night, after receiving some necessary instructions in etiquette, he dined with the men of the Household. Breakfast next day was at half-past nine, followed at eleven by the Service.

Punctually at eleven the door opens—"The Queen"—all rise. I was conscious of a little black figure supported by an Indian servant and followed by children. The little figure sat down at once, opposite the priest, and scanned the text placed on her table, Princess Beatrice and her children surrounding her!

The Service then started. Liturgically, Lang comments, it was "a somewhat mangled affair," but gained "dignity through its circumstances." Lang preached on the text: "Lord, to whom shall we go? Thou hast the words of eternal life." He had written out his sermon, but did not use the script. "I never can read a sermon," he wrote to his mother; though there is not the least doubt that he could and often did read one. Later he found that the Queen generally sent afterwards to ask for the manuscript, and when, as sometimes happened later, he spoke from notes, he had to sit down and try to reconstruct what he had actually preached.

He had arranged to spend the rest of the day with the Rector of Whippingham, but just before luncheon he had the Queen's command to dine with her that evening and to stay on till Monday. So, after preaching at the evening service at Whippingham, he returned to Osborne for dinner at nine o'clock.

I can never forget the impression made when, before dinner, the door opened, the page announced in a loud voice, "The Queen," and she entered, so small in stature, yet clothed with such unconscious but unmistakable dignity. I have been present at many great State occasions during the last half century, but I do not think that I have ever been so immediately and deeply impressed as by that simple entry of "The Queen."

The party was quite small, consisting of Royal relatives, a few people in waiting, and Lang himself. "The dinner was exactly like any private family party, except that, of course, the Queen did not actually speak except to the royalties next her." They were waited on by "a supply of very stout and somewhat bibulous-looking Scotch menservants, two in kilts, the rest in scarlet, with an Indian to boot."

After dinner the Queen sent for Lang and talked to him for twenty minutes or half an hour.

It was difficult to realise that the little figure over which one bent, with the soft kind voice and simple manner, was the Queen and Empress whom a year ago one had watched passing through crowded and jubilant London, the centre of the greatest pageant in our history, the embodied spirit of the great Empire. Certainly she has the royal art of putting people at their ease. The grace and simplicity of her manner, the native kindliness of her smile made nervousness vanish.

With one exception all the portraits and photographs of her give a very one-sided picture of the expression of her face. No doubt in repose and on great occasions it was severe and masterful. But in conversation, unless she was bored or annoyed, it was lit up by a very charming smile. The one exception to which I have referred was a photograph taken of the scene at the steps of St. Paul's Cathedral on the day of the Diamond Jubilee. When the huge crowd surrounding the steps began to roar "God Save the Queen!" she turned towards it with a radiant smile, like a sudden shaft of sunlight. Happily it was just at that moment that the photograph was taken.

Moreover, when she was amused—and she had a very real if very simple sense of humour and fully relished any good story or any amusing turn of phrase—her voice would break into a soft, gentle, and very delightful laugh, a sort of gurgle of pleasure.

Well, at that first conversation with her she asked many questions about my parish and the way in which it was managed. And here a fragment of the conversation may be worth recording, as somehow —I know not how—it got into the Press in many versions and has been repeated there *ad nauseam* ever since. I had been speaking of my fifteen or sixteen curates who lived with me.

Queen: "Don't you think you ought to marry? A wife would be so great a help."

Myself: "I fear I cannot afford one: my curates cost too much."

Queen: "But surely a wife would be worth more than one or two curates."

Myself: "No doubt, ma'am, but there is this difference: if a curate proves to be unsatisfactory I can get rid of him. A wife is a fixture."

Queen (laughing): "I can see you have a very poor idea of matrimony."

Then she asked much about the alleged lack of religion and the Socialism of the working classes. I told her what I had observed, of good rather than of evil. "But," she said—and I remember still the simplicity, almost the naïveté, with which she looked up and asked —"all this is combined, is it not, with great personal loyalty to the Throne?" Of course, I could only reply that whatever may have been thought about the Throne, there was no doubt about loyalty to the Queen.

At about eleven she rose, gave an arm to the Indian servant, and with a stick in the other hand passed out of the room. "The Queen will now spend perhaps two hours writing letters," remarked Lord Edward Pelham Clinton, the Master of the Household.

The experience had not been as alarming as Lang had feared it might be.

She had the reputation of being a very formidable person. Indeed, I remember a curious episode on another visit. An officer in the South African War had been distinguished by such conspicuous bravery that he had been, by the Queen's own express wish, summoned to Osborne to receive his Victoria Cross from her own hands. But as he approached the door beyond which the great Queen was awaiting him, all his valour failed. He fainted and had to be "gingered up" in order to face the ordeal.

I remember on another occasion watching an eminent person . . . accustomed to all the demands of public and social life, whom the Queen, rather against her will, had invited to dine, being brought up to speak to her. It was at once plain that owing to his nervousness the conversation was "making very heavy weather." Very soon there was the very slightest droop of the Royal mouth, the very slightest but stiffest inclination of the Royal head. But these signs sufficed to say, "This is enough and—never again!"; and the poor man retired discomfited.

Lang evidently made a good impression, as the Queen's journal contains the following entry under the date January 30th, 1898:

Spoke to Mr. Lang some time after dinner. He is a very interesting and clever man, a Scotchman, and was at Oxford. He has a very hard time at Portsea, having 40,000 parishioners, and the population is not very pleasant, particularly the artisans, who are very difficult, sceptical, and full of prejudices. The sailors are true and warm-hearted, but, as well as the soldiers, somewhat difficult to manage. Mr. Lang has thirteen curates to assist him, and they all live together.

Lang's next summons was in August. He was on holiday at Largie and by some mistake the command did not reach him until the Wednesday before the Sunday on which he was to preach. This time he was asked to stay from Saturday till Monday, and hurrying south found a large party at Osborne—several royalties, the Prime Minister (Lord Salisbury), and the Cranbornes. On Saturday night he was unwell, with internal pains, and did not sleep at all. This was the more disconcerting because he had omitted to prepare a sermon, hoping for two quiet hours on Sunday morning, and when it came felt too stale and jaded to put anything on paper. In the end, he says, he gave up the attempt and preached extempore on "The Name of Jesus," the day being August 7th. In the afternoon he walked and talked with the guests, and after preaching once more at Whippingham attended the Royal dinner-party.

After dinner he talked with Princess Beatrice and the Duchess of Connaught, "a very straight and good woman and moreover a good Churchwoman." They discoursed on the desirability of joining the work of Nurses with the discipline of the Religious Life and the need for an order of Mission preachers. "Lord Salisbury joined the conversation and threw in some characteristic touches of good-natured sarcasm, which the less subtle-minded Princesses seemed not wholly to understand." In fact, Lang adds, they appeared to be rather afraid of the Prime Minister.

The conversation was interrupted by the Queen's summons to Lang.

I told the Queen that I had been reading a sermon by Principal John Caird delivered before her in Crathie Church [1]; and greatly daring I added that I had noted that the sermon must have lasted at least three-quarters of an hour, whereas I had been told that sermons delivered before her in England must not exceed twenty minutes. She took this with great good humour and said drily: "When English dignitaries and clergy can preach as well as the Scottish ministers I will let them go on as long as they like." We agreed Mr. John Caird was probably the most powerful preacher to whom we

[1] The parish church of Balmoral.

had ever listened, though she preferred the broad human sympathy of her favourite Norman Macleod.

On the differences between English and Scottish religion she said: "I like the solemnity of the Scottish Communion. In England people seem to treat the Sacrament too easily. Why, I am told that many receive it as often as once a week. This seems to me a very mechanical view of the Sacraments. I wonder how much preparation they can give. For myself, three months seems not too long to prepare." I tried to show the other side, though I did not think it necessary to say that in *my* Church there was a daily Celebration! Yet was there not something worth pondering in those no doubt very one-sided words?

The third visit was in January 1899. This time the Empress Frederick was staying in the house.

It was interesting and amusing to watch the way in which Mother and Daughter, *Queen* and *Empress*, settled the question of precedence. *Both* sat at the head of the round table; at the end both rose together. The Empress Frederick, as Empress, went out first, but as daughter and guest turned round as she went and curtseyed to the Queen!

In the drawing-room I had a long and very touching conversation with the Empress. A few days before she had paid a private visit to Portsea Parish Church, the foundation-stone of which she had laid ten years ago; so that the ice had already been broken. She began to talk at once about her sorrows. I do not think that I ought to put down even here all that she said, for I am sure it was not meant for other ears. Her words about the change in her destiny—the difficulties of a woman ambitious to rule, prepared for it by long thought and study, versed intimately in all European affairs, and now excluded from all authority—the sadness of "separations from the living far harder to bear than even separation from the dead"—the loneliness of her life, "left more and more alone as one draws nearer the last gate, where there is room for nothing but the solitary soul to pass"—all were inexpressibly touching. Her emotion was very real; and the tears were in her eyes and on her cheeks. It was the talk of one of whom sorrow is an abiding companion. It seemed so hopeless to *say* anything to one so high in position, yet so humbled by sorrow: it seemed best to let her speak: what feeble words one did say did not seem to offend, as well they might have done. She has a most

134

wonderful simplicity of speech and manner, and a perfect ease . . .
disturbed only by a curious nervous habit of moving continually in
a side direction as she speaks. It seemed difficult to believe that this
simple-feeling, simple-speaking woman was one of whose cleverness
and influence even Bismarck was afraid.

This conversation was followed by some talk with Princess Beatrice,
who exchanged with him books of devotion and thoughts about Prayers
for the Dead. "The Princess showed that she really was in many ways
an instructed Anglican." The Queen then sent for him. She spoke of
her love for Balmoral and of her attachment to the Church of Scotland,
undiminished by the incident she went on to relate.

It happened once that the people of Crathie Church in the election
of a Minister had rejected the Queen's wish about a candidate and
had elected one of their own choice. "It is the only place," she said,
smiling, "where the Queen's wish seems to count for nothing. However, I determined to show that at least I could submit and be civil."
Then she added some rather remarkable words: "After all, it made
one feel that if people who depended on me for everything could be
so independent, I could trust them all the more fully." I could not
help reflecting how different the history of this island might have
been if Charles I had had the same respect for the ecclesiastical independence of the Scots.

On these visits the Queen talked much of Scotland, and once,

Knowing my devotion to the Highlands, she asked why I never went
to her own Aberdeenshire Highlands. I replied—again *very* greatly
daring—that there was one reason which I could not mention in her
presence. "That is all the more reason why I should know it," she
said. It was, I was bold enough to say, because that part of Scotland
was associated with the final defeat of Prince Charles Edward, for
whom I had a sentimental loyalty. "Oh," she said, "you need not
be afraid to speak about him. His history has always touched me
deeply. I will never allow my gentlemen or ladies to speak of him
as 'the Pretender,' but only as 'Prince Charlie' or 'the Chevalier.'
Indeed, I added his name to the names of one of my sons." (Prince
Leopold.[1])
"Then may I keep my sentimental loyalty?"

[1] This is not correct. The Duke of Albany was Leopold George Duncan Albert.

"Certainly," she said with a laugh; "provided, of course, that it is strictly sentimental."

Regularly twice a year the summons came. One visit took place just after Black Week in the South African War, when we had suffered reverses at Stormberg, Magersfontein and Colenso. He had two long conversations with the Queen.

She had special maps prepared on a large scale to suit her eyesight, and with these she followed every word of the despatches. She would not rest satisfied till she had located every farmstead where a skirmish had taken place. She took the warmest interest in all messages of loyalty which came from different parts of the army. I remember at dinner a telegraph message came in from Kimberley, then under siege. It was a few words of fervent and cheerful loyalty. "The dear fellows!" said the Queen, in just the tones in which a mother would hear the greetings of her absent sons. In conversation she said something worth remembering which explains the sort of instinctive sympathy which had sprung up between the army and the Queen. "When I was a little girl," she said, "I remember that they used to laugh at me because of my excitement when soldiers passed. I remember very well wishing that when I grew up I might be known as the Soldiers' Queen. I have had that wish ever since."

Certainly it has been abundantly fulfilled. It seemed strange to think that this resolute and determined old lady, keen and alert about all the battles, was the Queen who was said to have made up her mind that she would never sanction a war. I can never forget the tone and manner with which she said : "It was now not only necessary: it is just. It must, it shall be fought out to the end. These brave fellows shall not be allowed to suffer in vain. There is no place for panic"—or the way in which she stamped her foot as she said : "I will hear of no complaints against my generals till the war is over. They have my confidence. They will do their utmost." It was touching indeed to look down on this simple little old lady and to feel that here was *Britannia at bay*! All the strength and self-control and determination of the Empire seemed really and literally to be personified in her. She dealt very faithfully with President Kruger. "The man's parade of religion annoys me. I don't think much of a religion which is used to justify such self-aggrandisement and wilfulness and corrupt government."

"What I most dislike about President Kruger," she went on to remark, "is the way he brings his politics into his religion and his religion into his politics. I am bound to say that in Mr. Gladstone also I disliked this mixture of politics and religion, which"—with emphasis—"is of course quite intolerable."

These reflexions led her on to John Morley, whose character she admired, while lamenting many of his opinions. James Bryce, whom she also greatly respected, was shaky about the war; on the other hand, Lord Curzon's despatches from India were giving her much pleasure. She went on to comment upon the Church of England, which was passing through one of its recurring crises, and upon the policy of the Bishops.

The Bishops could not be surprised if men resented any sudden forbidding of practices which had long been tolerated. More than once she had plainly expressed her concern about the consequences of a policy of *laissez faire*. It must never be forgotten that, whether we call it "conviction" or "prejudice," the one thing which the mass of the English people would never stand was any belittling or apparent undoing of the Reformation.

This was one of many conversations Lang had with the Queen about religion, sometimes upon the subjects with which he had dealt in sermons and sometimes upon the ecclesiastical troubles of the time.

Her position might, I suppose, be described in ecclesiastical language as "Broad Church." On some subjects, such as Prayers for the Dead, she differed widely from the point of view of ordinary Protestantism. She knew, and was very suspicious about, the Oxford Movement and its followers. But there could be no sort of doubt as to the sincerity and simplicity of her personal faith and trust in God.

Lang visited the Queen for the last time in the autumn of 1900.

I could see a very marked change. At dinner she was very silent and at times seemed to have some difficulty in keeping awake. When I talked with her after dinner, she was less bright than usual and was plainly soon tired. Though we did not then realise it, the shadow of the approaching end was drawing near.

Looking back, Lang recalled one touching memory of her.

I had been telling her about the drowning of a sailor in one of the Royal yachts, and of the poverty in which his wife, one of my parishioners, had been left. Next morning I was summoned to the Queen's private room. She was, as usual, sitting writing letters or signing papers at her desk.

"I want," she said, "to give you something from me to help the poor sailor's widow you told me of last night." Then she took a bundle of keys from a girdle, just like any ordinary housekeeper, went to a cupboard and opened it. The contents were curious—papers, parcels, and chiefly toys kept for presents to her grandchildren. In one corner was a small tin box, like a schoolboy's cash-box. Fumbling somewhat owing to her shortsightedness, she opened it, and very carefully took out five sovereigns. "Please give these," she said, "to that poor woman. But," she added with a whimsical smile, "you mustn't tell Sir Fleetwood Edwards" (the Comptroller of the Privy Purse). And this was the Queen-Empress!

"It has been an anxious Sunday," Lang wrote in his diary on January 20th, 1901. The old Queen was dying, and swiftly the end came.

It was with a profound shock that the people heard that the Queen had passed away. It seemed impossible to realise that the reign of over sixty years, which had meant so much in the destiny of her country, of the Empire, of the world, was over. Immediately after her death I was asked, as one of her Chaplains, to go over to Osborne and to give what help I could to the Bishop of Winchester (Randall Davidson) in making arrangements for the Funeral.

Immediately on arrival I was taken to the temporary chapel where the Queen's body lay. My first impression was of the stillness of the Guardsmen standing around the bier with heads bent and rifles reversed. They seemed to be statues representing the sorrow of the Empire and the solemnity of death. In the middle of a mass of flowers, under a white pall with a small crown at its head, was the coffin where the Queen's body was lying.

As there was no one else in the chapel (except the Guard) I was able to have some minutes of quiet thought and prayer, realising what the passing of the great Queen meant. Soon after, as I was talking with the Bishop of Winchester in one of the corridors about the religious services for the Funeral, a small erect figure, quietly dressed, came up. I thought it was somebody's servant until the Bishop turned round and bowed. Then I noticed the upturned ends of the moustache and realised that it was the German Emperor. He very humbly apologised for his intrusion, asked if he could be of any help, and said that his own wish was to be useful and to show his veneration for his grandmother. I was told afterwards how tactful and useful he had been. Here is one instance. It was said by some of her family that the Queen's wish had been that any pictures in the temporary chapel should be *domestic*, of herself with her husband and children—a very characteristic trait. Others thought that this would be inappropriate and that the pictures should be of sacred subjects. It was the Emperor who suggested that the points might be combined by putting on the walls pictures representing the Holy Family and Our Lord in the home life of Nazareth. And this was done.

The funeral followed.

It must have left an indelible impression on those who in any way witnessed it. I can only write about the scene on the Solent and at Portsmouth. I went to the Fort at the entrance of the harbour. The two long shores converging on the harbour-bar were crowded by masses of people, all in black. There was the strangest silence I have ever known. It could literally be *felt*. It was so deep and tense that when two children talked at a distance of some 300 yards it seemed an intolerable intrusion. The German Emperor afterwards said that nothing of the kind had ever impressed him so deeply as that wedge of black silent humanity through which the Royal yacht passed into the harbour.

It was a beautiful day, a day of summer rather than of January, the sky clear and the sea blue. Suddenly the silence was broken. A sound smote upon the heart. It was the sound of the guns from Osborne across the water telling that the Queen's body was being saluted by the Fleet. Then, through the long lines of battleships, stretching in a curve from Cowes to Portsmouth, came the little yacht *Alberta* bearing the body. The yacht was preceded by six torpedo-destroyers moving black and silent like dark messengers of Death sent to summon the Queen. The *Alberta*—small, slight, but dignified, passing through the huge ironclads, seemed strangely like the Queen herself. I shall never forget the booming of the great guns as the little ship with its precious freight moved slowly down the lines. The sound was varied only by the strains of Chopin's Funeral March, played by each ship's band as the body passed. Then —the most moving thing of all—just as the *Alberta* entered the harbour, the sun set in a rich glow of tranquil glory. I heard an old General behind me cough, clear his throat, and say as it were to himself, "No one will persuade me that Providence didn't arrange *that* !" So the sun set over the haven where the Queen would be.

Next morning, very early, about 7 a.m., I went out to the *Alberta* as she lay off the Clarence Pier with the Admiral (Sir Michael Culme-Seymour) in his pinnace. It was a very different day, raining, cold and squally. After robing in a cabin I had to wait some time till all the Royalties assembled. The last to arrive was the German Emperor. His arrival was characteristic : out from the side of the great *Hohenzollern* shot a steam launch. The Admiral, who was standing beside me, said : "Yes, that is the Emperor steering; he expects to bring her alongside; he doesn't know the tide or the currents." On came the launch, swaying hither and thither with the currents, but with admirable precision and without the loss of a second the Emperor steered her exactly alongside, threw aside the rudder-cords, and stepped up the steps looking every inch an Emperor.

Only the Royal Family with the Kaiser were present at the service. At its close, when all had left for the train and before the sailors came to carry out the bier, I was the only witness of an episode which I have every reason to remember vividly. The new King, Edward VII, a man always of warm emotion, paused for a minute or two and knelt silently at the foot of the coffin. The Emperor, turning round, saw this, and quietly knelt at the King's side. The German Emperor and the English King kneeling together, side by side, by the body of Queen Victoria—how could I fail to think, "What effect may this have upon the future relations of England and Germany ?"

Thirteen years later, in an unhappy moment, this memory was to bring Lang into great trouble.

Then followed an experience which moved me more deeply than I can express. It had been arranged that officers of the Navy and Army of, I think, or above the rank of Captain in the one case and Colonel in the other, might volunteer to form a Guard of Honour lining the long covered passage from the yacht to the train. It fell to me to walk in my robes immediately in front of the coffin. I could therefore see the faces of these men who had served or fought for the Queen in all parts of the world, as they turned towards her body to give their last salute. I do not think there was one of them who had not tears in his eyes, and certainly there were tears in mine. . . .

The train glided slowly out of the station; and Queen Victoria passed out of sight.

*　　*　　*　　*　　*　　*

The visits to Osborne introduced Lang to other members of the Royal Family. He had long and intimate talks with the Empress Frederick, Princess Beatrice, Princess Christian, Princess Victoria, and the Duke and Duchess of Connaught. "They make the most of a parson when they have him," he told his mother; and no doubt they soon discovered the sympathy with which he listened and the wisdom and comfort of his counsel.

He also made the acquaintance of the Prince of Wales (King Edward VII) and his family. During the South African War Lang had written a letter to the *Times* about the overlapping of military and naval relief funds. The letter made a stir, and presently Lang was summoned to a conference at Marlborough House, over which the Prince of Wales presided, and later to serve on a Committee which was to deal with the whole matter. The Prince took a strong interest in the administration of war funds and, at the suggestion of the Duke of York, invited Lang to Sandringham, to stay and to preach on the Sunday appointed as a National Day of Intercession for the War.

Lang travelled down on the Royal special train and was presented to the Prince in the waiting-room at Wolfercot Station.

The Prince summoned me and said: "I think this is the first time you have been my guest at Sandringham. All the others know their way about. I am going to give myself the pleasure of taking you with me in my own carriage." This to the most obscure of his guests —surely the thought of a great gentleman.

The informality of Sandringham contrasted with the rather rigid etiquette of Osborne.

There was all the ease and homely comfort of an ordinary large country house. After tea the Duke of York came in and embarked on a lively discussion on the War Charitable Fund (on which I had written an article in the *Nineteenth Century*). The Prince arranged for the Form of Service next day, taking earnest apparent interest in it. Mr. Goschen arrived later, very pleasant for me, as I had known him and his so long and so well. The Princess had a cold and was unable to come to dinner. We dined at a round table, the Duke of York and his Equerry, Derek Keppel, joining the party. After a short time in the drawing-room the Prince took me to the smoking-room. There he smoked endless cigars and talked most affably to everybody on all sorts of subjects.

Next morning the snow lay thick upon the ground. The service at the little church of Sandringham was at twelve (11.30, the time being kept half an hour fast of set purpose). The Prince and Princess were there with the Duke of York and the two Princesses, Goschen, etc. Unfortunately snow came on and made the church very dark. I had foolishly written a good deal of what I meant to say. So the darkness put me out, as I could not see to read. This spoiled the sermon (it was on much the same lines as the Osborne one), so far as I was concerned. But at least it was a strange experience to have spoken on two consecutive Sundays on the great subject of the War —a war which has meant so much to the whole Empire—to the Queen, the Heir-Apparent and the Heir-Presumptive of the Crown (sic): possibly three generations of Kingship. How odd that such an experience should have fallen to an obscurity like me!

At lunch I sat next the Princess of Wales. She is certainly still very beautiful and looks marvellously young. I could not see any signs of "art" in the picture, except doubtless the masses of fair hair: the complexion, wonderfully clear, seemed simply admirably tended. But the charm of her beauty is spoiled by her deafness: it is not serious deafness, but it is enough to make talking, especially to such an exalted Personage, difficult and to produce in her a certain diffidence, almost awkwardness of manner. . . . I had to be both discreet and faithful in her very bitter remarks on the Charity Organisation Society. She may well dislike it and, good lady! her estimable spirit of charity ignores its first principles. Miss Knollys told me it was simply heartbreaking to know the ways in which she was duped by beggars of all descriptions: the kindness of heart is out of all proportion to her discretion of head in discernment of human nature. She can't resist any highly pitched tale of distress or appeal to her heart.

After lunch, in spite of the snow, the Prince invited us to walk. The Duke of York joined us and I spent most of the time with one or other of them. They were both charmingly kind, and simple and genuine in their kindness. We went with all the religious conscientiousness of a Sunday walk through all the stables, visiting each of the stud. The great Persimmon [1] received a special visit. His Magnificence dwells in a separate house padded with yellow leather and carefully regulated in temperature, with his own establishment of tutors and governors. He is a thing of beauty certainly, and it was amusing to watch the disdainful and complacent pride with which he treated his Royal Master. We then went through the magnificent conservatories built of Persimmon's Derby winnings, under the guidance of the inevitable intelligent Scottish gardener. . . . Returned to tea, dispensed by the Princess. . . . The little York children were there—quite fascinating. I played with little Prince Albert and stuck him up on the top of a pillar, but he was evidently not accustomed to such robust amusement!

The Duke of York then took me to York Cottage to see the Duchess (who would not come out, as she was expecting another Royal babe). She was, as usual, very pleasant, in spite of a certain shyness. I like her personality very much, very sincere and genuine. They showed me over their little house with a quite charming and almost naïve keenness. It might have been a curate and his wife in their new house! The Princess was at dinner. I sat next Princess Victoria, who was most lively and original. We discovered a great common (sentimental) devotion to Prince Charlie. She was most amusing about the boredom of Royal life and about her various and unconventional ways of escaping from it. One episode of the dinner . . . was an experimental discussion between the Duke and his mother as to whether the mites in a Stilton cheese could move! . . .

The Prince is evidently a man of the widest interest, large, though perhaps not deep, knowledge of affairs, and very shrewd judgment of the worth of men. He spoke very highly of the late Bishop of London (Creighton), specially praising the sermons he preached to "my difficult nephew," the German Emperor. . . . I have rarely enjoyed a country visit more. . . .

The Prince I saw again repeatedly at Marlborough House during all the delicate and disappointing negotiations concerning the War

---

[1] Winner of the Derby in 1896.

Funds, but that is another story. In these matters I found him very alert, prompt, punctual and dexterous on the surface of the subject, but showing admirable tact in discerning the limits of his own personal action.

★　　　★　　　★　　　★　　　★　　　★

At the outset of Lang's long friendship with the future King George V, when the latter, as Duke of York, was commanding the *Crescent*, the omens were far from propitious. Lang tells the story with the hope that it will be treated with "fitting discretion."

He (the Duke) was staying over a Sunday at Admiralty House. He had commanded me to preach at the Dockyard Chapel. The Collection was to be for the Korean Mission and the work of old Bishop Corfe, who had been a great naval chaplain. During the Saturday evening when I was preparing my sermon, a message came to me at the Vicarage (from dear, kind Lady Culme-Seymour) to the effect that during dinner H.R.H. had roundly denounced the loss of *Corfu* to the Navy and the futility of Missions, and had said in his warmth that if Lang were to preach on the subject next day, he thought he would go out. The message only decided me to change my sermon and to preach in defence of Christian Missions. At the Dockyard Chapel next day I began my discourse by saying bluntly: "I propose this morning to consider the obligation of Christian Missions overseas." I noticed that H.R.H. shifted restlessly in his pew, but I went on. After the service, as I went to Admiralty House for luncheon, I passed through the garden. H.R.H. was waiting for me. With characteristic frankness he at once said: "I believe you preached that sermon at me. I don't agree with it." I proceeded respectfully to indicate that it seemed to me that belief in the world-wide mission of Christianity was involved in being a Christian. "Then," said H.R.H., "you tell me that with my views I can't be a Christian?" I replied that I could only state the premises: it was for him to draw the conclusions. To which he retorted: "Well, I call that damned cheek," and left me. Needless to say, it was but a passing breeze; and I afterwards sent him the history of the Oxford Mission to Calcutta.

Certainly either the incident had been forgotten or Lang had been forgiven by the time of his visit to Sandringham.

With considerable abbreviation and the omission of a great deal of comment and reflexion, these accounts of Lang's early relations with the Royal Family are given much as he wrote them down. To some they may appear to disclose a streak of courtier and even of snob. In later years people often imputed to him this little weakness, enlarging upon it at the expense of finer qualities that should have outweighed it in their judgment. Lang himself seems to have been not unconscious of snobbery. When he became Archbishop, he was accustomed, as he motored to his summer retreat at Ballure, to spend a night or two at some of the great houses on the way; and he used to term this gilded pilgrimage "the Snob's Progress." That may have been the comment of the man in the stalls upon the man on the stage: it is certainly not a comment that any true snob would pass upon himself. Again, his notes continually allude to someone or other as one of his "dearest and closest friends," and it is to be observed that someone or other is very often Lord This or Lady That. Most of these allusions are omitted because the repetition is tiresome; but whatever the conclusion drawn, the fact remains that Lord This and Lady That were indeed his close friends and valued his friendship fully as much as he valued theirs.

If there is any substance in the charge, to make it one of snobbery and to leave it there were to do him less than justice. For him the social ascent was a necessary part in the play of the poor Scots boy who made good, of the drama—"From Woodlands Terrace to Lambeth Palace"—which one Lang was acting and the other Lang was watching. The contrast must be accentuated. The audience must be constantly reminded how strange and wonderful it was that an obscure youth from Glasgow should reach such remote and shining heights, should stay with Kings and Queens and call Earls and Countesses by their Christian names. The theatre made its demands and he complied.

There is perhaps this also to be said. Lang, like many of his fellow Scots, had a firm belief in the functional structure of society. "The rich man in his castle" is entitled to a meed of respect, not because he is a rich man and has a castle, but because he has been placed in a position of especial responsibility. This does not make him any better than "the poor man at his gate": rather it demands more from him and involves him in a sharper judgment; but the position does entitle him to an esteem above his fellows. Lang had none of the true snob's unlovely shame for a humble origin, in which rather he gloried, nor, of course, contempt for those who might be regarded as social inferiors. He had a genuine care for the poor and outcast, that "love of souls" which, when first he heard the phrase from Scott Holland, so puzzled him. He prized exceedingly his contacts with them; he threw himself whole-heartedly—at Leeds, at Portsea, and at Stepney most particularly—into the work of winning them; but probably he would not have conceded that, *ceteris paribus*, the friendship of a dustman was as delectable as that of a duke. Nor probably would most men, if the truth were told, though they might not avow their preference so plainly.

There are other senses, too, in which Lang's attitude was not snobbery, as the term is commonly understood. He had a strong feeling for the romantic, either in history or in contemporary life; as in history for the lost cause of the White Rose, so in contemporary life for the Royal Person, and all that Kingship represented. (In this he could have claimed the company of Sir Walter Scott and Lord Beaconsfield.) Monarchy meant something to him that it has ceased to mean to the majority in the modern world—not altogether to that world's advantage. The fervour with which he spoke was by no means uncommon in an age that has gone, though to our ears it may seem forced and unreal. Lang's loyalty had a religious as well as a romantic quality, and what he venerated so sincerely drew majesty and radiance from a high and sacred office. This is reflected in the reverence with which he writes of his relations with the Royal Family, and especially in that emotional response which emerges so clearly from his narrative of the solemn pageantry of Queen Victoria's funeral.

To some extent, though much less of course, it may account for his unconcealed deference to those who bore ancient and historic names. Though here, it may be suggested, another powerful sentiment came into play. He was naturally attracted to a new and gracious world whose gates had been opened to him. He liked it, and the people, and their way of life, and made them his, so far as he could. They spoke to the artist in him, the lover of tradition, of culture, and of dignity. In them he found his temporal home and much happiness; but it should not therefore be assumed that he ever forgot the home was temporal and not spiritual, or that Hatfield and Welbeck counted for as much in his life as Cuddesdon and Ballure. Nor, either with monarch or lesser notability, did he show the servility which is the hallmark of a certain kind of courtier. At the beginning of his acquaintance with the Royal Family he deliberately preached on the claims of Missions to the annoyance of a future King; and at the end of his life he found himself obliged to uphold Christian principles at the cost of a more serious displeasure.

Chapter XV

STEPNEY AND ST. PAUL'S

THE work of a bishop—or of a priest, for that matter—is what he likes to make it, without an end or without a beginning. Lang's work was always to be of the first kind, but at no time in his life were his energies more heavily taxed than in the seven and a half years when he was Bishop of Stepney and Canon of St. Paul's; nor, perhaps, did they ever yield so high a return.

He was consecrated Bishop by Archbishop Temple at St. Paul's Cathedral on St. Philip and St. James's Day, May 1st, 1901, the sermon being preached by his old friend Scott Holland, not without recollection of "the young lawyer who had come shyly to consult him about being ordained twelve years before." Dr. and Mrs. Lang came down from Scotland to see their son a Bishop, and they too, no doubt, had memories of a child's games in a garden at Morningside and of a boy plodding away at his home-work in the house in Woodlands Terrace. A little earlier Lang had been installed as a Canon of St. Paul's by Dean Gregory,[1] now a very old man, who by a strange trick of memory insisted on naming the new Canon "Charles Gore." Fortunately nobody raised any objection.

Lang now plunged headlong into the limitless waters of his new work, as Bishop and as Canon. He was immensely proud of his association with St. Paul's in the days of its greatness, when a series of notable Deans had raised it to a position of unrivalled influence in the religious life of London. The latest of the line, Dean Gregory himself, still led the Chapter, and "though his rugged body was losing strength, his mind, in spite of some lapses of memory, was full of robust vigour and strong good sense."

> The sight of the old man conducted across the traffic by a faithful policeman twice a day was one of the familiar sights of the City. He was the father of the family and we were all devoted to him, though a man less sentimental never was.

> Then there was Scott Holland, "our dear 'Scotty' . . . to St. Paul's its very life and soul; to me the dearest and most beloved of friends."

[1] He was appointed Dean of St. Paul's in 1891 and died in 1911, aged ninety-four.

He was, Lang added, "the most delightful of companions," and in spite of the stress of nerves and the fits of depression to which he was subject, "he seemed to possess and radiate 'the joy of the Resurrection.'" During the coming years he was Lang's spiritual counsellor and confessor.

William Newbolt [1] had succeeded Liddon,

> preaching, and exhibiting in his own life, the traditions of the Tractarians—the light of a sense of humour, sometimes grim but always delightful, breaking through his severity—a good old Tory in most effective contrast to the ebullient liberalism of Holland.

With the Archdeacon of London (W. M. Sinclair [2]) Lang found his relations less easy. The Archdeacon had been a young man of promise, never fulfilled, and disappointment, Lang thought, had soured him and given a rougher edge to a formidable temper.

> He stood apart from his colleagues, but he had a kind heart and there was never any breach. We took his occasional "tantrums" simply as a familiar feature of our united family life. He was proud of St. Paul's and he had his own following and many admirers of his huge voice, which, to his own delight and to theirs, boomed into all the corners of the Cathedral.

The Organist was the "gentle, cultivated, truly Christian" Sir George Martin, [3] who lived in and for the music of the Cathedral; and his assistant, Charles MacPherson, [4] was a gifted and fervent Celt, whose "MacPherson in D," then and later, moved Lang more deeply than almost any other rendering.

> The Choir was still at its zenith. It still had a thrill within it, as of some vital power moving through the music and lifting it, so to say, beyond itself. It was to me a continual joy and refreshment and made me, day by day during my residence and as often as possible at other times, glad to go into the house of the Lord. I have a real compassion for those, like Dean Inge, who are deaf to music and for whom the daily service is a duty rather than an uplifting joy.

As at Magdalen, Lang took especial pleasure in the boys of the Choir. Relays of them would come to his house on Sundays after the afternoon

---

[1] He died in 1930.
[2] Archdeacon of London 1889-1911. Died in 1917.
[3] Sir George Clement Martin, M.V.O., Organist at St. Paul's 1888-1916, when he died.
[4] He succeeded Martin at St. Paul's and was Organist till 1927, when he died.

service, to be regaled with tea and tales. Once, when he was telling one of his stories, he dramatised the entry of the villain by a series of knocks and was much gratified by the reaction of one of his small hearers, who called out: "Oh, please, sir, don't let him in!" One summer he took some of the boys to Largie for a fortnight.

His months of residence were February, June and October, when, by an unbroken law, he attended all the services and preached on the Sunday afternoons. In those days, before the week-end habit had so largely emptied London, a large congregation would assemble and fill the Dome and transepts. Lang followed his custom of preaching courses of sermons. While still at Portsea, he had published, first in *Good Words* and afterwards in volume form, his sermons on *The Miracles of Jesus*, which were and remained his most popular literary achievement. The sermons, vivid, closely argued and felicitously phrased, are a model of their kind and deservedly went into six editions. *The Parables of Jesus*, a course he preached at St. Paul's, was nearly as well received; and in 1905 he brought out a third book, *The Opportunity of the Church of England*, a series of lectures delivered during the previous year in the Divinity School at Cambridge. They dealt with the dissolution of belief and the indifference of the great masses of the people towards religion, and were a challenge, firstly to those who had already taken, or were about to take, Orders, and secondly to all men who were willing to give their service.

William Temple, then an undergraduate at Oxford and later to succeed Lang, first as Archbishop of York and then as Archbishop of Canterbury, described Lang's preaching at this time in a letter to his mother.

I am just back from a sermon by the Bishop of Stepney on "Fervent in spirit, serving the Lord." I think he is very great. . . . When I hear the Bishop of London, I get very much excited, rather hysterical perhaps, and feel ready to do anything: all of which is done away by. the next excitement, a concert or reading *The Critic*: and when I come to his text in the Bible, I remember that I was excited and have a vague sort of conception why. But when I hear the Bishop of Stepney I am not moved at all: I have to listen for fear of losing the inevitable connexion of his points, and the pleasure is intellectual and not emotional: but when I come to his text afterwards, I can remember all his points, just because their connexion is inevitable, and can then see whether I am following the precepts so obviously implied in the text. And for me there is no doubt that this is the more edifying by far.

One of the duties of a Canon in Residence was the ordering and arranging of special Services. This task brought Lang into a renewed contact with the Royal Family, and once into a less agreeable encounter with the Archbishop of Canterbury.[1] A Service of Thanksgiving for the recovery of King Edward VII from his illness and for his Coronation was to be held at St. Paul's. Lang went to Balmoral to discuss the details with the King, who expressed a Royal wish that the prelates and other officials taking part should "wear their best clothes."

"Copes?" suggested Lang.

"I don't know what you call them," replied the King. "I mean their best clothes—the sort of things worn at the Coronation."

This was good enough for Lang.

Accordingly, when the time came, I asked the Archbishop to wear a cope. He bluntly refused. As I knew that the Archbishop of York, the Bishop of London, the Dean and Chapter would be wearing their copes, I felt it would never do for the Archbishop himself to be otherwise apparelled. But he was adamant. On the very eve of the Service I made a last effort. I wrote to his chaplain begging him to get a cope from Westminster Abbey and to try to persuade the Archbishop even at the last minute to wear it. Unfortunately— I can't tell why—I put the word "Chaplain" on the outside of the letter. As ill luck would have it, the Archbishop, seeing the letter and judging from that word that it was on business, himself opened and read it. Then he sat down and wrote me a letter in his own hand, striking straight from the shoulder.

"All the particulars," wrote Archbishop Temple, "of such ceremonies as the Thanksgiving of to-morrow have been governed by precedent. The last precedent was that of Queen Victoria, when Her Majesty went to St. Paul's to give thanks for the recovery of the Prince of Wales, now His Majesty the King. On that occasion no Bishop wore a cope.

"To depart from precedent in these cases is highly dangerous at all times. To depart from precedent in this case will unquestionably

[1] Frederick Temple, father of the late Archbishop of Canterbury, William Temple.

be held to be taking sides in the present controversy concerning Ritualism.

"It is not loyal to the King to let him step into this position."

On the day the Archbishop came uncoped; but he bore no grudge, and when he saw Lang, remarked: "Well, I wouldn't do what you asked, but I've crammed on everything else I could."

The answer illustrated with equal clarity the essentially kindly nature of the Archbishop and his misunderstanding of the Catholic position.

Another task of a Canon in Residence was the conduct of parties round the Cathedral. These tours sometimes brought refreshing and unusual experiences, one of which Lang recorded.

This party had been arranged by the good Misses Dalton, sisters of the Rector of Stepney, for some rough girls, most of whom had never been inside a church. It was hoped that St. Paul's would duly impress them. I met them at the West door. At once one of them —I shall call her "A"—exclaimed: "What an awful plaice! It's like the graive!" Presently the good verger, Skinner, appeared in his robes. "Wot's that?" asked "A." "It's a verger," I said. "Wot's a verger?" "Oh, he stays here all day and looks after the Cathedral." "Wot! Staise 'ere all dai! Well, I 'spec he taikes it out o' nights." Thoughts of the blameless Skinner recovering from the tedium of St. Paul's by night orgies!

As I took the party down the steps to the Crypt, Miss "A" lingered. In a fatherly way I put my hand on her shoulder to hasten her. She turned to her companion and whispered: "Oh my, 'Liza, ain't he free!"

Afterwards, at tea in the Chapter-house, I spoke to the party, said I had taken many parties over St. Paul's, but never any that were so . . . and here I paused for the word. At once "A" interjected, "Spicy, ye mean." It was exactly the word.

Soon after this—so I heard—"A" was conducted to a Mission Service at Stepney by Miss Dalton. As the preacher was discoursing on some common faults and sins, she turned to Miss Dalton and whispered: "'E's talkin' abaht me sister." Then, as the preacher proceeded, she whispered again, now with some awe in her voice: "'E's talkin' abaht *me* now." Months passed. I was taking a Con-firmation at Stepney Church. I had been told that after much hesitation "A" was one of those to be confirmed. It so happened that I was standing at the vestry door as the girls in their veils passed. I recognised "A." She turned to me and said: "Oh, Bishop, pray for me: I'm afraid." A year passed—another Confirmation at Stepney Church. I was at the Rectory when the girls were having their veils put on. I saw "A" assisting one of them. I said to her: "Is this your friend?" With a smile and a bright glance she said: "Yuss. When I was confirmed you said we was to try to bring someone else in. Well, this is my friend and I've brought *her*." I was long enough in the East End to know that this was not the only girl that "A" "brought"; that she was a faithful and eager communicant, still "spicy," but with a new joy and purpose in her life. And this was the girl who thought that dear old Skinner must need a night's dissipation to recover from spending a day in St. Paul's!

The Canonry brought Lang other duties—the weekly meeting of the Dean and Chapter, at which all the business of the Cathedral, and in particular the vexed question of its structural stability, was discussed; Bible Classes for the Cathedral workmen; addresses to the St. Paul's Lecture Society; meetings of the Amen Guild for Young Warehousemen.

In addition, a "special and delightful" work fell to him. Some "West End" ladies approached him with a request that he should prepare their daughters for Confirmation. He agreed, and organised classes at which a band of girls, from thirteen to sixteen years of age, shepherded to and from Amen Court by their parents or governesses, appeared for instruction. The classes, which were known as "No. 2 Company" (from No. 2 Amen Court, where Lang lived), were "happy and informal," and the girls' weekly papers "gave me some insight, not always reassuring, into the religious instruction which girls of their class, who were not sent to schools, received from their parents and governesses at home." By the time Lang left London, about fifty of these girls had passed through his classes. Many of them became and remained his firm friends and, after his translation to York, by the kindness of Mrs. Randall Davidson he was allowed to entertain them once a year at a garden-party at Lambeth Palace.

In all this, it might be thought, was enough work to keep any ordinary man fully employed; but the Canonry of St. Paul's was the lesser of Lang's twin burdens. He was also Bishop of Stepney. The district included within its borders practically the whole of the vast area conveniently designated the "East End"—Bethnal Green, Stepney, White-chapel, Limehouse and Poplar; Hackney, Clapton, Stoke Newington up to Finsbury Park; and for a short time the part of East Central London which lies around Gray's Inn Road and Holborn. Here lived two million people, nearly all working folk, poor and badly housed, grouped into 208 parishes, a city within a city, an East that had a life of its own and seldom met the West.

As Suffragan Bishop, Lang had a measure of independent juris-diction. Apart from occasional visits, the transaction of legal business, and final decisions on grave questions, the Bishop of London left him to do the work in his own way. In a very real sense, to the clergy and people of the sub-Diocese he was "our Bishop," as Winnington Ingram had been before him.

Since the position of a Suffragan, in relation to his superior, has often been debated, Lang's views are of interest.

I am convinced that where there can be more than one Suffragan Bishop, it (a minimum of interference) is the right policy and the best way of using the Suffragan system. The Suffragan is able to feel in all his work that he is, and is regarded as, a real Bishop and not merely as an episcopal curate to his diocesan. He can have all the joy of a Bishop's work without the strain of final responsibility. Through the monthly meeting of the Bishops and Archdeacons the Bishop was able to keep his hand over the whole administration, and by being free to visit when and where he pleased, to make his influence felt throughout it. During all these eight years there was never the very slightest strain in the relations of friendship, comrade-ship and trust which bound the Bishop of London and his Suffragan of Stepney together.

To follow Ingram at Stepney was in one sense an advantage, in another a difficulty. Most people would probably agree that in Stepney Ingram found his true kingdom. His simplicity and warm-heartedness won him a host of friends and gave to the office of a Bishop a new meaning among the toiling masses of the East End. Later, as Bishop of London, he never quite fulfilled that early promise. He was no states-man; he had the innocence of a dove without the wisdom of a serpent; and he was far more at home when surrounded by a throng of grimy children than when he was presiding over the complicated discussions of a committee. Yet, at the outset at least of his new voyage, he sailed to a favouring wind; and to the end of his days he kept the affection of his people in Stepney.

He was already known and beloved through the whole East End as Head of the Oxford House and then Rector of Bethnal Green and Bishop of Stepney. His services at St. Paul's, when he was Canon there, had drawn great crowds. He was well known in the West End pulpits. Everywhere his almost boyish frankness and simplicity, his cheerfulness, his overflowing kindness of heart had charmed the heart of the people. And now here was a Bishop of London who came simply preaching the Gospel of the Kingdom of God; and crowds followed him wherever he went. As I once said of him, he seemed to be the Chevalier Bayard of the Church, *sans peur et sans reproche*. True, he had not then, and never had, any contacts with the intellectual or artistic life of London: he was a Bishop of the ordinary people. True, even then, the wiles of ecclesiastics set traps for him which he was too guileless and sanguine to detect. True, even then, men, and still more women, who were unworthy of him exploited his undiscerning goodness of heart. True, he had not much influence in the world of public affairs, though he always had a power of going straight to the main point in any public matter and expressing it with unconventional force. But in these early years of which I am writing, people did not care to mark such defects: they took him as he gave himself to them, an apostle of the Gospel, a friend whose spontaneous goodwill flowed over all sorts and conditions of men. Even though the glamour and glow of these early years have been somewhat dimmed, this fact remains: no Bishop of the Anglican Church has ever shown such loving kindness to all who were in need and trouble. Certainly, in this springtide of his episcopate it was impossible not to rejoice in his vivid and radiant personality; and all one's work under him and with him was warmed by the glow of his own fervour and hopefulness and joy of service.

Ingram would have said as much of his relations with his Suffragan. "I don't think that you have any idea what a blessing and help you are to me," he told Lang; and, only a few months before he died, he wrote with feeling of the "very happy years when we worked together like two brothers." Those who knew both men best in those days would have testified, too, how heavily the Bishop of London leaned upon the judgment of his Suffragan, who supplied so much that was lacking in

Ingram, with all his shining qualities of head and heart. After Lang had left London, the Bishop was noticeably more often the victim of some unhappy *contretemps*, which would probably have never occurred when his wise young Suffragan was at his side.

Lang himself was no stranger to Stepney. While a layman, through his interest in Toynbee Hall and Oxford House, he had "already touched the fringe of its life and problems."

I have always considered that the years—say 1890 to 1914—were the Golden Age of parochial work in the towns of England. In spite of all controversies—the growing pains of the Church—the ideals of the long and steady Church Revival had taken hold. What may be called "the social consciousness" of the Church had been roused by Maurice and Kingsley and their friends, and more recently by men like Gore and Scott Holland. The work of the Church had grown both in the intensity of faith and worship and in the extent of its range. There were able and devoted men in charge of industrial parishes everywhere; and the public schools and universities and theological colleges were still sending out full supplies of keen and healthy young men to help them. In East and North-East London in my time there were great parish priests, like "Algy" Lawley at Hackney, a true *Domini Canis*, following the trails of his people with his nose on the ground in dogged fidelity; Dalton at Stepney, vigorous, cheerful, unsparing in toil; Frank Gurdon at Limehouse, afterwards my trusted and beloved Suffragan of Hull, shepherding his flock with a broad smile and a firm will; Eck of Bethnal Green, modest, wise, devout; Chandler at Poplar, somewhat rigorous and detached, but a real power among the Socialists there; and afterwards Mozley, wise and trusted, later to become himself Bishop of Stepney and the Bishop of Southwell; and—a man of a different ecclesiastical position—Watts-Ditchfield of St. James the Less, Bethnal Green, who drew crowds of men from East and North-East London around him and built up a congregation, a real community, of singular zeal and loyalty. The great traditions of Charles Lowder were still upheld at St. Peter's, London Docks, with wonderful devotion and self-sacrifice by old Wainwright, and by men of like views at St. Augustine's, Stepney. Dolling was for a short time at St. Saviour's, Poplar, though his old force was then somewhat spent. Gerald Marshall was the centre of a really remarkable Church family at St. Simon Zelotes, Bethnal Green. The names and faces and churches of other valiant parish priests rise before me as I write. I cannot even mention them : I can only say it was a privilege to be among them as their Bishop. There were, of course, black spots, but not more than one or two. There were a few parishes where the priests had lost heart or grown slack. But my memory is of a Church life humming with activity and hopeful persistence in its task.

The parish priests, by their own acknowledgment, received from Lang leadership of a rare quality.

"Few Bishops that I have known or heard," writes the present Dean of Lichfield (Dr. Iremonger), "were better able to lift up a Confirmation Service and make it something that would stand out in the memory of the candidates in the years to come, or to invest with its full significance the institution of an incumbent. One such service I recall vividly, when he was instituting a new Vicar at All Hallows, East India Dock Road. The congregation was small, tired and apathetic; even the least sensitive could not help being affected by the terrible depression in the church; and I wondered whether even Lang could put any heart and hope into the few faithful people who had come to welcome their new Vicar. But when he began to speak, the whole atmosphere changed. I do not recall any particular sentences of his address, but I do remember how the depression lifted and the tired seemed to draw new life and spiritual energy from what he said that evening; and there was a look of new hope and resolve in the faces of the congregation when they left the church for their homes in the mean streets."

Then there were the people themselves.

In spite of all the poverty, of much squalor, of weary men and worn-out mothers, of ailing children, of tired, ill-paid home-workers, of drab streets and dirty yards, the main impression left upon my mind is their astonishing patience and good humour. Of course, I could only see the surface, only occasionally penetrate the sin and shame and misery which too often lay beneath it. But I knew enough of all this to feel both a heavy burden of conscience and a flame of indignation that such things should be in the midst of our boasted civilisation. It almost *hurt* to go into the West End, and it was difficult to have the patience with which the poor of the "other City" endured their lot. When in the streets and parks and houses of the West I thought of that patience, I could not but mutter, "How long? How long?" It was a sad patience which one often saw on the faces of the older men and women in trams or buses. Yet I repeat the main impression was one of a patience lightened by cheeriness and humour. In the young—the lads and working girls—these qualities broke out in a noisy hilarity. For liveliness of chaff and quickness of repartee, commend me to the Cockneys of East London.

This noisy gaiety was at that time the special mark of the East End working girls. I can see them now, with their ostrich feathers and sham plush coats, linked arm in arm, rollicking along the streets. But it was an ordeal for me in my episcopal attire to encounter them. Such a figure excited not reverence but ribald mirth. Noticing my hat, one of a band of them in Old Ford remarked with a sniff as I passed: "Law, what a smell of 'ats!"

On another occasion I was greeted by the cry, aroused by the sight of my short episcopal apron, "Fie for shaime! Let down yer petticoat!" (these were the days before short skirts!). Where have these noisy yet so attractive hoydens gone? I see them no longer in these once familiar streets. I only see spruce young ladies, dressed exactly as one's own girl-friends anywhere. The change after twenty years may be due partly to the levelling of education: is it partly due to the invention of artificial silk stockings? Yet I miss the sight of the plush-and-feather damsels and feel that one of the glories of the East End streets has departed. I only hope that the new generation keeps something of the lively humour of the old.

These were the days before Bishops journeyed in motor-cars. I was a "bus and bag Bishop," carrying my own robes-bag in train and tram and bus. I confess I miss the contact with plain folk which this mode of travelling brought, and the humour of the old bus driver who, like the East End girls, has gone. I can't forbear from telling one story. I was sitting on the box-seat of the Poplar bus, next the red-faced driver. He collided with another bus. The drivers exchanged a volley of mutual reproaches, made ruddy by their oaths. Foolishly, no doubt, when the buses were disentangled, I remarked to my driver that all this language was a bad habit. "'Abit?" he retorted, "'tain't a 'abit—it's a bloody art." He was proud to practise it.

In my very last year, a number of my friends presented me with a small car. At first I doubted whether a Bishop in a car—they were new things then—would not be misunderstood by the East End folk. I consulted a working-man in one of the clubs. He reassured me. "Why shouldn't a Bishop have 'is car as well as the tuppenny-pill man?"—his word for a doctor. It so happened that in one of my very first journeys my chauffeur, through no fault of his own, overthrew a very elderly couple in the Hackney Road. They were a bride and bridegroom returning somewhat unsteadily from the bridal feast. They were not really hurt, but a crowd assembled. Said one of them, voicing the general indignation: "I s'pose 'e was 'urryin' back to the 'Ouse of Lords."

His chaplain, the Rev. Lumley Green-Wilkinson,[1] has given some diverting details of this first motoring venture. A few of the Bishop's friends, he says, wished to provide him with a motor car, but Lang, although touched by their kindness, refused the offer. Then, one night in Poplar, happening to meet George Lansbury and some fellow-Socialists, he told them of his decision and discovered, much to his surprise, that they thought he had made a mistake. He withdrew his refusal, and presently a Belsize coupé turned up, complete with chauffeur. The first journey, however, was nearly a disaster. The Bishop had a Confirmation at Stoke Newington and, thanks to the Belsize, the time of departure was later than it would have been for a journey by bus or train. At last the moment arrived. Lang and his chaplain got into the car. The chauffeur began to operate the starting-handle. Nothing happened. Lang, who never liked mechanical novelties, felt that his first suspicions were being amply confirmed. "This car of yours will make me late," he said reproachfully to his chaplain and, seizing his bag, hurried off to catch a bus in St. Paul's Churchyard. With his departure the car at once started. The Bishop was retrieved and off he went, to collide a few minutes later with a whisky van. Out jumped the chaplain to take the names and addresses that would be required by the insurance company, and presently returned to find an irate Bishop, shrinking back in his seat in the car, which had become the centre of a large and critical crowd. As the result of this mishap Lang—for the first time, he claimed—was late in arriving at the Church, and Mr. Green-Wilkinson was told that it was all his fault for insisting upon a car.

[1] Vicar of St. Peter's, Bournemouth, 1921-1927.

To be unpunctual for anything was a lapse: to be late for such an engagement was almost intolerable, for Confirmations were a particular joy and privilege to him. "It was wonderful to see the faces of the lads and girls, often of men and women, with a new expression on them. . . ." The ceremony at an Anglo-Catholic church, with its band of carefully instructed candidates, was always impressive; but so, too, was the evangelical fervour to be witnessed at a church like St. James the Less. The teaching, it is true, whether Catholic or Evangelical, did not always percolate unpolluted among the mass of the population. Once Lang was on his way from St. Columba's, Haggerston, to confirm a sick person near by. As he passed in cope and mitre, he heard a small boy say to another, "It's the Pope of Rome."

"'Tain't," replied his companion, proud of his superior knowledge. "It's a Confirmaition: it's the 'Oly Ghost!"

This was one of many memories of those days, amusing, touching, and often lightened by flashes of Cockney humour.

Once I had promised to celebrate in the very early morning in a Mission church in Poplar. I stayed the night before with the priest-in-charge in his tiny flat in a great block of workmen's dwellings. My presence there caused some excitement among the other dwellers in the block. One of them knocked at our door and presented two (very smelly) kippered herrings wrapped in a newspaper. "We thought," she said, "as the Bishop might like them kippers for 'is supper."

The Church spread its net wide, with Missions and Settlements, with Clubs and organisations of every kind, with addresses in the open air and a multitude of charitable projects, but only too many of the fish were missed altogether and some that were caught slipped through the meshes. Yet for those that stayed in it, Lang insists, life had a new happiness and purpose, lifting them above the monotony of toil and care; and always in the East End was the contrast between the drab streets and the light, the colour and the music of the churches, between "the noise of toil outside and the peace within, between East London and the City of God."

I don't think I can better summarise all that the Church brought to East London than in the words of a cobbler of Bethnal Green who had worked for long years shut up in his single room. I think I recollect them fairly accurately. "For years," he said, "I seemed to be in a kind of dungeon, no light, no hope. But when I joined the

Church and heard what it was all about, I got free and found meself in a world full of all sorts of wonderful things I had never dreamed of before."

That vision was not for all men and the going was sometimes far from easy in days when large sections of the people of East London were not indifferent but actively hostile to the Church. "You evidently think it fun," Lang once retorted to a noisy meeting in the Isle of Dogs, "to bait a Bishop." But at the end of the meeting he said: "I have heard to-night of all the things which you would like to take from the Church and from myself; but there is one privilege of which not even the most revolutionary of you can rob a Bishop. So I ask you all to stand while I give you my blessing." The men who a few moments before had been shouting abuse at him stood up in complete silence while he gave them his blessing, and as he left, each man shook his hand.

Yet on the whole Labour and its leaders were by no means unfriendly. There was Will Crooks, the "Father of Poplar."

No one could speak so forcibly to East Londoners in their own language as he, or out of a more kindly heart. I remember, for example, a big meeting of working men. Crooks put aside his politics and spoke to them about their home life and their treatment of their wives. "Do a bit o' courtin' of them sometimes. Go 'ome and give them a kiss, just as you did when you were walkin' out with them in the old days."

He used to hold a sort of family gathering of his neighbours in the Poplar Town Hall on Sunday afternoons. During Lent he gave his audience to the Rector—"to give the Parson a run"—as he said. Though he was not a practising Churchman (his family were), this was one of his ways of showing friendliness to the Church. One Lent I took some of these addresses. He always presided himself. One Sunday afternoon I gave the best I could give. When my address was over, Crooks said: "Well, we've 'eard things to think about this afternoon. Go 'ome and think about them. Of course, you're free to ask any questions. Any fool can do that. Does anyone want to ask any questions?" And there was silence.

George Lansbury was another friend.

One Sunday afternoon I was to preach at Bow Church. The Rector, Manley Power (once curate at Leeds), sent me word that a very

THE VICAR OF PORTSEA AND HIS STAFF

THE BISHOP OF STEPNEY

interesting man with whom he had been having some talks might be there and would meet me at supper afterwards. He was a secularist lecturer, by name Lansbury, who seemed to be feeling his way back to the Church. He came to Bow Church, very shamefacedly, and sat in the back behind a pillar. After supper he poured out doubts, questions, desires, as out of a long-corked-up bottle; and I was much moved by his sincerity. Thereafter he threw in his lot with the Church, taking St. Francis of Assisi as his ideal Christian. For some time, until increasing political work made it difficult, he held a class for lads on Sunday afternoons. Shortly after our talk at Bow Rectory, I asked him if he would give his witness to the Christian faith at a big men's meeting to be held at Bow Baths. He said it would not be easy, but he would do his best. It was advertised that he would speak. There was a great crowd—hundreds of the kind of collarless men not usually seen at such meetings. They listened quietly to me, but when Lansbury rose there was an outcry—shouts of "Traitor!", "Judas!", and so forth. I shall never forget the way in which Lansbury turned on them—"Is this the freedom of speech you claim for yourselves?" etc.—and gave his witness and impelled silence.

About the year 1905, when the problem of Unemployment became very acute, the Government and local authorities formed a new public organisation which was called, "with a deficient sense of humour," "The Central London Unemployed Body." The Chairman was Russell Wakefield, afterwards Bishop of Birmingham, and Lang was an active member. So was Mr. Keir Hardie.

On some point he and I took different views, and we were commissioned to refer the matter to the Local Government Board, of which John Burns was then President. When we arrived, the President entered with a bevy of secretaries. We put our cases. The President obviously agreed with mine. He kept on saying to Hardie, his old comrade, with great official gusto: "The Board is of opinion . . ." etc. As we left, Keir Hardie was in high dudgeon, and said to me in his native Doric: "Did you ever hear the like of that! The *Board* think this and the *Board* will do that. And I mind the time when I was hangin' on to the Board's coat-tails in Trafalgar Square to keep it from talkin' treason!"

Much of Lang's work took him outside the diocese. The financing all these activities depended to a very large extent on the East London

Church Fund, and to obtain support for this he continually preached in the West End and throughout Southern England.

No doubt it was a great privilege to speak on behalf of my East End Folk, but it became a somewhat wearisome task to bring the East End into every sermon on every subject. It seemed as if the whole issue of the Christian Faith was the support of the Fund. I used to say that I had to add a new clause to the Creed—"And I believe in the East London Church Fund." At some meetings, as in the Mansion House and at Bournemouth, the Bishop of London would give his powerful help. Fervour and humour were stronger in his speeches than accuracy. I remember on one occasion he claimed that there were so many thousands of regular Church workers in East London. The excellent secretary of the Fund whispered to me : "He's put on a nought." On the next occasion he repeated his enthusiastic figures. "He's done it again," whispered the secretary. "Never mind," I replied ; "a nought is naught to a Bishop." And so it was.

Last, but far from least, of Lang's labours at this time was his service to the Church of England Men's Society. Shortly before he came to London, representatives of the principal Church organisations for men were summoned to Lambeth by Archbishop Temple. "You all seem to be doing the same work," he said in his characteristically blunt way. "Why can't you do it together ?" His injunction took effect, and the various organisations were amalgamated into The Church of England Men's Society. The Bishop of London was its first Chairman, but a little later, at his express request, Lang succeeded him.

The infant Society, when I took charge of it, was a very sickly infant ; indeed it might almost have been called "stillborn." Whatever vigour there may have been in the old societies had gone : none had taken its place. The Society scarcely knew what its objects or purposes really were. I well remember its first annual meeting. It was held in, I think, the St. Bride's Institute, off the Strand : perhaps a hundred or so were present. The only effective personality was G. A. King [1] (afterwards Sir George), a doughty Evangelical, who became one of the stalwarts of the Society and its Treasurer. He had his little ways, which were sometimes a trial to me, but he was a really good man and always loyal and affectionate. The first task was simply to keep the infant alive. But very soon I came to the

[1] Chief Master Supreme Court Taxing Office 1921-1928, when he died.

conclusion that the vital need was a first-class Secretary. I refused to be in any hurry about getting him and maintained that we must wait and pray for the right man.

The right man duly appeared in Gordon Savile, who had just come home after a strenuous ministry at Kalgoorlie, in Western Australia. When his zeal and powers of organisation were matched with the ardour, the driving force and the eloquence of Lang, the Society moved forward rapidly. "Suddenly," Lang told a meeting, "a power seemed to come behind them that lifted the whole thing out of their hands."

Indeed, it became rapidly a movement rather than a Society. This is no place in which to record its history. Suffice it to say that I threw myself heart and soul into the movement. It was a summons to the men of the Church to enlist in its active service. I went all over the country, addressing meetings of men, sounding this call. I shall never forget those gatherings, their numbers, their enthusiasm. It really seemed as if the men of the Church had been waiting for this call and were ready to respond.

It was the chance he had always sought, for which he had long waited; and in all modesty he claims that between the years 1904 and 1914 no one can have passed, or even reached, his record in the numbers of men addressed in England and Wales. The movement, in these days of its prime, had the fire and fever of an election campaign; and conferences all over the country culminated in a meeting of men which completely filled the Albert Hall and, by its size and enthusiasm, amazed the Archbishop of Canterbury, who presided over it. More than 600 branches of the Society were formed and more than 20,000 members were enrolled; but Lang was for ever uttering warnings against the lure of numbers, of the danger of quantity as compared with the need for quality. Those were certainly great days, when the Society counted for much in the life of the Church. Lang kept up his connexion with it after he had left Stepney, but at York his time and opportunities of service were necessarily restricted; and with the war of 1914-1918 it suffered the fate of many other societies. It still exists and does good work, but the ferment has gone from it.

When I look back on the great years, 1904-1914, I am still convinced that the movement was real and strong and God-intended. But I don't think that the Bishops and clergy showed the sympathy and imagination needed to make use of all this readiness for service which was offered to the Church. As I have often put it, the molten flow of zeal (of which I was the witness, as no one else in like measure could be) was allowed to cool before it had been shaped and used. No doubt, also, the members, for all their apparent enthusiasm, often fell below their professed ideals, though I am sure Bishops and clergy might have done more to encourage and train them. There are times when I think that the movement of 1904-1914 was one of the lost opportunities of the Church of England.

Chapter XVI

A BISHOP IN RESIDENCE

SO unceasing was the work and so fierce the pace during the seven and a half years at Stepney and St. Paul's, that it might be thought little time or scope was left for any sort of private life and home would be merely a place of abbreviated nights and hurried meals. But the position was not quite as bad as it might appear.

My new London home was No. 2 Amen Court, the little court tucked up within the warehouses near St. Paul's, the abode of Canons and minor Canons and Organist. I think it must be the quietest spot in London. During the day the roar of the City traffic is shut out by the high encompassing buildings, and during the night the City is as still as the grave. Numbers 1, 2 and 3 date from the days of Wren: No. 2 had one treasure, a bit of Chinese wall-paper dated from the 17th century, and its drawing-room had a charming design on its ceiling. It is not a large house: how the Gregory family, who once lived there, were fitted in I can't imagine. On the ground floor were a good hall, a small room which, with its furnishings most kindly left by my predecessors, I retained as a Chapel, the dining-room with windows opening on the court, and a little side-room which I used as my own oratory. On the first floor were the drawing-room, my study and a bedroom; on the second floor my bedroom, two small bedrooms, and a small sitting-room where my chaplains were installed, a servant's room and a bathroom. The kitchen was in the basement. It was an ideal bachelor's house. I was very proud of it and, as I have said, it was quiet and peaceful; so still that whenever I spent a night in the country the country noises were an unwonted disturbance. Here I settled, with much content.

The content was enhanced by a faithful and efficient staff. Martha Saville, who came to Amen Court as a parlourmaid, remained with Lang until the bombs drove her from Lambeth Palace in 1940. She died three years later. Annie Loosemore was housemaid at Amen Court, and afterwards housekeeper at Bishopthorpe until her death. A cook and a boy completed the establishment, which was, Lang says, "a most

165

harmonious family." In those days, as always, his relations with his staff were such that he never lacked willing and loving service.

Lang had long decided, after a good deal of reflexion and talk with his friends, that he would not marry. His notes do not mention the subject, but his motives are reasonably certain. They were not, in the stricter sense, ecclesiastical. It is true that when he was at Leeds he told Fred Farrar, one of the men in his class, that if ever he became a vicar he would never allow one of his curates to marry and would get rid of him if he did. But this was an opinion which he later revised. He did not, as the straiter Anglo-Catholics did, hold that the clergy should be celibate : he did, however, believe that marriage was not the right course for him, that he would work and serve better without the ties and complications of family life. He would never advise—still less attempt to press—this personal view upon others. On the contrary, he rejoiced in the marriages of his chaplains, in the friendship of their wives, and in the companion-ship of their children, for whom he had a particular affection. Nor did he in the slightest degree shun the society of women : he welcomed and took the greatest pleasure in it. Some of his closest friends were women and they were as attached to him as was he to them. But while once or twice gossip may have allowed itself to play round the person of a young, good-looking and single Bishop, there is no evidence that he ever thought seriously of marriage.

Yet he was essentially a social person, dependent, despite the reserves that have so often been noted, upon companionship. Except for that depressing interlude between Balliol and the Bar, when he lodged alone in Bloomsbury, he was accustomed to a more or less communal life—at Cuddesdon, then at Leeds, where one of his first actions had been to establish a modest Clergy House, at Magdalen, where he shared the life of the College, and at Portsea, where he dwelt with a small army of curates. His new home at Amen Court was therefore a departure from precedent ; but the first of a long line of chaplains and secretaries arrived to break his solitude and to give him something of the companionship with which he could never dispense without unhappiness.

Stafford Crawley,[1] his first chaplain, had been an undergraduate at Magdalen when Lang was Dean of Divinity, and while staying at Largie one summer was persuaded to take Orders. He was a part-time secretary and was also attached to Stepney Parish Church. In 1905 he married—Lang performing the ceremony—and brought his wife back to Amen

[1] Canon A. S. Crawley, Canon and Precentor of Windsor. Died in October 1948.

Court for six weeks. Thereafter, so far as his work in the Church allowed, he was continually in and out of Lang's life. When he was not actually with him in some capacity, the two wrote regularly to each other; Mrs. Crawley became as firm a friend as was her husband; and the children, as they grew older, became a kind of adopted family.

Then in 1903 came C. S. Donald,[1] "that quaint lovable creature," who was also on the staff of Stepney Parish Church and later was "a heroic worker among the rough lads of Notting Hill." He was followed in 1906 by Lumley Green-Wilkinson, attached to Holy Innocents, Hammersmith, afterwards Vicar of Bournemouth, and still later "my invaluable 'Controller of the Household' at Lambeth." Finally there was "dear Wilfrid Parker," the present Bishop of Pretoria, another firm friend of a lifetime; and from 1905 to 1907, sandwiched between chaplains, was "a layman-secretary and companion, Dick Sheppard, who delighted me by his wilful, wayward, whimsical ways, and whom I tried gently to steer towards Ordination."

These were far more than chaplains or secretaries to a Bishop. They were, one and all, devoted friends, who supplied a little of the family life that would otherwise have been missing in Amen Court. So much Lang, always deeply conscious of his dependence not only upon the service, but upon the affection, of those about him, would have been the first to allow. The chaplains also fill in some of the gaps in Lang's notes; for there is much that a man cannot say of himself or of his work. They are witnesses to his immense correspondence, mainly conducted in his own hand; to the crowded congregations in St. Paul's on the Sunday afternoons when he was preaching one of his Courses; to his impact upon the intellectual life of London; to his influence on the committees he joined; to the effect of his oratory upon the mass meetings he addressed; and, above all, to his wisdom in counsel, which brought many leaders in Church and State to the house in Amen Court. Those were the days of the Education controversy, when Mr. Balfour's whip was soon to be followed by Mr. Birrell's scorpion; and while Lang had as yet no vote to give and no seat in the House of Lords to fill, his advice already carried weight, not only with men like the new Archbishop of Canterbury (Randall Davidson), the Bishop of London and Lord Hugh Cecil, but with others outside the inner circle of the Church. Mr Green-Wilkinson goes so far as to declare that "almost every person of importance came to Amen Court to consult him from time to time."

[1] Afterwards Head of the Rugby School Mission, Notting Dale, 1905-1926.

The picture is one of unremitting labour.

"It was a marvel to me," Canon Crawley writes, "how he found time to prepare the sermons and addresses which he had to give on so great a variety of occasions and to master the details of the committees ... over which he presided. ... He worked late into the night, sometimes as late as 2 a.m. I think he never went to bed without saying his prayers in his little oratory next his study, where I often found him at other times in the day. He almost invariably attended the daily Eucharist at eight o'clock in the Cathedral. I sometimes accompanied him to some of his great meetings, at the People's Palace or at some special service where were gathered great congregations, at which he preached with great eloquence, often without notes or with notes on a half-sheet of paper, made in his very indecipherable writing."

While Stafford Crawley was away being married, his place was taken by another Magdalen man, the Hon. and Rev. H. E. S. S. Lambart (now the Ven. the Earl of Cavan). Lang, he says, "lived an almost 'inhuman' life of concentrated work : early at St. Paul's, a silent breakfast opening letters, consultations almost daily with the Bishop of London, Sidney Webb and such to lunch, Stepney and East End till ten p.m., and while he read the *Times*, I would cook him some poached eggs and implore him to eat. I remember two or three walks along the Embankment when he weighed, near emotion, the joys of married life against the demands of *his* life and possibly his future. His life was lived hard then, and his bedroom was like a Victorian servant's, with a horrible painted iron bedstead and scarcely a decent bit of furniture ; but the other rooms were well furnished for Amen Court."

His only diversion was a very occasional game of golf. For years he played with unvarying ill-success, exclaiming "Lamentable !" as he fluffed one shot after another.

"He had little or no social life—just work," writes Mr. Donald. Professedly a day off was taken once a week ; but too often it slipped by unheeded, and when it did not, the scramble to clear up work before leaving made the holiday as bad as any ordinary day. As time wore on, the upper millstone of the East London Church Fund and the nether millstone of the Church of England Men's Society ground his spare time into almost imperceptible fragments.

So *Punch* could write of him in those days that he

> Finds tracts in trams, texts in the running bus,
> Sermons in trains, and work in anything.

A scrap of paper, dated January 10th, 1903, torn from a letter written possibly to his mother, gives some idea of the life he was leading.

Drove over to Cuddesdon and refreshed my soul by a short visit to my Holy Place—my Mecca. Ah me! What memories of early days it brought back! Then on the Saturday I travelled to Torquay, once again to beg for East London. Again it was mostly very wet. Sunday afternoon and evening it poured and so considerably affected my "bag." I preached three times. Last Tuesday I went on to Plymouth and spoke on behalf of the Exeter Diocesan Mission, and preached, and addressed a meeting of men in the evening. Next day had a beautiful day. I preached at Dawlish for East London and spoke at a meeting at Exeter, also on behalf of East London. Next day, Thursday, I went in sheets of rain to Ilfracombe for East London —in spite of rain a good meeting and a good collection. Friday, went to Seaton in Devon for a meeting of the Diocesan Mission, returning to Exeter to preach for East London and to address a meeting of men.

This was before the C.E.M.S. took its toll from his time. Afterwards, of course, the strain was even heavier. Mr. Green-Wilkinson describes how the Bishop would be out speaking many evenings each week for the Society, returning very often after midnight, when his faithful chaplain would fry him eggs and bacon over the study fire.

When he was not travelling and talking, the trickle of visitors to Amen Court went on through the day—clergy from the East End; politicians; members of one of his innumerable committees; people who wanted him to speak for some cause they cherished; people who wanted to consult him about something. And scattered among them were the time-wasters and charlatans: the callow youth from Peckham in a blazer of Cambridge blue, whose "auntie" wanted him "to go in for the clergy"; the "curate" who was discovered on enquiry to have done time for writing the wrong name on a cheque; the "engineer" who tried to collect carriage on a non-existent caribou head, alleged to have been sent by Lord Strathcona; the "doctor from Portsea," who had unluckily been robbed and wanted his fare home; the vicars who, more innocently, had something to be dedicated or unveiled and thought they had only to ask the Bishop. The chaplains could dispose of some, but not all, of these callers.

Almost any day, when Lang was in Amen Court, someone would

arrive for luncheon, generally bringing with him a request for advice or a problem to be solved. Occasionally the parties were larger, more social, and sometimes more difficult for the host; as the luncheon when, during a sudden lull in the conversation, a distinguished lady, who had been discussing with her neighbours the careers of some boys they both knew, remarked, "Geoffrey? Ah, poor Geoffrey, the fool of the family! He is, of course, destined for the Church"; or the other occasion when, in a similar lull, Mrs. Barnett (of Toynbee Hall) was heard to declare with emphasis, "I *hate* curates!"

Holidays, of course, there were, fleeting visits to friends, or to Cuddesdon, and each summer the weeks at Tavantaggart,[1] without which Lang would say he could not have supported life at all. In 1905 he stayed with Lord Halifax,[2] at the villa he had taken on the Italian Riviera, the first of many similar visits and the beginning of a long and treasured friendship. But a holiday with Lord Halifax was always in danger of becoming a busman's holiday for Lang, since his host could seldom abstain from discussing ecclesiastical politics. The guest at length was driven to negotiate a "gentleman's agreement" to avoid the subject, but subsequently had cause sometimes to complain that Lord Halifax was not sufficiently scrupulous in observing the pact.

Another visit, to be regularly repeated in the coming years, was to Balmoral in the autumn of 1902. The Castle was full of guests and at dinner the first evening Lang's diplomacy was taxed to the full by a Royal cross-examination on the relative merits of the Episcopal and Established Churches, with Lord Balfour of Burleigh, a pillar of the Kirk, listening in across the table. On the following evening there was a torchlight dinner, with reels and toasts in whisky to follow. On Sunday Lang was confronted with a problem which never ceased to embarrass him. Should he or should he not accompany the King to the service in Crathie Church? If he did, his action might offend and even prejudice the Episcopalians. If he did not, the King would be annoyed. In the end, he told his mother, he followed his "rule"; and since the Episcopalians offered no service within a reasonable distance, to Crathie he went, complaining afterwards that the proceedings were "too Anglican. Too few of the old Psalms and Paraphrases for *my* taste."

The "rule" did not save him from the reproaches of his old friend "the Prophet," who presently wrote that a Presbyterian of his acquaint-

[1] See Chapter XVII.
[2] The 2nd Viscount Halifax, for more than fifty years President of the English Church Union.

ance had twitted him on the presence of a High Church Anglican Bishop at a service of the Kirk. Lang replied rather curtly, the sharpness of the letter revealing the unsureness of the writer.

In 1904 Lang was to have made another journey—no holiday this time—to South Africa, whither his brother Norman had gone. His plans were made, his ticket was taken, and then, two days before he was to sail, he saw his doctor, who forbade the trip. After years of overwork Lang's heart was showing signs of trouble. The threat was not serious and nothing came of it, but in the circumstances the doctor advised him to cancel a tour which would mean much strenuous travelling and constant preaching.

A man is as likely to be a hero to his valet as is a Bishop to be a saint to his chaplains. But Lang's young men retained the most agreeable memories of their Bishop. In perspective the little foibles, which the world saw only too well, were overshadowed into insignificance by the finer qualities of head and heart of which they had had so much experience. Some of the foibles they have themselves recorded with an amused and affectionate tolerance. There was, for example, Lang's dislike of novelties, and in particular those of a mechanical kind. He did not understand them and therefore mistrusted them. Until they had won his confidence by long and faithful service, he disowned proprietorship. It was "*your* car," "*your* typewriter," "*your* telephone," until he was persuaded that his chaplain had not introduced into the house a monster of evil and unpredictable propensities. New doctors, new butlers, or new pipes came under the same rule of probation; but when every test had been successfully passed, Lang would admit the innovation, human or mechanical, into his affections, acknowledge ownership with the word "my," and thereafter treat the person or thing with uncritical loyalty. Even this had its embarrassments, for when he became thus attached to some inanimate object, he would refuse to be separated from it, even when it had reached an unserviceable and decrepit old age. In 1913 he bought a Wolseley touring car, in which for twenty-one years he made all his journeys by road. Towards the end of its career King George V told Lord Wigram that it was a positive danger and must not be allowed to come to Balmoral again; but Lang's regard for it was undiminished by the Royal displeasure. He only consented to part with it when the cost of replacing the parts became prohibitive, and was extremely indignant when he discovered that this old and tried retainer had gone for a pittance of five pounds.

The pipe was at least as important as the doctor, the butler or the car. Lang was a happy and persistent smoker, but he had a horror of receiving people in a smoke-filled room and always sought privacy for his pipe.

The ordinary tasks, transactions and "gadgets" of modern life were mysterious and baffling to him. He knew little, and cared less, about his private finances. So long as he kept out of debt he did not worry; and although over a great many years he disposed of a substantial income, his savings were negligible, he had only the vaguest idea how he was spending his money, and once when he was Archbishop of Canterbury and had a stipend of £15,000 a year, had to confess that he did not know where he banked. A chaplain or a secretary handled these matters for him, and provided a little pocket money was forthcoming when he needed it, he was unconcerned. Shopping was another dark and dangerous business, to be avoided at almost any cost. When he was an old man he used to say that after he became Archbishop of York he never entered a shop, and even in the days at Amen Court his clothes and other necessaries were all bought for him and his tailor and haircutter came to the house. Time-tables and journeys were another trouble. He was a last-minute starter and an uncertain traveller; and once, when he was proposing to take his annual holiday in Norway, he missed his steamer because, in the teeth of his chaplain's protests, he insisted on trying to travel to Hull by a non-existent train from Liverpool Street. The Duke of Portland once presented him with a Gillette Safety Razor. This looked inviting, but its complications proved insuperable and Lang eventually reported that it was "quite useless." When its mysteries were explained to him and he understood that after shaving with it he would have to take it to pieces and clean it, he would have nothing more to do with it. Another friend gave him a beautiful gold-mounted fountain-pen. Lang never used it because he could not master the intricacies of filling it, but he liked the look of it and carried it about in his attaché-case for twenty-seven years.

Foibles such as these were trivial stuff, and if sometimes they made life a little more difficult, they also made it much more amusing. What mattered chiefly to the chaplains was that Lang was the easiest and most pleasant of masters. "Only once," writes Canon Donald, "did he see red with me, and that was when in his name I sent his heartiest good wishes for a merry Christmas to a clergyman whom he had buried a few days before with some ceremony and outpouring of tears." Indeed, Lang's attitude towards the young men was very much that of a man towards his younger brothers. He felt deeply responsible for their well-being and happiness, and while pathetically grateful for anything they did for him, was ruthless in his self-criticism when he thought he might have done more for them.

"You have been an unfailingly cheerful and unselfish companion for these two years," he wrote to Green-Wilkinson on the latter's departure. "It isn't for my kicks and grunts that I am sorry. They are only 'my little way.' What I am sorry for is that during two years of your ministry I have been able to do so little to help you yourself."

Kicks and grunts there may have been, but they were of little consequence, scarcely noticed at the time and unremembered afterwards. Mr. Donald goes further in his tribute :

> Those who lived close to Bishop Lang knew him to be a saint. Christian defeated Apollyon after a strong struggle, and in Lang there seemed to me to be a constant struggle, crowned with victory. His ideal of the self-giving Good Shepherd was constantly at variance with his quick brain and powerful intellect. The Good Shepherd always won, and that is to be a saint. Shallow people sometimes thought him pompous. Really it was the big man retiring into reticence when he could have hurt with the *mot juste*. Lang never hurt us weaker ones. He had a very tender heart and a deep understanding and compassion for the sinful. His friendship had depth. We small fry of the Church at times suffer from a genial prelate who expresses pleasure at seeing you—you knowing that he does not even remember your name. Lang never had to remember, for he never forgot.

The quality of Lang's friendship was never more faithfully reflected than in his relations with his lay secretary at Amen Court. In 1905 Dick Sheppard, at twenty-four, was still very much at a loose end. He had been working at the Oxford House, where his success had been immediate and spectacular; but although to others his vocation seemed plain, he could not bring himself to take Orders. Then, one day in Holy Week 1905, his father, Sub-Dean of the Chapels Royal, wrote to Lang to ask his advice. What did the Bishop, who had seen Dick in Bethnal Green, think of him? Could he suggest for him any sort of secretarial work? Lang at once pounced. He knew and liked Dick and needed a lay secretary. The thing was done, and in the summer of 1905 Dick Sheppard began his work at Amen Court. He became at once much more than a secretary; he became a friend, almost a son to the older man. They played golf and took their holidays together; and above all they talked. Dick Sheppard had abounding vitality and the kind of temperament that always appealed to Lang, who saw in him as in a mirror his own younger self, with the same enthusiasms and uncertainties. Even the violent changes of mind delighted him, as when Dick came back from the Oxford House, "declaring one evening that the East End working man was a hero, and the next that he was a swine." On his side, Lang gave exactly the tonic Dick Sheppard needed to dissolve his doubts and to brace his will. He had begun by making it clear that he had no intention of taking Orders; but Lang, who once too had had no such intention, could speak to him on the subject with a humility, an affection, and a moral authority which were irresistible. The persistent voice, which years ago had asked a young lawyer, "Why shouldn't *you* be ordained?" now began to put the same question to Dick Sheppard, and in the end the same answer was given. So it was settled and Dick went to Cuddesdon, commending his successor, Wilfrid Parker, with the typical message—"You'll find him clean about the house." The rest of the story is Dick's rather than Lang's, and has been told by his biographer, Mr. Ellis Roberts. His verdict can surely be accepted: "There is no doubt that, as far as man's influence counted at all, the Church of God owes Dick Sheppard to Cosmo Gordon Lang."[1]

All through the year at Cuddesdon Lang kept his eye on Dick, advising, encouraging, sympathising. Was life there so very difficult? Was so much uncongenial? Then "Make an offering of your time there; and don't in thought take your offering back." Dick finished his training and was to be ordained on October 6th, 1907. When he died, thirty years later, "Cosmo's Ordination letter" was found among his papers.

I must send you a word to greet you in this most momentous week. I want you to know how much my heart goes out *to* you and goes up *for* you in prayer. I try to put myself back 17 years to the time when I was preparing for the great venture; and set myself at your side as an older comrade in the service, conscious, alas!, of many failures, defeats and surrenders, knowing something of the toils and trials of the long campaign, seeking to recover his own early faith and ardour at the side of the young knight waiting for the first call. So in spirit, old boy, I kneel at your side, and pray both for you and

[1] Ellis Roberts: *H. R. L. Sheppard.*

with you, as I remember kneeling at the altar of Cuddesdon Church those 17 years ago in the stillness and darkness of that sacred place, on the eve of my ordination.

Recalling those days, then, what I would say to you is just this—during this week, *let yourself go.* Let yourself go in a simple, sustained, trustful surrender of yourself to the great Captain and offer all your services. Don't let any doubts or apprehensions enter your mind *now.* The time for them is over. Probably you have already made your last and full confession of all your sins and poverty and weakness. When that is done, then, I repeat, let yourself go. Let the thought of the great Love which has chosen you, called you, enter into you—open yourself out to It as arid sand lies open to the inflowing tide—realise all it means to be thus chosen by the Infinite Love to go out and witness to It and fight for It, and let all your manhood welcome It and give itself over to It.

> " O Love, I give myself to Thee,
> Thine ever, only Thine to be."

Those simple words of the hymn, I repeated so often to myself just before ordination, that they always come back to me, bearing the associations of that happy time with them, recalling me from the dryness and dullness of work to the freshness and fullness of the first consecration. Bathe yourself now, dear old boy, in the spirit of them. By God's grace you know something—more than many—of what love, and loving, means. Try to think of all you can conceive of Love, at Its highest, fullest perfection and reality, giving Itself to you now—the Love which is seen in the Life and Passion of Jesus giving Itself in all Its promise of strength and inspiration for the years and the work that are to come—giving Itself in the very call of your ordination—and give yourself over to It.

> " O Love, I give myself to Thee,
> Thine ever, only Thine to be."

Don't *now* check your emotions and the words in which they clothe themselves; don't stop to question and test their reality. The time for that, as I said, is over; and there will be plenty of time for it again. But for this week let yourself go. Then the memory of these days of Love, welcomed and accepted and given, will often come back in later years, to rebuke sometimes, but also to cheer and refresh.

And, lastly, if sometimes during these days you feel tired and the fount of feeling does not run quickly, don't be distressed and don't attempt to work up your emotions. You can quietly say, "Lord, Thou knowest all things, Thou knowest—even if I cannot feel—Thou knowest that I love Thee."

And may God the Holy Spirit be with you to prepare and then to empower you.

Forgive these words. As you know, I don't often let *myself* go. Perhaps I ought to oftener than I do; but this perhaps may make my words more real—let yourself go now.

I shall expect you any time on Saturday.

A few days later, when Dick Sheppard was kneeling in St. Paul's Cathedral, his fingers were clutching a half-sheet of paper in the pocket of his cassock.

Don't worry any more, dear old boy. You have prepared yourself as carefully as you can. Now lean back on a Father's love, and say over and over again in St. Paul's Cathedral, just these words:

"O Love, I give myself to Thee,
Thine ever, only Thine to be."

They were, of course, the words which had brought such help to Lang himself seventeen years earlier in the parish church of Cuddesdon.

"Very seldom," writes the present Dean of Lichfield, "did Lang put a foot down wrong in giving personal advice." On a day in 1904 Mr. Iremonger, a young man eating his dinners at the Middle Temple, went to see the Bishop of Stepney to tell him of his decision, against the wishes of his parents and the remonstrances of his friends, to study for Holy Orders as soon as he had passed his Bar Examinations. What he wished to do was so like what Lang himself had once done that possibly he came to Amen Court looking for a warm, even an enthusiastic, welcome. But "I was not drawn to him at all: he was very official and episcopal." The Bishop did not tell his visitor that he was a fine fellow and should go on in the face of every objection: he warned him that a vocation to the priesthood demanded discipline and preparation and that he ought to spend the next eighteen months fitting himself for it, spiritually and intellectually. Afterwards the young man realised that the Bishop "had done for me—in his own shrewd and inimitable way—exactly what was then needed."

Spy.

"A BISHOP OF DECISION"

THE VIEW FROM BALLURE

Such episodes show not only Lang's influence and the soundness of his personal judgments, but his readiness to accept the responsibility of grave decisions. Another example, of a rather different kind, belongs to the Portsea days and is told by Lang himself in a short memoir of Charles Deveber Schofield, afterwards Bishop of British Columbia.

Charles, as we always called him, was ordained Deacon in the parish church by Bishop Fisher, then Bishop Suffragan of Southampton in the Diocese of Winchester. The story of his Ordination is so unusual that at this distance of time it may well be recorded. There was a great congregation at the Ordination service and Charles was the only man to be ordained. I was myself the preacher, and very naturally I tried to impress upon the congregation the great responsibilities of Ordination to the Ministry of the Church. My words, together with his feelings of solitariness in the presence of the many people, seemed to affect his nerves, already highly strung by his own very intense preparation. When, after the sermon, I was conducting him to the Sanctuary for his Ordination, I heard a very pathetic voice at my side saying, "I cannot go on. Please let me go." I told him to come with me to the vestry. He repeated his plea. Knowing what the Principal of Leeds Clergy School . . . thought about him, I had no hesitation in saying frankly, "This is just a temptation due to your nerves. You must fight and overcome it now and I will stand by to help." We returned to the church. I knelt beside him during the Litany. Now and again he whispered, "I cannot go on. Let me go"; and I whispered in return, "No." In a scarcely audible voice he read the Gospel. Then came the questions. In a feeble voice, while I stood beside him, he managed to say the responses, until the last question came—the promise of obedience, etc., when he stood mute. I suppose he thought this was his last chance of escape. The Bishop repeated the question. Still no answer. What was the Bishop to do? It was his first Ordination, and he turned to me obviously perplexed and distressed. Being myself wholly sure about Charles, and resolved to see him through his trial, I said to the Bishop: "I take full responsibility, and request you to proceed with the Ordination." The Bishop consented. I do not think anyone heard what was passing. And so Charles was ordained. Immediately afterwards I sent him off for a day or two of rest. When he returned he was fully himself again and most grateful to me for rescuing him from his overwrought nerves. I do not know whether he ever afterwards alluded to this very singular Ordination.

Incidents like these largely explain the devotion with which so many of the younger men in the Church came to regard Lang. Not only was he a friend, but quite possibly at some critical moment in their lives he had come forward with a wise head and a firm hand to help them through some difficult decision. In after years Dick Sheppard was to have many moments of impatience and disagreement, but he never forgot what Lang had done for him during his years of uncertainty.

      ★   ★   ★   ★   ★   ★

One morning, in the autumn of 1908, when Lang was sitting at breakfast in Amen Court, a cable arrived with the startling news that he had just been elected Bishop of Montreal. The message further begged him to defer his reply until he had had letters of explanation from the Dean and Chapter and Lord Grey, the Governor-General, and had also seen Lord Strathcona, who was then High Commissioner for Canada in London.

A few days later the promised letters arrived. The Dean described how the Synod, when it met to elect a new Bishop, had been hopelessly divided. Since there seemed little hope of agreement, he had suggested an adjournment for prayer; and during the day that followed the thought of the Bishop of Stepney had come to him in a flash. When the Synod reassembled, he made the suggestion to it, and then and there the Bishop of Stepney was unanimously elected. Lord Grey wrote strongly supporting the offer and urging its acceptance, and Lord Strathcona in person made the same plea.

Lang was quite bewildered at this sudden siege. He consulted the Archbishop of Canterbury and was asked to wait. He went again to Lambeth and had the same reply; a third time, and was still asked to wait. But some answer had to be sent to Montreal, and presently, driving with the Archbishop to a meeting in Queen's Hall, he repeated his question. "It is very difficult," said Dr. Davidson, "but I am afraid I must advise you to refuse." He gave no reason, no sort of explanation, but Lang felt bound to obey and sent a regretful refusal to Montreal.

A few days later, just after his forty-fourth birthday, a second bomb-shell burst on his breakfast-table. This was a letter from Mr. Asquith, the Prime Minister. Lang knew him, for he had been introduced to him at the Prime Minister's express request by the Bishop of London;

but so far his only definite association with him had been slightly unfortunate. Preaching one afternoon in St. Paul's, he had caught sight of Mr. Asquith in the congregation and had realised with a pang that not long before, when he had preached an almost identical sermon in quite a different place, Mr. Asquith had been in the church.

The letter he now opened, however, had no reference to this incident, and was to ask him, in restrained though complimentary terms, to allow himself to be nominated for election to the Archbishopric of York, which Dr. Maclagan was vacating at the end of the year.

Recovering from his surprise, Lang went to see the Prime Minister to discuss the offer, consulted Dr. Davidson and the Bishop of London, and wrote a formal acceptance. His next action was to inform his father and mother, under pledge of the strictest secrecy, of what had happened. The secrecy, it turned out, was hardly necessary, for the newspapers had had word and the reporters were on the parental doorstep demanding photographs and details before the letter reached Aberdeen, where Dr. Lang was now Vice-Chancellor of the University.

The world received the appointment with agreeable surprise. The *Times* described it as "courageous"; most of the comments made much of Lang's extreme youth for so high an office; and, when he visited Windsor later in the month, Queen Alexandra exclaimed in amused dismay that she had not hitherto thought herself old enough to be the mother of an Archbishop. (On the same visit he received a short and simple charge from King Edward—"to keep the parties in the church together and to prevent the clergy wearing moustaches.")

More than two thousand letters of congratulation poured into Amen Court, their variety showing the range of Lang's acquaintance: from Lord Curzon, the Society of Friends, Sir Squire Bancroft, the York Federation of the C.E.M.S.; from Oscar Browning, wishing "that King's could claim for itself the honour in which Balliol is now rejoicing"; from Princess Beatrice, Lord Roberts, the Borough Councils of the East End, the Bishop of Lincoln, who had confirmed him; and from his old friend Hensley Henson, who even then sometimes dropped a little acid into his ink. "I am, of course, surprised," he wrote, "that you go *straight* to an archbishopric. . . . But you are too meteoric for precedent. I am sorry, of course, very sorry that you are so stiff a High Churchman."

Two letters probably gave Lang particular pleasure. One was from Watts-Ditchfield, the Evangelical Vicar of St. James-the-Less, who might be presumed to have little sympathy with Lang's ecclesiastical opinions.

> You have helped me spiritually far more than you can ever know. . . .
> During the past seven years the Church has become more keen, more
> alert, realising more fully her mission, and for this, under God, we
> have to thank you.

The other letter was from Dick Sheppard.

> Take nearly all my heart with you to York. I expect even Archbishops
> need human love at times, and since you can never realise what East
> London is to me without you, I must tell you that I shall never cease
> to pray for God to give you the greatest power and the biggest "guts"
> in Europe and the knowledge, in times of depression, that a young
> freak of a deacon, who owes the intensest joys of his life to you and
> who finds he loves you even more than he loves the East End boy,
> is often on his knees, trying to switch on a little light and love to
> penetrate the loneliness of His Grace's study at York.
> This is written as I think off the reel and it may sound all rot.
> Like my rotten sermons, it admits of no reply.—Your ever grateful
> and devoted   Dick.

Chapter XVII

THE HIGHLAND HOME

ON the very first Sunday that Lang, as the new Dean of Divinity, celebrated in Magdalen Chapel, he noticed a very tall boy among the communicants. Next day the boy called and introduced himself. He was John Ronald Moreton Macdonald of Largie Castle in Kintyre, and his visit was the beginning of the friendship referred to in an earlier chapter.

In the late summer of the following year (1894), possibly at the suggestion of Macdonald, Lang took his holiday at Machrihanish, his companion being Winnington Ingram, with whom he played some strenuous but undistinguished golf; and as they were only some twenty miles from Largie, a visit was paid to the Castle. Next year Lang returned to Kintyre, where he spent most of September as the guest of the Macdonalds, celebrating Holy Communion in the Castle chapel on the mornings of the 8th, the 15th and the 22nd.

He had always been a lover of the Highlands, and this particular country, where in older days Macdonalds and Campbells brawled and broke each other's heads, enchanted him. He looked across the sea to the islands of Cara and Gigha, with behind them the high hills of Jura and Islay, and in the far south-west, like a cloud upon the horizon, the coast of Ireland. As he gazed over the water, and then at the woodland and heather and peace of the Highland hillside, he turned to Ronald Macdonald and said, "This is where I want to be." Macdonald, who was already warmly attached to him, at once declared he would build him a house. He chose a site on a low hill a little to the north-west of the Castle. Here he and the men on the estate, working with timber supposed to have been taken from a wreck, built a little house. It was a very simple structure of wood and stone, with a dining-room hall, a sitting-room and two other rooms, one of which was fitted with bunks, on the ground floor, and upstairs two small bedrooms, one for Lang and one for a guest. Either then or a little later an outside hut with more bunks was added. Lang's new home was completed in April 1896 and was named Tavantaggart (The Priest's Rest) or "The Tave" for short.

Here he came, year after year, sometimes at Easter and always for his summer holiday, when as a rule he stayed for from four to six weeks. He brought his friends, lay and ecclesiastical, choirboys from Magdalen first—"very bright, boisterous and obedient"—choirboys from Portsea afterwards, and chaplains when he was at Stepney and York. They must be ready to lead a simple life, to walk and sail, talk and read, and if possible not to trespass too much upon the time of their host. The walks were and remained a particular delight. There was the long tramp up the glen to the loch in the hills behind, through a charmed land where, in their several seasons, were yellow irises in great clumps, orchids, field gentian and butterwort, bog myrtle and bell heather; without a sound to be heard but the crying of the curlew or living thing to be met but the black-faced sheep. The return would be seawards, and if the day was clear, the Paps of Jura rose, quite close as it seemed across the water, but actually some twenty miles distant. There were other and shorter walks which Lang was to continue taking when he was an old man and unable easily to climb the hill. He would go down to the shore across the turf and short heather, turn northwards to "the Point," and from there inland past the last of the Burnet roses. Or he would take a field path along the hill, skirting a wood, towards a farm where the Macdonalds stayed when Largie was let; and so down to the sea and home across the grass. This he called "going to church." On this and on all his walks—and there were many variations—he had one sovereign rule—as far as was possible to avoid the road.

Father Talbot, who stayed with him, recalls that a walk was punctuated every few hundred yards by exclamations of delight and admiration. Lang treated the view of the islands from his house "very much as the producer of a play might regard its performance." It was as though he were personally responsible for it and must apologise if the weather obscured or dulled its beauty. Nor was the guest "allowed to admire anything but the scene in its full glory. A tribute to something less was as if you had praised unduly an understudy to a *prima donna* and by so doing had diminished the eminent excellence of the latter. Any movement on your part which had not received his sanction was regarded with suspicion and disapproval. To steal off on your own and climb the hill behind the house was, as it were, to assume rights of membership in a club to which he alone could properly introduce you." On the other hand, if these *droits de seigneur* were duly observed, all was well. Lang, Father Talbot concludes, was at his best and happiest on these holiday visits. "He seemed to put off all pomposity and to be a delightful and most entertaining host."

Then there was the chapel at Largie, where Lang was enlisted for the family events, the weddings and the christenings. Indeed, to regularise his position he took a title in the Episcopal Church of Scotland and, as he liked to remind his old friend Canon Simpson, became a Domestic Chaplain with the right to attend meetings of the Representative Church Council. When Largie was let and the tenants were reputed not over-sympathetic, the use of the chapel at the Castle was no longer easy; and for such seasons Macdonald built of rounded logs a rough little hut in the wood near the Macdonalds' farmhouse. This was named St. Hubert's Chapel and became a place of many sacred and happy associations.

"A vivid impression of Our Lord *there*," Lang wrote after celebrating one morning, "coming fresh from the Eternal Holiness, Truth, Beauty, Love, and drawing me—this mere man—drawing those present, Daisy [1] and surely John and her children, drawing the Church of England now, drawing the Church Universal, drawing the whole world—into communion with God through Himself, and communion one with another in Him."

In summer there were excursions by sea and land. Some of his guests have left recollections of these. Canon Crawley recalls a visit to Cara with a boatload of Balfours, one of whom let off his gun by mistake and shot the mast. Or there was a night on the same island in a shepherd's hut, when Lang drew tales out of the shepherd and his wife. There were longer and more adventurous voyages—particularly to Iona, for many years a place of pilgrimage for Lang. He responded very readily to its charm and only gave up his visits when people became tiresome and said he was trying to proselytise.

Another chaplain, Mr. C. S. Donald, tells of an excursion to "Columba's Coif," a cave at the head of Loch Coalisport, some twenty miles from Largie. By tradition St. Columba stayed there on his way from Ireland to Iona, but left when he found that from it he could see the coast of his native land. In the cave are a rock-hewn altar and a cross, reputed to date from the Saint's time; and Lang, then Bishop of Stepney, formed the plan of celebrating Holy Communion in this spot of sacred associations. A party from Largie, headed by Bishop and Laird, was to

[1] Mrs. Macdonald. This was after the death of her husband.

sail up the coast, land and sleep at the house of the owner of the cave, and next morning attend the service. "A grudging wind" brought the little yacht at sunset to the loch's entrance and then died. Rain began to fall. At the water's edge lanterns were waved to show the landing-place, but the yacht was becalmed. Macdonald decided to spend the night on board, but Lang was resolved to sleep ashore, and with some difficulty he and Donald and their suitcases were put in the dinghy and landed. The lanterns were gone, the night was dark, the rain poured down. They missed the path, which was blocked by a fallen tree, and at first every track they followed took them back to the shore. At last, after a long trudge through dripping pine woods, they stumbled on what was clearly a garden wall, and climbing over this fell with their suitcases into a bed of saturated rhubarb. By this time they were soaked to the skin and their tempers were slightly frayed, but persevering they at last found shelter.

The service, which had to be postponed for twenty-four hours while clothes were dried, was memorable in itself, and also for the loveliness of the morning, with the sun shining into the cave, and a robin singing at the moment of Consecration, and a black cock and a grey hen who sat in the heather near by, as though part of the little congregation.

Mr. Donald also recalls the occasion at Largie when David Dhu, the big Highland bull, was starting for the Perth show by road on a float. The bull contrived to prod the horse with an immense horn; the horse bolted; the factor in his best black Sunday clothes was rolled down the brae; the terrier bit the waggoner; and the Bishop and the Laird, hanging on manfully to the ropes which held the bull, were nearly carried over the side, with horse, bull and float, into the stream twenty feet below. However, all was well, control was re-established, David Dhu went off to Perth and won his medal, and a Bishop of Stepney survived to be Archbishop of Canterbury.

Impatient though Lang was of interruptions to his summer holiday, for many years in succession he went to Balmoral for a few days. He avoided if possible a Sunday there, since monarchs were slow to understand why bishops and archbishops hesitated to attend the Presbyterian Kirk at Crathie, whither royal guests were expected to go. Lang knew too much about the religious situation in Scotland to pretend that there was for him any easy way out of an old and unsolved problem.

When he became Archbishop of York, Macdonald laughingly suggested that "The Tave" hardly fitted the new dignity and offered to build an extra storey, but in 1914 another solution appeared. Ballure, a dower-house of the Macdonalds about three miles from the Castle, fell vacant through the death of the tenant. Lang was offered and accepted the lease; and so for the rest of his life Ballure was his retreat, "my beloved place of peace." It is a small grey house, standing well above the road and looking out between trees over the sea and the islands. To the right, as you enter, is a small drawing-room, not greatly used by Lang except when ladies were staying with him. On the left is the dining-room, beyond it Lang's study, and beyond that "the Cell," so often mentioned in his notes, a tiny place, with an altar, a prie-Dieu and two or three chairs.

In Ballure, from 1914 to 1945, he made his Highland home, keeping, in his methodical Scots way, to a routine more strict as he grew older. Most of the morning was spent in "the Cell." He would take a nap after luncheon, and then there would be a walk or an excursion in the car or by water. On his return he would sit in the summer-house and read the *Times* or his book of the moment. It was, to outward view at any rate, a pleasant, pottering life. No one bothered him; and to a wandering visitor the elderly gentleman wearing what was known as "the stockbroker suit" might have been a business man on holiday from Glasgow.

Such was his rule, for a month or more in every year; and in talk and in writing he repeatedly recorded his conviction that without this time at Ballure he could never support the drudgery and cares of his office.

At Largie, "The Tave" and Ballure, Lang found a little of the family life he could not have at Portsea, at Amen Court, or even later at Bishop-thorpe, when he had the Crawleys for company in the north wing of the house. Ronald Macdonald himself was one close friend; his wife, after his marriage, became another; and the children, as they appeared, were his by christening, confirmation and general adoption. Among his papers was found a letter, dated April 30th, 1906, the Macdonalds' wedding-day.

My more than ever dear Taggart,[1]—I must send you a line before this great day is quite over to say what a very great difference it made to us both—and to me of course in particular—to have you to marry us; and to thank you for your help. I don't think I realised before what a difference it would make to have you; but I do now. Perhaps

[1] Gaelic for "priest." Lang was always called Taggart by the Macdonalds and their friends.

I never really understood before to what an extent I was bound to you and dependent on you.

I would like to take this opportunity to thank you for your loyal friendship through these years; but somehow friendship is not a thing of yea and nay, and perhaps I would do better to thank God for it; and that I *will* do before I go to bed to-night.

Rather as Tupper-Carey had done many years before, he ended by asking Lang—"From Daisy as well as from me"—to break in on the honeymoon for a night.

In the late summer of 1921 Lang was at Ballure as usual. On the night of September 2nd he was visiting on one of the islands when he was recalled by a telegram. Macdonald, who was then staying in Ballure, had been taken seriously ill with an internal ulcer. Lang returned the next day. Mrs. Macdonald, who had also been away, hastened back and a specialist was summoned from Glasgow. On September 7th, after a blood transfusion, Macdonald collapsed, and on the 10th he died. It fell to Lang, in the midst of his sorrow, to make all the necessary arrangements, on a dull dark September day to follow the coffin (of timber from the Largie woods) as it was piped to the family burial ground, and to read the funeral service over the body of his friend; and thereafter, from year to year, as September came round, he would try to set aside any business that might keep him from Largie and the annual commemoration.

But Ballure was something more to Lang than a beloved home, which each year he rediscovered with delight and left with an ache in his heart. It was even more than a part of his life. With Cuddesdon it was, by his own judgment, the most important part of it; and whatever may be the truth of that verdict, it is quite certain that to know him properly it was necessary to have known him at Ballure, or at least to have some idea of the life he led there. It was not merely that in Ballure he shed the cares of the Church and the circumstance with which, as Archbishop, he protected himself, the self-consciousness which hardly ever left him in the world outside. Something more than that happened to him at the end of his long journey, when he drove up the steep little drive and put on "the stockbroker suit." The journey itself was part of the drama of transformation; for he made of it the long and leisurely business of "the Snob's Progress," during which he was very much a Prince of the Church. But "here again in blessed Ballure" all that was over; and the world that had watched a busy prelate, perhaps thinking him proud, self-important, ambitious and worldly-minded, would have seen a very different man.

"The Cell" was the heart of Ballure. During the first days of his holiday he would contrive, if he could, to be alone, so as to be able to spend his mornings in uninterrupted prayer and meditation.

In this sacred little place, by God's mercy, watersprings break from a dry and thirsty land. It is a marvel to me that in spite of all my prayerlessness in the busy months of the years, all my forgetfulness of the lessons learnt in the Cell year after year, God does not take His Holy Spirit from me. . . . It is here that my real self—at least what ought to be my real self—*lives*.

So he wrote in one of the many little notebooks which he covered with pencil jottings, even more illegible than the writing in his letters. Much of their content may be thought too private for publication, and yet to understand him something must be given, for these books are far more revealing than is anything in his autobiographical notes. Did he even in these jottings, rid himself entirely of the curse of self-conscious-ness of which he was so well aware? Some will doubt it. He doubted it himself. "It is so difficult," he wrote, "to exorcise the thought that some other eye than my own may read." Yet he tried, and the trail when followed takes us nearer to him than we are likely to get by following any other path. Sometimes, surely, the thickets in which he hid himself so persistently are torn aside and we have a glimpse of the man—not as the world saw him, not even as, at other times and in other places, he saw himself, but as he was.

For he came to "the Cell" each year in an agony of contrition, oppressed by a sense of his failures and shortcomings. This appears again and again in the notes, where his meditations—on St. Mark's Gospel, on some particular psalm, on a text from that old favourite of his mother's, *Daily Light*, or on some book he was reading like C. F. Andrew's *Christ in the Silence*—are mingled with confession and prayer; always returning to the same cry of humility and shame—"*Domine, non sum dignus.*" He was unworthy to be bishop, unworthy to be priest, unworthy of every spiritual privilege God had given him.

In 1926 he wrote:

In Cell this morning read with some humiliation the record of 1924 and realised how pitifully I am the same "yesterday and to-day" and wondered whether I shall be the same for ever. . . . Reflected on my work after twenty-five years. Am I losing initiative, hope, adventure ? Yes.

Later still, after he had become Archbishop of Canterbury, he had to confess :

I come in penitence, after a year's lack of prayer and meditation . . . of sadly incomplete surrender of self to God. . . . What have I really *achieved*, in my own soul or in the life of the Church—leaves, leaves, leaves, mostly falling now, but how little fruit ! God forgive me !

Why was it so with him ? It must be, he thought, through "an incompleteness of self-surrender" that he had "after all these years . . . such a poor, broken, maimed, inconstant offering to make to God."

He wrote at greatest length in 1924, shortly before his sixtieth birthday :

Let me record again my thankfulness for God's merciful and wonderful goodness to me in the Cell for these last ten years. Year after year its peace abides, welcomes, tranquillises, inspires. It has become filled with a sense of the Divine Presence—laden with sacred association, a sense, an atmosphere, which it seems to keep ready for me when I return to it. So it has become like Cuddesdon Church— how I wish Bishopthorpe Chapel could gain the same atmosphere !— and when I ask myself whether I still wish every year to come back to this place, what makes me answer "yes," even more than the ever fresh beauty of the West Highlands, are these precious memories and gift of the Cell. Yes, sixty years. Divisions of time are arbitrary and conventional. Yet somehow I have always felt that sixty would make a very special sign in life. It means at least that in years, whatever it may mean in spirit, one passes from middle to old age. Very definitely the longest part of the way through this earthly life is behind. What remains must be the closing scenes.

I come burdened with the thought of manifold failure. In spite of Cuddesdon at Easter I know . . . that I have been "letting myself down." So the thought uppermost in my mind when I re-entered the Cell was that of the Prodigal Son. I had been in a far country, too often not ashamed to eat husks fit only for swine. And seldom have I used the old words, "Father, I have sinned . . . and am no more worthy to be called thy son," with more sincerity and shame and great desire for the Father and His House. And once again the wonder was brought back to me of the Father seeing His prodigal *a long way off*, and running to meet him, and covering him with the robe of forgiveness.

I have been reading afresh the book which helped me much before my ordination, thirty-four years ago—*Méditations sur les Saints Ordres* by Henri Perreyve. *There* he gave expression in passionate French to thoughts and desires and emotions which I then genuinely had and which it was difficult for a Scot to put into words. When I remember how real then was all this—this desire to be a saint, this prayer for detachment from the things of the world, for chastity, for the "love of souls," for this ardent service of Christ and His Kingdom, this abandonment of self to the Lord Jesus—and then think of these thirty-four years since, I am really *overwhelmed* with shame—there's no other word. To think of the thing that I am now at nearly sixty being all that I can bring to God as the result of His Love and Grace. What must have been His Purpose, when all those years ago He changed my life and revealed something I had never known before—the "joy and peace of believing," the sense of His Love and the peace of His Presence? When in a way I cannot doubt He called me to His Service, what (was His) purpose for me in my own character, in my life for this Church and Nation? And yet this, this poor and shoddy thing, is all that I can show for their fulfilment! . . .

I have tried hard to *rationalise* those early experiences. . . . But it won't do, unless the whole of one's inner life and the highest and truest part of the life of man is a delusion and a mockery. No: if I am called to swear my conviction of the truth of anything, I will swear that behind these experiences there is a Reality—God in Christ. I must stake my life on that truth. Else indeed it is "a tale told by an idiot . . . signifying nothing." . . .

It is all I have really to live for, so I must simply get back to it, rebuild these few remaining years on it, be reconverted, and trust that even yet I may be able out of the fragments left to give God a love, a life, which has not actually failed for His purpose. . . .

So in the Cell this morning . . . I came back and renewed my desires and dared to repeat again the old refrain of Scheffler's hymn—

> " O Love, I give myself to Thee,
> Thine ever, only Thine to be."

It did not seem to be a mere "crying in the night." There did seem to be a Presence, still, calming, enfolding me as with a robe of Love and Mercy. And curiously enough, in the stillness after I had made my prayer and offering, I heard some small bird—I don't know what—singing . . . what sounded like a song of spring. Spring in the autumn of sixty years! So be it—Amen.

Ronald Macdonald once said: "He might have been Cardinal Wolsey or St. Francis of Assisi, and he chose to be Cardinal Wolsey." That was perhaps an over-simplification of a complex character. Lang, as will have been observed, was for ever harking back to early life. He once told Canon Simpson that when he was born his mother found herself unaccountably repeating the words addressed by Pharaoh's daughter to the mother of Moses when the baby was drawn from the water: "Take this child, and nurse it for me, and I will give thee thy wages." From the beginning he was as one marked out for a high destiny. So, as a boy and a young man, he had been immensely ambitious, absorbed in the business of getting on, carving a career, making a name. He could and must win his way to the top; his will was fixed on success, all his thoughts revolved round it. It was his life, which he watched unfolding, like a drama, himself both actor and audience. Then one day everything seemed to be changed by a question—"Why shouldn't *you* be ordained?"—and the answer he found to it in Cuddesdon Church; but when the dust of the upheaval had settled, stage, actor, audience and theme were back almost as they had been: only the detail was different. The end was to be Convocation and not the House of Commons, Lambeth Palace and not No. 10 Downing Street. One part of him still acted, posed a little, was intensely preoccupied with the play and with keeping the rules of the theatre. It was the part the world saw and did not always like. Yet the other part was there too, the boy who rode on the Downs with "Tupper" on a spring afternoon, and prayed in Cuddesdon Church, and made a choice. Here in Ballure he was bitterly conscious of this conflict of Ormuzd and Ahriman, of the ambitious, forceful, histrionic prelate and the man of prayer and penitence; conscious too that those things which counted for so much with him during eleven months of the year—to be the successor of St. Wilfrid or St. Augustine, to walk with kings, to be on easy terms with the famous, to stay in the houses of the great—in the cool accusing stillness of the Highlands all this was no more than the stuff that men hang on Christmas trees for the delight of children.

Yet even in the depths of his contrition he must have known in his heart that when his car had swung out of the little drive on the journey back to Bishopthorpe or Lambeth, and "the Cell" lay behind him, he would be back in that old life of incessant toil and ubiquitous temptation, when prayer was so difficult and sin was so easy. "*Video meliora proboque, deteriora sequor.*" Once he had meant it all to be quite different, but now it was too late to change the play. Presently the curtain would go up on a new Act which he could neither cut nor revise. The plot must march inexorably on; or rather, having reached its climax, must mark time. The poor Scots boy had become a Prince of the Church, and the gods in the gallery had clapped and stamped, and everyone had been satisfied—except a man on his knees in a little Highland house.

What was the matter with him? He could not and would not distrust his vocation. He believed that he had been repeatedly "disobedient unto the Heavenly vision," but he could not doubt the reality of his experience and his call to the priesthood. For if these were not true, his whole life was a monstrous error, a parody that was nearly a blasphemy.

His thoughts continually went back thirty or forty or fifty years to a young man on a Sunday evening in the parish church at Cuddesdon. They might have gone back further still to the boy of eight or nine who walked westward from Ardrishaig towards the setting sun, seeking something, a discovery, an adventure, an ideal, the unknown which at all costs he must follow and find; until, tired and hungry and disappointed, he had sunk on a bank and surrendered himself to pursuers and punishments from the workaday world.

So the argument went on, year by year. It was marked by those who knew him best that if, as he grew older, he became less forceful and dynamic, he also became gentler and more lovable. Was this simply the mellowing that comes with age, or was it the answer to his prayers in "the Cell"? This at least is certain. Many men, as time slips by, take themselves for granted. They are not continually searching themselves for sins, weighing and examining their lives and finding them wanting. Without necessarily condoning their weaknesses, they come to accept them as part of themselves, finally perhaps to forget all about them. Lang was preserved from such complacency partly by his self-consciousness and a lifelong habit of introspection; but far more by a spiritual flame which might flicker and die down, but could never be extinguished. It is not the ordinary unregenerate man, but the saint or one not far from sanctity, who is most conscious of sin, of the fearful disparity between God's Will and his own way of life, of his utter failure to keep to or even near the course he once had plotted. Because Lang was essentially a man of prayer, his remorse was the more extreme. Because he set his standard so high, his failures to reach it appeared to him so pitiful. Because he never lost the vision he once had seen, his judgments on himself were so harsh.

Above all, in spite of every failure, he would go on trying. One afternoon, in the Chapel at Bishopthorpe, he was speaking to a small group of young people of the active desire for spiritual progress which each should have. "If," he told them, "I were to think that I could never advance beyond the point I have now reached, I should be un-utterably depressed. It is only the thought of what I may some day become that keeps hope in me." It was that thought which upheld him in Bishopthorpe, in Lambeth, above all at Cuddesdon and in "the Cell" at Ballure, through setback and disappointment to his life's end.

Chapter XVIII

ARCHBISHOP OF YORK

THE new Archbishop was forty-four. In eighteen years from Ordination he had risen to the second highest position in the Church of England, so that Hensley Henson's description of his career as "meteoric" was fully justified; and since Dr. Maclagan, his predecessor as Archbishop, had just retired at the age of eighty-two, the contrast between past and future was likely to be marked. Maclagan would probably have described himself with Bishop Wilberforce as "a High Churchman on an Evangelical basis"—a label which Lang would not have rejected for himself. But Maclagan's High Churchmanship found no outward expression in ritual, which he disliked, whereas Lang had a strong sense of the value of ceremonial, not so much perhaps to express doctrine as to give dignity and beauty to the worship of the Church. Mr. Kensit and his followers, at any rate, were conscious of a contrast in this respect too. They denounced the appointment on the grounds that the new Archbishop was a "Romaniser," and appeared in force to make their protest at the confirmation of the election. The Archbishop of Canterbury, however, not for the last time, adroitly and politely manœuvred them off the scene, leaving them possibly with a vague sense of a lost opportunity, though they could scarcely have said how and why they had missed it.

The enthronement at York was on St. Paul's Day (January 25th), 1909.

I cannot say it was a very well-conceived ceremony, e.g. it had been arranged that the Bishops of the Province should be attended by their Chapters, which made a great muddle. The clergy of the diocese were placed with civic dignitaries and the mass of the people in the nave. The best places in the choir were given by the Dean to his friends, old ladies and the like who were devoted to him. I was placed on my throne symbolically—as the old alleged Saxon chair was used—by the Dean, my dear old friend Purey-Cust.

The night before the ceremony the Kensitites staged a demonstration in York, but the City was not tolerating outside interference of this kind, and the discomfited demonstrators, chased by a crowd of six thousand people, retired to the safety of the police station.

Next day the Minster was filled with six hundred clergy and more than five thousand people. The Archbishop's chaplain, Wilfrid Parker, was kept in London by illness, but Lumley Green-Wilkinson took his place and carried the pastoral staff, while the Rev. W. G. Pennyman, the vicar of Bishopthorpe, was also in attendance and bore the primatial cross. The ceremony, as Lang noted, was not as impressive as it might have been, the arrangements having an air of amateurishness to anyone accustomed to the precision of St. Paul's; and the music, Lang told Wilfrid Parker afterwards, was "too finicking."

It was a bitterly cold January day, but the weather did not daunt the crowds in and around the Minster. Along a path lined by members of the Church of England Men's Society the new Archbishop made the traditional approach to the West door, where a zealous policeman, unfamiliar with the rites of the Church, anticipated him by knocking on it himself. As Lang passed up the nave into the choir, to be surrounded by a great concourse of ecclesiastics, most of whom were elderly, he looked young to be there at all, let alone to be the eighty-ninth Bishop since Paulinus. This thought may have been in his own mind. A sense of the responsibility he was assuming weighed on him, and one who was present noted the mixture of strength and anxiety on his face.

So the ceremony went its course, watched with deepest interest by an old Scots lady who had come all the way from Aberdeen to see her son enthroned and was given a favoured place close to the altar rails. Dr. Lang should have been there too, perhaps to remind his wife of their first and only previous visit to York Minster, when as a young couple, not long married, they had stood there in wonder and awe, and without a thought so absurd as that one day a son of theirs would be Archbishop. But at the last moment Dr. Lang was taken ill. He could not make the journey and the family was represented by his wife and his sons, Patrick and Norman.

Some people expected that I would follow the London use and wear cope and mitre. But I deliberately did not do so, as I had no wish even to seem to play to any section within the Church. And there was a consequence of this worth noting, of which I did not learn until long after. It seems that the clergy of Sheffield, who were then almost wholly Evangelical, had been discussing the new Archbishop, about whom they had serious apprehensions, with the worthy Rural Dean, Gilmore. After the manner of the British Bishops on the advent of Augustine, they decided on a sign which would determine their opinion of what they might expect in the new *régime*. It was whether or not the new Archbishop would wear a mitre! As I did not, they were reassured; and from that time onward the good Gilmore, distinguished by his long patriarchal whiskers, was my most devoted henchman, and all his clergy were most loyal and cordial.

Here I may add that later on, quietly and without any fuss, first at an Ordination in the Minster, I wore cope and mitre, certainly the first to do so either there or in the whole Province since the Reformation. The custom was gradually extended and indeed welcomed, and I never had one single word of protest or remonstrance—an illustration, I think, of the wisdom of doing these things quietly and gradually. Some years after, an anonymous donor—it was the late Lord Halifax—presented to the Minster for the use of the Archbishops, a gorgeous cope and mitre of cloth of gold, which I used on great occasions. I lived to see vestments in ordinary use in the Minster, and again no word of protest ever reached me.

In the choir and again in the nave the Archbishop spoke, first on the history of the Church and its significance, and then on the work that lay before clergy and laity alike. Many have witnessed to the drama and thrill of his appeal: "Men of the North, we are calling upon you to rise and work with new zeal and force for your Lord and for His Church."

So he passed out of the Minster, "installed, inducted and enthroned Archbishop of York"; and as the early winter darkness fell he drove out to Bishopthorpe, the village two and a half miles from the city, where he was to live. Here too he was royally received, for the bells of the village church were ringing, the horses were taken from the carriage, and a team of sidesmen and choirmen drew the Archbishop through an avenue of torch-bearers to his new home.

The house was already quite prepared to receive me. This was due to a man for whom I have many reasons to be grateful, Harry Dixon, introduced to me first by Lumley Green-Wilkinson. He was a man of most cultivated taste and expert knowledge of furniture and furnishings of all sorts, at that time connected with the firm of White,

Allom & Co. He had bought everything for me, either in London or from the sale of the Maclagan furniture, chiefly in London. People wondered how a bachelor could furnish a big house, and all I can say is that, thanks to Dixon, it never gave me a moment's trouble. Yet I settled everything, except for the minor articles which Dixon settled, and this without ever entering a shop. The result was admirable. The furniture for the drawing-room, now at Canterbury, was mainly of the William and Mary period, exact copies of existing and well-known pieces. The study was furnished amply through the pence of the East End. The dining-room, with its rich Renaissance ceiling and the portraits of my predecessors, had a very fine long refectory table of oak, rescued by Dixon from the servants' hall, which I afterwards left as a gift to the house. So all was ready, from curtains and carpets down to dust-cloths. It was a delightful and most comfortable home.

Then there were the grounds and the garden. The grounds were

some eight or nine acres (I suppose) of lawn and trees with a small lake or fishpond at the end, bounded by the curving River Ouse. I know of no more delightful grounds round any episcopal house, though Cuddesdon has its noble view and Chichester its outlook on the Cathedral. The trees are good—two noble larches in the centre of the lawn, a famous hornbeam (now, alas! blown down), several deodar cedars and Spanish chestnuts, a fine Austrian pine, a splendid plane tree (one of the largest I have ever seen), a group of magnificent beeches, and an avenue of limes. Next the garden. When I came there were very few flowers, except in some beds on the main lawn. There was a very large kitchen garden, with fine old brick walls, some distance from the house. In an early fit of economy I let this for a market garden; but I soon found that the tenant merely exhausted the ground and made it most untidy. I therefore determined to take it into my own hands. I got a new gardener, Budden, a Dorset man, who came from Bramham Park. It proved a most happy choice. He showed at once a real love of flowers and something like a genius for colour. Under his guidance I soon determined to give at least half of the kitchen garden, including a delightful walled garden, to flowers. The result was the creation of a garden with a long herbaceous border which became famous in Yorkshire. It opened out a new life for me and was a source of unending interest and delight. Also, the terrace on the river became a paved garden filled with all manner of flowers which bloomed in the spring and early summer.

To this account some particulars may be added.

Bishopthorpe has been incorrectly called a palace. It is a large and rambling house, begun in 1240, with many additions of different periods and merits. It might almost be described as three houses, with a north wing so distinct that a separate family can easily be housed there. Lang lived in it while the main building was being altered, decorated and furnished; and later on it was occupied successively by the de Boinvilles and the Crawleys.

Much needed to be done at Bishopthorpe and much was done, either at the outset of Lang's primacy or in the course of twenty years. He removed the canopy over the porch as dangerous, dismantled the stables, reorganised and extended the central heating, put in three new bathrooms, and replaced the clock in the gatehouse. The actual decorations and furniture were appropriate, if rather too prelatical for the liking of everyone. The drawing-room was the *chef d'œuvre* and the Archbishop was not allowed to see it until it was quite finished. When the moment arrived, a small party of friends accompanied him, holding their breath in suspense as they awaited the verdict. The door was flung open. The Archbishop walked in and stood for two minutes surveying the room. Then he turned to Dixon and said with unusual emphasis: "Yes, my dear Dixon, I think it is quite *admirable*." So all was well. Into the midst of all this new magnificence Lang imported, as a relic or a reminder of earlier days, the horrible iron bedstead which gave Tupper-Cary such a bad night at Leeds and at Amen Court provoked the unfavourable comment of the future Lord Cavan. A friend at last conspired with the chaplains to replace it with something more comfortable and less repelling; and a new bedstead was bought and smuggled into the Archbishop's bedroom while he was at dinner. He meekly accepted the change, although next morning he accused the conspirators of having destroyed his "last link with the Apostles."

In meditation at Ballure he reflected wistfully on his failure to find in the chapel at Bishopthorpe the spiritual atmosphere of "the Cell." Yet he describes it as

one of the most beautiful and satisfying of the episcopal chapels. It was pure early thirteenth-century, built by Archbishop Walter Gray.

The stained-glass windows, quite good, had been placed there by Archbishop Maclagan—the Incarnation over the altar and figures representing the Church in the North, Aidan and Bede and St. Andrew, patron saint of Bishopthorpe. I soon put in an "English altar"—a *memorial* I called it of my time with my beloved first chaplain there, Wilfrid Parker. The services there were a great joy— an almost daily Eucharist, for which I used white vestments. Would that I could have used the chapel more for private prayers and meditation!

The grounds and gardens were to give him some of his happiest hours. In addition to the improvements he has noted, he cleared the grounds near the house, planted many trees and shrubs, and later, when the Crawley family were in the north wing, made two tennis-courts for their entertainment. But the glory of the garden, as he himself claims, was the great double herbaceous border, nearly a hundred yards long, which people would come many miles to see. This, to reach its full perfection, was the work of years. Lang was not a gardener when he came to Bishopthorpe: he was when he left.

Such a setting demanded grace and dignity of living.

It was made more easy by the blessing of good and faithful servants: till the end of the War, Raymond, best of butlers, friendly without presuming; as housekeeper, first, till her health gave way, the gentle and anxious Annie Loosemore, whom I brought from Amen Court, then Mrs. Opie, still (1937) happily with me at Lambeth; Martha Saville, also from Amen Court, first as head housemaid, then, after the War, when I gave up men servants, as head parlourmaid.

Finally there were Budden, "my wholly admirable gardener, creator of the gardens both at Bishopthorpe and at Lambeth," and Walter Wells, "I think the best chauffeur ever known," he wrote in 1937—"a skilful driver and mechanic, who in spite of my constant motoring has so far, after twenty-seven years, preserved me from any accident." "Few men," he concluded, "have been more blessed in the possession of 'good and faithful servants.'"

He added a note about "that remarkable man" his secretary, Mr. R. A. D. Booker.

He had been employed by Archbishop Thomson; he was with Archbishop Maclagan for eighteen years; so that when I left he had been Archbishop's secretary for more than forty years. He had a wife and family in York, but he kept his private life, which was not very happy, rigorously and obstinately to himself. Every day, whatever the weather, he walked the two and a half miles from and to York: he never missed a single day all my twenty years. All day he was glued to his desk: it was his life. He was fairly good at shorthand and typing, but his system, or rather want of system, of filing was lamentable. I tried with some success to reform it. But what he lacked in his method he made up for in his memory. It was amazing. Though he never left his desk, he could tell me all about every parson in the diocese, and had his own somewhat cynical view of the clergy. Take this for an example: "Do you know anything about Mr. So-and-so?"—"Well, your Grace, he wants watching: he writes poetry!" Impenetrable, indefatigable, a sort of automaton, he passed his days without either enthusiasm or complaint, but unfailing in his industry and fidelity. It would need a Trollope to describe him.

At the gates was the village of Bishopthorpe.

It was when I came, and during all my twenty years, in the main, though so near York, a country village. Though I could not often visit the homes of the villagers, in one way or another I saw much of them, and the "Lower Hall" at the Palace (built by Archbishop Maclagan) was a centre of their social life. I liked them, good-hearted Yorkshire folk, and they were always most friendly to me. The parish church was modern, built in the time of Archbishop Maclagan, in place of a very poor old church on the river bank: light, roomy and of good proportions. I used to preach there on the great festivals and on many other occasions; and I have many happy associations with it.

Of the Minster itself Lang writes little, not, it may be said with certainty, from any lack of appreciation, but perhaps because he felt that where others had written so much, his own tribute was superfluous. It was the first and greatest church in the Diocese: that went almost without saying.

Disraeli may have been overstepping the mark when he said in his youth, after travelling abroad: "I have seen the three greatest buildings in Europe—the Parthenon of Athens, the Alhambra of Spain, and the Minster of York." But assuredly it is a most noble thing. It would be tedious to write about it here—about the glory of the transepts and the unique beauty of the glass, etc. Suffice it to say that for two things I am thankful: one, that it was my Cathedral Church for twenty years; and two, that there is no place for comparison between it and Canterbury: they are wholly different in style and spirit, each with its own supreme excellence.

Participation in services at the Minster was to be the more agreeable from the friendliness of the Dean and Chapter. The relationship between a Bishop and a Dean is not always easy, but Dr. Purey-Cust was the old friend who many years before had circumvented the regulations in order to get a young deacon from Leeds into the Minster pulpit.

He was already what is called an "institution," a fine old aristocrat, beloved by all. I was once walking beside him in the street at York and overheard one workman say to his mate, pointing to the Dean: "A s'pose it taakes about three hundred years to make *that*." His relations with Archbishop Thomson had been notorious. It was the old case of Bishop versus Dean within the Cathedral, both obstinate about their rights. In Convocation, when Thomson was President and Purey-Cust was Prolocutor, the disputes between the two were habitual. Is it not on record that when the Lower House, to avoid deadlocks, proposed that a committee should be appointed to consider the relations of the President and the Prolocutor, the Dean said that such a committee was unnecessary, as these relations were well known: the President seemed to consider that the Prolocutor was only a doormat on which he was pleased to wipe his shoes? No doubt there were faults on both sides. But in justice to the Dean it has to be said that there was never the slightest friction between him and Thomson's successors, Maclagan and myself. How often it proves true that if rights are not asserted they are in fact conceded, and that the best solvent of disputed rights is a little genial good humour, not unmixed with chaff! Certainly as long as the old Dean lived, nothing ever disturbed our mutual harmony and affection.

So the rule of twenty years began, with almost every auspice favourable. Irrespective of ecclesiastical opinion, the appointment of the new Archbishop was undoubtedly an act of daring. The criticism has often been heard that the high places of the Church are filled with "safe men," the sort who, making no mistakes, do not make anything else that matters very much. But Lang was not in this sense a "safe man." He had ideas and the forcefulness which can carry them out. In those days there was something about him of a Man of Destiny. His rapid rise to authority, the ease with which he dominated each new position, and above all his remarkable achievement with the Church of England Men's Society suggested that here at last was a man of God who would bring His Spirit into the dry bones that they might stand upon their feet, "an exceeding great army." To a generation which only knew the Archbishop as an old man such a picture may seem far-fetched; in 1908 it was no fantasy, but a reasonable forecast of things to come. Lang's arresting appearance, his physical and intellectual vitality, his magnificent voice, his power to seize and hold an audience, his talent for affairs were apparent at once to all who saw him.

Mrs. Lionel Ford, whose husband was presently to be Dean of York, describes his English as "glorious." "He could paint word pictures and touch the imagination and emotions in a wonderful way"; and she recalled her husband pointing out to her "his masterly use of substantives, which boomed through his discourses like themes in a fugue." Some of the effect was lost when the spoken became the written word, separated from the voice and presence of the speaker. Lang was an orator; and it is the rarer sort of oratory that passes with undiminished effect through the transformation into prose.

In more intimate talk among friends he had the rare quality of the spellbinder, who compels not so much by argument as by the sheer power of personality. Some indeed, as Lord Cavan has recorded of himself, avoided him for that very reason, fearing to be driven into decisions which they would wish to repudiate when no longer under the magic of his presence.

"I came to think later," writes Father Talbot, "that there was a certain danger in his capacity to dramatise your life for you and to impose a picture of your potentialities. Encouraging it was, no doubt, but it sometimes inclined you to accept a rather fictitious valuation of yourself. More than once I have had to resist the magnetic pull of his influence and the cogency with which he sought to fit me into a pattern, alluring indeed to vanity as he presented it in vivid colour, but misleading. I have sometimes wondered whether some of the men who in early days were swept into Holy Orders under his influence were reacting too readily to the spell of his persuasion and found themselves misfits. But this perhaps is a presumptuous surmise."

It was a side of Lang hidden from the great majority, who never saw him at close quarters. They were more aware of an Archbishop, playing the part in the grand manner, often a little too self-consciously for their taste. "I think," wrote Dr. Webb, "that some of the misunderstanding of him . . . arose from the Englishman's tendency to suspect *acting* of insincerity. Lang's instinctive sense of the dramatically or spectacularly appropriate made him a wonderful performer in great ceremonies and the like; but of course a wonderful performer is not in the least of necessity a humbug or without a deep and serious interest in what he is doing. Yet it is not always easy to convince a certain kind of man that this is so." Lang was fully aware of his gift and of its uses. His sense of the theatre never left him. But to say that he was a great actor [1] is very far from saying that he was a great humbug. Indeed, the opposite is true, for without an essential sincerity no acting can be great. He had a clear picture of what an Archbishop should be, how he should look and behave and live. As a man might school himself to play Hamlet or Othello he schooled himself to play the part; and in time, like any good actor, he merged himself in it and became what he was playing. That is, in large measure, the story of the next twenty years.

[1] Dramatic talent may have been in his blood. Matheson Lang, the well-known actor, was a cousin.

Chapter XIX

THE DIOCESE AND THE PROVINCE

WHEN I became Archbishop, York was a huge diocese alike in population and in extent. For at that time, and for five years after, it contained what is now the Diocese of Sheffield and, until a year or so before I left, another part of the West Riding now included, to its great benefit, in the Diocese of Wakefield. There must have been, I suppose, some six hundred benefices, always the real token of what a diocese means to its Bishop. There were two great cities, Sheffield and Hull, manufacturing towns like Middlesbrough, crowded colliery districts in the West Riding, seaside resorts like Scarborough, Whitby and Bridlington, the old City of York, and masses of country parishes. The Diocese then contained the whole of the East Riding and large parts of the West and North Ridings. It extended from Sheffield in the south to Middlesbrough in the north; from Castleford in the west to Hull in the east. What was always most attractive about it was the variety in conditions and character of its people; the wide range, from great cities and crowded colliery districts to the quietest and most remote country regions; its scenery—the smoky West Riding, the great moors of the North Riding, the plain of York, the wide fields and the open spaces of the Wolds in the East Riding. The variety and beauty of the scenery was always a delight and refreshment to me as I went about the Diocese. I cannot think now without emotion, say, of the road across the moors from Pickering to Whitby, or the views of the Plain of York from the Wolds, or of Cleveland from its hills, or of Rievaulx Abbey nestling in its wooded valley, or the great vale stretching from Helmsley to Scarborough.

Was there any diocese, he asked, more rich in beautiful churches? There was York Minster itself, Beverley with its "matchless choir," and Selby Abbey. The last had been badly burned just before his time. He saw it first in its desolation, and in September 1912, when it had been rebuilt, he came again, to enjoy its recovered loveliness and to dedicate the restoration. Beverley and Selby were supreme, recalling the old days when Ripon and Southwell Minsters were also in the Diocese of York. There were others, such as Holy Trinity, Hull, and the Priory Church at Bridlington, and Hedon, and Patrington, rightly called "the Queen of Holderness," or Howden, even in its ruins; and of quite another sort, remarkable rather for old-world quaintness than for beauty, the old Parish Church of Whitby, with its three-decker still in use and a family pew still across the chancel screen, where I found myself blessing the backs of its occupants! I remember assuring the churchwardens that if anyone attempted to modernise its oddities it would be over my dead body! And there were many country churches full of beauty and history, like Lastingham. All these were a continual joy.

Of course, it was far too large a diocese for the Archbishop with all his added duties in the Province. I can't imagine how, even in more recent times, before the advent of the motor car made transit so infinitely easier, and before Sheffield was separated, my predecessors, Thomson and Maclagan, managed to get any real hold of it. Even after the Diocese of Sheffield was created the task was, as Dominie Sampson would say, "prodeegious." When I look back I cannot but be amazed at the way in which somehow I managed to get about the Diocese and ultimately to pay at least one full personal visit to every parish within it. I suppose this was largely due to my wonderful health, which never failed during all these twenty years.

The Archbishop's past health was a subject on which he was not a reliable authority. He was determinedly oblivious of minor indispositions and was genuinely convinced of the truth of the statement, which he sometimes made, that during the whole of his time at York he had never spent a day in bed. His health was not quite as flawless as this claim suggests, but was good enough to enable him to carry out an ambitious programme of visits, which took him into every corner of his wide diocese and to every one of its 659 parishes.

Of these he has left fairly full notes, which begin with an account of the officials with whom he had most frequent dealings.

First and foremost there was dear old Crosthwaite,[1] the Suffragan Bishop of Beverley and also Archdeacon of York. I used to say—and it was scarcely an exaggeration—that the Diocese of York was distinguished by having as one of its Bishops the best—in the sense

[1] Bishop of Beverley 1889-1924. Died in 1925.

of the "good-est"—man then living in the Church of England. No words can fitly describe the affection, the admiration, the gratitude I had from the first, and increasingly, for this truly good old man. For the last ten years of Archbishop Maclagan's time, when the Archbishop was already failing, he had been practically the Bishop of the Diocese. And he was a very able man, clear-headed, concise and direct in speech, admirable in the conduct of business, utterly unselfish and devoted in his service, and possessed of a delightful dry humour. He had won and kept the unqualified confidence, trust and affection of the whole Diocese. I was profoundly touched by the way in which from the first, though so much older and more experienced and accustomed for so many years to the chief place in the Diocese, he accepted me as his chief who might well have been his disciple. Among all my memories of my time in York there is none so fragrant as my memory of this wonderful old man. I cannot write of him now without emotion; and I bless God in the gifts He gave me in the help and friendship and loyalty of the Bishop of Beverley.

The other Suffragans were the Bishop of Hull and the Bishop of Sheffield. The former (Dr. Blunt[1]), "tall, handsome and genial," had been a most popular Vicar of Scarborough, where his Bible Class for the ladies "had been thronged." He was "a good type of the acceptable Victorian Churchman," and although neither in temperament nor in opinion of a sort to make particular appeal to the Archbishop, his energy and success were fully recognised.

The Bishop of Sheffield (Dr. Quirk[2]) was a "wide-minded Evangelical." "Somewhat reserved, but most kind-hearted," he had had considerable parochial experience, was sound in judgment, much trusted by his people, wielded a good whip and drove a pair of chestnut horses. When Sheffield was made a new diocese, many in the city expected and hoped he would be the first Diocesan Bishop.

Certainly he worked indefatigably and most disinterestedly for the creation of the Bishopric. I thought, however, that a fresh mind and fresh energy were needed; and they were abundantly supplied by the man whom I recommended—the excellent Burrows[3]—still working with undiminished vigour. A happy solution of the

---

[1] Died in 1910.
[2] Afterwards Suffragan Bishop of Jarrow. Died in 1924.
[3] Bishop of Sheffield 1914-1939. Died in 1940.

difficult problem of Quirk's position when the See of Sheffield was created was found when the Bishop of Durham (Moule) chose him to be Bishop Suffragan of Jarrow and Canon of Durham. He, too, like his brother Suffragan, was always generous in his kindness and loyalty to me.

Then there were the other two Archdeacons.

The Archdeacon of the East Riding was Mackarness, son of the former Bishop of Oxford, a devout inheritor of the Tractarian tradition, a most able and faithful parish priest in his Scarborough church of St. Martin's, kindly and wise, a man in whose company it was good to be.

The Archdeacon of Cleveland (Lindsay) was a trusted henchman of Archbishop Maclagan's. He had been a vigorous and able Vicar of St. Paul's, Middlesbrough, and if a little too gaitered for the liking of some of the clergy (including his new Archbishop), was a tremendous worker and "a vigilant framer of schemes."

In the course of years death or preferment wrought changes in this "admirable team."

The first to go was Bishop Blunt. In his place I secured Kempthorne, the Rector of Liverpool. He made a great impression : his face alone counted for much, and his preaching and speaking were admirably clear and strong. Everybody liked looking at him and listening to him. For myself, I found him a little hard to know intimately ; but he was a great help, and his wife also. His gifts marked him out for appointment to a diocese, and after three short years he was translated to Lichfield, to our loss and its gain.

After Blunt the good Mackarness passed away ; and in his place I appointed Lambert, an incumbent in Hull and its Rural Dean, much trusted by its clergy. He was born and bred in the East Riding, and what he did not know about its people, their speech, their ways, their character, was not worth knowing. He belonged to no party, a simple, straightforward, somewhat old-fashioned Churchman, shrewd in judgment and abounding in quiet humour ; he scorned gaiters and was as little typically an Archdeacon as Lindsay was much. He was with me to the end and I found him a tower of strength.

When to my deep sorrow dear old Crosthwaite died, I appointed Cooper, then Vicar of Scarborough (later Dean of Carlisle), to be

Archdeacon of York. It proved to be an excellent appointment. He was very different from Lambert, sensitive, apt to overstrain his nerves. But he had a way with him which led him into the hearts of clergy and laity, and was invaluable in cases of parochial worries or disputes. He was well-read and thoughtful, Catholic in his ideals, Liberal in his sympathies. At his side, while I was Archbishop, he had his delightful wife, daughter of Dean Stephens of Winchester, granddaughter of Vicar Hook of Leeds.

When Kempthorne left for Lichfield, a "special Providence" gave me Frank Gurdon [1] to be his successor as Bishop of Hull. I had known him well in my East End days when he was the admirable Rector of Limehouse; and to my great joy I persuaded him to leave Christ Church, Lancaster Gate, and to adventure himself into the strange land of Yorkshire. What I owe to him for friendship, help and example cannot be estimated. There was a certain sternness in him, in his ideals for himself and others; and people sometimes felt it for their good. But it was concealed by a radiant smile. In the East Riding, as in the East End, it might be said that he ruled by his smile. It overcame all resistance, all suspicion, and won even hearts that his severity might have hurt. His sheer goodness, his combination of high spiritual ideals with a rich and full humanity gradually gave him a remarkable sway over the clergy and the stiff, cautious folk of the East Riding. To me his help was unfailing and his companionship a continual joy.

When at last death closed the life here of the beloved Bishop of Beverley and the good white head was no more seen, I chose as his successor my young friend Harry Woollcombe, whom I had known as the Head of Oxford House in Bethnal Green and for a time as my chaplain at Bishopthorpe, and who was now Vicar of the great parish of Armley, Leeds. There could have been no greater contrast than that between him and his predecessor. He looked a mere boy; he had all the qualities of a boy; cheerful, frank, outspoken, disliking all conventionality. But I knew well there was a deeper side, a real faith inspiring his enthusiasm; and he had knowledge of and sympathy with all sorts of folk, and very great gifts of ready speech, which would have been even more effective if he had held them under greater restraint. I felt that the Diocese and his bit of it needed a stimulant, and he admirably provided it. Certainly, while I was

---

[1] Bishop of Hull 1913-1929, when he died.

his chief . . . his own freshness was a constant refreshment. As there was no longer any connexion between his sphere of work and the East Riding, the title of Beverley was abandoned and he was called Bishop of Whitby. Indeed, there could only, can only, be one Bishop of Beverley : no one else must bear his title.

Strengthened by his experience in London, the Archbishop resolutely maintained the principle of giving each of the Suffragans a sphere of his own into which the others never intruded. He believed the system worked well.

The Bishops and Archdeacons came once a month to Bishopthorpe, when we discussed fully and frankly together all the business of the Diocese—the exercise of patronage, cases of discipline, and the various spiritual enterprises by which we tried to keep its life moving and true to its real mission. Never, except once, during all these twenty years was I conscious of the slightest difficulty or friction in what we called "the Staff." There is no need that I should describe that one exception. For the moment it was painful, but it passed and never hindered the loyal service of the man who was hurt. Suffice it to say that it was a disappointment about preferment. Strange how that poison gets into the blood even of good and earnest men ! When it does, it works havoc. But it is not for me to criticise my brethren for yielding to a temptation from which no virtue of my own but the mere force of circumstances has kept me free.

Yet it was no more than a "passing jar" and must not qualify the gratitude Lang felt for "these long years of unbroken and happy fellowship in the Staff, with each other and with me."

This account hardly does justice to the tact and consideration with which, as a newcomer and a young man, the Archbishop managed his relations with men so much older than himself in years and in experience.

Bishop Gresford Jones, who was Archdeacon of Sheffield from 1912 to 1914, recalls the regular gatherings at Bishopthorpe, when the Archbishop "was at his most intimate and most charming."

Each month for a night we met there, a congenial band : his three Suffragan Bishops, Crosthwaite of Beverley, Quirk of Sheffield, Kempthorne and later Gurdon of Hull ; his four Archdeacons, Lindsay of Cleveland, Mackarness of the East Riding, Sandford of Don-

BALLURE. THE "CELL" IS ON THE EXTREME LEFT

THE ARCHBISHOP OF YORK

Macdonald.

caster; and myself: wholly delightful gatherings. Yet here too, amid surroundings so engaging, there was the same onward sweep of work, the same austere self-discipline, the same commanding leadership. Each day began with one whole hour in the beautiful chapel, each day closed with Evensong. . . . Each one of us he saw separately, and at our joint conference each Diocesan need, each curate's claim was in turn reviewed. "I marvel not," he once said to me, "at the defects of the clergy: what I do marvel at is their lack of discipline." "The holy spirit of discipline" was, I should say, one of the outstanding beauties of his memorable life.

He wrenched the very best out of himself. He drew the best out of those who served under him. Everything for the Church of Christ must be of the very best. Hence the dignity of all his great moments in the Minster, the level of his speeches up and down the land. His inner self was not easily reached, yet I know he was sustained by a most tender Evangelical faith.

In 1916, the old Dean of York, Dr. Purey-Cust, died. His place was taken by Dr. Foxley Norris, who went to Westminster in 1925, being succeeded in York by Dr. Lionel Ford, who had married a daughter of the old Vicar of Leeds. No appointment could have been more agreeable to the Archbishop, and "intercourse between the Deanery and Bishopthorpe was constant and delightful."

Lang goes on to give some account of his journeys about the Diocese.

I soon discovered that there were many of the country churches which had never, or almost never, been visited by the Archbishop; and as soon as the Diocese of Sheffield was separated, I formed the ambition of paying at least one visit to every church. Accordingly, I made a new plan of episcopal visitation. Instead of summoning all the clergy and churchwardens to some one special place and delivering a formal Charge, I issued careful questions to the incumbent of every parish, and then, with the answers before me, visited the parishes one by one, deanery by deanery. In each deanery I first summoned the clergy to some central church, prayed with them, spoke to them about their spiritual life and work, and entertained them to lunch. Thereafter I went to each of the churches in the deanery, two or even sometimes three in one day, held a service for the parishioners, who usually attended well in spite of inconvenient hours, and spoke specially to the churchwardens and later, when they came into being, to the Parochial Church Councillors. It was a long task, begun and continued in spite of the War, and lasting after the War was over. But gradually it was accomplished [1] and I had the satisfaction of knowing that every parish, however remote, had been visited at least once by the Archbishop.

Even in the first months, before he had started episcopal visitation on the lines he has described, the pace was often that of a whirlwind election campaign. In a very short time he had been to most of the towns of any importance, occasionally darting over the borders of the Diocese into the wider field of the Province. He was at Bradford, Hull, Sheffield, Scarborough, Burnley, Middlesbrough, Rotherham, Guisborough, Driffield, Goole, Whitby, Stokesley, Liverpool and Mirfield. In July he reached Leeds, recalling old times, meeting old friends, speaking in the Town Hall and preaching in the Parish Church. Wherever he went he was beset with functions, luncheons, dinners, civic receptions, mass meetings, and of course at least one sermon in at least one church. Everyone, it seemed, wanted to see the Archbishop; still more, to hear him. In January 1910, when he was back in Bradford, the visit, according to Bishop Gresford Jones, was "a veritable adventure." The people "rose to him," and queued four deep outside the Parish Church. At the big evening meeting, St. George's Hall was packed to the ceiling, with the rival Parliamentary candidates sitting on the platform. "There he stood, with his light youthful figure, every gesture, every word, in place, keeping the vast audience spellbound by his surprising oratory"; so that after nearly forty years one of his hearers can still recall his feeling that "here at last was one who, not by his gifts only, but by his character, his courtesy, his dignity, represented my idea of what a clergyman of the Church of England should be and could be."

Yet the Archbishop's memories were perhaps less of these larger functions, which necessarily tended to conform to a pattern of rather formal hospitality, than of visits to village churches and encounters with the folk of the Yorkshire countryside.

On one occasion, visiting a parish in the East Riding Wolds, I found two churchwardens, one aged about seventy-five, the other about eighty-five and almost wholly deaf. They evidently regarded me and my business with some suspicion. I began to get on well with the younger man, which only increased the suspicions of his older

[1] In 1921.

and deaf colleague. Suddenly the latter asserted himself and said: "If tha's coom here for money, Ah tell tha there's nowt to be 'ad." Then, having faithfully given his testimony, he relapsed into silence.

In another parish one churchwarden apologised for the absence of his colleague on the ground that he had felt obliged to fulfil his duties as a judge at the Fat Beasts' Show at York. But before I left, the colleague, stout and rubicund, drove up in his gig and said: "Ah thowt Ah ought to coom. Ah had to choose between the Fat Beasts and t'Archbishop. The woon was pleesure, and t'other was duty. So Ah've chose me duty."

At Leeds he had had his first taste of Yorkshire outspokenness. Now he renewed acquaintance with it, to his never-failing delight.

The excellent vicar of a North Riding parish had retired after eighteen years. He had every reason to know that he had been respected and liked, and was just a little surprised that when he left little notice was taken. A year afterwards he had a letter from his old church-warden asking him to come, as the parishioners wished to give him a testimonial. When he came and met them in the school, he was surprised to see that his successor was not present. The reason was soon obvious. This was the speech of the churchwarden who presided: "When you were here, Mr. So-and-so, we often said: 'Well, we might 'ave a worse.' *And so we 'ave.* So we thowt we'd like to give ye a testimonial."

This was the reward for eighteen years of most faithful service, but, as often in Yorkshire, more was meant than was said.

The country people were not always responsive to new enterprises.

To a parish which had gone asleep I appointed an energetic young incumbent. The Rural Dean was returning from a visit to the parish, driven by a farmer churchwarden in his gig. The Rural Dean asked how he liked the new Vicar. The good man replied: "Afore 'e coom we were left to ourselves. But now it's woon thing woon day and another thing the next. Ah'll tell tha what Ah think of him"—here he took his whip and flogged his old horse—"Ah say, damn him—damn him—damn him"—and pointing each "damn" with a stroke of his whip. But I think the young Vicar gradually won his way.

In spite of rural opposition of this sort, after "the very quiescent years of the later times of Archbishop Maclagan," much was needed in the way of diocesan reorganisation.

After the Report of the Selborne Commission on Church Finance, I instituted a diocesan Board of Finance with all the business, necessary but irksome, of parochial questions and the like, and started or re-organised all sorts of diocesan activities. At one time I raised a considerable sum—I think about £30,000—for the increase of the stipends of the poorer clergy, and was encouraged by the contribution of £5000 at the start from my good friend, Sir Hugh Bell. He was one of the last of the consistent Liberals of the old school. Though professedly agnostic, he and his wife were, as I always said, in active generosity two of the best Christians in the Diocese and I greatly valued their friendship.

Change and reform were needed, not only in the villages where incumbents, after long years, had become drowsy, but in the cities and larger towns as well. "Some of the Hull churches are rather depressing," the Archbishop wrote to his mother in 1910. "The old-fashioned Low Church spirit is hopelessly inadequate for modern needs. It is a sort of dead hand, chilling and binding the progress of the Church." In 1912, as a daring expedient, he sent Dick Sheppard for a short time to a church at Middlesbrough, and presently was telling Wilfrid Parker of the remarkable change from debt, depression and a dilapidated vicarage to the hope and buoyancy of a new order.

Much was undoubtedly accomplished by the visits, and more, perhaps, by the knowledge that at any moment a youthful and tireless Archbishop might swoop down on the smallest and sleepiest parish and call for an account. Lang was not satisfied: he seldom was with anything he did or tried to do; but he kept his criticisms for himself rather than for his clergy.

On the whole, in the Diocese of York I was impressed by the steady level of quiet, unobtrusive fidelity to their charge among the clergy in the country parishes. No doubt in very many there was more pious routine than vitality, and still less any capacity for adventure. But there were very few black spots; and perhaps patient continuance in well-doing is all that can be expected. And there were many instances of men holding to a high ideal in spite of continual difficulty and disappointment. Before such men, as I have often said, I stand hat in hand. Yet how far it all was from the ideal of the living, active Body of Christ!

York was less troubled than were some other dioceses by the extremists on either side; but during Lang's long episcopate the waters were occasionally ruffled, though on such disagreements or disturbances the notes are silent. The Kensitites continued to rumble intermittently, their most publicised eruption being in 1912, when they stole the statue of Our Lady from St. Matthew's, Sheffield, and delivered it at Bishopthorpe. But they by no means represented the generality of Low Churchmen who, while dissenting from the ecclesiastical views of the Archbishop, found him a tactful and sympathetic superior. They soon learned that he was ready to adapt himself to the type of service he found in any church he visited and had no intention of forcing the clergy into vestments or of inundating the parishes with "spiky" curates.

With the more advanced of the Anglo-Catholics his relations were more difficult, perhaps because he was nearer to them in opinion and understood, better than some of his brother Bishops, the points at issue. The chief contention was about Reservation of the Blessed Sacrament, on which Lang took the view that while it was beyond the power of a Bishop to forbid the practice, he was entitled to regulate it. One dispute was very like another, and the Archbishop's views on the subject may be left to a letter which he wrote to his old friend Lord Halifax in August 1918. It was in reply to a protest against the treatment of the Vicar of Clifford, near Bramham, the home of Lord Halifax's daughter-in-law, Lady Bingley (Mrs. George Lane-Fox).

In your letter you lay all your stress on the value of the permanent Reservation of the Blessed Sacrament for the communion of the sick. But that is not now the point on which the main stress is laid. Beyond question, Reservation is now desired and claimed mainly for purposes of worship: and, following on this, is the determination widely expressed to introduce into our churches the use of Exposition, Benediction and other devotions which are customary in the Roman Church. This claim cannot be ignored, and it is only the logic of events that compels my regulations for the use of the Reserved Sacrament for communicating the sick to be affected by it. . . .

It was a point of view which never failed to anger Lord Halifax. But indeed the Archbishop, sorely against his wish, was always paining and disappointing his old friend. "I cannot conceive," Lord Halifax would say to him, "anything more splendid than that your Grace should be executed on Tower Hill. Nothing but the martyrdom of an Archbishop can save the Church of England. I crave the honour of it for you and that I should live to be there, so that I might plunge my handkerchief in your blood, and pass it on to Edward [1] as the most precious of heirlooms." But martyrdom was not in this Archbishop's stars.

There was similar trouble with other recalcitrants, such as Fr. Ommaney of Sheffield and Fr. Burn of Middlesbrough, but the disputes, as a rule, were carried on quite amicably, even when disagreement ended in "discipline." Characteristic of Lang's policy was his approach to All Saints, Middlesbrough, a church with a long record of rebellion. The visit was preceded by a telegram—"May I come to preach for you next Sunday evening? Cosmo Ebor." He came in peace, took tea in the Vicarage, praised the marmalade, and had a short talk with the Vicar. Afterwards, in church, he wore his cope and did everything asked of him except bless the incense. ("There are some things I don't do," he explained with a smile.) Then, service and sermon over, he went to the back of the church and shook hands with everybody. "The effect was naturally tremendous and lasting."

Beyond the Diocese was the Northern Province, in which the Archbishop, as *primus inter pares*, had to walk with some delicacy. The ecclesiastical complexion of most of his episcopal colleagues emphasised the need for circumspection.

The Upper House of the Convocation of York, when I first presided over it, was an Evangelical preserve. . . . Moule at Durham, Chavasse at Liverpool, Diggle at Carlisle, Knox at Manchester, Boyd Carpenter at Ripon, Straton at Newcastle, Drury at Sodor and Man—all of the same colour, though in varying hues.

Eden at Wakefield "stood apart," representing the Cambridge tradition of Lightfoot; but Jayne [2] at Chester, who had once been Vicar of Leeds, had moved away from his earlier opinions and "was becoming increasingly eccentric."

But though seven out of the nine were definite Evangelicals and all were so much older than I was, nothing could exceed the kindliness with which they all received me and the generous loyalty which they gave me. This happy friendliness was helped by the fact that for the meetings of Convocation they all stayed with me at Bishop-

---

[1] The present Lord Halifax.   [2] Bishop of Chester 1889-1919. Died in 1921.

thorpe—except Jayne. Nothing to the end of my time could persuade him to join his brethren as my guest. It was one of the strangest of the many kinks which marred the episcopate of that very able man.

The "kink," it may be hazarded, came from an old grudge. In 1891, when Leeds Parish Church celebrated its jubilee, Lang wrote its history in which he was injudicious enough to remark that Dr. Jayne, when Vicar, had the Napoleonic art of retrieving a failure by an appearance of success. Jayne was gravely annoyed by this quip from a curate, and a little later, when he was in Leeds and Lang was introduced to him, said "How do you do" in the chilliest of voices and turned his back on the impertinent young critic. Nor, twenty years later, would he accept the hospitality of Bishopthorpe.

In the first years the Archbishop found the rather unbending Protestantism of the Northern Province a little trying. In time, of course, new men arrived, among others Burrows to Sheffield, Strong (afterwards Bishop of Oxford) to Ripon, and Hensley Henson, "my old friend from All Souls days," who had moved away from earlier opinions, to Durham, all of whom brought added authority and distinction to their sees. In the early days the most congenial colleague was the Bishop of Wakefield. "It is a blessing to have *one* Bishop with whom one can confer whole-heartedly," he wrote to Wilfrid Parker a month after the enthronement. Again, at his first Convocation, when the question of vestments was discussed, he complained of the strange ignorance of the northern Bishops. "But for Wakefield, who at least understands, all the others seemed to live in a different world from mine."

At York, though not at Canterbury, it was the custom for the President to address Convocation in full Synod, and the Archbishop regularly availed himself of the opportunities so afforded of guiding the deliberations. The presence of the Bishop of Beverley as Prolocutor of the Lower House was a guarantee of happy relations between the two Houses. The debates were often "prolix" and generally rather hum-drum, until the Revision of the Prayer Book began to be an active issue, when they became longer than ever, but much more animated.

> I have a recollection of the good wives of Bishops Moule and Chavasse leading their lords up and down the lawns at Bishopthorpe on the morning before the question of permitting white vestments was to be decided, pleading with them to be faithful to their true evangelical tradition.

Happily the day of Mrs. Proudie was past and the white vestments won.

I always felt it to be my duty as Archbishop to pay frequent visits to the great cities of the Province—Liverpool, Manchester, Bradford, dear old Leeds, Sheffield, Newcastle—and the large towns such as Bolton and Bury and Doncaster and Preston and Wakefield; and also the various Cathedral churches. It was a peculiar pleasure to be present at the consecration first of the Lady Chapel and then of the Choir and Transepts of Liverpool Cathedral. At the latter consecration, by the way, the Archbishop of Canterbury was present, but the dignity of York was maintained by his (Canterbury's) being separately escorted robed as a mere Doctor of Divinity to a pew opposite the pew occupied by the King and Queen. I think I may say without boasting that no previous Archbishop of York had been so well known throughout the Province.

The consecration at Liverpool impressed him as "a very wonderful religious drama, full of spiritual movement and significance." Some of the visiting ecclesiastics were less responsive. The Bishop of Gloucester (Dr. Gibson) wrote that he had come away "very thankful that his Cathedral had already been consecrated and that it was not built in the twentieth century"; while Durham (Dr. Hensley Henson) dismissed the whole ceremony as a "pageant of irrelevant mediaevalism."

Although no part of the official business of either Province or Diocese, the Royal tour of the North in 1912 touched the Archbishop himself very closely. Indeed the idea was his, having been suggested during a visit to Balmoral in the early days of the new reign. He was asked to submit a memorandum, and in it "I urged the importance of his (the King's) coming into contact with the masses of his people, that it was not enough that they should assemble in the streets on ceremonial occasions to see him, but that he might, so to say, go to see them—move about with as little ceremony as possible through their own towns, villages and workshops."

The tour took place in June and July, and on much of it the Archbishop accompanied the King and Queen.

I can testify to the delight of the people on seeing him and Queen Mary in the midst of them in their own familiar surroundings. I feel sure that these tours did much to create and sustain their sense that he belonged to them and they to him in a very human and personal way.

Nothing quite like it had happened before and the response was immediate, overwhelming, sometimes a little unexpected. As the Archbishop was driving with Their Majesties through South Yorkshire, crowds of workers held up the cars near Rotherham. The Archbishop overheard the following conversation:

"Na then, which is t'King?"

"It's t'little chap i' the front wi' a billycock hat."

"Nay, he ain't seech a fine man as Teddy (King Edward VII)."

"Well, anyway, he's gotten him a fine ooptstanding wife."

At first, Lang records, the King and Queen "seemed to be somewhat disconcerted by such free remarks," but soon they saw the humour of the situation and the genuine warmth of the welcome.

In July, while the tour was still in progress, the disaster at Cadeby Pit brought bereavement and gloom to the South Yorkshire countryside. The next day the King was to have gone down a pit not far away. The Royal party was lunching at Hickleton with Lord Halifax, the Archbishop being among the guests, and there was some uncertainty whether, in view of the disaster at Cadeby, the King would be wise to keep to his plan. Neither Lord Halifax nor the Archbishop had any doubt what he should do, and their advice prevailed. He went down the pit without mishap and with profound effect on the feelings of the mining population; while he and the Queen further endeared themselves by a visit to the scene of the tragedy and by the genuine sympathy they showed.

"I had a long and earnest talk with the King," wrote the Archbishop, "about his conception of his duty to his people. He is really splendidly high-minded about it." So thought the people too and, despite the disaster, the tour was deemed a striking success. "All my hopes," Lang told his mother, "have been more than fulfilled."

Other Royal journeys to other parts of the country followed. "I often say," wrote the Archbishop in 1914, "that if I have done nothing else worth doing in my life, I have at least the credit, I hope, of originally suggesting these tours."

Chapter XX

BISHOPTHORPE

"I WILL not disguise from you, my dear Lang," said Lord Curzon when writing to the Archbishop not very long after his enthronement, "what pleasure it gives me, as the years advance, to see my friends inhabiting spacious places."

People were naturally curious to see what a bachelor Archbishop would do with so spacious a place as Bishopthorpe, and also what Bishopthorpe would do with him. Lang, with his strong sense of dramatic and historical fitness, never hesitated in his answer to either question.

> I think I succeeded in making my home a social centre. Certainly I did not neglect hospitality—dinner parties, luncheon parties, dine-and-sleep parties for clergy and laity and their wives, a large annual garden party for each Archdeaconry in turn, children's parties about Christmastide, etc., etc., as well as entertaining my own friends from London and elsewhere. I was anxious to show that for this sort of hospitality a wife is not indispensable!

He began in March 1909 with a house-warming, at which his guests included Lord and Lady Balcarres, Mr. George Lane-Fox (afterwards Lord Bingley) and his wife, Sir Ian Malcolm, and Mr. Edward Wood (afterwards Lord Halifax). The garden was full of crocuses, snowdrops and aconites, and the party, with its nice balance of old friends and new neighbours, was a "triumphant success." It was the first of many. His chaplain, the present Bishop of Pretoria, describes the unending stream of visitors—Bishops, Ordination candidates, Rural Deans in conference, former members of No. 2 Company at Amen Court,[1] men in public life, friends from All Souls and Magdalen, and "an occasional Bohemian, such as John Tweed the sculptor."

On his merits as a host the opinions given vary. Tupper-Carey, not always the kindest of critics, says that on many people he had a "numbing" effect.

> Often when I was having lunch at Bishopthorpe and among the

---

[1] See page 152.

guests were people whom he only knew slightly, his pomposity was so awful that I felt I could have screamed or told some *risqué* story to relieve the tension : nobody seemed at their ease. I am quite sure it was nothing but shyness. . . . But on the other hand, with people whom he knew, or who were on the same intellectual level, such as Judges or K.C.s, he was quite delightful and opened out. The society of young people who were not afraid of him seemed to bring out the best side of him. I was in the smoking-room at Bishopthorpe talking to two or three Bishops in front of the fire when the door suddenly opened. They at once paused in their talk, shot round to see who it was, and when they saw it was only a footman at once resumed their conversation. It was exactly the same with the Ordination candidates. When they were by themselves with one of his chaplains, there was a buzz of conversation ; but directly he came into the room there was dead silence. And I well remember his saying to me afterwards, "What is the use of my coming to see these fellows if they stop talking directly I enter ? I had better keep out of it altogether."

The truth probably is that, like most men, he was at his best when his guests were congenial ; neither then nor at any time in his life did he suffer dullards patiently, and his dramatic repertory lacked the gift of appearing to be vastly entertained when in fact he was being profoundly bored. If the company was shy or irksome and conversation flagged, his tendency was to withdraw behind the outer defences of archiepiscopal dignity.

But all agree that in favouring conditions he could be the most charming of hosts, particularly to the young of either sex. He took an especial delight in entertaining children, such as the young Fords or Crawleys. The Crawley children regarded him as "a sort of uncle or grandfather." "They were and are part of my life," he wrote of them. "I look upon them as my own, the nearest and dearest of the families whom I have adopted." He once invited Aidan, aged three, to have luncheon with him alone at the long refectory table. Aidan came, but either the dignity of the occasion or the absence of any control over his diet was too much for him and he was sick. A Ford infant, aged eight, was asked to go and sit at the head of the tea-table. "Oh yes, Archbishop, I should like to," was the immediate reply. "You and I always wink at each other, don't we ?" Stories of this kind could be multiplied.

Whatever the Archbishop's other guests may have thought of him, the children loved him.

For the older visitors there were the glories of the house to be explored. Lang was an admirable if rather exacting guide: as at Ballure, his friends had to mark his footsteps well and be ready with their tributes of discriminating praise. Fr. Talbot tells of a visit of Lord William Cecil [1] (later Bishop of Exeter), who had just been to China to survey the work of the Christian missions and came to Bishopthorpe to report on what he had seen.

> The Archbishop's mind was absorbed in the beauties of his newly acquired palace. Lord William's mind was full of nothing but China. After luncheon the Archbishop said, "Now, Fish (Cecil's nickname), come and tell me all about China, and as it is so fine let us walk in the garden." (He turned to me and invited me to join them and hear the account of the Chinese Missions from Cecil.)
>
> When we got into the garden, Cecil began: "Now the salient fact is that the main railway lines have their junction at Ping-Ting. That then is obviously a strategic centre for all educational work."
>
> Archbishop: "Quite so. Fish, forgive me, but I must draw your attention to the house as seen from this point. The red brick and grey stone make an admirable ensemble."
>
> Cecil: "Very nice. On the other hand, the Baptists are already *in situ* at Ping-Ting. We should not wish, therefore, to trench upon their sphere of work."
>
> Archbishop: "Exactly. Archbishop X added that chimney to the house. It is not in itself beautiful, but it adds a certain interest to the whole construction."
>
> Cecil: "Very interesting. All the same, for educational purposes co-operation with all Christian bodies is very desirable."
>
> Archbishop: "That would certainly be wise. Fish, will you look, etc., etc.?"
>
> "It was," Fr. Talbot concludes, "like watching two croquet balls colliding and separating."

The incessant work which had become Lang's habit kept entertainment within narrow bounds. He was perpetually on visits to the parishes of the Diocese or the larger cities of the Province, going up to London to confer with the Archbishop of Canterbury or to attend a debate in

---

[1] 2nd son of the 3rd Marquess of Salisbury. Died in 1936.

the House of Lords, or fulfilling some engagement outside the Province altogether. A letter to his mother on October 26th, 1913, gives a view of a fortnight in his life at this time. He left Bishopthorpe on the 13th of the month to stay with Lord Glanusk at Crickhowell, to speak at the St. David's Diocesan Conference at Brecon, and to address a great gathering of Welsh country folk, meeting to protest against the Bill to disestablish and disendow the Church in Wales. On the 15th he motored on to Cardiff and a Conference of the Men's Society, attending a service and speaking at two meetings of 4000 and 2500 men respectively. On the 17th he spent a night with one of his old curates near Chichester, and on the 18th he was at Portsea, which he had not seen for four years. Next day, being Sunday, he preached in the parish church in the afternoon and to an "overflow" crowd in the evening. The 20th found him staying at Lambeth, talking to the newly formed Cavendish Club; and on the 21st and 22nd he was occupied with long sessions of the Bishops' meetings. On the 23rd he was at Sheffield for the Diocesan Conference and a meeting of 2000-3000 church-people. The 25th saw him at Manchester, for another demonstration of nearly 8000 people against the Welsh Church Bill. He got back to Bishopthorpe late that evening after a fortnight which for him was merely busy and for most people would have been, in his own favourite phrase, "quite intolerable." When he was back at Bishopthorpe he had very little respite, as he had then to deal with the business of the Province and the Diocese, which the faithful Booker had been accumulating during his absence; and even when he had guests in the house, it was his custom to bid them goodnight at ten o'clock and to retire to work till midnight or later in his study, on the right of the entrance hall and immediately in front of the chapel.

At Cuddesdon, Magdalen and Portsea Lang had been one of a community, even if each in turn lacked companionship of the quality he was always seeking and seldom finding. At Amen Court, it is true, he had lived alone with a chaplain, but the work was unremitting, the house was small, and outside it were London and a multitude of friends; so that there was no sense of isolation. Bishopthorpe was another kind of life altogether, and during the first years, at any rate, he suffered a lot from loneliness. A friend recalls how, visiting him one evening, he found him seated silently at dinner at one end of the refectory table, with a silent chaplain sitting at the other end. He did not see much of his family, although his mother was a fairly regular visitor and his brother Norman generally came to him for Christmas. In May 1909 his father died, having never recovered from the illness which had prevented his presence at the enthronement. "I am very thankful," Lang wrote, "both for his noble life and for his peaceful end"; and although after Ordination he had seen little of him, and still less since the parents' move from Glasgow to Aberdeen, the death broke another link with those old times of holidays in the Highlands and the workaday life of the Barony.

He had neighbours, of course, some of whom became good friends, but Yorkshiremen are slow to admit a stranger to intimacy. For ordinary human companionship he had therefore to rely most upon his chaplains; and on them he became, and remained, extremely dependent. The first of these was Wilfrid Parker, who had been with him in Amen Court and was unable through illness to join him at Bishopthorpe until the spring of 1909. "Come back when you *safely* can," the Archbishop wrote to him in February. "Soon, says my heart, but my hand underlines 'safely.'"

In his notes he wrote:

He was a most delightful companion and an admirable chaplain, not least in his genuine interest in the social side of my life, the one of all my chaplains who helped me there, fruitful of suggestions as to persons who ought to be invited and most agreeable to them. He came to be as much liked by the laity as by the clergy and made many friends among them, sometimes among the least "churchy." It was a great grief to me when after three years he felt called to give himself to the Church in South Africa.

Thereafter the Archbishop would write to him almost every week in his own hand, long, intimate and confidential letters. To no other man did he unburden himself so completely.

The Bishop of Pretoria, on his side, describes the Archbishop as "the kindest and most affectionate of chiefs. The impression of stiffness and austerity which he sometimes gave masked his real character and may have been a form of protective armour of shyness. At the same time it is true to say that he never forgot the dignity due to the great position of Archbishop of York; his keen historical sense and dramatic instinct would always have prevented that."

Possibly at the time Wilfrid Parker hardly realised how much his help and companionship meant to the Archbishop. "Do let me thank you with all my heart," Lang wrote in July 1910, "for all the help you give me. It just makes *all* the difference to my life. You shield me from all the domestic worries which might be such a nuisance." But the chaplain was more than just a shield; and a little over a year later, when Parker decided he must go and gain wider experience, the Archbishop, who was in Iona at the time with Dick Sheppard, wrote to Canon Crawley: "I come back with a broken heart. I can't bear to think of the home life at Bishopthorpe without him."

"You see," he wrote to Parker himself,—"or rather you don't see, for these are not things one ought to wear on one's sleeve—my life is really rather a lonely one. It needs, not friends—I have plenty of them: not work—I have too much of it: but just that old simple human thing —someone in daily nearness to love. The fact that, for reasons sufficient to me, I am not and do not propose to be married, does not make the need less." From the moment of the first meeting in All Souls he had known that Wilfrid Parker would supply that need. He might, he added, get a better chaplain: that was not the point. He would not have the companionship he wanted so badly. Wilfrid must forgive his selfishness.

He was to have other chaplains; to some of them he was to be devotedly attached; but possibly none of them quite filled the empty place which Wilfrid Parker left behind him. His immediate successor was Harry Woollcombe [1]—"not a very reliable student of Bradshaw," but nevertheless regarded with deep affection. His flippancies were sometimes disconcerting. Once, after luncheon, having been told to show the guests the pictures, he was heard to remark, as he pointed to the portrait of a past Archbishop, "Look at that old boy, with what looks like a bottle of Bass under his arm." The Archbishop of the day, overhearing, muttered indignantly, "It is intolerable that I should be surrounded by a pack of buffoons!" Doubtless this was one of the times when Woollcombe was considered not to have held his gift of "ready speech" under proper restraint.

After Woollcombe's departure Maurice Ponsonby came for a short time, until he went off as a Chaplain to the Forces; and in 1914 Edward Gibbs, a cousin of Mrs. Crawley, arrived. He had a special place in the Archbishop's affections.

I loved him dearly as a younger brother, and I had ordained him to a curacy in a mining village and brought him back. He had no intellectual gifts: the preparation of sermons in Bishopthorpe Church, when he acted as curate to Crawley and afterwards, when S. C. went

[1] He became Bishop of Whitby in 1923, Bishop of Selby in 1939, and died in 1941.

to the War, as curate-in-charge, was an agony to him. Like all his family, he loved a horse and was always eager for a mount; but his sheer goodness was transparent and the people of Bishopthorpe loved him and preferred his very simple sermons to most others.

The relationship was rather that between a father and his son than that between two brothers, much more than that between an Archbishop and his chaplain. "Once," records Canon Crawley, "when leaving the scene of a busy day and night's work, Edward sank beside the Archbishop in the car, saying of the processional Cross in its heavy case, packed on the top with the other robe-cases: 'I hope your old bag of tricks is up above.' To which the Archbishop replied: 'That, dear Edward, is really more your affair than mine.'" Gibbs was devoted, often critical, fearlessly outspoken, quick-tempered. After some disagreement or rebuke he would flare up and leave the room, banging the door behind him like a naughty child; and a little later, when he came back to apologise, would find the Archbishop almost in tears with contrition at having upset him.

Besides the regular chaplain there was the Vicar of Bishopthorpe, who was almost a supernumerary chaplain. In 1910, when Mr. Penny-man left, the Archbishop persuaded Stafford Crawley to take his place. He stayed until 1915, when he went to the War, and soon after his return resigned his benefice and left the Diocese. But he returned to Bishop-thorpe in 1924 as domestic chaplain and secretary of the Diocesan Board of Finance, he and his family living in the north wing for the last four years at York. The Archbishop thoroughly enjoyed the occasional parties when the north wing invaded the main building.

He entered with zest into our games and foolery and would laugh most heartily at it all, at the same time preserving some measure of the dignity of his office, which he never quite forgot. I think he was rather glad to see the fine stables half full of horses and ponies, and even to have his garden cut up by a cricket net and two lawn-tennis courts. In the Easter holidays the children made a regular steeple-chase course all round the grounds, neighbours came to a great party, and the young people, young and old for that matter, ran races over the course, the Archbishop hurrying from jump to jump and cheering them on.

Finally there was Dick Sheppard, almost the "problem child" of the early years at Bishopthorpe, who could pull the archiepiscopal leg as

BISHOPTHORPE FROM THE RIVER

THE CORONATION OF KING GEORGE V

REV. A. S. CRAWLEY   REV. E. L. A. HERTSLET   REV. WILFRID PARKER   REV. CLAUDE JENKINS   REV. JOHN MACMILLAN no one else could, "whose unfailing love and sympathy is a great treasure," and whose future was an ever-recurring question. In October 1910 he resigned the headship of Oxford House and the problem re-appeared. "Keep quiet now," the Archbishop wrote to him, "and don't worry either about the past or the future. You are in the strong sure hands of Love." He had a scheme. Dick was to come to Bishopthorpe as secretary; and Dick, protesting that the office was "mere charity," agreed. He was the most agreeable of companions, if a rather incalculable secretary. Mr. Ellis Roberts tells of the time when he wanted to play golf with Raymond, the butler. The Archbishop did not care for the plan and said so. That day there was a procession in the Minster in which Dick, carrying the primatial Cross, walked in front of the Archbishop, leading him to his throne. As they started, without turning his head, Dick muttered, "May I play golf with the butler?" There was no reply, but he could "feel a certain vexation" behind him. "May I play golf with the butler?" he repeated. "If you don't say 'yes,' I'm going to take you all round the Minster *and* into the Crypt." This time an answer came in a sharp undertone: "Don't be ridiculous, Dick." "Well, here goes! I'm off to the Crypt! May I play golf with the butler?" And the Archbishop, knowing that Dick was quite capable of carrying out his threat, capitulated: "Oh, very well, Dick; but it is scandalous, your behaviour is disgraceful!"

Or there was the minor *contretemps* at the Church Congress at Middlesbrough in 1912, when, while the Archbishop was "looking dignified and splendid," Dick was caught by a photographer roaring with laughter at "an old fussy who was in the procession in a top-hat, umbrella and surplice."

The post of secretary was a manufactured job, to allow time to look round. There was talk of a mining town, and for a short time Dick actually went to Middlesbrough, but in the end his way took him back to London, to Mayfair first and then to St. Martin-in-the-Fields, where he did what many will claim was his finest work. After illnesses and between jobs he was often at Bishopthorpe and took no important step without asking the Archbishop's advice, even though he did not always take it. Lang was continually damping his many mutually conflicting schemes with gentle douches of cold water. "I cannot see," he wrote once, "how what we both accepted as God's purpose for you in February can be regarded as no longer His purpose in April." Dick wilted and grumbled, but usually decided that his "dearest Grace" was right. His "dearest Grace" was certainly the most disinterested of counsellors, and much as he wanted to capture Dick for the Northern Province, would not allow his personal wishes to interfere with what he believed to be Dick's appointed and proper career. In 1913, when Dick offered to throw up Grosvenor Chapel and come to Bishopthorpe as chaplain, the Archbishop refused. Instead, Dick came to stay, and while with him nearly collapsed. "I don't know what we are to do with Dick," the Archbishop wrote in despair to Wilfrid Parker. "He can't go on like this and is impervious to reason; yet he is doing a great work."

The Archbishop delighted in the companionship of these young men. They were not overawed by his dignity and with them he could be more natural than he was with anyone else. He could talk freely to them, chaff them, and even, within limits, be chaffed back. He tolerated hunting in moderation and encouraged them to play cricket, taking it as a personal grievance if one of them got out while he was watching. The young men were also a constant reminder of his own days at Oxford, for which his loyalty, so far from abating, grew as the years passed; and in June 1913, when his old University gave him an Honorary D.C.L. (the Public Orator dubbing him "wise as the serpent and harmless as the dove"), he declared that the degree was "one of the few honours I really value." To a young man thinking of being ordained his advice was unvarying. If not already at Oxford, he must go there (Cambridge being just permissible as an indifferent alternative), and then it must be Cuddesdon and a title in the Northern Province. In 1912 he was writing gleefully to Wilfrid Parker, "We have now over thirty Cuddesdon men in the Diocese, instead of twelve when I came."

To Cuddesdon he himself went, whenever he could, for Holy Week, and occasionally at other times. He usually lodged at the Bishop's Palace until, with the coming of Dr. Kirk, this was handed over for the use of the Ecclesiastical Commissioners. Thereafter he stayed with the Principal of the College or—at the end of his life—in the guest's flat in Liddon Building. In the church he always occupied the little oak pew in which he had sat on that summer evening in 1889 when his perplexities were answered. It was the second and is now the front pew on the north side of the nave, a pew having been taken away when the pulpit was moved to the south side.

"It was a great joy," he told his mother after one of these visits, "to have those four undisturbed and quiet days at Cuddesdon. It is a place full to me of the most sacred memories: there I made up my mind to be ordained: there I learned something of the meaning of Christ, His Life and Death and Abiding Presence: there I was ordained deacon: there I celebrated for the first time as priest."

"Once again," he wrote in one of his notebooks, "I could not resist the chance of spring-cleaning and renewal. Ought perhaps to be addressing my own people in Holy Week and on Good Friday, but I can't be always talking—others do it better—and I can only give what I receive; and this is really the only time and the best place to become passive and to receive. . . ."

But there was Largie in late summer too, "The Tave" during the first years, and then Ballure. Every August saw him on the road to the north, with Walter Wells to drive and Mrs. Wells to cook and "do" for him—the "Good Companions," as he liked to call the party. That was the necessary relief to the tension of life at York; and Tupper-Carey, seeing him one year on his way back to Bishopthorpe, reported him as glum as a schoolboy at the end of the summer holidays.

Chapter XXI

THE CHURCH AND THE WORLD (1908-1914)

IN making choice of a man to be Archbishop of York, the Prime
Minister had taken the view that the ensuing twenty years would be
critical for the Church of England, particularly in its connexion with
the State; and that the new Primate must therefore be a man of outstanding ability and also young enough, by reasonable expectation, to
lead and guide the Church over a quarter of a century. With this
opinion the Archbishop of Canterbury warmly concurred. In the
increasing infirmity of Dr. Maclagan little help had come from the
North; and during the rule of Dr. Davidson's predecessors relations
between the Provinces had been polite rather than co-operative, each
apparently preferring its own path. But the expansion of the Anglican
Communion overseas and the emergence of many new and difficult
problems demanded a fresh outlook. Old Provincial rivalries must be
discarded and be replaced by a close unity of policy.

> "I pray that by the blessing of God," wrote Canterbury to York,
> "you and I may have the right opportunities and the grace to use
> them rightly in the coming years. Perplexities are neither few nor
> far between. I grow increasingly sure as time runs on that the
> simplest of the old Gospel truths and lessons of our childhood are the
> most effective too for our daily need. 'When I am sometimes afraid
> I lift up my heart unto Thee.' . . . It is surely of the essence of your
> position and responsibilities that you should next session be to the
> fore as *Archbishop* and make up for my manifold 'lack of service' to
> Church and Realm. It is part of your service to *North* as well as to
> South, that the Primate of England should cease to be an unusual
> figure in the forefront."

For the collaboration thus required, the Church of England was
fortunate in its two Primates. Lang has put on record his

> thankfulness for all I owed to the wisdom, the counsel, the example
> of my great and good predecessor at Canterbury, Randall Davidson.
> He had been my Bishop when I was Vicar of Portsea and had shown
> me great kindness when I was Bishop of Stepney. During all my

time at York, Lambeth was my London home. I always had a room there where I could do my own work—in Morton's Tower and then in Cranmer's Tower. I cannot be sufficiently thankful for the never-failing kindness and hospitality of the Archbishop and his dear wife; it made my visits to London so easy and comfortable; I could not have been, or have been made to feel, more at home if I had been a member of the family.

To this may be added the testimony of the Bishop of Chichester, who had unequalled opportunities for witnessing the working of the partnership.

No small part of the wonderful harmony and trust which bound the older and the younger Archbishop together to the very end may be attributed to the fact that Lang was for nearly twenty years an intimate member of the household, with his own bedroom and sitting-room always ready and as sure of Mrs. Davidson's friendship as of her husband's.

Archbishop Davidson was a prince of co-operators. He knew from long experience (and training) exactly how to get the maximum contribution from another. Archbishop Lang was more self-reliant, and also less skilled in the art of delegation. It was of first-rate importance, therefore, for the principal affairs of the Church, and also (where their spheres overlapped) of the State, that the two Primates should naturally and regularly see much of one another. Their consultations were regular before the Bishops' meetings three times a year, and not only were any matters of special importance on the Agenda talked over between them (where necessary) in advance, but the visits to Lambeth afforded the opportunity for discussion on a hundred other things as well; and quite often one or the other (sometimes both) had their own private list of subjects for private debate. In addition, debates in the House of Lords, where Davidson was an almost unfailing attendant, brought Lang to Lambeth many a time before and after the First World War. And apart from these and similar more or less regular occasions—ecclesiastical, political or social—Davidson would often urgently ask Lang to make a special journey to Lambeth or Canterbury when something of particular importance required mutual counsel. Lang used sometimes to say that the Archbishop of Canterbury did not seem to realise that it was just as far from Bishopthorpe to Lambeth as the other way; but he never demurred, and thoroughly understood the advantage both of a common policy and of his having a full say in its framing.

Lang in his earlier days was less patient than Davidson, less cautious, and showed at times a marked independence. He was more "radical" in his politics, and this led to his taking an entirely opposite line to that taken by Davidson and the Bench as a whole in his famous speech in the House of Lords on the Lloyd George Budget. Lang, again, took an active part in the Royal Commission on Matrimonial Causes. Davidson was not a member of the Royal Commission, and while it was a subject on which he had his own fairly clear views, there is little evidence in his correspondence of an overriding and unyielding concern such as Lang undoubtedly showed. Yet here also the two Archbishops had a common link . . . in Sir Lewis Dibdin,[1] Dean of the Arches, Davidson's trusted adviser in Church law and also not only a member of the Royal Commission, but also with Lang a signatory of the Minority Report. . . .

Perhaps an illustration of the difference in method between the two men, when holding the same post of responsibility, in dealing with a similar problem, may throw a little light on their difference generally. When Davidson met conferences of Free Churchmen and tried to find a solution of the educational religious problem, he would open the proceedings by explaining to the company the difficulties of his situation with his own constituency and invite their help. He then let them do all the talking, but in the end got out of them the lines of the solution on which he himself had determined. When Lang held similar conferences (he being then at Canterbury) he did all the talking and propounded his solution at the start. He was the cleverer and academically the abler man; but though much trusted at the end, he lacked the sympathy of his elder and the elder's capacity for winning as much as could be won from the other side.

The collaboration was none the less complete because of these differences in temperament, mind and method. That Davidson and Lang should have worked together so closely, continuously and harmoniously during twenty years is creditable to them both, and particularly perhaps to the older man, who had the major responsibility and the initiative; and to him his colleague pays the warmest of tributes.

Randall Davidson was always in his heart a somewhat old-fashioned

---

[1] Dean of the Arches 1903-1934, First Estates Commissioner 1931-1938, when he died.

Victorian Churchman, with strong leanings in a Broad Church direction. On his intellectual side he was a disciple of Lightfoot and very specially of Westcott. On his devotional side the old Prayer Book fully satisfied all his needs. He had no personal desire for any change in it. During the long discussions on its revision I do not remember any single proposal or suggestion which he himself made, except his one desire to make the use of the Athanasian Creed optional : he was content to be merely the Chairman, seeing that the business got done. He believed in the Church of England as a Reformed Catholic Church, but in his own mind he laid more emphasis on "Reformed" than on "Catholic." Gradually indeed, possibly through the influence of Mrs. Davidson, partly through his friendship with Edward Talbot and Charles Gore, chiefly through his own essential fair-mindedness and generosity of outlook, he came to appreciate more fully the place of the specifically Catholic movement in the Church. But he always looked at it from without rather than from within. Its modes of worship made no sort of appeal to him and he was uncertain about its ultimate purpose. For himself I think he was content in his own fair and generous way to maintain the comprehensiveness of the Church and to recognise the place of the Catholic movement within that large ambit. He set himself to maintain that comprehensiveness and to give fair play to its elements. This he did not only with characteristic skill, but also because he genuinely believed that comprehensiveness was a true note of the Church of England. Let me put it this way. Seated as Archbishop on the box, he handled the three horses, Evangelical, Modernist and Catholic, fairly and adroitly, but he always seemed to me more concerned to get them together round the next corner than to envisage what the ultimate course of the journey was to be. He did not care to "see the distant scene"—that he left to God : one step—the next step—was enough for him.

No episode of his life was more typical of his mind and policy than his handling of the Malines Conversations. I do not remember any matter about which he was more anxious or took more trouble. It certainly showed his courage. It also showed his concern that there should be no minimising or bartering of the fundamental issues of the Reformation.

He had a whole-hearted belief in the Establishment of the Church as the expression of its national character and of its place in the national life. It was this which led him to "magnify his office" as Archbishop. He felt that he had, and he was zealous to maintain, his position as the holder of a national and not merely an ecclesiastical office. So he loved the House of Lords and was never more, so to say, at home than when he was there. He liked to be in his place whatever the business in hand might be. He became an institution there, a "House of Lords man." Few things gave him more pleasure than the peerage conferred on him when he retired. He was no orator: his speeches were apt to be too long and diffuse; but he took immense pains over them, never spoke without having mastered his subject; and a House which sets no great store on oratory always listened to him with attention and respect. His chief pleasure in life was to have talks with important persons on important affairs; and after these talks he was careful to make memoranda of them. He was always pleased and excited when he was consulted on matters of State. He valued all this not only because it suited his temperament, but because it emphasised the national character of the Archbishop and the Church.

The association, Lang went on to say, had been "one of the main elements" in his life as Archbishop of York.

I can never be sufficiently thankful for those twenty years during which I watched him at work and for his goodness and generosity to me, for the lessons I learned from his mind and above all from his character. . . . The main impression left upon me as year by year, month by month, I watched him at work and shared fully all his thoughts and plans, was not only or chiefly his almost uncanny wisdom, or his marvellous memory, or his stores of knowledge and experience, or his thoroughness, or his power of handling men, but his essential goodness, his deep though unobtruded piety, his constant remembrance of God in all his ways. He was not only a great Archbishop: he was in the truest sense of the words a good man.

The Bishop of Chichester, in his remarkable Life of Randall Davidson, has recorded fully and definitively the events of twenty years in the history of Church and State. His book is at hand for all to consult, and as the story of one man is in so large a measure that of both men, in these pages little more will be attempted than to discuss the various issues as they especially concerned Lang.

Education was a serious preoccupation of the first years of the new Liberal Government, the controversy rapidly reaching a climax with the Bill which Mr. Augustine Birrell, the mildest revolutionary who ever came out of the University of Cambridge, introduced in April 1906. The Bill was drastically amended by the Lords and the amendments were rejected by the Commons. Two further and abortive attempts at agreement were made by Mr. Birrell's successors, Mr. McKenna and Mr. Runciman. They failed, not through lack of goodwill on the part of Davidson, but through the intransigent spirit of the extremists, the House of Laity in the Representative Church Council voting down by a large majority the solution at which the Archbishop and Mr. Runciman had arrived. Lang at this time was Bishop of Stepney: he had no seat in the House of Lords and consequently took no public part in the Parliamentary struggle. But if he was not an actor, he was a prompter behind the scenes. The Archbishop consulted him freely, and even enlisted his support for a critical interview with the "stiff men" in the Church. Davidson's policy, so unpalatable to the Old Guard, was to get a settlement which, while it might not give the Church all it wanted, was likely to be very much better than anything obtainable in ten or twenty years' time, when the position of the Church schools would probably have further deteriorated. So, while the "stiff men" were for mobilising all their forces in defence of their own schools, Davidson thought it more important to get satisfactory terms for the teaching of religion throughout the whole national system, and to this end was even ready if necessary to sacrifice the denominational schools. Lang agreed with this view and with the proposed solution. "I am *sure* it is right to try to bring peace," he told his mother, and peace could only be by compromise. But since the selected compromise was unacceptable, the whole question was laid upon the shelf for a few years.

In the matter of the Marriage Laws, Lang took a leading part. In 1909, after some years of preliminary argument, a Royal Commission on Divorce and Matrimonial Causes was set up. The Prime Minister wished to exclude ecclesiastics altogether, but gave way when Davidson threatened to "say openly that I thought the Church had been most improperly treated." So Lang, who was now Archbishop of York, was appointed to "a most tiresome and unpleasant Royal Commission on the Divorce Laws of which I felt bound, *much* against my wish, to become a member." A little later, after the Commission had met, he wrote again, bewailing this burden that had been thrust upon him.

Since most of his fellow-members regarded Our Lord's words on the subject as "irrelevant," a Minority Report was almost inevitable. His prophecy was proved correct in 1912, when the Commission completed its labours.

At the very beginning I was doomed to work for two years on the Royal Commission on Matrimonial Causes, of which the late Lord Gorell was the able, genial and generous Chairman. It meant constant visits to London, reading of endless papers, examining and cross-examining witnesses. In this cross-examination the Chairman and my colleagues were wont to say that it showed what I might have accomplished at the Bar! In the result three of us—Sir William Anson, my Warden of All Souls, Sir Lewis Dibdin and myself—were compelled to present a Minority Report. It was drafted almost entirely, with suggestions from Anson and myself, by Sir Lewis Dibdin, and was, I think it may be said, a very able document. The *Times* printed it as a special pamphlet. It remains, I suppose, the best argument against any additions to the legal causes of divorce. On many points, especially of procedure, the majority and the minority agreed.

These were that men and women should be put on an equal footing, that the law should be the same for rich and poor, so far as this could be secured through a decentralisation of Courts, that publication of the proceedings might be restricted, and that the grounds for nullity should be extended. The Minority dissented from the recommendations to add five new grounds for divorce to adultery, already allowed by the State (though not admitted by the Church) under the Act of 1857.

The guiding principle of the Minority Report, as the Archbishop explained in his defence before the Convocation of the Northern Province, was that "any Christian society should be at liberty to give or withhold its own religious sanction to marriages to which the State reluctantly, but under pressure of social facts, feels compelled to give its civil consent." To those who felt that even the Minority had sold a pass, the Archbishop wrote his apologia in the *York Diocesan Gazette*. It had been "a very distasteful task" and he had had "to consider not what might be in theory desirable, but what is in practice possible."

The Reports made a stir, but in the press of competing legislation no immediate action was taken by Parliament. Eventually, in November 1918, Lord Buckmaster introduced an unsuccessful Bill incorporating two of the Majority's proposals. In 1920, with the formidable support of Lord Birkenhead, he brought in a more comprehensive measure which embodied practically the whole of the recommendations of the Majority Report. It fell to Lang to open the case for the opposition, which he did in a powerful and effective speech affirming the view of the Church, but arguing his case in the main on public welfare. After he had spoken, Lord Haldane, who was supporting the Bill, sent him across a note, declaring that his speech was "one of the best bits of advocacy I have ever heard." Although, largely as the result of the brilliant oratory of Lord Birkenhead, the Bill passed its Second and Third Readings, it was not pursued by the House of Commons; and no effective step was taken by Parliament until the Bill of 1937, sponsored by Mr. A. P. Herbert.[1] On this the Archbishop has left a note, explaining an attitude which at the time came in for criticism.

Rightly or wrongly, I came to the conclusion that it was no longer possible to impose the full Christian standard by law on a largely non-Christian population, but that the witness to that standard, and consequent disciplinary action towards its own members or persons who sought to be married by its rites, must be left to the Church. I was put in a very painful position as a result. I said that I could not as a citizen vote against the Bill, but that I could not bring myself as a Churchman to vote for it; and I announced that I would not vote. This seemed to some an unworthy temporising position and was rather fiercely denounced in the House of Lords by Lord Russell of Killowen, a fervent Roman Catholic. Others whose judgment I respected, such as Robert Cecil, thought it was the only course I could well take.

On Education, the Marriage Laws and other points of contention in the borderland of Church and State, there was a wide tactical difference between the policy of the extremists in the Church and that of the two Archbishops. The first were for contesting to a finish every position that was attacked, without compromise or surrender. They would have a pitched battle, even if its outcome would almost inevitably be a defeat. Randall Davidson, on the other hand, was in mind and temperament a man of settlement. He would, it is true, strongly resist a secular assault upon the territory of the Church. But if the attack were pressed, he would come to terms and retire in good order to the next

---

[1] Now Sir Alan Herbert, Burgess of Oxford University.

position; and as he was a master of rearguard action, he generally contrived to extract some substantial advantage from an adverse situation. With some justice he might have criticised the extremists as lacking in realism; and equally they might have accused him of "defeatism," on the ground that a rearguard action, however skilful, has never yet won a war. Lang was of Davidson's mind; and for good or ill, for nearly forty years, from 1903 to 1942, the official policy of the Church was guided, first by Davidson alone, then by both jointly, and finally by Lang alone, upon the tactical principles of this second school of thought.

That Lang would be prominent in the debates of the House of Lords was to be expected, if only because he was there fulfilling an old ambition. "The Earl of Norham," it may be recalled, made his first appearance in the Upper House in 1912, so that the Archbishop of York, taking his seat in February 1909, defeated the forecast by three years. After an introduction which, he told Wilfrid Parker, was "extraordinarily like a scene from *Alice in Wonderland*," he made his maiden speech (November 30th) on the famous "People's Budget."

> On one of the days of the discussion I opened the debate and so had a crowded House. . . . The Press reported the speech in full with such headlines as "A Daniel comes to Judgment." It was praised (I saw in his *Reminiscences*) by John Morley and as a speech seemed to make some impression. I think my brother Archbishop was doubtful of the wisdom of such an excursion into the purely political arena. Was it, I wonder, a resurgence of my old political ambitions? I imagine it caused some perturbation among the very conservative laymen of the north, and I was rebuked for it by the redoubtable Theresa, Marchioness of Londonderry.

The Lords, Lang declared, would be justified in refusing to pass the Budget only if the method were unconstitutional or the proposals revolutionary. Neither charge was true, and in the circumstances to reject the measure would jeopardise the claim of the Lords to control legislation and would disturb the balance of the Constitution. He spoke with some hesitation, as the Archbishop of Canterbury had advised the Bishops to take no part in the debate. But "I was too deeply convinced of the unwisdom of the course the Lords proposed to take," he wrote to his mother. "I think the other Archbishop really agreed, but he felt bound by what he had previously said to many of the Bishops who were absent." His words, he knew, had offended many, but "there it is, I said what I thought and the consequences must take care of themselves."

The speech, which drew a stately reproof from Lord Curzon, was greeted with respect by the Press, even by those organs which were opposed to the Budget, and was generally regarded as one of the most important contributions to the debate. Its maiden success must have recalled an occasion twenty-six years earlier, when a young undergraduate defended the Scottish Kirk in the Oxford Union.

Long afterwards Lang wrote :

I never felt from the first the difficulties of which others, notably Archbishop Benson, have been conscious in speaking in the House of Lords. True, it is not a lively or outwardly encouraging audience : was it A. J. Balfour who, fresh from the House of Commons, said it was like speaking in a tomb ? But after long experience I have become independent of applause and satisfied with attention. Indeed, I have often noticed that the passages in a speech which were most loudly applauded were apt to be just those which one afterwards regretted. True also that the audience is coldly and politely critical. But if one has anything to say it is always attentive, and their Lordships are always more ready to praise than to blame a speech, especially if it is made by one "of their own sort." They are put off by anything irrelevant or confused or over-rhetorical (except in the case of masters of rhetoric like Buckmaster). What they seem to like is the sort of speech which the Chairman of a Limited Company makes to its shareholders. But all this only puts one on one's mettle and compels one to be sure of one's matter and careful of one's form.

Next year came the crisis Lang had foretold, a Bill he greatly disliked, and ultimately a vote which was widely condemned. After the second indecisive election of 1910 he, like his brother of Canterbury, hoped and worked for a settlement of the Constitutional quarrel by negotiation and compromise. When all hope of this had vanished, the Archbishops were agreed that of two evils the threatened creation of peers was the greater and the passage of the Parliament Bill the lesser ; or rather that it was better for the Bill to pass without than with an inundation which would have destroyed the House of Lords altogether. Both therefore spoke in the debate, opposing rejection ; and both, when it seemed that the revolt of the "Ditchers," led by Lord Halsbury, might prevail, voted for the Bill. As 11 Bishops joined them in the lobby and the majority for the Bill was only 17, their intervention was of real, and perhaps of decisive importance.

"The 'Ditchers,'" Lang wrote to his mother a few days later, "were beside themselves with excitement. Apparently, to judge from the letters which I have received, they are very bitter. I never knew men so 'possessed.' There was a nasty flavour of party intrigue behind the action of a good many of them; the others seemed incapable of argument. But I was never so sure that my vote was right. But I did not like it."

Nor did many of his Conservative friends, some of whom neither forgot nor forgave his action in voting for a Bill which he disliked in order to avoid a result which he disliked still more.

The corollaries of the Parliament Act followed. Lang spoke and voted against the Home Rule Bill, while arguing vehemently and persuasively for a settlement by compromise. Much of what he said in his three speeches on the subject sounds like common sense to-day, but at the time his appeals were unavailing. His last word was nearly never uttered, not because he had changed his mind, but because, as he told his mother, he had discovered that his capacity to win the attention of his exalted audience "stirs some of the embers of the political ambitions of other days." He was so alarmed by this thought that he had almost made up his mind not to speak at all. In the end, however, he kept to his first intention, contenting himself with the warning that "the snare wants watching"; and the speech, in which, while loving neither the Bill nor the methods of the Government, he confessed to "a strong bias in favour of some measure of self-government for Ireland," enhanced his growing reputation as a debater.

His attitude, both on the platform and in Parliament, towards the Disestablishment and Disendowment of the Welsh Church needed neither explanation nor defence. He was one of its stoutest and most effective opponents in demonstrations all over the country and continued to resist it in the House of Lords until, through the mechanism of the Parliament Act, it reached the Statute Book. The War of 1914-1918 then broke out, the operation of the Bill was suspended, and in 1919, when the suspension was lifted, the bitterness it had aroused was diminished by a considerable mitigation of the financial clauses.

The Bishoprics Bill of 1913 was another measure in which the Archbishop of York was necessarily interested through the inclusion of

Sheffield among the new dioceses to be created. It might be thought that so blameless a Bill would have had an easy passage through Parliament, but a number of members of the House of Commons set themselves to obstruct it, not so much because they disliked the Bill as because they disliked Bishops. In the end it passed as the result of a Parliamentary deal, its supporters having intimated that if its career were again blocked, they would serve the same treatment to a number of Charity Bills in which the Nonconformists were deeply interested.

The years from 1908 to 1914 were charged with industrial troubles, which particularly concerned Lang as the Bishop of a great industrial diocese. He was never to be as far to the Left as was his friend and first mentor, Henry Scott Holland, his views remaining very much those of the Tory Democrat of Oxford days or perhaps of the young curate who had introduced Tom Mann into the Clergy House at Leeds. As an advocate of an "enlightened capitalism," he deplored the resort to strike or lockout, while always a supporter of improved social and working conditions. It was an attitude which satisfied the extremer men of neither side and occasionally disappointed those who wished the Church to give a constructive lead. When the Coal Strike of 1912 brought the industrial trouble to his own front door, he steadily refused either to offer arbitration or to pronounce upon the justice of the claims of masters and men, continuing to maintain that it was "within the power of reasonable men" to adjust the apparently conflicting contentions and to "devise some means by which both the rate of a fair day's wage and the output of a fair day's work can be ascertained." On March 17th he went to Sheffield in "pitiless rain" to address large meetings, mainly of miners, and to plead the cause of conciliation. The men listened to him, but do not appear to have been much moved by his words of peace.

He repeatedly returned to the social and economic problem, both in his sermons and at public meetings, putting his general position most clearly and characteristically in some words he spoke at a Coronation meeting for men in the Queen's Hall in 1911.

"The nineteenth century," he said, "was concerned with the creation of wealth: the twentieth century will be concerned with its distribution. There is none of us, whatever may be his political views, who does not feel that this is a problem which needs adjusting. We cannot but be appalled by the contrast of increasing prosperity and great wealth and of great poverty, of increasing luxury and of great squalor. . . . That contrast between the London of the West and the London I know so well of the East is a contrast which may be seen over the whole field of our English life. When I think of that great multitude of our working folk among whom I have laboured, whom I have learnt to reverence, I cannot but see the picture of the monotony of toil which they are called upon to bear, of the uncertainty of employment which haunts them day by day, of the overcrowded houses in which we ask and expect them to rear British homes, of the mean streets from which every sign not only of the beauty of God's earth but of the comforts and conveniences that are common to ours are shut out. . . . Our best self in the contemplation of this inequality says that these things ought not to be."

Parliament and the claims of secular questions were not the sum of the duties to be discharged outside the Province. In 1911, when the King was crowned, a minor but troublesome point of controversy arose. At the previous Coronation, owing to the frailty of Archbishop Temple, Dr. Maclagan had crowned the Queen, thereby, in the view of some, creating a clear precedent in a matter disputed (sometimes in a very unedifying fashion) between Canterbury and York. This view, however, was questioned and finally rejected. Lang accepted the return to the earlier custom with good grace, explaining and defending it in the *York Diocesan Gazette*. As a salve to Provincial pride he had been assigned the task of preaching the short sermon at the ceremony. This he did with admirable skill, and by general consent his homily, apt, concise, simple and perfectly phrased, had never been surpassed or even equalled at such a function.

"The ceremony at the Abbey," he wrote to his mother, "was . . . most wonderful and splendid. The King and Queen went through their long ordeal with great dignity and devotion. The Queen especially looked really beautiful, very quiet and recollected. There were hardly any hitches. On the whole the atmosphere was very reverent, but I am told that in the nave, where so little was seen or heard, people seemed to lose the spirit of worship."

There were other events, too, which touched the whole Church. There were the Church Congresses, notably the meeting in 1912 at Middlesbrough, where the Archbishop, being on his own ground, was host and Chairman.

My opening address, afterwards printed and published, was on "The Church and Nation," on the national responsibility and mission of the Church. Returning to Ormesby Hall (the home of my good friends the Pennymans, where I used to stay so often), Charles Gore in one of his petulant moods said crossly: "How *can* you go on believing in an Established Church?"

On the same occasion, and in the same mood, Gore was heard to remark: "Lang would be a dear, delightful boy if he were not so terribly archiepiscopal."

There were the beginnings of the long task of revising the Prayer Book, the subject of a later chapter, but in these years one of the principal preoccupations of Convocation. There was a sharp recrudescence of old controversy when in 1911 J. M. Thompson, a successor of Lang's as Dean of Divinity at Magdalen, published *The Miracles of the New Testament*, in which he arrived at conclusions that gave grave offence to the orthodox. His licence was withdrawn by Dr. Talbot, who had become Bishop of Winchester, and there were signs of restlessness from Gore, who in the same year succeeded Paget as Bishop of Oxford. In 1912 two more books of modernist tendency made their appearance: *Foundations*, a collection of essays edited by Canon Streeter, and *The Creed in the Pulpit* by Hensley Henson. A private meeting of Bishops to discuss the situation did nothing to reassure Gore, who (perhaps in another of his "petulant moods") began to talk of resignation, and a war of pamphlets followed. The dispute dragged on rather indecisively for two years and ended with a Resolution in the Upper House of the Convocation of Canterbury which reaffirmed belief in the historical facts of the Creeds. In all this Lang had a minor part, being content to offer counsel and perhaps to do some "back-seat driving" while his brother of Canterbury got his three restive horses round another difficult corner. Lang's letters to Wilfrid Parker tell something of his personal opinions. There would, he feared, be trouble over Streeter's contribution on the Historic Christ, and he anticipated with dread another "ignominious heresy hunt," but he had read *Foundations* on the whole with appreciation: Neville Talbot's [1] Introduction was quite brilliant. "I am more a 'modernist' than you," he told Parker, "and nothing in the book shocks me. . . . It is only *Lux Mundi* a stage further on." He had no sympathy with Gore's fulminations against the contributors: "he treats them just as Liddon treated him."

[1] 2nd son of Dr. E. S. Talbot. Bishop of Pretoria 1920-1932. Died in 1943.

Kikuyu, another almost forgotten controversy, threatened more serious consequences. The trouble arose out of a gathering of Protestant missionaries of many denominations at which the Bishops of Mombasa and Uganda and a number of Anglican clergy were present. The conference drew up a scheme of federation for the East African Missions and closed with a service of Holy Communion at which the Bishop of Mombasa administered the Sacrament to all the delegates with the exception of those from the Society of Friends. These proceedings were sternly challenged by Frank Weston, the able and saintly Bishop of Zanzibar, and his indictment to the Archbishop of Canterbury was strongly supported by Gore and the bulk of the Anglo-Catholics. Those who wish to rake the ashes of this old, but not uninteresting, dispute will find a full and fair account in Dr. Bell's *Randall Davidson*. Since the Bishop of Zanzibar owed canonical obedience to Canterbury and not to York, Lang was not so closely concerned as was Davidson, whose diplomatic handling of a very difficult and delicate situation was characteristic and won the admiration and complete concurrence of his colleague. When Lang visited Hickleton in January 1913, he found Lord Halifax most warlike and unwilling to be edged off this ecclesiastical topic of the hour. For himself he thought the administration of the Sacrament had been a "great mistake." The whole business promised to be the "toughest job" of 1914 and it would be "for the wise to try to undo the mistakes of the good." Nevertheless he had a lifelong sympathy with the cause of Reunion, and when in the same month he preached at St. Mary's, Edinburgh, he described the conflict as one of "two great principles, each in itself high and noble."

Lang was a member of the Consultative Body which Dr. Davidson called to his aid. It met in July 1914 and, without any kind of preliminary conference, arrived at a unanimous conclusion, which was the substance of the Archbishop's eventual answer. "By disappointing *both* the outside extremists," Lang wrote to Wilfrid Parker, "we shall probably prove to be in the way of truth—that we have stood up for principles and yet recognised that in spiritual things equity is higher and truer than logic."

In Province and Diocese, Church and State, there was more than enough in these six years to keep a man fully occupied. The standard of unremitting labour which Lang had set himself at Leeds, and had fully observed at Magdalen, Portsea and Stepney, was not only maintained but even raised during those years at York. Escape from this treadmill of work was rare and brief. There was "blessed Ballure," which began to beckon him as summer turned to autumn; there was the sanctuary of Cuddesdon in Holy Week; there was the welcoming gate of All Souls, twice or three times in the year; and there were evenings in London, when he fled from Lambeth and the cares of the Church and dined congenially at Grillions or the Club, of both of which he had become a member. So he found himself, overdriven yet conscious of some achievement, when in the summer of 1914 the world fell into the catastrophe of war.

Chapter XXII

THE WAR (1914-1918)

PARTLY perhaps because Lang was a Lowlander who had "adopted" the Highlands, tales of curses, dreams and the like were a never-failing entertainment. One of his favourite stories, illustrating his own powers in this mysterious province, doubtless gained something during years of much telling and certainly should not be taken at all seriously. He would sometimes stay, the tale ran, with a friend who had a little house on the edge of a loch, with an island in it so beautiful that anyone who came to those parts was taken to see and admire the view. But one year, when the Archbishop went to see his friend, the latter told him with a long face that the view was gone. Someone had bought the island and built on it a large red terra-cotta hydropathic hotel. Lang responded suitably with sympathy and indignation, and that evening, when the talk happened to be of birthdays, he disclosed that he had been born on Hallowe'en. "Then," said his friend, "you must have the power of cursing. Do come and curse the Hydropathic." "Certainly," replied the Archbishop; "but first you must teach me an old Gaelic curse." A form of words was found and the Archbishop cursed the hotel. Three months later he had a grateful letter from his friend to tell him that the offending building had been burnt down. Time passed and suddenly he got a telegram. "Your curse not much good," he read. "They have built up Hydropathic again and worse than before. This time of yellow terra-cotta and covered with decoration." The Archbishop at once replied, "I will curse it again." He did so; and six weeks afterwards the new hotel too was burnt to the ground. Being very proud of this hitherto unsuspected power, he used frequently to tell the story, and one day repeated it to a clergyman with whom he was staying in the South of England. His host said, "That's a useful gift. Do come and curse my East window: it's of unexampled ugliness and I can't get rid of it." The Archbishop at once obliged; and next Sunday, when the clergyman was in the middle of his sermon, without warning or visible cause the East window fell in with a crash and broke into a thousand fragments.

Some examples of the Archbishop's dreams have already been given.

244

People usually avoid the man who insists on relating his dreams to them, but the Archbishop's had about them a quality which lifted them above all tedium. Two of his favourites are related by Father Talbot. The first concerned King George II. His Majesty, so the dream had it, for some offence had been put to a penance, consisting of a fast, and arrived at St. George's, Hanover Square, to have it remitted. Descending from the Royal coach, he went on his knees up the steps of the church, followed by two pages, one of whom was so amazed to see the King in such a posture that he pointed at him, crying, "Pussy, pussy!" Whereat the King turned round and cuffed him. Crawling on up the aisle, His Majesty at length reached the altar rails, within which stood an eighteenth-century prelate, complete with wig and ballooning lawn sleeves and holding a basket. The Bishop declared the penance duly performed and absolved the King, taking from his basket an apple for the Royal breakfast. Whereupon the King in a fury jumped to his feet and exclaimed, "Damn your apples! Give me a mutton chop!"

Shortly before 1914 the Archbishop dreamed that war had broken out with Germany and that he was summoned to Lambeth, where he found the Archbishop of Canterbury walking about the garden in some distress of mind. The War Office had just sent him a message that five thousand German women had landed on the coast of Essex. With the news was a request from the Government that the Archbishops, supported by the clergy of London, should go forth to meet the invaders and try to turn them back by "moral suasion." So the Archbishops, at the head of a long procession of clergy, marched out of London, which was filled with troops and every kind of vehicle, mobilised for war. They reached Epping, and on coming to the top of a rise saw on the opposite slope a horde of Amazons, gnashing their teeth and brandishing knives. When the clergy were within earshot, the Archbishops went forward to practise "moral suasion," but the women only gnashed their teeth and brandished their knives more ferociously. Finally an enormous parson from the ranks pushed roughly past the Archbishops saying, "Damn your moral suasion! Let's get at 'em!" Whereupon the Archbishop awoke.

Father Talbot would sometimes point out the frequent appearance of bad language in these dreams, remarking that a psychologist would probably suggest a sinister explanation, but the Archbishop brushed aside any such modern theory, maintaining that dreams are "purely the play and frolic of the human mind amusing itself."

Not long after this dream of an invasion by Teutonic Amazons, war with Germany did in fact break out.

How well I remember those tense days at the beginning of August 1914: preaching to a huge crowd in the Minster on the Sunday before war was declared, when dear Scott Holland was with me; the discussions at Bishopthorpe with my old All Souls friend, Sir John Mowbray, and Professor Goudy, the Lyttons (with young Knebworth, then a little boy, afterwards killed in an air accident in the fullness of his strength and promise), and Lady Jane Lindsay, who was staying with us, and who all at once left when the momentous declaration was made.

Lang was perplexed and troubled, not only by the particular circumstances in which war had come, but by the larger question of the part, if any, the Church should take even in a just war.

I was harried with anxiety as to the rightfulness of the Church in any way supporting war; and I well remember the real torture of mind when I tried to think out the problem in September while in retreat at Cuddesdon. But I was driven to the conclusion, right or wrong, that the War was righteous, that we were bound in honour to enter it, and that the Church could not rightly oppose it. Even now, with all the bitter disappointment which has come, I am still convinced that no other course was possible.

One question immediately arose, to be till the end a major preoccupation with the Archbishops.

What was to be the position of the younger clergy? After full consultation the Archbishops decided that every effort should be made to liberate them for work as Chaplains to the Army and Navy, but that they should not be encouraged to enlist as combatants. Some of them insisted that they must, and it was not possible to forbid them. Most of them in my Diocese were eager to go out as Chaplains, and many did, including my own Vicar at Bishopthorpe, Stafford Crawley. The Chaplain-General (Bishop Taylor Smith) was unfortunate in his handling of the whole problem. He was, at least at first, resolved to choose Chaplains of his own way of thought, and even afterwards, when the demand increased, annoyed keen young men of another type by his methods of questioning them. But ultimately things came right, and I don't think the Church has any reason to be otherwise than proud of its Chaplains in the War. Certainly, when in the summer of 1917 I visited all the fronts in France and Flanders, the testimony of all the Commanders of the Armies with whom I stayed was emphatic. When people talk now about the place of the Church in the War having been "unfortunate" and "negligible" they forget the work of its Chaplains.

But not all, even of the younger clergy, who were in charge of parishes could be spared. I encouraged some of them (like Alan Don, the Vicar of Norton) to stay at their posts, even when this meant real self-sacrifice. I was indignant when later on I discovered that some of the Chaplains resented the position of their brethren who had thus held the fort at home, for I knew that for them this was by far the harder course.

Later on in the War, when a call for organised national service at home was made, I drew up a scheme for the service of the clergy at home, at least of all but the older men, obtained the approval of the Bishops, took it to Neville Chamberlain, who had been put at the head of the National Service campaign (his first Government work), and he accepted it As a result—I speak only of the Diocese of York—practically every parson in the prime of life was engaged in some form or other of National Service, in agriculture, even in munition factories, in Government and other offices, in hospitals, etc. Early in the War I summoned all the clergy of the Diocese to the Minster and spoke to them about the duties of the clergy in a time of war—words which were afterwards published. It was a very memorable and impressive gathering.

Lang never shifted in opinion from the position he took up in Convocation on July 21st, 1915, that "the proper point of view of the man in Holy Orders was that his place in national service was the ministry of the Word and Sacraments and influence among his own people in the place where he was appointed to serve." Those who could be spared from the parishes should go as Chaplains or might undertake some other form of non-combatant work ; but it was not their duty to fight. People might murmur and point to France, where the priest served in the ranks, and some of the younger men who wanted, like the clergyman in Lang's dream, to "get at 'em," might fret ; but the War Office accepted the views of the Archbishops. It is true that in the spring of 1918, when man-power problems had become grave, a new Bill in its first draft included the clergy in the general conscription, but this provision was soon withdrawn. In return, the Archbishops conceded that under a special dispensation the clergy were to be allowed to enlist for combatant service. The numbers involved, of course, were negligible : for both parties in the controversy it was the principle that mattered.

Having made up his mind that the Church was right to give its full support to the national effort, Lang threw himself wholeheartedly into the recruiting campaign, addressing meetings in most of the cities and larger towns of the Diocese. In this he walked ahead of his brother of Canterbury, who was warier—and perhaps wiser—in keeping himself a little detached from the more secular enterprises of the early days.

One of the meetings brought Lang into serious trouble, arising out of an incident, apparently trivial, which nevertheless pursued him through all the years of war and even afterwards was remembered against him. Not only did it give him great personal pain and a sense of misrepresentation and injustice ; but he felt that it was impairing his influence at a time when this might have had the best effect.

He gives his own version of the episode :

I was speaking at a great gathering of York citizens in the Empire Music Hall on the ideals which lay behind our part in the War, of the spirit in which it ought to be carried on, and on the duty of supporting the cause. I was anxious from the first and always to mitigate all bitterness of spirit against our enemies ; and speaking as I did without notes, and annoyed by recent words and cartoons about the Kaiser, I remembered at the moment what I had seen in the *Alberta* in Portsmouth harbour before the body of Queen Victoria was taken to London and Windsor, and of the Navy service on the deck of the *Alberta*—the Kaiser kneeling beside King Edward VII at the bier of Queen Victoria—these two alone,[1] and I said something to the effect that for my part I had a "sacred memory" of the Kaiser which made me sure that he could not lightly have embarked on a war with England. I did not notice that, as soon as this doubtless ill-chosen phrase had escaped my lips, several reporters left. Before many hours were over I learned to my cost that the phrase, without any of its context, had been telegraphed to all parts of the country, indeed of the world. Immediately there descended upon me a vast spate of letters, protesting and denouncing. It was a sad revelation of the hysteria already working in the public mind. One letter was

[1] See page 140.

significant: "That the Kaiser's soul may rot eternally in Hell is the daily prayer of yours truly, A. B., Churchwarden and communicant for twenty-five years."

Lang's own letters, and those of his friends, give some further facts about an incident which had an entirely disproportionate effect upon himself, his work, and the way in which people regarded him. It appears that as he was entering the hall where he was to speak, a youth pressed into his hand "a vulgar lampoon about the Kaiser." He glanced at it, and in his indignation inserted an impromptu passage, reported as follows the next day:

> He resented extremely the coarse and vulgar way in which the Emperor of Germany had been treated in some of the newspapers and so-called comic illustrations. His Grace had a personal memory of the Emperor, very sacred to him, which made him feel that it was not without great reluctance that he felt himself compelled to accept the fact that his conduct, and the conduct of his ministers, had involved his nation in a war with Great Britain.

Neither in substance nor in phrasing was this a happy interpolation. It followed an indictment of the militaristic spirit of Germany and preceded a forthright attack upon the Emperor's advisers. The Archbishop could have made his point more effectively in other language and without allusion to a "memory" which could mean nothing to his hearers and, in the prevailing temper, was more likely to exasperate than to persuade them.

"Hundreds of letters and scurrilous postcards, a perfect hail of de-nunciation," he complained bitterly to Wilfrid Parker. "I am supposed to be a sycophant of the Kaiser, a pro-German, and goodness knows what else. The abuse doesn't affect me; but this storm may affect some of the other big men's meetings arranged at Sheffield, Bradford, Hull, etc. It is really monstrous that one's chance of rousing the spirit of the people should be prejudiced by the tricks of these reporters and the monstrous injustice of these fanatics. But the worst thing is that the storm has been a really woeful revelation of the spirit of hatred and malice which the War seems to have aroused. It is terribly hard to get even a hearing for some faint voices of the Christian spirit." According to Canon Tupper-Carey, he received twenty-four Iron Crosses by post. "I doubt," he wrote again, "if we can throw stones at those German 'Hymns of hate.'"

It was a great fuss about what was at worst a verbal indiscretion; and the agitation ignored not only the Archbishop's conspicuous service, but also the effect of the speech upon those who actually heard it. Later in the War four soldiers, all of whom had enlisted in the first few weeks, were sitting in a dugout in France and discussing their reasons for joining up. One of them said: "I happened to go and hear the Archbishop of York speak on our aims in the War. It was a very fine effort and I was so carried away that I went to the Recruiting Office next morning." This was, it appeared, the very meeting that aroused the storm.

But the thing was done; and attempts which he made at once to explain his words were neither well-conceived nor successful. Worse than the snapping of newspapers were the cold shoulders of acquaintances in the Yorkshire Club; even more, the estrangement of some of his friends in the Diocese; and worst of all, perhaps, a temporary coolness at Windsor and Balmoral. He might and did console himself with the thought that a friend of his was the victim of a similar persecution. He had long known and liked Lord Haldane, whose career up to a point had borne some resemblance to his own. He had stayed at Cloan and been under the charm of old Mrs. Haldane. "A most wonderful old lady," he wrote. "It's like being in retreat to talk to her. She is so quietly and strongly 'in the Spirit.' When her son, the Lord Chancellor, is away from home, she sends him a text as her special message every day. She makes one realise how much a modern Christian loses in forsaking this steadfast study of the Bible." Yet, despite the daily text, Haldane halted on the threshold of religious belief. "His philosophy is a good bridge to religion. He encourages one to cross, but prefers himself to live on the philosophic side." In March 1915 Lang dined at Grillions, with Haldane as a neighbour—"very interesting on the foolish attacks on his supposed pro-German sympathies—a foolish hysteria propagated by Leo Maxse and the *National Review*." Haldane too was the victim of an unhappy phrase, having once alluded to Germany as his "spiritual home"; and his detractors, ignoring his indispensable achievements as Secretary of State for War, were not satisfied until they had driven him out of office. Lang may have had Haldane's fate as well as his own in his mind when he wrote:

With all respect to the natural feelings of men and women who lost those who were dear to them, we cannot look back without shame to the widespread anti-German hysteria, both during and immediately after the War. There were disgraceful instances, even in my own Diocese, of the persecution, often most bitter, by women of those who were known or supposed to have some German blood or German relations. Nor, I think, can we feel happy about the treatment meted out to *really* "conscientious objectors." It was all an instance of the way in which any war wrecks the ordinary instincts of humanity.

At intervals during the next four years the "sacred memories" were brought up against the Archbishop. In 1918, after his visit to America, he was a target once more.

"Owing to a misreport of a sentence quoted from a New York paper," he wrote, "I have been again the centre of attacks and letters to the *Daily Mail* and in the columns of the gutter-press. Being compelled to drop that cry, the old cry of the 'sacred memories' has been stirred again, and the pack has been yelping after it. What hurts is the monstrous injustice of it all and the effect it has on the working folk and soldiers who read these newspapers." A little later, when he went to Middlesbrough, he found that his meeting had been boycotted and that hardly anyone was there. "I have tried hard to be of service to the nation and this is my reward," he commented ruefully. . . . "I think I must give up this public work."

So for the first time the wind of popular disfavour blew on him, chilling him to the bone. A sensitive man like Lang will always feel the blasts more keenly than will others of tougher fibre, and nothing had happened in his life before to prepare him for the experience. In the past he had had his full share of publicity, and so long as it was favourable or not unfriendly, he welcomed it. But he shrank from the rough-and-tumble of a public controversy.

Added to this personal trouble were his anxieties over the course and probable issue of the War. In August 1915 he had a long and depressing talk with Lord Curzon, who took the gloomiest of views. The Russians, he declared, had been so battered that they could hardly continue. On the Western Front we had fought to a stalemate, while the French were unlikely to face a third winter of war. The shadow of failure already hung over Gallipoli. In one of his notebooks Lang set down his reflexions. He was critical of the Government, even of the Prime Minister, whose gifts he admired and whose friendship he prized. "The nation needs for leadership something more than the lawyer's power of

putting his case and managing the Court and jury. It needs force, fore-
sight, the glow of conviction and the sense of disciplined energy. . . ."
Only Mr. Lloyd George had "that glow in the soul" so necessary for
victory.

Always dependent on companionship, he lacked it most in these
days when his want of it was greatest. Maurice Ponsonby and Stafford
Crawley went off as Chaplains, and Edward Gibbs, with some help from
Tupper-Carey, now a Canon of York, took charge of the parish of
Bishopthorpe. Then Gibbs too left, glad to be quit of the sermons
which caused him so much agony, but sorrowful to be leaving the
Archbishop.

"Your letter just made me cry like a child," Gibbs wrote a few days
after the parting. "You always pretended to think I didn't care, but
I believe you know perfectly well I love you with all my heart, and
the parting knocked me out. I couldn't even say thank you or ask
you to forgive me all my loss of temper, disrespect and rudeness.
You say in your letter you hardly could get through your giving me
your blessing and the goodbye at the station, but I didn't get through
either. My self-control, never over-strong, just broke down completely."

"I did not quite know," wrote Stafford Crawley of his return
from France in 1917, "how bad a time the Archbishop had been
going through. . . . He had borne with great fortitude and without
resentment the wave of unpopularity that had surged up in the
nation, irritable and strained by reason of the War, and ready to find
a scapegoat for its ill-humour. I did not quite know how strained
and lonely he had been, and think that in leaving him we acted rather
cruelly. He was very patient and kind about it, though he gave no
outward sign in his behaviour of the distress he felt. . . ."

Yet one outward sign there was. In 1914 he was still in appearance
a young man, with an abundance of black hair. Two years later, when
he was still only fifty-two, his hair began to fall out in patches. He
consulted a specialist, who told him that he was suffering from alopecia
and sent him to a dentist; but there was nothing wrong with his teeth.
Soon most of his hair had vanished and what remained had turned
completely white. He started wearing a wig, but, by a credible account,
gave it up when it caught in a chandelier at Bishopthorpe. "So the
bald head with its white fringe," he commented ruefully, "had to be

accepted at the age of fifty-two." So drastic was the change that at first he was unrecognisable even to those who knew him well. He had been young; and in a few months he was an old man.

I remember that when I went to speak at some big meeting in Sheffield, no one seemed to realise who I was, and some thought I was the old Bishop of Beverley. I expect there was more astonishment at the transformation of the Archbishop than attention to his remarks. One of my old Leeds lads who was there wrote afterwards: "Well, you always played the Archbishop, now you look it." I also remember the astonishment, followed by characteristic guffaws, of King George V when I entered the Royal train, which had been drawn up at some station.

But the work of the Church went on, with new tasks added and an increasing shortage of clergy to cope with them. One heavy but necessary work was the preparation and issue of Forms of Service for use in the churches. Lang records that in this the Archbishops had little help from the so-called liturgical experts. With the exception of the Dean of Wells [1] (Dr. Armitage Robinson), who made some useful contributions, they "produced Forms and prayers culled from mediaeval sources or expressed in language wholly foreign to the real needs of the human heart"; and the better part of the work fell on Lang himself, who compiled most of the prayers issued. "No doubt they might have been better, but equally they might have been worse."

More than once the War came very close to the Diocese.

York itself was twice bombed by Zeppelins. I vividly remember seeing the first of them coming over Bishopthorpe—an unclean thing moving through the clean skies—and suddenly hearing the crash of bombs. I could not think of my own safety, though many of the villagers rushed into the basement of the Palace. My one dread was for the glorious Minster, and indeed one bomb fell within a few hundred yards of it next day. I went to the old Dean (Purey-Cust) and insisted that at once he should begin to remove the beautiful and priceless glass from the windows and bury it in some place of safety. He pled, and with tears, that he was too old to face the task; but I said I would not leave him till he had promised. So the long work began, first of removing such of the windows as could be removed, and then of cleaning and releading them. Good came out of evil.

[1] The Very Rev. J. Armitage Robinson, Dean of Wells 1911-1933. Died in 1933.

It became plain that if this had not been done, many of them would soon have suffered or been lost from natural causes. Thus the War brought not destruction but preservation to this glorious heritage of the Minster.

German warships bombarded Whitby and Scarborough. It was a "cruel and wanton raid." Archdeacon Mackarness was celebrating the Eucharist when two shells crashed into the roof of St. Martin's. He told the people they were as safe there as they would be anywhere and, to Lang's admiration, went on with the service. Hull had several raids, the first of which killed some eighty people in a crowded centre.

Thereafter, whenever the weird siren sounded, giving warning of the approach of Zeppelins, crowds of the poorer people streamed out into the fields. I saw one of these treks: it was a pathetic sight, though on the whole there was commendable fortitude. Yet if the object of these attacks *was* to shatter the nerves of the population, it had some success in Hull.

The Archbishop took the leading part in the National Mission of Repentance and Hope which was launched in 1916.

"It is not enough," he told Convocation, "that the Church should call its people to prayer and endeavour to cheer and comfort those who have been called to suffer sacrifice and sorrow. Those duties we have tried, and are trying, however imperfectly, to fulfil, but we recognise perhaps more clearly than at first we did that there are vaster and deeper issues involved in this most mighty and moving time. We are seeing with increasing clearness that we are living and fulfilling our ministry in one of the great days of the Lord, when the secular powers are being shaken to their very foundations. There is a call to the Church to bear witness to the things that remain unchanged, the sovereignty of God and the claim of Jesus Christ to the lordship of all human life." (He himself had called together the clergy of the Diocese, and nearly six hundred of them had met in the Minster for two days.) "We have called it a National Mission of Repentance and Hope," he went on to say—"Repentance because plainly we are called to bid men and women everywhere to repent of the sins which have stained our civilisation and brought upon it the manifest judgment of God, and Hope because, during the closing period of this terrific ordeal in the midst of increasing strain and sacrifice and sorrow, our people will need the strength of Hope, and in those difficult days that are coming, when the old order will have gone and the duty will be laid upon the nation of seeking a new order in a new world, we must present before the minds of the nation the one hope, Christ, His mind, His Spirit, for the rebuilding of a new world."

At the time, and still more afterwards, the Mission came in for criticism; but into it Lang threw all his eloquence and powers of organisation.

I still believe that it was right. Without it the Church as a whole would never have had the chance of witnessing to the moral and spiritual lessons of the War and to the hopes of a better order of national life. In spite of all the disappointment of these hopes, it was right then to uphold them. I have little sympathy with the war-weary, disgruntled spirit which depreciated this National Mission. Certainly in the Diocese of York, where the best available clergy were sent out, two by two, into all the towns and villages, at least a witness was given to the call for both repentance and hope. It meant very elaborate organisation and I am sure it was worth while.

The Mission, however far short it fell of the first expectations, at least gave birth to the Life and Liberty Movement, which helped to bring about an important change in the constitution of the Church. The Movement sprang largely out of the impatience of some of the younger clergy, and particularly the Chaplains serving with the Forces. They felt that the Church had lost touch with the people, that it lacked resolute leadership, that it was impeded by the shackles of the Establishment, and that it was spending far too much time on unessential matters, largely connected with all the business of temporalities, to the neglect of those larger issues, spiritual and social, on which the nation looked for light and guidance. The protagonist of the Movement was William Temple, and among its most enthusiastic originators and supporters was Dick Sheppard, whose presence was itself a guarantee of vigorous and unconventional action. The first demand was for "a forward move," a rather vague expression which was presently translated into an attempt "to win for the Church the liberty essential to fulness of life." The Archbishop of Canterbury, who had a habitual distrust of phrases when he did not know exactly what they meant, was cautious and even a little discouraging. He felt it was unfair to charge the Archbishops with a lack of leadership when they had lately, on their own initiative, launched the Mission which begat the Movement. Nor did he feel that the Government, beset by the claims of the War, would be very sympathetic towards a peremptory demand for the terms on which the Church should be allowed her freedom. Lang was more in touch with the younger priests and was temperamentally more inclined to sympathy with their discontents, though he too was critical of the sledge-hammer tactics they favoured. He was with Davidson on October 24th, 1918, when a deputation came to Lambeth.

"To our surprise," he wrote, "some eighty men and women came, evidently determined to let those two wily old men have it! . . . Of all the speeches, except Temple's, I can only say that the vigour was more conspicuous than the good taste. Dick's, which he read, was, I am bound to say, both full and petulant. . . . It is a thousand pities these good fellows have worked themselves up into this state of feverish excitement. They will only spoil their good case. I think some of their supporters must have inwardly blushed at the taste and spirit of their remarks."

But His Grace of Canterbury was not a man to be hustled, and handled the impatient clergy with masterly skill. In 1913, as the upshot of a Resolution in the Representative Church Council, the Archbishops had appointed a Commission on Church and State, under the Chairmanship of Lord Selborne, which published a unanimous Report in 1916. In effect its proposal was that the Representative Church Council, with certain changes, should receive statutory recognition and, subject to a Parliamentary veto, have real legislative powers in Church matters. The scheme received the general approval of the Church, but was put in cold storage till the end of the War. Meanwhile an Association was founded to watch over the plan and ensure its eventual emergence in legislative form. The Archbishop of Canterbury now arranged a match between this official and respectable Church Self-government Association and the lively and more emancipated Life and Liberty Movement. The Association's plan, he urged, gave nearly all the Movement demanded: let the two work together and not separately. So the turbulent torrent of Life and Liberty was drawn off to supply the power which would drive the wheels of the official machine; and at the end of 1919 the Association's scheme found its fulfilment in the Enabling Act, under which the Church Assembly was constituted. This outcome, which gravely alarmed the Erastian-minded, also disappointed some of the more ardent spirits of Life and Liberty, who would probably have preferred the completer freedom of Disestablishment; and even before the scheme had become a Bill, Gore, objecting to the Baptismal franchise, for the last time sent in his resignation.

Lang's approach to these questions may have been guided to some extent by his affectionate admiration for Dick Sheppard and the work he had begun to do at St. Martin-in-the-Fields. The Archbishop did not altogether approve when in 1914 Dick, without consulting him, abandoned his parish and went to France; but through the letters which soon began to arrive at Bishopthorpe, the horror, the suffering, but also the opportunities of the War came closer than by any other medium. "I've sat in a dugout," Dick wrote, "expecting the Germans at any moment all through one night. I've held a leg and several other limbs while the surgeon amputated them. I've fought a drunken Tommy and protected several German prisoners from a French mob. I've missed a thousand opportunities and lived through a life's experience in five weeks." Later Dick was with the French, had his baptism of fire, and joined in an infantry attack. "He says," Lang wrote to Wilfrid Parker, "he only knows that he ran towards and not away from the enemy, but could only say his prayers, shut his eyes and run."

The Archbishop, too, was to have a glimpse of the realities of war. In the summer of 1915, on the invitation of Lord Jellicoe, he visited the Grand Fleet at Scapa, Invergordon and Rosyth. He spent about a month with the sailors, going from ship to ship and speaking at crowded gatherings of officers and men. In the opinion of the lower deck he was "a nice sort of cove" and "a good plain speaker," adjectives more suited to a cook than to an Archbishop. He described his visit in an article to the *Times*, and the general view (as given by the *Church Times*) was that "the right man had said the right thing."

Two years later he visited the Western Front, staying with each Army Commander in turn. Once more he addressed a large number of meetings, but his "main business" was to attend the Chaplains' Conferences. "It is good to see the discontent which prevails with the conventional ways of the Church," he wrote. Life and Liberty were moving and the Chaplains were outspoken, one of them describing the Bishops as "like hens, who laid eggs, but could not hatch them." "They have not much of a sense of proportion," was Lang's comment, "and are very ignorant of the position and problems of the Church at home." Consequently they were "in some danger of adjusting the Church to the Army rather than of lifting the Army to the Church. Here and there there were signs of a rather carping sort of criticism, and of an attitude towards the Bishops which is unjust and not very seemly among men who ought to be learning the discipline of respect to superior officers."

The occasions that remained most in his memory were the addresses he delivered to six brigades of the Vth Army, just before they made an attack; a Sung Eucharist to more than a hundred Chaplains at Toc H in Poperinghe; a meeting of about five hundred Generals and Staff Officers of the Ist Army; his visits to the battlefields of the Somme, Messines and Vimy, during one of which he came under fire, a shell dropping some fifty yards away; his service at Bapaume and the talk he gave to about three thousand men; and finally the Confirmation of thirty Kaffirs at Abbeville.

He brought away with him one or two agreeable stories. A Brigadier of the Vth Army had just told his men that a live German was a curse to civilisation and that therefore they must take no prisoners. After Lang had spoken, he amended his instructions. "You heard what I said. Well, after the Archbishop's words, you may take a few prisoners."

As Lang was returning in a small steamer from Boulogne he had a curious experience.

> Just as the steamer was leaving—the hawsers let loose, the paddle wheels beginning to turn—suddenly a gangway was thrust across, so hidden by men that it was impossible to see what it contained: was it a horse, or what? Curious to see what the creature was, I went down to the hold, and behold! it was Ramsay MacDonald! He had gone out to see the Red Cross work. His views about the War —very creditable to his conscience—were notorious. When he had left Dover, the crew had struck and were with difficulty persuaded to go on with such a passenger. What I had seen was the way in which he was at the last moment smuggled on board on his return. Yet within seven years he was Prime Minister of England.

On the home front of the Church not much was to be recorded of the years of war. The appointment of Lang's old friend, Hensley Henson, to the See of Hereford provoked an angry agitation; but that trouble belonged to Canterbury and not to York. In 1918 the Government at last succeeded in getting an Education Bill through Parliament, Mr. Fisher's Act receiving the steady support of both Archbishops. Lang, in face of every difficulty, continued his Visitation of the Diocese.

With the increasing pressure of work his spare time was cut still further, but he managed an occasional escape to Cuddesdon, with all its memories of "a clear call I could not resist"; and each summer he was able to spend a short time at his new Highland home of Ballure, where for the first years Norman and his wife were regular guests.

He had his opportunity of carrying out what was perhaps his most eminent service in the War early in 1918, when the Episcopal Church of the United States invited him to pay that country a visit. "I don't want to go," he wrote. "It is hard to leave home at this time. I dislike American fuss and publicity." But with warm encouragement from Mr. A. J. Balfour and Mr. W. H. Page, the American Ambassador in London, and after an assurance that his meetings would not be limited to church-people, he accepted the invitation. "He was not," he told Convocation, "so much afraid of being killed by the malice of the enemy as by the kindness of one's friends." He asked Dick Sheppard to accompany him as his chaplain; and Dick, unable to go, recommended Mr. F. A. Iremonger, a most successful choice.

They had a stormy passage across the Atlantic. Mr. Iremonger "existed on 'Mothersill' and apples," but Lang himself was unaffected. On arrival in New York he stayed at the house of Mr. Stuyvesant Fish, sleeping in a room "fit only for a Pope"; and at once he plunged into a programme of sermons, speeches, luncheons, dinners and interviews, enough to daunt even the most insatiable of workers in the Church of England. At one of the first luncheons he met "a charming-looking young man, who greatly took my fancy": his name was Franklin Roosevelt. He took tea and talked with a then more celebrated kinsman, Theodore the ex-President, who had just come out of a nursing home after a serious operation to one of his eyes. After the interview Lang recalled and confirmed the Oxford verdict— "Matter $\beta-$; Man $a+$." There was an inevitable and impressive Pilgrims' Dinner at the Waldorf-Astoria, and during his week in New York he made sixteen speeches.

A whirlwind tour followed round some of the principal cities of the Atlantic seaboard and the Middle West. At Washington, which he reached on Holy Saturday, he heard of the death of "my dear old friend and spiritual guide, Scott Holland. It is glorious to think of what the other world will be bringing to him—all the longings of his eager spirit being satisfied; but his going leaves a great blank in my life." No one ever would or could fill that blank. There was a day when a freshman from Glasgow went to church in Oxford to hear a preacher who looked like "a mediaeval monk" and had "a good English style." There was another day when a very perplexed young man arrived with a letter of introduction from Lord Robert Cecil and enquiries about a vocation for the priesthood. There were later days of close and happy association in Amen Court. There were, finally, fleeting visits to Bishopthorpe, when the Archbishop would put aside Diocese, friends and engagements, to walk up and down the garden with his "dear Scotty." Scott Holland was one of the very few men who knew Cosmo Lang through and through.

But he had little time for mourning. He was in the toils of his American programme, and in Washington the work was important and interesting. There was his "cousin" at the White House, to whom Walter Page had written: "The Archbishop is a man and a brother, a humble, earnest, companionable fellow, with most charming manners and an attractive personality, a good friend of mine . . . you will enjoy him." Lang paid a formal call at the White House and dined there the same evening. He had a long conversation with the President, about literature and life, war and the coming peace. "Felt all the time I was talking to a man with some great qualities rather than to a great man." Indeed, he had a slight sense of a rebuff when he told Wilson how in New York he had spoken to the Chamber of Commerce and it had seemed to him that the souls of its members had been moved. "It is something," replied the President drily, "to know that these gentlemen have souls."

At Washington he was being photographed on a lawn with a group of prominent persons when the operator noticed that the Archbishop's pectoral Cross was caught in his belt. Running across the grass, the man flipped it free with his finger, saying, "I guess you'd look a durn sight better if you showed your charm." This was an occasion when the Archbishop was not amused.

On April 2nd Lang was at the Capitol and was asked to open a meeting of the Senate with prayer, a graceful compliment to a visiting ecclesiastic. On the 3rd he was at Baltimore and on the 4th at Pittsburg, where he addressed seven hundred business men, one of whom Mr. Iremonger overheard saying, "I wish we had a bit more of that kind of talk: it blows the froth off this job."

So the tour went on, very much to the pattern of a hundred programmes for visiting Britons of distinction. The Archbishop was without any doubt a success: the intention was always complimentary, even behind the statement of a reporter that "the Archbishop of York, though not of particularly striking appearance, has a much more refined voice than the average Englishman." In forty days Lang visited sixteen cities and delivered eighty-one addresses to about a hundred thousand people; and in the opinion of the British Ambassador, Lord Reading, wherever he went, his personality made an impression equalled by no European visitor except perhaps Marshal Joffre.

He ended with a short visit to Canada, to Ottawa, Montreal and Toronto. At Ottawa, where he was the guest of the Governor-General (the Duke of Devonshire), he was dressing for dinner when a cable was handed to him. It was from the faithful Booker—"Chaplain Gibbs killed 29th March." It was, Lang told his brother Norman, "literally as though I had lost my own son"; and although he brought himself to go downstairs and dine and talk as though nothing had happened, for some weeks Edward's death was seldom out of his thoughts. His sense of loss was even more poignant on his return to Bishopthorpe, where there was so much to remind him of his beloved chaplain; and early in June he was writing to tell Wilfrid Parker of a "charming" dream he had had "about Edward—coming to me, smiling and radiant, and saying, 'Thank God, there are no sermons here!'"

On April 10th he was back in New York. He spent the week-end with J. P. Morgan on Long Island, where Sunday, in spite of his grief, was "one of the happiest days of my life." That week-end began a friendship "for which I have a gratitude no words can express": it was one of the most valued gifts of the American tour and was to last until Morgan's death in 1943.

Lang returned to New York for a few last engagements, including a luncheon with Colonel House, where with ex-President Taft, Elihu Root and others he discussed the new design for a League of Peace; on the 15th he was aboard the *Cedric*; and early next day the skyscrapers and the Statue of Liberty melted out of sight behind him in the morning mist.

On Sunday the 28th he reached York after an absence of nearly three months. The Minster bells rang a chime of welcome, and at Bishopthorpe the whole village was waiting in front of the house to greet him. "It seems to me now like a wonderful dream," he wrote of his journey. There was, it is true, an ugly uprush of the old criticism, when something he had said in New York at a Three Hours' Service on Good Friday about the need to forgive our enemies was misreported and misinterpreted by the Press. The "sacred memories" were exhumed and some of the comments distressed the Archbishop. Eventually the *Daily Mail*, which was leading the hunt, was dismounted by a daring sortie from Iremonger and was even induced to a not very gracious recantation. Apart from this episode, the success of the tour was generally recognised. "It was," said the *Westminster Gazette*, "one of the most moving and memorable visits ever paid by an Englishman to the United States." To a degree unsurpassed by any previous visitor he had brought home to a vast variety of audiences "all that Great Britain had contributed to the common cause, her achievements by land and sea, her sacrifices, her labour, and her wealth"; while, "with insistent emphasis," he had urged Americans to remember how great were the moral issues involved. By an American verdict "his visit ranks along with those of Marshal Joffre and Mr. Balfour as those which have produced the greatest impression upon our people."

With the failure of the German offensive, the brilliant British attacks of the summer, and the growing weight of American intervention, the War was drawing to a close. For Lang the four years had been a time of some achievement, but even more of setback, of sorrow and of disappointment. Till 1914 his ship had sailed forward steadily to a favouring breeze. The weather was fair and every omen was propitious. After 1914 it was checked by adverse winds and roughly buffeted by the waves; so that progress, if progress there might be, was slow and grudging. But on November 11th relief at the ending of the sorrow, carnage and sacrifice predominated over any feeling of frustration and failure. He was in London on Armistice Day, and on November 12th attended St. Paul's for the Solemn Te Deum. "Even I, who thrill less and less as the years pass, was stirred," he wrote to Wilfrid Parker.

So the awful shadow of these four bad years passed. When I look back, in spite of all the horrors and the barren fruit they brought, I cannot think, as I have said, that we could honourably have kept out of the War. But the course of it proved that once war is let loose, all sorts of evil passions are let loose with it, that it is in *itself* futile as well as horrible; and that mere victory is barren. Two things trouble my conscience: one, that perhaps more heed should have been paid to the proposals of the famous Lansdowne letter; the other that, like others, I was too blind to the character of the final Versailles Treaty, its lack of the true wisdom of magnanimity, its obsession with the past, its failure to foresee the future. Certainly the dregs of the War poisoned from the first the hopes of bringing in some better order of human life.

Yet I cannot bring myself to believe that mere negative pacificism is right in this mixed and perverse world. I still maintain, as I used to do in those now distant days, that peace in itself is not an ideal: it might be a state of things attendant upon the achievement of ideals, of justice, of freedom, and—in its widest sense—of love. The thing to labour for is not the mere abolition of war but the transformation of the conditions, social, political, international, which lead to it. This must be the witness and work of the Church of Christ. Would that it could speak and act as one body, that even now Christians in every part of the world could put the patriotism of the Kingdom of God before every other!

Chapter XXIII

"AN APPEAL TO ALL CHRISTIAN PEOPLE"

AMONG the prayers and resolutions which Lang jotted down on the eve of his Ordination was an intention "to promote the unity of the Church in Great Britain." By this he surely meant more than merely a lessening of doctrinal and ceremonial differences within the Church of England. Very much in his mind, then and always, was the Church of his forbears and his youth. Long after it had ceased to claim him, his respect and affection for it were strong; and any approach to Reunion which should overlook the Established Church of Scotland would have been inconceivable to him. He was conscious of an intellectual kinship which to the end of his life found frequent expression in word and phrase. His own associations, too, had been, through his father, with the "High Church" element in the Kirk, which neither in belief nor in practice was very far from Anglicanism. Nor was he without experience of the practical disadvantages of separation. It irked him to be unable, save on some exceptional occasion, to worship in his mother's Kirk; and the "Balmoral problem" was with him to the end of his days. It is perhaps not an unfair conjecture that in his heart of hearts lurked a faint and muted regret that across the Border his place was in the Episcopal Church and not in the Established Kirk.

With the former his relations were correct and perfectly cordial; but, so far as is known, he never had a thought of making it his own Church by anything more than formal acknowledgment. When he left the Kirk he joined the Church of England; and though later, through his chaplaincy at Largie, he had a licence from the Episcopal Church of Scotland, he otherwise stood a little aloof from its life and activities, almost as though he were an English visitor. This attitude may be accounted for partly by a desire not to make difficulties for his father; and partly possibly by a recollection of the slight resentment felt by many Presbyterians at the very large claims of a very small Church. More than once he protested against the air of patronage assumed by some priests of the Episcopal Church, and particularly by those—more numerous then than now—who had been imported from England and were liable to forget that in Scotland they were the Nonconformists.

So at Leeds, when a visiting Bishop of Edinburgh delivered an address on the Episcopal Church of Scotland, Lang commented, severely and rather audaciously, "on those assumptions of superiority which hindered sympathetic relations with the Established Church, giving as an instance the recent transformation of incumbents into rectors."

One of his fellow-curates at Leeds was J. G. Simpson, "the Prophet," whose background was not unlike his own. He came of a Border family; he claimed an ancestor hanged in Edinburgh for resistance to prelacy; and he was a son of the Manse who had taken Orders in the Church of England. Naturally, therefore, the relations between Prelacy and Presbytery were often discussed by two young men each of whom, as Simpson recalls, had "the Kirk in his bones."

Lang went on to Magdalen, and Simpson to St. Mary's, Edinburgh, but they corresponded regularly for some years, often about "the Scottish question"; and in October 1894, with Simpson's encouragement, Lang accepted an invitation to address the Representative Council of the Episcopal Church at Aberdeen, where, as he told his friend, he proposed to hold "a 'watching brief' for the Kirk." The point of view he put in his address is of especial interest as differing little, if at all, in essentials from the point of view he was to express more than a quarter of a century later at a Lambeth Conference.

Episcopalians, he said, should work for union, not by individual conversion, though this might sometimes be necessary, nor by absorption, but by a sharing of the good things possessed by each Church. The process neither should nor could be hurried: it was not yet the time for "official overtures between organised bodies." But preliminary steps should be taken. The first of these was to find and emphasise points of agreement: the points of difference could be dealt with later. (Here again he anticipated his later technique.) Anglicans, he maintained, had more in common with Presbyterians than was generally allowed, particularly with the school of thought represented by the Scottish Church Society and of course by his own father. Then there must be "recognition that for a hundred and thirty years after the Reformation, Episcopacy and Presbyterianism flowed together in a confused stream." Although at the Revolution of 1688 their courses had separated, signs were not wanting that "these two main currents are again approaching." But before there could be serious talk of reunion Episcopalians must change their attitude towards Presbyterianism. They must show tact, considerateness, a clear and large aim.

The reactions, if any, to this plain speaking are unrecorded. By the custom of those days an address of this sort was not subsequently debated; and in any case the speaker was no high authority in the Anglican Communion, but a young and almost unknown Dean of Divinity from an Oxford College. Yet that the paper was not regarded as altogether without significance may be deduced from the fact that in the following year it was printed and published in Edinburgh. It fairly expressed an opinion from which the author was never seriously to deviate.

While Lang might have moments of impatience with the Episcopal Church of Scotland, he was always punctilious towards it. When, two years after the address, he was invited to preach to the students of the University of St. Andrews, on discovering that the sermon would have to be delivered not, as he had supposed, in an academic building, but in a kirk, he wrote to the Bishop of St. Andrews for approval; and when the Bishop objected, Lang refused the invitation, not because he agreed with the Bishop's point of view, but because he believed that on a matter of this kind the opinion of the relevant authority in the Episcopal Church must be final.

Although in 1894 Lang could speak of Reunion in terms of an approaching issue, in the following quarter of a century it moved very little nearer the foreground of men's minds. The Church of England was still chewing the cud of its domestic troubles, and the Church of Scotland was rather too busy accomplishing a reunion of Presbyterians to look beyond its borders. Such impatience of Christian divisions as was manifested was mostly in the mission field, as at Kikuyu in Africa or among the Churches of South India. It was true that the Bishop of London had had talks with Wesleyans, that the American Episcopal Church had been considering a proposal for the Ordination of Congregationalist ministers, that in 1910 an International Missionary Conference met at Edinburgh, and that in the same year there was a plan for a World Conference on Faith and Order. But these faint stirrings of conscience were all that could be recorded.

The War of 1914-1918, however, brought the whole question forward and gave it urgency; in part from a consciousness that religious division was one of the circumstances which had made such a catastrophe possible, in part perhaps from a sense of shame that in every belligerent country the Church had given almost unreserved fealty to the secular power, and in part through an attraction to the idea of religious unity equivalent to the attraction towards secular unity which was bringing to birth a

League of Nations. However this may be, in the contemporary phrase Reunion was "in the air." Other and equally vexing questions were bound to come before the Lambeth Conference of 1920—the bounds within which the Modernists should be restricted, Marriage and Divorce, Theosophy, Spiritualism, Christian Science, the Ministry of Women; but before all and overshadowing all was the problem of Reunion. What line should the Conference take, or should it take any line at all? Should it content itself with a procession of blameless generalities, which would win the unanimous assent of three hundred and fifty Bishops and in fact not advance the cause of Reunion by an inch? Or should it attempt the apparently impossible task of securing a wide measure of agreement on some action which would transport the whole question from the realm of distant ideals into that of practical politics?

That the second and not the first course should have been followed was owing mainly to Lang, the Chairman of the Reunion Committee. He did not come to his task in a very hopeful spirit. "It seems humanly impossible," he wrote to his mother, "to get a crowd of Bishops representing every possible point of view, and already disclosing great cleavages of principle, to unite in any proposals short of mere platitudes." Since the "crowd of Bishops" included those of Zanzibar, Mombasa and Uganda, who had collided so recently and violently at Kikuyu, besides such pertinacious controversialists as the Bishop of Durham, the obstacles may well have seemed insuperable. No one, in fact, expected much more from the discussions than a reaffirmation of the Lambeth Quadrilateral, first enunciated in 1888, accompanied possibly by some unimportant concessions to local or sectarian opinion. Nor in the first sittings of the Committee did any larger result appear to be materialising. Various schemes from different parts of the world were presented and criticised, but no real progress was made; the only hopeful portent being the unexpectedly sympathetic attitude of the Bishop of Zanzibar. Some of his episcopal brethren, with Kikuyu fresh in their memories, had been filled with foreboding: to the more timorous it was as though a lean alley cat had stalked into a company of plump pigeons. At the least, his appointment to the Committee dealing with Reunion had seemed to guarantee a minority of at least one against any favouring decision that was likely to be reached. To the general surprise, however, he showed himself readier than some of his colleagues to envisage an arrangement by which non-Episcopal Churches might be brought within the framework of a united Church.

Yet it was Lang who suddenly and dramatically lifted the whole question to another plane with the idea of "An Appeal to all Christian People." "I took the line from the first," he wrote to Wilfrid Parker, "that it was useless to consider projects and proposals in different parts of the world until we had agreed upon the ideal of unity that we must seek. . . ." This ideal was to be expressed in a letter addressed not to Churches but to people, and to be not so much an argument or an attempt at negotiation as an appeal for co-operation in overcoming the sin of disunity. The first draft was largely the work of some of the younger Bishops who gathered for the purpose in the Lollards' Tower, and Dr. Bell has given the Archbishop of Canterbury's description of the subsequent crucial meeting on July 18th, in the garden of Lambeth Palace, when

A little group sat all the afternoon under the tree on the lawn. It consisted of the two Archbishops, Bishop Rhinelander of Pennsylvania, Bishop Brent, the Bishop of Peterborough. . . . We went through the various drafts, Resolutions, etc. which had been suggested, but on the whole decided to transpose it into an Appeal of a consecutive sort.

"For the first week," Lang wrote to his mother, "I seemed like a skipper, sitting at the tiller attempting to keep his boat going on a bit of water where cross tides and currents moved it to and fro and prevented it from making any headway; then after a week there came a puff of a fair wind and I put on all sail and finally reached the harbour of a unanimous Report."

When the Report came before the full Conference, the puff became "a mighty rushing wind," and in less than a day carried the Report right through. It was inexplicable unless God had some purpose in the Appeal. "We may ourselves bungle that purpose and the world may be blind to it, but none the less I shall remain convinced that some purpose was there."

The Appeal was prefaced by an Encyclical Letter which claimed that men had begun to think of the Reunion of Christendom "not as a laudable ambition or a beautiful dream, but as an imperative necessity." The Appeal itself began with an admission that the Lambeth Bishops were conscious of sharing in the sin of disunion. "We acknowledge this condition of broken fellowship to be contrary to God's will, and we desire frankly to confess our share in the guilt of thus crippling the Body of Christ and hindering the activity of His Spirit." The times called for "a new outlook and new measures." The separated groups of Christians must "agree in forgetting the things which are behind and reaching out towards the goal of a reunited Catholic Church . . . within whose visible unity all the treasures of faith and order, bequeathed as a heritage by the past to the present, shall be possessed in common, and made serviceable to the whole Body of Christ." The unity foreshadowed by this vision of the future must rest upon a "whole-hearted acceptance" of the Holy Scriptures, the Creeds, the Sacraments of Baptism and Holy Communion, and a Ministry with Apostolic authority—practically a reaffirmation of the Lambeth Quadrilateral. It was recognised that while the first three conditions might present little difficulty, the claim that an Episcopate was "the one means of providing such a ministry" would not easily be commended to the non-Episcopal Churches. While thankfully acknowledging the working of the Holy Spirit in these, the Appeal nevertheless urged that the Episcopate "is now and will prove to be in the future the best instrument for maintaining the unity and continuity of the Church." It went on to make one of the most significant proposals that had ever come from a Lambeth Conference.

> If the authorities of other Communions should so desire, we are persuaded that, terms of union having been otherwise satisfactorily adjusted, Bishops and Clergy of our Communion would willingly accept from these authorities a form of commission or recognition which would commend our ministry to their congregations, as having its place in the one family life.

The offer was made "in all sincerity as a token of our longing that all ministries of grace," episcopal or otherwise, would be enabled to serve together in a united Church. It was hoped that "the same motive would lead ministers who have not received it to accept a commission through episcopal ordination, as obtaining for them a ministry throughout the whole fellowship."

The action, therefore, was to be reciprocal. No one was asked to repudiate his past : everyone was asked to enlarge the scope of his future service, non-Anglicans by episcopal Ordination, Anglicans by some equivalent commission.

Appended to the Appeal were a number of Resolutions dealing with some of the questions which were bound to arise. While the Conference could not "approve of general schemes of inter-communion or exchange of pulpits," it suggested two important concessions, "in view of prospects and projects of reunion."

(1) A Bishop is justified in giving occasional authorisation to ministers, not episcopally ordained, who in his judgment are working towards an ideal of union such as is described in our Appeal, to preach in churches within his Diocese, and to clergy of the Diocese to preach in the churches of such ministers;

(2) The Bishops of the Anglican Communion will not question the action of any Bishop who, in the few years between the initiation and the completion of a definite scheme of union, shall countenance the irregularity of admitting to Communion the baptised but unconfirmed Communicants of the non-episcopal congregations concerned in the scheme.

"The Appeal and the Resolution," wrote the biographer of Randall Davidson, "were almost unbelievable after everything that had been said before the Conference began. Not only were the lions in the path overcome, but something new and creative had been done, and a great blow struck for the Reunion of Christendom."

Lang gave some account of the proceedings in his private letters.

"I think all will agree . . ." he told Wilfrid Parker on August 10th, "the memorable occasion of the Conference was the reception of the Report of the Committee on Reunion, of which I was Chairman, by the full Conference. You can understand how impossible I thought it would be to get any kind of common mind when I found myself presiding over a Committee of 70 Bishops, representing every sort of problem and conviction from Zanzibar to Durham, but gradually in a very wonderful way we seemed to be drawn together. . . . Having got things through the Committee, I was afraid that the remaining 200 Bishops, who had not worked together as we had for a fortnight of ceaseless toil, would cut the thing to bits. Instead of that, when I presented the Report it seemed to be taken out of my hands and what Neville [1] called 'a rushing mighty wind' seemed to sweep away difficulties and criticisms, and instead of days of anxious discussion, the Appeal and its accompanying Resolutions were adopted in less than one day, with only a handful of Bishops

---

[1] Neville Talbot, Bishop of Pretoria.

objecting. I think most of us who were present will not forget that day, for it was difficult—to me impossible—to think that this wind was other than the wind of the Spirit; anyhow, I must believe that somehow God has a purpose in a thing which comes with so much unanimity from 200 Bishops who really prayed and asked for guidance at a critical time. Of the younger Bishops both Neville and your old friend, Nassau,[1] were on the Committee and both were very useful in different ways. Perhaps the most useful person was Zanzibar, who, unless he yields to some fit of reaction, is whole-hearted in support of the principles of our Appeal."

He wrote again on August 21st:

Remembering as I do all the difficulties of our Committee, and all the care and thought that went to the framing of every sentence, knowing as I do the many difficulties of a practical kind which underlie the words that are used, I am surprised, not to say awed, by the way in which first the Conference itself received and adopted it with practical unanimity, and, second, by the response which it has so far had in the Christian world. Here is dear old Halifax writing that few things in his life have given him more pleasure. And on the other hand here is Scott Lidgett [2] saying that it is the most remarkable document issued since the Reformation; Shakespeare,[3] saying that "it is the finger of God"; Horton,[4] that it creates a new epoch; and Zanzibar pleading with all his fellow-Catholics that they will make it their guiding vision for years to come. How can one doubt, with all this in mind, that there is some purpose of God in this thing?

When, in Dr. Bell's words, every allowance has been made for Lang's "immense influence in the shaping of the Appeal, and in its presentation to, and acceptance by the Conference," the great surprise was the attitude of the Bishop of Zanzibar. Incalculable he would always be, at least to the majority who did not fully follow his thought. Difficult he would often be, as when he told his colleagues grimly that "to-day might be the last day on which he could attend the Committee." But his champion-

[1] The Rt. Rev. Roscow Shedden, Bishop of Nassau 1919-1931.
[2] A prominent member of the L.C.C. and Editor of the *Methodist Times*.
[3] Secretary of the Baptist Union.
[4] The Rev. R. F. Horton (Congregationalist), President of the National Free Church Council 1927.

ship of the principle underlying the Appeal was as eloquent as it had been unexpected, and he carried over to its support many who were wavering and might have drifted into opposition. He and the Bishop of Durham became firm friends, and towards the close of the Conference the Bishops of Zanzibar, Uganda and Mombasa were photographed, grouped round the Archbishop of Canterbury, an agreeable footnote to Kikuyu and a propitious omen for the cause of Reunion.

The Appeal, as Lang wrote to Parker, was carried through the Conference by almost universal acclamation, the Bishops rising and singing the Doxology. Nor was its reception in the world outside less favourable. It was translated into six languages, was widely read in many lands, and attracted an attention never before accorded to the pronouncements of a Lambeth Conference.

But the real test, as the Archbishops were the first to recognise, was in what was to follow. The Appeal was to be no passing proclamation, lightly made and soon forgotten. Nor, on the other hand, did any rational person expect it to sweep the world into religious Reunion on a tidal wave of enthusiasm. What was hoped for was rather a gradual but steady approach of separated bodies, a process of discussion and explanation, leading to a better understanding and a firmer desire for fellowship, no sudden blaze, but a slow fire on which the instruments of future union would be forged. Nor by this test may the achievement of 1920 be written off a failure, as many, including that most candid of friends and acidulated of critics, Dr. Hensley Henson, have written it. It gave an impetus to Reunion, the force of which is not yet spent. Indeed, its various sequels are a sufficient theme for a separate volume. The South India Scheme, although its starting-point was a meeting in Tranquebar in 1919, received powerful reinforcement from the Appeal. There have been recurring Conferences with the Free Churches, resulting, it is true, in no plan of Union, but fostering a new and happier relationship. There were the Conversations at Malines, in which the zeal of Lord Halifax harnessed itself to the Appeal. There has been a continuing *rapprochement* with the Orthodox Church, between whom and the Anglican Communion no insurmountable barrier can be said to exist. There has been a growing friendship between Canterbury and York on the one side and some of the Churches of the Continent on the other. The Conference on Faith and Order at Lausanne in 1927 and at Edinburgh in 1937, although not in a direct line of descent from the Appeal, undoubtedly derived from it an effective encouragement. Nor do these by any means exhaust the consequences, direct and indirect, of the Conference of 1920, at home, in Europe, and in countries overseas.

During the twenty years that followed the Appeal, Lang as Archbishop, first of York and then of Canterbury, had his full share in all this work. Truly the Appeal itself and its aftermath may be said to be his greatest contribution not merely to the Church of England but to Christendom. The Bishop of Chichester, who is in a position to judge, has given a verdict upon his work.

It (Reunion) was a cause particularly dear to Lang, and he played his full part in the Lambeth Conference of 1920 and its sequels. Here beyond doubt his was the master mind. It was Lang who conceived the Appeal and in the main put it into words, after what seemed an *impasse* in the Reunion Committee's proceedings. It was Lang who commended it to the full Conference. It was Lang again who followed it up with the Church of Scotland and the Free Churches. He took the labouring oar. And there is no man in the whole Anglican Communion who has left a deeper impression on the Unity movement in that Communion between 1920 and 1947 than Lang. Temple in certain special respects extended its influence more widely, for he went far outside *Ecclesia Anglicana*; but Lang, especially by his promotion of the Appeal of 1920, by his leadership in the Joint Conferences with Free Churchmen, and by setting his seal on the Oecumenical Conferences in 1937, took the significant decisions for the Church of England and its sister Churches. And certainly it was Lang, rather than Davidson, who gave it the principal impetus while the two were Archbishops together.

The Free Churches of England were the first to respond to the Appeal. In September 1920 a Provisional Statement was issued under the joint authority of the Federal Council of the Evangelical Free Churches and the National Free Church Council. This was followed on December 8th by a Conference at Lambeth, when the two Archbishops, supported by six Diocesan Bishops, met a special committee of Free Churchmen. At this stage the danger, the Archbishops noted after the meeting, was that people in their eagerness would try to move too fast. But there were no short cuts to Reunion, which could only come when the Lambeth principles had been "thoroughly understood and assimilated."

Early in 1921 the two Free Church Councils published *The Free Churches and the Lambeth Appeal*, an important pronouncement which

S   273

indicated a readiness to carry the discussion further. In April 1921 Lang spoke to the Assembly of the Baptist Union, and in May to the General Assembly of the Presbyterian Church of England.

"I am afraid both proceedings would be a great shock to your Anglican orthodoxy," he wrote to Wilfrid Parker. "In both cases the reception was very cordial to me personally, but I do not think these good people have any real care about a visible Church at all. I am afraid that they are still content if only they can preach at St. Paul's and communicate at our altars. A great deal of thinking about the meaning of the Church must come before any union worth having is at all possible."

Nevertheless the movement went on. A series of conferences between representative Anglicans and Nonconformist leaders was projected, and at the first of these, on November 30th, 1921, both Archbishops and nine Diocesan Bishops met twenty-five delegates from the Free Churches. This was the forerunner of twenty-two meetings, extending over four years. Their importance perhaps lay not so much in anything that was said or in the measure of agreement discovered, as in the fact that they were held at all. Two hundred and sixty years had passed since the Savoy Conference brought Anglicans and Nonconformists to the breach; and now at last, in happier circumstances, the debate was being resumed.

The work of these conferences was controlled by a sub-committee, of which Lang was Chairman. "The outstanding personality," wrote Dr. Bell, "was the Archbishop of York, whose conciliatory spirit came as a surprise to some who had supposed him to be the most rigid of orthodox ecclesiastics. . . ." On him, too, fell the major share of the work of expounding the Appeal at meetings of every kind throughout the country; and this he did in a campaign which must have recalled the old days of the East London Church Fund and the C.E.M.S. But now he was speaking not only to church-people, but to Nonconformists of all the leading denominations, and on them the impact of his eloquence and personality was impressive. After the Annual Assembly of the Baptist Union in 1921, Dr. Shakespeare wrote to Lang: "Your address was so persuasive that I said afterwards that if someone had risen and moved that we accept episcopal ordination, it would have been carried. I think perhaps this is an exaggeration, but something very near it would have been reached."

On the Free Church side Dr. P. Carnegie Simpson [1] for the Presbyterians, Dr. Scott Lidgett for the Wesleyans, and Dr. Garvie [2] for the Congregationalists were most prominent. Although the intercourse was always amicable, wide differences of opinion between Anglicans and Nonconformists soon appeared, on the nature of the Church, on the need for episcopacy, on the proposal for Ordination, and on the minimum of common faith that would serve as a foundation for union. Having discovered where the principal points of difference were likely to arise, the Conference turned to those of agreement. A number of Articles, dealing with the nature of the Church, the Ministry and the Creeds, which Lang had drafted with many misgivings, to his astonishment were adopted with very few changes by his sub-committee. He could write with restrained enthusiasm to his brother Norman of

a most remarkable meeting with my sub-committee of Bishops, Divines, and Nonconformists on Reunion, at which I submitted a number of propositions on which we seemed to have been agreed, expecting that when they saw them in a definite shape they would jib. Instead of that, most amazingly they were practically unanimously accepted. It remains to be seen what will happen to them when they are reported to a fuller Committee which meets on May 24th. Whether they will ever see the light I don't know, but if they did I think people would realise how much progress could be made if only leading Divines could get together and cease to think about their tails!

To his "thankful surprise" the propositions were subsequently accepted with "almost complete unanimity" by the Joint Conference, and on the 26th he was again writing to his brother:

It certainly exceeded all my expectations or anticipations that the Conference with almost complete unanimity accepted the draft which I had prepared for the sub-committee, and which was adopted with some amendments by them. It is certainly strange how step by step we seem to be led on, and I cannot believe that having got so far we are not meant to get further. But, as you say, the trouble both among ourselves and these good Nonconformists is that our

[1] Moderator of the Federal Council of the Free Churches of England 1926-1927 and of the General Assembly of the Presbyterian Church of England 1928.
[2] The Rev. A. E. Garvie, Chairman of the Congregational Union of England and Wales 1920, President of the National Free Church Council 1923, Moderator of the Federal Council of the Free Churches 1928.

Ministers and people are a long way off the new spirit which is moving in their leaders; and I have a somewhat uncomfortable feeling that the Bishops did not take sufficient steps to spread the vision which they saw at Lambeth effectively among our own people, so that they could share it and take it up with enthusiasm as a real call, and give it expression in constant and fervent prayer. I don't feel somehow as if we had really appealed to the imagination of the Church as we ought to have done.

Yet there were grounds for sober thankfulness, if not for satisfaction. "I was particularly struck," he wrote in his notes, "by Dr. Selbie [1] saying that though of course he might have expressed himself differently in some respects, he was prepared whole-heartedly to accept them (the drafted Articles) and to stand by them." They certainly represented a notable advance towards agreement, and though, when published, they were severely criticised by the *British Weekly* on one side and the *Church Times* on the other, from this conjunction, Lang remarked drily, "the usual inference may be drawn."

The Episcopate was accepted by the Free Churchmen, without subscribing to any especial theory of its origin and character, while the Council of the Presbyters and the Congregation of the Faithful were accepted by the Anglicans as "permanent elements in the order and life of a future United Church."

The Federal Council of the Free Churches, meeting in September, received the Report with sympathy, although some misgivings were expressed. It asked for a clarification of a number of doubtful points, and particularly of the proposal for Ordination. Were the Anglicans ready to recognise the Free Churches as corporate parts of the Church of Christ? Would they consent to accompany the discussions with "acts of unity" between the Churches?

Lang answered the first of these questions in April 1923 when he said that "we must regard these ministries as ministries of Christ's Word and Sacraments within [2] the Universal Church of Christ which is His Body." Three months later his statement was confirmed at a meeting of the Anglican representatives at Lambeth, the ministers being there described as "within their several spheres real ministers in the Universal Church."

---

[1] The Rev. W. B. Selbie, Principal of Mansfield College, Oxford, 1909-1932, Chairman of the Congregational Union 1914-1915, President of the National Free Church Council 1917.

[2] In his private notes Lang emphasises the importance of the use of the word "within" and not "of."

The difficulty, however, remained of determining who was a minister and what was a ministry within the meaning of the admission. The point was possibly of greater moment to Nonconformists than to Anglicans, as "even among the Free Churches themselves there may be ministries exercised by one which are regarded by another as in some respects, more or less important, irregular or inadequate." However regular or adequate a ministry might be, Ordination would still be required, and however irregular or inadequate, by Ordination entry into full communion would be possible; although, as Lang had said in April, the process by which the different ministries could be admitted into a United Church was another question.

The Federal Council, in its reply, regretted that no distinction was made between those who claimed to be already exercising a regular ministry and those who did not, and that for all, ministers of every kind and ordinary laymen too, the same procedure was suggested. Why, they asked, was it necessary to ordain men who were already in "real ministries of Christ's Word and Sacraments in the Universal Church"? "The way of reunion is not yet clear to any one of us," they concluded.

The Anglicans had some difficulty in meeting this question, and in fact did not return an answer until two years later, when they pointed out that the matter was one not of spiritual efficacy but of due authority. They made two suggestions, either of which might, they thought, satisfy the Free Churches. One was to substitute for Ordination some form of solemn authorisation by a Bishop; the other was for conditional Ordination. But on fuller reflexion the Bishops did not greatly favour the first idea, and the Free Churches were emphatic in rejecting the second. There for the moment the matter rested. The deliberations were suspended, and to many it seemed that a promising beginning had come to a disappointing end. Yet, if the discussions had no other result, they had brought together the representatives of Churches long separated and once deeply estranged. These had met and talked and prayed together, and thus the friendship and fellowship which are essential conditions to a union had been begotten. Nor was this all, for in meeting they had discovered an extent of agreement on doctrine hitherto unsuspected.

Neither of the Archbishops, therefore, was disposed to acknowledge failure. Better than to marry in haste and to repent at leisure was such a slow process as they had seen unfolding. The ground won must be consolidated. The leaders must advance further in mutual understanding, and the laggards, whose backwardness was so often the target of Lang's comments, must be brought to share their knowledge and sympathy. Later the discussions could be taken up at the point where they were suspended; as indeed they would be after the Conference of 1930.

In all this it is of some interest to note how closely the technique had followed that proposed by Lang at Aberdeen some thirty years earlier. The avoidance of all hurry, the emphasis on points of agreement, the more generous interpretation of history, the "clear and large aim," and the establishment of friendlier personal relations—all had played their part in the discussions.

In addition to his work as Chairman of the sub-committee, Lang had been assiduous in expounding the Appeal to the Free Churches. He was perhaps not quite so forward as his brother-Archbishop in promoting the "acts of unity" for which the Nonconformists pressed. The Lambeth Conference, while not approving of "general schemes of Communion and exchange of pulpits," gave its opinion that ministers, not episcopally ordained, who were working towards the ideal of Union, should occasionally be authorised to preach in Anglican churches; that clergy, under a similar dispensation, might preach in Free Churches; and that non-Anglicans, in special circumstances, might be admitted to Communion. These concessions went rather further than many Anglicans liked, but not as far as most Nonconformists wished. Lang stood loyally by them. He was firmly against intercommunion, apart from the especial circumstances in which the Conference gave its approval, not only because this was something which the general mind of the Church of England would not accept, but also because he saw intercommunion not as an antecedent to Union but as its crown. "Intercommunion," he had told the Convocation of York in February 1919, "should be the result of Reunion and not a means to it," and to this opinion he adhered.

In Scotland the position was rather different, as the Established and United Free Churches were in process of completing a union first projected in 1908 and only finally consummated in 1929. In these circumstances both Churches were too preoccupied with a practical and immediate scheme to lift their eyes more than momentarily to the wider horizon opened up by Lambeth. Nevertheless the General Assemblies of both Churches gave very cordial welcome to the Archbishop of Canterbury when he brought the message and interpreted the Appeal to them in person. Although he was careful to avoid touching upon the thorny topic of Ordination, he did not escape an invitation to preach in St. Giles' Cathedral, a test, as it appeared, of the reality of his desire for better relations. Dr. Davidson, had he had only his own feelings to consult, might have accepted, but he was well aware of the heartburning his presence in the pulpit of St. Giles' was likely to arouse among Episcopalians. A master of tactics, he contrived to evade the invitation without offence.

To the Evangelicals in the Church of England the Appeal meant chiefly an approach to the Church of Scotland and the Free Churches: to Anglo-Catholics it would mean little unless it led to at least an attempt to end the breach with Rome and to create a more official and intimate relationship with the Orthodox Church.

On September 19th, 1921,[1] Lang heard from his old friend Lord Halifax.

"I shall have a very important letter to write to you and to the Archbishop of Canterbury in a few days," Halifax told him, "touching a matter which may really have by God's blessing the greatest consequences. It relates to an interview which through no seeking of my own I am likely to have with Cardinal Mercier. I believe despite my eighty-two years and my eyes I shall be going to Brussels in October for this purpose, but that is only a part and a small part of what is involved."

That momentous interview was the starting-point of the Conversations at Malines. The story of them has been told at some length, by the Bishop of Chichester and others, and need not here be repeated. The idea undoubtedly originated with Portal, the gifted and indefatigable Lazarist who was Lord Halifax's colleague thirty years earlier in the affair which ended in a formal condemnation of Anglican Orders. The Appeal, with its declaration of the readiness of Anglicans to receive from the authorities of other Churches "a form of commission or recognition," indicated a way of getting round the Bull *Apostolicae Curae*, hitherto accounted an insuperable obstacle, and probably suggested to Portal that the moment had arrived for a further attempt at reconciliation. This he proposed to make through the medium of Cardinal Mercier, who was not only a hero to the Belgian people but also a man of considerable influence with the Holy See.

Portal found it easy to kindle the zeal of Lord Halifax, who bore

---

[1] The date on the letter is 1920, but this is surely an error.

lightly his eighty-two years and his growing infirmities and plunged enthusiastically into this new and congenial adventure. A meeting was arranged at Malines and, before leaving for the Continent, Halifax succeeded in extracting letters from the Archbishops of Canterbury and York to the Cardinal. They both wrote guardedly,[1] for their position was by no means easy. They would never, of course, have assented to any suggestion that the Roman Catholic Church lay beyond the orbit of the Appeal. On the other hand, they knew that Lord Halifax represented only a section of opinion in the Church of England and that there were plenty who would resent and resist any appearance of a concession to the Roman claims. The Protestant drum still hung on the wall, in readiness for those disposed to beat it. Moreover, the shadow of the Revised Prayer Book fell heavily upon Lambeth. The long labours of Convocation and the Church Assembly were coming to a climax. Presently the new Book would be before Parliament, where it would find its sharpest critics, and Dr. Davidson had no wish to supply them with ammunition. Lang was of the same way of thinking. His sympathy with the purpose of his old friend was tempered by memories of a still youthful impetuosity. Before Halifax left, Lang wrote to him privately:

> You will now have received my letter as well as that of the Archbishop of Canterbury about your journey. I am greatly relieved and pleased that you are not disappointed with his letter. For the reasons I have given I think it deals with the situation in the best possible way at the present stage. I agree with you that formal conferences are almost useless unless they have been preceded by informal and private conferences to pave the way.
>
> Once again let me send you Godspeed.

Cardinal Mercier received his visitors and listened to them sympathetically; and so the Conversations had their beginning. They went on intermittently from 1921 to 1926, the fifth and last Conversation being held after death had taken from the scene the two ruling spirits on the Roman side, the Cardinal himself and Abbé Portal. As in the discussions with the Free Churchmen, negotiations began hopefully with the discovery of a greater community of thought than had been presumed. Later, difficulties and differences forced themselves into the

---

[1] The Archbishop of Canterbury's letter appears in full in *Viscount Halifax*, by J. G. Lockhart, Vol. II, p. 269.

foreground, and to some of them no clear answer could be found. The high authorities of both Churches became nervous of admissions and commitments which their representatives might be led into making in their name and to their embarrassment. The Anglicans were more and more apprehensive for the fate of the Revised Prayer Book, the English Roman Catholics more and more suspicious and resentful of negotiations which at once profoundly concerned and had the appearance of ignoring their existence. In the circumstances, even if Mercier and Portal had lived, the Conversations could hardly have continued much longer; although it is conceivable that they would not have ended, as they did end, on a note of some disappointment and with a regrettable argument about the publication of the proceedings.

Yet the episode should not be dismissed as barren of result.

For the first time since the Reformation Anglicans and Roman Catholics had met round a table, spoken with complete candour, argued but not quarrelled, and parted with a heightened mutual esteem. Many old misunderstandings had been cleared away, some points of agreement reached. Apart from the mere fact of the meetings, the most important results were the discovery, firstly, that while doctrinal differences could not be rushed or jumped, there was a prospect of bridging them; and secondly, that if this bridging were successfully achieved, the administrative difficulties were not likely to be insuperable. Doctrinal differences, of course, remained, and it cannot be claimed that the Anglicans made much progress in obtaining from the Romans any admission of a possible distinction in authority between what was originally *de fide* and what had come through development. But a good deal of undergrowth had been cleared away, and the nakedness of the rocks was not so uncompromising as the friends of Reunion had feared to find it.[1]

On the Anglican side the greater burden fell on the Archbishop of Canterbury. Lang, who took the lead in the discussions with the Free Churches, was here content to be a loyal lieutenant. While ecclesiastically he may have been more sympathetic with the Roman Catholic position than was Dr. Davidson, he was no less firmly rooted in the Church of England. That early dream, in which Cardinal Newman had drawn him into a third-class compartment, never, so far as is known, returned to trouble him. Indeed, he was capable of occasional irritation

---

[1] *Viscount Halifax*, by J. G. Lockhart, Vol. II, p. 341.

when he considered that the Church of Rome or its dignitaries were asserting unwarrantable claims or casting the net of their propaganda too persistently in Anglican waters.

But of more effect than any transitory annoyance of this kind was Lang's complete accord with Davidson's view of the Conversations. The Archbishops did not go as far as Lord Halifax wished, and Cardinal Mercier could speak impatiently of "la grande réserve des deux Archevêques de Cantorbéry et d'York"; but they went quite as far as the temper of their constituents would admit and a good deal further than many of them liked. (The Bishop of Durham was especially disquieted.) Lang's own correspondence with the Cardinal was mostly an exchange of friendly messages: his personal contribution to the Conversations was more through his friendship with Lord Halifax, to whom he could write with candour and understanding. For the first Conversation Halifax had procured the attendance of Dr. Frere,[1] the Superior of the Community of the Resurrection and later Bishop of Truro. Another Anglican representative, however, was required, and preferably someone who was closer to the central stream of thought in the Church of England. Dr. Armitage Robinson, the Dean of Wells, was clearly the man, for in addition to his qualifications of character and scholarship, he was an intimate friend of the Archbishop of Canterbury. The Dean was unwilling to go, and only yielded when Lang added his persuasions to those of Halifax. Again, when, to the consternation of the cautious, the second Conversation produced the proposal of the *pallium* for Anglican metropolitans, Lang stepped in to make peace between Lambeth and Hickleton.

"If, my dear old friend, you were a golfer," he wrote to Lord Halifax, "I would point out the danger of 'pressing,' a fault which is very apt to spoil the game. But indeed I know how natural it is for you, with the years shortening, to 'press.'"

To Lord Halifax "The Appeal to all Christian People" was chiefly, if not entirely, a means of reconciliation with Rome. The Archbishops worked with a wider background. While the emissaries were journeying to and from Malines, absorbed in their task, discussions were going on not only with the Nonconformists of England, but also with the Orthodox Church of the East. One of the principal cares of the Archbishops was therefore to prevent one set of negotiations prejudicing the

[1] The Rt. Rev. W. H. Frere, Superior of the Community of the Resurrection 1902-1913, Bishop of Truro 1923-1935. Died in 1938.

others; and this was not always easy. At Christmas 1923 the Archbishop of Canterbury issued a Letter to the Metropolitans of the Anglican Communion, reporting the responses of the different Churches to the Appeal. In describing these, he gave an account of the Conversations at Malines on "a question which has features of paramount importance." The report was friendly and encouraging, yet gave offence to Mercier and his colleagues. They objected to this treatment of the Conversations as a kind of appendage to the Appeal; nor would they admit that advances to other religious bodies were in any sense comparable with the overriding and all-important matter of a reconciliation with Rome.

The incident marked a difference in outlook which was never dissipated. Yet the approach to the Orthodox Church, at any rate, was something which could not be ignored, if only because it proved to be one of the most successful of the sequels to the Appeal. A delegation from the Patriarchate of Constantinople had come to Lambeth in 1920 and been present at meetings of the Committee on Reunion. Returning, it had produced a Report, accompanied by a treatise upholding the validity of Anglican Orders, the work of one of its members who was a leading Orthodox theologian. Accordingly, in July 1922 the Oecumenical Patriarch and Holy Synod of Constantinople put forth an official declaration stating that "as before the Orthodox Church, the Ordinations of the Anglican Episcopal Confession of Bishops, priests and deacons, possess the same validity as those of the Roman, Old Catholic, and Armenian Churches possess, inasmuch as all essentials are found in them which are held indispensable from the Orthodox point of view for the recognition of the 'Charisma' of the priesthood derived from Apostolic Succession." This declaration was subsequently affirmed by the Patriarch of Jerusalem and the Church of Cyprus, and still later by the Patriarch of Alexandria. It inaugurated a new era in the relations of the Anglican Communion with the Orthodox Patriarchates. While of course it did not establish the full inter-communion which was the ultimate purpose of the Appeal, it was a notable and necessary step towards it. The process received a remarkable endorsement in 1925, when the 1600th anniversary of the Council of Nicaea was celebrated in Westminster Abbey, in the presence of the Patriarchs of Alexandria and Jerusalem, two Russian Metropolitans, and representatives of the Greek and Rumanian Churches. The Archbishop of Canterbury preached and the Nicene Creed was solemnly recited, first in its Western form and then according to Orthodox use, without the *filioque*. The occasion, the

Bishop of Chichester points out, "was unique, not only in the history of the Anglican Communion, but in the story of the whole Church of Christ."

The other non-Roman Churches of the Continent presented rather different problems as, with the exception of the Old Catholics, their Orders, where they claimed to possess them, were often of doubtful validity. With the Old Catholics relations had already become close and, under the future primacy of Lang at Canterbury, were to become even closer. The Church of Sweden had been prompt in its response, and in September 1920, on the invitation of Archbishop Söderblom, an outstanding figure among the Continental upholders of Reunion, the Bishops of Durham and Peterborough took part in the consecration of two Swedish Bishops in the Cathedral of Upsala.

In countries overseas the Appeal had a similar welcome. In South India the negotiations between the South India United Church and the Anglican Church received a new impetus; and from the United States, Canada and Australasia, from Asia and from Africa, came reports of inter-denominational conferences and of "a new spirit of fellowship, a new readiness for understanding and co-operation."

"The vision which Our Lord, as we believe, has set before us," were the concluding words of the Archbishop's Letter of Christmas 1923, "points the road to Reunion. The road may not be short; but we believe it will be sure."

Chapter XXIV

LAST YEARS AT YORK

THE War tired and aged Lang. In 1914 he was young and vigorous. His hair was dark and plentiful, and people could still wonder that a man of his years was an Archbishop. But in a few months his hair turned snow-white. As he has related, at one great meeting he found himself unrecognised; and more than once he was mistaken, to his amusement, for the Bishop of Beverley or, to his slight annoyance, for Canon Tupper-Carey. Newspapers which continued to reproduce in 1918 photographs of the Archbishop which had been taken in 1914 were confounded by the reproaches of their readers.

Nor was the transformation an illusion, an outward sign with no corresponding interior meaning. Although his energy appeared unabated, some of the spring had gone out of him. His whitened hair was a symptom of change inside. His own notes reveal the difference. He was thinking more about the past; he was hoping less from the future; and those who knew him best detected a mellowing, a greater gentleness, something of a kindliness more common in age than in youth.

He was weary from the stress and anxiety of war, from the lingering prejudice of the "sacred memories," from four and a half years of grappling, short-handed, with the needs and problems of a Diocese and a Province. He was also more conscious of the loneliness, the lack of companionship, in which he lived.

"I feel very much isolated here," he wrote to his mother in January 1919—"so few really able and leading men in the Diocese with whom I can take counsel, so few people with whom one can get any really helping talk. This isolation is not eased by my private life."

He was missing Wilfrid Parker and Edward Gibbs. He felt prematurely "aged and dull and stupid, and I expect more tired inwardly even than I think." The state of the world after the War—the uncertainties abroad, the rising discontent in industry at home, the recoil from Christian standards of conduct, the attrition which seemed to be destroying the influence of the Church—all added to his depression.

Sometimes he longed to get "free from official responsibilities and say and do what seems to matter."

Possibly, too, he was a little stale. Since his Ordination he had not been so long in a single place. He was three years at Leeds, three at Magdalen, five at Portsea, seven at St. Paul's and Stepney. In 1918 he had been ten years at York. Short of resignation and retirement, which few men of fifty-four would contemplate seriously, there was only one more move he could make; and at Canterbury the old Archbishop had settled himself back in the saddle, to ride the Church through the Lambeth Conference of 1920 and another troubled decade of her history. The very rapidity of Lang's rise now worked against him. He had come to York too soon and was to go to Canterbury too late. The critic who watched the drama might have written down this third Act as anticlimax, too long, repetitive, and almost dull. Something had gone wrong with the story: it lagged and lost itself; the rhythm and sureness of move-ment had left it. Lang went on doing his work conscientiously and well. He discharged the business of a bishop with all his old industry and efficiency. He assiduously kept up his visits in his own Diocese and his excursions into the other Dioceses of the Province. He took his full part in Convocation and the new Church Assembly. He preached and spoke with all his former felicity and eloquence. It may be that after twenty-five years of incessant sermons a man loses fire and freshness of thought and expression; or perhaps the new world was less receptive of the kind of message Lang continued to offer, that it was expecting something from the Church—what it hardly knew—which it was not getting, and from Lang something which he could not give. During the last ten years at York his public appearances did not always command the attention they had had in the first ten years. Yet the quality was not perceptibly different, and sometimes he regained his highest level. He was at his happiest, perhaps, not when preaching, but when speaking outside the routine of the Church's year, as in dedicating the memorial in Winchester Cathedral to his old friend John Moreton Macdonald, or in making an after-dinner speech to some secular society. All his life, indeed, even in the prime of his preaching, he would feel the restraint of the pulpit, with its convention of what might and might not be said and the lack of any audible response from the listeners. Notable as many of his sermons were, like his father before him he was more at ease on a platform.

A good example was his address as the spokesman of Cuddesdon men, past and present, when they gave a gold watch to that old retainer of the College, George Belcher, on the completion of fifty years of service. His speech not only illustrates the grace and ease of phrase Lang had at his command, but also conveys something of the depth and warmth of his feeling for Cuddesdon.

We all know that this is one man's day. We are here to offer the love and gratitude of fifty generations of Cuddesdon men to Mr. George Belcher. . . . You will let me represent the old students because I remember sadly the length of time which has passed since a very doubtful brand, pulled from the Balliol and All Souls burning, entered this College thirty-seven years ago; and I may speak for the young students because for the last five years I have been allowed to spend four Holy Weeks here, and be readmitted each time by the Principal. And one thing at any rate qualifies me to speak for all of you who are here; it is that there is no man at this festival who could say more fully from his heart and with more increasing fervour that he owes to this College more than he can either express or repay. When we think of the memories of this dear place, there is at once a special and abiding place given to the man whom this day we delight to honour.

It has happened in the history of many great schools and colleges that faithful and wise servants have been raised up to be guides, philosophers and friends to successive generations, such as, I am specially bound to remember, Hancock the porter at Balliol, and "Gunner" the steward of the Junior Common Room at Magdalen; but George, our own, our incomparable George, is the chiefest of them all. For these fifty years, principals, vice-principals, chaplains have come and gone, but like the stream George goes on for ever; and the stream which has flowed from him, from his large and loving heart, has been a stream of pure disinterested loving-kindness, which has for all these years made glad this corner of the City of God. From time to time at rare intervals we have had "spikes" among us. George as a man of humour understood them, but he never liked them. Happily in larger numbers we have had saints, and as a Christian man George esteemed and revered them. But I do not think that they ever quite got George's heart, because he never felt that they needed him as much as some others. George's place has been to remember that most of us are neither "spikes" nor saints, but very ordinary human beings, imperfect human creatures, and for all these years he has had human nature in this College under his especial charge. He has had a unique power of discerning abashed, suspicious, even rebellious humanity in most of those who came here, and he has taken it into the arms of his cheerful sympathy and nursed it into quietness and peace. . . . Frederick Douglass, who has given his life to India, told me that when he came here he said to George that he despaired of himself because he knew that he could never be as good as the others who seemed to be able to talk about Church things all day long. George replied, "Lor' bless you, sir, it isn't their goodness, it's only their little way!"

For fifty years to this great family of Cuddesdon men George has been the nursing father. All the time we have known that there is one man here who has taken charge of our unregenerate humanity. It is the same motive which prompts George to take charge of our bodies. Others have to take care of our poor souls for what they are worth. It is for George to look after our bodies, and he knows how much the one depends upon the other. That has been his Christian philosophy. When the door of the refectory is opened we pass at once into the kingdom of our "most religious and gracious King George." When a boy invited Mr. Squeers to give him more, Mr. Squeers was astonished; but George's heart always goes out to the man who asks, or even looks as if he wished for more. The same spirit spreads over that admirable set of boys to whom the Principal has already most justly referred, who have waited upon us for these years. George has given them his spirit so that they put our modest meals before us as if they were the feasts of kings. Even in those old ascetic days in which the students were reared, those days when dear old Ducat, thinking no doubt of the glass of very moderate sherry that was to reward at the Easter luncheon our Lenten abstinence, preached his cheerful Easter sermon on the text, "Mortify your members"—even in those days George enabled us to give thanks for our few small fishes. And now that a different régime has been introduced by our genial Principal, while some of the old students may shake their heads, George smiles because he knows that at last he has come into his own.

We think of all these fifty years of unselfish, cheerful, disinterested service, of the kindness which he has shown even when the shadows of his own sorrows were upon his life. We think of

THE ARCHBISHOP OF YORK. 1918 *Macdonald.*

AT LARGIE CASTLE. 1920

THE ARCHBISHOP   C. R. L. FLETCHER   REV. A. C. DON   J. R. MORETON

this man girding himself day by day during these fifty years for his
ministry of kindness; we think of him washing our feet stained by
some of our imperfections, bruised sometimes by the hard road of
discipline which it was difficult for us to tread, with the water which
flows from his own kind and loving heart. When we think of this
there are some words which come unbidden to our memory, "I am
among you as he that serveth." There we know who George's
Master is; and we know something more, we know that in one and
perhaps the greatest of all Christian lessons our teacher and our
example has been George. There are indeed no words that can
describe the love which all our generations of men have for him.

On occasions of this kind Lang excelled; and because he could be
relied upon to say the right thing and to say it so perfectly he was in
persistent demand from societies and organisations of every kind. He
could be grave or gay by turns, adapting himself without effort to the
situation and the audience. In 1928, when he was the guest at the dinner
of the Royal Literary Fund, he was able to tell how Lewis Carroll had
once suggested they should write a book together. Lang was to give
an account of the religious problems that beset the Victorian mind and
Carroll was to solve them by Symbolic Logic. When Lang got Carroll's
first solution, however, he cried off the collaboration, feeling, he said,
that the only possible title for the book would be "The Faith of a March
Hare."

But this was the small change of ecclesiastical currency; and in those
larger matters that touched the life of the Church his influence was less
marked. "Lang was a great speaker and preacher," the Bishop of
Chichester has written; "a superb draughtsman in many ways and a
most diligent administrator; but he was not a reformer with a policy,
wise, patient, conciliatory, but determined and inflexible, that the
Church of England even more urgently required."

A like criticism was voiced more frequently as the years passed, not
least by those, like Dick Sheppard, who loved Lang best. They were
critical because they were disappointed. They had begun by pitching
their expectations too high and were loth to admit, even to themselves,
that their Archbishop was not of the stuff of a Lanfranc or a Becket.
It is an interesting speculation whether, if it had been Lang's lot to work
with some other Archbishop of Canterbury, the story would have been
different. Davidson had his own policy, which he pursued with tenacity

and patience. It may have been both wise and necessary, but those who esteemed him most would hardly assert that it was either spectacular or heroic. Lang made that policy his own. From the outset he had resolved to render loyal collaboration, and for twenty years he kept his resolution so strictly that he was, as Dr. Bell has written, "the closest counsellor and most trusted of all." He made a choice which none can doubt brought manifest and valuable advantage to the Church; while it is equally certain that a separate and vigorous policy at York would have been attended by the gravest drawbacks and dangers. But the good lieu-tenant does not always make the best commander. It may be that Lang paid the price of his loyalty by a surrender of some of the initiative so necessary in a leader. Or it may be that he was lacking in the originality that would have framed a policy of his own, and the power that would have driven it on. The first is probably the more likely answer, for against the second is the witness of "An Appeal to all Christian People," which, although encouraged and endorsed by Davidson, was essentially Lang's policy, conceived and applied in the main by him.

Those who thought him self-confident, even arrogant, were equally wrong. "I care little," he used to say, "what people think of Cosmo Gordon Lang, but I care very much what they think of the Archbishop of York." The reproaches and sorrowful meditations in "the Cell" at Ballure show the depth of his self-distrust and disappointment. Else-where, too, the truth sometimes escaped through the curtain of his reserve. In 1924 a number of friends arranged for him to be painted by Sir William Orpen, so that his portrait by a contemporary master might hang with the likenesses of his predecessors at Bishopthorpe. The picture is there now and shows, at first glance, the kind of man so many thought he was. "They say in that portrait I look proud, prelatical and pompous," the Archbishop, who had brought some people to see it, remarked in the hearing of Dr. Hensley Henson; and that old and candid friend is reputed to have interjected, "And may I ask Your Grace to which of these epithets Your Grace takes exception?" Nearer to the mark was the comment of Archbishop Söderblom, when he, too, was shown the portrait: "That is what the devil meant him to be, but thanks be to God it is not so."

Lang himself thought it "a very fine picture"; and if he told Wilfrid Parker it had "too much of the proud prelate" about it, he added that he did not want to be "handed down to posterity with an amiable smile on my face." There is, indeed, on closer inspection, the ghost of a smile, almost as if the Archbishop's tongue was in his cheek and he was telling his friends that this was a portrait not of Cosmo Lang the man, but of Cosmo Lang playing the part of an Archbishop of York. The picture was given to him at Bishopthorpe by Lord Halifax, the oldest of the subscribers and one of the oldest of the friends who had come for the occasion. The Archbishop's words of thanks, as revealing as the portrait itself (though in another sense), were not formally recorded, but one who was there has remembered some of them. "When I sit here in this dining-room," Lang had said, "and look up at the pictures on the walls, I often wonder what were the hopes and aspirations of my predecessors, what they worked for, what were their prayers for their people. We cannot tell, but I can tell you here to-night what this picture means. It is a portrait of a very hard-working, very well-meaning, very lonely and very disappointed man." And he sat down.

On his own achievement, as on his own character, he was habitually the harshest of judges. Because the ideal he set himself was so high, the inevitable failure to reach it was more pronounced and more poignant; but the failure was more noticeable to him than it was to others. Much that he did, too, was of a sort that for obvious reasons eludes the attention of the outside world. Few men can have had so large a number of friends and acquaintances who claimed his advice and help.

"He must have had a large correspondence with a great number of people," Canon Crawley has written. "He invariably answered letters almost by return of post and very often in his own handwriting, even in the crowded days of his later life (yet when were his days not crowded?); but he never seemed too busy to give personal consideration to the problems of the least prominent and indeed the humblest of the men who in any way came under his influence, and so maintained a lifelong contact with some men who as boys had come to know him when he was a curate at Leeds."

They may not have been, in the technical sense, his "penitents," but they leaned heavily and never vainly on his wisdom and sympathy; and what passed between them was mostly *sub sigillo*. One of the younger men who went to him in this way has given his testimony that "you could tell him anything"; that he would devote to a personal problem so put to him his absolute and undivided attention, as though it were the only matter in his mind; and that his counsel was beyond comparison or price. An elderly lady, whom he predeceased by two years, would often say that nothing had "been the same since 'Taggart' died." In this fashion he helped large numbers of men and women, and their experience should not be overlooked because their witness is not available.

In January 1921 he lost his mother, the member of his family nearest and dearest to him, for, far as he had travelled from the old life at Woodlands Terrace and the holidays on Arran, the affection and understanding between them had survived unbroken. To the end he wrote her long, regular and intimate letters. He usually managed to stay a night or two with her in Edinburgh on his way to or from Ballure, and she was a fairly frequent visitor to Bishopthorpe, usually staying there for Christmas.

"You will be sorry to hear . . ." he wrote to Wilfrid Parker, "that my dear old Mother has passed away in her eighty-first year. I was staying with the Sandwiches at Hinchingbroke on January 4th, enjoying a very happy visit, when I got a telegram saying that she had passed away suddenly that morning. When I got home I found a letter from her written the day before with more than her usual strength of handwriting and of spirit. I think it was the last letter she wrote. She slept well that night, and in the morning quietly said to the nurse that she felt a certain dizziness in the head. The nurse went to the telephone to tell the doctor, and when she returned the old lady had already passed to the other side. It is of course rather sad that none of us was able to be with her at the time, but she cannot have missed us as she cannot have known that the end was near, and there can have been no pain for there was no time to feel it. She was, as you will remember, a woman of great force and decisiveness of character, and it would have been distressing to her and all of us if she had been doomed to years of infirmity of mind or body. As it was, in the last year of her life she just had so much physical restraint due to rheumatism as to bring into her forceful character a rather beautiful patience and resignation. Up to the last year she was always full of life, and you will remember that when she was (I think) seventy-six she went off with dear Edward Gibbs for a jaunt in the side-car of his motor bicycle! That was characteristic of her spirit. Now we can only be thankful for the life she lived and for the way in which she was called to the fuller life elsewhere. We laid her body to rest beside my Father's in the shadow of the old Cathedral at Aberdeen, with the kindly light of the winter's sun shining upon us."

In 1924 Lang's loneliness was mitigated by the return of Stafford Crawley with his family. He came back "as a sort of missioner as well as Clerical Secretary to the Diocesan Fund, and came to share my home at Bishopthorpe with his family." So for the rest of the time at York the Crawleys lived in the north wing, to the Archbishop's great content.

"The next four years," Canon Crawley writes, "were very happy ones for us and, I hope, for him. He was able to share a great deal of our family life."

"I can't write here about them," was the Archbishop's own tribute to his tenants: "they were and are part of my life. I look upon them as my own, the nearest and dearest of the families whom I have 'adopted.'" The "adoption" was no empty formula: the children had a very special place in his affections, and in 1928, when Janet Crawley married, the Archbishop not only performed the ceremony, but did the honours afterwards on the grand scale.

It seems strange that a great wedding should take place from the house of a hardened bachelor like myself; but everything went with a great swing; the house was crammed; I had dinner parties of over forty people on two successive nights; the flowers, which were wonderful, came from my own garden, and the food from my own kitchen. Budden covered himself with glory. I am fairly expert in these weddings, but I have never seen one more beautiful in arrangement, in colour, or in spirit. . . . I am told that the bridal procession through the old gateway in the sunshine was a thing not to be forgotten.

The garden, under Budden's expert management, remained Lang's predominant delight, the great herbaceous border, after a wartime eclipse, blooming with all its old glory. He treated his flowers almost as if they were children, blessing the first snowdrops and saying good-night to his "dear delphiniums."

So the years slipped by, neither uneventfully nor unhappily. In the late summer there was always the haven of Ballure where, after some first solitary days, he liked to entertain a few specially selected guests, such as Fords and Talbots, the Archbishop of Canterbury and Mrs. Davidson, or his own brother Norman. In 1922 his old Leeds Vicar himself paid him a visit. "The Bishop is a quaint fellow," Lang wrote, "swinging about with a large stick and his stiff leg, and getting somewhat deaf." There were Holy Weeks at Cuddesdon, visits to Balmoral and friendly houses such as Welbeck, and rare excursions to the Continent. But for most of the time he was caught in a ceaseless round of work, which on any day began after breakfast and often did not end till midnight or even later.

The years inevitably brought changes both in Province and in Diocese. In 1920 Bishop Knox retired from Manchester. He and his Metropolitan had had their battles, but their personal relations were "always cordial and indeed affectionate." "We have fought often enough," the Bishop wrote, "but we have never quarrelled, because you have always fought fair, even when I have been most tiresome." Later, when Bishop Knox was living at Beckenham, he wished to dedicate his Reminiscences to Lang. "Though he acknowledged the force of some reasons which I urged against his wish, I always like to think he had it. It was characteristic of the genial kindliness which underlay his combative vigour." He was succeeded at Manchester by William Temple, once, as an undergraduate, an unqualified admirer, now to be the most loyal of colleagues, and finally to follow his old leader first at York and later at Canterbury. "We are looking forward," Lang wrote, "to William Temple's Consecration on the 25th (January 1921). I shall have a large number of people there. I think he will do well. With Henson and him in the Upper House of York, we shall have lively times."

Hensley Henson had been translated from Hereford to Durham in 1921, and Lang, once invited by him to be his curate, now became his Metropolitan. By contrast with the storm which attended the appointment to Hereford, the translation passed off peacefully enough. The Archbishop, although not unprepared for ructions, was glad to have a man of Henson's calibre in the Province. "I expect a good deal of mischief and worry from Durham," he wrote, "but that again cannot be helped and I often rather agree with him." He once remarked that Henson would first provoke and enjoy a controversy, and then lament it.

Henson, on his side, has recorded his verdict, in which compliment and criticism are nicely blended. The Archbishop's occasional speeches, he says, were "always felicitous," but "his handwriting was atrocious. . . . Lang shared with Dicey and Headlam the reputation of being the least legible of the All Souls Fellows." Like Dr. Davidson, he had "a tendency to prolixity," probably caused by an anxiety to escape behind a cloud of "prophylactic verbiage" from any inconvenient commitments into which he might drift.

He loved beautiful things and stately surroundings and moved with natural ease, and was himself not the least impressive feature in the grand public pageants in which he was required to be a central figure. He was also a great actor, and merged himself in the parts which he was required to play. The details of religious ceremonial were to him important and significant. He could never have been at home in the bleak simplicity of a Presbyterian church, but it was easy to conceive of him as a Mediaeval Pontiff. . . . He was not as great a statesman as Davidson, nor a philosopher like Temple, but he had distinctive qualities of his own not less considerable than theirs. . . .

Dr. Henson ends by avowing his belief that Lang "must be ranked among the greater figures of ecclesiastical history."

In the Diocese the Archbishop had a new Dean at York. Dr. Purey-Cust had been followed by Dr. Foxley Norris [1]; and the latter, when he moved on to Westminster, by Dr. Lionel Ford.[2] Ford was a friend and his wife was a Talbot, one of the children of the Vicarage in the old days at Leeds, so that by natural process the Fords became another of the "adopted" families.

Towards the end of his time at York the Archbishop would reflect with surprise, tinged with melancholy, that of all the leading men of the Diocese who had welcomed him in 1908 hardly one was left; while many of the best of the parish priests, including some of his own Cuddesdon men, had died or gone elsewhere. "It is rather tragic," he wrote as early as 1921, "that practically all the men of the sort I care for, whom I brought into this Diocese, have gone or are going." Other good men were arriving, but they did not quite replace the old friends, like Father Burn of Middlesbrough, whose departure or demise he deplored, even when they had been recurring problems.

"You would see the news of the death of dear old Burn of Middlesbrough," he wrote in 1925. "One cannot think without emotion of these forty-one years of continuous pastoral work among all sorts and kinds of people. He was, so far as I am concerned, very often most tiresome and troublesome. But it was always possible to get

---

[1] Dean of Westminster 1925-1937. Died in 1937.
[2] Dean of York 1925-1932. Died in 1932.

at the man's heart behind his words, and I had a real affection for him, and I think in some ways he had for me. Whatever else he was, he was a great lover of souls, and I am not surprised that Middlesbrough gave at his funeral an overwhelming testimony of its respect and gratitude."

An outstanding event of those last years at York was the celebration in 1927 of the 1300th anniversary of the founding of the Minster, an occasion that appealed strongly to Lang's imagination and sense of drama. In 627 King Edwin of Northumbria, yielding to the persuasions of his wife and of Paulinus, became a Christian and built a small wooden shrine to enclose a font. Here on Easter Eve he was baptised; and on the site of this modest building the Minster grew and now stands.

The celebrations began at midnight on December 31st, 1926. The Minster was filled with people and thousands more were standing outside in wintry weather. "It was difficult," Lang declared, "not to believe that a great cloud of witnesses—all the builders and makers of the Minster, known and unknown—was, as it were, overshadowing the multitude." On the stroke of twelve and to a fanfare of trumpets the Archbishop arrived, to knock thirteen times on the door. In spite of a severe cold in the head he went through his part and delivered an address at the West door to the multitude assembled outside. "I am thrilled," wrote Lord Halifax next day, "by the accounts of the function at York last night. It is all wonderful, and not the least good part of it was that most excellent and admirable address which His Grace of York, one day to be 'His Eminence the Cardinal Archbishop of York' or more probably 'H.E. the Cardinal Archbishop of Canterbury,' the 'Alterius Orbis Papa,' delivered on the occasion." With the Archbishop in cloth-of-gold cope and mitre and all the canons in copes of brilliant colours, with torches and trumpets and vast crowds, the spectacle was deeply impressive. Afterwards Lang told Mrs. Ford that he thought the great Anniversary services which followed had reached a climax of beauty and were a pattern of worship in the Church of England.

The celebrations culminated in a week of ceremonies during the Octave of St. Peter.

"They have been devised on rather a large scale," the Archbishop wrote, "and I only hope that the organisation will be equal to the task. That remains to be seen. There has been a great deal of interest shown in the matter throughout Yorkshire. I am breaking many of the traditions of the past by inviting the Archbishop of Canterbury to bear his Cross within York Minster, when the rival Archbishop is present. I think many of my predecessors will shiver in their graves; but people were all most anxious that he should come, and we have arranged so that my position should not be compromised!"

About the success of the celebration and of Lang's part in it there was general agreement. One untoward event slightly marred the harmony of the proceedings and brought him some annoyance. At Easter the Roman Catholics of York had their own commemoration of the anniversary, and Cardinal Bourne, who attended it, delivered a polemical and provocative speech. He was thinking more of Mercier and Malines than of Paulinus and York, and the reply of the successor of Paulinus was both dignified and effective.

Apart from the duties of Province and Diocese, of Church Assembly and House of Lords, of Church Congresses and Royal Christenings, the Archbishop was Chairman of two Commissions of some importance. One was the Commission on the Ecclesiastical Courts, the upshot of a long contention dating back to the days of the prosecutions under the Public Worship Regulation Act.

"I had to spoil a good part of my holiday," Lang wrote in October 1925, "by attempting to draft the Report of the Commission on the Ecclesiastical Courts of which I am the Chairman, a most thorny and difficult matter when you have Darwell Stone [1] on the one side and the Bishop of Durham on the other, and lawyers like Dibdin and Phillimore quarrelling as experts always do. Whether I can shake anything through worth producing remains to be seen."

More congenial perhaps were his labours for three years on the Cathedrals Commission. Here again his was the hand that drafted the Report—"a very difficult bit of work," he told his brother Norman, "as the subject is so huge and complicated, and after all our enquiries and deliberations for three years not very much seems to have emerged from it all, and I have rather to make bricks without straw."

"The great trouble about the Cathedrals," he told Wilfrid Parker, "is the lack not of ideals or efforts, but simply of money; and until the Church understands that if the Cathedrals are to be what we

[1] Dr. Darwell Stone, the Principal of Pusey House, Oxford, was an Anglo-Catholic leader.

wish they ought to be much more largely supported, we cannot make the revival which we would wish."

The Cathedrals Measure, which was the fruit of these labours, at first met with a good deal of opposition in the Church Assembly. But this gradually weakened, under Lang's adroit handling, and when the Measure went before Parliament it was approved without a division in either House.

Chapter XXV

THE PRAYER BOOK

IN the background of these years was always the Revised Prayer Book, which was climbing slowly and painfully through Convocations and Church Assembly, through innumerable meetings and conferences, through revisions and concessions and more revisions and fresh concessions, to the top rung of the ladder in Westminster. The battle of the Prayer Book was the last of a great partnership, a Malplaquet with a less fortunate issue. The story belongs to Davidson rather than to Lang and has been superbly told by the Bishop of Chichester. In this record, therefore, little more is necessary than to describe the particular part of the Archbishop of York, at the beginning the loyal lieutenant, although in the last stages the commander.

Controversy, of course, was mainly concerned with the new alternative Liturgy, about which in the beginning Lang had some qualms. As early as April 1923 he told the York Diocesan Conference:

"We are to enter a period of permitted alternatives: only, these alternatives must have behind them the sanction of authority. There is a great deal to be said against the inconvenience and confusions of such a period, but it is inevitable. It is impossible to know what changes will really stand the test of conformity to the life and needs of the Church except by their being used." It was a period of experiment by which we should discover "the lines along which we may hope to approach the final revision and recasting of the Prayer Book of the Church of England." There were some, he went on, "amongst whom I must be included, who thought that the changes (in the Order of the Holy Communion) were too meagre to be of much use to the Church and that we had better wait till a time had come when it might be possible to suggest to the Church that if there were to be any alternative rite of Holy Communion it might be one with associations so venerable and with liturgical beauties so marked as the First Prayer Book of Edward VI."

Three years later, before the same body, he made his claim to understanding and sympathy with the three separate schools of thought within the Church, each of whom approached the question of the Prayer Book from a different angle.

The Evangelical tradition is in my bones, a part of my very being. I pray I never lose the fervour of its appeal, of its adoring gratitude to a Divine Redeemer and of its remembrance of the continual presence of a personal Lord and Master. I owe to the Liberal tradition a new sense of reality in the study of the Bible, an inspiring conviction that God upholds both His mind and His presence through the discoveries of science. The Catholic tradition has stirred my imagination, given a sense of the beauty of worship, the wonder of the Sacraments, the majesty of the Creed and the glory of the Holy Catholic Church, which, however feebly grasped, have brought to life, in the midst of heavy labours, its glory and strength and peace.

The Prayer Book baby can hardly be said to have had very satisfactory godparents, since one Archbishop did not really want it at all and the other Archbishop would have preferred something else. The First Prayer Book of Edward VI was, and had been for some years, with Lang's permission and that of his predecessor, in use at Hickleton, the domain of Lord Halifax, and the Archbishop on his visits had become familiar with it. He abandoned it with genuine reluctance, when he found the majority would have none of it.

Failing the Liturgy of 1549, Lang was at first inclined privately to think that "if we are content to wait for a bit it will be possible to make a change much more adequate and satisfying." But these were early thoughts, and when it became clear that there must be an alternative Liturgy, and that this could not be that of 1549, Lang fell into step. Thenceforward he took his full part in the compilation and revision of the new Book and in commending it to Convocation, the Church Assembly and other gatherings.

Accepting Davidson's view that "it was a question, in the good sense of the word, of expediency," he joined in the task of trying to discover what was, ecclesiastically speaking, at once the Highest Common Factor and the Lowest Common Denominator.

"Speaking for myself," he told a joint sitting of the Convocations at Church House, Westminster, in February 1927, "there are things included which I would rather have excluded, things excluded which I would willingly have included. But let the test of our proposals be not whether they go beyond or fall short of what any party would desire, but whether they give a fair and generous place to each and all—a place which will strengthen and not strain that fellowship in one Body to which we are called."

Yet to dismiss the matter as one of expediency, even in "the good sense of the word," is to do less than justice to Lang's sentiments. The Communion Office was holy ground, not to be trampled upon by warring bands or bargained about for the sake of peace. One afternoon, when he was having tea at Lambeth, the talk turned on the Prayer Book and particularly on the new Liturgy. A silence falling, Lang, as it were unconsciously, began to think aloud about Eucharistic worship, speaking for several minutes. Later, when he had left, Mrs. Davidson said to someone who had been present, "It was very wonderful for you and me to hear Ebor talking this afternoon, wasn't it?" Then she added: "Remember always that *that* was the *real* Cosmo."

As the Archbishops approached the last stages of their long labour, Lang's apprehensions grew. They are shown best perhaps in his letters to his brother and Wilfrid Parker.

> "What will happen I don't know," he wrote in October 1925. "I want to keep an open mind, but I have my own ideas pretty clear. The tiresome thing is that there are so many Bishops now who have got very cantankerous on the whole matter. However, it would be lacking in faith if one did not believe that honest-hearted men in such a matter will get help from the Holy Spirit. I think there is a disposition on the part of the best sort of people—Anglo-Catholics among them—to trust the Bishops and to be willing to accept what they propose."

Both then and later he and Davidson were a little inclined to over-estimate the confidence of the country in the wisdom of the episcopate. In the same letter Lang went on to deplore some recent activities of the Bishop of Birmingham,[1] which were likely to jeopardise the Book.

The Convocation of the Northern Province was the least of the Archbishops' troubles. Under Lang's adroit and conciliatory Chairmanship the Upper House gave unanimous approval to the Prayer Book Measure, while the Lower House passed it by 68 votes to 10. The figures hardly reflected the doubts and apprehensions of a large body of church-people. The Book was a compromise, incapable of kindling much

---

[1] The Rt. Rev. E. W. Barnes, appointed Bishop of Birmingham in 1923.

enthusiasm. The more extreme Protestants disliked it, because they thought it gave too much, the more extreme Anglo-Catholics, because it did not give enough; while a middle opinion voiced a doubt whether the Book, if passed, would command loyal obedience, and a question, to which no satisfactory answer was ever given, as to what would happen if it did not.

In March 1927 Lang was writing to Wilfrid Parker:

That wonderful Archbishop is keeping extraordinarily well. True, I left him in bed, but he always recovers from these chills, and though I can see a good many signs of age, he has been wonderfully vigorous and clear about at least the main principles of this Prayer Book business. . . . Of course the extremists on both sides are up in arms. That was to be expected. Plainly no Book for the Church as a whole could be one that satisfied either of them. I think the question for your Anglo-Catholic friends is whether they go on in a more or less lawless and combative way, or are willing that the whole corporate worship of the Church should be raised by authority to a higher level; in other words, whether they care more for themselves or for the Church, though that perhaps is rather a crude way of putting it. . . .

Of course the labour involved in this business has been very great and I have had to do a good deal of the detailed drafting work and general watching over details, which my brother of Canterbury cannot and indeed ought not to undertake. It is difficult to know what the final issue will be, but we must leave it in God's hands. I think of the little girl who, when faced by a bulldog, said, "Oh God, if you *really* care for little girls, now's your chance!"

In July, when the new Book had been before the Church Assembly, Lang wrote to his brother Norman:

The Archbishop of Canterbury excelled himself in the Chair, so shrewd, so patient, and keeping things in hand without seeming to exercise any undue pressure. His opening speech was very weighty and impressive. The rest of the debate was, of course, somewhat disappointing; everything that could be said had been said before. Joynson-Hicks [1] made a good speech from his point of view, keeping himself well in hand and speaking with charity and good temper. There were several deplorable speeches from ——, showing ignorance

---

[1] The Evangelical leader. He was Home Secretary and afterwards became Viscount Brentford. Died in 1932.

of theology and of the teaching of the Prayer Book. On the second day the speeches had to be reduced to five minutes, except in the case of Inskip,[1] who had to wind up the opposition, and myself, who had to wind up for the Book. Inskip's speech was very long and rather ineffective; it was rather a poor type of the House of Commons speech. It was too late, and the House too tired to make it possible for me to make an effective close. My speech seemed to go down all right, but it was in my judgment a poor speech and not worthy of the occasion, although I dare say others will not agree with me. Anyhow, the result was most satisfactory. I was very apprehensive all the time, from various indications, lest the majority in the House of Laity should be so small as to make it very difficult to know what course to take in the future. If there had been an indecisive majority it would have taken the heart out of the whole business and made it very difficult to approach Parliament. As it is, the majority, even in the House of Laity, was so decisive that it must have a great effect not only on the Church but on Parliament. At the same time I am well aware of the strength of the opposition that will be engineered in the House of Commons, and I cannot but be apprehensive about the attitude of the House of Lords. These good people are full of their own prejudices, which will be exploited and stimulated by the agitation which Knox and company are now to let loose through the country. However, we can only hope that, everything having had so much encouragement, our future difficulties may be overcome. It is a very long and anxious business and I wish it were over.

Parliament was now the principal worry. Lang was frankly afraid of the politicians. They were prone "to act upon their own personal likes and dislikes or grudges against individual clergy or Bishops" and could not "forget the Bishops who dabbled in the Coal Strike."

"I am concerned," he wrote to his brother Norman in August, "by the kind of influences which seem to work upon members both of the House of Commons and the House of Lords:—their readiness to be suspicious, shown in an absurd agitation about the alleged treatment of prayers for the King, their readiness to regulate their vote by their own personal likes and dislikes, their blindness to the gravity of the issues that would arise if the Measure were rejected. Meanwhile Knox and company are carrying out a great campaign of

[1] The Solicitor-General; afterwards Lord Caldecote. Died in 1947.

prejudiced literature, and it is difficult to say how the poor Bishops can undertake, even if they ought to do so, any propaganda. On the other side, we can only say our prayers and hope for the best, but I wish I could begin my holiday without this burden of anxiety upon my mind."

He was particularly fearful because, as he told Wilfrid Parker, "in the House of Commons there are so few Churchmen who carry weight. My own hope is that the motion in favour of its receiving the Royal Assent may be moved by Willie Bridgeman." [1]

On December 12th the Parliamentary battle began in the House of Lords, "filled from end to end with such a crowd as I can hardly remember seeing there, great animation and interest, and much uncertainty as to how the vote would go." Next day he wrote to his brother:

> On the whole, I think it looks as if the Lords will pass it, but there are many unknown and irresponsible Peers. I shall have to wind up on Wednesday. I hope I may convert any who are still doubting and that I may not say anything that would turn them the other way. But I expect most people have already made up their minds.

He spoke at the end of the three days' debate—"well, but . . . perhaps a little too long," the Bishop of Durham commented. Lang himself was not very satisfied with his effort, "but it seemed to hold the House and many others seemed more than pleased by it." On the division the Resolution commending the Prayer Book Measure was carried by 241 votes to 88, a hopeful augury for its fate in the other House, where, for some reason, an easier passage was expected.

> The night after the vote in the Lords I had a very vivid dream. . . . I was looking down from the Strangers' Gallery on the brilliant scene I had just left. Suddenly there emerged from beneath four black and sinister figures. They solemnly passed through the crowded Lords towards the Woolsack, and then the light went out. I was to see them again when I looked down from the Peers' Gallery in the House of Commons after the fateful division there. They were the four tellers advancing to the Speaker to announce that the Measure was lost.

[1] As it was. The Rt. Hon. W. C. Bridgeman, First Lord of the Admiralty. He became Viscount Bridgeman. Died in 1935.

The rest of the story is told in a letter to Wilfrid Parker.

During the last few days I knew that a rather anxious drift the wrong way had set, but we were assured that there ought to be no doubt of at least a small majority. But at once I felt that there was some-thing wrong in the atmosphere. Your brother-in-law, dear Willie Bridgeman, who had most chivalrously consented to move the Measure, did his best. We relied on him as a good typical Church of England man influencing the average House of Commons member. In ordinary circumstances he would have done so, and he really did very well and put his case quietly and sensibly, but it was evident that something more powerful was needed for the temper of the House. Then Joynson-Hicks followed and with great skill reached and inflamed all the latent Protestant prejudices in the House. It was not a very scrupulous speech, but it was extremely effective. I felt at once that unless it could be effectively answered, the chances of the Measure were small. Unfortunately there was no one in the House of Commons on our side who could really make an effective answer. Hugh Cecil, who once would have been able to hold the House and lift it to a higher level, completely failed to do so. I know his position was very difficult, but somehow he did not impress the House; he was too agitated and subtle, and never really struck a high note which might have appealed to the really religious, as distinct from partisan, spirit of the House. With very able speeches by Simon[1] and Douglas Hogg,[2] Attorney-General, on the other side, the drift set quite plainly steadily against the Measure. Even the Prime Minister, who in a few earnest and thoughtful words expressed his own intention to vote for the Measure, but was obviously re-strained by his inability to exercise any party pressure, was quite unable to arrest the drift. When Inskip spoke with great force I saw that the chances of the Measure were gone, and poor Top Wolmer[3] could only scream a few concluding words, very earnest and sincere, to a House which was already eager in talk and straining for the division. When the tellers came in, it was plain that all was up; and the labours of twenty years and the demand of all the representative Assemblies of the Church were thrown down, by 238 to 205. It was of course a great blow to my dear old brother Archbishop and friend:

[1] Now Viscount Simon.
[2] Afterwards Viscount Hailsham and Lord Chancellor.
[3] The present Earl of Selborne.

I felt deeply for him this reverse at the end of his twenty-five years' labour as Archbishop. The worst of it was that the vote was largely determined by the pressure of the debate, and there was no one who could really answer, and we were sitting there impotent and feeling that things were going steadily wrong.

Lang does not mention a speech which, even more than the eloquence of Sir William Joynson-Hicks or the disappointing performance of Lord Hugh Cecil, turned the House against the Measure.

"The most effective speech of all as regards votes," noted Dr. Davidson, "was, I think, Rosslyn Mitchell's.[1] It was a simply ultra-Protestant harangue, with no real knowledge of the subject, but owing its power to a rhetorical presentment of no-Popery phrases and arguments of the sort which are to be found in *Barnaby Rudge*, when the Lord George Gordon Riots set London aflame."

"My brother of Canterbury," wrote Lang again, "though in many ways showing signs of his great age (he will be eighty on April 7th), is wonderfully well and keeps, outwardly at least, very calm. Anything more ridiculous was never written than all that sob-stuff in the Press about his being taken by me from the House of Commons after the division with tears in his eyes! But of course the shock in many ways has told upon him."

As for Lang, he retired to his quarters in Cranmer's Tower and solaced himself by reading Gertrude Bell's *Arabian Letters*.

The verdict placed the leaders of the Church in an extremely painful position. The new Prayer Book had received ecclesiastical sanction by a series of substantial, almost overwhelming majorities. Even in Parliament the House of Lords had recorded its approval, and so, on an analysis of votes, had a majority of the members of the House of Commons who belonged to the Church of England. The rebuff was an assertion of spiritual prerogative which many, like the Bishop of Durham, thought intolerable: it brought into question not the Prayer Book only, but the whole relationship between Church and State. The Bishops were in the further difficulty that, hard as they had hitherto found it to discipline a clergyman who took liberties with the Book of Common Prayer, in the future their task would be impossible, especially if the liberties were

[1] M.P. for Paisley.

those which had received synodical sanction and were embodied in the new Book.

In discussing the next step that should be taken, for almost the first time in the history of the long partnership the two Archbishops disagreed. The Parliamentary opposition had fastened upon the provision (under conditions) of perpetual Reservation of the Blessed Sacrament: this was, or appeared to be, the head and front of the Book's offence. Dr. Davidson, therefore, was for eliminating the provision altogether and seeking the necessary Parliamentary approval for a bowdlerised Book. Lang, however, believed that to do this would be to surrender, to acknowledge the overriding authority of the State on a matter of spiritual importance. His first feeling therefore was against any immediate further attempt to obtain Parliamentary sanction for the Book; his second that, while it might be right to make the attempt, it would be wrong to try to placate the opposition by excluding either Reservation or the new Canon. He pressed his point hard, and eventually Davidson, possibly influenced by the thought that the days of his reign at Lambeth were numbered, gave way to the man on whom, as his most likely successor, the burden of the decision would fall.

In the revised version of 1928 the conditions for Reservation were made more definite and therefore less palatable to Anglo-Catholics, while the Black Rubric was inserted at the end of the Alternative Order. When the new Measure was brought before Convocations and the Assembly, every attempt was made to minimise the changes, as being "merely for the purpose of removing, if possible, some avoidable misunderstandings which may have influenced at least some members of the House of Commons." The amended Book had an uneasy passage, but eventually went through. Once more Lang brought the Upper House of York to a unanimous decision, but in the Lower House the majority dropped from 58 to 31. In the Convocation of Canterbury and the Church Assembly the reductions were heavier.

"Many who felt a good deal of strain in supporting the Book," Lang wrote, "found that this last twist was enough to break it. . . . If people knew the difficulties, of which I have personal knowledge, in securing an inclusion of continuous Reservation at all, they would be more generous."

The new Measure was reintroduced into the House of Commons on June 13th, 1928. This time its supporters managed the debate better, but again failed to carry the House with them, being beaten by 46 votes, a slightly larger majority than before. An impression of disingenuousness explained, at any rate partially, this second defeat. The Church was told that the changes were unimportant, the House of Commons that they were serious enough to warrant a reversal of its previous verdict. Neither took the assurance in good part and the compromise gave little pleasure to anybody. It affronted the Anglo-Catholics and appeased very few Evangelicals. In the view of many who were by no means extremists, it neither defended the spiritual rights of the Church nor, in the event, gave it a new Prayer Book.

Lang must shoulder his share of the responsibility for this second defeat, for it was his advice which had finally prevailed with the Bishops. It is easy in retrospect to blame his judgment, to suggest that after the first failure the leaders of the Church should at least have done at once what they did later. But as between Davidson and Lang this was not the issue; and, apart from the further surrender of principle involved, it is questionable whether the former's policy, if it had been adopted, would have prevailed. The current of opinion in Parliament was running strongly, and behind the arguments of the debate was a deep distrust both of the Bishops and of their ability to keep the clergy within the limits of any Book that was passed.

Lang wrote with deep disappointment of the result.

The debate was conducted on a high level, especially by the supporters, and was much better than last time. Hugh Cecil really held the attention of the House and lifted it, at one point, to really high ground. Two of the best speeches were by women—Lady Iveagh and the Duchess of Atholl—but the Prime Minister, though he wound up, was not very effective. His line of thought was entirely right, but it was, so to say, too good for the temper of the audience. As soon as any impression seemed to have been made by reason, the gusts of Protestant convictions, suspicions, fears, prejudices swept through the House, and ultimately prevailed.

But it is no use denying that one cause of the temper of the House, at least certainly among a large number of quiet English members—especially from the country—was the long-accumulating resentment against too many Anglo-Catholics who have thrust their ways upon quiet country folk entirely unprepared for them. This resentment has now, so to say, exploded. When some of their stalwarts say, "All we have gained has been gained by fighting," this strong resentment on the part of multitudes of quiet folk is the price that has been paid. It is extremely difficult for the Archbishops and Bishops to continue to do their utmost to give a generous place within the Church to the ideals of the Anglo-Catholic movement when many of its leaders, and not least its organ the *Church Times*, are perpetually sneering at their authority, treating their efforts almost with contempt, and enormously increasing the difficulties with which they are faced.

When the House of Bishops met to consider the results of this second reverse, they agreed unanimously on a statement proclaiming the inalienable right of the Church, in the last resort, to formulate its Faith and to order the expression of it in forms of worship.

"The Church," Lang told the Convocation of York on July 11th, "is responsible for meeting the spiritual needs of each generation, and for securing the ordering of its own life. The Church, therefore, is thrown back upon its only available resource, the administrative action of the Episcopate. . . . The knowledge which is given to us in the Revised Book must needs be a guide as to what may be rightly permitted or prescribed in the present situation."

The new Book was published, without prejudice, at the end of the year; and in 1929, when a new Archbishop was at Lambeth, a further statement declared that "during the present emergency and until further order be taken," the Bishops would not treat as disloyal any additions or deviations within the limits of the rejected Books, while refusing to countenance any practices outside those limits. Further, they allowed the use of any of the Forms and Orders of 1928, provided such use was approved by the Parochial Church Councils concerned.

A full and fair judgment of this unhappy episode in the history of the Church is given by the Bishop of Chichester in his *Life of Randall Davidson*. It was the old Archbishop's last battle. He had been eighty in April, and although still hale and alert, tired easily and responded with increasing strain to the heavy and growing demands of his office. The decisive consideration, however, was the approach of 1930 and another Lambeth Conference. He himself had no thought of presiding over it, and it was only fair that his successor should be allowed plenty of time for preparation. Accordingly, in July he sent in his resignation. Few doubted that the new Archbishop would be the man who had worked so well with Davidson for twenty years. "I could not but have a foreboding," Lang wrote modestly, "that it might fall to me to be his successor." In the notes he scribbled at Ballure that summer he described his feelings more fully. He had been fairly successful in banishing the idea from his thoughts until Davidson began to talk about his resignation. Then "It became clear that a big trial would await me —either to accept a *very* difficult position if some other Bishop were appointed and to try in the circumstances to 'play the game' rightly and honourably; or to face, knowing my shortcomings, the tremendous responsibilities of the office." He would leave the issue in the hands of God, and asked grace and strength to meet whatever might be the decision. But he found it hard to go on with his work at York as though no other prospect lay ahead, and to make arrangements and engagements for the future.

He was appointed to the Commission which was to receive the Archbishop's resignation, and on July 26th, the day after it was made public, had come up to London to attend a garden party at Buckingham Palace. After the party he was told the Prime Minister (Mr. Stanley Baldwin) was coming to Lambeth at 9.30 p.m. that evening and wished to see him.

He (the Prime Minister) told me that he proposed to recommend me to the King as the next Archbishop of Canterbury and that the King had given his ready assent. It may be worth noting (1) that I doubt whether any such communication had ever been made by a Prime Minister by word of mouth and not by letter, except the famous case of George III's direct offer, apart from Pitt, his P.M., to Manners Sutton; (2) that certainly no Prime Minister had ever conveyed such an offer smoking a pipe! He was very kind and cordial about it. Of course I asked whether I might have some time to consider his proposal. He at once said: "No, it is inevitable. I won't hear of any refusal. You are the only man. Your one and only duty is to say Yes at once, and before I leave." I could only submit, suppressing my feelings, which indeed could scarcely be expressed. Archbishop Davidson was then summoned to the study; and at once the Archbishop, the Archbishop now designate, and the Prime Minister settled the other consequent appointments—William Temple to be translated from Manchester to York, Guy Warman to be translated from Chelmsford to Manchester, and Wilson to be appointed to Chelmsford. It was quick work! Then the P.M. left, and after a few very moving words with Randall Davidson I went to my room, knowing that this heavy burden of responsibility was to be laid upon me. The public announcement immediately followed. It was arranged that the vacancy should occur in the late autumn, on November 12th, the Archbishop's Golden Wedding day.

In the rough notes Lang pays high tribute to the sincerity and simplicity with which the Prime Minister, puffing away at his pipe, discussed the new appointments. Lang was emphatic in commending Temple to York. If London had been vacant, he might have gone there "to clean out the situation in that Diocese." But Dr. Winnington Ingram "had clearly intimated that he was not disposed to resign or to take a less arduous Diocese." Besides, "Temple's marked ascendancy of mind, his large outlook, his vigorous personality, and his power of writing and of speech made him the right man" for York. His youth would balance Lang's maturer age "in the united work of the two Archbishops which my friendship with him would continue."

No sooner was the news published than Lang was "deluged with a huge tidal wave of letters." Notable among these was "that word of Charles Gore . . . to me, the only word of so many in those countless letters that went like an arrow to this conscience, 'Keep loyal above all things to Jesus of Nazareth.'" He was troubled by doubts of his fitness, by a sense of his weaknesses, "spiritual, and also intellectual and temperamental. I am under no illusions as to this—in spite of all the human promptings of ambition, I know myself not to be in the same class as my immediate predecessors on the Throne of St. Augustine."

He could not but be pleased by the note of personal affection in the letters, or by the wider prospect which was now opening. It would, he told Wilfrid Parker, be a terrible wrench to leave the North, and the work of twenty years, and his home at Bishopthorpe—"and you cannot understand what a hold the garden, which is now really famous in the North of England, has got upon my life." Yet he would have been less than human had he not been conscious of the honour that had come to him.

In August he had to accompany a pilgrimage of the British Legion and the British Empire Service League, led by the Prince of Wales, to the Menin Gate of Ypres, where he delivered his first address since his translation had been announced.

Then, as soon as he might, he escaped to the peace of Ballure, where he spent the better part of a fortnight alone, praying, meditating, and writing in his little notebooks. Afterwards, as he hoped, his future colleague, Temple, was coming with his wife to stay for a week; and then he must return to Bishopthorpe for all the sad business of goodbye, for gatherings of clergy and people and for the ceremony at which he was to receive the Freedom of the City of York.

I look back in these notes to the beginning of my time as Archbishop of York and think of all the hopes and plans with which I began. And now after twenty years the ending. Certainly there was enough and to spare of *doing*. Yet, after all the ceaseless process of doing, what was *done*? Again I cannot tell. God knows. Church life somewhat encouraged and invigorated, I hope; but the Church is ultimately only a means—to use the old word—of winning souls to God. How many souls were brought nearer God by all this *doing*? The words of the Methody hymn come to my mind—"Doing is a deadly thing." What is certain is that much more of true value might have been done if I had cared less for doing and more for *being*. If the inner life had been kept more true, the outer life would have borne more fruit. "He that abideth in Me and I in him," said the Lord, "the same bringeth forth much fruit: for apart from Me ye can do nothing." But for my Holy Weeks at Cuddesdon and my months in "the Cell" at Ballure, truly my soul would have withered. I can only with deep penitence leave these years to the merciful judgment of God. Yet it would be wrong not to give thanks for all the health and help given to me, for all the kindliness and loyalty which surrounded me, for the beauty and refreshment of my home at Bishopthorpe. Otherwise—"God be merciful to me a sinner."

So he felt as he looked back; and as he looked forward he began to feel the weight of years, for he was approaching his sixty-fourth birthday. Yet he stood on the threshold of what must needs be his last and greatest office, and in "the Cell" at Ballure, despite misgivings for his fitness and a sense of past failure, some of the old buoyancy and hope and exhilaration came flooding back. "After all," he wrote to Dick Sheppard, "I think I have some invincible youth hiding within me, and a late lark singing."

Chapter XXVI

ENTHRONEMENT AND ILLNESS

MY confirmation took place with all the customary forms at Bow Church in Cheapside, and without any sort of disturbance.[1] The first person, outside the officials, to greet me as Archbishop was the Lord Mayor, the good Kynaston Studd, whom I always thereafter called "*my* Lord Mayor." For this confirmation I stayed with my friends Ian and Jeanne Malcolm,[2] signing his visitors' book as I left the house as "Cosmo Ebor," and when I returned as "Cosmo Cantuar." This has always seemed to me, and to others, a very happy and euphonious signature—C. G. Lang—C. G. Stepney —Cosmo Ebor—Cosmo Cantuar.

The enthronement of the 95th Archbishop of Canterbury followed on December 4th.

The Dean, George Bell (now Bishop of Chichester), had taken infinite pains about all the arrangements. He had given full play to his vivid imagination in order to make the ceremony symbolic not only of ecclesiastical life, but of the national life, including "the Arts." Hence the series of independent representative processions, admirably marshalled. Never certainly had any previous Archbishop been enthroned on a scale of such colourful and symbolic magnificence.

Two memorable changes marked the proceedings. In the fifteenth century the Mandate to Enthronement was issued to the Prior, but after the Reformation to the Archdeacon or his proxy. An unexpected letter from Dr. Brightman[3] to the Dean suggested the desirability of trying to revert to something like the earlier practice; in other words, that the Mandate should go to the Dean and Chapter and that the Dean should enthrone. The ground was delicate, as it must always be when any change is contemplated affecting the prescriptive rights of ecclesiastical

---

[1] There was the usual objection by Mr. Kensit and his friends, which had the ludicrous result of sending the new Archbishop down into "the vaults"—in fact the coal-cellar— while the substance of the protest was examined.

[2] Sir Ian Malcolm, M.P., and Lady Malcolm.

[3] Fellow of Magdalen College, Oxford, Examiner in Theology. Died in 1932.

313

offices. Dr. Bell consulted the Bishop of Truro and the Dean of Wells, who both favoured the change, and also discussed the matter with Archbishop Davidson, the Archdeacon of Canterbury and Sir Lewis Dibdin. It is a tribute to the Dean's diplomacy that eventually, with the concurrence of all concerned, a satisfactory compromise was reached. By this the Mandate was issued to the Dean and Chapter without prejudice to the Archdeacon's rights. They then appointed the Archdeacon to enthrone in the Archbishop's throne and the Dean's stall, while the Dean enthroned in the Marble Chair and the Prior's seat in the Chapter House.

The other important alteration was in the placing of the Marble Chair of St. Augustine, which, after the advice of the Bishop of Truro and the Dean of Wells had again been sought, was removed from the Corona to a special platform on the top of the steps at the east end of the nave. The removal had something more than a ceremonial significance. In the past an Enthronement had been treated rather as a domestic occasion at Canterbury; the new arrangement, by the closer association of Church and people with the proceedings, symbolised the changed status of the Archbishop. He was more than the Bishop of a Diocese or the Metropolitan of a Province: he was the first spiritual leader in the land, in old Lord Halifax's favourite phrase, "Alterius Orbis Papa," the senior Bishop of a world-wide Communion.

The same interpretation appeared in the composition of the congregation, which included representatives of the Church of Scotland, the Free Churches, the Churches of the Continent, and, so far as was possible, every element in the nation's life. It appeared also in the Order of Service, which, while based on ancient forms, reflected the new and wider office of an Archbishop of Canterbury in the twentieth century. The Service was the result of the collaboration of the Bishop of Truro, the Dean of Wells, Dr. Brightman, Dr. Percy Dearmer, and Canon Dwelly of Liverpool; and the Te Deum was especially composed by Dr. Vaughan Williams.

The ceremonies met with general approval, but displeased the *Church Times*, whose criticism, neither for the first nor for the last time, annoyed the Archbishop. His own address, by the judgment of the Bishop of Durham, "pleased everybody, and alarmed nobody." It lacked the vigour and fire of his speech in York Minster twenty years earlier and perhaps he did not say very much; but what he did say was perfectly phrased and delivered.

I have never been a favourable, perhaps never even a fair, judge of my own performances in the way of addresses and sermons. This address was mainly a plea for unity within the Church of England. As for myself, the words which were in my own mind and heart . . . were Ps. 118, v. 14—"The Lord is my strength and my song."

So with pageantry and silver trumpets, and in the perfect setting of the Cathedral, the long ceremony drew to its close and the new Archbishop stood bareheaded outside the West door to give his blessing to the people.

Unhappily the Enthronement coincided with a crisis in the illness of King George V.

Indeed, till the very day itself it was doubtful whether it would become a great act of national grief and mourning rather than the Enthronement of the Archbishop. All the morning I was at one end of the telephone, with Lord Stamfordham at the other end, to get the latest account of the King's condition. To my immense relief, just before I went over to the Cathedral, Stamfordham was able to assure me that the King had had a good sleep, that the crisis was past, and that there was every hope of his recovery. This I was able to announce to the great congregation. But this anxiety prevented the Prime Minister (Mr. Baldwin) from being present, as he had fully intended to be. He was represented by the Lord Chancellor and one or two other Ministers.

The Archbishop added a note on his own apparel.

I decided not to wear cope and mitre, as I was anxious not to seem to be making at once a departure from the ways of my dear and honoured predecessor. But, as at York, I waited; and very soon quietly and without "advertisement" appeared at an Ordination fully vested in cope and mitre. The custom thus begun was established. It is certain that since the Reformation no previous Archbishop had ever worn a mitre either in the Cathedral or elsewhere. I carried on the custom in London, when desired, and in other places. I. cannot remember having ever received a single word of protest, hardly ever of comment. I can't but think that if the Anglo-Catholics had in this way bided their time and been patient and considerate about some of their practices, their efforts, especially in country places, would have excited far less controversy.

The move from Bishopthorpe to Lambeth and Canterbury was an arduous and melancholy business. The Archbishop felt acutely the wrench of leaving the beautiful house that had been his home for twenty years and, even more, the garden he had loved and tended so well. He was glad, he told Mrs. Crawley, to have been too busy to "moon about" Bishopthorpe during the last days. "Your picture of the desolate house went to my heart."

The change was the sadder because it ended the close association with Crawley and his family. Lambeth Palace, unlike Bishopthorpe, did not admit of two separate establishments under the same roof, and reluctantly Crawley came to the conclusion that his family should have a life of their own, unbroken by the intrusions of public work. The Archbishop lamented losing the companionship they had given him in his rather solitary existence, the liveliness of the children, and not least the presence of Mrs. Crawley, from whom he used to say that he would take in the way of plain speaking what he would allow from no other woman.

To him once more in his perplexity came Lumley Green-Wilkinson, who had almost a habit of reappearing at difficult moments in the Archbishop's career. He was with him at Amen Court. He joined him again for his initiation at York. Now, ill health having led him to resign his post as Vicar of St. Peter's, Bournemouth, he came back once more, to be, in the Archbishop's words, "a very special providence."

True, he was only an extra-non-resident chaplain; but he was very often an acting chaplain on all sorts of occasions, Consecrations, etc., including the Coronation; and his ever cheery presence came constantly like sunshine into Lambeth. He took over all my financial affairs, paid the wages, kept the accounts . . . and so took off my shoulders a burden which by nature I am very incapable of bearing. I can never express what I owe to his service, then and ever since.

The first regular chaplains were the present Bishop of Winchester and the present Archdeacon of Canterbury.

I was from the first and all through my time "singularly blessed" in the matter of chaplain-secretaries. The first was Mervyn Haigh, whom I inherited from Archbishop Davidson. He "saw me in." The change of masters made no difference in his loyalty. From the first days I could rely on his swift, critical and clear brain. In all the business of the Lambeth Conference of 1930 his help was invaluable. I can't think how I could have got through without it. I knew that

Baldwin, the P.M., had been much impressed by his abilities, so I was not surprised when in 1931 he was appointed Bishop of Coventry. I expect many people *were* surprised that a man should go straight from the office of Archbishop's chaplain to be Bishop of a Diocese. I thought it was a fitting recognition not only of his great abilities, but of the ever-increasing importance of that office.

Alec Sargent, whom I had known when he was chaplain at Cuddesdon, joined Haigh from the sub-wardenship of St. Paul's College, Grahamstown, South Africa, in 1929. His duty was to look after the Diocese. He could not resist the lure of the Diocese, for he had been born and bred within it, at the King's School, in his Ordination and first curacies, and loved everything in it. When later, in 1939, I appointed him to be Archdeacon of Maidstone and Canon of the Cathedral, and afterwards Archdeacon of Canterbury, the senior Archdeacon of the Anglican Communion, he was delighted. Whatever else I may have done in my life, I knew that I had made one man blissfully happy. He gave me ten years of devoted service—at first rather shy and self-contained, but growing each year in confidence. His knowledge and love of the Diocese were a great help.

There were also the secretaries, and pre-eminent among them Mr. A. J. Clements and Miss Gwen Fuller, who had both been with Archbishop Davidson and were both to stay with Lang for all his time at Lambeth. Mr. Clements

went his own way, remote, I think rather cynical, perhaps not unnaturally, about ecclesiastical persons and affairs. . . . He was always *there*, always efficient, with no other interests in life.

Miss Fuller—"truly one of a thousand"—dealt with much of the Archbishop's official correspondence and with all his private letters.

The making ready of two large houses was in itself a considerable labour. At Lambeth Palace a group of generous laymen bought from Dr. Davidson all the really valuable furniture, much of which for long years had been handed on by purchase from one Archbishop to the next. More, of course, was necessary, and after a twenty-five years' tenancy much redecoration was required. Once again Mr. Harry Dixon, who had dealt so well with Bishopthorpe in 1908, came to the rescue, the arrangements he made being, as before, much to the satisfaction of the new tenant. To the Old Palace at Canterbury, which was more easily prepared for occupation, went most of the furniture from Bishopthorpe.

The Archbishop took with him many of his old staff, including Martha Saville, who had been with him at Amen Court, Mrs. Opie, Budden the gardener and Walter Wells the chauffeur. The garden at Lambeth was a difficult problem, with few of the natural advantages of Bishopthorpe and a soil soured by centuries of London soot. But presently, with the help of a handsome present of six hundred tons of earth from Mr. J. Pierpont Morgan, wonders were worked, and for many weeks in the year the garden at Lambeth, although never quite competing with the glories of Bishopthorpe, was an oasis of beauty and colour in a wilderness of bricks and ferro-concrete.

At Lambeth he was to have his garden : at Canterbury he had the Cathedral.

To me the building was a constant joy and inspiration. How fortunate I was to have had my "seat" in two such splendid churches as York Minster and Canterbury Cathedral; and happily they are so different that comparisons were out of place. Surely the view of the choir and apse at Canterbury is one of the most beautiful pictures in stone in England, perhaps in the world.

It has what I can only call a *witchery* of its own, especially when the sunlight gleams from the windows. . . . It was itself worship in stone and colour.

Scarcely was the new Archbishop enthroned than he was struck down by the first serious illness he had known. Ailments of a milder sort he had occasionally had, despite his protestations to the contrary; for in one of his notebooks he makes the extravagant claim that "until December 23rd, 1928, I had never remembered being in bed for a whole day in my life" and that this was his first experience of nurses and of having his temperature taken. On December 23rd, however, and for many weeks afterwards, the malady was too grave to be forgotten or minimised.

On the eve of Advent Sunday [1] (1928) I was sitting at dinner with the Ordinands reading aloud to them (as had been my custom for many years) selections from Bunyan's *Pilgrim's Progress*. I had no sooner entered the river with poor Christian . . . than I was seized with a sudden internal pain, a pain more acute than I had ever experienced. I was just able to put the book into the hands of Vernon

---

[1] It was the eve of the Fourth Sunday in Advent, December 23rd.

Storr,[1] then my examining chaplain, and struggle to my room. Mervyn Haigh sent an urgent message to the Canterbury surgeon-doctor, Whitehead Reid. He said that in nineteen cases out of twenty he would operate immediately, but he had an instinct that this might be the twentieth case. Accordingly he telephoned to the eminent surgeon, Sir Henry Rigby, to come to Canterbury at once. He did so, straight from the bedside of the King, whom he had been attending, and arrived about 1 a.m. in his car, bringing with him his two nurses and all the apparatus for a major operation. He at once examined me, probed the body where the pain had been for a considerable time in complete silence, then quietly said: "I agree that in nineteen cases out of twenty your doctor would have been right to operate, and so would *I*, but I think this *is* a twentieth case and I will not operate." Meanwhile I could hear the nurses making their preparations in the adjoining room. They remained and Sir Henry returned. . . . Very shortly afterwards he came back with Lord Dawson of Penn for a consultation. So began my close association with Dawson, which ripened into a most real friendship. Neither seemed quite clear as to the cause of the pain, though they were sure it must have been very severe. I gathered afterwards that probably a small clot of blood had wandered over my body and through my heart, and Rigby told me that if either my doctor or he had operated that night I would probably have died, as the heart could not have stood the strain. How much I owe to the courageous decision of these men! The only result of it all was a mild form of pleurisy; but both Dawson and Rigby agreed that I must be a prisoner in bed for some time and not return to full work for four months!

He was a bad patient and a difficult convalescent. Green-Wilkinson records how in January the Archbishop, still bedridden, insisted upon supervising the hanging of his pictures and the sorting of his papers at the Old Palace. In the hiatus between the departure from Bishopthorpe and the arrival of the new "manager" affairs had fallen into some confusion and a suitcase bulging with unpaid bills and unanswered letters clamoured for attention. Meanwhile the Archbishop was exasperated by his enforced inactivity and fretted ceaselessly over an absence from duty in the first days of his rule, worrying himself and all about him

[1] Canon V. F. Storr, Archdeacon of Westminster 1931-1936. Died in 1940.

with his anxieties. Green-Wilkinson had his hands full and his patience tried to breaking-point; yet the Archbishop, despite all the grumbling and surface irritation, was full of gratitude. "Lumley here is most devoted," he wrote to his brother Norman. "I tell him he has mistaken his vocation. He ought to have been either a valet or a nurse."

When the time for convalescence came, Dawson was most kind and assiduous in trying to find a suitable place in the South of England. Finally he arranged with Lady Cowdray that she should offer me a small house of her own at Bognor (The Moorings). I hesitated, lest I should seem to be intruding on the King, who had just been moved to a house almost next door. Lord Dawson told me that he had consulted the Queen and that she hoped I would come.

Being thus the King's neighbour, I saw him frequently at Craig-weil House, where he was convalescing. Thus I was thankful to be able to give the spiritual ministration which had not been possible during his illness (though dear Archbishop Davidson had gone almost daily to Buckingham Palace in the hope that he might be called in—the old queer English custom that the "parson" only came when death was imminent!) Thus I had with him and the Queen a short service of Thanksgiving for his recovery, and gave him and her—no one else present—their Easter Communion in his room. I doubt whether this would have happened unless I had been there as a personal friend rather than officially as the Archbishop. . . .

In a notebook Lang describes the King as looking "like his old self—only thin and speaking with unwonted gentleness." For the Easter Communion Green-Wilkinson's wartime altar was used and "the King seemed much moved by the thought that so many of his army had received their Communion from this altar." A little later Lang and William Temple, the new Archbishop of York, in the presence of the Prime Minister (Mr. Baldwin), were admitted to make their long-deferred homage.

Lang describes The Moorings, to which in after years he was to make eight separate visits, as "a charming little house, beautifully fur-nished, at the end of a quiet avenue and on the very beach, with its long stretches of sand."

By another "special Providence" the last stage of the Archbishop's convalescence was a voyage in the Mediterranean on board Mr. J. Pierpont Morgan's yacht *Corsair*, "the first of three cruises which, as

I have often said, brought me more happiness than any other events in my life." He kept a careful diary of each of these voyages.

He joined *Corsair* at Venice on April 2nd, 1929. She was a comfortable yacht of 2000 tons and the Archbishop had a cabin "as large as an ordinary bedroom, with its own bathroom attached." His fellow-passengers were Mr. Pierpont Morgan and his daughter Mrs. Nicholls, Lord and Lady Buxton and Lord Clarendon; but the host, being summoned to Paris to take part in a Reparations Commission, was absent during the first part of the cruise.

After five days in Venice they sailed down the Dalmatian coast, calling at Zara, Sebenico, Trau, Split, Dubrovnik and Cattaro, before returning to Venice to pick up Mr. Morgan. He arrived from Paris with a copy of the *Daily Telegraph* containing a *canard* which caused the Archbishop some annoyance. There had been talk of a visit to the Holy Land, and although the idea was abandoned, apparently when Mr. Morgan was called to Paris, the story had got round that the Vatican had made representations on the subject to the Foreign Office, which had asked the Archbishop to omit Palestine from his itinerary. This was quite untrue, but a little later, when the party was in Greece, the story reappeared with embellishments.

The yacht's course was through the islands to Athens, where the Archbishop had to lay aside the clothes of convalescence and don a purple cassock. After luncheon at the Legation, he was driven to the Cathedral and, in the presence of a large crowd, was received by Archbishop Chrysostom, attended by fifteen of the Metropolitans and Bishops of Greece. He was conducted to a chair of state in front of the Ikonostasis, where he sat while a hymn and a Litany were sung. This ceremony was followed by a reception at the Archbishop's house, when His Beatitude read an address in Greek, recalling the translation of Theodore in the seventh century to Canterbury. As a memento of this return visit Athens presented Canterbury with a gold cross, and in a further tour of the Cathedral large numbers of the faithful knelt to kiss the visitor's ring and to receive his blessing.

Two more days, mostly given to sightseeing, were spent in Athens, followed by a run to Nauplia, Mycenae and the islands, to Athens again and the battlefield of Marathon, and then back to Venice. Such was the magic of the voyage that the Archbishop almost forgot his vexation and was disposed even to feel grateful to his illness for giving him such an experience.

Two years later he had another illness and another cruise.

> Early in 1931 I became aware of considerable pains in my head. Dawson said that it was the beginning of that most painful of maladies known as "Fifth Nerve" and that I must give up all work and retire to bed and submit to the care of two nurses. Strangely enough, I have no *memory* of all the usual excessive pain. This was due to a "doping" by Dawson so skilful that it dulled the sense of pain and yet left me entirely conscious, able to see people sometimes and even to do a little necessary business. I only remember visits from various medicine men—Dawson's well-known team work. The result was that when I came through and read many of the letters which had arrived, kindly telling me about the dreadful pains of this malady, I could not realise that I had suffered them.

Nevertheless this second illness, coming so soon after the first, depressed him to such an extent that at times, even when he was clearly on the mend, he began to fear he would never regain his old health or be well enough to carry on with his work. This feeling explains a short conversation at the luncheon table in 1932 between him and the faithful Martha Saville.

> C. C.: "What's this?"
> Martha: "Them's brains, Your Grace. You haven't had any for a long time."
> C. C. (grimly): "No, I know I haven't."
> Martha: "Oh, I didn't mean that, Your Grace."

For his convalescence he had another cruise. On March 24th he joined the ship at Monte Carlo, where he had a glimpse of his old friend Tupper-Carey, who was shocked by his appearance as he went aboard. *Corsair*—a new yacht under the old name—took him first to Naples and Sicily. On Good Friday he was at Athens, where the Archbishop gave him a "very cordial and indeed affectionate" welcome. After touching at Nauplia and Epidaurus, *Corsair* dropped anchor at Patmos, where the Archbishop climbed up to the great monastery and was received by the monks with hymns and an address of welcome. Bad weather prevented a landing at Rhodes and the next port of call was Beirut, whence the party took train to Baalbec and Damascus—"a jewel set in a rich plain of gardens and fruit trees with the desert hills surrounding it. As we looked down upon it a brilliant, almost dazzling, shaft of sunlight fell on the road to Damascus just where St. Paul saw the light that blinded and converted him."

Without protest or rumour of protest, he moved south into the Holy Land, through Capernaum and Tiberias to Nazareth, Nablus, and finally Jerusalem, where he was the guest of Sir John Chancellor, the High Commissioner.

Wearing my purple silk cassock, cape and cap, I was met at the Jaffa Gate by the Deputy Commissioner, the Chief of Police, and the Bishop in Jerusalem (MacInnes), in scarlet doctor's gown, with Archdeacon Stewart and others, and conducted ceremoniously up the narrow cobbled street to the Church of the Holy Sepulchre. In the courtyard was a considerable crowd and representatives of the various ecclesiastical authorities (except the Latin)—the Metropolitan of Philadelphia (Timotheos), who had been at Balliol and at Lambeth and spoke English fluently, representing the Orthodox Patriarch of Jerusalem; the Locum Tenens of the Armenian Patriarch; the local head of the Coptic Church. Then I was conducted by all this company through the various sites within the Church. In spite of this crowd I felt that in this central shrine of Christendom there was a real spirit of reverence. I say nothing about the historical authenticity of the sites: enough that they have been for centuries symbols of faith and reverence and devotion.

I was then conducted to the Orthodox Catholicon, within the Holy Places but independent and under the sole charge of the Orthodox Church. It had been intended that after an address from Archbishop Timotheos, as representing the old Patriarch who is ill, I should reply and give a blessing. But immediately before the ceremony the Deputy Commissioner intervened, saying he had given a pledge—I presume to the Latin authorities—that I would not even seem to be disturbing the *status quo* by speaking, and that I must be silent. As the Catholicon is in the full control of the Orthodox Church, this seemed to me real pedantry: the intervention was much resented by its representatives and was afterwards objected to by the High Commissioner. But at the moment it was impossible to do otherwise than acquiesce.

So Archbishop Timotheos put me in a chair of state, a welcome was sung by the choir just as in the Cathedral of Athens in 1929, the Archbishop read his address, I merely bowed, was taken inside the

Ikonostasis where I knelt in silent prayer, and was then conducted formally out of the Church.

Formal visits to the three Patriarchates followed, the Latin Patriarch, Monsignor Barbassina, notwithstanding the episode in the Catholicon, receiving the Archbishop not merely affably but with some pomp, and later unbending so far as to attend the reception at Government House, which previously he had not entered. A long day ended with a call on the old Patriarch Damianos, who "lives, or rather declines to die, in a charming little house with its own courtyard on the top of the Mount of Olives." He gave the Archbishop on leaving a mother-of-pearl patriarchal staff, "which he evidently intended to mean his recognition of my status as a Patriarch!"

After these more formal functions the Archbishop was permitted to see the sights of the city and the neighbourhood, visiting Jericho, the Jordan, the Dead Sea, and of course Bethlehem, where he replied to an address of welcome in the Church of the Nativity. The party rejoined *Corsair* at Haifa, and after a leisurely voyage across the Mediterranean and up the Adriatic came to Venice, whence a special train took them to Calais. "So ended what I think were the happiest six weeks of my life."

The third and last cruise was in April 1939. The Archbishop undertook it with hesitation and after consulting the Prime Minister (Mr. Chamberlain) and the Foreign Secretary (Lord Halifax), for the clouds of war were banking up heavily over Europe. At last he decided to go, and on April 2nd he and the rest of the party joined *Corsair* at Monte Carlo. At first they voyaged over now familiar seas, touching at Naples, Athens and Nauplia, where Easter Day was spent. Athens, although shaken by the Italian invasion of Albania, gave a ceremonial welcome, the new Archbishop doing the honours. The next call should have been at Mount Athos, but there the sea was too rough to allow a landing and *Corsair* went on through the Dardanelles into the Sea of Marmora, reaching Istanbul on April 12th. On the 13th Santa Sophia was visited in the morning, and the old palace of the Sultans in the afternoon. On Friday the 14th the Archbishop paid his formal call on the Phanar, an event, he remarked, of some significance in ecclesiastical history, as marking the first visit of an Archbishop of Canterbury to an Oecumenical Patriarch.

The first ceremony was at the little Cathedral. On arrival I was met by the Holy Synod, some twelve Metropolitans, richly robed, and was conducted with great pomp to the Church. It is highly decorated with a very elaborately carved wooden Ikonostasis. I was placed on a seat opposite the Patriarchal Throne, where the Metropolitan of Chalcedon, as deputy of the Patriarch, who was too frail himself to attend, presided. Then followed the usual ceremonies for the reception of an Archbishop or Patriarch. . . . At the close, with a Cross in my hand, I gave a blessing to the considerable crowd. I was then conducted with much state to the Patriarchal Palace. There the Patriarch awaited me, welcomed me with the usual salutations, and took me into his "Throne room." There he proceeded to read to me an allocution in the presence of the Synod and other officials. I gave a very much less flowery reply. The Patriarch then gave me ceremonially a jewelled encolpion (if that is the right word) with a gold chain, the symbol of a Metropolitan, and less ceremonially a bundle of Easter eggs! We then sat down for our informal conversation. At first the old man (he is not really old, about seventy, but looks much older) was somewhat shy and embarrassed, but soon became quite cordial and lively. I spoke to him about my proposed united Whitsuntide Appeal (for peace), with which he agreed, and of course about the relations of our respective Churches. Then, as I was leaving, came the tedious business of being photographed, the Metropolitans chattering like excited jays about their places; and after more embraces I left and returned to Istanbul.

The whole visit was both intensely interesting and also pathetic. It was hard to realise that this frail old man held an office which once had rivalled, and sometimes eclipsed, that of the Pope at Rome. Now, in spite of his great position, he has little authority. The various autocephalous Orthodox Churches regard him with formal deference or even reverence, but with great jealousy lest he should interfere with their independence. He is kept in a state of somewhat humiliating subservience by the Turkish Government, indeed as practically a prisoner within the Phanar. There he lives with his Synod of Metropolitans, a shadow of former greatness. The position of these good men is also mainly titular, for though they bear the most ancient titles in Christendom, they have now no real jurisdiction, as the Greeks in Asia Minor have been transported to Greece.

Later in the same day the Patriarch paid a return call at the British Embassy. The cruise should have continued to Smyrna, Ephesus and other places, but the news was now so menacing that it was decided to return home. So, after steaming through the Bosphorus to give the passengers a glimpse of the Black Sea, *Corsair* turned round and headed for Monte Carlo.

These three cruises, which the Archbishop always recalled with delight, were not mere holiday jaunts; nor were they undertaken solely for the sake of convalescence. They had a valid connexion with that work for closer relations with the Churches of the East which will be discussed in a later chapter. Indeed, the Archbishop ends his account of his journeys by insisting that they had "some measure of importance not only in my own life, but in the long-drawn efforts to strengthen the ties between the Anglican and Orthodox Churches."

Chapter XXVII

THE NEW TASK

DURING those first three years at Canterbury illness, breaking into the routine with which Lang had always ordered his working life, limited his activities both in range and intensity and, to some extent, affected his judgment of men and affairs. Apart from the two major attacks, he had lesser ailments. In June 1930, just before the Lambeth Conference, he began to feel "some internal discomfort," diagnosed by Lord Dawson of Penn as denoting the presence of a duodenal ulcer, not as yet formed, but "growling." As a precaution and to ensure that the claims of the forthcoming Conference would be satisfied, he banished the Archbishop for a month to The Moorings, where he put him on a strict diet. Next year, after the appearance of the "Fifth Nerve" and before the second cruise in *Corsair*, Lang was taken in charge by Green-Wilkinson at his home in Windsor Forest. He began his visit unpropitiously by falling in his bath and striking his head with such violence that, when help arrived, he was almost unconscious. Strangely enough, from that moment the pain of the peccant nerve began to abate. The cruise followed, with a continuing improvement, but on his return he developed a new trouble in the shape of fibrositis. For recuperation he went to Cannes, where Lady Gladstone lent him her villa; and after Cannes to Harrogate, where "I lived luxuriously in the Hotel Majestic and submitted to every sort of treatment at the Baths." These he regarded with suspicion, refusing to enter unless Green-Wilkinson went in too. Still the acute rheumatism persisted, and when he left Harrogate for Ballure he could hardly walk and found that his inability to kneel in "the Cell" was a bar to the concentration he tried to practise. Ballure perhaps brought to his body the healing it had so often given his spirit, as when he returned to Lambeth his malady vanished as quickly and mysteriously as it had appeared. A sharp attack of shingles in 1932 was the last of his troubles. Thereafter, he wrote at the end of his time, "I have had almost unbroken health"—a statement on his medical history which for once was near enough to the truth!

During those years of intermittent illness and interrupted labours, irritability was never far from the surface. Big troubles found him

327

unshaken: the minor misadventures of life exasperated him. (Years earlier he had noted the same foible in his mother.) He was a sore trial to his chaplains, attached though they were to him. Sargent, until he got to know him better, found him "a most alarming and disconcerting person." Lang's health seemed to have forsaken him at the very moment of reaching the place where he would be; and he was haunted by the fear of breaking down completely. This drove him to efforts which he would have been wiser not to make, to work when he should have been resting, and to worry when he should have sought to put business out of his head; and the more he tried, the harder the labour became. "Cosmo Cantuar, Cosmo Cantuar," he once muttered as he signed some letters. "What's the good of calling yourself that, when it's all dust and ashes?"

Yet somehow the work went on. He was, as Sargent remarks, "an *inexhaustible* person," not only in his industry, but in his resource, the sweep of his mind, the charm of his company, his "comicality," and above all his devotional life. These overshadowed the little defects on which so often first opinions were formed—his "prelatical" side, his weakness for people of rank or importance, the sardonic humour which occasionally exploded in some shattering comment. "And now—and now—the heart of the Primate is filled with pastoral joy, as he prepares to address his faithful people. Oh dear, give me my hat." Or, as he watched the Cathedral bedesmen in their Tudor gowns mustering for a procession, "Oh, these ridiculous old men! Oh, these ridiculous old men! All this fuss, how I hate it, how I hate it!" But he did not really hate the fuss or think the bedesmen ridiculous. He liked both it and them. Or again, as he entered the Albert Hall to address a gathering of the Mothers' Union at the end of a "Week of Renewal" and caught sight of the vast concourse of women, he was heard to mutter: "Bless my soul! Look at all those renewed women." None of these comments reflected his real feelings.

He wrote at length in his autobiographical notes of the work as he found it in 1928 and of the men with whom he had to do.

One of the most difficult problems for any Archbishop of Canterbury must always be to strike the right balance between his duties as Archbishop and his duties as Bishop of his Diocese. . . . During my time it was my custom to spend the middle of the week at Lambeth and the week-end at Canterbury, but of course this custom was liable to constant interruptions for all sorts of special occasions in London. I tried to do my best for the Diocese and . . . succeeded in visiting every parish at least once—many more than once. I always made the journey from Lambeth to Canterbury and *vice versa* in my car with the *Times* and the companionable silence of Alec Sargent—an immense saving of time and energy. I don't think I travelled by train more than once, and thus I was a complete stranger in the station at Canterbury.

On that solitary occasion, when his car had broken down and he had to go by train, he was caught in a queue of passengers at the station barrier and was overheard by his chaplain saying to himself, "Never again, never again!" And never again it was.

The Archbishop added a note on the debatable question of a head-quarters staff.

It is difficult to criticise a proposal which has taken many shapes, none of them very clear and most of them based on ignorance of the actual facts about the Archbishop's work. There has been the grandiose conception of a sort of "Abbey of Cardinals"—a precedent which I don't think would commend itself to Anglican Churchmen; or it has been advocated that there should be experts in various branches of the work of the Church at home and abroad to assist the Archbishop with their knowledge and counsel. Passing over such technical matters as their payment, etc., I would say that I could always get such expert advice when I wanted it without creating this special sort of staff. For the Church's work overseas there was always available the Secretary of S.P.G., a Society always regarding itself as in close relations with the Archbishop.[1] I appointed a Committee to advise me on more difficult or constitutional questions, of which Bishop Palmer, formerly Bishop of Bombay, was the most active member and on which he took infinite trouble. For relations with other Churches abroad there was created the Council on Foreign Relations, of which the Bishop of Gloucester [2] (Headlam) was a most competent Chairman. This did a great deal of very useful work, though I was always careful to insist that it could not take the place of that personal action or advice on the part of the Archbishop which these Churches always particularly valued. As to the affairs

[1] The Archbishop also consulted the Church Missionary Society on overseas questions.
[2] The Rt. Rev. A. C. Headlam, Bishop of Gloucester 1923-1945. Died in 1947.

of the Church at home, on executive questions there were always available the leaders and officials of bodies such as the Ecclesiastical Commission and Queen Anne's Bounty; and on questions of policy it would have been very unfortunate in my judgment if it were considered that they were decided, or even strongly influenced, by particular individuals and not the Archbishop himself. If they were not known, there would be inevitable suspicion and gossip as to who they might be. On legal questions there were always ready to hand and in frequent consultation my legal Secretary and on exceptional matters the Vicar-General. (Here I would refer most gratefully to the ever willing and valuable assistance of my legal Secretary, H. T. A. Dashwood.[1]) Thus there was always a Headquarters Staff in fact, if not in form, and one much wider in range and abler in *personnel* than any ever suggested by "reformers," whose fertility of suggestion was greater than their acquaintance with the facts. Anyhow, I seemed to get on well without the apparatus of any of those fancy schemes.

On the Diocesan Staff proper he wrote:

They were the Suffragans or Assistant Bishops and the Archdeacons. We met regularly at the Old Palace at least once a month and dealt with all matters of diocesan administration, chiefly of patronage. At the beginning of my time the Suffragan Bishop of Dover was the good and wise John Macmillan, till he was called to be Bishop of Guildford. Then I personally and the whole Diocese had the invaluable help of Alfred Rose,[2] who came from the Vicarage of Brighton. He proved to be an almost ideal Suffragan for an Archbishop whose time was necessarily much, even chiefly, occupied by the general affairs of the Church. He was indefatigable in his visits to the clergy personally and to their parishes, who greatly appreciated his cordial and genial approach and his pastoral talks, and in arranging almost too readily for confirmations. He most generously made his services voluntary. Croydon is a place entirely unique in the ecclesiastical organisation of England. It belongs to the Diocese, yet is not part of it geographically. It is a separate *enclave*. . . . Both church and town value their connexion with the Archbishop; they have no wish to leave his Diocese and no other Diocese has shown any

[1] Mr. H. T. A. Dashwood, Registrar of the Court of Arches and of the Court of Faculties, and Principal Registrar of the Province and Diocese of Canterbury.
[2] The Rt. Rev. A. C. W. Rose, now Bishop of Dover.

great wish to have them. . . . I felt strongly that the Bishop of Croydon ought to live in the midst of his See. Accordingly I persuaded the always genial, popular and able Edward Woods (now Bishop of Lichfield) to come, and made him Vicar of the Parish Church. Moreover, as it seemed undesirable to have too many dignitaries crowded into this small space, he became a sort of Pooh-Bah Bishop, Vicar, Archdeacon and Rural Dean. . . .

Then there were the Archdeacons of Canterbury and Maidstone, who by virtue of their Archdeaconries were also Canons Residentiary of the Cathedral. For most of my time the Archdeacon of Canterbury was Edward Hardcastle, of whom I used to say that he was the Archdeacon whose type is laid up in the heavens. He looked and was an ideal Archdeacon, with whom anyone delighted to work. The Archdeacon of Maidstone was the Bishop of Dover (Macmillan) until he left for Guildford.

He was succeeded by Canon T. K. Sopwith, who in 1939 left to become Archdeacon of Canterbury and was followed by Archdeacon Sargent. "No Bishop," Lang concluded, "could have had a better team. They were all most real friends and nothing could have been happier than my associations with them all."

The heart of the Diocese was the Cathedral itself, a never-ending interest and delight.

When I first knew it in the days of the vigorous Dean Wace, the human worship offered was rather cold and dull. But George Bell had made great improvements in his short tenure of the office of Dean. The music was still at best scholarly, but without any thrill. Before I left and before the War, Gerald Knight had begun to transform it and to give his choristers a lovely purity of tone. Perhaps it might be said that it tended to be too "precious," but it was a joy to hear it.

With the departure of Dr. Bell to Chichester in 1929, Canterbury had a new Dean in Dick Sheppard. Much as the appointment delighted Lang, he feared for Dick's health, which had broken down during his last days at St. Martin-in-the-Fields. The anxiety was only too well founded. Although the doctors were reassuring, scarcely had the new Dean arrived than his old enemy, asthma, gripped him again. He had to spend most of his time at Broadstairs, the climate of which suited him better than Canterbury's; but after two years of struggle, worn out by illness, he resigned.

Yet in spite of all this, even in the two short years he had greatly improved the Cathedral and city by his so lovable personality. Crowds came to hear his simple vivid messages of the love of God. He endeared himself to everyone in the Cathedral, from the Chapter to the vergers and the workmen. He passed like a meteor of light and love.

Under his successor, Dr. Hewlett Johnson, improvement continued, copes being worn and vestments being in use at the side altars.

The relations between Dean Hewlett Johnson and some of the Chapter were not always harmonious and his ceaseless propaganda on behalf of Russia somewhat provocative. Owing to perversions abroad, and even at home, I had to make it plain that the Dean and the Archbishop were not the same person and that the Archbishop had no control over the opinions of the Dean. But my own personal relations with him were always most cordial; there was never a trace of the faintest friction between Bishop and Dean within the Cathedral. I only wish that the Chapter had been always immune from that strange disease which I was accustomed to call "the Cathedral blight."

Among the less agreeable of Lang's duties was the task of presiding over the Upper House of the Convocation of Canterbury. The Convocations, he reflected, appeared, like the American Constitution to the eye of an outsider, to have been devised for the express purpose of preventing anything being done.

Certainly there could not be a more cumbrous proposition than one which requires any major matter affecting the spiritual life of the Church to secure the assent of two separate independent bodies, the Convocations of the two Provinces, and of the separate Houses of Bishops and Clergy within each. Something has been done, and more could be done, to mitigate this grievous practical inconvenience. Thus within each Convocation the two Houses have often met together in full Synod, as it is called. At York when this was done, the matter in hand was debated by the two Houses together, though of course the voting was always separate. In Canterbury meetings in full Synod were assembled not to have a joint debate, but to hear some statement by the Archbishop as President on his own behalf and on behalf of the Bishops of the Upper House. There are exceptional occasions when in my judgment the York plan might be adopted in Canterbury. Again, it has been ruled that there is no constitutional objection to the two Convocations meeting together. This was done before the final adoption of the Revised Prayer Book. This might be done on any equally important occasion. But if so, it is clear that in voting the separate identity of each Convocation must be preserved, otherwise York would always be out-voted by the Houses of Canterbury, so much more numerous. Even with this safeguard, York has always been jealous of such joint Sessions, on the ground that York would be, if not out-voted, yet out-debated, by Canterbury.

On the whole, notwithstanding the manifest disadvantages of the existing arrangement, he thought the old constitution, adjusted or modified, must continue. Between North and South the difference was real, and the independence of the Convocations and their separate Houses had roots which struck deep into the history of the Church. Sometimes, however, he would liken himself to a man trying to drive four horses abreast, and never knowing when one might lie down or another kick out at its neighbours.

I confess I found it more agreeable to be President of the York than of the Canterbury Convocation. York, being much smaller, was more intimate. The Bishops always stayed with me at Bishopthorpe; the clergy met constantly together in social intercourse. My relations with both Houses were, unlike those of Archbishop Thomson, always most cordial. On the other hand, to be frank, I often found the Lower House of Canterbury a real difficulty. Things went smoothly enough when dear Archdeacon Gibbs [1] was Prolocutor, at the beginning of my time. The spirit of a true gentleman seemed to pass from the Chair to the House. But they tended to become more awkward when Dr. Kidd [2] was Prolocutor, and certain officious and insistent Proctors (whom I shall not mention by name) made it their business and pleasure to show a meticulous jealousy of the privileges of the House, or to search out minor awkward points and make a great fuss over them, and to manœuvre their fellow-Proctors into a tug

[1] Prolocutor 1925-1932.   [2] Prolocutor 1932-1936.

333

with them. The atmosphere was better under the very capable management of Cranage,[1] Dean of Norwich. Yet always I had some reason to ask the Prolocutor in a chaffing way: "What mischief has your House been up to to-day?"

"Clergy," as the Archbishop wrote to Wilfrid Parker, "are very troublesome people."

The Church Assembly was a more congenial body.

When it was first established after the Enabling Act, there were many who thought that it would inevitably supplant Convocation, for it consisted of the four Houses of Convocation sitting together as a House of Bishops and a House of Clergy, reinforced by a House of elected laity. But, partly through the wise handling of Archbishop Davidson, a real if not clear distinction of function came to be realised, that matters directly concerning the spiritual life of the Church were for the Convocation, matters concerning legislature, finance and the like were for the Assembly. Of course, it belonged to the nature of the Church that this distinction could not always be clearly drawn or observed, but on the whole it worked; and the Convocations have continued as before, though the Bishops especially, and some of the clergy, jibbed at being obliged to attend so many extra meetings.

The Assembly soon got into its stride, though the stride was somewhat slow and unsteady. One proof of its good work is the record of legislative Measures to which Parliament gave the force of law and which would never, or without infinite delays, have got through the ordinary procedure of Parliament. It had its own procedure, elaborated by the care and skill of Hugh Cecil (Lord Quickswood); and though for long this procedure mystified the members and suffered from the over-pedantic supervision of its creator, it soon became understood and kept the business in order. But it demanded constant vigilance on the part of the Chairman, and I always tried to interpret it on lines of common sense. The Assembly became on the whole a fairly business-like body.

Of course, like all such Assemblies, it suffered from its bores; but it suffered them, if not gladly, at least with even excessive patience. The chief sufferer was the Chairman, who had to sit through all their tedious speeches and interruptions, but I hope I kept any signs of irritability in due check. On the whole I thought the level of speaking

---

[1] Prolocutor 1936-1945.

was high, higher than in Parliament. On great occasions, in spite of the intrusions of the bores, it reached a really high level. A special feature of the debates was the orations by my old friend Henson, Bishop of Durham, never indeed constructive, but entertaining and sometimes impressive, and if rarely followed, always admired. Not the least effective speakers were often women, such as Lady Bridgeman and Lady Cynthia Colville.

There is, and always must be, a special difficulty in the dual rôle of the Chairman, on the one hand as Chairman, with the duty of guiding the business and keeping order, and on the other hand as Archbishop, with the inescapable duty of acting as a responsible leader. I tried to keep a just balance between the two rôles. As to the first, the Assembly was always very responsive and I cannot remember anything in the nature of what the Press calls a "scene." As to the second, it was always only too generous in following the Archbishop's "lead." Indeed, there were, I knew, critics who thought that his "lead" unduly influenced the course of the debate. It may have been so, but the fault was not his.

On the whole I enjoyed the Assembly, though the demand on my patience was sometimes very exacting. Perhaps I was fortified by my habit of taking a humorous view of my fellow-creatures.

Later he was to add a comment upon both bodies.

I fear the Church is not at its best in these ecclesiastical assemblies; and though I always tried to take them seriously and to do my duty to them, the fact that they were never really congenial seems to show that I have never been an ecclesiastic in the narrow sense of the word —at heart.

However uncongenial the duty may have been, by general consent Lang made a most skilful and effective President, the only criticism of him being that he was inclined to double the parts of Speaker and Prime Minister!

Hard as the work had been at York, at Canterbury it was even harder. He had not known before how heavily the burden of Convocation, the Church Assembly and Bishops' Meetings would press upon an Archbishop. When Lang was at York, he had journeyed frequently South for consultation with Davidson; but when the talks were over and he had gone back to York, an immense and hitherto unimagined amount of tidying up remained to be done. This task now fell to him; and in addition there was all the business connected with the Churches overseas, which was almost entirely for the attention of Canterbury. The routine work, too, increased in his day, largely by his own choice. He could never understand how Davidson found time to sit through debates in the House of Lords when he had no intention of speaking; or often in the afternoon to look in at the Athenaeum for an hour or two. Lang hardly entered the House of Lords unless he meant to take part in a debate or, until his retirement, made any use of his membership of the Athenaeum.

"I have never been inside the Athenaeum for a year!" he was to write in his notebook in 1936. "Certainly dear old Holland's kindly gibe about the influence on Davidson of the old gentlemen in that Club can never be levelled at me."

Besides his duties as the senior Metropolitan, there was the Diocese, in which he worked indefatigably, visiting parishes, addressing clergy, and being accorded civic receptions—a rather old-fashioned compliment for which he had a particular regard. He did not enter easily into this new kingdom. The first year was difficult; he was ill, shy, self-conscious, oppressed with the arrears of work at Lambeth, and missing the outspoken kindliness of the North. Presently, however, people and country alike found their way to his heart. At first, after Yorkshire and Scotland, he thought the Kentish countryside a little tame, but after a while he discovered the charm of its quiet beauty. Soon he had his favourite views—from the top of Charing Hill, from Stone Street to Dungeness, the spaces of Romney Marsh, and the first glimpse of the Cathedral on the road from London.

"I do want to emphasise," writes the Archdeacon of Canterbury, "that he was a good Diocesan, diligent, painstaking, genuinely sympathetic. . . . All the clergy revered him as a great man; most were afraid of him; some really loved him. I think they all felt that he listened with his whole being to them when they brought a problem to him, and that he understood, from experience and from his realistic view of human nature, how difficult their task was."

Sometimes, if the "prelatical" side were uppermost, he might show a lack of the "common touch," comparing in a village sermon the great affairs of Church and State, which were his habitual care, with the short and simple annals of his hearers. On better days he would preach with simplicity and power, using some scrap of local colour or history to give life to his words; and in his references to persons he seldom tripped up.

"I think, too," the Archdeacon adds, "that his impartiality was recognised in matters of controversy. By training and temperament a High Churchman with a keen sense of history and of beauty in worship, he never became 'Anglo-Catholic' in the party sense; but he understood what the Anglo-Catholics meant and deprecated merely destructive criticism of them. . . . His Presbyterian birthright and wide experience of Evangelical churches in the North made him at home in a simple 'Gospel' atmosphere. I have heard him preach in churches of all descriptions, and the *substance* of what he said was the same; but he varied the emphasis and the language. What he disliked was anything in the nature of flat disobedience to his directions and high-falutin' made-up prayers in place of the Prayer Book. More than once I have heard his, 'Oh, good gracious!' when the parson mouthed an elaborate utterance to the Almighty."

Although in conversation with friends he would sometimes describe the doings of the Anglo-Catholics as "quite intolerable," he stood firmly by the principles of the Catholic Revival and looked on his coming to Canterbury as in a sense an official endorsement of it. That there were differences between him and its later protagonists he recognised when he wrote in September 1929 to old Lord Halifax, in reply to a letter about the secession of Father Vernon:

I know well how constantly I must disappoint you and come short of what you would wish to be and do if you were in my place. But you can scarcely realise how constant are the limitations imposed by that care of all the churches which presses upon me daily—*all* the churches in this strange Anglican Communion, all the sorts of men and activities which have found a place within it. I confess I often find myself wishing that I could have been, or could still be, a free-lance, able to speak out my whole mind without the restraints of responsibility. It must be a great thing to be a prophet, even to be a priest with one's own sphere of quiet teaching and worship. It is a very different thing to be a ruler; but one can only trust in the guidance of the Divine Ruler of His Church and do one's best.

I like to think that our ultimate ideals are not widely different. Yours is a Catholicism more tinged perhaps than mine by the traditions of the Latin Church of the West; mine a type of Catholicism, not, I hope, heedless of that great tradition, but of a wider and more inclusive kind, one which is not yet realised, perhaps never can be realised, but in my dreams I seem to see more capable of realisation in the Anglican Church than elsewhere.

"He comes to his throne at an evil time," wrote Dr. Hensley Henson gloomily. "Since Cranmer's accession was there ever a darker outlook for the Church of England?" Of immediate and critical concern was the action that should follow the second rejection of the new Prayer Book, of which some account was given in Chapter XXV. The Archbishop, in what is clearly his final judgment on the whole matter, carries the tale a little further. Parliament, he points out, in refusing legal sanction to the Book had severely set back the relations of Church and State.

The question which immediately faced me on becoming Archbishop of Canterbury . . . was "What now was the Church to do?" There were three possible courses. The first was to take the decision of Parliament, so to say, lying down and to abandon the use of the Revised Book. This course was for many reasons really impossible. It would have left unchanged the problem which the Church had set itself to meet. The vote in Parliament in no way met it. The Royal Commission had acknowledged that the Act of Uniformity . . . was too strait and that the need of authorising supplementary services and of modification of the rubrics to meet the conditions of a new time ought to be met and had, so to say, directed the Church to endeavour to meet this need. It would have been inconsistent with the self-respect of the Church to abandon that endeavour. With what I then thought, and still think, was an act of great courage, Archbishop Davidson in his last speech to the Church Assembly had taken a step very remarkable for a man of his former outlook: he had declared that the Church had an inalienable right to determine its own modes of worship when its mind and will had been fully ascertained. If ever in the confused history of the Church of England that mind and will had been ascertained, it was in the consents of its representative bodies to the permissive use of the Revised Book. . . . Merely to acquiesce would have been expressly to disavow that right.

Secondly, there was the possibility of the opposite extreme course of ignoring the action of Parliament and boldly authorising the use of the Revised Book. This, indeed, was the course advocated, strangely enough, by Lord Birkenhead in a letter to the *Times*. But this would have been in my judgment a very undesirable direct defiance of and challenge to Parliament. I have always maintained that if Disestablishment were to come, it should come from the State itself, and that it might be the duty of the Church to make its own decision and go its own way and leave it to the State to determine what action it would take if it disapproved. But on this matter the Church had expressly asked the State to do what the Church wanted. Having done this and been refused, merely to ignore the refusal as if the request had never been made would have put the Church in the wrong and seemed indeed to be an act of undignified petulance.

There was a third possible course; and it was this which was ultimately adopted by the Bishops. It was generally admitted that they had by virtue of their office the duty of meeting the patent needs of the Church to implement the Act of Uniformity from time to time, by sanctioning or permitting additional services or variations from the text of the Book of 1662, and to do this by their administrative action. This had constantly been done for long years.

Accordingly, in Convocation of the summer of 1929 they had passed the resolutions given on page 309.

No doubt it was a somewhat makeshift course, but it has been at least in practice successful. Parts of the Book of 1928 have been widely followed in every Diocese; for example, the alternative offices of Baptism and Holy Matrimony are in very general use, though the whole of the alternative order of Holy Communion is not. And this has provoked no action on the part of either Parliament or the Courts of Law.

The Archbishop recognised with gratitude the restraint of the Book's antagonists in not challenging the Bishops' action and so provoking "a most awkward, even fateful, collision between the Church and the Law."

This third course was, I think, the only right one in the circumstances and it was justified by comparative success. But I have also called it "makeshift." It leaves big questions . . . unanswered. One of the most obvious of these is, What is really the true source of Authority in the Church of England? What is really the meaning of the words in the declaration made by every clergyman before Ordination or institution, that he will obey the Book of 1662 "except so far as may be ordered by lawful authority" ? What is this "lawful authority" ? The question touches every parson's conscience. Many answers may be and have been given. Archbishop Davidson used to tell his Ordinands : "For you it is sufficient to say 'the Bishop.'" I myself have always thought that the answer is what it would have been when the words were first used—the Privy Council.

For convenience, the rest of the story, with its inconclusive ending, may be taken here. In 1930, as the result of a Resolution of the Church Assembly, a Commission on the Relations between Church and State was appointed. It made a unanimous Report, in which it suggested that a Round Table Conference representing the various schools of thought should be convened. This was to consider, among other matters, permissible deviations from the Order of Holy Communion and the use and limits of Reservation. The other recommendations of the Commission, which concerned legislation, the Ecclesiastical Courts and a Synodical declaration, were not pursued. In 1938 the Archbishop summoned the Conference, which consisted of theological experts and representatives of every party. It met several times at Lambeth, under the Chairmanship of the Archbishop of York.

In some respects it seemed to make some progress, and on some points there seemed to be unexpected agreement. But . . . the old fact emerged that men were afraid of what they called "those with whom we are accustomed to associate"—in other words, that it is the tail that wags the dog, not the dog that wags the tail. Moreover, there was a perhaps natural tendency to wander off the point. Thus the going was hard, rather confused. Then the War broke out and the Commission had to be . . . suspended. So the point remained unsettled ; but sooner or later it must be tackled afresh.

The policy may have been "makeshift" ; it gave no final settlement to the Church ; but Lang remained convinced that in the hard circumstances of the time no other course had been possible. In a letter he wrote to Dr. Carnegie Simpson in 1943 he claimed that it had brought variations from the Prayer Book within reasonable and defensible limits and had given more peace than the Church had known for many years.

In May 1930 Lang's old comrade and chief in this bygone battle was
dying.

His (Davidson's) resignation had been a real pain to him, and he
always frankly confessed to me that he was never able to adjust
himself happily to the complete change in his life which it involved.
All his days he had been absorbed in his work. He had given his
whole being to it. His interests were almost wholly in affairs—the
affairs of Church and State—and in his contacts with the men who
were concerned in them. When he laid down his control of them,
he felt lost, as though he were moving in a strange world. He was
too old to take up new interests. He was pathetically eager, as long
as he had the strength, to preach or speak or attend meetings, to talk
to people about what was going on. Few things had given him more
pleasure than the peerage which enabled him to keep his place in the
House of Lords, and he would be seen day by day on the cross-
benches. He did not seem ready even to deal with his own papers
and memorials. . . . It was only when his strength finally failed that
quietly and simply he laid him down to die.

I saw him often in those last days, celebrated for him in his sick-
room, and gave him news about men and things such as he was always
eager to hear. The last time I saw him before consciousness left him,
the old man gave me his blessing, saying, as he laid his hand on my
head, in a faltering voice, "God give you judgment"—the gift he
had so abundantly received; was Elijah handing on his mantle to
Elisha?—and then added, "judgment—and mercy—and peace."
When I next saw him, on the eve of his final passing, he was unconscious. . . . The word which almost at once came to me was:
"He served his generation according to the Will and the Counsel of
God." It was only afterwards that I learned that this was the very
word which he had chosen in his address on his enthronement as
Archbishop to describe the ideal he put before him. I think it well
sums up the purpose of his life.

"I shall miss him terribly," Lang wrote to Wilfrid Parker, "as my
job is at best very solitary, and it seems more so now that I can no longer
resort to his wisdom and quite unrivalled experience."

In January 1932 he bade goodbye to an even older friend, Charles
Gore, with whom long ago, in his time of uncertainty, he had walked
and argued in Christ Church meadows. Since then, in friendship and

mutual respect, they had had many arguments. Standing by Gore's bed, Lang heard him say twice, "Transcendent glory!" before he died. Later, reading Dr. Prestige's Life, Lang lamented that Gore had ever shackled his prophetic gift by becoming a Bishop. "The restraints brought out all his testiness and petulance. Yet what a noble life! It humbles me."

In the same year old Lord Halifax paid his last visit to Lambeth. At ninety-three his balance was uncertain, while the Archbishop, barely recovered from his several illnesses, was nearly as shaky. As his guest was leaving, he gave him an arm down the flight of steps leading to the front door. Lord Halifax leaned with unexpected weight for so fragile a figure, the Archbishop stumbled, and the two of them rolled unceremoniously together to the bottom of the stairs, where they picked themselves up, unhurt and overcome with laughter.

Despite Lang's own sickness and the death of friends, he must plod on with his work, never sparing or satisfying himself. At Ballure that year he was once more overcome by a sense of his inadequacy and personal failure.

I ought to have thought and pondered more about the problems of Church and State at this very critical time. Perhaps the lack of mental energy is a sign of increasing years. But it is dangerous: it leaves me too dependent on meeting each call as it arises, too content to keep the ship moving somehow without a clear sense of the journey it ought to be taking. . . .

On October 31st he would be sixty-eight.

The thought humiliates, as I realise painfully how little progress and growth I can show in the inner life, how little I have been able to achieve in the life of the Church and the people. My chance is rapidly passing—how poorly used!

He was resolved to make his inner life more worthy, to give a steadier and stronger devotion to God's service, so that when his time came he might have less cause to be ashamed of what he had to offer.

Well, well, it is easy to feel all this, to desire it all. But I must do more, with God's help, to attain.

Chapter XXVIII

LAMBETH CONFERENCE (1930)

HOWEVER minor a landmark a Lambeth Conference may be in the history of the Church, in the rule of any Archbishop of Canterbury its importance is beyond dispute. He may look to preside once, and hardly more than twice, over the assembled Bishops of the Anglican Communion; and the Churches overseas at any rate are likely to assess him as an Archbishop largely by his success or failure as a Chairman during a few short weeks. Perhaps it is as well for him that the opportunity is limited, as the organisation of such a gathering is necessarily formidable. Davidson's resignation was dated to allow his successor time to prepare for 1930; and much had still to be done when the "growling" duodenal ulcer banished Lang to The Moorings for a month. Afterwards he was grateful for the respite, irksome as at first he found it. "I tremble to think," he wrote, "what might have happened, apart from health, if I had emerged into the Conference from that overcrowded June." As it was, he entered it with collected thoughts and weathered it without illness or even undue fatigue.

The strain of the Conference threatened to be so severe and the Archbishop's health was so uncertain that those nearest to him were full of apprehension. But their fears proved groundless. The Bishop of Chichester reported him as "rather frail and timid about himself at first, and pessimistic (apparently) as he had been the previous months about the likelihood of the Conference doing much useful work." But when it began to go well, the Bishop adds, "he grew better and stronger himself."

Behind him at Lambeth he left Mervyn Haigh to give the last touches to the arrangements, while Green-Wilkinson prepared for the entertainment of the 307 Bishops who were expected. Apart from the agenda, the appointments to committees, and all the minor multifarious details which needed attention, for the Archbishop there was the onerous responsibility of the host. The Conference had not quite discarded its character as the occasion when the senior Metropolitan of the Anglican Communion invited the other Bishops, in comparatively manageable numbers, to confer with him at Lambeth. In sixty years of steady and

343

continual expansion the numbers of Dioceses had risen to 146, and that of the Bishops attending from 76 in 1867 to 307 in 1930; so that the tax upon the resources of Canterbury had greatly increased. In 1930, for the first time and despite some doubts, financial assistance was officially offered to the Archbishop to enable him to discharge his duties as host, the Church Assembly voting two grants of £1000, out of which the cost of entertainment, printing, extra salaries and so forth was to be defrayed. The sum was of course quite inadequate. The expense of entertaining the Bishops to luncheon and tea every day over a period of five weeks alone amounted to £1400; and that was but one item in the Bill. Each overseas Bishop (with his wife, if he had one) was invited to spend a night at the Palace; and every evening there was a dinner party. The total expenditure under all headings amounted to much more than £2000, the balance being met by the Archbishop himself.

The catering was Green-Wilkinson's most stubborn problem, as none of the firms at first approached was ready to undertake the work at any price that was possible. At last he discovered some racecourse caterers, who accepted the contract and carried it out to the general satisfaction, the waitresses subsequently declaring that they "preferred Bishops to bookies."

The gathering opened with a devotional day at Fulham Palace. The address was given by old Bishop Talbot, "as almost the last survivor of those who had personal links with the Oxford Movement and the friend and disciple of Dean Church." He was eighty-six and had recently fallen, breaking his thigh; but he came, practically carried by his large son, the Bishop of Pretoria (Neville Talbot), and "the mere sight of the old man, with his rugged head and beard and clear voice, was more moving than any words."

On Saturday, July 5th, the Bishops were given a ceremonial welcome at Canterbury Cathedral, especial honour being paid to the Orthodox Delegation, headed by Meletios, Patriarch of Alexandria. Lang stood at St. Augustine's Chair to receive his guests.

> It was indeed moving to see this great company of Bishops from every part of the world slowly and with ordered dignity passing before me as I stood at that Chair.

The subject of the Conference was to be "The Faith and Witness of the Church in this generation"; and in the address which Lang gave he tried to strike the note he hoped to hear throughout. "It cannot be," he said, "that He means us to come and go and leave nothing but a string of platitudes behind us."

The ceremonies ended with a hymn, in which choir and congregation joined. "To me the most moving part of the service was the singing, strong, full, exultant, of Heber's hymn, 'Holy, Holy, Holy, Lord God Almighty,' immediately after the Creed."

Next day it was the turn of St. Paul's, the purpose being to associate the Conference with the reopening of the Cathedral after the extensive repairs to the Dome. "The Archbishop of York preached a fine sermon, well-delivered and closing with a noble passage which left its imprint on the mind of the Conference, repeating the words 'God reigns' like the sounding of a bell."

On Monday, July 7th, the Conference began with a plenary session of the 307 Bishops. The library, in which by tradition they met, could only just hold them all when some of the bookcases had been removed. Among the first necessary decisions were the appointment of the Bishop of Chichester as Episcopal Secretary and of Mervyn Haigh as his assistant; both of whom Lang was later to commend in the warmest terms.

As I surveyed the long rows, I thought of all the preparations which had been made, all the prayers which had been offered—my own constant prayers in the quiet of The Moorings—the great circle of intercessions which had surrounded us, the expectations, the long journeys which most of these men had made. And here at last was the Conference assembled. What would come of it?

He had approached the Conference with apprehension, expecting sharp divisions of opinion, particularly over Unity and South India. Much, he believed, would depend on the start, and this brought him some reassurance. "Very soon I began to feel that quietly, almost insensibly, a right spirit was moving."

The general theme of "The Faith and Witness of the Church" had been divided into six separate parts, each of which was to be the business of a Committee—The Christian Doctrine of God, The Life and Witness of the Christian Community, The Unity of the Church, The Anglican Communion, The Ministry, and Youth and its Vocation. During the first week set speeches were delivered on these different subjects. Lang thought these a little disappointing, although he excepted from criticism the speeches of the Archbishop of York and the Bishop of Gloucester (Dr. Headlam) on Unity, and the Bishop of Winchester's speech on Moral Witness. Some of the speakers were inclined to exceed the time allowed them, the worst offender being the Bishop of Pretoria, who went on for so long that the Chairman had to cut him short.

On Tuesday the 8th the Orthodox Delegation was formally received. This was a distinguished body, headed by the Patriarch Meletios and consisting of representatives of the four ancient Patriarchates and of the Churches of Rumania, Jugoslavia, Greece, Cyprus and Poland. Through some rather delicate diplomacy Bulgaria, which was in technical schism with the Oecumenical Patriarchate, was also represented, a circumstance which, Lang believed, contributed to an improvement in its relations with the other autocephalous Churches. In view of the continuing *rapprochement* between Anglicans and Orthodox, which had received so notable an impetus in 1920, considerable importance was attached to the presence of such a full and powerful Delegation. Alone among the Orthodox Russia was unrepresented. "It proved impossible—and I did not encourage the attempt—to get any representative of the Russian Church. The difficulties with the Soviet Government and the rivalries of the two sections of the Church among the *émigrés* in Europe (Evlogie and Antonin) stood in the way." Lang records his debt to Canon J. A. Douglas for his advice and help. "He spared no pains, and his expert knowledge of the internal ways of these Easterns was invaluable."

On the 16th the Old Catholics arrived and were welcomed. Their representatives were the Archbishop of Utrecht and the Bishops of Haarlem and Deventer—"very humble-looking little gentlemen in their frock-coats, in contrast with the resplendent Orthodox." They were entertained to dinner that evening, Lang feeling very much ashamed that the rustiness of his French and German, much neglected since the days of his youthful journeys on the Continent, made conversation difficult with these and with his other foreign guests. However, he got through fairly well, supplementing the efforts of his interpreter with nods and smiles, and for the Orthodox the inevitable embrace.

On Monday, July 14th, the Committees began their work, which was to last for a fortnight, during which the President was left fairly free to look after the entertainment of his guests. He was, of course, available for consultation and paid an occasional visit to any Committees which found themselves in rough water; but for the most part he left them to pursue their labours undisturbed. On Wednesday the 23rd the Bishops were received by the King and Queen at Buckingham Palace. Afterwards Lang suggested to the King that the visit had been a good lesson in geography; to which His Majesty replied: "I know more about it even than you—you see, I collect stamps!"

As the Committees began to send in their Reports, the points of possible contention appeared. The Report on "The Christian Doctrine of God" was, Lang thought, a little disappointing, that on "The Anglican Communion" was good. The Committee on "The Ministry" had produced a useful piece of work, though Part I was "rather inconclusive about Voluntary Clergy." Part II, dealing with a more controversial question, "had, as it left the Committee, a long paragraph, the work I believe of Truro, about the 'theological' grounds of objection to the admission of women to the priesthood, which got the Report into trouble at the Conference and was finally omitted." "Youth and its Vocation" was "perhaps inevitably disappointing," in Lang's view largely through weak handling by the Chairman, the Bishop of London.

The two critical Committees were those on "The Unity of the Church" and on "The Life and Witness of the Christian Community." The Committee on Unity had seventy-three members and was presided over by the Archbishop of York. It separated into two sub-committees, one to study relations with non-Episcopal Churches, under the Chairmanship of Dr. Temple himself, the other relations with Episcopal Churches, the Chairman being the Bishop of Gloucester.

The Archbishop of York's Report was "a wonderful example of his power of pouring out lucid statements on any subject." If a little long, it was very able and "held the Committee." Over South India, on which Lang had anticipated the most serious trouble, a remarkable unanimity was reached, the *deus ex machina* being the Bishop of Chichester, "who brought all round," and the decisive point being "the discovery that the South Indian Church was to be a province not of the Anglican Communion, but, independently, of the Universal Church." Lang had himself invited Dr. John White of the Barony, first Moderator of the united Church of Scotland, and introduced him to the Committee, with agreeable though not very conclusive results. "The one unsatisfactory feature of this Committee's work was the reception of the delegation of the Federal Council of Evangelical Free Churches in England. It was not successful and left an unhappy impression." The failure, Lang thought, was partly due to the timing, the delegation arriving before some of the Bishops had become sufficiently familiar with the background of the problem, and partly to the insistence of Dr. Carnegie Simpson in pressing the logical point that if the Free Churches

347

already possessed "real ministries of the Word and Sacraments," they had nothing further to gain from Episcopal Ordination. "This so annoyed and perplexed the Committee that it left out from its final Report a balanced endorsement of the memorandum on existing Ministries in our 1921-1925 Conferences and fell back simply on the words of the Appeal of 1920 about 'spiritual efficacy.'" Dr. Carnegie Simpson retired to underline the omission in an article he wrote for the *British Weekly.* "All this will make resumption of these conferences difficult. Some of the Bishops were so distressed by this interview that they formally begged me to invite the delegation to the concluding Service in the Abbey. But on reflexion—especially as I would have had to point out that only the Bishops could communicate and this might create fresh misunderstandings—I did not do so."

The Report on the Episcopal Churches, which was mainly the work of the Bishop of Gloucester, was "admirable."

All were loud in praise of Gloucester's handling of the matter and of Chichester's drafting of the summaries. On the last day of the Committee's interview with the Orthodox Delegation I went into the drawing-room to express my gratitude to all. Meletios replied, showing that he was greatly pleased and would go away with high hopes that further steps towards fuller unity would soon—and especially at the proposed Pro-Synod—be taken. Then we all went into the Chapel. I offered Thanksgivings at the Altar, robed and with Cross and Pectoral Chain. Meletios (with me in the Sanctuary) offered prayers in Greek and we each gave a Blessing. A very sincere and rather moving Service.

When the complete Report went before the Conference in full session, it had a most favourable reception, the Resolution on South India in particular arousing satisfaction that "where division had once been feared, there should be unanimity."

The Committee on "The Life and Witness of the Christian Community" fell into the gravest trouble. The Reports of the sub-committees on Race and on Peace and War called for little comment. The first was "good up to a point, but not very effective," the second was "well arranged and well put." The sub-committee on Marriage and Sex, after recalling the teaching of Our Lord, recommended "that the marriage of one whose former partner is still living should not be celebrated according to the rites of the Church"; and that when the innocent party in a divorce remarried under civil sanction and subsequently desired to receive Holy Communion, the case should be referred for consideration to the Bishop, subject to provincial regulations.

It is perhaps a reflexion on the attitude of the Press towards the Conference that a single paragraph in the Report of this sub-committee was given more attention than anything else that happened at Lambeth. The paragraph dealt with Birth Control, and whatever view may be taken of its wisdom and rightness, it suffered by removal from its background and a certain amount of misrepresentation. In view of the widespread criticism that followed and still survives, it may be not out of place to recall what the sub-committee actually said. This was that "there are circumstances in married life which justify, and even demand, the limitation of the family by *some* means." What mattered, of course, was the motive. If this was the evasion of parenthood, it was wrong; if it was "pleasure or self-indulgence," it was wrong; but equally it was wrong for intercourse to take place "which might lead to conception, where a birth would involve grave danger to the health, even to the life, of the mother, or would inflict upon the child to be born a life of suffering; or where the mother would be prematurely exhausted, and additional children would render her incapable of carrying out her duties to the existing family." In such circumstances the proper course was abstinence; yet moral situations existed "which may make it obligatory to use other methods." While this obligation must be affected by medical and scientific advice, "the final decision must still be determined by reference to the spiritual ends for which marriage was ordained." Therefore married people should ask themselves: "Would conception be for any reason wrong? If it would clearly be wrong, and if there is a good moral reason why the way of abstinence should not be followed, we cannot condemn the use of scientific methods to prevent conception, which are thoughtfully and conscientiously adopted." In the sub-committee's view the principle was: "Children are the primary end of the intercourse to which marriage leads. Married people do wrong when they refuse to have children whom they could train to serve God and add to the strength of the nation. But intercourse has also a secondary end within the natural Sacrament of marriage. Where for any morally sound reason the first end is to be ruled out, it does not necessarily follow that the secondary end must be ruled out also, provided that self-control is exercised and husband and wife have truly examined their consciences upon the matter."

Without entering into argument on a much-disputed question, it is to be observed that opposition, both inside and outside the Conference, was chiefly to the claim that "moral situations" do or can exist "which make it obligatory to use other methods" than abstinence. Some members of the Committee itself dissented to the point of asking the Archbishop either to omit their names from the published list of those taking part or to allow their individual disagreement to be recorded. Lang appears to have been curiously uninterested in the points at issue. As President, he interpreted his duty as being rather to arrive at a conclusion satisfactory to a substantial majority than to give a clear lead on a grave moral issue. The final form of the Resolution was only reached after some very exhausting negotiations, and having, as it were, discovered the highest (or lowest) common denominator, he was ready to give it his official support. He refused the dissentients' request, because he thought it would be unfair to the Committee to imply that the opposing opinion had not been represented on it, and also because a record of dissent by giving names or by a minority report would be an undesirable precedent. The full Conference, however, referred back the controversial paragraph for redrafting, eventually passing it in its amended form by 193 votes to 67. The verdict so displeased the Bishop of Bloemfontein (Dr. Walter Carey) that he withdrew in protest and was impervious to Lang's persuasions, not only refusing to attend the final Service in Westminster Abbey, but even sending a petition on the subject to the King.

Dr. Carey was the only casualty, but just when it seemed that every obstacle had been cleared and the course was open, some of the other Bishops, on quite different grounds, threatened to follow his example.

Meanwhile a trouble had been brewing, leading to the most awkward incident in the Conference. It arose over Resolution 42, dispensing from the rule that Anglicans must only receive the Holy Communion from priests in or in communion with the Anglican Church, in special areas. . . . York conveyed to me an intimation from the Metropolitans and Presiding Bishops that several Bishops had told them they were so greatly concerned about the passing of that Resolution that they meditated withdrawal and absence from the final Service in the Abbey. The only inkling of this I had had was a letter from Korea (Dr. Trollope) written from Cuddesdon, saying he had gone and could take no further part.

Apparently some thirty or forty Bishops were feeling uncomfortable and wanted the Resolution reconsidered. When Lang objected, pointing out that it had been carried by a large majority, the Bishops replied that the atmosphere created by the South Indian Resolution had "rather hypnotised" them. After some parleying with the Metropolitans, Lang decided he would not try to reason with the "rebels," but would leave it to the Conference to settle whether the question was to be reopened. The Conference, after hearing a very forthright speech from its President, agreed with him by a large majority, an explanatory note was added to placate the malcontents, and there were no further withdrawals.

During these last days, with all the coming and going, protest and counter-protest, departures and returns, the Archbishop must sometimes have felt as though he were playing croquet with the Queen of Hearts. It will be recalled that when Alice got the flamingo-mallet into position, she would find that the hedgehog-ball had crawled away; and that by the time she had retrieved it, the soldier-hoop had moved off to another part of the ground. However, more fortunate than Alice, the Archbishop at last reached the happy position when flamingo, hedgehog and soldier were all in place and the ground was clear for publication of the full Report and the Encyclical Letter which was to introduce it. The Letter was the work of several hands, and particularly those of Bishop Palmer and the present Bishop of Winchester, but the structure and phrasing owed much to the Archbishop himself. In 1920, it suggested, the pervading idea had been *fellowship*; in 1930 it was *witness*. So the appeal of the Conference began with a short restatement of the Christian doctrine of God, passing from that to the life and witness of the community. It reasserted the sanctity of marriage, of the family, of sex, and of parenthood. It condemned racial discrimination and "war as a means of settling international disputes." Passing on to the question of Unity, the Letter recapitulated the sequels to the Appeal to all Christian People, particularly welcoming the presence at Lambeth of the Orthodox and Old Catholic Delegations, and commending the proposal to appoint commissions of theologians with a view to the restoration of Communion. It described the South Indian scheme and rejoiced "that one part of the Anglican Communion should be found ready to make this venture." It was, broadly speaking, a plan for unity into which the Churches coming together would gradually grow. "It will have a very real inter-communion with the Churches of the Anglican Communion, though for a time that inter-communion will be limited in certain directions by their rules." By comparison, the reference to the approaches to the non-Episcopal Churches in Britain were brief and appeared a little tepid. On the Anglican Communion, the Ministry, and Youth the Letter had less to say. The Conference recommended that while the work of women should be enlarged, they should still be confined to the Order of Deaconesses. In conclusion the Letter returned to its opening theme of the corporate witness of the Church.

To this summary Lang's comments may be added.

Friday, August 8th, was given to the Encyclical Letter. Palmer with great vigour and his usual patience and sometimes humour piloted it. On the whole, the Bishops dealt reasonably with it. Only very few tried to get in edifying thoughts which had occurred to themselves. Some real improvements were made. Poor Croydon had to see his glowing appeal to Youth cut short. Bishops have a dislike of what seems "high-falutin'." I think they might have spared those few flowers. I had concluded with "Arise, shine, for Thy light is come," etc., to which the preceding words were meant to lead; but Norwich got the present last words substituted—quite good.

The Letter had a more favourable reception from the leading newspapers than I expected, and it has some merits. But it is too long and wordy. Ten years hence the character of this Letter should be reconsidered. That of 1920 and this of 1930 fall between the two stools of exhortation or edification and information—too much of the former, too little of the latter. When this Letter of 1930 is read, ordinary people (who won't read or can't really understand the Resolutions as a whole) will have little idea of what the Conference actually did. I think that the main things which the Conference really decides should be tersely stated in a framework of exhortation.

Of the Archbishop himself the Bishop of Chichester records the general feeling that he had been "an admirable Chairman," if perhaps a little too indulgent to some of the more lengthy speakers.

As part of the concluding business the Conference presented its President with a Pastoral Staff; and on Sunday, August 10th, the Bishops, except Dr. Carey and those who had already had to leave by sea for their distant Dioceses, met in Westminster Abbey for the parting Service.

The main impression left on my mind was the good *spirit* of the Conference. The Bishops represented every type of Anglican churchmanship. Differing views were frankly expressed. As I have shown, there were some moments of rather acute strain. But I cannot remember a single word lacking in charity or considerateness. It was difficult to discover any clear divisions into "Catholic," "Evangelical" or "Modernist." On the few occasions when strain was felt, there was with it an immediately felt desire to prevent the strain getting near a real breaking point. I can say quite simply that it was a company of Christian gentlemen; and I was proud of the tone and temper of my brethren. The letters I have received, the words spoken to me, made it clear that the Bishops left for their distant parts with the sense that a real fellowship of spirit had bound them together. The difficulties of a very few made the contrast with the general feeling more marked. If the future of the Churches of the Anglican Communion follows at all the lines that seemed to be foreshadowed in this Conference, the link of the Bishops in Council will become all-important; and in view of this future it is encouraging to know that the Conference of 1930 proved that this link is real and strong.

As to the actual work of the Conference, I am no good judge; I write too soon after our meeting. The history of the next ten years will test it. Certainly, the clearer conception, realised and expressed, of the ideal and future of the Anglican Communion was of great value. On some delicate matters, such as Birth Control, the majority of the Bishops showed courage and gave advice which, when it is understood, will prove to have been timely and worth giving. Strong and true things were said about Race and War. There was certainly a remarkable strengthening of our relations with the Orthodox Churches, which may have important consequences; and the lines of the advice about South India may bear fruit, perhaps with some acute difficulties added, in other regions. In this quest for Unity, to which the Lambeth Conference, and I hope the Anglican Communion, is pledged, we certainly did not simply stand still and repeat old aspirations. We took definite steps forward. And—to repeat the thought again—it was shown that beneath and behind all its divisions of place and problems and outlook and opinion, the Anglican Communion, at least as represented by its Bishops, has a character and ideal and unity of its own. I do not say that we rose to all expectations. I dare say we made some mistakes. I am sure that, being very fallible men, we missed many opportunities. We may

z

have shown little prophetic power. But I hope we did not wholly fail to fulfil whatever purpose God had for our Conference.

This contemporary comment, written at Ballure immediately after the close of the Conference, was naturally influenced by the emotion of the moment. The critics outside were more dispassionate, some disliking what had been done and others what had been omitted. Mr. T. S. Eliot, in his "Thoughts After Lambeth," gave a balanced judgment. "The Church of England washes its dirty linen in public . . ." he wrote. "In contrast to some other institutions both civil and ecclesiastical, the linen does get washed." With some of the conclusions reached and many of the opinions offered he disagreed, but added that the Conference "has affirmed, beyond previous Conferences, the Catholicity of the Church; and in spite of defects and dubious statements in detail, the Report will have strengthened the Church both within and without."

It is hard to assess the lasting value of the Conference of 1930, especially as, before the Bishops could meet again at Lambeth, a new war was to shake the world and largely to destroy the secular pattern on which they had worked. Old problems were to recede: new problems were to appear. The decision on South India was obviously important; the relations with Orthodox and Old Catholics were carried a stage further; the much criticised Report on Youth has paternal rights in the Youth Council of the Church; but nineteen years after the event any larger claim to visible results is not easy to support.

Yet this may be to underrate the achievement. The guidance of such a gathering, representing men of opinion so varied coming from every quarter of the world, must tax the ability of any Archbishop; and at times Lang's notes almost suggest the thought that any Conference would be a success which neither contented itself with "a string of platitudes" nor broke up in a disorder of conflicting views. By such a test—and in the circumstances it may not be dismissed as negligible— the President did his part and the Conference had no cause to be ashamed of its work. If it had said less, it would have said very little; and if it had tried to say more, it might have ended by saying nothing.

Chapter XXIX

REUNION

DURING twenty-five years of renewed opportunity the cause of Reunion owed much to the presence, first at York and then at Canterbury, of so faithful and persevering a champion as Cosmo Lang. His service to Christian unity was his greatest contribution to the Church. That is the judgment of those who knew him best; and he would, we may assume, have accepted the verdict. Amid all the business and care of his office, the cause was never far from his mind or his prayers; nor did he fail to seize any chance he saw of furthering it.

In Chapter XXIII some account was given of the "Appeal to all Christian People" and its sequels in the years that followed. The approach to Rome had ended for the time with the death of Cardinal Mercier and the close of the Conversations at Malines. The *rapprochement* with the Orthodox, on the other hand, had gone steadily forward. The Delegation which had been at Lambeth reported back, and two years later the Oecumenical Patriarch informed Archbishop Davidson of the Holy Synod's conclusion, after examination of the Anglican Orders, that they had the same validity as those of the Roman, Old Catholic and Armenian Churches. An Encyclical to this effect was sent to the heads of all the autocephalous Churches, and the same opinion was given by the Patriarch of Jerusalem and the Archbishop of Cyprus.

Although in their relations with other Communions the Orthodox Churches always insist on the importance of full dogmatic agreement as the first essential step towards inter-communion, in practice they do not take up a legalistic attitude. By virtue of the principle of Economy they are able to set aside the regular rules and customs of the Church when such action appears necessary to its good or the welfare of individual souls. According to the Report of the Lambeth Conference of 1948, Economy is "a technical term representing administrative action to meet a temporary situation without prejudice to any principle of administrative order." The region of dogma is outside its scope. By the exercise of Economy, therefore, a verdict favourable to Anglican Orders had been given by the Oecumenical Patriarch, who holds a primacy of honour among the Orthodox, and by the Churches of Jerusalem and Cyprus; to be followed later by that of Alexandria.

It is to be noted, however, that the other autocephalous Churches still held their hands; and also that recognition itself, while a necessary stage on the road to inter-communion, is not the end of the journey. The next event of importance was the celebration of the anniversary of the Council of Nicaea in Westminster Abbey in 1925, when representatives of several of the Orthodox Churches were present. Canon J. A. Douglas, who took so prominent a part in the movement towards unity and had been sent on a preliminary reconnaissance of the Eastern Churches, emphasises the significance of this occasion. The arrangements for it had been far from easy. On the advice of Archbishop Germanos, *apokrisarios* of the Oecumenical Patriarch, and by what was probably an error of judgment, the Orthodox were asked to the celebrations through Constantinople. From there the invitation to Russia went not to the Metropolitan Sergius in Moscow, but to the Metropolitan Antony of Kiev, the head of the Russian Council of Bishops at Karlovci, who recognised neither Sergius nor the Soviet régime. Whereupon the Serbian Patriarchate, which was especially sensitive on the subject, took umbrage and refused to send a representative. Elsewhere, however, the idea was received with enthusiasm. The Service was an unequivocal success. The Patriarchs of Alexandria and Jerusalem, the Metropolitans Antony and Evlogie, Archbishop Söderblom of Upsala (Sweden) and the Mar Shimun of the Assyrian Church were in the company at Westminster Abbey. No formal discussions were attempted during the visit, but an atmosphere was created favourable to further developments. These, it was hoped, would come from the Lambeth Conference of 1930, which eventually was attended by a Delegation representing all the autocephalous Churches except Russia.

With the Old Catholics the road was easier and the pace was faster. In 1925 the Archbishop of Utrecht wrote to the Archbishop of Canterbury:

The Old Catholic Church of Utrecht has hitherto been in doubt as to the validity of Anglican Orders. . . . After long enquiry and serious deliberation, and after consultation with our clergy, we have reached a decision which we hereby communicate to Your Grace. . . . We believe that the Church of England has wished always to maintain the episcopal rule of the Church of antiquity and that the Edwardine formula of consecration must be accounted valid. We therefore declare without reservation that the Apostolic Succession has not been broken in the Church of England.

Later in the same year this decision was endorsed by the Old Catholic Bishops of Germany and Switzerland and by an International Congress of Old Catholics at Berne; and in 1930 a Delegation arrived at Lambeth.

Other Churches of the Continent had also heard the Appeal. In 1920 the Bishops of Durham and Peterborough had assisted at the Consecration of two Swedish Bishops at Upsala, and seven years later a Swedish Bishop took part in the Consecration of the Bishop of Dover (Dr. John Macmillan) at Canterbury—acts of inter-consecration which opened a new relationship between the Church of England and the Scandinavian Churches.

As was related in Chapter XXIII, conversations with the Free Churchmen of England went on for five years, some advance in understanding and agreement being recorded before the exchanges ended on a note of controversy about Ordination. They had not been resumed, partly possibly because during the next four years the Church of England was preoccupied with the new Prayer Book; partly, too, because it was felt by many that while some progress had been made, a "cooling off" period was desirable, to enable the arguments on either side to be properly considered and to allow the rank and file to catch up with their leaders. At the same time the South India Scheme, in which both the Church of England and the Free Churches were interested, had continued to move forward.

The Church of Scotland, it will be recalled, had been polite but non-committal in its response to the Appeal. At the time the union of the Established and the United Free Churches was nearing consummation; and in 1929, when this was finally effected, Lang, as Archbishop of Canterbury, attended the celebration in Edinburgh. His presence and speech were little more than a courteous gesture, and privately he showed some disappointment at the degree of dignity accorded at the ceremonies to the successor of St. Augustine—or, he might have said, of William Laud.

Such was the position at home and abroad when the Bishops came to Lambeth in 1930 with the hope and purpose of a further advance. Little as Lang mentions the matter in his notes, there is no questioning that he gave the whole subject a great deal of thought and careful preparation. The forward movement was to continue to follow certain broad principles. To some extent he may be said to have formed these when first the problems of Reunion claimed his attention, but undoubtedly the experience of ten years had strengthened some and modified others.

The first of these principles was the need to avoid undue haste. Lang could sympathise with those, like old Lord Halifax, who were anxious for quick results; but his historical sense warned him not to try to find a short cut to the goal he sought. The divisions were too old and deep, and it was futile to hope to change the work of centuries in a few years. The leaders themselves were nervous, still rather suspicious of each other, and very ready to recoil if they believed they were being "rushed"; while the people often lagged far behind them in thought and opinion. A position, when reached, must therefore be consolidated before any further advance should be hazarded. Lang would sometimes recall the advice Jowett had once given him in a different context—"Don't expect too much and don't attempt too little." The work must go steadily on, without remission, without hurry, and without disappointment at setback or an apparent slowing of the pace. Under Divine Providence Reunion, as Lang saw it, would come not by a sudden conversion, but through a slow growing together of the separated Churches.

A second principle has been described by Canon Douglas as *Nihil Christiani a me alienum*. Some Churches were obviously nearer unity than were others; some indeed were so remote in faith and order from the Church of England as almost to forbid the thought of any immediate approach. But Lang would exclude no one from the opportunity of sharing in this adventure of "growing together." The upshot was beyond his power to foresee or to determine; but in the Universal Church of his dream and desire were many mansions.

His third principle was tactical. It was always tempting, when a negotiation was started, to use for it those most likely to be in sympathy with it, to send Anglo-Catholics to meet Latins or Orthodox, and Evangelicals to treat with Lutherans, Presbyterians or Free Churchmen. Lang believed that any advantage so gained would be illusory, since delegates, chosen in this fashion, were always liable to exceed their instructions and to lead where their constituents—or a large section of them—were unwilling to follow. They might also, quite unconsciously, convey to those they met a false impression of the Church of England, that it was predominantly Catholic, with an insignificant Protestant rump, or mainly Evangelical, with a scanty Catholic fringe. Sooner or later a halt would be called and a negotiation, ending abruptly in this way, might leave behind it a resentment, even a feeling that duplicity had been practised. That was the lesson of the Conversations at Malines; and Lang was therefore emphatic that any future approach from the Anglican side must be made not by a section, but by the whole Church.

A fourth principle naturally followed. The right hand must not only know what the left hand was doing, but must never spoil its work. One set of negotiations must not prejudice another or even be inconsistent with it. At the root of the problem of Reunion everywhere lay the question of the Ministry, to Orthodox, Old Catholics and Anglicans the very gate of the Church, but to those with less or no regard for the Apostolic Succession an awkward if not an impassable barrier. To overlook this difference in outlook in any negotiation that might be attempted was to court an unhappy, possibly a disastrous, breach in a renewed relationship elsewhere.

From all this, if accepted, it followed that nothing was to be gained and much might be lost by trying to secure concessions for which opinion in another Church was as yet unready. A concession so made and later repented would be an obstacle to further progress. The most difficult man is always he who suspects, rightly or wrongly, that he has been "out-smarted." Inviting opportunities might therefore have to be forgone and an immediate benefit sacrificed to the ultimate advantage.

With these ideas in the forefront of his mind, the Archbishop laid his plans for the Conference of 1930. He was anxious not to force the issue of Anglican Orders with the Orthodox. Meletios's action after 1920 had not been an unmixed blessing. Some of the other Orthodox Churches had resented it as an exercise of a quasi-papal power to which he was not entitled and as a breach of the principle of oecumenicity, by which all the Churches should be consulted before important decisions are taken. Some did not even reply to his invitation to concur with the verdict of the Holy Synod of Constantinople.

Two distinct lines of approach were now possible. The first was the direct method of obtaining an assent gradually, and as the result of an expanding relationship, from the different Churches. The second was by an extension of mutual consecration, especially with the Old Catholics, whose Succession was recognised by the Orthodox, so that eventually, whatever view might be taken of the original validity of Anglican Orders, they might in time acquire a footing identical with that of a

Church whose Orders were not questioned. Lang was, and remained, more than a little dubious of this second course. He would never have admitted that Anglican Orders required any external reinforcement, but he was quite ready, for the quieting of uneasy consciences abroad, that the method should be explored. The first need, he felt, was to go slowly. "In all this perplexity," Canon Douglas writes, "Lang's cautious wisdom held us back from rushing things."

The ground had to be properly prepared. Opportunity had been taken at the World Conference on Faith and Order at Lausanne in 1927 to broach to Orthodox and Old Catholics the idea of sending Delegations to Lambeth in 1930. The representatives of both Churches were sympathetic, the Old Catholics in particular intimating a readiness to enter into an agreement for full intercommunion of a kind which would not disturb the Evangelicals. The position with the Orthodox was unlikely to be quite so easy, and once more Canon Douglas was sent out on reconnaissance. At Alexandria he obtained a promise of attendance from Meletios, formerly Patriarch of Constantinople; and among the Balkan Churches he found a general readiness, under Economy, to accept the validity of Anglican Orders and Sacramental Ministrations and to authorise resort to the latter in spiritual emergency or isolation. Everywhere, however, it was impressed on him that the Conference must offer an interpretation of the Anglican formularies which would make it plain that the dogmatic tradition of the Church of England was not inconsistent with that of the Orthodox Church, especially in regard to the nature of the Sacred Ministry.

In all the preparations that followed some inconvenience was caused by the Archbishop's illness; and to this may perhaps be attributed the lapse by which invitations to the Orthodox were again sent through the Oecumenical Patriarch. However, since this time the Russian Church was not asked, the complication of 1925 was not repeated. A powerful Delegation, headed by Meletios of Alexandria, came to Lambeth, where it held four Conferences with the Sub-Committee on Relations with Episcopal Churches, of which the Bishop of Gloucester was Chairman. The choice of Dr. Headlam to preside over this important branch of the Committee on the Unity of the Church was in accord with the Archbishop's third principle, but was a cause of some anxiety. The Bishop's Bampton Lectures were susceptible to the interpretation that all Orders, however conferred, episcopally or otherwise, were valid, and such a view, if pressed, would gravely disturb the Orthodox (among others).

The risk, however, was taken and all went well. The Orthodox were undisturbed and the Evangelicals, who might have been suspicious with another Chairman, were satisfied.

Accord was reached on a number of important points. It was proposed and agreed that a Joint Theological Commission, appointed by the Archbishop of Canterbury and the Oecumenical Patriarch ("acting in conjunction with the other Patriarchs and Autocephalous Churches") should examine the "theological relations" of the two Communions, subsequently reporting upon them to the Pro-Synod of the Orthodox Church, which was due to meet shortly,[1] and either to the Lambeth Conference or to the Synods of the Anglican Churches.

It was further proposed that the Terms of Inter-Communion drawn up at the request of the Eastern Churches Committee and published in 1921 should be taken as the basis of discussion. The Orthodox Delegates, while disclaiming power to accept these terms, agreed that they were a satisfactory basis of discussion, but stipulated that additional information should be given on the subjects of the Holy Eucharist and Ordination.

Some questions were mutually asked and answered on these, and also on authority in the Church, on discipline, and on the negotiations with non-Episcopal Churches. Lang's occasional intervention was required in these discussions, his continual anxiety being to allay the qualms of the Evangelicals. Some of them, for example, led by the Archbishop of Armagh (Dr. D'Arcy), were disquieted by the Orthodox statement that the Eucharist is a sacrifice for the living and the dead; but Dr. D'Arcy yielded to Lang's exposition so far as to say, "If that's all they mean, I see no objection." As to the negotiations with non-Episcopal Churches, Meletios volunteered the opinion that that kind of activity was fairly covered by the practice of Economy.

The explanations being found satisfactory, the conversations closed very happily, the Orthodox Delegation, subject to the verdict of the forthcoming Pro-Synod, expressing a favourable view both on Orders and on the use of the Sacramental Ministrations of the Anglican Church in cases of need and when no Orthodox priest was available.

The Committee's Report was unanimous and was accepted by the full Conference with only five dissentients. The various Orthodox Churches also gave its contents a cordial reception; and on December 25th, 1930, the Patriarch Meletios wrote to the Archbishop to report the decision of the "Holy Synod of the Metropolitans of the Apostolic and

---

[1] It never did meet.

Patriarchal Throne of Alexandria" to recognise "the validity, as from the Orthodox point of view, of the Anglican Ministry." A small minority of theologians, especially in Rumania, were critical, but the great majority assented. Yet Canon Douglas on his next journey discovered that resentment at the action of the Oecumenical Patriarch in 1922 was still an impediment; that the Serbs and Bulgars were unwilling to act without Russia; and that in Athens a strong body of opinion was inclining to the view that the points raised could only be settled by a Pan-Orthodox Conference. To this the objections were obvious. No one but the Oecumenical Patriarch could properly convene such a Conference, and the Turks were most unlikely to give him the necessary permission. The Serbs and Bulgars would not come without the Russians, and the Soviet Government would certainly refuse to allow the Metropolitan of Moscow to attend a gathering where he would meet and talk with all sorts of undesirable and unfriendly foreigners.

The next step was the Joint Theological Commission proposed by the Lambeth Conference. It met in London in 1931, all the Orthodox Churches except Russia sending Delegates. The Archbishop had carefully chosen the Anglican team. Dr. Headlam was Chairman and the Evangelicals were well represented. The findings did not amount to very much, but some doubtful points were cleared up and the Orthodox members went away satisfied. In accordance with his third and fourth principles, the Archbishop was careful to prevent the Evangelicals being pressed further than they—or their supporters outside—wished to go, particularly over the authority of Holy Scripture as compared with the tradition of the Church. When Canon Douglas showed him the draft of an agreement which Headlam had actually accepted, he read it with "a glint in his eye" and said, "We can't betray our historic position. The Church of England stands or falls by the paramountcy of God's Word. I won't let you give it away."

Two years later an important move was made on the Anglican side when the Council on Foreign Relations was set up by vote of the Church Assembly. The project had been long in debate, but Davidson never favoured it, feeling that relations with Continental Churches were the personal responsibility of the Archbishop and that a Council of the sort proposed might develop into an ecclesiastical Foreign Office. Lang was at first inclined to the same view, but accepted the opinion of the Assembly. As he mentions in his notes, he "was always careful to insist that it (the Council) could not take the place of that personal action or advice on the part of the Archbishop which these (Continental) Churches always particularly valued." Within this limitation, and with Dr. Headlam as Chairman and Canon Douglas as Honorary General Secretary, the Council "did a great deal of very useful work." Canon Douglas adds that the Archbishop kept it to its functions as a discussing and advisory body and was always in the background of its deliberations. The arrangement worked admirably. "In all my life I have never had a leader who so knew how to use his subordinates and make them feel that they were not pawns but members of teams."

Meanwhile the quiet, steady approach went on. In 1935 the Archbishop commissioned a Delegation to visit the Rumanian Church, which was one of those that had not signified its recognition of Anglican Orders. Canon Douglas having prepared the ground with another journey, the Delegation, which was led by the Bishop of Lincoln (Dr. Hicks) went to Bucharest, where it was hospitably and even enthusiastically received and entertained. The discussions were long and difficult, as some of the more rigorous of the Rumanian theologians were reluctant to concede anything. Nevertheless a settlement was reached, recognising the Anglican Orders, by Economy and in accord with the Lambeth meetings. When this agreement came before the Convocations of Canterbury and York for ratification, it encountered some opposition, due, in Canon Douglas's opinion, to the fact that the Evangelicals had been inadequately represented in the Anglican Delegation. With acceptance, Rumania joined Constantinople, Jerusalem, Cyprus and Alexandria in an acknowledgment by Economy of Anglican Orders and Ministrations.

In 1936 Miron Cristea, Patriarch of the Rumanian Church, paid a visit of courtesy to Lambeth. Lang made an excellent host on such occasions, Canon Douglas noting that the Orthodox were attracted by him and "sensed in him a kindred mystic soul under the severe, official, formal mask of his face and in spite of his apparent lack of effusiveness. Somehow or other he disliked kissing and the other gestures which are to the Easterns what handshaking is to us."

As to the other Balkan Churches, which were slower in moving, the exchange of visits continued, Anglican and Orthodox theologians meeting and conferring at Sofia, Belgrade and Athens. From Jugoslavia and Bulgaria recommendations were forthcoming for a recognition of Anglican Orders; and in Greece an exhaustive enquiry undertaken in 1939 by members of the Theological Faculty of the University of

Athens, an extremely influential body, gave a similarly favourable verdict. The whole process was then interrupted by the outbreak of war, which not only postponed the Lambeth Conference of 1940, but necessarily halted the exchange of visits and negotiations. Lang sent a last Delegation, led by Dr. Headlam, to the Balkans in 1940, but this had a political as well as an ecclesiastical purpose, being partially designed to counteract Axis propaganda. In this it seems to have met with some success. "Everywhere," Canon Douglas writes, "Lang's name was a talisman."

The cruises in *Corsair* had a part—in Canon Douglas's view a very important part—in this business of "growing together." The journeys to Athens, Constantinople and Jerusalem were far more than sightseeing and left a lasting impression on those cities. In the eyes of the Orthodox the Western Patriarch was paying a formal, ceremonial visit to his brethren of the East. Almost as helpful was the continual entertainment at Lambeth of visiting Orthodox dignitaries. Lang may have found the frequent exchange of the kiss of peace a little irksome, but he was too good a host to omit any compliment that might gratify his guests.

Unhappily he was not allowed to finish the story and to set the seal upon the work of twenty years. He was planning a further move forward in the Lambeth Conference of 1940, when the ragged ends would be tidied up. Canon Douglas believes that had not the War destroyed all these plans and preparations, an "all-round advance" would have been recorded.

The relationship with the Old Catholics was closer and the task less complicated; so that the Conference of 1930 had no difficulty in agreeing that there was nothing contradictory in the Anglican and Old Catholic dogmatic traditions and formularies. A further conference to consider inter-communion and inter-consecration was held at Bonn in July 1931. True to his policy, Lang saw that the Evangelicals were sufficiently represented on the Anglican Delegation, which was led by the almost inevitable Dr. Headlam and carefully briefed by the Archbishop himself. Dr. Graham Brown, afterwards Bishop in Jerusalem, was the chief Evangelical watchdog and would pass nothing that might be unacceptable to those whose interests he was charged to protect. After a brief negotiation the Delegates arrived at the following agreement:

1. Each Communion recognises the catholicity and independence of the other and maintains its own.

2. Each Communion agrees to admit members of the other Communion to participate in the Sacraments.

3. Inter-communion does not require from either Communion the acceptance of all doctrinal opinion, sacramental devotions, or liturgical practice characteristic of the other, but implies that each believes the other to hold the essentials of the Christian Faith.

This felicitous result was endorsed first by the Synod of the Old Catholic Church and later by the Convocations of Canterbury and York, nearly all the other Anglican Churches following suit. It established inter-communion and—of perhaps even greater significance—carried the necessary authority for inter-consecration. So in 1932, in the primacy of Archbishop Lang, the Church of England for the first time since the Reformation entered into full and formal relationship with a Continental Church. Apart from the historical interest and intrinsic worth of this achievement, it had two external consequences. It served to dispel some of the doubts of Orthodox theologians about Anglican Orders; and through the participation of Old Catholic Bishops in Anglican Consecrations, as in those of the Bishops in Jerusalem and of Gibraltar, the ministerial succession of the Episcopate of the Old Catholics began to be merged with that of the Church of England.

The visible results which flowed from the negotiations with the Orthodox and Old Catholics must give them the first place in any estimate of Lang's work for Reunion; but the other approaches which he sponsored and encouraged should be neither ignored nor underestimated. Indeed, it is true to say that much as he prized the outcome with Orthodox and Old Catholics, he would not have accepted this as the only test of his policy. Let it be repeated that Reunion, as he saw it, neither should nor could be some sudden and spectacular reconciliation. It would be a growing together in understanding and purpose, slow, and sure because it was slow. Only less heinous than the sin of doing nothing was the blunder of trying to do too much too quickly; and results which seemed meagre enough to the contemporary eye might well be found to have genuine value for the future.

With the Roman Catholics no progress was made; and after Malines, where the method departed from Lang's principles, little was attempted. In 1928, shortly after the Lausanne Conference, Pope Pius XI issued an Encyclical warning his fellow-Catholics against participation in movements "by which non-Catholics seek to bring about the union of Christian Churches. There is but one way in which the unity of Christians may be fostered, and that is by furthering the return to the one true Church of Christ of those who are separated from it: from that one true Church they have in the past fallen away."

But while the official attitude of the Vatican was unchanged, during Lang's Primacy, and particularly during the Second World War, the Roman Catholic Church in Great Britain showed a greater readiness to co-operate with Christians of another allegiance on matters outside the frontiers of Faith and Order. This new spirit owed something to the stress of the times, but at least as much to the simultaneous presence of Archbishop Lang at Lambeth and of Cardinal Hinsley at Westminster. Fifty years earlier Lang had emphasised the error of trying to deal with the Church of Scotland over the head of the Scottish Episcopal Church. Privately, it may be assumed, he would have criticised the Conversations at Malines for the omission to take proper account of the Roman Catholic community in Great Britain. It was another of those short cuts or circuits which he mistrusted. His own relations with Cardinal Hinsley were mostly unofficial, but of a cordiality without precedent. He attached considerable value to "the private wire," as he called it, between Lambeth and Westminster; and while there were no formal visits, there were times when he discovered a new use for his neglected membership of the Athenaeum.

"He had to my mind," wrote Bishop Mathew, Auxiliary Bishop of Westminster, "a quite remarkable knowledge of the ecclesiastical temper, which enabled him to understand both the world of the Roman Curia and that of the different national episcopates which are in communion with the Holy See. I am left chiefly with the memory of his persistent, patient and undimmed charity. This, I think, arose from his deep, humble sense of the supremacy of the spiritual factor in man's troubled life. . . . He was kind to the young, and I was very young when I was first received in his study at Lambeth in 1935. To me he will always remain the embodiment of the great tradition of Andrewes, Laud and Cosin."

With the Protestant Churches of the Continent the "growing together" went on at a slow but appreciable pace, Anglicans taking a leading part in the World Conferences on Life and Work and on Faith and Order. At Oxford in 1937 Lang was President of the Conference on "Church, Community and State." In accordance with the Resolution of the

Lambeth Conference and by permission of the Bishop of Oxford, the Archbishop celebrated Holy Communion in St. Mary's Church, the delegates having been previously informed of the hope "that not only such of them as are members of the Anglican Church, but also others who are Baptised Communicants in their own Churches, may come to the Service and partake of Holy Communion." Later on in the same year the Conference on Faith and Order, successor to Lausanne, met at Edinburgh. It belongs less to Lang's history than to Temple's, as it was he who there inspired and promoted the design which brought the various streams of the Oecumenical Movement into the broad river of a World Council of Churches. Owing to the War, the Council was unable to hold its first meeting until August 1948, when the representatives of a hundred and forty-eight Churches—Anglican, Orthodox, Old Catholic and Protestant—assembled in Amsterdam.

In 1939 a Commission, led by Dr. Headlam, visited the Churches of Latvia and Estonia, Convocation subsequently authorising its recommendations for participation in the Consecration of Bishops, for a measure of inter-communion, and for mutual recognition of the validity of the Sacraments of Baptism and Marriage. These arrangements did not imply full inter-communion as with the Old Catholics, but established an interim relationship, which would last until the Orders of the Baltic Churches were regularised. A similar agreement had already been reached with the Church in Finland.

By comparison the *rapprochement* with the Free Churches of Great Britain, which had made so promising a start after 1920, was a little disappointing. In 1925, it will be recalled, the discussions were broken off by a failure to agree on the vital question of Orders. They were to have been resumed after 1930, but as Lang discloses in his notes, the Delegation to the Conference from the Federal Council of the Evangelical Free Churches was "not successful and left an unhappy impression." Doubtless both sides were at fault, but the Free Churches could perhaps be pardoned for contrasting their polite but unenthusiastic reception with the warmer welcome given to the Orthodox and for finding significance in the failure to repeat or to endorse the recognition of 1923 that their Ministries were "real Ministries" in the Universal Church. Nevertheless the Council accepted the invitation to renew the conversations and appointed a sub-committee for the purpose. Not much was to come of the meetings, but in 1935 and 1938 two documents of some importance, *A Sketch of a United Church* and *An Outline of a*

Reunion Scheme, appeared. The *rapprochement* may also be credited with some indirect results. The first was the gradual advance of the South India Scheme, which was not, of course, the immediate concern of the Provinces of Canterbury and York or of the British Free Churchmen, but leaned heavily upon their approval and encouragement. Another was the concordat of 1941 between Anglicans and Nonconformists over the vexed question of Education.

"On August 15th, 1941," the Archbishop wrote, "I took a very remarkable deputation to the new President of the Board of Education (the Rt. Hon. R. A. Butler) on the subject of better Christian teaching in *all* Schools. The basis was a statement previously issued by the Archbishops of Canterbury, York and Wales after consultation with the other Bishops, putting forth five main points concerning Elementary Schools. For the first time in the history of English education, the deputation, instead of representing division among Christian Churches in England and Wales, represented their unity; for it consisted of not Anglicans only, but of the leading Free Churchmen. . . . This measure of unity was the result of long conferences with Free Church leaders, under Scott Lidgett,[1] and held under the auspices of the National Society. It reflected the new attitude forced on people by the evidences of widespread ignorance of the Christian Faith and the challenge of Nazi Germany to any sort of Christian civilisation. As the President was new to his office and had to consider other interests, he was guarded in his reply. But he was much impressed by the character of the deputation and showed that he personally was in much sympathy with its aims. . . . I ought to add another quite unprecedented fact: at the end the President asked me to offer prayers for guidance."

The Archbishop appended a note under the date August 1943:

In the White Paper containing the full programme of Educational reconstruction issued by the Board of Education, all these five points are accepted:

1. Religious teaching in *all* schools, primary and secondary, to be a statutory obligation.
2. Schools to be opened daily by an act of corporate worship.

[1] President of the Uniting Conference of the Methodist Churches, and first President of the United Church, 1932.

3. Religious teaching to be given at any hour of the school day, not merely at the beginning.

4. Religious knowledge to qualify for Teachers' Certificates at Training Colleges.

5. Religious teaching in the schools to be inspected as to method and competence by H.M.'s Inspectors.

All these points, he adds, were embodied in the Education Bill of 1944.

The Bishop of Chichester, whose book *Christian Unity* and series of *Documents on Christian Unity* should be studied for the whole story of the movements of these years, believes that since 1914 the relations between the Church of England and the Free Churches have been transformed. While disagreement still persists over the Ministry and Episcopal Ordination, a real advance is to be recorded in the whole field of Faith and Order, as well as in that of social and international action.

Dr. Carnegie Simpson, who had not always been easy in conference, has given his testimony to the Archbishop's share in bringing about this better relationship. While he looked back "with much disappointment" to the results of the various meetings, he recalled Lang's part in them with admiration and respect. He had been warned that Lang was a diplomat and needed watching, but "I found him straightforward and always fair." Through his Presbyterian upbringing he was quicker than were some of his brethren to appreciate the position of the Free Churchmen. "His mind," Dr. Simpson concluded, "was skilful in adjusting truth rather than original in discovering it or powerful in stating it."

There remains the Church of Lang's own birth and upbringing. Dr. John Whyte, who came to Lambeth in 1930, reappeared in the following year with Dr. Archibald Fleming, the Minister of St. Columba's, Pont Street. Their purpose was to discuss the idea of initiating negotiations on the lines of the "Appeal to all Christian People"; but they wanted to deal direct with the Church of England and not with the Episcopal Church in Scotland. Such a procedure, of course, ran contrary to Lang's method and was another of those short cuts he disliked. He therefore stipulated that the Episcopal Church must not be left out of the negotiations, and parted with his visitors on a compromise by which both Scottish Episcopalians and English Presbyterians were to be included. In April 1932 Dr. Whyte returned to Lambeth, bringing with him

Principal Martin of the United Free Church and Professor Curtis of Edinburgh. Lang was supported by Archbishop Temple, and after some discussion it was agreed that the matter should be brought before the General Assembly of the Kirk in May. Lang then suggested that he might be asked to come to Edinburgh, bringing with him the proposal for a conference between the various Churches. The Presbyterians thought this a good idea, and in due course an invitation arrived from Professor Mackintosh, the new Moderator. Lang went to Edinburgh, but unfortunately his presence was not the olive branch it was meant to be. Some of the Presbyterians were irritated and suspicious, smelling a backstairs intrigue. While they received their visitor politely and listened to him with deference, among themselves they were asking by whose authority he had been invited. The slight chill in the atmosphere was so perceptible that, as Lang left the General Assembly with Bishop Reid of Edinburgh, the latter remarked ruefully, "Nothing will come of it." Something, however, did come of it, for the Assembly appointed a Commission to negotiate with the Church of England, the Episcopal Church of Scotland and the English Presbyterians, as had been agreed at Lambeth.

But at next year's Assembly, when the first report on the meetings was made, other counsels prevailed and a motion, introduced by Dr. Fleming and passed by a narrow majority, declared that before the conferences went any further the Churches must mutually recognise the validity of each other's Ministry. "Am I still *persona grata*, Your Grace?" enquired Dr. Fleming a little nervously, on his next visit to Lambeth. "*Persona grata*, my dear Fleming," was the reply, "but not *persona gratissima*." From the point of view of the Church of England, and still more from that of the Episcopal Church, the motion begged the whole question; and so the meetings came abruptly to an end.

Of little specific relevance to Reunion, but possibly as a small contribution to the "growing together," was the Archbishop's later visit to the Assembly in 1935. In that year Marshall Lang was Moderator, so that by a singular chance Canterbury and Edinburgh were represented by two brothers. The exchange of solemn courtesies between them provoked some merriment, and on this occasion the visit gave general satisfaction.

So this long and complex story reaches its ending, or rather is broken off unfinished. No man may tell what might have happened at a Lambeth Conference which was never held. For Lang it was one of the tragedies of the War that the plans he had laid so carefully and for which he had worked so indefatigably were brought to nought. Others might take up his pen and finish the tale, and when they did so would find the earlier chapters written by a firm and sure hand. But he would neither complete the book nor live to read it. He had been allowed a glimpse from Pisgah of the living green of the Promised Land; but his people must follow another leader into their inheritance.

Chapter XXX

"ALTERIUS ORBIS PAPA"

"THE job is really impossible for one man," the Archbishop wrote in 1935, "yet only one man can do it"; and at a public dinner next year he described the life he was leading as "incredible, indefensible and inevitable."

In earlier chapters something has been written of the nature and extent of his labours in Diocese and Province and the central affairs of the Church. Yet with these his duties were by no means ended. An Archbishop of Canterbury is a national figure and, apart from such special or unprecedented occasions as an Abdication, a Coronation or a war, his presence is expected, almost of right, at many functions which appear to have little connexion with his ecclesiastical responsibilities. When, in addition, he has the oratorical gifts that were Lang's, the demands on him are redoubled. Their nature and variety may be best appreciated from a few of his engagements in the early days of his rule. He spoke at the Bunyan Tercentenary, where he paid tribute to a religious community whose work and quiet devotion he had long admired, a meeting of the Church Army, the Royal Academy Banquet, the College of St. Nicholas (Church Music), the City of London School, the Friends of Canterbury Cathedral, the unveiling of the Memorial to Lord Curzon, the Pilgrims of Great Britain, the Newspaper Press Fund, a meeting at the Guildhall on Slum Clearance, an International Boy Scouts' Jamboree, and Cheltenham Ladies' College. These are a sample of his engagements, picked almost at random from a long list. Some of the societies, organisations or functions he addressed more than once. He was on the Council of the Boy Scouts' Association and spoke at many of the big Jamborees. He was a Vice-President of the Pilgrims of Great Britain, presiding and speaking at the luncheon on June 24th, 1931, when the Pilgrim Trust was founded, and speaking again at the Society's Coronation Celebration in 1937. He was a frequent guest at the Royal Academy Banquet, the kind of occasion on which he found his best after-dinner form.

In between he was talking on subjects so diverse as the plight of the Jews in Germany, the Centenary of the Oxford Movement, the influence of films, Miss Gertrude Bell (daughter of his old friend in the North), disarmament, the legal profession, the repair of Boston Stump, and the destruction of sea-birds. These, too, are an almost fortuitous collection of some of the subjects on which he was expected to prepare and deliver an informed and often a constructive address. The *Church Times* could justly refer to "the almost inhuman activity of the Archbishop of Canterbury"; and his own notebooks, penned almost entirely in his fastness of Ballure, abound in laments at the absence of any breathing-space when he could, as it were, sit down and think out some of the major problems of the Church.

Lang's oratory was as distinguished in its quality as it was wide in its range.

"I think," writes Lord Quickswood, no mean judge, "Archbishop Lang was one of two or three whom I should call the best speakers I have ever heard. The most remarkable feature about his speaking was its admirable many-sidedness. There was hardly any kind of speaking which he could not do very well indeed. Whether it was exposition or narrative, exhortation or argument, anecdote or humour, he was pre-eminent in all these arts. I have never heard him attempt passionate rhetoric and I suppose it to have been uncongenial to him, but his technique was so excellent that I think if he had felt the emotion necessary, he would have been able to express it with the incomparable felicity which marked his speaking in any manner. I think I have never heard him speak badly, though there was a period, when he was in bad health, when he tended to be a little diffuse. That was in the early 'twenties, when he had not fully recovered from the nervous illness which he had during the 1914-1918 War.[1] But even this trifling defect completely passed away.

"When he became Archbishop of Canterbury and presided always in the Assembly, he had to deal with a great variety of occasions for speaking, and it was always supremely well done. To anyone accustomed to make speeches himself, perhaps the most wonderful thing seemed the effortless ease with which he always found the right word. And his speaking was not only delightful to listen to, but always very effective for the object he had in view. Unlike some speakers who dazzle and even charm, yet do not convince, he was extraordinarily persuasive. Indeed, one of the criticisms

[1] This is not quite correct. The Archbishop was never ill, although he suffered from alopecia.

sometimes made upon his Chairmanship was that, speaking at the close of a debate, he would put his point of view so well that it prevailed, to the disappointment of those who were opposed to him and felt that he used with too much power the prerogative of the last word.

"In the technical work of Chairman, he was exceedingly careful and painstaking and not in the least indifferent, as too many ecclesiastics are, to the importance of regularity. He had not got that rather strange power, a natural sense of procedure, which resembles an ear for music, but his unfailing address as a speaker enabled him to smooth out any difficulties and make good any casual slips that he might make. To his gift of words he added a wonderfully dignified manner which was at the same time entirely free from pretentiousness or pomposity. He could always act as an Archbishop without giving the least impression of self-assertion."

Lord Quickswood adds that while he had seldom heard the Archbishop preach, he thought his sermons were not so brilliant as his speeches.

Looking back on his labours, the Archbishop gave generous acknowledgment to the services of his chaplains. Mervyn Haigh saw him through the first two years and the Lambeth Conference.

Then on Haigh's departure in 1931, a great good fortune—or rather God's Providence—brought me Alan Don from the Provostship of St. Paul's Cathedral, Dundee. He had been a resident at the Oxford House, where he was one of the band of young men who would have followed Dick Sheppard to the ends of the earth. I had ordained him at York to his curacy at Redcar and given him the benefice of Norton near Malton before he went to Dundee, a most loyal and enthusiastic son of the Scottish Church. I am thankful to say that he stayed with me for ten years, during which, in 1936, he became Chaplain to the Speaker of the House of Commons until he was made Canon of Westminster and Rector of St. Margaret's. . . . I cannot dwell here on the blessings which he brought me—of companionship, of steady judgment, of faith, of goodness, of width of interests, and of the ability to get on good terms with all sorts of people, officially and personally. What Haigh was in the affairs of the Lambeth Conference of 1930 he was in all the preliminary business of the Conference which but for the War would have been held in 1940. It was a real sorrow to me when he left in 1941 after ten years of service.

The present Archdeacon of Canterbury went in 1939, to be succeeded by the Rev. Ian White Thomson, son of the Bishop of Ely.

To my great content he was with me to the end of my time, and in the midst of all the turmoil and confusion of the War gave me eager and unruffled help. He saw me out and has seen two successors in. He has had the strange, certainly unprecedented, lot of having served three Archbishops within four years.

Lang was not always an easy master. He had a reluctance to delegate, a determination to keep his eye and his finger on everything, which a chaplain was bound to find occasionally irksome. There was that surface irritability, which his mother too had had, disconcerting and even alarming to anyone who did not know him well. Yet he could also be the best of company to those who served him, kindly, affectionate, amusing. "If one treated him quite naturally," writes the Dean of Lichfield, "and was not afraid of or awed by him, he really could be great fun."

Dick Sheppard, to the Archbishop's sorrow, left the Deanery in 1931, to struggle with failing health, to be, for a short and unhappy period, a Canon of St. Paul's, and to die in 1937. On October 31st, the eve of Lang's seventy-third birthday, he found on his table a letter and some flowers from his friend; and an hour later a telephone message came to tell him that Dick was dead. "We shall never see his like again," he wrote sadly to Wilfrid Parker, now Bishop of Pretoria. "How I wish," he wrote again a little later, "that somehow the course of his life had been different and that the dear man had never written those very tiresome and unhelpful books, but simply allowed his unique personality to radiate its influence of love and goodwill." On either side the affection was deep and enduring, but each man had his private portrait of the other and was distressed whenever the original appeared to fail in fidelity to the likeness. "There!" said Dick Sheppard once, pointing to a portrait of Lord Curzon. "That's the man who has been his curse." The Archdeacon of Canterbury recalls Lang's words at the unveiling of the Memorial to Lord Curzon in 1930. The address was generally hailed as a masterpiece of insight. If Dick Sheppard was right, it may also have been a piece of self-revelation; it certainly showed the side of Lang which his friend liked least.

A few very big issues or events may befall an Archbishop, but his working time is mostly taken up with the care of innumerable matters which seem very important at the time, but less so ten or twenty years afterwards; with Measures pregnant with possibilities, but in result neither so beneficial as their supporters hoped nor so dangerous as their adversaries feared; with disputes about fundamentals, which pass and leave the foundations of the Church unshaken; with decisions so critical that a false step would appear fatal, but in effect so ephemeral that in a short time they are forgotten; with movements, controversies in the Courts, secular encroachments and the like, on which to-day the dust lies thick; and above all with the ceaseless routine of a Diocese.

Lang, it will be recalled, was resolved that the last should be no formal or delegated duty. As at York, so at Canterbury, the Diocese had a high priority among the claims on his time, and by 1935, when he held a Visitation of the Clergy, he was able to say that he had prayed and preached in exactly half the two hundred and ninety-six parishes. Following his practice in the North, he had sent round a questionnaire to all the incumbents, and he spent most of a holiday at Ballure studying the replies. "Very laborious," he commented, "yet full of interest and on the whole not discouraging." At the Visitation he delivered a Charge in which he gave his conclusions, which were appreciative of the devotion of his clergy, but outspoken and disquieting on the situation revealed. New ideas and habits, the motor car, the wireless, the film and so much else were coming like a mist between people and "their vision of a personal God."

Do not misunderstand me. This is no sort of Jeremiad of a man of elderly years. I ask you and myself to look upon all these things not as menace but rather as a challenge. There is none of them wherein there is not some good as well as evil. It is for us to overcome the evil with the good. We have not to entrench ourselves against them and make our Church life a refuge. Rather we have to go out from it as from a fortress to meet and redeem them, trusting still in the redemptive power of the Gospel of Christ. They may be the travail pangs of some new birth. Pray God it may be the birth of a better life both in the Church and in the world.

He went on to give practical advice to the parish priests, warning them of the dangers of Accidie and urging them at all costs to find time to escape from the racket of their work and "go apart to be with Christ in prayer and stillness." "Then, sometimes," he ended, "even in the dull and dusty way of our labours we can make our own the words which I dared to put before myself as a motto when I was enthroned as your Bishop: 'God is my strength and my song.'"

Lang's years, as he travelled down his own "dull and dusty way," were memorable for the Lambeth Conference, the Abdication, the Coronation and the War. They also saw an advance in the cause of Christian Reunion. But when they passed, the mark they left on the history of the Church was comparatively small. Some have felt that it should have been larger and deeper; that the Enabling Act opened new possibilities which were not firmly and adventurously grasped; that the rejection of the Prayer Book was a challenge evaded; in short, that the moment had come when the relations of Church and State should have been revised and the spiritual authority and autonomy of the Church asserted, even at the cost of Disestablishment. Yet on all this ground Lang did little more than mark time. He led the way in laying down the rules for Bishops and clergy to follow on liturgical questions; and in 1938 he convened the Round Table Conference to discuss authority and order. But the rules have been unevenly observed and the Conference was moving to an unpromising finish when the War ended it. Sooner or later, Lang concluded, the question must be "tackled afresh." He added, "It is not for me to say when."

"Where Lang failed in my opinion," writes the Bishop of Chichester, "was after the rejection of 1928. Many brave words were spoken in the Assembly debate. An Archbishop's Commission was appointed and reported, but from 1929 to 1947 no effective steps whatever have been taken to enable the Church of England to revise its forms of worship, to frame its laws on spiritual matters, to exercise its discipline through proper Church Courts, to have an effective voice in the election of its Bishops."

To accept an unsatisfactory situation without making much attempt to put it right may suggest, as it suggested to the Bishop of Chichester, a lack of the qualities of a reformer, even perhaps of a leader. But it is also possible that, after the exhausting controversies of the Prayer Book, the Church needed a respite, and that the comparative quiescence of Lang was wise and timely. Or it may be that both views contain an element of the truth, that the days were unpropitious for the radical reforms the Bishop wanted, and that in any case Lang was not the man to bring them about.

Whatever judgment be correct, the truth is that Lang continued the rearguard action which Davidson had fought so skilfully and for so long. The main question of spiritual authority being unresolved, the defensive continued on the dependent questions, such as Education, the Marriage Laws and Tithe. In 1935 Convocation received the Report of the Joint Committee on Church and Marriage. It declared the right of the Church to make its own rules about admission to the Sacraments and its freedom to forbid the use of its buildings for the remarriage of divorced persons, while allowing that in certain special cases these might subsequently be allowed to make their Communions. Two years later the Archbishop declined to vote either for or against Sir Alan Herbert's Bill, which emphasised the growing opposition between the Marriage Laws of Church and State.

Tithe had long been a grievance, always most vocal in years of agricultural depression, and although the final settlement was the work of a predominantly Conservative Government, it was such as seriously to impair the finances of the Church. A Bill was introduced and withdrawn in 1934, a Royal Commission being then appointed to re-examine the question. In 1936 a new Measure, commuting Tithe with compensation, was presented and passed. The Archbishop was inevitably prominent in the Parliamentary debates. He took the line that the Church would not oppose commutation in principle, but was entitled to a more generous rate of compensation than either of these Bills allowed. He thought the terms were harsh and told the House of Lords that they would involve clerical Tithe-owners immediately in a loss of eleven million pounds and ultimately in one of about sixteen million. He secured some modification of the terms allowed, but the second Bill went through substantially as it was introduced. The Archbishop, as the chief mouthpiece of the Tithe-owners, came in for some obloquy from the agitators in rural areas, and in 1935 his effigy, with that of Queen Anne, was ceremonially burned in a demonstration at Ashford, Kent.

More satisfactory for the Church were the two Measures of 1931 and 1934, passed first by the Church Assembly and subsequently by Parliament, dealing with the recommendations of the Cathedrals Commission, of which Lang had been Chairman. It appointed a body of Cathedral Commissioners, who were to assist the Dean and Chapter in revising old and drawing up new statutes, and in preparing schemes and adapting buildings to the needs of the times. All land, except the actual sites and fabrics of Cathedrals, was transferred to the Ecclesiastical Commissioners in return for a fixed annual income.

A minor but tedious controversy of the early days was the dispute over St. Aidan's, Small Heath, Birmingham, where the patrons had presented an incumbent whom the Bishop of Birmingham (Dr. Barnes) refused to institute. The patrons, among whom was the Bishop of Truro (Dr. Frere), eventually applied for a declaration that their candidate, the Rev. Doyle Simmonds, had been duly presented and asked for an order compelling the Bishop to accept him. This they obtained, but the Bishop continued contumacious, refusing either to admit the authority of the High Court of Chancery in such a matter or even to appear before it. In the end the Archbishop was driven to admit Mr. Simmonds himself. The incident involved him in an argument with the Bishop of Birmingham, who took the opportunity to attack the doctrine of the Real Presence in a letter which made it plain that he did not really understand what the doctrine was. Lang, like Davidson before him, dealt politely but firmly with Dr. Barnes and so closed a rather unedifying incident.

More serious and protracted was the problem of "my poor Assyrians," as he used to call them, which was to be with him for as long as he was at Lambeth. Theirs was an old, unhappy story. They were a community of Nestorian Christians, the remnant of a once numerous and powerful people, who until the First World War lived precariously in the highlands of Hakkiari and the adjacent country, with Turks as their masters and Kurds as their neighbours. They then rose, abandoned or were driven out of their settlements at Hakkiari, and joined the British, to whom they gave some assistance in the fighting. When the War ended, they wanted to return to their homes, but these were still in Turkish territory and the Turks, not unreasonably, would not have them back. On the other hand, they were not at all welcome in Irak, and between Turks, Irakis and Kurds, their future was most uncertain. Their only friends were the British, who employed them as military levies in Mesopotamia, thereby diminishing still more their popularity with the Irakis, especially after the Arab rising in 1920. Since 1886 they had looked to the Archbishop of Canterbury for protection; an Anglican mission had worked among them; and they had had help and encouragement in their difficult life as a Christian island in a Moslem sea. Although their future was unsettled, they were unmolested so long as the British Mandate in Irak lasted, but when it ended in 1932, the problem at once became acute. While the Government of Irak gave guarantees for the fair treatment of its minorities, the Assyrians were not specifically mentioned in the Anglo-

Iraki Treaty. Were they to stay in their temporary quarters, or to return to Hakkiari, or to go somewhere else? No one could answer this question. The Irakis professed readiness to retain their uninvited guests, provided they would behave like any other minority and cease regarding themselves as a separate nation. The Turks continued to refuse to take them back, and the Kurds were only waiting for a chance to pay off old scores. The Assyrians—and particularly the disbanded levies—became impatient. In 1933 some of them attempted an unauthorised migration into Syria and on their return fought with Iraki troops. This so-called rising was the signal for a massacre. The Iraki army ran amok. The Kurds were called in. Numbers of innocent Assyrians, who had had nothing whatever to do with the migration, were butchered. Villages were looted and largely destroyed.

In a welter of conflicting evidence it was plain that something would have to be done quickly, or the Assyrians might be exterminated, and that the real issue between them and the Government of Irak was their claim to remain a nation within a nation. Their ecclesiastical head was the Mar Shimun, who also claimed certain secular powers which were the stumbling-block in the negotiations. Eventually the British, by a rather high-handed action, which they claimed was as much in the interests of the Mar Shimun, whose life was threatened, as in those of an agreement, deported the young man to Cyprus. There he remained for some time with his family, in poverty and under protest, before he was allowed to leave for the United States. Meanwhile the League of Nations had become busy with the Assyrian problem. Various plans were produced and came to nothing. At one time it seemed likely that the French would allow a settlement on the Orontes in Syria, but this project, too, was abandoned and the Assyrians stayed on where they were.

The Archbishop was heavily involved in all these events, as the Mar Shimun repeatedly appealed to him to use his influence on behalf of the Assyrian people. On November 28th, 1933, he spoke at length on the subject in the House of Lords, giving the whole story and calling upon the Government to recognise its obligations.

"I have had one continuous worry," he wrote in his notebook that year, "over the plight of the poor Assyrians in Irak—endless correspondence with the Foreign Office, with Sir John Simon, Vansittart and others on the staff, with Sir Francis Humphrys at Baghdad, with poor Mar Shimun himself, deported to Cyprus, with various people in Irak (very secretly) and in England. What will happen it is impossible to say. I have done my best and can't do more, but it has been an endless worry."

So it continued to be. He had an almost paternal affection for the Mar Shimun, who had been educated in England, and a strong sense of responsibility towards the Mar Shimun's little people. In 1936 he returned to the attack, speaking in the House of Lords and comparing the massacre of the Assyrians with that of the Macdonalds of Glencoe; and some months later, when the Syrian scheme gave promise of a solution, he made an appeal at the Mansion House for funds to finance the settlement of 21,000 Assyrians on the Orontes. His efforts were in vain. The Mar Shimun stayed in exile and the Assyrians remained unsettled. In the Second World War the British again recruited them and they did loyal service, especially during the troubles of 1941, when they fought bravely in defence of Habbaniya. Their feats did them credit, but made their position in Irak even more difficult. They are still an unsolved problem and an undefined commitment of Church and State in Britain.

Another and much larger community also claimed the Archbishop's interest. The persecution of religion in Russia drew from him repeated protests in the House of Lords. In 1930 he appointed a day of intercession for Russian Christians and objected strongly when the War Office tried to forbid the use at parade services of a prayer for the Russian Church. He gave his sympathy and active support to the Russian Church Aid Fund, and when the choir from the Russian Academy at Paris visited this country, preached at a special service at St. Martin-in-the-Fields, at which it was present and sang. Neither he nor anyone could do much to counteract the persecution, but if the criticisms did little, or nothing, to better the position of Christians in Russia, there is evidence that they touched a raw spot. The Soviet Government treated the Archbishop's interventions with anger and answered them with abuse. He was pilloried as one of the principal enemies of the Soviet Union, and in the Museum of the Godless at St. Isaac's Cathedral, Leningrad, was accorded (with the Pope) the honour of an insulting cartoon.

At the same time he was condemning in the House of Lords the treatment by the Nazis of Christians and Jews in Germany. Here again he could only argue and protest to men who were impervious to words, however eloquent. In Germany, too, he became a target for abuse. In 1934 a letter to the *Times* denouncing the revival of the old and dis-

credited story of ritual murders won him the attention of *Der Stürmer*.
Streicher followed up with other attacks, but in these was not always
fortunate in his facts, as first he confused the Archbishop with the Dean
of Canterbury and later with the Dean of Westminster.

The criticisms may not have affected the policy of the Reich, but
undoubtedly annoyed the Nazis. On October 10th, 1934, the German
Ambassador, von Hoesch, came in person to Lambeth. The Archbishop
did not mince his words. He told the Ambassador that Christian opinion
in Britain was outraged both by the way in which the unification of the
Protestant Churches was being carried out and by the principles underlying the policy of the Reich, as manifested by the Aryan Clause and the
writings of Rosenberg, von Shirach and Dr. Burgmann. He warned
von Hoesch that unless within a week "some effective signs of a change
of policy" were shown, he would lay the whole matter before the
Bishops of the Church of England, the Protestant leaders, and the non-
Roman Christian leaders on the Continent. There was no change of
policy and another unheeded protest was the only result.

With von Hoesch's successor, von Ribbentrop, the Archbishop also
had his brushes. On June 5th, 1935, the Ambassador arrived for luncheon
and received a lecture. He took this quite amiably, but showed, the
Archbishop commented, very little understanding of what all the fuss
was about. Nearly three years later, when von Ribbentrop came to say
goodbye on leaving his post, the Archbishop spoke even more plainly
of the disgust felt in Britain at the persecution of both Roman Catholics
and Protestants, and in particular at the imprisonment of Pastor Nie-
möller. The retiring Ambassador may have been a little preoccupied,
as that day the news of the Anschluss reached London.

On Abyssinia, again, the Archbishop had something to say. He
condemned the Italian aggression in Parliament and at the Church
Congress at Bournemouth in October 1935. He followed up his words
by sponsoring an appeal for a British Ambulance Service to accompany
the Abyssinian troops; and a little later, when the unit was equipped
and ready to leave, he gave it his blessing.

In 1933 he had an onerous but not unwelcome addition to his duties.
Two years earlier he had spoken effectively in the House of Lords on
Indian policy. "To govern India," he said, "has been the greatest
achievement this country has ever attempted. . . . It will be an even
higher achievement, an even nobler task, to assist India to govern itself."
His sentiments and the impression made by this speech may have given

the Secretary of State, Sir Samuel Hoare (now Lord Templewood) the idea of asking him to serve on the Joint Committee upon the Indian Constitution appointed in March 1933. The proposal was not without its critics, Lord Salisbury among others holding the view that the work was not suitable for an Archbishop of Canterbury. But the Prime Minister, who was responsible for the appointments, agreed with the Secretary of State and the invitation was sent. "If Your Grace is able to accept," Sir Samuel wrote, "I can assure you that your action will be very reassuring to thousands of men and women in the country who are not looking at this question through the spectacles of any party. If you are doubtful, I would venture to ask you on no account to refuse until you have had a talk with Irwin (the present Lord Halifax) or me or both of us." Whatever the Archbishop's intentions may have been, he saw Sir Samuel before yielding to his arguments. The Chairman of the Committee should have been Lord Peel, a former Secretary of State for India, but illness prevented him from presiding and Lord Linlithgow, afterwards Viceroy of India, took his place. The Archbishop was a conscientious and useful member. "Looking back at the part he took," Lord Templewood has written, "I am convinced that the broad issues of Federation were just the kind that particularly interested him. He himself seemed to regard the work as some of the most interesting he ever undertook." In fact, the experiment of appointing him "was in every way satisfactory. The Archbishop, so far as I remember, attended practically every meeting and took the closest possible interest not only in the question of the Indian Christians, but in the whole field of constitutional reform."

After the Committee had reported, the Archbishop heard from a friend in India : "I was talking to an educated Hindu, who told me that he followed all the proceedings of the Select Joint Committee, and that he felt that when the Archbishop intervened he lifted the proceedings from the realm of politics to a higher plane."

In his notebook the Archbishop called the Committee his "chief tyranny" and declared that "had I known what the work would mean I certainly would not have consented"; but undoubtedly he valued the compliment and was absorbed by the subject. "The business is of course of supreme interest, but of a difficulty which grows as one gets further into the problem—a problem, I suppose, of constitution-making more novel and intricate than any set of men have ever had to consider." Therefore he did not grudge, though he could ill afford, the toll it levied on him. "The Committee met in the King's Robing-room at Westminster at first three mornings in each week, then three afternoons as well, then four days a week morning and afternoon! And this with all my ordinary work, heavy enough at all times, added. It was a gruelling time."

Not so gruelling, but of much longer duration, was his work, *ex officio*, as a Principal Trustee of the British Museum. He attended the sessions of the Standing Committee with commendable regularity, being present and presiding at no less than 187 out of 227 meetings during his time as Archbishop.

"He was an ideal Chairman," writes Lord Macmillan, "and dealt with the long and varied agenda not only with admirable tact and judgment, but with zest and interest. Apart from the actual meetings of the Committee, he concerned himself constantly and sympathetically with the solution of the Museum's problems, and especially with the elimination of the personal frictions inevitable in the working of an institution staffed by experts. When asked how he contrived to find time for all that he did for the Museum, he confessed that he found the work enjoyable and its atmosphere congenial by way of a change from his other duties. He liked to meet round the boardroom table interesting colleagues from walks of life so different from his own, including personal friends such as the late Lord Crawford, Lord Ilchester and others. And perhaps, too, he rather enjoyed showing how efficient a man of business an Archbishop could be."

An enterprise especially attractive to him, both as Archbishop and as Principal Trustee, was the purchase in 1934 of the Codex Sinaiticus.

When his time came to leave Lambeth, the end of his Trusteeship was among his more poignant regrets. However, by a happy solution he was elected a member of the Standing Committee and, as his successor "was very willing, for the present at least, to be relieved of the duties of Chairman," Lang continued to preside at the meetings.

A Governor of the London Charterhouse and of Charterhouse School since 1910, the Archbishop was elected Chairman of both bodies when he went to Canterbury. "His love for the London Charterhouse," writes the Master, the Rev. E. St. G. Schomberg, "with its ancient buildings and historic traditions, became something very real." He took an active part in all that concerned it, particularly in the appointment of new Governors; and "I soon realised that I had in him a friend upon whom I could rely for unfailing support in any difficulty that arose." Difficulties there were, to be surmounted largely through the tact and firmness of the Chairman; and once, when a very unpleasant situation had to be faced, the Archbishop took upon himself the burden of it, carrying it with marked success. When during the War the old Pensionary hospital was completely destroyed, many thought it should be rebuilt elsewhere; but Lang was resolved to retain the traditions associated with the old site and in the end he had his way. Equally notable was his Chairmanship of the School. Although himself educated in Scotland, he had a deep sense of the value of the English Public School in the life of the nation. Early in 1939 a fall in the number of boys seeking admission began to cause some anxiety, and under the Archbishop's Chairmanship two important meetings were held in the London Charterhouse between representatives of the Headmasters' Conference and of the Governing Bodies. These meetings, for the discussion of problems which presently received additional emphasis from the War, led to the formation of the Governing Bodies' Association, bringing the Public Schools for the first time, according to Canon Spencer Leeson, then Headmaster of Winchester, "to some measure of conscious co-operation." Here, he remarks, was "one more illustration of the Archbishop's power of mastering in an astonishingly short time a mass of complicated technical detail and his service in wisely directing two rather difficult meetings." Charterhouse, like the British Museum, was loth to lose the Archbishop's help when he retired. By statute his Chairmanship of the Governing Body of the School had to end, but the Governors of the Hospital, on the single precedent of Archbishop Sancroft the Non-Juror, asked Lang to continue to preside over them. He gladly consented and remained Chairman of Charterhouse until his death.

With all this business, he could usually find time for the visitor, the man who wanted to talk to him about Russia, or Church music, or the progress of Slum Clearance, in which he had a never-failing interest born in his days at Leeds, or the new Church House, begun in 1937 and opened in 1940, or the Abyssinians, or anything else that might concern an Archbishop whose intellectual province was as wide as Lang's. The picture may be a little bleak, of a life of incessant activity and of a man engaged in a constant struggle to keep his head above the waters of his work. But even in his busiest months he had interludes of relaxation and refreshment at All Souls, where he was now Visitor, and also in his Lambeth and Canterbury homes. The garden at Lambeth, in its summer glory of hollyhocks, dahlias, snapdragon and salvias, was an abiding interest, and his pride in and affection for the historic Palace grew with the years. He enjoyed having his friends there and showing them round, whether they were the leaders of the land or his old Leeds boys like Steve Gould, Fred Farrar and Will Todd, who paid him an annual visit. He had a strong sense of the dignity of the Palace and treated the intrusion of a burglar in the summer of 1933 almost as an affront. The man climbed in through Lang's open bedroom window, later admitting astonishment at finding "an old man in bed" where he had expected a drawing-room. He was caught and identified as the recent robber of Miss Betty Nuttall's lawn-tennis cups. "And *who* is Betty Nuttall?" asked the Archbishop indignantly, when the capture was reported to him.

Each Holy Week saw him at Cuddesdon, where "the old church, with its 'patient peace,' never ceases to cast its old spell upon me." The Bishop of Brechin (the Rt. Rev. Eric Graham), who was Principal from 1929 to 1944, recalls that in Holy Week 1930, Archbishop Temple turned up at Cuddesdon too, under the mistaken impression that Canterbury had gone elsewhere. "Where is this interloper from the Northern Province?" demanded Lang thunderously; and although relations were most affectionate and the two Archbishops conferred fraternally between devotional exercises, neither particularly wanted to see the other at that time and in that place, and thenceforward Canterbury was left in un-disputed possession.

"On these Holy Week visits," writes the Bishop of Brechin, "he (Lang) made it clear that he was at Cuddesdon for purely private and personal purposes, his 'annual soul-cure,' to use his own phrase. He would celebrate on one morning in the Parish Church, which all the students attended in Holy Week, but he would never preach either there or in the College chapel. He was invariably present at all the services in church, and at Compline in the College chapel. And he spent long periods in church alone. Dr. Strong, whose own de-votional habits were of a different pattern and who found he could pray best at high speed, was once heard to make the somewhat puzzled comment: 'He spends a lot of time in church, you know.'[1]

"It took us a little time to adjust our relationship with the Arch-bishop on these occasions. At first, in deference, as I supposed, to his

---

[1] According to a ribald and purely legendary tale of the times, the two prelates were said to have remarked on each other's habits as follows: "Poor old Cosmo: he hasn't read a book for years." "Poor old Tommy: he hasn't said a prayer for years."

expressed wish to be left to himself, I told the students not to pay him any special attention. They followed this injunction faithfully; but then I heard, indirectly, that they had incurred His Grace's criticism for complete disregard of 'the Primate of All England.' So the next year they were instructed to rise whenever he came into the room and be as deferential as possible on all occasions. This proved (as I had expected) to be more than the Archbishop really wanted, and he told them to take no notice of his comings and goings. So we reverted to the original scheme by his own authority; and all was well. . . .

"The constant and deep impression which he left upon us was wholly delightful. He was a son of the College coming home to the place where he had begun to learn his deepest lessons and glad to share its life once again; a holy and humble man of heart seeking quite simply to be alone with God and to strengthen his discipleship. It was obvious that he greatly valued these visits himself; but their value to the College, Staff and Students alike, deserves a grateful mention. It was an inspiration to find that the great ecclesiastic was also a simple Christian of deep piety, whose life was 'hid with Christ in God.'"

He spent Christmas at the Old Palace at Canterbury, his usual guests being the Ford family.

"He had a special corner in his heart for Christopher, my six foot seven son (later killed in action at Anzio)," writes Mrs. Ford, "who was a great raconteur and mimic and was always entirely at his ease with him and amused him greatly. Every Christmas the Archbishop had a big children's party and a feature of this was a variety entertainment organised by the Hardcastles and my family. Christopher came in as a ballerina, Madam Fatima by name, the world's largest woman, in a stiff muslin skirt sticking out round his waist over pink pyjama trousers, his chest enlarged by a pillow and draped with shawls, his face heavily made up with cosmetics, and on his head a black curly wig crowned by a wreath. He went round the hall . . . blowing kisses to one and all. The Archbishop literally laughed till he cried."

With the beauty of the Cathedral and its services in the background, the children's party, the music or reading aloud in the evenings, the Canterbury Christmases were "true delights." Once he took his guests round the Cathedral. He stopped before the wooden panel on which are inscribed the names of all the Archbishops and remarked, "Here, children, you see the place of my humiliation." "Why, Archbishop?" enquired Mrs. Ford. "Because the panel is so ugly?"

"*Really*, my dear May," was his reply, "cannot any of you do better than that? Lanfranc, Anselm, Becket, Laud, Davidson—and then, at the end, my unworthy self, Cosmo Gordon."

In August each year he obeyed the beckoning finger of Ballure, looking forward, like a schoolboy before his holidays, to the hour when he would put one of his beloved Waverleys and the last John Buchan into his bag and take the road to the North. In 1935 the ancient Wolseley, which had served him since 1914 and was finally banned from Balmoral as a public danger by the King, was replaced by a new Armstrong-Siddeley. First came "the Snob's Progress." A visit to Hinchingbrooke, the home of Lord Sandwich, had an almost invariable place on the itinerary. Afterwards he would stay at Welbeck, where the "Duchess Winnie" [1]—"unchanged and unchangeable"—occupied an especial niche in his affections. Then he might move on to Garrowby, to visit the son of his old friend Lord Halifax, or Castle Howard, or Lumley Castle, or Alnwick, or Howick; and so across the Border to the first exciting glimpse of the Highland Rampart; and on to Kintyre, to the ever-welcoming Macdonalds and the ever-welcome "Cell." There he prayed and read and walked and had a few selected friends to stay, such as the Temples, who came twice, or Jack and May Talbot—"the good companions," as he called them.

There too, in 1934, he had "a great exhilarating experience"—his first flight in an aeroplane. He had always wished, he said, to see Largie Castle from the air, and his chance came when a friend of the young Macdonalds arrived with his own machine. By present ideas it was not, it would seem, very reliable and some misgivings were felt at the Archbishop's venture. He himself was chiefly anxious lest news of his flight should leak out into the papers, and insisted on Simon Macdonald putting on the archiepiscopal cloak and impersonating him while he was in the air. Fortunately the flight was uneventful and the young pilot's forebodings that death would come to the Archbishop were unfulfilled.

I very soon got over the first inevitable sense of dizziness and was greatly excited to see the islands and Arran and the moors, with Largie and Ballure, from a great height. . . . Indeed, the experience seemed to anticipate a little what death might be like—old familiar objects becoming fainter and fainter as one rose into another world.

[1] The Duchess of Portland, wife of the 6th Duke.

Chapter XXXI

THE DEATH OF THE KING

YEAR after year at Ballure the rough diary told of the annual visit to Balmoral. The Archbishop's memories of King George and Queen Mary went back to the distant days when the King was Duke of York and Cosmo Lang was Vicar of Portsea, and they had a brisk difference of opinion about Korea and foreign missions. That cloud had passed very quickly, and soon Lang was writing: "I really like him very much—frank, unaffected, outspoken to a fault." As time went on, his love and reverence grew and deepened. The Royal office, of course, had and would always have his loyal respect; but for the King as a man, for his kindliness, simplicity, religious spirit and single-hearted devotion to his duty, Lang had much more than a formal feeling. King George and Queen Mary too, for whom his regard and admiration were equally high and as repeatedly expressed in his private jottings, became in a genuine sense his friends. In the scale of worldly values nothing stood higher than this friendship. He valued it above price and was especially proud to be treated as a trusted counsellor, to be admitted into the little affairs of the family—as a family and not as King, Queen and Princes—to share its jokes, its anxieties, its sorrows and its many memories. He would recall days on the hill when the King was stalking—the time, for example, when a heavy shower came down on them as they were close to an overhanging rock which could only shelter one; and the King lay down under it, and the Archbishop, claiming the privilege of a subject to cover the person of his Sovereign, lay down on the top of him. There were the long talks and consultations and family councils. "You know my mind," the King once said on some rather difficult occasion, and went off for a long walk, leaving the Archbishop to take his place at the table.

The King returned Lang's regard, leaning often upon his judgment and discretion and talking freely to him of all that was happening. In Lang's scanty collection of letters are several subscribed by "your sincere old friend G.R.I."; in 1923 he received the Royal Victorian Chain, an especial honour; and in 1933, when the office of High Almoner fell vacant, the King insisted, with the support of a single precedent, upon the Archbishop filling the post.

In September 1935 Lang paid his usual visit to Balmoral. The King seemed fairly well, but depressed by his inability any longer to shoot or stalk and by "certain family troubles" on which he unburdened himself to his guest. On December 30th came a last "charming letter." A fortnight later the Prime Minister (Mr. Baldwin) told Lang "he was troubled by news from Sandringham," adding a word about his fears for the future. The Archbishop left a very full account of what followed, apparently written immediately afterwards; and from this are taken any quotations in this chapter not otherwise attributed.

On January 17th the people were warned by a bulletin that there were "signs of cardiac weakness which must be regarded with some disquiet." During the earlier Royal illness in 1928 the Archbishop had received a long letter from Lord Stamfordham on the question whether, if the King were dying, the Primate should be officially present. "Apparently there is no precedent for this, as an official duty of the Primate, since George III." The Archbishop now telephoned to Lord Stamfordham's successor, Lord Wigram,[1] "telling him that I hoped that, if the anxiety grew, I might be allowed to come as, apart from the call of personal friendship, I felt the country would expect it." The Queen, on being consulted, agreed, and on Sunday the 19th the Archbishop travelled to Sandringham, to be met by Lord Dawson of Penn with the melancholy news "that he had little hope, but that the chances were seventy-five per cent. in favour of the King's lasting for days or even weeks, twenty-five per cent. in favour of hours."

The Queen was wonderfully calm and talked freely on all sorts of subjects. After dinner I went with her to the King, but he was asleep. So I did not rouse him, but said some prayers over him at his bedside. He looked very frail and the failure of circulation had discoloured his face. Next morning, Monday, 20th January, he seemed slightly better. I went to him about eleven. He was sitting on his chair propped up by pillows—very thin and weak and unable to speak much, but quite conscious. He spoke quietly and gently about our old friendship—"Yes, very old friend—how long?" "Yes, thirty-eight years"—and said he was glad to see me. I asked if I might pray with him and give him my Blessing. "Yes, please do— I would like it." So I offered some simple prayers, laid my hands on his head, and blessed him. He thanked me and said goodbye.

[1] Permanent Lord-in-Waiting since 1936.

The Privy Council then arrived to receive the King's approval for setting up a Council of State.

There was much discussion as to what would happen if the King were unable to sign with his own hand. We agreed that if he could only make his mark, we who were present would sign an attestation that he had done so in our presence and that we were satisfied that he had done so with clear and conscious intention to sign. We were then summoned to his sick-room. . . . The King was in his chair, looking pathetically weak and frail, but fully conscious. He smiled as we entered. The President read the Order in Council. With a clear voice the King gave the reply so familiar to him, "Approved." Then Dawson, kneeling at his feet and watching his face, said, "Sir, do you wish to sign yourself?" "Yes," said the King, rallying for the last time to the old call of duty. "I have always signed in my own hand." Dawson tried to put the pen in his fingers, but owing to the failure of circulation they could not hold it. Then the hands moved most pathetically over the paper in the effort to sign. This took some minutes. Then the King turned to his Councillors and said, "I am very sorry to keep you waiting so long"; adding shortly after, "You see, I can't concentrate." Once again the hands moved impotently up and down. Then, with great adroitness, Dawson put the pen in his hand and guided it, saying, "Make a mark, Sir, and you may sign afterwards." So two marks, X X, were made. Then the King turned again to his Councillors and dismissed them with the old kind, kingly smile. It was his last official act: we were all deeply moved. Then downstairs we all signed the attestation.

After luncheon Lord Dawson told the Archbishop, who had been thinking of returning to London, that the end might come very soon and that he should stay. Other members of the Royal Family had now arrived.

We all met at tea. The Queen was still amazingly calm and strong, the Prince of Wales full of vitality and talk, and touchingly attentive to the Queen. I went again to the King's room: his breathing showed that the end was coming. This evening the Queen and her family dined quietly apart. It was just after the household dinner that Dawson consulted us about the famous bulletin—"The King's life is moving peacefully to its close." The idea of it was entirely his own. . . . Shortly afterwards I went up to the King with the

Queen, and then went to my room to be quiet and await my summons to the King's side for the last minutes. It came through Sir Frederick Willans [1] about 11.15 p.m. I put on my cassock and went with him to the King's room. The Queen and Princess Mary were there, with the doctors and nurses. The sons were together downstairs. No one seemed to think of calling them, and for this I was sorry. Then, after some time of quiet waiting, as the King's breathing grew more slow, I read the Twenty-third Psalm, some passages from the Scriptures such as St. Paul's great "I am persuaded . . ." and some prayers at quiet intervals, and then, going to the King's side, I said the Commendatory Prayers—"Go forth, O Christian Soul"—with a final Benediction. As it was plain that the King's life could only last for a few minutes, I felt that I must leave the Queen and her family alone, and retired. I was told afterwards that the sons, especially the Prince of Wales, were painfully upset—I suppose they had seldom if ever seen death—and that it was the Queen, still marvellously self-controlled, who supported and strengthened them. Finally, within a few minutes, the breathing ceased and, in the words of the last bulletin, "Death came peacefully to the King at 11.55 p.m." Within five minutes a new day, a new King, a new reign. So passed my King, my friend of these long years. God grant him rest and peace and light!

King Edward, the Archbishop noted, began his reign at once.

After midnight he ordered all the clocks, which by long custom at Sandringham were kept half an hour in advance of the real time, to be put back! I wonder what other customs will be put back also!

The Archbishop wrote with feeling as, owing to the unheralded change in time, he was nearly late in the morning at Sandringham Church, where he was celebrating Holy Communion.

Later he saw King Edward and

was thus the first of his subjects (outside his household) to greet him as "Your Majesty." I spoke a few hasty but deeply felt words about his great responsibility and my desire to give him loyal service. He was very cordial. After saying goodbye to the Queen—her fortitude still marvellous—I went to the King's room alone : there was no one there. I lifted the veil from his face and looked upon it for the last time. It had a light upon it of most beautiful serenity and peace. So with a final silent commendation of his soul to God I left.

[1] Sir F. J. Willans, K.C.V.O., Surgeon-Apothecary to H.M.'s Household at Sandringham.

That afternoon the Privy Council met at St. James's Palace to witness the declaration of accession. King Edward "read a short and admirable speech, closing, as I was glad to hear, with words expressing the hope that God would guide him. He went through these ceremonies with great simplicity and dignity. . . ."

The Royal funeral was to be a week later, so that there was little enough time for the arrangements to be made. These were interrupted, for the Archbishop, by the meeting on the 22nd of the new Convocation, which claimed his attention for the procession, the Latin sermon, the election of the new Prolocutor, a speech in Latin, and other duties. His chaplains meanwhile were kept busy telephoning and moving rapidly between the Earl Marshal, the Lord Great Chamberlain and Westminster.

On Thursday the 23rd, King George's body was brought from Sandringham to lie in state in Westminster Hall.

On Tuesday the King had said to me that he did not wish any religious service to be held, as—said he—he was anxious to spare the Queen. But I insisted that, however short, there *must* be some such service. Certainly the whole ceremony would have been, as it were, blank without it; and it was at the Queen's own wish that the one hymn— "Praise my soul, the King of Heaven"—was to be sung. I borrowed from Westminster the purple cope used at the funeral of Charles II. . . . I have been present at many great ceremonies, but I cannot remember any more impressive. On each side of the Hall the two Houses of Parliament stood; at the south end on the steps the choirs were gathered; in the midst on a crimson platform the trestle awaited the bier. I have never felt such a silence, helped by the fact that a great soft grey carpet had been stretched along the Hall, so that not even a footfall could be heard. A few minutes before four, with the Earl Marshal and other officials, I went out to receive the body.

In the procession to the catafalque the Archbishop walked immediately before the bier, the Royal Family following it.

In tense silence it moved up the Hall. After the bier had been set in its place, I took my place on the low platform below it, facing the King and Queen. The service I had drawn up was very simple: it began with "O Saviour of the World," etc., then the Lesser Litany and Lord's Prayer, and a prayer of thanksgiving and remembrance of the dead King, the hymn, and my Blessing. I was so profoundly moved that it required a great effort to control my voice. . . . Then we conducted the King, the Queen and the Royal Family to the North door, and bade them farewell, the Queen still wonderful in her self-control.

Afterwards in the House of Lords the Archbishop made a simple and very moving speech, describing the last Privy Council at Sandringham and ending with Milton's "Nothing is here for tears . . ." On Sunday the 26th he preached at the Abbey, which was filled, multitudes being turned away; and that evening he broadcast an address at a memorial service arranged by the B.B.C., in which leaders of the different religious communities took part. "It was significant to hear Prayers for the Dead read with full unction by a Moderator of the Kirk."

Next day, the eve of the funeral, he had "one of my vicious catarrh colds." In the afternoon he went down to stay with the Crawleys, his old chaplain being now a Canon of Windsor, arriving with a temperature of over a hundred. "He complained bitterly at having been made by us to see the doctor," wrote the Archdeacon of Canterbury, "as the medicine he gave him had only postponed the cold's development! When we got there Mrs. Crawley, the only person in the world who can really do anything with him, sent him to bed and made him have his dinner there."

Tuesday the 28th, the day of the funeral, began with a damp mist, which cleared later. Owing to the unexpectedly large crowds in London, the train was forty minutes late in reaching Windsor and there was a cold and draughty wait in St. George's Chapel, this and the Dean's arrangements moving the Archbishop to caustic comment.

At last came the sound of advancing troops and words of command. The sailors, in marvellous order, drew the gun-carriage to the foot of the steps. Then followed two most poignant sounds, the bos'n's whistle, "Admiral on board" and "Admiral over the side," and the pipes playing "The Flowers of the Forest"—it was this sound that went straight to my Scottish heart.

So the solemn and beautiful service began and went its course, with Goss's Sentences, the Twenty-third Psalm, "Abide with me," the Lesson, and Walford Davies's "God be in my head . . ."

Winchester read the Lesson from the closing chapter of the Book of Revelation; then I advanced and stood before the coffin. It was slowly lowered as I said the Solemn Sentences. At the committal the King, at his own suggestion, advanced and himself threw in the dust. It was not easy to control my voice, but I learned afterwards that it was clearly heard throughout the world. The Archbishop of York read the concluding prayers. Then Garter King of Arms (Sir Gerald Wollaston) in his regalia announced the styles of the dead and of the living Kings, with some nervous hesitation. Finally I pronounced the Benediction.

He had had a terrible week of mental and emotional strain. "Looking back, it is difficult to think how I was able to 'win through,' but by God's grace I was, in the old words, 'wonderfully sustained.'"
On the 29th he went to Buckingham Palace to see Queen Mary.

I had a long talk with her and dear Princess Mary—her (the Queen's) fortitude still unbroken. Let it not be supposed that this unfailing self-control was due to any sort of hardness. On the contrary, her emotions were always ready to break through; only her courage restrained them.

Then I had quite a long talk with the King. I told him frankly that I was aware that he had been somewhat set against me by knowing that his father had often discussed his affairs with me. But I assured him—which was true—that I had always tried to put the most favourable view of his conduct before his father. He did not seem to resent this frankness, but quickly said that of course there had always been difficulties between the Sovereign and his heir. He said, naïvely, that he understood he had now to appoint Bishops, and asked me to tell him how it was done! I tried to enlighten him. He spoke of one or two clerics whom he had met; but even of these his knowledge was very faint. It was clear that he knows little, and, I fear, cares little, about the Church and its affairs. But I was impressed by his alertness and obvious eagerness to know and to learn; and he was very pleasant and *seemed* to be very cordial. As I left, I spoke once again, as at Sandringham, about his great responsibilities and promised to give him all the help and service I could. Well, we shall see. But I feel that a long and greatly valued chapter in my life, associated with the constant kindness and friendship of King George, is closed. There is not only a new reign, but a new *régime*. I can only be most thankful for what has been, and for what is to be, hope for the best. God guide the King!

Chapter XXXII

THE ABDICATION

THE Archbishop kept a diary during the weeks of what he liked to call "The King's Matter." Although he edited it afterwards, he evidently wrote it from day to day, when the end was still obscure. He intended it as a guide for his biographer and a record for the historian, but not for publication, at any rate in its entirety, during the lifetime of those about whom he wrote. The treatment of this document, therefore, presents some difficulty. On the one hand, the Archbishop's wish must be respected, but on the other, his own part in these events having been misunderstood and exaggerated in some quarters, a fair record is owing to himself and to history.

In the present account, therefore, while many details of a personal character are necessarily omitted, the main outline of the story will stand as he wrote it; and the reader is assured that nothing has intentionally been left out which might affect his judgment of the Archbishop. Where no other source is given, the quotations are from the diary.

For some time the Archbishop had been aware of the attachment of the Prince of Wales to Mrs. Simpson. When he was staying at Balmoral in 1935, he had a "long and intimate talk" with King George on the subject; and probably there were other unrecorded conversations. As the Archbishop told the new King a few days after his father's death,[1] he was conscious that these talks might have worked to his prejudice. The Prince of Wales would not unnaturally dislike the thought that a comparative stranger (to him) should be allowed to share in a matter so private, and would suspect that advice, which he would regard as disagreeable, had been offered, or at least that an attitude unsympathetic to him had been shown. We have the Archbishop's word that these suspicions were unfounded; but the fact that the conversations were held at all, and were known by the Prince to have been held, was bound to embarrass the relations of King and Archbishop.

No one could have described Lang as a harsh critic of Royal persons. The divinity that hedges a King was very real to him and, in addition, his genuine admiration and affection for King George V as a man and

[1] See page 395.

for Queen Mary as a woman would naturally predispose him to a favourable, or at any rate a tolerant, judgment on their children. In his notebooks he makes occasional comment on the Prince of Wales, on his gifts, his charm and his promise, with sometimes a note of regret that these were not always wisely directed. The fault, he felt, lay not so much with the Prince himself as with some of the people who were round him. Yet he must have known that while these were not at all the sort who would hobnob happily with Archbishops, the Prince himself, in thought and tastes and temperament, was very far from him; that he could never be the friend his father had been. Yet he would still have had the Archbishop's loyalty and service, even his affection, had not a barrier risen between them.

In the summer of 1936 there was of course no visit to Balmoral, but by a generous thought the Duke and Duchess of York invited the Archbishop to their Highland home at Birkhall. "The kind Yorks bade me come to them at Birkhall," he wrote in his notebook. . . . "It was a delightful visit. They were kindness itself. The old house is full of charm and the Duchess has done much with the garden." After tea on the second day,

> The children—Lilliebet, Margaret Rose and Margaret Elphinstone— joined us. They sang some action-songs most charmingly. It was strange to think of the destiny which may be awaiting the little Elizabeth, at present second from the Throne! She and her lively little sister are certainly most entrancing children.

When he left he was told he must come again, "so the links with Balmoral may not be wholly broken." Family life of that quality was something the Archbishop had honoured in King George and Queen Mary, who had given a pattern and example to all the families they ruled.

He had graver cause for uneasiness in conversations during the summer with some of those who were near the person of the King and had an inkling of his intentions. Next year the King was to be crowned, in a solemn act of dedication, the significance of which no man felt more deeply than Lang. Yet in Court circles, and indeed outside them, it was already common knowledge that Mrs. Simpson was contemplating a divorce from her husband, with the plain inference that this would be followed by marriage with the King. So here—to put it plainly—was the possibility that at a time when the Church was reasserting its Marriage Laws with some vehemence, the Archbishop might be required to crown and to administer the Sacrament of Holy Communion to a man married, or about to be married, to a person who had twice divorced her husband. Such a surrender would shake the foundations of the Church's influence and teaching.

Nor was this all. An Evangelistic campaign was being planned for 1937, in association with the Coronation, the people being asked to dedicate themselves with their King to the service of God and their country. At the end of 1936 the Archbishop was to open this campaign of "A Recall to Religion" with a broadcast. But if this looming possibility was realised, with what force or sincerity could he speak and, above all, how could he allow the appeal to hinge on a ceremony which had become a mockery? Time was passing and some decision must be taken on this point, which was of grave importance to the Church and the Archbishop, however subsidiary it might seem in the eyes of the world.

Beyond lay the Archbishop's personal difficulty of crowning the King at all, if he persisted in his purpose. Some have suggested that he should have refused, others that he would have refused. He has left no record of a decision, if indeed he ever made one; and it is perhaps profitless to discuss what would or would not have been his action in circumstances which were necessarily hypothetical. A passage in his diary gives some indication of the working of his mind.

I had hoped—little knowing what was impending in the autumn—that when the time came for me to go into the Coronation Service more fully and to prepare him (the King) for it, I might use this opportunity to speak to him frankly about his private life and ask him to reconsider it in the light of these solemn words. But as the months passed . . . the thought of my having to consecrate *him* as King weighed on me as a heavy burden. Indeed, I considered whether I could bring myself to do so. But I had a *sense* that circumstances might change. I could only pray that they might, either outwardly or in his own soul.

These words may be taken to imply that if, with the consent of Parliament, the King had been able to have his way, the Archbishop, despite the heaviness of his heart, would neither have refused his services nor himself have abdicated. He might have pointed to the complicating relationship of Church and State, arguing that in clearing himself from complicity he would merely be passing the burden on to someone else; the Coronation would nevertheless take place; some more complaisant prelate, with a different view of the respective claims of the Establishment and the Law of the Church, would be found; an irreparable harm would still be done; and at a most critical time the leadership of the Church might well be in fumbling and suspected hands. But this is conjecture. What is certain is that he concealed neither from himself nor from others that the ceremony in the circumstances would be unreal and meaningless. It would, he said, be "pouring all those sacred words into a *vacuum*." He had a presentiment, however, that the decision would be taken out of his hands.

As summer passed into autumn and an announcement of the impending proceedings for a divorce was published, his anxiety grew. By a "gentleman's agreement" the Press of the United Kingdom made no mention of an issue which had become a common topic of conversation in the country. But the Press of the United States and the Continent was under no such obligation. Some of what was published was false, like the statement in an American paper that the Archbishop had refused an invitation to a Court function on learning that Mrs. Simpson was to be there; but much was only too true, and Lang felt that the Monarchy was being vulgarised and degraded, that mud was being thrown on sacred things. With the Press cuttings came the letters from overseas, mostly expressing dislike and dread of what appeared imminent and urging the Archbishop to "do something." But he could do nothing. He could only wait and watch.

"I made repeated suggestions about seeing him (the King),"[1] he told Wilfrid Parker, "but he was very emphatic that on the subject of his relations with Mrs. Simpson he would listen to nobody but Mr. Baldwin, who had a right to speak to him and advise him."

But afterwards he had qualms.

On looking through these notes among my papers, I am disposed to think that I might have *written* to Edward VIII, if only to liberate my conscience. Yet almost certainly this would have invoked, even if any reply had been given, the sort of slight which *I* personally might have understood, but to which the Archbishop of Canterbury ought not to be exposed.

[1] Evidently not directly to the King himself.

He was assuredly right that no letter would have had any effect.

On Sunday, November 1st, when the Archbishop was at Hatfield, he saw the Prime Minister, who told him that on October 19th he had at last spoken to the King. He said that "he had approached him as his confidential counsellor and hoped he might always do so with perfect frankness. His Majesty cordially assented." The Prime Minister had urged the King "to realise that this was a matter which was affecting and might come to affect even more gravely his own position and the prestige of the Monarchy. They parted cordially, and both seemed relieved that a frank opening had been made."

A few days after this conversation with the King, Mrs. Simpson was given a decree *nisi*. The silence of the Press was still unbroken. On November 19th Lang saw the Prime Minister again, who told him that the King adhered to his intention of marrying Mrs. Simpson, even if this meant retirement into private life. However, a visit followed to the depressed areas of Wales, where the King was much moved by the warmth of his reception; and when the Archbishop saw Mr. Baldwin again on the 26th, he found that once more all was uncertainty. A man prominent in newspaper circles had approached the King with a proposal for what would have been in effect a morganatic marriage. A disquieting possibility was that such a plan, if put forward with the King's approval, might be strongly supported by a section of the Press.

During the anxious days that followed Lang saw and talked with many of those principally concerned. There was no argument, for there was no disagreement; nor did he make any attempt, as superfluous as it would have been futile, to impose a point of view upon the Government.

I had another long talk with the Prime Minister, who had again seen the King. The P.M. had meanwhile secured the unanimous support of the whole Cabinet and the promise of support from Attlee on behalf of the Opposition. He had told His Majesty plainly as to the suggested compromise that it would require special legislation and that neither the Government nor the Opposition would introduce it; and that he must choose between Mrs. Simpson and his throne.

Meanwhile the Bishops had come to London, so that the Archbishop might place before them that subsidary but vexing problem of the "Recall to Religion." He felt that before deciding whether, and if so how, the campaign was to be launched, they should know what was happening. The meeting of the Bishops at such a time naturally provoked speculation, some sensational and erroneous explanations appearing in the American newspapers.

Then on December 2nd the Press published fully an address by the Bishop of Bradford [1] to his Diocesan Conference, in which, after admirably describing the significance of the Coronation Service, he had spoken of the part of the King in self-dedication and of his need of Divine Grace, adding that it could be wished that he showed more awareness of this need. He explained next day that the address had been composed *six weeks before*, that he had no intention to refer to the rumours which had become current, but only to his negligence in church-going. But these last words had already been taken as referring to these rumours and proved to be the leakage which at last burst the dam; and the newspapers broke their restraint. The *Times* had a long article on December 3rd, and the *Daily Mail* and the *News Chronicle* had articles favouring "the compromise."

Actually the first comment in the Press appeared in a leading article in the *Yorkshire Post* of December 2nd. This had been circulated on the previous evening by the Press Association to all other newspapers.

The story that the Archbishop was privy to the Bishop's speech and had even instigated it was totally untrue. On the contrary he was extremely annoyed by it, since it looked as though the leakage had come from Lambeth. Actually the Bishop's words merely anticipated something that was bound to have happened within two or three days. The newspapers were waiting for a cue and the Bishop of Bradford gave it them.

The Prime Minister had a long interview with the King on the evening of December 2nd, the purport of which he passed on next day to the Archbishop. Before seeing the King he had consulted further with the Cabinet and had communicated with the Governments of the Dominions.

They had one and all (except de Valera, who had difficulties of his own) stated that they would not support the legislation necessary for the compromise. There was a particularly strong telegram from the Prime Minister of the Commonwealth of Australia (Mr. Bruce), [2] stating that in his view His Majesty could not now re-establish his prestige or command confidence as King. Baldwin did not hesitate

[1] The Rt. Rev. A. W. F. Blunt.
[2] Mr. Bruce (now Lord Bruce of Melbourne) was High Commissioner. The Prime Minister was Mr. Lyons.

to show H.M. this telegram. He told him that there were only three alternatives :—(1) Give up Mrs. Simpson. This H.M. said he would not do. (2) Marry her, but not make her Queen : this was ruled out by the impossibility of getting necessary legislation in this country and the Dominions through. (3) Abdication.

He left H.M. with this last course plainly before him. H.M. must now come to a decision.

On December 4th Mr. Baldwin told the House of Commons the position. The King must choose.

That afternoon I saw the Moderator (Aubrey) and Secretary (Berry) of the Federal Council of Evangelical Free Churches and gave them as much information as I thought it was possible to give. I discussed with them the reactions of public opinion. They believed the mass of the people would support the Government, but acknowledged that a large proportion, especially of the young to whom the King was a popular hero and who knew little of the real circumstances, felt a strong sympathy with him. "He is doing the honourable thing. He wants to marry the woman he loves. Why shouldn't he ?" etc. I suppose that those who, like myself, have known the whole business for two years can scarcely realise the effect of this sudden crisis on minds wholly unprepared for it and ignorant of all that had led up to it. Letters from and talks with all sorts of people showed how widespread this ignorance and consequent surprise were.

I may add that on the same afternoon, December 4th, earlier, I had lunched with the Crown Prince of Sweden at the home of the Swedish Minister and had a long talk with him. He was distressed for and by the King and said that this was a matter which affected not this Empire only, but all the countries where the Monarchy survived.

That evening the Archbishop made an appeal to the clergy, by newspaper and broadcast, to "refrain from speaking directly on the King's matter" in their sermons on Sunday, but asked that "everywhere prayers should be offered for him and his Ministers." That night, when listening to the wireless in his study at Lambeth, he was dismayed to hear that "the Archbishop of Canterbury had gone to Fort Belvedere," a statement demanding an immediate contradiction.

On Saturday, December 5th, he went down to Canterbury to hold Confirmations next day, but on the Sunday afternoon was recalled to

London by the Prime Minister. The King had put forward a new proposal on which Mr. Baldwin desired his opinion. It is to be observed that this was the only occasion on which the Archbishop's advice appears to have been asked or given, and as later the Cabinet took the same view as he had put to the Prime Minister, the suggestion was stillborn. In any case, it had no effect upon the issue, which was already certain.

It is to the credit of the King that in these hectic days and hours he has cancelled all his engagements and refused to come to London, so as to avoid all demonstrations and do as little as he could to divide the country. . . . Hours passed—all sorts of suggestions and rumours in the Press. On Tuesday, December 8th, the Prime Minister had his last interview with the King, who now accepted abdication as the only way by which he could justify his wish to marry Mrs. Simpson. On December 9th the Queen went to the Royal Lodge at Windsor to see the King. Every sort of official was by this time busy in preparing for an abdication. I saw the P.M. on Thursday, December 10th. The Cabinet in the morning sent a last request to H.M. to reconsider. He answered at once that his decision was irrevocable, and at Fort Belvedere he signed an Instrument of Abdication witnessed by his three brothers and sent to the P.M. for announcement in Parliament with a message.

That afternoon (December 10th) the message was read in both Houses of Parliament in crowded Houses. In the Lords Edward Halifax told the tale shortly and simply; Snell spoke well for the Opposition; then Crewe for the Liberals. Then I spoke, and what I said seemed to move and impress the House. Salisbury followed with a few words about the moral seriousness of an abdication. In the Commons the P.M. made a full statement of all his conversations with the King, in words characteristically simple and sincere. As Garvin said in the *Observer*, it proved that nothing in literature or oratory can exceed in effectiveness a plain tale well told. There was almost complete unanimity in the House in support of the P.M. Even Winston Churchill, who had played for a time with the idea of a "King's party," acknowledged that the abdication must be accepted.

This account should have shown how small was the Archbishop's part in the conclusion. He was deeply concerned; he was kept fully informed; but, except for one occasion, when the result was no longer in doubt and his opinion was asked on a contingent point, he neither

403

influenced, nor tried to influence, the course of events. Satisfied that the Prime Minister's attitude was substantially identical with his own, he was content to leave him the hand to play, without an ecclesiastical interference which was unnecessary and might even have been embarrassing. This view was confirmed by no less weighty an authority than Lord Baldwin himself. A few weeks before his death in December 1947 he told the present writer that the Archbishop had made no attempt to force an issue, or even to press his point of view, and that the decisive factor was the uncompromising stand of the Dominion Premiers, and especially of the Prime Minister of Australia.

On December 11th both Houses of Parliament passed the Abdication Bill.

That evening the late King, on his own responsibility, broadcast a message from Windsor Castle. It was well done: his voice was under good control. It had some real pathos, but there was one passage which jarred: it was when he said that he had been "denied" the happiness of his brother in having his wife and children—as if he might not at any time have honestly possessed this happiness if he had chosen. But he ended on a right note—"God save the King."

On Sunday, December 13th, it was the Archbishop's turn to broadcast. His words had a very mixed reception.

It was a difficult task. I felt that I could not in honesty and sincerity merely say kind, and of course true, things about the late King's charm and manifold services; that in my position I was bound to say something about the surrender of a great trust from the motive of private happiness and about the social circle in which he had thought that that happiness could be found. . . . But I added some words, most sincerely, about that charm, about those services, etc., and then went on to speak of Baldwin's place in the crisis, of Queen Mary, and of the new King and Queen. The address must have been listened to by millions at home and overseas. It was next day published in full in the leading newspapers, and more or less fully in all the others. As I fully expected, my words about the late King let loose a torrent of abuse from the less reputable Press and from a multitude of correspondents. On the other hand, there were just as many letters of gratitude.[1] The one which for me was sufficient was

---

[1] This is not correct. The majority of the letters were critical or abusive, but the Archbishop did not see most of them.

a letter which next day the Prime Minister sent, written by his own hand, in which he warmly praised what I had said, and ended with the words, "It was the voice of Christian England."

These were the passages on which comment was concentrated:

What pathos, nay what tragedy, surrounds the central figure of these swiftly moving scenes! On the 11th day of December, 248 years ago, King James II fled from Whitehall. By a strange coincidence, on the 11th day of December last week King Edward VIII, after speaking his last words to his people, left Windsor Castle, the scene of all the splendid traditions of his ancestors and his Throne, and went out an exile. In the darkness he left these shores.

Seldom, if ever, has any British Sovereign come to the Throne with greater natural gifts for his kingship. Seldom, if ever, has any Sovereign been welcomed by a more enthusiastic loyalty. From God he had received a high and sacred trust. Yet by his own will he has abdicated—he has surrendered the trust. With characteristic frankness he has told us his motive. It was a craving for private happiness. Strange and sad it must be that for such a motive, however strongly it pressed upon his heart, he should have disappointed hopes so high and abandoned a trust so great. Even more strange and sad it is that he should have sought his happiness in a manner inconsistent with the Christian principles of marriage, and within a social circle whose standards and ways of life are alien to all the best instincts and traditions of his people. Let those who belong to this circle know that to-day they stand rebuked by the judgment of the nation which had loved King Edward. I have shrunk from saying these words. But I have felt compelled for the sake of sincerity and truth to say them.

Yet for one who has known him since his childhood, who has felt his charm and admired his gifts, these words cannot be the last. How can we forget the high hopes and promise of his youth; his most genuine care for the poor, the suffering, the unemployed; his years of eager service both at home and across the seas? It is the remembrance of these things that wrings from our hearts the cry— "The pity of it, O, the pity of it!" To the infinite mercy and the protecting care of God we commit him now, wherever he may be.

The Archbishop went on, as he has said, to pay tribute to Queen Mary, to the Prime Minister and to King George VI. "A King has gone. God be with him. A King has come. God bless him, keep him, guide him now and ever."

He had spoken with genuine unwillingness and from a compelling sense of duty. A chaplain going into his study while he was preparing the broadcast found him on his knees by his desk.

For a few days the dimensions of Lang's mail recalled the "sacred memories." Some of the critics were stung by a rebuke they rightly felt was intended for themselves. Others, wrongly regarding the Archbishop as the chief agent in the Abdication, chided him for ungenerously exulting over a beaten adversary.[1] Yet others, unmindful of the office of an Archbishop and of what was due from it, felt that the King might have been suffered to go in silence, without any attempt to point the moral.

The broadcast was composed in haste, and no doubt, if the Archbishop had had more time, he might have phrased it a little differently. His sense of pathos, of tragedy, of historic contrast, was always strong, sometimes overpowering. As his anxiety lifted, he was gripped by the drama of what he had witnessed and so alluded to the flight of King James II and used such words as "In the darkness he left these shores." Nor, perhaps, was "a craving for private happiness" a fair and adequate interpretation of the King's motive; while the allusion to "a social circle" was liable to misunderstanding. But these are minor reproaches. It was right that, as Archbishop, he should say something at such a moment and should not confine himself to a few amiable platitudes. How far some of his words might have been better chosen is a matter of taste on which opinions may legitimately differ.

At least, there was no foundation for the charge that he had spoken in a vindictive or triumphant spirit.

"My heart aches for the Duke of Windsor," he wrote in his diary, "remembering his childhood, his boyhood, the rich promise of his services as Prince of Wales. . . . I cannot bear to think of the kind of life into which he has passed."

The sequel was happier.

On Monday, December 21st, I was bidden by the King and Queen to go and see them at their house, 145 Piccadilly, at 5.30 p.m. They

---

[1] As—   "My Lord Archbishop, what a scold you are !
          And when your man is down, how bold you are !
          Of Christian charity how scant you are !
          And, auld Lang swine, how full of cant you are !"

were, as they have always been, most kind and cordial. I had already received a long and delightful letter from Queen Elizabeth, dated December 12th, signing herself "for the first time and with great affection, Elizabeth R." She wrote . . . "I can hardly now believe that we have been called to this tremendous task and (I am writing to you quite intimately) the curious thing is that we are not afraid. I feel that God has enabled us to face the situation calmly." The King was in good spirit; and for an hour we talked together with the utmost ease about "the crisis," about the poor Duke of Windsor, and then about the arrangements for the Coronation. What a relief it was, after the strained and wilful ways of the late King, to be in this atmosphere of intimate friendship, and instead of looking forward to the Coronation as a sort of nightmare, to realise that . . . I was now sure that to the solemn words of the Coronation there would be a sincere response. At Christmas the King wrote to me most kindly, and I noted that it would be difficult to see in his handwriting and specially his signature, "George R.I.," any difference from that of his father. Prosit omen!

Chapter XXXIII

THE CORONATION

THE Archbishop may not have been alone in his presentiment that he would not be called upon to crown King Edward.

I had had some talk with King Edward in the spring (1936) . . . about his Coronation. I noted at the time—and the facts seem strangely significant now—that he summoned his brother ("Bertie") to be present, and when in the course of our talk I gave him a book of the Service as used at his father's Coronation, he gave it to his brother, saying, "I think *you* had better follow this." I wonder whether even then he had in the back of his mind some thought that the Coronation might be not his, but his brother's. I was fearful lest he should wish to shorten or cut the Service about, and indeed he began by saying he hoped the *whole* service might not be used. But when I tried to explain its significance, and the close relations of all the parts, he acquiesced. What I think most impressed him was my pointing out how wonderful it would be, and would seem to the whole world in the midst of its confusions, that he would be crowned with the same ceremonies with which his predecessors had been crowned for a thousand years. He contented himself with saying that he hoped there might be *some* shortening, and I said I would consider omitting the sermon and the Litany. But he seemed, I noted then, strangely detached from the whole matter.

When the trouble was past, the Archbishop went to see the new King and Queen, who were still at 145 Piccadilly, to discuss with them the arrangements for the Coronation. "It was indeed like waking after a nightmare to find the sun shining," he wrote. "No words can describe my relief, my burden, like Christian's, falling from my back."

But before he could apply himself to the multitudinous claims of the ceremony, he had to inaugurate the Recall to Religion with a broadcast. Lang had at first regarded wireless, as he regarded any mechanical invention, as one of those mysterious and perilous devices which the prudent man avoids. He soon changed his mind, "that thing of yours" becoming "my wireless set." A reluctant convert, he became an enthusiastic adherent, his recognition that by its agency a man's words could be carried simultaneously to many millions of people all over the world being undoubtedly reinforced by the discovery that he was himself the possessor of a perfect broadcasting voice. So he had spoken several times, and with marked success, before delivering what he regarded as his most urgent and important charge on December 27th, 1936.

> It had seemed to me—quite apart from the Abdication—that the time had come to ask the nation to consider whither it was tending —whether in view of the haste and confusion of the times it was keeping or losing its hold on the Christian Faith.

His purpose was not merely to bring home the meaning of the Coronation to the people, but to try to associate them with it in a way never before attempted. He would without doubt have accepted the description of the ceremony's significance given by the Archbishop of York in his book *The Claims of the Church of England*. At the Coronation, Dr. Garbett points out, the King represents the State and the Archbishop the Church. The Archbishop presents the King to his people, delivers to him the Orb, places in his hand the Sceptre, and receiving the Crown from the Altar sets it on his head. "All through the Service the Archbishop blessing and exhorting the King is also hallowing the State." The King, on his side, seeks God's help for his high office, is anointed, and kneels for the Archbishop's blessing and to receive the Body and Blood of Christ. The ceremony is therefore the commissioning of the State, through the King, by the Church, through the Archbishop.

By the light of such an interpretation Lang approached his broadcast.

> "In the pressure of those anxious days at the end of the year I had had no leisure to prepare it. I ought to have gone into retreat; but this was impossible." His words were to be a solemn appeal to people to stop and ask, "Whither are we going?" They were "a summons to refound our life, personal and national, on the Fear of God, on the Revelation of Himself, of His Will and Purpose for the human race in Jesus Christ, on the standards of human conduct which Jesus Christ has set."

There was, he told his listeners, a drift away from religion. "God is not so much denied as merely crowded out"; and the result was "a slackening, sometimes even a scorning, of the old standards of Christian morality." This was particularly noticeable in the loosening of the ties of marriage and in a lack of restraint upon the impulses of sex.

At the same time there was, he believed, "an instinct of religion and of sound morality in the common heart." There was also an awareness of the value of spiritual things, springing from the "deep, ineradicable needs of human nature which nothing material can supply." Therefore the need was for "a new, deliberate, and sustained endeavour to arrest the drift, to arouse and strengthen the interest, to satisfy the longing." A King was to be crowned. "Let him not come alone to his hallowing." Let it mark the "beginning of the return of the nation to God." This might take, for all men and women, irrespective of their specific beliefs, the outward form of a daily prayer, of "an act of worship in God's House on God's Day." On those who were already practising Christians a special obligation was laid. To be a Christian is "to accept a vocation," and this a man must show continually by the witness of his life.

When the Archbishop had spoken, encouraged as he was by the immediate response, he was, as usual, disappointed in the final results and self-reproachful about his own part. He felt that with more careful preparation he could have done so much better; yet how, amid the anxieties and stresses of the past months, could he have found the time and serenity of mind he had needed? While conscious of failure and of the loss of an opportunity which might never recur, he allowed no hint of his vexation to reach the outside world or discouragement to slacken his own efforts. During Coronation Year and for many months afterwards he spoke and preached assiduously on his chosen theme, beginning with a meeting of the clergy of the Diocese in Canterbury Cathedral. Indeed, he persevered with his task until the clouds of war began to settle over the land and to darken the minds of men. Nor, for all his misgivings, did he look on his labour as a ploughing of the sands. "I cannot doubt," he wrote, "that the Appeal did stir the common mind and conscience."

The lasting results of such an enterprise are always hard to assess. It will fail to fulfil any expectation of a sudden and dramatic conversion; but it may leave a more durable though less spectacular mark upon the lives of individuals. "I am sure the Appeal was worth making," he insisted. "Would God I had made it better!" Once more the Archbishop was the sternest judge of himself and of his work, where an impartial court might have returned a more favourable verdict.

In addition to the Appeal, during the first months of 1937 the Archbishop was necessarily and constantly occupied with the preparations for the ceremony. In the account he left among his biographical notes he shows his interest in and attention to the minutest details of an occasion which called for all the drama and pageantry which, with him, were so strong an expression of religious feeling. But he is best left to tell the story himself.

In the previous summer at Ballure I had given a close study to the Coronation Rite, reading through Wickham Legg's huge volume on the records of the Coronation Services and other books, including that of Ratcliff, Fellow of Queen's, with whom I had several talks. As a result, I decided to make only four considerable changes. The first was to remove the litany from its place within the Service and to have it chanted by the Westminster Canons and Choir as they moved down from the Altar before the Service, after their procession up to the Altar bearing the regalia. . . . The second change was to put the Oath in its old place immediately after the Recognition and before instead of after the beginning of the Communion Service. . . . The third change was to omit the sermon, as had been done for other reasons at the Coronation of King Edward VII. I had myself preached the sermon at the Coronation of King George V, and I had realised how little could be profitably said within the limits of five or six minutes. True, many had then spoken kindly about my discourse, and I remember Lord Morley writing to me that it was a "model of concentration"; and when I proposed the change to the Privy Council there were several, including Winston Churchill, who, recalling that sermon, said they wished something of the kind could be repeated. But I knew that I would be broadcasting an explanation of the inner significance of the Rite on the Sunday before the Coronation, and I felt that it would be superfluous to have another discourse within the Service. And though I was sorry not to give His Grace of York this part in the ceremony, events proved that I was right; and on the day the whole Rite itself seemed so wonderfully to unfold its full meaning both in the Abbey itself and to the listening multitudes everywhere, that any sermon, however excellent, would have been felt to be an unwelcome intrusion. The fourth change was to restore the old order of the Anointing, rising from the hands to the head, instead of descending from the head to the hands. This also, I am sure, proved itself to be right.

But a more substantial change was constitutional, not liturgical. It was imposed by the wholly new position of the Dominions created by the Statute of Westminster. This involved first a change in the form of the Recognition, as hitherto prescribed since the Coronation of William III and Mary—the simple form *"your* undoubted King."

The principal change—one of historic importance—was in the form of the Oath. The differences can be seen by comparing the form for George V with the new form for George VI. Each of the Dominions was mentioned by name after Great Britain, thus putting them on an equality and implying that the English King was King also of Ireland (Eire), Canada, Australia, New Zealand and South Africa. At first I was disposed to think and at first some of the High Commissioners were disposed to think, that rather than import into the ancient Rite difficult constitutional issues it would be better to keep its old character—the Consecration and Crowning of the English King by the English Church—the representatives of the Dominions merely "assisting" by their presence. But further reflexion showed that they wished *their* King to be crowned and consecrated at the same time and in the old way. The question then arose : What was the form of Oath which the Dominions would accept ? This proved to be a question of the utmost intricacy and difficulty. Letters, telegrams, telephone messages passed between the Dominions Office in London and Governments of the Dominions. For weeks the air was thick with these messages. Two or three times a week Malcolm MacDonald, the Secretary for the Dominions, came to Lambeth to consult as to the various suggestions made. He handled the matter with great patience and tact. The chief difficulties came, of course, from the Irish Free State and from South Africa. But at long last general consent was obtained for the form which was actually used. No sooner, however, had this difficulty been overcome than another emerged. The Dominions discovered that this Oath was followed by the promise to maintain the "Protestant Reformed Religion as by law established." The Irish Free State, the Roman Catholic Prime Minister of Australia, the French Canadians insisted that *their* King must not be required to make such a promise. New and even more intricate negotiations began. There were times when MacDonald and I were at our wits' end to discover some way out of the dilemma —how to reconcile these most natural objections with the Protestant convictions—or prejudices—at least of Great Britain. But here also in the long run patience, forbearance and considerateness won their way. I had objected to a good many suggestions, but the new form ultimately adopted seemed to me to be an actual improvement on the old. The King was required to maintain "the true profession of the Gospel" (there was no objection to *that*) and to maintain the Protestant Reformed Religion only as it is by law established *in the United Kingdom*; and this constitutional requirement was separated from the promise to maintain the rights and liberties of the Church of England. Perhaps only MacDonald and myself realised what labour had been involved in extricating the Oath from all these entanglements.

The official preparations for the ceremony, which was fixed for May 12th, 1937, began in the summer of 1936, long before the Abdication. There were three main Committees, with many Sub-Committees. The chief one was the Executive Committee, of which the Earl Marshal, the young Duke of Norfolk, was the official Chairman. Let me say at once that, young as he was, he fulfilled his duties admirably, combining modesty with authority. There was also the Privy Council Committee, to which decisions of the Executive were referred for confirmation. Of this the President of the Council, Ramsay MacDonald, was the not very effective Chairman. There was thirdly a special Committee, of which the High Commissioners of the Dominions were members, to consider the interests of the Dominions and Colonies. I was a member of all the Committees and attended as regularly as I could, and this took much of my time. The co-ordination of the work was not easy, but the General Secretary, R. U. E. Knox,[1] one of the secretaries of the Privy Council, did it well. . . .

The rehearsals of the ceremony in the Abbey began early in the year. There were about eight fixed rehearsals. I attended them all. It was not easy to bring what at first seemed chaos into order. The ordinary Englishman will not take ceremonies seriously when he is in his ordinary clothes. I had perforce to take the leading part in these rehearsals, for the Earl Marshal, though always in command, was too quiet and modest to be sufficiently peremptory and decisive, and Garter (Sir Gerald Wollaston), though master of all the details, was too much occupied by them to take any general control. I saw at once that somebody must get things done, and I had to do it.

[1] Of the Treasury. Now Sir Robert Knox, K.C.V.O.

It was said afterwards with some truth that the Archbishop "produced" the Coronation! And there are some stories about his voice being heard—"Dukes, please stop talking," "Ladies, please attend," "Where is that Dean?" "Garter, where *are* you?" etc. The part of the King was taken first by Gwatkin of the Lord Chamberlain's department and then by young Hunloke, who did his part with quiet dignity, the part of the Queen by Lady Rachel Howard, the Earl Marshal's sister. (I chaffed the two "Kings" about their having been actually crowned in Westminster Abbey.) The King and Queen came twice to special rehearsals. Gradually things got into order; the final full dress rehearsal went well; and on the great day there was not a single hitch, and everyone from the King to the smallest page played his or her part without fault.

A new and special difficulty was created by the fact that for the first time in history it would be possible for people in every part of the world to listen through the wireless to the whole ceremony. . . . It was arranged that there should be no microphones *seen* in the Abbey —they were all concealed—and that the B.B.C. observer should be housed in a little hut in the triforium just behind the main Altar, so constructed that his voice could be sent through space yet not heard within the Abbey.[1] I advised that the whole Service should be broadcast, except the actual Communion. It was comparatively easy to arrange about photographs, but what of the films? Some thought that they ought not to be allowed; but I felt that if all the world were to *hear*, it would be well that so far as possible it should *see* at least some parts of the ceremony which would mean so much in the world's thought. After many consultations with representatives of the film industry and the Office of Works (Lord Stanhope), it was finally settled that there must be no special lighting, no turning on of high lights, during the ceremony; that I should decide and tell the representatives of the industry what parts might be and might not be filmed—this I did, ruling out the most sacred parts, the actual anointing and the Communion of the King and Queen; and that to prevent any possible breaches of this ruling, the Earl Marshal and I should inspect the proposed films on the afternoon or evening of the Coronation Day, before they were released.

---

[1] "It was a dreadful place," the Dean of Lichfield (Dr. Iremonger) recalls. "I could not even see the Altar, and much of what I said had to be calculated not by what I could see, but by the stop-watch timings I had taken at the rehearsal."

At this point Lang broke off to note the handicap he was under during the months of preparation from the absence of any summary record of the arrangements at the preceding Coronation. Archbishop Davidson was known to have kept, *more suo*, all the relative correspondence, but when it was wanted it could not be found. Eventually, a month before the Coronation, three bulging boxes were discovered "hidden away" in the "muniment" room. But so voluminous was the collection and so late the hour that it was extremely difficult to extract any clear or succinct account of what had actually been done.

As to the Service, it was left to the King's Printers and the Presses to come to some mutual arrangement, which was satisfactorily done. . . . The Presses agreed with themselves that Cambridge should present the Dean and Chapter with a special copy of the Service and that Oxford should present the Bible itself. When the time came, only a few days before the Coronation, Sir Humphrey Milford brought me a magnificent Bible, but of a size which would prevent its being carried in the Procession or indeed used in the Service. To his manifest disappointment I had to insist on his producing another Bible of a more manageable size. To his credit, this was done on the very eve of the Coronation Day. I have arranged that the Bible actually used should, according to precedent, be deposited in the Lambeth Library, and that I should give the huge and sumptuous Bible, specially prepared but not used, to the Dean and Chapter of Westminster on permanent loan.

On the top of deciding and preparing the proofs of the actual Coronation Service came the task of drawing up services in connexion with the Coronation for use in all the churches of the realm. . . . They seemed to give general satisfaction.

A word as to the allocation of seats in the Abbey. It was a difficult problem to allot 8000 places among the many more thousands who might have some claim, personal or official or representative. Many of us on the Committee were anxious to give more places than heretofore to representatives of the great body of working folk. I tried, only partially successfully, to limit the number of the wives of all sorts of minor persons and officials, and was much chaffed for the prejudices of "the premier bachelor of England." To find some more room for wider interests a departure from tradition was made by not inviting the eldest sons of peers and their wives, except when their fathers were not able to attend. The Earl Marshal very kindly put some 12 places at my own disposal.

One preliminary trouble caused me a good deal of anxiety. The Federal Council of the Free Churches in England put forward to the Coronation Committee a formal request to have some "part in the Service" given to them. The matter was put in my hands. I was obliged to tell the Moderator (M. E. Aubrey) and the Secretary (S. M. Berry) that this request could not be granted. I said frankly that I could not share my traditional duties with other persons; and that the whole Service was within the Order of Communion of the Church of England. But I was the more anxious to give some special place to the Free Churches and also to the Church of Scotland as representatives of the religious life of the country. Accordingly I arranged that for the first time a place should be given to their representatives in the Great Procession and in the "theatre" in the Abbey. Thus seven of the Free Churches and four of the Church of Scotland [1] followed the Royal Chaplains and preceded the Chapter of Westminster in the Procession, and had good places on the north side of the "theatre" immediately in front of the Peeresses. . . . The result gave much satisfaction; and after the Coronation I received many expressions of gratitude. There was also some trouble about the representation of the King's Chaplains in Scotland, about which the "Auld Kirk" showed itself very sensitive. In the end four, I think, of them were included with the English Chaplains selected to head the Procession. I found S. M. Berry and Dr. John White very helpful and considerate in all these rather tiresome and delicate negotiations. What the position of the Church of England will be at another Coronation who can tell? But if it remains the Established Church, I hope that the decisions and arrangements made in 1937 may be followed.

Next a word as to the position of the Dominions, not merely in the change of Oath, but in the ceremony itself. It was decided that their Prime Ministers, with the Prime Minister of Great Britain, should have a place in the Procession. But I had hoped that more than this might have been possible. There was an idea that they might join the Peers spiritual and temporal in the homage. But fortified by a memorandum on the meaning of the Homage by Garter, I came to the conclusion that this was impossible: it would

---

[1] Actually six representatives of the Free Churches and three of the Church of Scotland.

be importing a modern constitutional position into an old feudal ceremony with which it had no sort of connexion. But I suggested to the High Commissioners that at the Recognition each Prime Minister might step forward and on behalf of his Dominion signify its consent by saying in the traditional form "God save King George." At first they seemed to be in favour; but on reference to the Governments it was found that South Africa, to say nothing of the Irish Free State, objected. So the suggestion was dropped and only the place in the Procession remained.

And so the great ceremony itself drew near. At Eastertide, while staying at Windsor Castle, I had gone through the Service quietly with the King and Queen and found them most appreciative and fully conscious of its solemnity. On the Sunday before the Day I went to Buckingham Palace for a more spiritual preparation. The King and Queen readily concurred in my suggestion that this should take place about the same time in the early evening as multitudes of their subjects would be assembled in the churches both at home and overseas. So at 6 p.m. I met them in their own room in Buckingham Palace. . . . After some talk on the spiritual aspects of the Coronation and of its spiritual meaning for themselves, they knelt with me; I prayed for them and for their realm and Empire, and I gave them my personal blessing. I was much moved, and so were they. Indeed, there were tears in our eyes when we rose from our knees. From that moment I knew what would be in their minds and hearts when they came to their anointing and crowning.

I was with them for about an hour and a quarter, and then went straight from Buckingham Palace to Broadcasting House. There, after a Service admirably arranged by F. A. Iremonger . . . I sent out to the world my message explaining the character and the spiritual meaning of the Coronation and the spiritual share in it which the people ought to take with the King and Queen. . . .

And now the great Day itself, Wednesday May 12th—to me, I suppose, in a sense the culminating day of my official life, the day on which the Archbishop of Canterbury fulfils his highest office in the national life, on which through him the Church of God consecrates that life in the person of its King.

Through the personal kindness and care of Sir Philip Game, the Chief Commissioner of Police, I was saved from the long waiting to which others in the Abbey who had to be in their places by 8.30 a.m.

had to submit. Escorted by a superintendent of police on horse-back, I left Lambeth about 10 a.m. and drove in a few minutes from Lambeth to Westminster through streets from which all vehicles had been cleared and past the crowded stands round the Abbey. I was accompanied by my chaplains, Alan Don,[1] Alec Sargent and Lumley Green-Wilkinson, clad in the mulberry-coloured robes such as were worn by the Archbishop's chaplains at the last Coronation. My own robes and Primatial Cross were already in the Annexe at the Abbey. I wore the white cope with its gold bullion which had been given to me at Bristol by Mrs. Fry. I had decided not to raise the question of wearing a mitre. True, of course, I had constantly worn a mitre, at York, in London and at Canterbury, the first Arch-bishop, either of York or Canterbury, who had done so since the Reformation. True, also, that by King George V's somewhat reluctant permission I had worn it at the great State Service at St. Paul's on the day of his Silver Jubilee. But on this special day, when it was necessary to keep close to precedent, I decided, rightly or wrongly, not to introduce an innovation to the precedents of certainly three hundred years. I am rather sorry, but so it was.

From the Annexe I could see the Nave with its crowded tiers of people, the galleries clothed in the really beautiful drapery which the Office of Works had provided after the greatest thought and care. I had arrived just after the Litany had been sung in procession, and just before 11 a.m. I went with the Earl Marshal to receive their Majesties at the door of the Annexe, and so was able to see something of their procession and the arrival of the golden coach with its grey horses. At about 11.15 the Great Procession began to move, and the choir began Parry's noble anthem "I was glad." . . . By Order of the Privy Council the conduct of the music was given to Dr. Ernest Bullock, the organist of the Abbey, "in consultation with" Sir Walford Davies, the Master of the King's Music; and it was left for me to arrange with them what the music should be. . . . Our plan was to include representatives of English Church Music from Tudor times to the present day. In order to get a wider choice, we agreed to substitute for one long anthem during the Homage six short "Homage Anthems" (though only four of these were actually sung). Thus the music ranged from Byrd with his noble Creed, through

---

[1] This is incorrect. Dr. Don, as Chaplain to the Speaker, drove to the Abbey in the Speaker's Coach and only joined the Archbishop in the Annexe.

Tye, Wesley, Stanford, Parry, to Walford Davies, Harris and Vaughan Williams, who composed the very fine Te Deum. There were, besides the large orchestra, about 400 voices in the choir, placed above and around the screen, including some specially selected singers, men and women, from the Dominions. Common consent applauded both the selection and the performance of the music. It seemed to me more splendid than at either of the two previous Coronations at which I was present. A special word of praise is due to the Fanfares, for which credit must be given to Bullock. When I sometimes now listen to the gramophone records of the Coronation given to me by the B.B.C., I can never hear the strains of Parry's anthem which ushered in the great ceremony without deep emotion.

The Great Procession moved along in good order, though there were some gaps due to the fact that the movement of the King and Queen was slower than that of others. On arriving at the Sanctuary, I went to the Altar, knelt in prayer, and then turned westwards, so that I could see the arrival of the King and Queen passing from the Choir to the Sanctuary. Like everyone present, I was at once deeply impressed by their demeanour—so dignified, so plainly conscious of the solemnity of the occasion. The little Queen, the only woman present with an uncovered head awaiting its anointing and its crown, advanced with a real poetry of motion, her dignity enhanced rather than diminished by the tall and beautiful figure of her Mistress of the Robes (the Duchess of Northumberland). The King (as many said afterwards) looked like a mediaeval knight awaiting his consecration with a rapt expression in his eyes, which turned neither to right nor to left. Their demeanour, sustained through the whole long ceremony, seemed from the first to invest it with a spirit of reverence.

I cannot and need not write about all its stages. To me personally, and I know to many others, the most moving scene was the King's Anointing, when, as the glorious music of Handel's "Zadok the Priest" rang through the Abbey, he was stripped of all his official garments save a simple white tunic, and then after his anointing knelt, this slight white solitary figure, at the faldstool to receive my Blessing.

I may recall one or two episodes, trivial indeed and scarcely worth mentioning, but perhaps of some human interest. For example, it so happened that when Lord Salisbury presented to me the King's

Crown and the Duke of Portland the Queen's, the fringes of the cushions on which the Crowns were placed got entangled with the Garter chains round their necks, and Garter standing by had to tear the fringes off. Then there was the episode at the Crowning which, insignificant in itself, was recorded by the merciless accuracy of the film and therefore was noticed by millions, sometimes I am told with amusement. The facts are these: the King was very anxious that the Crown should be placed on his head with the right side to the front. Accordingly it was arranged that a small thin line of red cotton should be inserted under one of the principal jewels on the front. It was there when I saw the Crown in the Annexe before the ceremony. But when the Dean brought the Crown to me on its cushion from the Altar and I looked for my little red line, it was not there. So I had to turn the Crown round to see if it was on the other side; but it was not. Some officious person must have removed it. This turning round of the Crown took only a second and did not in the least perturb me; and but for the film it would not have been noticed. Yet when the film was produced there were comments like "the Archbishop fumbles with the Crown." However, some dear old lady wrote to me that "the most beautiful thing of all was to see the dear Archbishop blessing the four corners of the Crown before he put it on the King's head!" Another and more serious instance of the meddlesomeness of some official was this: Before the Service begins the Dean and Chapter of Westminster have to carry such of the Regalia as are not carried in the Great Procession from the Annexe to the Altar, including the Imperial Crown, to be deposited in St. Edward's Chapel, where the King puts it on instead of the heavy King Edward's Crown, for his recession. The Dean had given his receipt that all these Regalia were in his possession. But when he came to take the Imperial Crown from the Annexe it was not there! As every moment was carefully timed, he could not wait to search for it; and, poor man, he had to move up to the Sanctuary without knowing what on earth had happened to the Imperial Crown. Imagine his relief when on going into St. Edward's Chapel he found it deposited on the Altar there! Some tiresome official underling, thinking he was very wise, had taken it from the Annexe and put it there.

Let me return to the great Rite itself, the great drama. From first to last it moved on, stage by stage, scene after scene, with unbroken tranquillity, dignity and beauty. I may quote the words of a German witness, Dr. Schramm, the Professor of History at Göttingen University. He has made a lifelong study of the coronation rites of Europe, of which ours is the only survivor, and had written an admirable book on the subject in its historical and constitutional aspects. I asked him what his impression of the actual ceremony was. He said, "Sir, I have lived in this theme; I have given my life to the study of it; but when I saw the ceremony with my eyes in the Abbey I can only say it was overwhelming." For myself I can only say that I never had a moment of nervousness or hesitation. I seemed to be sustained by some Higher Power Who was in control. I know that this was the experience of the King and Queen, for they wrote to me afterwards with touching simplicity about it. . . . It was impossible not to realise that in the midst of the splendour of things seen and temporal there was the reality of things unseen and eternal. . . . It was this sense of the religious reality and solemnity of the ceremony which filled the Abbey, and distinguished this Coronation from the previous two at which I had been present. Many who had shared this experience with me agreed as to this difference. It was partly due, no doubt, to the fact that for the first time, owing to the skilful placing of microphones, everyone in every part of the Abbey could hear the words of the Rite. I cannot doubt, as I have said, that it was partly due to the demeanour of the King and Queen. Nor can I doubt that in spite of all appearances there is now a deeper religious sense, a quicker religious imagination, than in the days of a more conventional religion. But behind all this surely God Himself was in our midst.

It is wonderful that in some measure the spirit which was felt in the Abbey, as well as the sounds that were heard, seem to have been brought through the wireless to the millions who were listening. That this was so I had the testimony of letters sent to me by all sorts of people in every part of the world—Europe, China, Africa, America, Australia, etc. It is a matter of mere thankfulness, not of any kind of boasting, that my voice was everywhere clearly heard. Take the United States: Nicholas Murray Butler [1] told me that every business man that he had met had been out of bed at about 4 a.m. to listen. I wonder whether any event in history has ever been so *realised* throughout the whole world; and everywhere some impression of

[1] President of Columbia University, New York. Died in 1948.

the religious solemnity of the ceremony seems to have been given. For all this much credit is due to our B.B.C. All its technical arrangements were admirably conceived and carried out. The commentator within the Abbey, whose voice was unheard there, but heard throughout the world—F. A. Iremonger—by his quiet and reverent explanations enabled the multitude of listeners to get some idea of the scene, as well as to hear the words. During the long pause, while the King and Queen were making their Communion, he said some most suitable prayers and the hymn "Let all mortal flesh keep silence" was taken in from a choir singing in St. Margaret's Church near by. It was a wonderful opportunity for broadcasting, and full and excellent use was made of it.

When all was over I was not in the least tired, only filled with thankfulness that all had passed so well. By the kind arrangements of Sir Philip Game, I was back at Lambeth actually before the King and Queen had left the Abbey for their great Return Procession through the streets of London; and though, alas, I could not see that wonderful procession, I was able through the wireless to hear the description of it and the cheers of the crowds.

The weather throughout the day had been dull but cool, a fact for which the police, fearful of the effect of heat upon the crowds, were thankful. It was sad that rain fell before the Procession reached Buckingham Palace and during the evening. But this did not seem to affect the spirits and the enthusiasm of the vast crowds who filled the streets and surged round the Palace.

In the evening, according to arrangement, at 8 p.m. the Earl Marshal and I met at the small private theatre of the British Movietone Company in Berners Street, to see and if need be censor the films of the ceremony in the Abbey. But happily there was no need of censoring. . . . The films on the whole are good. But they suffered from the light in the Abbey and from the fact that they could only take very short and limited views. The ordinary photographs give a better conception of the splendid setting of the ceremonies.

So the great day passed. All the elaborate preparations for it and its own splendid events are over. Very soon the Abbey will be stripped of its galleries and draperies and restored to the Dean and Chapter and its wonted uses. Besides writing the moving letters that I have mentioned, the King and Queen a few days after asked me to have tea with them at Buckingham Palace, and we went over the day again in retrospect. I can only be thankful to God's over-ruling Providence and trust that the Coronation may not be a mere dream of the past, but that its memories and its lessons will not be forgotten.

Little need be added to Lang's account of an occasion which, as he himself has said, he looked on as the climax of his ecclesiastical life. He had played his part in other solemn and splendid ceremonies, such as the 1300th anniversary of York Minster and the Silver Jubilee of King George V, but the Coronation was pre-eminent. It is significant how again and again in his description the language of the theatre slips from his pen; and it was surely the country's good fortune that in 1937 the Archbishop of Canterbury was not only a churchman who took an exalted view of the Rite, but also an actor and producer of the first order. That the effect of the Service would largely depend upon the flawlessness of the organisation is obvious, but men might overlook that at a Coronation the second "lead"—in terms of the theatre—is played by the Archbishop, and that in 1937 the casting was beyond reproach or possibility of improvement.

There is a comment from Lang's old friend and critic, Dr. Hensley Henson: "The Archbishop was in excellent spirits and performed his duty to perfection, only making two unimportant faults, viz. fumbling with the Crown before he could get it the right way round,[1] and omitting the prayer of the blessing of the bread and wine offered by the King."

Innumerable letters pay tribute not only to the Archbishop's personal performance, but also to the success with which he had conveyed, *urbi et orbi*, the religious significance of the ceremony. His friend and doctor, Lord Dawson of Penn, had feared that the physical strain of so long and exacting a Service would be too much for a man of his years. He accordingly sat in the south transept with a hypodermic syringe, ready charged, prepared on a signal from a chaplain to hurry forward and administer an injection. Happily this dramatic and unrehearsed addition to the ceremony was unnecessary. When all was ended the Archbishop was not even very tired. "Once I saw it was going well, I enjoyed every minute," he said. "Thank God that is over!" remarked Lumley Green-Wilkinson, as they got into the car to leave the Abbey Precincts. "Lumley, how can you say such a thing!" was the Archbishop's retort. "I only wish it was all beginning over again."

---

[1] This is explained by the Archbishop on page 420.

Chapter XXXIV

THE WAR

THE Archbishop was "in the best of spirits, 'enjoying the Papacy' with a vengeance. Moreover, in spite of his unintermitted labours, he seems to be in abounding vigour." So wrote Dr. Hensley Henson in May 1937; and so Lang might appear to anyone who saw him occasionally. But his chaplains had their misgivings, and in August, when he was established at Ballure, Don sent him a long admonitory letter.

"Ever since last October," he wrote, "you have been subjected to a pressure of work and to a weight of responsibility such as would have broken most men of your age. Your physical constitution has stood the strain wonderfully. Your mental vigour has remained unabated throughout. You have in fact, if I may say so, come through with flying colours. Your gluttony for work is a source of perpetual amazement to those who know what you get through in the course of a week. And you have your reward. The name of the Archbishop of Canterbury is to-day a household word throughout the inhabited globe—honoured and revered by most, hated and feared by some, but acknowledged by all to stand for something that counts in the affairs of men."

Some plain speaking followed.

"You are daily growing older. You have passed by some three years the Psalmist's allotted span. You are in fact (though you hate to admit it) an elderly man and your physical frame is showing signs of wearing out. . . . Seven years ago your doctors thought that you had come to the end of your tether—they have told me so. You cheated them and have been crowing over them ever since, but you cannot go on cheating old Father Time. You are seven years older than you were in 1930, and those seven years have inevitably told their tale."

The letter ended with some practical suggestions. The Archbishop should try to keep clear of engagements during the week-ends before and after meetings of the Church Assembly or Convocation. He should reduce his activities in the Diocese. He should accept fewer invitations to public dinners, "with their rich food and cigar smoke and interminable speechifying."

The Archbishop took this "filial admonition" in a very amiable spirit. His chaplain had been over-generous in his tribute. "I can't recognise myself in any of these descriptions. I know myself too well—my sins, failure, ignorance, weaknesses—to be able in any sort of way to associate myself with such words as 'great.'" He allowed the truth of much of Don's indictment, but "I can't indeed admit that in one sense I am growing old; for my spirit is, I think, far younger than it once was." He could not deny he had been overworking, yet it was not the big events that tried him, but

> the everlasting invasion of all the cranks and busybodies and ecclesi-astical partisans and the sons and daughters of Zeruiah, all over the world, which you introduce day by day. This is what wearies me, and I fear you also. Yet I can't escape it. I am only sorry that it induces a certain surface irritability for which I apologise. But you know well enough that my barks are not bites: they are only a relief to my feelings.

As for Don's suggested remedies, he agreed that before and after important meetings he should try to keep his week-ends free. He did not agree at all that he should restrict his work in the parishes. "Apart from duty, these visits, especially in country parishes, are really a refresh-ment." They "keep me in touch with the real work of the Church and with ordinary humanity." He only partly agreed about the public dinners. He had been going to too many, but

> "I regard them as ways of keeping the Archbishop not detached from, but in contact with, lay folk. I don't want his office to be side-tracked into a purely ecclesiastical line, apart from the main lines of national life.
>
> "The real remedy you don't mention, though I am sure you have it in mind. It is to find more time for thought and above all for prayer. This goes to the root of the evil. What would become of me if I had not this yearly time of greater quiet here in my little 'Cell' and amidst the beauties of sea and sky and hills I can't imagine.
>
> "So the firm must carry on its business," he concluded, "doing its best and trusting in God's help."

In short, the Archbishop must go on working and his chaplains must go on worrying. More than once he seemed on the edge of a complete collapse; yet after the troubles of his first years at Canterbury he had no serious illness. He slept badly, or rather went to sleep late and woke with difficulty in the morning. At Holy Communion or Mattins each day in the Chapel at Lambeth, which he insisted on attending however short his night had been, he was often almost drunk with sleep. Once he appeared to have some kind of seizure. He became unconscious, was revived and helped to his room. Presently, to the astonishment of his chaplains, he appeared in the dining-room as though nothing had happened and ate a hearty breakfast, before carrying out without noticeable effort a formidable programme of engagements for the day. His recuperative power was extraordinary. Sometimes his weariness and exhaustion would alarm his household. Then he would retire to his room, to re-emerge a little later a new man, fresh, brisk and ready for business. It was as though the actor had merely changed his part; and yet the recovery was as genuine as the tiredness had been. With it all his general health was unaffected; he was as punctilious and efficient as ever; and his judgment of men and affairs was as true.

The summer of 1937 was an unusually taxing time, with all the work of the Coronation. Besides the routine of his office there was a big party for the overseas visitors, when the garden at Lambeth came to a climax of glory, and the beginning of Church House, of which Queen Mary laid the foundation-stone on June 26th, and the Marriage Bill in the House of Lords. The autumn, when he was back from Ballure, brought little relief. October took him to the Albert Hall for a monster meeting of protest against "Japan's war on Civilians," his strong words drawing angry comments in German and Japanese newspapers.

The outlook abroad was threatening and, by no merit of his own, he was soon to obey some, though not all, of his chaplain's injunctions, for a time was coming when there were to be very few public dinners and the parishes of Kent were to be more familiar with visiting aeroplanes than with visiting Archbishops. Next year brought the anxieties of Munich, which drove Lang prematurely back from Ballure. His reactions were very much those of the vast majority of his fellow-countrymen—relief tempered by misgivings. He had a strong liking for the new Prime Minister, Neville Chamberlain, and in the dark months that followed the two men met and corresponded when opportunity offered. It grieved Lang that Chamberlain, by his own confession, was a "reverent agnostic," but from talks with him he believed that "in the inner sanctuary of his spirit he came increasingly, as anxieties and responsibilities grew, to rely upon the help of God and the guidance of His Spirit."

A few days after war broke out Chamberlain wrote in anguish of "those gallant fellows who lost their lives last night in the R.A.F. attacks" and of the need to put them out of his mind. "Thank you again for your constant thought and prayer." At the end of the year the Prime Minister wrote again: "I find war more hateful than ever and I groan in spirit over every life lost and every home blasted."

In little things as in big the War was breaking up the old ordered life. The balloon barrage invaded the garden at Lambeth, much to the detriment of the lawn, the Royal Air Force quartered itself in Morton's Tower, and the Crypt under the Chapel was turned into a shelter for some two hundred people. In 1940 he told his brother:

Of course it has been quite impossible for me to get to my beloved Ballure, though my heart *aches* for it. It is the first time I have not been in that blissful region for, I suppose, 45 years.

He consoled himself with a visit to Newtimber Place, the Sussex home of Lady Buxton and Dame Meriel Talbot, where he took long walks on the Downs.

A notebook diary describes some of the events of the summer of 1940.

At the end of May I got the King to consent to express his own desire that Sunday, May 26th, should be observed as a National Day of Prayer. It seemed to me that this was the best way of investing the day with a fully national character, avoiding the procedure of a Royal Proclamation, which is really obsolete, and of an Order in Council, to which there are many objections in principle and which is formally directed to the Established Church. By all accounts it was generally observed, with very large congregations in all our own churches and elsewhere. I also called for a day of Thanksgiving after the marvellous rescue of the B.E.F. from Dunkirk, and for special prayers for France in her extremity on Sunday, June 16th.

July 4th. I have just returned from the House of Lords where Halifax described to a tense House the steps taken about the French fleet. . . . I am told that Winston Churchill's statement in the House of Commons was followed by the whole House rising to its feet and cheering, recalling the great scene when Neville Chamberlain announced that he was flying to Munich—a scene which seems to belong to another world.

I had a long talk with Hankey,[1] who knows all about everything. I found that he entirely agreed with me in thankfulness that the Act of Union with France proposed as a last-minute effort to rally France has failed. It was evidently Winston Churchill's own plan; and it was regarded with grave misgivings by Edward Halifax and others in the Cabinet. . . .

Hankey also told me that having been Weygand's colleague on the Suez Canal Board he had observed that he was really a sick man, kidney trouble, etc., which may account for much; that it could not honestly be said that the French Army had fought well—British officers had told him that though it had not run away, it had *walked* away; that he put this and other sinister happenings down to the extent of Communism in France, and in recent tours there had found evidence of Communist activity even in the remoter country villages. . . .

July 29th. The country has been kept in a state of tense anxiety about the threatened invasion. . . . When I was visiting some of his troops and speaking to them at Eastwell Park, the general in command of the division for the protection of Kent, General Liardet, showed me confidentially his map of the defence system. It was amazingly thorough, and I find it difficult to conceive how a German army and air force could get through it. Meanwhile the visits of German aircraft to our S.E. coast have been intensified. The towns on the coast from Whitstable to Hythe are almost derelict. . . . The population has left, though so far no orders of compulsory evacuation have been issued. I have just issued orders for the closing of seven churches which are really now wholly redundant, though of course at least one church in each town is left. . . .

In spite of the turmoil I have visited six country parishes this month and held two services for the troops. The latter seem much more intelligent and therefore attentive than those I remember addressing in 1914.

Winston Churchill continues to be the man of the hour. All his colleagues testify to his qualities of drive and courage, and his powers

---

[1] Lord Hankey, Secretary of the Cabinet 1919-1938.

of glowing speech are a great public asset. Most of the team he has collected seem to be doing well—not least the two Labour men, Morrison and Bevin. In the latter I seem to see a possible Labour dictator of the future. . . . I am very sorry for Neville Chamberlain, with whom I have a real personal friendship. He bears the cloud on his fortunes with great dignity. I am told that his coolness and judgment still tell in the War Cabinet. . . .

August 1st. I had a long talk with the Prime Minister. He had just awakened out of his afternoon sleep, which he regards as the best protection of his health. It was his first introduction to his ecclesiastical duties — the appointment of a new Bishop of St. Edmondsbury and Ipswich. Evidently he knows almost nothing of the Church and its personalities, but his comments were entertaining. He said very little about the business in hand, but discoursed on things in general with immense vitality, as he puffed the inevitable cigar, as inevitable as Stanley Baldwin's pipe. He seems confident that things are going well, though as ignorant as any of us about Hitler's intentions, and pleased with his team. He spoke very generously about Neville Chamberlain and has no wish to lose him. He told me he had just finished a book about—Henry VIII! *What* a man he is—such amazing vitality and confidence! But before I left I could see there was depth beneath this brilliant surface, when he spoke with real emotion about the honour of being alive at this greatest moment in British history, and when, remembering his immense responsibilities, I said, "God bless you and guide you."

August 8th. . . . I managed to escape for sixteen days to Newtimber. It was a really blessed time, in spite of the intrusions of correspondence. I think Newtimber is the most satisfying and one of the loveliest of English homes. The ladies of Newtimber (Mildred B. and Meriel Talbot) were the best of company. . . .

August 26th. I lunched at 10 Downing Street with the Prime Minister—Geoffrey Dawson [1] also there. The P.M. was in great form, but with an undertone of seriousness. The main topic was the arrangement with the U.S.A.—destroyers on the one side, naval and air bases in our Colonies on the other. He was very anxious that it should not be regarded as a mere bargain—rather as a spontaneous

[1] Mr. Geoffrey Dawson, editor of the *Times*.

recognition of mutual interests. It may be the first of many epoch-making events. The P.M. was greatly pleased by his one independent ecclesiastical act—bringing Henson back to the Abbey. I told him that in policy it was all wrong—a canon of 77 etc., but in person it was all right; and Henson may have something to contribute by his forcible eloquence. Winston showed his hopes by arranging for a service in the Abbey on September 3rd, the anniversary of the declaration of war, at which Henson preached. I went to the Abbey on the morning of the National Day of Prayer, when he preached again; but I was rather distressed to see signs of age—the mere speaking seemed laborious.

As to that Day of Prayer, I broadcast an address from Broadcasting House in the evening, the Scottish Moderator, Dr. Forgan, reading the prayers. I had taken an immense amount of trouble over it—probably too much, as I tried to put into sixteen minutes more than they could stand. But some subsequent letters seem to show that there were some who appreciated it. Anyhow, I did my best and must leave it there. I ought to add that on the previous Sunday evening I broadcast a message to the people of the United States.

How wearisome is the constant and petulant cry for "strong leadership"! In the stress of events people either don't notice or forget all the things one tries to say. But I dare say I lack the strident tones which some people think "leadership." And in truth I am conscious of a certain lack of pushful ardour, which no doubt is a sign of growing old. Yet my constant prayer is, "Forsake me not when I am old and grey-headed; until I have shown forth Thy truth to this generation and Thy strength to them that are yet to come."

Sept. 6th and 10*th.* I visited the towns on the S.E. Kent coast, Dover, Folkestone, Margate and Ramsgate, seeing in each case the Mayor and Town Clerk and learning what I could of the plight of these sorely tried towns. It was sad to see towns in former years thronged by happy holiday crowds almost completely deserted—Margate especially, though not so badly damaged as Ramsgate, was like a city of the dead, shops shut, hotels empty, street after street of comfortable houses uninhabited.

During the summer months the War brought other new problems. Lang argued with Sir John Anderson, the Home Secretary, about the treatment of enemy aliens, and with Mr. Anthony Eden, the Secretary of State for War, about the order forbidding the ringing of Church bells except as a warning against parachutists. He was greatly concerned at the closing of the Burma Road and the other concessions to Japan; and at a secret session in the House of Lords he spoke strongly about the Government's policy, chiefly, however, "in order to give Halifax the opportunity, which he fully used, to tell the House what he had told me." But he still thought the appeasement of Japan was doubtful wisdom. "How hard it has been and will be in this struggle to be compelled to choose so often some lesser evil in order that some far greater evil may be averted! I wish I had some of the qualities of the fanatic, who is always prepared to 'damn the consequences.'"

Lord Halifax, who "goes on his serene way, often tired, but always unrattled," had made a great impression with his speech, "revealing as it did his grasp of affairs." He had also broadcast, much to the Archbishop's approval.

He told me that he meant to use it (the broadcast) to sound a more definitely Christian note than has been heard in recent statements, and he fully used his opportunity. Yet I am told that there were many who seemed to think that such words should only come from Archbishops and the like; which only makes them more timely.

Early in September the bombing of London began. Lang spent the nights of the 11th, 12th and 13th at the Palace. A large bomb fell in the garden, uprooting some trees, while another destroyed part of St. Thomas's Hospital close by. Lang suffered these disturbances with unimpaired equanimity, his reluctance to allow them to interfere with his usual activities rather alarming his chaplains. One evening, when the *blitz* was at its noisiest, he moved them to vigorous expostulation by a proposal to retire to an upper room of the Palace to discuss the affairs of the Church with the Archbishop of York, who had come to see him. But he had the safety of his household as well as of himself to consider.

Sept. 17*th.* In view of all this strain and danger I decided that Lambeth must be closed down as a residence; that the older servants, Mrs. Opie, Martha and Matheson, the head housemaid, should leave by the end of the week, McDade and Alan Don remaining in charge; that I should mainly reside at the Old Palace, Canterbury; that if I come up to London for occasional duties or if the Old Palace were damaged, or in view of invasion I should be ordered out by the military authorities, I should live in the Lollards' Tower as the safest part of Lambeth. Accordingly I had to write to the Bishops who have rooms there, telling them sorrowfully that I must resume possession and asking them whether for the time I might use their furniture. I then went down to the Old Palace.

Hardly had he gone than Lambeth Palace suffered its first damage.

On September 19th,[1] 1940, a bomb crashed through the big oriel window into the large drawing-room, exploded there, ruined the room and most of its contents, the bedrooms above and the rooms in the basement below, and badly damaged the parlour and the small drawing-room on either side and their contents. The household, except McDade the butler, had already arranged to leave the next day. It is fortunate that no one was hurt. Some men of the Balloon Barrage . . . had a marvellous escape. . . . The windows in the study were broken, but the three adjacent rooms for chaplain and secretary were undamaged, and happily my bathroom.

"The living part (of Lambeth)" he wrote to Margaret Ford (now Mrs. Lane), "has been literally cut in two. . . . I have a presentiment that I shall never live there again."

When I have to be in London, and this is frequently, I make use of the old housekeeper's sitting-room in the basement as a bedroom and use the chaplain's room for writing and interviews. But it is impossible to have meals except breakfast. . . . Often I have to use the Athenaeum, which I had scarcely entered for thirteen years.

On September 27th

I saw things which I had long wished to see. I was visiting the hop-fields (the first time I had ever seen this so characteristic Kent industry) at Boughton near Faversham, and specially the homeless East-Enders who have flocked there. Then in swift succession I saw (1) a German bomber being brought down by our R.A.F. fighters. (2) A man descending through the air in a parachute, swaying hither and thither. He was a German: his plane had evidently been destroyed higher up. I learned after that when he landed, the soldiers and police had great difficulty in preventing the women hop-pickers, maddened by the loss of their homes in East London, from surround-

---

[1] September 20th.

ing and lynching him! (3) A Messerschmitt just destroyed lying in a field with the dead German covered with a cloak lying beside it.

Next month he had luncheon with the King and Queen.

The War has fully secured the affection they had already won. The fact that they had been bombed at Buckingham Palace brought them close to humbler folk who had gone through much more terribly the same experience. They both seemed well and full of eager spirit, and it was delightful to have a long gossip with them about all the happenings of these tremendous times. I met them again later (November 10th) when I had escaped for a Sunday night from London and was staying with May Ford at Windsor. I was walking with Christopher Ford in the Park when we met them, with the young Princesses, and I was able to congratulate Princess Elizabeth on her quite admirably spoken broadcast to children—her first address, strange to think, to what may be her future subjects!

In October, Church House, so lately completed, was struck.

Alas! my presentiment has been confirmed. On or about October 14th [1] a large bomb went right through the beautiful hall (of Church House), the centre of the great building, from the roof. On its way it destroyed one of the club rooms and within it my dear friend Lionel Hichens [2] and Alfred Buxton, who had both been invaluable members of the Council in the building of the House, and I think three others. Then it dashed the hall to pieces, made matchwood and rubble of all its so carefully designed furnishings and decorations, including pitifully the chairs from which the King and Queen had opened the House only last June. It is sad to think that the Church Assembly had only once used the hall specially intended for it. . . . I am specially sorry for Partridge, Bishop of Portsmouth, to whom the House had been his life's work, and for the architect, Sir Herbert Baker, who had devoted all his skill and imagination to this hall.

Lang, when in London, had first used the Bishop of Blackburn's rooms in the Lollards' Tower. Later, after the Tower had been twice set on fire by incendiary bombs, he moved into the basement of the Palace.

The caretakers, Mr. and Mrs. Berry, go on and are very efficient. My invaluable butler, McDade, rules over the ruins of the Palace and

---

[1] The night of October 13th-14th.   [2] Chairman of Cammell, Laird & Co. Ltd.

watches over the old parts still left, and acts with admirable good sense, humour and efficiency as Chief Warden of the shelter in the Crypt. He has made himself the father of a happy family.

Lang was particularly sorry for Budden, whose garden was now given over to vegetables.

For myself I think of the days when I used to walk round the garden and see the great house and recall the memories of 700 years which cling round it, and the hopes of using it well for the good of the Church, and all those who have gone forth from it to their labours in every part of the world.

The Archbishop was at Lambeth on the night of May 10th, 1941, when the worst damage was done.

Four bombs fell in the courtyard, wrecking the chauffeur's house and making big holes elsewhere. One of them exploded in the yard below the Lollards' Tower. I was quite near at the time, in the basement, and the blast induced me to fall flat! Fortunately, a brick blast-wall had just been erected in front of the door where I happened to be, which took most of the blast force. Otherwise I might not be alive now. Then I saw flames breaking out in the roof of the library. They spread quickly over half the roof before the Fire Brigade could send an engine. Then incendiary bombs set the roof of the Chapel on fire. Next morning the roof had gone; charred beams littered the Chapel. Only the walls remained, with much of the stained glass. Good may come out of evil, for when the Chapel is some day restored, the nineteenth-century Gothic spandrils will, I hope, have disappeared, the old flat roof may be restored, and all the bad stencilling on the walls may vanish. About the same time incendiary bombs attacked the Lollards' Tower, and though the old walls stood firm, the interior was largely gutted. A dreadful night of screeching bombs and crackling flames.

Fortunately most of the pictures and other treasures had been sent to a place of safety. Lang was deeply distressed by the virtual destruction of Lambeth Palace, where only the basement, which he continued to occupy when he was in London, was now fit for habitation. Canterbury—now his headquarters—was only a little less unquiet than London. On September 9th, 1940, just before the first attack on Lambeth,

As I was sitting at tea with the Bishop of Croydon and Mrs. Anderson, there was a sudden terrific screech and swish as a huge bomb struck Alec Sargent's house next door to the Old Palace—that lovely old house which I used always to call "the Church of England," so fully did it seem to embody the old-fashioned C. of E. of Trollope. The greater part of it—happily not the oldest—was destroyed.[1]

"I can only hope," he wrote to his brother Norman, "that if any disaster comes to *that* house (Lambeth) or to this (the Old Palace), I shall bear it with the fortitude that Alec Sargent has shown." Several of the old buildings were damaged or destroyed, some of the bombs falling quite close to the Cathedral.

Meanwhile, so far as was possible, Lang went about his duties in the Diocese. His presence in Kent was a source of some embarrassment to the military authorities, not so much perhaps from a fear for his life, as from the possibility, with invasion threatening, that the Germans might have the satisfaction of capturing the Archbishop of Canterbury. In May 1941 he took a little house at Ramsden, "partly as giving some relief from the monotony and cramped spaces of Canterbury and partly as a refuge for my household if the once expected invasion had come." That year and the next he spent Holy Week at Cuddesdon, his last visit to his "Mecca" being from April 2nd to 6th, 1942. The College was then closed and did not reopen until the autumn of 1945.

On July 23rd, 1941, he lunched again with the Prime Minister.

After lunch I had half an hour with him about the four sees soon to be vacant: Hereford, Worcester, Newcastle and (if Parsons is moved) Southwark. In these matters the P.M. is a difficulty—in some ways more of a difficulty than other P.M.s with whom I have had to deal. (1) Of course he is immensely more preoccupied with incessant affairs of great importance; (2) He knows nothing whatever about the Church, its life, its needs or its personnel; (3) To his credit he will not let (1) and (2) interfere with his own sense of responsibility: where his hand has a right to be, he will put it in, and he is going to be P.M. all round. The result is much provoking delay and un-

---

[1] This is a slight exaggeration. The bomb was not large and only one end of the house was destroyed.

certainty as to what motives or how much knowledge may determine his decisions. But he has an admirable Secretary (Anthony Bevir), who knows more, learns more, and takes more pains than any other Secretary I have had to deal with; and he has always given full deference to my recommendations and has almost always accepted them. And, like other P.M.s, I am sure he would never advise any applicant of whom the Archbishop really disapproved.

That summer the Diocesan Bishops of England, Wales and Scotland met in St. Edmund's Hall, Oxford. "The conferences were well sustained. All the speakers said just what they thought, but there was throughout a delightful atmosphere of harmony and fellowship." The Archbishop found his position as President a little exacting, but in his opinion the experiment was fully justified. "It was a sort of very minor Lambeth Conference. It was so much appreciated, in spite of many previous doubts, that I hope that some day the precedent may be followed."

Lang was in no uncertainty about the justice of the country's cause or of the Church's right to give it every spiritual reinforcement. In the years before the War he had sometimes received deputations of pacifists, but while hearing them with respect and sympathy, he always refused to endorse their arguments. He could, of course, have appealed for technical justification to the Articles of Religion or to Catholic theology; but he was more inclined to found his conviction on the plain truth (as he saw it) that when a man is confronted with two evils he must choose the lesser. After 1939 he interpreted his primatial duty as largely one of refusing to allow spiritual values to be lost in the welter of conflict and of pleading for an honourable war and a just settlement. He did not see entirely eye to eye with his brother of York, who, while acknowledging the necessity of the War, felt unable to encourage people to "pray for victory" and was horrified to find his name officially associated with an exhortation to that end. Lang explained afterwards that he had had no time to consult Temple and had assumed his agreement!

On December 21st, 1940, both Archbishops were among the ecclesiastical leaders who signed a joint letter to the *Times* on the "Ten Points of a Christian Order," a statement combining the Pope's Five Peace Points with the Report of the Conference at Oxford. Despite the discouragements of those first years, he corresponded continually about

436

the future peace. He was resolute on the need to refrain from making an overture, or anything that might be construed as an overture, to the enemy, until a decisive military victory had been won. Here he did not altogether agree with the Bishop of Chichester's distinction between "good" and "bad" Germans. "I fear all this means," he wrote to the Bishop, "that—to use the language of the day—you are an optimist and I am a realist."

He took a sympathetic interest in "The Sword of the Spirit," a movement initiated by the Roman Catholic Church with the purpose of uniting all men of good will in a crusade of prayer and of combating the totalitarian systems. Roman Catholics alone could be full members, but the help of others was invited. With the encouragement of the Archbishop and the leaders of the Free Churches, meetings were addressed from a common platform, and a joint committee was set up for "parallel action in the religious, and joint action in the social and international field." The movement made a considerable impact upon public opinion, incidentally manifesting a new friendliness and co-operation between Canterbury and Westminster; but with the death of Cardinal Hinsley it lost much of its impetus.

Nor, despite the difficulties of those days, was Lang inactive in the Diocese.

> During the past two years I have addressed great numbers of Church Parades of the troops, crowded in the villages of Kent, in the country churches. These smaller parades are much more satisfactory than larger gatherings of the troops: it is so much easier to keep their attention. I have been much impressed by their unfailing attentiveness. . . . Best of all, I think, were the London Scottish in Bridge Church.

Of these he added in his diary:

> It was delightful to hear the old Scottish paraphrases, and being rather picked men they were so intelligent and attentive that it was an inspiration to speak to them.

At the same time he steadily pursued his aim of visiting at least once every parish in the Diocese, however small or remote, and actually completed his task on Sunday, March 22nd, 1942.

During the early months of the War he spoke little in the House of Lords, but on October 23rd, 1941, he made two speeches. The first was on Russia, about which he said plainly that without forgetting or con-doning "the excesses and persecutions" he had so often denounced, in view of the uprising of the Russian people in defence of their country, they must now be regarded as allies against a common enemy. His second speech, in support of Lord Samuel, was on the danger of excessive restrictions on materials and labour needed for the production of books which were of value in sustaining the spirit of the people.

Ballure was out of reach, Cuddesdon was soon to close down, and All Souls, where he was now Visitor, was his last haven. On November 1st, 1941, he was there for a Gaudy, staying with the Warden, singing the Mallard's Song in Hall, and celebrating Holy Communion in the Chapel on Sunday morning.

Chapter XXXV

RESIGNATION

DURING the summer months of 1941, and particularly during walks at Ramsden, the Archbishop had been coming to a decision.

My bodily health was excellent. I was not conscious—whatever others may have been—of any serious diminution of such mental powers as I may ever have had. I had indeed been aware of becoming more easily tired than I used to be and of feeling with a greater sense of oppression the burden of problems constantly arising and of ceaseless and wearisome correspondence. I confess that I began to have a longing for relief from these burdens. But deeper down, and I hope stronger, was the growing conviction that these times called for qualities of mind and spirit in such leadership as the Archbishopric involves which I could not expect to have at my age, in my seventy-eighth year. It had become clear that this awful War would last longer than had once been expected, at the least till, say, 1944. I would then be eighty. At, and indeed before, the end of the War, great problems of reconstruction in Church and State would emerge which a man of that age could not be expected to be able to tackle. If so, the man who would be responsible for meeting these problems *then* ought to be responsible for preparing for them *now*. And there was the next Lambeth Conference due to meet as soon as possible after the War. . . . At such a time it would be perhaps the most fateful Lambeth Conference ever held. In view of the wholly new circumstances, all my full and careful preparations for the Conference which was to have been held in 1940 must be scrapped. Two things were plain : one that *I* would be too old to preside over such a Conference ; the other, that he who would preside ought now to be in a position to prepare.

All these considerations, as I thought and prayed about them, brought me before I left Ramsden to an increasingly clear conviction that I ought ere long to resign and to make way for a younger man. Of course, my one hope was that that younger man might be William Temple.

There were still two things which troubled me : (1) Was my real motive a selfish longing for relief from the burdens of office ? Motives are always mixed, and no doubt on the surface that motive was there. But, as I have already said, I hope that beneath the surface the real motive was public duty. (2) Ought I not to hold on till the great struggle was over and see it through ? This was what the Prime Minister pressed upon me when I told him what was in my mind. But, for the reasons given above, plainly to wait till the War was over would be too late.

Thus by November (1941) I had made up my own mind that I ought to resign and that my resignation, if approved, should be made public by a statement to the Convocation of Canterbury on January 21st (1942) and take effect on March 31st.

I spoke about it definitely to the Prime Minister on November 27th, and to the King when I spent a night at Windsor Castle on December 12th. The King and Queen were full of understanding sympathy—especially the Queen, who spoke about my intention with her usual quiet wisdom. She recognises that this is no time for the leadership of elderly gentlemen ! As there was some talk of his going to the United States, I had to tell the Archbishop of York what was in the wind.

Two personal difficulties had to be faced. How and where was he to live after resignation ? He would receive a pension of £1500, subject, of course, to taxation. At Bishopthorpe and Lambeth he had saved a little, a few hundred pounds in War Loan and a Life Insurance policy ot £9000 being his only assets. Apart from his own needs, "what troubled me much was that it would be quite impossible to make any financial provision for my old and faithful servants." He does not mention the further vexation of a claim for surtax for the last year at Lambeth, which he would have to pay after relinquishing the income of an Archbishop. A few of his friends, learning of this claim, raised £2000 and so enabled him to meet it. The larger problem was solved for him by the generosity of someone whose name, by the Archbishop's explicit direction, cannot even now be disclosed. This friend gave him £15,000. "I have no words in which to describe what I thought, and think, of this extraordinarily generous gift. My first instinct was to refuse it; but the way he put it to me, and my knowledge that his chief pleasure in life was to show kindness to his friends, made this impossible."

Then where was he to live? At first he thought his home would have to be a villa in an outer suburb, but the King dispelled this depressing prospect with the offer of a "grace and favour" house on Kew Green, adjoining the Gardens. These acts of kindness enabled him to put out of his mind the practical problems which could not determine, but must necessarily complicate, his decision.

The announcement of his resignation was to be made in Convocation on January 21st; but two days earlier he took the Diocesan Bishops of England and Wales into his confidence. On Wednesday the 21st he met both Houses of Convocation in full Synod. He was, he told them, in his seventy-eighth year and had been an Archbishop for thirty-three years. In resigning, he had no selfish motive or desire to escape from the burdens of office. But a younger man was needed for the great tasks of reconstruction which would await the Church after the War and for the crucial Lambeth Conference.

You can realise what it means for any man who for long years has been in the very centre of great affairs of Church and State to con-template a sudden withdrawal to some obscure place in the circum-ference, and to face the restraints and inconveniences of very slender means.

He was conscious of his own failures and therefore

must needs welcome the prospect of a few years when, by God's grace, I may be able to gain that communion with Him which has been so sadly broken by the incessant pressure of work, and to prepare aright for the last stage in the journey of life.

The phrasing did not show the Archbishop at his happiest, and the reference to "very slender means" was to be recalled and to provoke some private comment after his death, when what remained of his friend's gift was added to his insurance policy. The news of the resignation was a surprise to all the members except the Bishops, and both in Convocation and next day in the Press his decision was sympathetically received. "Assuredly," ran the leading article in the *Times*, "there is no soft cushion in the Chair of St. Augustine."

On February 4th he took his leave of the Church Assembly.

So I bade farewell to Convocation and the Church Assembly. I must frankly confess that this was not to me a very grievous loss. Convocation had always been a trouble and a trial, especially the

441

proceedings of the Lower House. And though in a measure I always enjoyed the duties of Chairman of the Church Assembly, it was often wearisome to be tied to the Chair during long debates in which the most frequent speakers were often the least able or useful; and it was difficult to suffer the inevitable bores gladly.

So it was settled. "The only thing that does trouble me," he wrote to Mrs. Crawley, "is the thought that my life-work is over and that I have done so little with it."
At the end of March he came to his last week.

On Sunday, March 22nd, I ended my long effort to visit every church in the Diocese publicly at least once, by visiting St. Peter's, Folkestone. This was the one church which I had been unable to visit at all, as the incumbent was one—the *only* one—of the clergy who had refused to obey my very tolerant injunction about the Reserved Sacrament. But I could not bear to leave it out at the end; and though the incumbent was still obstinate, I felt I must not penalise the people or refuse them a parting Blessing.

On the same afternoon he held the last of those Confirmations "which had always been the chief joy of my episcopate." On Tuesday the 24th he was in Canterbury Cathedral, with "a vast crowd filling and overflowing the Choir." After giving his Blessing at the High Altar, "I went out with the strains of thanksgiving for all God's undeserved mercies, the hymn which always moves me, 'Glorious things of Thee are spoken, Zion, city of our God.'" That night was his last in the Old Palace, and next morning, in the Crypt of St. Paul's, he consecrated, as his penultimate archiepiscopal act, the newly appointed Bishop of Willesden, son of his old friend from the North, Dr. Gresford Jones, the Bishop of Warrington. His very last act was the Confirmation of Princess Elizabeth on Saturday the 28th at Windsor.

I had always hoped that I might have this privilege. The night before I spent at the Castle and had a full talk with the little lady alone. She had been prepared by Stafford Crawley at Windsor, and though naturally not very communicative, she showed real intelligence and understanding. I thought much, but rightly said little, of the responsibilities which may be awaiting her in the future—this future more than ever unknown. The Confirmation itself was very simple—in the ugly private Chapel at the Castle—only a few relations and friends and the boys of St. George's choir present. . . . My address was just what I have so often given in country churches. And so the blessing of one who may be Queen was the last official act of this very unworthy Archbishop of Canterbury.

To move house after nearly fourteen years was a formidable business, but once more the invaluable Lumley Green-Wilkinson was at hand to shoulder the burden. Lang spent a few days at Fulham as the guest of the Bishop of London, but beyond trying to sort out the books he wished to keep from the accumulations of fifty years, he left most of the work to his chaplain. On April 1st he was no longer Archbishop, but the King, following his father's action with Dr. Davidson, had made him a Baron, so that he would still have a seat in the House of Lords. Next day (Maundy Thursday) Lang drove to Cuddesdon, where he stayed over Easter. Here he poured out his reflexions and meditations in one of his notebooks.

How strange to be here immediately after my resignation took effect on March 31st! I can only put on record one or two leading thoughts which have come to me. Of course, very constantly the thought of having been here at the beginning of all my ministry fifty-two years ago and being here now at the end. . . . And yet is it really an ending? An ending, yes, of outward activity, of ministry to others; but must it not be a new beginning, of inward activity, of ministry at last to my own soul? I see all along, so to say, two selves—the outer and the inner man, never wholly united. God knows the weakness and failure of the outer man—Priest, Bishop, Archbishop. Yet I cannot doubt that there has been all along the inner man, the man God meant me to be, deep down, often submerged, yet by God's Grace kept alive, from time to time coming forth, as here or in the "Cell" at Ballure. Even at the beginning, in my resolve to be ordained, how much there may have been of a mixture of motives on the surface—disappointment at the fading away of chances of a political career beginning at the Bar, etc.! Yet I am humbly sure there *was* an inward sense of vocation, that God was calling me and that I must obey. And then all the discovery here, those fifty-two years ago, of a new life for the inner man, a new and vivid sense of real communion with God in Christ, a new experience of the joy of that communion in the Holy Communion—something which I hope I may call a real conversion. And now at the end, doubtless the same mixture of motives, longing for the relief from the burden of office and all its heaviness. And yet beneath this, a real belief that it was God's Will for me and for the Church that I should make way for a younger man. It is this that I must trust.

So there must be not an ending but a new beginning, a new life for this inner man, a new remaking of my own soul. I know that here there may be a conflict of duties. The letters which have come to me from all sorts of people, high and low, rich and poor, express the hope that I may still be available for active influence in affairs of Church and State, and sometimes that I may have more time for personal influence on persons. There will be the temptation to turn from all this too completely to the inner life; and I must guard against making that an excuse for mere desultory idleness or self-chosen pursuits. And yet I feel sure that the real meaning of this change is that the inner man, God's man in me, who has always so fitfully but so constantly been alive in me deep down below the surface, may at last have his chance. And whatever personal influence I may have must come from this source. After all, it is that inner man, the inner soul, that will matter when the final change comes at death; and I must prepare for this other new beginning.

He attended the services on Good Friday, sitting in the pew where he had sat on a Sunday afternoon fifty-three years ago. During that day and the next the words of the old hymns, "Abide with me," "Just as I am," and "Rock of Ages" "keep rising in my heart"; and unmentioned, but surely with them, was "O Love, who formedst me to wear," with the refrain which ran through his head all through the days of his Ordination and recurred so often afterwards. On Easter Eve he made his Confession, spending most of the day either in the Parish Church or in the College Chapel. "Once again, by God's goodness, a very real and strong sense of the presence of my Lord with me . . . something of the old inward vision of the Lord stooping down from the Cross, laying His hands upon me, and drawing me into union with Himself." So he came to the great services of Easter. On Sunday evening he had supper at the Vicarage. Some of the students were there, and afterwards they all sang songs. The day closed with festal Compline, at the end of which he gave his Blessing.

The sight of the surpliced youths, the sound of the Compline psalms, recalling that night fifty-three years ago when I had, as I thought, heard in the Church the new call to turn from all my old ambitions, and then the walk back to Oxford and All Souls by Shotover in a quiet amazement and thrill. So again a new beginning where the old beginning was made.

He would never again spend Holy Week at Cuddesdon. Next day he left, making "my last journey in the car which has served me well since 1935, with Walter Wells, my 'good companion' on so many journeys for more than thirty-one years." "This," he added, "was one of the 'last times' which gave me most pain."

Chapter XXXVI

THE KING'S COTTAGE

ON April 13th, 1942, Lang moved into the King's Cottage. It was on Kew Green, almost opposite the parish church.

It had been bought by George III, and the last tenant had been the Infanta Beatrice of Spain, a sister of Queen Marie of Rumania, who had left it two years before. The King had taken a personal interest in the matter, had arranged that the Infanta's tenancy should cease, and had even visited the house with the Queen. Lumley Green-Wilkinson went to see it on January 16th (1942) and sent me a glowing report, and I paid my first visit to it on January 31st.

"It is not," he added, "a cottage, but a roomy Georgian house." It is a rambling building with many small rooms, some barely habitable attics, a number of almost unusable cellars, and a pleasant first floor, with a study overlooking Kew Gardens and a big room, which Lang divided into two, turning one half into a chapel. For staff he had McDade, the butler from Lambeth, his wife, and Gertrude Castle, who had been for many years in service at the Old Palace. In 1943, however, McDade was called up for munition work, and in the following year, to Lang's sorrow, died of heart failure.[1]

One of the greatest attractions of the new house was a private door into Kew Gardens, where Lang was never tired of walking by himself or with visiting friends.

"Day after day," he wrote in the first month of his tenancy, "the Gardens, radiant with blossoms and fresh green and daffodils and other spring flowers, unfolded their beauties. I wandered at will and almost in an ecstasy of delight through those lovely glades. I realise with continuing thankfulness what it means, and will mean, to have these Gardens at my door, compensating for the loss of my own gardens at Bishopthorpe and Lambeth."

---

[1] Mrs. Opie and Martha Saville, his servants of so many years, had retired with pensions, the latter dying in 1942, the former in 1948.

They were, he told the Bishop of Pretoria, "an unending pleasure"; he took a proprietary interest in them, and another friend has suggested that he "knew the name and history of every tree."

The new life, therefore, had its compensations.

"I fear," he wrote to Mrs. Crawley in May, "I am only too well contented with my charming house and the glories of Kew Gardens, and too reluctant to undertake any sort of public work again for the present. I do not in the least mind being alone. . . . The pictures, furniture, etc., do not suggest 'memories and ghosts' so much as thankfulness for good days I have had."

He missed his car and would have, he said, to accustom himself to becoming once more, as in the Stepney days, a "bus bishop." This transformation was quite unnecessary. Out of the proceeds from the sale of the Armstrong-Siddeley, supplemented by the gifts of some friends, a fund was formed to enable him to hire a car whenever he wished to go to London. But with a bus at his door and the District Railway a few minutes distant, the ineradicable Scot in him could not bear the extravagance. "My Scottish nature revolts," he said, "against paying two pounds ten for a car when I can go to the House of Lords and back for one and sixpence."

More serious was "the loss of frequent celebrations of the Holy Communion." Kew parish church was "a seemly Queen Anne building," and its Vicar, the Rev. A. L. Evan Hopkins, whom Lang himself had ordained, had Holy Communion on Sundays and Saints Days only. The relations between Vicarage and Cottage were extremely cordial, and at two Christmases Lang went over to a party, presiding with benevolent dignity over the children's bran tub. On Sunday mornings Lang would appear in the vestry with the question, "What are my orders for to-day, my dear Vicar?" The "orders" were generally to read the lessons, an unfamiliar task for Archbishops which he enjoyed and performed perfectly.

His own Chapel was ready in the autumn.

The Altar I had taken from the Chapel at the Old Palace, as it was my own, the money for it having been given to me by a generous personal gift from the Diocese of Leicester some years ago. The very beautiful hangings on the walls were the gift of many friends in the Diocese of Canterbury. The Chapel has a real beauty and a real atmosphere of devotion. At present I have not been able to have more than a weekly celebration, at which the Vicar and his curate form the regular congregation. But I rejoice in having this hallowed place for my own daily offices, prayers and meditations.

On April 15th he made his first appearance in the House of Lords as Lord Lang of Lambeth, being sponsored by Lord Macmillan, "an old friend and a brother Scot," and Lord Wigram. He was touched by the unwonted attendance of his colleague of Coronation days, the Duke of Norfolk, who appeared in the gorgeous raiment of Earl Marshal and conducted the proceedings. "The ceremony, with its elaborate bowings and putting on and off of three-cornered hats, always seemed to me to have the atmosphere of *Alice in Wonderland*." Returning as a junior baron to the House, of which he had been a member for thirty-six years, he declared that he felt like a boy who, after being top of the school, comes back to sit in one of the junior forms; and a reader of *Vice Versa* suggested that he should be called "Archbishop Bultitude." The House was now his chief remaining link with the world of affairs, and during the next two and a half years he attended and spoke fairly frequently— notably on the punishment of war criminals, in support of the Beveridge Report, in criticism of area bombing, and on the need to protect art treasures in the theatres of war.

There were also sermons, which showed no decline in his powers. On June 14th, 1942, he preached at All Souls, which, on his ceasing to be Visitor, had elected him an Honorary Fellow, thus preserving an association of more than fifty years. His sermon on the place of the Chapel in the life of the College was well up to the old standard and was afterwards printed. In the autumn he was at Eton Chapel. Subsequently the Provost, Lord Quickswood, wrote that he had been going through the preachers during the half with the Captain of School and the Captain of Oppidans, with the idea of discovering who should and who should not be asked to come again, and that they had marked Archbishop Lord Lang $a+$, a class which so far no other visitor had reached.

He had now more time to see his friends. Lumley Green-Wilkinson was a regular visitor and kept a watchful eye on the Archbishop's business. "It was," he said, "a delightful change to be *welcomed* to long talks about his affairs, in place of the struggles to get an innings of the Lambeth days when, after waiting about for ages to get his wishes on

AT THE PHANAR. 1939

THE ARCHBISHOP   THE ŒCUMENICAL PATRIARCH

THE LAST DAYS

Bassana.

really important matters concerning his personal affairs, I would be greeted with 'Go away, Lumley, I can't possibly spare you a minute.'"

Another occasional and most welcome caller was Don, who had left him in 1941 to be Rector of St. Margaret's, Westminster. Queen Mary and the young King Peter of Jugoslavia were other visitors at the King's Cottage. There were neighbours, too, whom he liked to see (in moderation), and in particular Gilbert Coleridge, his old collaborator in founding the Oxford University Dramatic Society.

These were some of the amenities of retirement. Lang had his moments of regret, when he contrasted what he had been with what he was.

"I listened two nights ago," he wrote to the Bishop of Pretoria on April 25th, "to a B.B.C. record of William Temple's enthronement at Canterbury with very mingled feelings. I remembered my own enthronement of thirteen years ago and realised very poignantly that another has taken my place in my glorious Cathedral. On the other hand, I am most thankful that that other is William Temple."

A month later he told Arthur Ford:

Here I am writing in the midst of the Kew Gardens, radiant in their spring beauty, and the contrast with this devastating war is bitter. . . . It is not easy to adjust myself to this new life and the thought that my life's work is now behind me with all my failures. It is hard to bear. But God is merciful and will, I trust, forgive ; and I must be thankful for all His goodness and mercy to me then and now.

But he was sure he had been right to go. "How wise I was," he wrote to the Bishop of Pretoria, "to resign when people were saying, 'Why should he ?' instead of waiting till they were saying, 'Why hasn't he ?'"

A year later, "I cannot deny, now that the novelty has worn off, I regret that retirement"; but he had not, he added, changed his mind about its wisdom.

Best of all was the return to Ballure, where now he could spend all the months of the summer. He was no longer the tenant of the little house.

Daisy Macdonald, since Jock and his wife entered into possession of Largie Castle, very naturally wished to make this house her home.

So she asked me and I most willingly consented to let her have it. So she is now responsible for it, has put much of her own furniture into it, manages servants and household affairs, the only condition being that I should be free to come whenever and as long as I wished in the years that may remain.

The arrangement suited Lang admirably and gave him the added advantage of Mrs. Macdonald's companionship—"a great blessing." The charm of the place and the peace of "the Cell" were unfading. "The more I know it the more I love it," he wrote to the Bishop of Pretoria, whose only fault in Lang's eyes was that he had never properly appreciated Ballure. Lang spent three months there in 1942 and again in 1943, when the weather was "consistently unfriendly." In 1944, when he was nearing his eightieth birthday, he was there for four months. "I can trudge the moors and hills," he wrote to Stafford Crawley, "not as if I were fifty, yet certainly not as if I were eighty."

At last he had time to read without interruption, and more and more he went back to favourites like Scott and Stevenson. Scott was his first and oldest choice. "I myself vividly remember," he had told the Sir Walter Scott Club of Edinburgh many years before, "as one of the landmarks of my life the day on which in my boyhood my father gave me *Guy Mannering* to read." Since then he had read the novels over and over again and "it is still one of the delights of preparing for a holiday to ask the question, 'Which of the Waverleys shall we take?'" He loved all, or nearly all, of them, giving the palm to *The Bride of Lammermoor*. Scott "wrote not because he was a literary craftsman, but because he was at heart a soldier and sportsman, a neighbour of all sorts and kinds of people, and a fervid Scot." Significantly, Lang praised his "superb absence of self-consciousness," adding, "Where he is greatest he is the possession of his own countrymen."

At Ballure, with a Waverley novel on his knees, Lang could almost forget the bomb-shocked world without and wander happily in a past which, as it receded, grew more and more alluring. He wrote and re-read the notes he had written on his Life and pondered often on that long and dusty road which had taken him from Woodlands Terrace to Lambeth. Even in remote Ballure, however, the War made occasional intrusion, as when the Admiralty put up a bombing range close to "the Point" and so intermittently interfered with a favourite walk.

Then, as summer turned to autumn, he would return to Kew, to the refreshment of the Gardens, and the House of Lords, and the visits of friends. He found the restrictions of wartime a little irksome, now that he had no chaplains to take the strain, and complained of the complexities and rigours of rationing (mitigated for him by Mrs. McDade and by regular gifts of marmalade from the Parkers in South Africa).

At the end of October 1944 he was shocked and distressed by the death of his successor, William Temple.

"I had a long letter from him two days before," he wrote to Mrs. Macdonald, "full of hope for his recovery. Then that horrid infection reached his heart. . . . Passing strange indeed that he, in the fulness of his power and influence, should have been taken, and I, old and out, left. I don't like to think of the loss to Church and Nation. . . . But I keep on saying two things—the bewilderment? 'God knows and God reigns': the personal loss? Think of his life rather than of his death, what it *was* and what it now *is*."

The appointment of Dr. Fisher to succeed William Temple was expected and appreciated, but Lang, mindful of his own aversion from being seen smoking in public, was mildly shocked by a photograph of the new Archbishop "with a pipe in his mouth." Dr. Fisher, however, brought the score level a little later when he came to All Souls as its Visitor. Lang, as usual, sang the Mallard Song, and the Archbishop, being unfamiliar with the habits of the College, was somewhat concerned by the spectacle of so venerable a figure chanting so ribald a ditty.

The next year saw victory and peace. "Strange," Lang wrote to Lumley Green-Wilkinson, "to be so completely out of all these celebrations, when I was so very much in the middle of them." He was back at Ballure, with the weather "better, I think, than I can remember." He reported that he was not so "gleg" on his legs as before, especially when he was going downhill; and those about him noticed a failure in strength. One afternoon, when he went to have a bath, he found that he could not get up and, the door being locked, was rescued with some difficulty and embarrassment by his hostess and a farm labourer. Afterwards he laughed over his predicament, and on November 1st, writing to Mrs. Macdonald, referred to it obliquely by reminding her of some verses in the 4th chapter of Ecclesiastes:

Two are better than one; because they have a good reward for their labour. For if they fall, the one will lift up his fellow: but woe to

him that is alone when he falleth ; for he hath not another to help
him up.

On October 28th he preached at King's School, Canterbury. No
record of his sermon was taken, for he spoke with such ease and perfection of phrase that the editor of the *Cantuarian* was sure there would
be a prepared text ; but when he asked for it, he was told there was none :
the Archbishop had been speaking from notes.

He was at Oxford for the Octave of All Souls and once again sang
the Mallard Song with all his old vigour. On the afternoon of
November 5th he took a walk with Sir Charles Grant Robertson, who
afterwards wrote :

> While we discussed many things from the late 'eighties of the nine-
> teenth century to the problems of November 1945, we turned into
> Magdalen and talked of that College too. Lang halted in the cloisters,
> pointed to the Tower, and then added : "It was here that I wrestled
> with the question whether I could leave this place, and St. Mary's,
> and All Souls, and go, as I was pressed, to Portsea. At times under
> that Tower I felt it was impossible. I must refuse and stay in Oxford,
> and work out the life I had planned as a don. And then with a great
> wrench I accepted." He paused. "I suppose," he said slowly, "I
> was right. What do you think ?"

On December 3rd he was in his place in the House of Lords for the
debate on hydro-electric development in Scotland.

> "I can speak," he said, "with some knowledge of the Highlands,
> especially of the West Highlands. I have had a home there for fifty
> years, and no words of mine can express what I have owed during
> a long and laborious life to the refreshment and recreation of the
> scenery of the Highlands."

He would surely have chosen no other theme for his farewell.

On December 4th Mrs. Ford came to him for the night. He was
looking very old, "especially the eyes," but seemed in good health and
spirits. They had so much to talk about, as their common memories
went back through Bishopthorpe and the Deanery at York to the days
when he was a curate at Leeds Parish Church and she was a girl at the
Vicarage. They spoke, too, of the havoc of war and the disorder of the
times. Mrs. Ford wished that she were twenty years younger and might

see the coming to birth of a new world. "No," Lang replied, "I don't think I feel like that. I think I have had enough of this one."

They said Evensong together in the little Chapel, and next morning, Wednesday, December 5th, before she went, Lang showed her a Christmas card he had just had from the Duchess of Kent. He put it on his writing-table, where later that day it was found. He took Mrs. Ford into the Chapel to give her his Blessing and to pray for the repose of the soul of Christopher, her soldier son who had fallen in Italy. Then he went down the stairs with her to see her off. "How lovely those Christmases were with you at Canterbury!" she said as she left.

He, too, had a train to catch, for he had an appointment at the Natural History Museum and in the afternoon the House of Lords was debating the distress in Central Europe. Saying goodbye to Mrs. Ford had delayed him a little and, disobeying his doctor, who had told him his heart was not very strong, he set off in a hurry. He went by his private door into the Gardens, and then along Kew Gardens Road. He reached the short incline which leads up to the District Station. About half-way up it is a fishmonger's shop. A queue of women were waiting there to be served, and as they stood, they saw an elderly clergyman come hurrying by. Just as he passed the shop he stumbled and fell. Lady Cynthia Slessor, who was standing in the queue, left it and helped him to a chair. He kept on saying, "I must get to the station, I must get to the station." Someone telephoned to the King's Cottage. An ambulance was sent for, but failed to come; and presently a large police car appeared. Lang, who by now was scarcely conscious, was lifted into it and driven to Richmond Hospital. When they arrived a lady doctor came out, looked at Lang, and said that he was dead. The hospital would not take in the body, so the car drove on to the Public Mortuary. Here, a little later, a post-mortem found that the Archbishop had died of heart failure. Lumley Green-Wilkinson, who had hastened to Kew, then took the body to the little Chapel at the King's Cottage, where, in the presence of Bishop Norman Lang and the household, he said a Requiem.

The funeral was on December 10th. The first service was at eleven o'clock in Westminster Abbey before a large company, a Requiem Eucharist being simultaneously sung in the Eastern Crypt of Canterbury Cathedral. The body was then moved to Canterbury, where that afternoon at three o'clock the leading clergy of the Cathedral and the Diocese escorted it in procession to the High Altar. After the funeral service the body was cremated, the ashes lying that night on the Altar in the Chapel of the Old Palace. Next morning they were taken to the Chapel of Our Lady Undercroft in the Crypt, where they remained during the Celebration of Holy Communion at eight o'clock. Afterwards, in the presence of the Dean and Canons, representatives of the King's Scholars and a few others, the Archbishop of Canterbury (Dr. Fisher) committed them in the Chapel of St. Stephen in the North-East Transept; and there they now lie, close to the tomb of Archbishop Chichele, the founder of All Souls College, within the Cathedral which Lang had loved so well.

Chapter XXXVII

COSMO GORDON LANG

L ANG would not have been the man he was if, in the time of leisure after his retirement, he had not constantly asked himself what kind of an Archbishop he had been; or if his answer had not shown the depth of his own disappointment. Once again it must be emphasised that his judgments on himself should not be taken as decisive. His sense of the theatre was far too strong. He would always see himself moving through a drama in which mighty forces contended for noble causes, going forward to resounding victory or down to total defeat. Even when he was an old man and knew that life was not like that, or was seldom like that, he never entirely rejected this pattern. "Lanfranc, Anselm, Becket, Laud," he had recited to his visitors. Where did he stand in such a company? What comparable achievement could he claim? He was sure of some purpose in the call he had had in Cuddesdon Church all those years ago. Yet he had not led his country back into an Age of Faith. No striking historical act had marked his primacy. He had been neither a great statesman nor a saint. Therefore he felt that he had failed.

In such an argument he must not be allowed the last word. Of course, if success is to be measured only by expectation, he was right: by any other yardstick he was wrong. It is true that he had no big constructive reforms to his credit. He was—especially in his later years—inclined to allow troubles to come to him and to deal with them as they arrived. He did not frame a policy and tirelessly push it through. He had presided over the Commission on Cathedrals and sponsored through Parliament the measure which gave them a new and more secure foundation. He had subsequently supported the venture of Church House, with its heavy financial commitment. But these were scarcely reforms of the first order. He did not settle a single one of the outstanding problems of the Church, such as the Prayer Book, the Ecclesiastical Courts, the doctrinal divisions, the relations between Church and State, Education, or finance. All these he left very much as he found them. But that in itself was more of an achievement than it sounds. He inherited a position of acute difficulty. The controversy

455

over the Prayer Book had embittered the various parties and dislocated the delicate balance of Church and State. In 1928 a great many people were saying that the Establishment must go and that the Church might disintegrate. Whatever may be thought of Lang's treatment of a menacing situation, when he retired in 1942 the talk of Disestablishment had died away and a much friendlier spirit prevailed within the Church. He may not have solved the problems he inherited; but at least he produced an atmosphere more favourable to an eventual solution, and in one instance, at any rate, that of Education, this improvement was to be of material assistance to his successor.

Something similar might be said of his work for Reunion, which was probably his most important service to the Church and to Christendom. What he actually did may not appear to amount to very much by comparison with what is still to be done. He did succeed in establishing a new and closer relationship with the Old Catholics, the Orthodox and some of the Scandinavian Churches. But more significant than any progress in inter-communion or inter-consecration was the impetus given towards unity, the general growth in mutual understanding, the marking of the lines of future advance; and what he began in 1920 he would have carried forward a further stage in 1940, if the War had not spoilt his plans and halted the whole movement.

More difficult to assess and therefore to appreciate is what can best be described as the "virtuosity" of his administration. The bulk of his work was with an infinity of detail, of letters to be answered, people to be seen, decisions to be made, meetings to be guided. The subjects may seem of little consequence now: they may not have been of much consequence even then; but cumulatively they form the business of an Archbishop, and the swiftness and success with which he manages them are one of the tests of a primacy. The passengers in a ship are usually unaware of what is happening in the engine-room. They know if their voyage is retarded by some mechanical breakdown and may drop a word of recognition if the ship comes punctually and flawlessly to port; but the multiplicity of processes behind either event is beyond their ken.

Lang's industry has often been observed. To the end of his time it never failed to astonish those who worked with or for him. His devotion to duty drove him on when others might have rested without any sense of default. He had exceptional administrative ability and was a most skilful chairman, as careful and effective in the larger affairs of the Church as he was heedless and helpless in the smaller affairs of Lang. His day by day decisions, his judgments of men and of issues, were very sure. He nearly always knew the right answer to any question that was brought to him; or it might be truer to say that he always knew the wrong answers and never gave them. People might and did complain of a lack of leadership on some particular point, and Lang was perhaps over-cautious, too reluctant to commit himself to a definite course, too ready, when face to face with some rocky protuberance, to float away from it on generalities. He would probably have admitted as much, but have explained that this manœuvre was necessary in the circumstances of the Church, or of any Church. "I am sometimes tempted to think," he told Father Talbot, "that the pronouncements from the Vatican are hardly less platitudinous than those which emanate from Lambeth." But temperament as well as policy inclined him to this attitude, for he disliked and distrusted the clear-cut, dogmatic decision, either on a con-temporary issue or on a religious belief. As he had once told Bishop Talbot, one half of his mind on the great questions of religion was a big question mark. He was content with mystery: indeed, he much preferred it to some unsatisfying elucidation.

He kept his particular caution for new and untried propositions, brought to him as a rule by an enthusiast who saw very clearly its merits, without weighing its influence upon the work of the Church in other spheres. Lang always had the whole landscape in his mind's eye and was careful to do nothing that might upset the balance of the picture. It followed that whatever disappointment he may sometimes have given to individuals, the Church in his time enjoyed a security it only fully realised when he was no longer there, a comfortable assurance that at Lambeth a wise head and a firm hand were in control.

As difficult to assess was the place Lang occupied in the national life. To this he attached the greatest importance. The present Dean of Westminster told him that his name was "a household word throughout the inhabited globe . . . acknowledged by all to stand for something that counts in the affairs of men." This may be thought an overstatement. That much-quoted person, the man in the street, may know little of and care less for any Archbishop of Canterbury, and what he knew of Lang was often neither true nor important—that he had a very large income and lived in a Palace, or that he had a lot to do with the abdication of King Edward VIII. What is both true and important is that many of the most influential people in the country respected and leaned upon his judgment; that his oratory made him a welcome and conspicuous guest at the meetings of innumerable learned societies and organisations; that his mastery of the broadcast brought him into occasional and fleeting contact with a wider circle of listeners; that he did inconspicuous but notable service to a number of institutions like the British Museum and Charterhouse and as a member of countless committees with a wide variety of purpose; that in the House of Lords, as in Convocation or the Church Assembly, he had an unusual talent for controlling a debate and bringing it to the conclusion he wanted; and that he knew nearly all the people who mattered most in the nation's affairs and knew some of them very well. At least it can be asserted that in his time the Archbishop of Canterbury was not "off the map." Contemporaries who watched him work have declared him with emphasis a great Archbishop. The claim is easier to assert than to justify, for it hangs not upon any single quality or achievement, but on a multiplicity of gift and merit, and of duties faithfully and often brilliantly performed. It is the greatness of the forest rather than of any particular tree in it.

The man himself remains, that complicated, introspective, emotional person who has been allowed, so far as has been possible in these pages, to speak for himself, to reveal his high standard and his sense of a failure to live up to it. Little, if anything, can advantageously be added. The biographer may be a judge, but is not a jury. So far as he can, he should see that the evidence is made available and is fairly displayed; but he must leave the verdict to others. Yet possibly, since Lang has not always been his own best witness, this much more should be said in amplification. He was a strangely unintegrated person, a jangle of warring personalities which never reached a working agreement among themselves. The prelate, the courtier, the priest, the actor, the man who had a fondness for society and the man who was nearly a mystic, the sentimentalist, the cynic, the ascetic, the tender and sympathetic counsellor, the lover of flowers and of scenery—all were there. "I see seven Archbishops," Sir William Orpen had said. "Which of them am I to paint?" Each Archbishop had a disconcerting habit of suddenly appearing and elbowing the occupant of the moment off the stage. To those who watched, it was outwardly the same man they saw, but inwardly it was someone quite different. One who knew him well has described how sometimes, at the dinner-table for example, a click could almost be heard as one Lang went off and another came on. The result has been a wide divergence of opinion about him. Some saw one Lang and some another, and what they did not see they can hardly be expected to recognise. Only a very few saw the whole man, with all those baffling changes of personality, the man who could by turns charm and exasperate, enthral and disappoint, but could never tire them; and those were the men and women who, understanding him best, loved and admired him most.

APPENDIX I

IMAGINARY ENTRY IN *WHO'S WHO*

William Cosmo Gordon Lange was born on the 31st of October 1864. His parents were the well-known Dr. Marshall Lang, of the Barony Church, Glasgow, and Hannah Agnes, daughter of the Rev. Dr. Keith, Minister of Hamilton. His birthplace was Fyvie, Aberdeenshire, where his father was clergyman, and where his godfather, Col. Gordon of Fyvie Castle, resided. His father then became Minister of Anderston Church, Glasgow, to w. city the family removed. Morningside Church, Edinburgh, was his father's next appointment, where the family resided for four years. Dr. Marshall Lang was then appointed successor to Dr. Norman McLeod in the Barony Church of Glasgow. Cosmo in Glasgow attended the school of the historian Dr. W. F. Collier, for whom he always had a great regard. Thence, at the somewhat early age of 14, he went to Glasgow University. There, after a successful career of four years, he graduated as Master of Arts. He then went up to Cambridge, graduated there, and entered the Law Classes of Glasgow University for three years. Taking the degree of LL.D., he was called to the Scotch Bar in 1888, aged 23 years. His business at the Bar being not at first remunerative, he turned to literature, where he has achieved a marvellous success as novelist, poet, historian. A few leading cases fell to his care, and this, with the fortune he had made in literature, settled him comfortably at the age of 28. Then in the year 1894 he married the younger daughter of the Earl of Kintore. Aged 30, he stepped forward into politics as candidate for North Ayrshire against the Liberal candidate. It was a Liberal seat, and he lost the contest. Fortune was kinder in a little, and in the General Election of 1897 he gained the seat for the Conservatives. At once he was a marked man. He moved the Address of 1897, and in a few months was Lord Beaconsfield's secretary. In the year 1900 he became Under-Secretary of State for Ireland. In 1902 he became Under-Secy. for Foreign Affairs. During the severe illness of Lord Salisbury in 1903-1904 he acted temp. Secretary, was appointed Secy. of State for War in 1907, Lord Claverton in the same year, Secy. for Foreign Affairs in 1908, Earl of Norham and Prime Minister in 1912. His career has been one long success. In literature, in oratory, in statesmanship, he has been equally successful, and equally admired.

The Rt. Hon. William Cosmo Gordon, Earl of Norham, K.T., D.C.L., LL.D.

Emily, sister to the Rt. Hon. The Earl of Kintore, Countess of Norham.

1. Lady Emily Gordon Lange, now Her Grace the Duchess of Richmond and Gordon, b. 1895. M. 1916, has issue—Alexander Douglas Gordon, Marquis of Gordon.

2. Hon. William Cosmo Gordon Lange, Viscount Claverton, b. 1897.

3. Hon. Douglas Kintore Marshall Gordon Lange, b. 1899.

4. Lady Anne Mary Keith Gordon Lange, b. 1900.

5. Hon. Keith Gordon Lange, R.N., b. 1901.

6. Hon. Norman Hamilton Gordon Lange, b. 1902.

7. Lady Hannah Buchanan Gordon Lange, b. 1903, d. 1910.

8. Hon. George Victor Albert Gordon Lange, b. 1905.

Seats : Norham Hall, nr. Norham, Norfolkshire.
Claverton Park, nr. Calne, Wiltshire.
Glendonald Castle, by Oban, Argyllshire.

Town Address : 10 Downing Street. Carlton Club, Conservative Club, Beaconsfield Club, Literary Club, London.

APPENDIX II

THE MALLARD SONG

Montagu Burrows, in *Worthies of All Souls*, gives the following version :

> The Griffin, Bustard, Turkey and Capon
> Let other hungry mortals gape on,
> And on their bones with stomach fall hard,
> But lett All Souls men have their Mallard.
>
> The Romans once admired a Gander
> More than they did their best Comander,
> Because hee saved, if some don't fooll us,
> The place named from the scull of Tolus.
>
> The poets faind Jove turnd a Swan,
> But lett them prove it if they can ;
> To mak't appeare it's not att all hard,
> He was a swapping, swapping Mallard.
>
> Then lett us drink and dance a Galliard
> In the remembrance of the Mallard,
> And as the Mallard doth in poole
> Lett's dabble, dive, and duck in bowle.

Burrows adds that a refrain, which does not appear in this version, is usually given at the end of every verse—

> O by the blood of King Edward,
> O by the blood of King Edward,
> It was a swapping, swapping Mallard!

He also states that in the early years of the eighteenth century the third line of the third verse was changed (and improved) to—

> As for our proof it's not at all hard . . .

though the reader will probably still find that All Souls might have done better.

Those who wish to explore the possible origin and meaning of this ditty should read Burrows' Appendix on the subject.

My mother, sister and I drove down to All Souls College in an old Oxford Cab about 10-oc. and stopped near the iron gate. We felt quite mysterious, waiting there quietly in that dark corner, surrounded by old buildings and walls, and could almost fancy ourselves to be taking part in some plot. Everything was still, except for the distant noise of the trams passing at the end of the street, and occasionally someone hurried by. A "Bobby" making his round evidently thought he had come upon something "fishy"; the silent "four-wheeler" roused his suspicions. He stood for some time watching us, but with this he seemed satisfied, for he finally moved on. Time passed quickly; we talked in whispers, listening all the time for the sound of singing from the College, which would be the sign that things were beginning. All the clocks round chimed and struck out the time—a quarter past ten, half past, and then eleven.

Almost on the stroke we heard voices in the quad, and driving up to the iron gate we looked through. There we saw groups of men with torches, and heard much discussion going on and laughter. They were evidently getting ready to start in procession. Soon someone gave the order and off they started.

A beautiful voice rang out on the night air singing the old Mallard Song which is peculiar to All Souls. We could hear every word distinctly as he sang in a rich clear voice, which seemed exactly suited for the occasion, and could never have sounded better than it did ringing out on the still night air. But the effect when the words were taken up by the whole College was magnificent.

> " O by the blood of King Edward,
> O by the blood of King Edward,
> It was a swapping, swapping Mallard."

The words echoed out again and again, sometimes faint, while the procession moved into the farther quad, and becoming louder again as the procession slowly approached us, and then the whole thing passed the gate quite close to us, and now I must give a description of it.

First came a few men with torches, one carrying before him on a long pole the stuffed mallard, then the Lord Mallard, carried on a chair shoulder-high by four men. At his side walked two others carrying wands in one hand, and with the other ready to steady his lordship should it be needful. Two more walked in front for the same reason.

It was the Lord Mallard who from his seat sang again and again the song before referred to. Following him came all the members of the College—all in gowns, some with caps, and here and there a top-hat, looking very much out of place. (As must have felt their owners, gambolling in the night air.) The procession passed twice round the quad, making the tour of the smaller quad in between, and then proceeded to mount to the roofs, which was the next item on the programme.

There was much laughter as they all disappeared from sight for a time, leaving us again in darkness, to emerge presently on a high roof near the chapel tower. Immediately in front of us, one by one they clambered up, and relit their torches at the top. Then again rang out the song as they slowly moved forward. It was a very pretty sight to see the lights winding about—sometimes disappearing for a minute or two behind a parapet or wall, only to appear again a little farther on. Once or twice we saw a light turn round and make its way slowly back again, evidently finding the onward progress too dangerous for an inexperienced climber at midnight.

The procession went all along the side of the quad, and then turned the corner to go along the bottom. Here there was a pretty effect caused by each man being obliged to mount a ladder—up one side and down the other, so that all the lights were on different levels. Having passed along the bottom they turned and walked up the other side—on the library roofs, and on reaching the front again each man extinguished his torch and after a good deal of delay and laughter (sometimes we could hear their words to each other quite distinctly), all were down and assembled in the quad again, where they relit their torches and once more walked in procession, singing until they reached the door. Here they all threw down their torches, which altogether made a great blaze, and taking hands walked round the bonfire singing "Auld Lang Syne." It was a curious sight—all their black forms outlined against the fire— and once I caught a glimpse of gaitered legs.

The Mallard Song was sung once again, and then everyone moved off, the time being 12.15.

M. J. LANCASHIRE
(née HOLLAND).

INDEX